Coming Together

THE INSTITUTE FOR EUROPEAN AND MEDITERRANEAN ARCHAEOLOGY
DISTINGUISHED MONOGRAPH SERIES

Peter F. Biehl, editor-in-chief
Sarunas Milisauskas and Stephen L. Dyson, editors

The Magdalenian Household: Unraveling Domesticity
Ezra Zubrow, Françoise Audouze, and James G. Enloe, editors

Eventful Archaeologies: New Approaches to Social Transformation in the Archaeological Record
Douglas J. Bolender, editor

The Archaeology of Violence: Interdisciplinary Approaches
Sarah Ralph, editor

Approaching Monumentality in Archaeology
James. F. Osborne, editor

The Archaeology of Childhood: Interdisciplinary Perspectives on an Archaeological Enigma
Güner Coşkunsu, editor

Diversity of Sacrifice: Form and Function of Sacrificial Practices in the Ancient World and Beyond
Carrie Ann Murray, editor

Climate and Cultural Change in Prehistoric Europe and the Near East
Peter F. Biehl and Olivier P. Nieuwenhuyse, editors

Water and Power in Past Societies
Emily Holt, editor

Coming Together: Comparative Approaches to Population Aggregation and Early Urbanization
Attila Gyucha, editor

COMING TOGETHER

Comparative Approaches to Population Aggregation and Early Urbanization

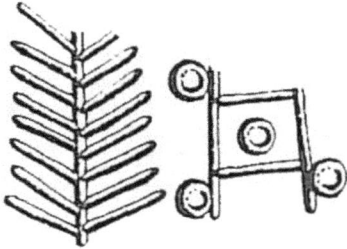

IEMA Proceedings,
Volume 8

EDITED BY
Attila Gyucha

STATE UNIVERSITY OF
NEW YORK PRESS

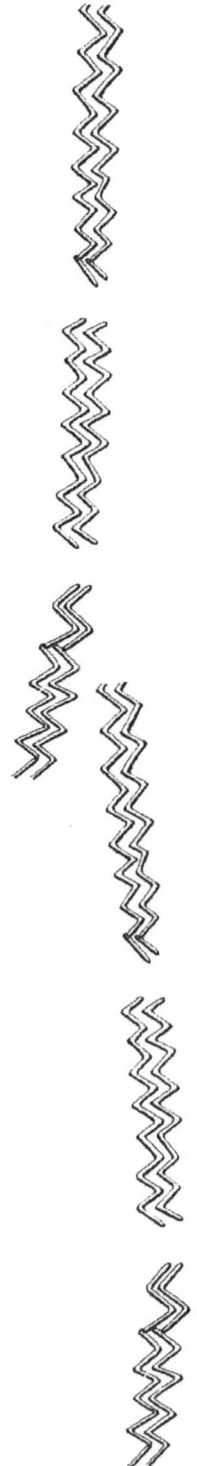

Logo and cover/interior art: A vessel with wagon motifs from Bronocice, Poland, 3400 B.C. Courtesy of Sarunas Milisauskas and Janusz Kruk, 1982, Die Wagendarstellung auf einem Trichterbecher aus Bronocice, Polen, *Archäologisches Korrespondenzblatt* 12: 141–144.

Published by
State University of New York Press, Albany

For information, contact
State University of New York Press, Albany, NY
www.sunypress.edu

Library of Congress Cataloging-in-Publication Data

Names: Gyucha, Attila, editor.
Title: Coming together : comparative approaches to population aggregation and early urbanization / edited by Attila Gyucha.
Description: Albany : State University of New York Press, [2019] | Series: SUNY series, the institute for European and Mediterranean archaeology distinguished monograph series | Includes bibliographical references and index.
Identifiers: LCCN 2018009221 | ISBN 9781438472775 (hardcover) | ISBN 9781438472768 (perf.)
Subjects: LCSH: Indigenous peoples—Urban residence.
Classification: LCC GN380 . C66 2019 | DDC 307.76—dc23
LC record available at https://lccn.loc.gov/2018009221

10 9 8 7 6 5 4 3 2 1

Contents

Illustrations

FIGURES

TABLES

CHAPTER ONE

Population Aggregation and Early Urbanization from a Comparative Perspective

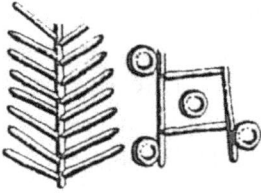

An Introduction to the Volume

Attila Gyucha

"The technological developments in transportation and communication which virtually mark a new epoch in human history have accentuated the role of cities as dominant elements in our civilization and have enormously extended the urban mode of living beyond the confines of the city itself" (Wirth 1938:4–5). Wirth's note penned 80 years ago is still just as valid today. Similarly to many others—particularly economists, such as Jacobs (1969)—Wirth called the growth of cities and worldwide urbanization as "one of the most impressive facts of modern times" (Ibid., 2), and states that "what is distinctively modern in our civilization is best signaled by the growth of great cities" (Ibid., 1). Yet, in the same paper, he goes on to describe the negative effects of urban life on humans by using one of the most extensive and eloquent vocabularies ever published to portray the calamitous impacts of urbanism. But if cities have such a miserable and devastating influence on the social and mental life of urban dwellers—as Simmel (1903) and others also so vividly described—why do people keep deciding to give up on living in small, dispersed communities and have moved into large settlements time and again for thousands of years? What do these "products of human nature" (Park 1925:1) offer that have always been so irresistibly desirable for people?

Wirth (Ibid., 10) argued that cities bring together people because they are different, and as a result, they are beneficial to one another. Likewise, Morris (2008:319) defined cities as sociopolitical mechanisms that produce human interaction, and Glaeser (2011:120) emphasized the importance of "connected creativity" that makes cities successful and productive social formations. Smith (this volume) notes that the increasing face-to-face interactions as population number and density grow stimulate a range of positive outcomes, including economic and urban growth as well as community formation. As Newman put it, the attraction of cities "lies in the opportunities that they create through networks of people" (2006:278). The dynamic interactions between these spatially condensed informal and formal networks—through individuals, groups, organizations, and institutions as nodal points—glue urban systems together. But why are these networks indispensable for the individuals?

Many sociological and anthropological studies conclude that although integration into multiple social networks may be attractive for several other reasons, it is the expected economic benefits—commonly, by taking advantage of previously established social ties and networks—that play a vital role in individual or group decisions about moving to cities (Bogue 1977; Browning 1971; Schiller and Çağlar 2009; Wang et al. 2015). These benefits are associated with a spatially concentrated population, socioeconomic heterogeneity, and an economy of scales, as cities are not only central places of services and functions for their immediate hinterlands but their external relations many times also include their participation in interregional and transregional networks (Capello and Nijkamp 2004; Hohenberg and Lees 1985; Orum and Chen 2003; Robinson 2005; Taylor and Derudder 2016). In addition to being "primary economic organs" (Jacobs 1969:6) for production, consumption, and circulation of goods, modern cities—partially through these external relations—are powerful and vigorous nodes for innovations and new ideas that give rise to cultural and political transformations at the global scale (Crane et al. 2016; Mumford 1961; Redfield and Singer 1954; Zeng and Greenfield 2015). Urbanization accounts for changes in the environment as well as in social order and practices, and cities are arenas to create, display, and reinforce social and economic inequalities (Colantonio and Dixon 2011; Gottdiener and Budd 2005; Musterd and Ostendorf 1998; O'Connor et al. 2001).

Taken together, the complexity of modern cities derives from a wide range of types and forms of interactions between integrative institutions and diverse social and economic networks of various scales. These interactions result in dynamic, constantly changing entities the rules and conventions of which are being continually challenged, reconsidered, and reconstituted by discovering formerly unexplored directions and introducing novel concepts.

Although this overview is a brief and simplified description of the current, highly urbanized world, some fundamental sociocultural dynamics in the development of past nucleated societies may have been similar. Therefore, in order to answer the question "How did our world become like it is today?" comparative studies between the present and the past must be applied. This conference volume approaches this question from the perspective of the ancient past using data from both prehistoric aggregated villages (*sensu* Birch 2013) and early urban contexts (see Smith 2007, 2016), collectively called "nucleated settlements" in this introduction. The 9th IEMA Visiting Scholar Conference brought together an international group of distinguished scholars to explore three major cross-cultural anthropological questions regarding variations in the trajectories of nucleated sites: (1) What factors and integrative mechanisms brought large populations together?; (2) What social practices and institutions facilitated the development and sustainability of these sites?; and (3) What were the impacts of permanent nucleations on sociocultural developments in ancient societies? With an overarching range of theoretical perspectives and methodological approaches, the chapters of this volume provide thoughtful insights into these matters through case studies from Europe, the Near East, and North America.

In the rest of this introductory chapter, following the initiatives of the conference listed above, I contextualize the chapters of the volume by discussing several theoretical and methodological issues related to the emergence, development, and sociocultural impacts of ancient nucleated settlements.

COMPARATIVE PERSPECTIVES IN THE STUDY OF NUCLEATED SETTLEMENTS

Comparative studies in archaeology are significant because they help to identify analogous and divergent patterns in the archaeological record, particularly in regard to cultural, social, political, and economic developments. Moreover, the constantly increasing quantity and quality of data can bring about more coherent explanations and models based on the recognized similarities and differences. As a result, comparative research also is complementary in nature, as this approach expands our interpretive schemes. Scholars agree that the systematic application of cross-regional and cross-temporal approaches results in a better understanding of past and present urban developments (Nijman 2007; Robinson 2015; Smith 2003a; Smith 2010; Smith et al. 2016; Ward 2008). In fact, many researchers convincingly argue for the prerequisite of comparative perspective in urban studies—as McFarlane put it, "When we make a claim about 'the city,' or about a particular form of urbanism, the claim is implicitly—and, crucially, inevitably—to some extent a comparative claim, because our claims and arguments are always set against other kinds of urban possibilities or imaginaries" (2010:725). Furthermore, systematic comparisons between past and present nucleation dynamics provide outcomes that help us understand current, many times pressing issues associated with modern urbanization trends.

Comparative research has documented common planning principles as well as regularities in social, economic, political, and religious mechanisms and practices in premodern urban settlements across the world. These studies, however, also pointed out a great deal of variation even in local and regional developments (e.g., Adams 1966; Blanton et al. 1993; Creekmore and Fisher 2014; Fernández-Götz and Krausse 2016; Smith 2003b; Storey 2006a). This dichotomy has been addressed and discussed from different angles. With regard to preindustrial urbanism, Storey concluded that it "is uniform throughout the world. Similar numbers of people could be fed and housed given the existing technology, transport system, hinterland productivity, and administrative structures available in the preindustrial era, which despite local variations, were similar all over the world" (1992:119). Renfrew (2008:36) noted that shared characteristics revealed in urban settlements are associated with the need to accommodate a range of similar functions. In addition to these functional approaches, others—such as Fletcher (1995) and Trigger (2008)—argued that cross-cultural regularities in the built environment of ancient cities indicate similarities in human behavior and thinking that may require various explanations. However, they may also act as launching platforms for comparative investigations.

Comparisons between ancient and modern cities had occurred in past urban studies, particularly with respect to architectural design (e.g., de Souza Briggs 2004; Kostof 1991; McIntosh 1991; Scargill 1979). The past 10 years, however, have witnessed the systematic application of a transdisciplinary approach based on, as Stanley and his colleagues (2015:122) stated, "the notion that urban areas throughout world history share commonalities" and "the guiding principle that present-day urbanism is better understood in the context of deep urban history." New comparative studies of premodern and modern cities—using theories and methods borrowed from multiple disciplines—illustrate "how different societies developed analogous suites of solutions to related problems" (Carballo and Fortenberry 2015:542). These studies already have yielded encouraging results in the investigations of timeless urban principles and characteristics (Dennehy et al. 2016; Smith 2010; Vis 2014; York et al. 2011).

Previous research commonly linked the emergence of cities to state-level political configurations (e.g., Adams 1966; Childe 1950; Manzanilla 1997; Trigger 1972). Nevertheless, recent archaeological investigations—largely based on comparisons between different trajectories across the globe—have stimulated arguments for decoupling urbanization and state formation processes. These studies have triggered the notion that urban settlement forms preceded the rise of states, and cities occurred within a broad range of sociopolitical contexts in many parts of the world (Cowgill 2004; Jennings 2016; Jennings and Earle 2016; Smith 2003a; Wengrow 2015). These findings further reinforce the efficacy of approaches to trajectories toward social complexity that go beyond unilinear evolutionary typologies (Fried 1967; Morgan 1877; Service 1962; Spencer 1990). A growing body of alternative perspectives addresses societal development and power relations in more complex societies through archaeological and ethnohistoric studies. The outcomes imply nonlinear social trajectories as well as tremendous variation in political structures, ranging from collective and corporate systems to rigidly hierarchical and autocratic political formations, sometimes even occurring in neighboring, contemporaneous polities (Blanton et al. 1996; Drennan and Peterson 2012; Ehrenreich et al. 1995; Fargher et al. 2011a; Feinman and Neitzel 1984; Feinman and Price 2010; Neitzel and Earle 2014). A particularly valuable finding of these studies is that the data from nucleated settlements indicate a great range of variation in the potential combinations of settlement form and political organization. These recent, interrelated theoretical advances underscore the importance of analyzing local- and regional-scale trajectories in their own cultural and historical settings when various pathways to social complexity are studied as they relate to ancient settlement dynamics (Falconer and Savage 1995; Smith 2016; see also Gaydarska, Harrison, and Bilgen, and Sastre and Currás this volume).

Another paradigmatic shift has emerged in the past few years that has placed the comparative investigations of ancient and modern aggregated settlements in a new dimension. In addition to mutual qualitative properties revealed by transdisciplinary studies, settlement scaling research has demonstrated that several quantitative attributes and patterns shared by recent urban settings also commonly occurred in ancient cities (Bettencourt 2013; Bettencourt et al. 2007; Cesaretti et al. 2015; Ortman et al. 2014).

Moreover, other related investigations indicate that sites classified as villages also tend to produce identical regularities (Ortman and Coffey 2015; Ortman et al. 2016; see also Smith this volume). Thus, scaling studies have provided empirical evidence for the operation of similar principal dynamics and mechanisms in the social development of nucleated settlements throughout human history to a considerable extent.

Apart from verifying the applicability of comparative studies into past settlement developments, the advances summarized briefly above have opened novel opportunities to explore prehistoric aggregated settlements and early urban sites using the same theoretical approaches. As previously urged by a number of scholars (e.g., Butzer 2008; Cowgill 2004; Smith 2003a; Storey 2006b), these advances also support the redirection of research focus from the threshold- and checklist-based separation of urban and non-urban sites—as well as related settlement typologies—to underlying principles and social processes in ancient settlement dynamics toward nucleation. An essential inspiration of this volume, these improvements also facilitate studies to model social, political, and cultural transformations generated by the coresidence of large populations in past societies.

This book is unusual in the sense that the aforementioned research questions are scrutinized through investigations of both prehistoric aggregated and early urban settlements. The nucleated settlements explored in the case studies encompass more than 7,500 years, representing tribal to state-level societies, and range from approximately one to several hundreds of hectares and from ca. 100 to possibly tens of thousands of inhabitants. As the chapters illustrate, the applications of different approaches permit us to assess the archaeological record from varying perspectives, contributing to a more sophisticated understanding of the developments of early demographic and political centers.

METHODOLOGICAL PERSPECTIVES IN THE STUDY OF NUCLEATED SETTLEMENTS

Although they profoundly affect which research questions can productively be studied and, along with those questions, what and how data can and must be collected, analyzed, and interpreted, the methodological opportunities and difficulties of nucleated settlements are rarely discussed in a systematic manner in the archaeological literature.

The horizontal extent of nucleated sites alone is commonly a major limiting factor that influences research for several reasons, including funding and time constraints. Even sites subject to intensive fieldwork for decades or sometimes centuries have been excavated only partially—for instance, approximately 67 percent of Pompeii has been recovered since the beginning of its official excavations in the middle of the eighteenth century (Laurence 2007:3). Nevertheless, as several chapters in this volume illustrate—including particularly Harrison and Bilgen's, and Kaiser's chapters—the unambiguous benefit of extensively excavated sites is that the available data allow us to explore specific aspects that cannot be addressed at sites investigated by small-scale archaeological fieldwork. This matter also relates to a frequently ignored area in scientific studies: the outcomes of cultural resource management (CRM) archaeological projects. Although the quick recovery and documentation of endangered sites characterize these field activities, the results from nucleated sites regularly provide valuable sets of information, particularly regarding settlement patterns, layout, and use (see especially Harrison and Bilgen, Kelly, Raczky, and Ryan this volume).

The past decades also have brought innovative field and analytical methods that let researchers overcome many of the challenges associated with the exploration of large sites. The application of noninvasive remote sensing techniques—including airborne (e.g., LIDAR) and satellite technologies (e.g., hyper- and multispectral imaging), as well as ground-based geophysical surveys (e.g., magnetometric gradiometry, ground-penetrating radar, electric resistivity tomography)—in combination with systematic field surveys, targeted excavations, and well-designed sampling techniques can facilitate in addressing specific research questions in a cost- and time-efficient way. Advances in multisensor systems in geophysical surveys enhance the speed of data acquisition in the field. In addition to outstanding examples such as research at Angkor Wat and numerous early urban sites in Greece (Donati and Sarris 2016; Stark et al. 2015), the productivity of large-scale geophysical studies is best illustrated by surveys conducted at prehistoric megasites in Ukraine (Chapman et al. 2014; Müller et al. 2016; Ohlrau 2015; see also Gaydarska this volume). Remote sensing techniques also have yielded groundbreaking outcomes in the assessment of site layout and organization at the local scale as well as settlement patterns and land use at the regional scale by using airborne LIDAR technology in areas where ground-based archaeological methodologies cannot or limitedly can be employed (Chase et al. 2011; Evans and Fletcher 2015; Fisher et al. 2016). Furthermore, geophysical techniques are beneficial tools in those cases where ancient nucleated sites are covered by modern settlements (Basile et al. 2000; Papadopoulos et al. 2009; Paz-Arellano et al. 2016; Tsokas et al. 2008).

The horizontal layout of settlements recorded by noninvasive techniques reflects the sum of archaeological features detectable through these methods. Thus, the resulting overall pattern manifests a palimpsest of the entire occupational history at nucleated sites—that is, a static image of many times hundreds or, on several occasions, thousands of years. When typochronologies of particular segments of material culture (e.g., architecture, ceramics) are available, they allow for pairing specific features and materials, as well as their spatial distributions, documented over the course of noninvasive surveys with chronological phases. In the majority of cases, however, a dynamic view of settlement development must be achieved by means of additional investigations. These investigations must focus on the temporal and functional relations between the recognized spatial units of any sorts—from individual features to the entire settlement—through the application of invasive archaeological methods.

The study of vertical stratigraphical sequences developed during long-lasting, continuous habitation within specific areas or across entire sites constitutes a major challenge in archaeological fieldwork. In regard to the latter, tell sites offer the most relevant examples (Hodder 2006; Kenyon 1981; Tasić et al. 1990; see also O'Shea and Nicodemus, and Raczky this volume). In addition to stratigraphic excavations, several geophysical techniques—including the use of ground-penetrating radar and electric resistivity tomography—and the analyses of systematically collected samples vitally can assist in the interpretation of social, political, economic, and cultural developments of the settlements. Recent advancements in radiocarbon dating (e.g., Bartůněk et al. 2017; Bronk Ramsey 2008, 2009)—in conjunction with increasing affordability that permits running longer series of samples—and sequences of tree-ring dates in some regions (e.g., Lipe et al. 1999) have resulted in the opportunity for more comprehensive and high-precision chronological assessments. This, in turn, brought about more sophisticated interpretations of long-term developments at nucleated sites.

Preservation matters also significantly impact the research possibilities and understanding of prehistoric aggregated and ancient urban sites. In many parts of the world, perishable materials were used for construction and since architectural features and the spatial organization of structures are among the most important sources for settlement studies, sites with non- or less perishable construction materials have better potentials to provide more precise and valuable data to evaluate settlement dynamics (see Kaiser, Pullen, and Ryan this volume). In addition, many major nucleated sites have partially or completely been destroyed or superimposed by later construction activities. For example, at the Aztec capital of Tenochtitlan or the Roman Age London (Londinium), research opportunities are profoundly limited, and only puzzles revealed by scientific programs and rescue operations can be used to make inferences regarding their evolution (Mundy 2015; Perring 1991a). As in the case of these two major sites, contemporary written accounts, as well as ethnographic and ethnohistoric sources, can contribute greatly to the study of the development of many nucleated centers (see Birch, Kaiser, Osborne, Pullen, and Sastre and Currás this volume).

Social scientists agree that the developments of past and present demographic and political centers cannot be explored without considering their broader social, cultural, economic, and political contexts in a diachronic framework. At the regional scale, analyses of the spatial distribution of sites—with strong emphases also on environmental variables—have brought about important outcomes regarding the origins of aggregation and dispersal processes as well as concerning variations and shifts in political structures both within and between individual regions over time (Drennan et al. 2015; Johnson 1987; Kantner and Kintigh 2006; McIntosh 2005; Peterson and Drennan 2012; Savage and Falconer 2003). The majority of chapters employ regional and diachronic perspectives in the present volume.

Finally, fundamental advances have occurred lately in computer-based analytical methods for studying settlement dynamics. A range of analyses on different software platforms are utilized to explore human–environmental and social interactions, political organizations, and behavioral characteristics as they relate to spatial patterns at the local, regional, and macroregional scales (Brughmans 2010; Cutting 2003; Golitko et al. 2012; Kantner and Hobgood 2016; Knappett 2013; Kosiba and Bauer 2013; Shapiro 2005; see also Harrison and Bilgen, and Kaiser this volume). Furthermore, mathematical and statistical techniques to assess qualitative and quantitative properties and regularities in datasets facilitate in modeling a plethora of aspects related to the development of nucleated settlements. These aspects include environment, demography, movement of people and goods, and chronological sequences (e.g., Contreras and Meadows 2014; Davies et al. 2014; Diachenko and Zubrow 2015; Griffin 2011; Johnson 1987; Rosenstock 2012; Walanus 2009). Several novel laboratory techniques also contribute to the study of population dynamics, economy, and health issues at these sites (Drake et al. 2014; Papagrigorakis et al. 2006; Price et al. 2007; White et al. 2009).

COMING TOGETHER: ORIGINS AND PROCESSES

Throughout human history, large settlements have occurred primarily through the agglomeration of individuals and groups, while internal population growth has typically contributed to their genesis to a lesser extent. Growth in the number and density of population at the regional scale regularly precedes the emergence of these sites. These demographic processes—as, for example, several recent studies on the Neolithic Demographic Transition (Bocquet-Appel and Bar-Yosef 2008) as well as Birch's and Kelly's chapters in this book exemplify—frequently are associated with shifts in subsistence and dietary practices. Additionally, the archaeological record indicates that the immigration of groups also could have contributed to regional transformations toward nucleation in both prehistoric and historic times (Álvarez-Sandoval et al. 2015; Manzanilla 2017; Wilshusen and Ortman 1999; see also Birch, Kelly, and Osborne this volume).

Major anthropological questions related to population aggregations in specific regions and periods include what pressures or opportunities triggered these processes and how agglomerations unfolded. In respect to these matters, Adler, van Pool, and Leonard (1996) have provided one of the most exhaustive overviews in the archaeological literature. The authors discussed push and pull models for aggregation and abandonment among ancestral Pueblo populations, considering potential exogenous and endogenous causal agents. Social scientists studying contemporary urban dynamics commonly view these same questions from the perspective of the participant groups and individuals, exploring the costs and benefits of aggregation (e.g., Abu-Lughod 1969; Body-Gendrot and Martiniello 2000; Brown and Wardwell 1980). Although the spectrum of potential causal agents that contributed to population aggregation in various past societies is broad, most of the relevant studies conclude that models for population aggregation and dispersal must consider the interplay of multiple push and pull factors (Algaze 2008; Kelly and Brown 2014; Leonard and Reed 1993; Smith 2014). Nevertheless, one of the common grounds that many scholars share with regard to both past and present societies is that the increased level and low cost of a large number of interactions is a major driver, as well as a benefit, of population nucleation (Gaspar and Glaeser 1998; Martín and Herrera 2014; Ortman et al. 2014; Tilly 1974; see also Smith this volume). The introduction of more regular and more intensive interactions is an adaptive, and productive, response to social, economic, and political challenges. These challenges may be associated with numerous endogenous and exogenous forces in a society, such as changes in trade networks, intensification of conflicts, an elevated level of social stress, or environmental pressures. This scenario holds equally for demographic and political centers that emerged through bottom-up and top-down mechanisms (for the former, see Birch, for the latter, see Kaiser and Pullen in this volume).

In this book, a particular stress is placed upon the study of *how* aggregation developed. Concerning this question, the relationship between places and people particularly must be explored. Several theoretical models and analytical approaches have been proposed to investigate why and how certain locations in the natural and social landscape become more prominent than others during the course of the formation of nucleated settlements. For example, the extended concept of central place theory, borrowed originally from geography (Christaller 1933; see also Mulligan et al. 2012), describes how functions—such as trade or exchange of information—supplying the members of a given polity bring about demographic, economic, and political centers at specific locations in order to minimize energy and time costs of travel (Blanton 1976; Crissman 1976; Smith 1979). Location theory and gateway theory—along with central flow theory used principally in urban geography—share the view of the presence of spatial patterns in the different placements of nucleated settlements in order to supply different functions as these functions relate to different scales and types of social interactions in a given polity (Johnson 1975; Kelly 1991; Portugali 1984; Taylor et al. 2010). Additionally, spatial interaction entropy maximization (SIEM) simulations address intra- and interregional causal factors in the growth or contraction of settlements in their geographic and sociopolitical settings (Bevan and Wilson 2013; Palmisano and Altaweel 2015; Wilson 1970, 2012). Regardless of how models based on these approaches explain the occurrence of demographic centers in past societies, all of them consider a geographic scope broader than the local scale in the study of the origins and processes of population nucleation.

Concerning environmental variables, in addition to the significance of proximity of specific, valuable raw materials, analyses regarding the placement of nucleated sites commonly have pointed out the importance of the density and diversity of natural resources to supply large populations in line with the available technology and possibilities of intensification in production (Read and LeBlanc 2003; Simmons et al. 1988; see also Kelly, Osborne, O'Shea and Nicodemus, and Sastre and Currás this volume). Yet, data on outsourcing of subsistence resources as a form of tribute regularly occur in historic documents of early cities in state-level contexts (e.g., Boardman 1999; Goodchild 2006) and also may have been present in prehistoric nonstate societies (Earle 1997; Kristiansen and Larsson 2005; see Gaydarska this volume). Furthermore, landscape features promoting social and economic interactions—such as major channels, bays, and valleys near passages—constituted fundamental settlement factors as well (Palmisano and Altaweel 2015; see Ault, Pullen, and Raczky this volume).

The social value of places prior to the emergence of nucleated sites is proposed in several papers in this volume (see chapters by Fernández-Götz, Gaydarska, and Kelly). In these schemes, sites subject to periodical communal gatherings, ritual ceremonies, or pilgrimages by multiple groups sharing common ideologies become settlements through permanent aggregation. In addition, the history and practices of the first occupants might decisively have influenced the settlements' appeal to immigrants (see O'Shea and Nicodemus, Raczky, and Ryan this volume). In these cases, similarly to sites that achieved their attraction through economic development, the place value was increased by social memory relating to the actual or imaginary transformative activities of the initial settlers.

Although the archaeological record indicates that in ancient societies aggregation tended to have been the outcome of a multistep, gradual development in which environmental conditions and the history of specific places played important roles, other processes that led to rapid aggregation also occurred. These processes affected both the location and the initial demographic composition of nucleated settlements and included the agglomerations of groups due to immediate threat (Kowalewski 2006; O'Shea 1989) or the establishment of relatively large settlements for economic or militaristic reasons (Stambaugh 1988; Tsetskhladze 2006). This latter example highlights that bottom-up and top-down mechanisms governed by sociopolitical organization also may have given rise to differences in the origins of centers. More hierarchical and centralized political structures commonly produced multitiered settlement systems in which an absolute (primary) center dominated subordinate, lower-level (secondary and tertiary) centers that supplied and coordinated special functions (Bard 2008; Fox 1977; Hansen 2008; Stone 1997; see also O'Shea and Nicodemus, and Pullen this volume). During the development of these sites, however, functional properties may have shifted by altering the initial or incorporating additional functions.

With the exceptions when immigration occurred from other areas (see Birch, Kelly, and Osborne this volume) or top-down political decisions determined the foundation of a site (see Pullen this volume), aggregation in ancient societies regularly unfolded through the agglomeration of multiple groups that previously had lived in smaller and more dispersed sites across the surrounding region (e.g., Birch 2012; Weiss 1986; see also Ault and Fernández-Götz this volume). Preexisting relations—based on common origins, history, and culture, as well as shared organizational structures—that had facilitated cooperation and perception of unity provided the sociocultural foundation to bring and bind these aggregates together (Jennings and Earle 2016; Kowalewski 2006; Ur 2014). Nevertheless, *synoikismos* resulted in substantial transformations, stimulating an increased degree of social, economic, and political integration through the introduction of novel institutions and practices (see Ault, Raczky, and Ryan this volume). These shifts gave rise to new concepts of community rationale and values, a sense of place and space, property and ownership, and identity (Düring 2013; Hutson et al. 2008; Isbell 2000; Kuijt and Finlayson 2009; Oosthuizen 2013; Yaeger and Canuto 2000). In those cases when aggregation unfolded through the coalescence of multiethnic and/or socially and culturally diverse groups with moderate or no preexisting affiliation (Birch 2012; Brett Hill et al. 2004; Manzanilla 2017; see also Birch and Kelly this volume), the achievement of a high degree of integration required fundamental changes in decision-making mechanisms and political structures.

The archaeological record frequently indicates constant or multiple periods of population influx to nucleated sites over a longer period of time, resulting in the spatial expansion and reconfiguration of these settlements (see Birch, O'Shea and Nicodemus, and Raczky this volume). These successive movements of people imply that—especially when immigration was generated by bottom-up mechanisms—integration, community building, and other developments during their initial phases rendered these settlements oftentimes successful social, economic, and political configurations.

Pathways to Sustainability: Challenges and Resolutions

Regardless of geographic and temporal contexts, the overarching and enduring tasks that each nucleated community encounters include the organization of settlement to create and maintain a single socioeconomic unit and to resolve challenges related to population number and density—as well as social and occasionally cultural heterogeneity—that frequently increase over time. Accordingly, nucleated settlements are characterized by multiple horizontal and vertical decision-making (i.e., structural) units that secure required actions at various levels, from single households to the entire site. These units commonly comprise kin-based structures of immigrant groups as well as institutions intersecting these structures. These developments result in a significant increase in structural complexity compared to preceding, more independent, smaller communities featured by spatially more dispersed settlements. Cross-cultural research revealed a high degree of correspondence between population number and the degree of structural complexity. These studies demonstrate that larger amounts of inhabitants correlate with greater numbers of decision-making levels (Blanton and Fargher 2008; Carneiro 1967; Dunbar 2011; Feinman 2013; Fletcher 1995; Lekson 1985).

Social relations between structural units at nucleated settlements are channeled through interactions that bring about the formation, maintenance, and perception of community (Kosse 2001; Marcus 2000; Roberts 2010; see also Smith this volume). As population size and, in turn, structural complexity increases, an increased degree of interaction administered by more intricate rules and mechanisms must be introduced in order to maintain settlement organization and community integrity. This suggests that an increased level of social interaction leads to a higher degree of organizational complexity at large settlements than at small sites.

Preexisting ties among aggregated groups tend to facilitate the development of the required degrees of structural and organizational complexities at nucleated settlements. When sites emerge abruptly, organizational principles encoded in the social structure of a given society, as well as shared ideology, social norms, and rules of conduct, commonly regulate the aggregation process (Kowalewski 2006). In some of these cases, latent social structures become actualized to ensure social and economic mechanisms toward community cohesion and economic productivity (O'Shea 1989; Parkinson 2006). Yet, when early nucleated centers emerged as a result of the steady or periodic influx of people, reconfiguration processes might have included recurring shifts in internal socioeconomic dynamics to counteract the close physical but gradually more distant social connections between residents (see Wirth 1938:14). After all, these reconfigurations aim to maintain constant levels of integration and interaction between structural units of different size and levels within the nucleated settlements.

The development and the achieved degrees of structural and organizational complexities—and, thus, community formation and transformation—may largely be driven by immediate local-scale dynamics. These processes result in the great deal of variability documented in settlement trajectories both in prehistory and history. Regardless of contexts, though, expected and actual sociopolitical challenges associated with population size, density, and sociocultural heterogeneity at nucleated sites are overcome through social innovations. The concept of social innovation in the context of ancient nucleated settlements denotes novel solutions specifically designed for and employed in a particular community in order to develop, sustain, or restructure sociopolitical organization and community integrity. Social innovations may be proposed by individuals or groups, but their introduction is approved by higher-order structural units at these settlements. A benefit of the social innovation approach is that it permits us to focus on specific, local-scale transformative forces and mechanisms in the developments of nucleated sites, even in those cases where sociopolitical configurations are dominated or largely influenced by top-down political mechanisms.

A majority of studies on the development of prehistoric aggregated and early urban sites explore the built environment, based on the commonly shared argument in social sciences that the organization and design of a physical space is the product of a dynamic interplay between cultural, social, economic, and political actions, practices, and processes (Hillier 2008; Hillier and Hanson 1984; Lynch 1981; Parker Pearson and Richards 1994; Rapoport 1994; Saunders 1981; Tonkiss 2013). Research on the relationships between the built environment, political configurations, and social interactions has resulted in numerous theoretical perspectives and methodological approaches to reveal, interpret, and compare spatial patterns both within and between ancient nucleated sites (Arnold and Ford 1980; Fisher 2009; Fletcher 1981; Kent 1990; Smith 2007, 2011a; Vis 2014; see also Ault, Harrison and Bilgen, Kaiser, Ryan, Sastre and Currás, and Smith this volume). Through spatial units, such as overall layout, sectors, boundaries, and communal places, these studies aim to identify structural units related to internal social interactions, power structures, and community building (Ashmore and Sabloff 2002; Keith 2003; McIntosh and McIntosh 2003; Morton et al. 2014; Perring 1991b). Transformations in the spatial organization and architectural design at nucleated sites over time manifest the materialization of social innovations stimulated by shifts in ideology and/or sociopolitical organization. Thus, diachronic archaeological data must be used to recognize and explain changes in these dimensions at the site level. For example, communal facilities through regular gatherings promote community integrity and sense of collective identity (e.g., Adler 1989; Moore 1996; Rautman 2013; see also Ault, Fernández-Götz, Harrison and Bilgen, Kaiser, O'Shea and Nicodemus, and Ryan this volume), and their size, structure, architectural properties, number, and locations can alter multiple times over the course of settlement development. These modifications may indicate subsequent innovations proposed and introduced to address recurring challenges in sociopolitical organization. Although sometimes the physical properties of these innovations alone may be indicative of the specific social demands that resulted in their introduction, more frequently additional components of the archaeological record must be consulted to single out causal factors.

Diachronic analyses of the built environment at the supralocal scale fundamentally contribute to the identification of social innovations and the assessment of their sociopolitical impacts. Through its temporal and geographic distribution, inferences can be made whether a given innovation ended up being a long-term resolution to specific organizational challenges in a particular settlement community, and was adopted also at other sites across a larger area as a response to similar problems, or whether the innovation in question failed relatively quickly. For example, the presence of a standardized architectural inventory at multiple coeval settlements implies the success and spread of social innovations at the supralocal scale (see Gaydarska, Pullen, and Ryan this volume). Thus, similarly to the spatial distribution of technological novelties, the adaptation of social innovations with respect to organizational principles—manifested by various features at and spatial properties of sites in the archaeological record—may have occurred at ancient nucleated settlements. Furthermore, these adaptations could have emerged through intercultural contacts as well (see Ault, Fernández-Götz, and Sastre and Currás this volume).

Based on recent scaling studies, Smith (this volume) notes that the larger the settlement the more per capita social outputs, both positive and negative ones, evolve. The advantages of increased social interactions include community formation, however, scale-related social problems associated with the given degree of structural and organizational complexities frequently occur in large settlements. This group of social phenomena—most commonly defined as "scalar stress" (Bandy 2004; Johnson 1982, 1987), and also labeled with similar meaning as "social stress" (Düring 2013), "communication stress" (Fletcher 1995), "intracommunity conflict" (Ur 2014), and "density-dependent conflict" (Birch 2013)—constituted major managerial challenges to secure daily operation and community integrity in both prehistoric aggregated and early urban contexts. Smith (this volume) extends the definition of scalar stress to incorporate all the negative effects related to growth in population size and density. Although significant variations occurred in ancient trajectories, scalar stress was resolved through two basic processes: fission or internal reorganization (see for example Birch, Fernández-Götz, Osborne, and Sastre and Currás this volume). As for the latter, measures through the introduction of social innovations to regulate structural and organizational complexities were major tools. Most commonly, these measures might have included the reconstitution of structural units as well as the development of new mechanisms and institutions to enhance social cohesion by means of shifts in the degree of social interaction; both increase and reduction in the degree of structural and organizational complexities could have occurred. In this scenario, the development or reorganization of social hierarchies—as one of the potential techniques to reduce scalar stress (see Bandy 2004)—may be related to the required degree of structural complexity.

Innovations to avoid or counteract social tensions and foster community cohesion through the management of social interactions among structural units in nucleated sites included novel, circumstantial initiatives and also ones that already had roots in past developments. In these latter cases, preceding resolution techniques were reconfigured and reinterpreted in new, nucleated contexts (see Raczky, Ryan, and Sastre and Currás this volume). The formation and manipulation of settlement layout are fundamental, cross-cultural and cross-temporal human behavioral mechanisms to override social challenges related to population number, density, and heterogeneity (Arnauld et al. 2012; Bray 2005; Hillier and Hanson 1984; Nishimura 2014; Rapoport 1977, 1990; York et al. 2011; see also Smith this volume). These spatial techniques include various configurations of spatial compartmentalization of structural units (i.e., house clusters, neighborhoods, quarters, districts, zones), as well as the construction and reconstitution of exclusive and inclusive settings. Many times, the intermediate structural units documented in ancient nucleated settlements—neighborhoods in particular—were equivalents of smaller-scale social units that previously had formed across the region and permanently aggregated at these sites (Rodning 2002; Smith 2011b; see also Ault, Fernández-Götz, Gaydarska, Kelly, and Ryan this volume).

Although context-dependent mechanisms to prevent and resolve intrasettlement conflicts were essential, growth in population number, density, and heterogeneity in nucleated sites also required an increased level of cooperation to promote social cohesion. In addition to regular public ceremonies, norms and measures to secure a certain degree of conformity in practices (see Osborne and Ryan this volume) and large-scale communal projects—such as the construction and maintenance of defensive and ritual structures— are among the most important and archaeologically best detectable social innovations that developed and advanced community integrity and group identity through collective actions (Adler and Wilshusen 1990; Carballo 2013; Carballo et al. 2014).

As this brief discussion above illustrates, although scalar stress could have resulted in crisis and decay at nucleated settlements, when immediate and complete fission as a response to internal pressures did not occur, these challenges encouraged the development and introduction of new social innovations to foster social cohesion through transformations in community organization. To a certain extent, scale-related tensions and pressures might have been beneficial social phenomena in the long run, constituting a major driver of sociopolitical transformations in past societies. Moreover, successful social innovations were incorporated into the organizational repertoire of these societies as potential techniques in the management of internal conflicts, and may have been spread as know-hows through supralocal social networks.

TRANSFORMATIVE EFFECTS: SOCIAL, POLITICAL, AND CULTURAL CHANGE

Studies of nucleation in past societies are remarkably important for understanding pathways to cultural change and the emergence of complex social and political configurations. Although aggregation processes could have been triggered by profoundly different causal factors and developments tended to take radically diverse courses, prehistoric and historic nucleated settlements were both products and producers of major social, political, economic, and cultural transformations. Moreover, a mutual characteristic of nucleated settlements in the past and present is that their trajectories vitally impacted developments in broader geo- and sociopolitical contexts (Cronon 1991; Redfield and Singer 1954; Wheatley 1972).

Sociopolitical organization is subject to continual negotiation and transformation in human societies. Growth in population number and density at the regional and local scales frequently has been considered as the preeminent impetus for fundamental shifts in sociopolitical configurations, including the genesis and evolution of social inequality and hierarchical political structures (MacSweeney 2004; Müller 2016; Roscoe 1993; Trigger 2003; Whitelaw 2001). When spatially dispersed groups decide to fuse with large settlements, social and political dynamics that previously regulated their more segmentary relations may alter radically. As the previous section exemplifies, when compared to preceding periods, aggregation in ancient societies commonly coincided with an increased degree of structural and organizational complexities that resulted in novel sociopolitical formations. Over time, more intensive, more regular, and more sophisticatedly structured interactions among individuals and subgroups within the sites, as well as processes and challenges associated with internal social dynamics and external forces, gave rise to additional, recurring renegotiation and reconstruction of the sociopolitical organization of these nucleated settlements. These modifications may have affected structural units of all levels represented at a given site, but alterations in higher-order structural units led to more substantial transformations.

From the emergence of the earliest permanent nucleated settlements onward, interactions between structural units assured that decisions were made and measures were taken to meet community requirements. Therefore, centralized management and political control of some sorts through higher-order structural units were present to a certain degree even in the earliest prehistoric nucleated sites (Billman 2002; Hayden 2001). Nevertheless, centralization did not necessarily correspond with profound shifts in preceding social configurations toward increased levels of social inequality and permanent hierarchies (see Ault, Birch, and Ryan this volume). In societies where institutionalized, hereditary social hierarchies did not emerge, bottom-up social mechanisms through distributed political power and consensual decision-making processes likely prevailed. Corporate political structures based on egalitarian ideologies assisted the achievement of community goals and ensured social cohesion in these contexts. However, the maintenance of egalitarian sociopolitical systems requires considerable community effort and necessitates an increased degree of organizational complexity through more collective political institutions and, as a result, their per capita social costs are high relative to more autocratic structures (Feinman 2011). Archaeological and ethnographic data from nonstate societies characterized by diverse sociopolitical organizations demonstrate that oftentimes direct leveling and limiting mechanisms were employed to impede the development of hereditary social inequalities and permanent social hierarchies (Boehm 1993;

Jennings and Earle 2016; Mitchell 1988; see also Ault this volume). Social innovations to regulate economic growth and prevent wealth differences also could have been used to counteract the constant claim for and the manipulation of individual and group privileges and statuses (see Fernández-Götz, and Sastre and Currás this volume). These mechanisms, developed specifically in the crowded and congested social arena of nucleated settlements, might have persisted to assure more collective forms of control over sociopolitical transformations and power relations even after the dispersal of nucleated sites in ancient societies.

By contrast, in many cases, aggregation coincided with the intensification of sociopolitical processes toward a pronounced increase in vertical social differentiation and the introduction of highly centralized power structures (see Fernández-Götz, and O'Shea and Nicodemus this volume). At these sites—and certainly also across their polities—varying forms and degrees of political authority and social inequality could have evolved. Interestingly, even in societies with rigid social ranking, stress resolution techniques to reduce the potential of wealth inequalities as well as various forms of resistance to dominance occurred (e.g., Fox 1977; Paynter and McGuire 1991). In other contexts, opportunities for the nonelites for personal advancements to integrate and overcome socioeconomic inequality were provided so as to avoid social tensions, violent conflicts, and outmigration (see Kaiser this volume).

Settlement duration may be one of the important variables in the development of social inequality, as differential access to power and resources may have occurred more frequently at nucleated sites where habitation was longer (Adler et al. 1996). However, as long-term occupation without the formation of institutionalized social hierarchy at sites such as Çatalhöyük illustrates (Hodder 2006, 2011), a great deal of variation must be considered in this regard. As many chapters in this volume imply (see for example Birch, Gaydarska, and Harrison and Bilgen), in addition to mortuary and dietary studies, the built environment is consulted most commonly to obtain relevant data to explore wealth and status differences among individuals and subgroups in nucleated settlements. These analyses are based on the premise that the location, function, construction properties, and spatial organization of structures and other features, as well as their transformations over time, provide information about social relations and political structure (Lawrence and Low 1990; Rapoport 1982). Yet, as Harrison and Bilgen's, and Kaiser's studies of visibility—as a tool to generate or claim shifts in social status—signify in this volume, research opportunities to investigate the emergence of social inequality are constantly developing, due to advances in theory and methods (see also Paliou et al. 2014).

Regional-scale, diachronic studies are productive instruments not only for reconstructing the dynamic relationships between population centers and their hinterlands regarding the origins and maintenance of nucleated settlements but also for making inferences about long-term social and political developments (see Drennan et al. 2015; Kowalewski 2008). Several processes may account for regional site size hierarchies, and the interpretation of these patterns in regard to the degree and nature of political centralization may be difficult for multiple reasons (see Duffy 2015). However, site size distribution properties in a particular polity tend to provide useful information about the regional political landscape and its transformations over time as they relate to the developments of centers (Altaweel 2015; Drennan and Peterson 2004; Falconer and Savage 1995; see Kelly, Osborne, O'Shea and Nicodemus, and Raczky this volume).

Recent research on the evolution of social complexity in ancient, particularly state-level, societies suggests convoluted processes. By consulting data from nucleated societies to a great extent (e.g., Blanton et al. 1996; Blanton and Fargher 2012; Fargher et al. 2011b; Feinman 2012; Liu 2004), these studies indicate that when changes in sociopolitical structures occurred, they did not always develop in a linear fashion through consecutive stages from less to more hierarchical and more centralized political forma- tions. Instead, the degree of sociopolitical complexity may have fluctuated over time even during the life span of ancient nucleated settlements. Moreover, egalitarian and more hierarchical power structures may have co-occurred at both the local and regional scale (Gearing 1958; Kuijt 2002; Leach 1954). Numerous chapters in this book illustrate a wide range of trajectories with repeating transformations in integrative mechanisms and sociopolitical organizations over time (for example, see the chapters by Fernández-Götz, Osborne, O'Shea and Nicodemus, and Sastre and Currás).

Shifts in sociopolitical structures frequently coincide with substantial changes in cultural traditions (Binford 1962; Hodder 1982). As permanent population aggregation increases the intensity and frequency of social interactions, nucleated centers become important settings for cultural transformations. In conjunction with shifts in social and political dynamics, ideologies, norms, and cultural practices shared by these communities also may alter. These changes are manifested in various, recurring elements of the material culture—ranging from architectural and spatial principles to decorative style—to express group membership and identity (Carr and Neitzel 1995; Hegmon 1992; Rapoport 1982; Riebe 2016; Schortman et al. 2001). Furthermore, the relationship between sociopolitical and cultural change is reciprocal, as modifications in ideologies and related practices also can account for transformations in sociopolitical configurations. For example, with a shift to cosmological principles that promote monumentality in architecture—a phenomenon frequently associated with the development of ancient nucleated settlements—managerial requirements, including design, organization, and mobilization of labor, offer opportu- nities to create and manipulate the status of individuals and groups within a society (Adler and Wilshusen 1990; Clark and Martinsson-Wallin 2007; Osborne 2014; Trigger 1990). Through social interactions within and between polities, the proposed alterations in cultural norms and practices may spread beyond the confines of nucleated settlements, and a great deal of them become approved and dominant over a larger geographic area, perceived as the spatial unit of "culture" in archaeology.

The termination of nucleated settlements and their polities oftentimes appears to have occurred within a remarkably short period of time at the regional and many times also at the macroregional scale (Borić 2015; Possehl 1997; Tainter 1988; Yasuda et al. 2004; see also Gaydarska, Harrison and Bilgen, O'Shea and Nicodemus, and Raczky this volume). Although the discussion of variation in causal forces and processes of settlement abandonment is beyond the principal scopes of this volume, as several papers illustrate (for example, see Fernández-Götz, O'Shea and Nicodemus, and Pullen) both external factors and internal socioeconomic transformations played vital roles (see also Adler et al. 1996; Buckley et al. 2010; Demarest 2003; Hoggarth et al. 2016; Knappett et al. 2011). More importantly in the context of this book, the abandonment of nucleated settlements and the formation of more dispersed and more loosely integrated village networks frequently is accompanied by a decreased degree of social complexity (see Fernández-Götz this volume), the introduction of new social practices (see Gaydarska this volume), and major transformations in material culture and symbology (see Raczky this volume).

Archaeological research incorporating long-term, diachronic perspectives into the study of sociocultural trajectories commonly identifies cycles of aggregation and dispersal, centralization and decentralization of power, as well as reveals periodic shifts in the degree of social complexity in ancient societies (Arakawa 2012; Gavrilets et al. 2010; Kowalewski 2008; Müller 2012; Parkinson 2002; Ur 2010; see also Fernández-Götz, Raczky, and Sastre and Currás this volume). As a matter of fact, the chapters focusing on ancient Greece in this book by Ault, Osborne, and Pullen illustrate that even in regions recognized as core areas of early urban developments and state formation in the world, urbanization and sociocultural change exhibit a nonlinear evolutionary pattern with cycles between growth and decay, florescence and collapse, and less and more complex sociopolitical configurations (see also Faulseit 2016; Marcus 1998; Schwartz and Nichols 2006; Wilkinson et al. 2014).

FINAL REMARKS

The latest edition of the *Global Trends Report*—a strategic document released by the National Intelligence Council of the United States (2017) every four years to assess major trends in the world during the next 20 years—envisions a radical increase in the role of large cities. In addition to a great deal of growth in the importance of metropolises as nodes in global networks, the study predicts that their local governance will have a tremendous impact on the political agendas of national governments. According to the report, innovations, entrepreneurship, and shared knowledge stimulated by "creative connectivity" (Glaeser 2011) and "energized crowding" (Smith this volume) as well as services provided at the local level will further enhance the significance of these centers as "social reactors" (Bettencourt 2013; see also Smith this volume). These predictions indicate the formation of more decentralized and more autonomous power structures, with a remarkable decrease in the degree of political integration. Compared to previous settings, in these systems, large cities' populations will rely heavily on local-scale initiatives and increased regional political power of their leaders, and on the cooperation with other similar centers through interregional networks. Along with these changes, lower-level centers would become economically and politically more dependent on the primary centers. From many points of view, the anticipated trajectory proposed in the *Global Trends Report* might appear to be familiar to archaeologists. Albeit at smaller geographic scales, analogous developments occurred in numerous cultural and temporal contexts across the globe (Hansen 2000, 2002; Nichols and Charlton 1997; Raczky 2015).

Nevertheless, as previously discussed, the historic pathways of powerful ancient nucleated settlements demonstrate that in addition to macroregional and regional factors, local social processes critically affected their development. A new initiative recently proposed in one of the most dynamically growing, current megacities perfectly exemplifies the significance of timeless, local-scale social challenges in nucleated contexts and provides me with the opportunity to return to my original question, with a bit of twist: What *should* cities offer people, in both the past and present, to make them desirable places of habitation?

In March 2016, the British newspaper *The Guardian* published an article about recent developments in the desert city of Dubai in the United Arab Emirates (Keenan 2016). The article reports that in order to obstruct a decreasing trend in "happiness inequality" in the city, the Emirates appointed its first Minister of State for Happiness, who started collecting data on how government services affect happiness in Dubai. A CEO of an investment holding summarizes the goal of the initiative in the article as follows: "Once we are able to manage and meet people's experiences, we will be able to rise on the happiness index. It is vital because if people are not happy, they don't stick around in the city; they leave." The simultaneous establishment of the Ministry of Tolerance to promote understanding and cooperation among the wide range of religious and ethnic groups in the United Arab Emirates, and particularly in Dubai, reflects the group aspect of social challenges with which large cities face.

These initiatives have occurred within the context of an absolute monarchy featured by autocratic leadership and a lack of general elections—the complete opposite of collective power structures. This example provides us with an important conclusion about the interplay between individual and group motivations and political power both in present and past nucleated societies. Regardless of social, political, and cultural contexts, the long-term and politically predictable participation of individuals and groups influenced by the dynamic relationship between social and economic costs and benefits determine the integrity and, thus, the future of a community. Importantly, this holds true even in societies with highly stratified sociopolitical configurations with domineering power and hegemony over each member of the society. Social innovations—such as the new ministries as structural units in the United Arab Emirates—have been crucial contributions to assure resilience and sustainability in the development of nucleated communities throughout human history.

Undoubtedly, one of the most important lessons that can be learned from the past is that cities are not everlasting entities—they are complex and, therefore, fragile configurations. Cycles of growth and decline reoccur, and the decay—and many times the complete disintegration—of even the most prominent and prosperous cities is just matter of time. As, for example, the Rust Belt cities in the American Midwest demonstrate, although we possess a great deal of tools and techniques to document and also change urban processes, the line between florescence and failure is still remarkably thin.

By presenting approaches, data, and interpretations regarding variation in societal trajectories, archaeology provides another essential dimension, the long-term perspective, to understand social, economic, political, and cultural principles and mechanisms as they relate to population nucleation. Edited volumes such as this are important steps in encouraging interdisciplinary dialogues and sorting out proper solutions to prevent and overcome challenges in modern urban environments.

ACKNOWLEDGMENTS

This volume is the product of the mutual and dedicated efforts of numerous people. I am deeply thankful to Peter Biehl, Stephen Dyson, and the other members of the IEMA board for their continuous encouragement and support that critically contributed to the success of the 9th IEMA Visiting Scholar Conference and made my stay in Buffalo productive and unforgettable. I am very grateful to the authors for their insightful contributions and exemplary cooperation during the conference and in the course of the preparation of this book. I am honored for the opportunity to work with such a prominent group of scholars and wonderful people. Additionally, I would like to thank the reviewers for their valuable comments. Lastly, I extend my appreciation to the administrative staff of the Department of Anthropology, many students, and my wife, Danielle Riebe, who all provided me with a tremendous amount of help in the organization and operation of the conference.

REFERENCES CITED

Abu-Lughod, J. 1969 *The City Is Dead—Long Live the City: Some Thoughts on Urbanity.* Monograph 12. Center for Planning and Development Research, University of California, Berkeley.

Adams, R. McC. 1966 *The Evolution of Urban Society: Early Mesopotamia and Prehispanic Mexico.* Aldine, Chicago.

Adler, M. A. 1989 Ritual Facilities and Social Integration in Nonranked Societies. In *The Architecture of Social Integration in Prehistoric Pueblos*, edited by W. D. Lipe and M. Hegmon, pp. 35–52. Crow Canyon Archaeological Center, Cortez, Colorado.

Adler, M. A., T. van Pool, and R. D. Leonard 1996 Ancestral Pueblo Population Aggregation and Abandonment in the North American Southwest. *Journal of World Prehistory* 10:375–438.

Adler, M. A., and R. H. Wilshusen 1990 Large-Scale Integrative Facilities in Tribal Societies: Cross-Cultural and Southwestern US Examples. *World Archaeology* 22(2):133–146.

Algaze, G. 2008 *Ancient Mesopotamia at the Dawn of Civilization: The Evolution of an Urban Landscape.* University of Chicago Press, Chicago.

Altaweel, M. 2015 Settlement Dynamics and Hierarchy from Agent Decision-Making: A Method Derived from Entropy Maximization. *Journal of Archaeological Method and Theory* 22(4):1122–1150.

Álvarez-Sandoval, B. A., L. R. Manzanilla, M. González-Ruiz, A. Malgosa, and R. Montiel 2015 Genetic Evidence Supports the Multiethnic Character of Teopancazco, a Neighborhood Center of Teotihuacan, Mexico (AD 200–600). *PLOS ONE* 10(7):e0132371.

Arakawa, F. 2012 Cyclical Cultural Trajectories: A Case Study from the Mesa Verde Region. *Journal of Anthropological Research* 68(1):35–69.

Arnauld, M. C., L. R. Manzanilla, and M. E. Smith (editors) 2012 *The Neighborhood as a Social and Spatial Unit in Mesoamerican Cities*. The University of Arizona Press, Tucson.

Arnold, J. E., and A. Ford 1980 A Statistical Examination of Settlement Patterns at Tikal, Guatemala. *American Antiquity* 45(4):713–726.

Ashmore, W., and J. A. Sabloff 2002 Spatial Orders in Maya Civic Plans. *Latin American Antiquity* 13(2):201–215.

Bandy, M. S. 2004 Fissioning, Scalar Stress, and Social Evolution in Early Village Societies. *American Anthropologist* 106(2):322–333.

Bard, K. A. 2008 Royal Cities and Cult Centers, Administrative Towns, and Workmen's Settlements in Ancient Egypt. In *The Ancient City: New Perspectives on Urbanism in the Old and New World*, edited by J. Marcus and J. A. Sabloff, pp. 165–182. School for Advanced Research, Santa Fe, New Mexico.

Bartůněk, V., K. Dobrovolný, M. Švecová, P. Matějka, P. Šída, P. Pokorný, M. Kuchař, and E. Černá 2017 Obtaining Black Carbon—A Simple Method for the Safe Removal of Mineral Components from Soils and Archaeological Layers. *Archaeometry* 59(2):346–355.

Basile, V., M. T. Carrozzo, S. Negri, L. Nuzzo, T. Quarta, and A. V. Villani 2000 A Ground-Penetrating Radar Survey for Archaeological Investigations in an Urban Area (Lecce, Italy). *Journal of Applied Geophysics* 44(1):15–32.

Bettencourt, L. M. A. 2013 The Origins of Scaling in Cities. *Science* 340(6139):1438–1441.

Bettencourt, L. M. A., J. Lobo, D. Helbing, C. Kühnert, and G. B. West 2007 Growth, Innovation, Scaling, and the Pace of Life in Cities. *Proceedings of the National Academy of Sciences* 104(17):7301–7306.

Bevan, A., and A. Wilson 2013 Models of Settlement Hierarchy Based on Partial Evidence. *Journal of Archaeological Science* 40(5):2415–2427.

Billman, B. R. 2002 Irrigation and the Origins of the Southern Moche State on the North Coast of Peru. *Latin American Antiquity* 13(4):371–400.

Binford, L. 1962 Archaeology as Anthropology. *American Antiquity* 28(2):217–225.

Birch, J. 2012 Coalescent Communities: Settlement Aggregation and Social Integration in Iroquoian Ontario. *American Antiquity* 77(4):646–670.

Birch, J. 2013 Between Prehistoric Villages and Cities: Settlement Aggregation in Cross-Cultural Perspective. In *From Prehistoric Villages to Cities: Settlement Aggregation and Community Transformation*, edited by J. Birch, pp. 1–22. Routledge, New York.

Blanton, R. E. 1976 Anthropological Studies of Cities. *Annual Review of Anthropology* 5:249–264.

Blanton, R. E., and L. F. Fargher 2008 *Collective Action in the Formation of Pre-Modern States*. Springer, New York.

Blanton, R. E., and L. F. Fargher 2012 Neighborhoods and the Civic Constitutions of Premodern Cities as Seen From the Perspective of Collective Actions. In *The Neighborhood as a Social and Spatial Unit in Mesoamerican Cities*, edited by M. C. Arnauld, L. R. Manzanilla, and M. E. Smith, pp. 27–52. The University of Arizona Press, Tucson.

Blanton, R. E., G. M. Feinman, S. A. Kowalewski, and P. N. Peregrine 1996 A Dual-Processual Theory for the Evolution of Mesoamerican Civilization. *Current Anthropology* 37(1):1–14.

Blanton, R. E., S. A. Kowalewski, G. M. Feinman, and L. Finsten 1993 *Ancient Mesoamerica: A Comparison of Change in Three Regions*. 2nd ed. Cambridge University Press, Cambridge.

Boardman, J. 1999 *The Greeks Overseas: Their Early Colonies and Trade*. 4th ed. Thames and Hudson, London.

Bocquet-Appel, J.-P., and O. Bar-Yosef (editors) 2008 *The Neolithic Demographic Transition and Its Consequences*. Springer, Dordrecht.

Body-Gendrot, S., and M. Martiniello (editors) 2000 *Minorities in European Cities: The Dynamics of Social Integration and Social Exclusion at the Neighborhood Level*. St. Martin's Press, New York.

Boehm, C. 1993 Egalitarian Behavior and Reverse Dominance Hierarchy. *Current Anthropology* 34(3):227–254.

Bogue, D. J. 1977 A Migrant's-Eye View of the Costs and Benefits of Migration to a Metropolis. In *Internal Migration: A Comparative Perspective*, edited by A. A. Brown and E. Neuberger, pp. 167–182. Academic Press, New York.

Borić, D. 2015 The End of the Vinča World: Modelling the Neolithic to Copper Age Transition and the Notion of Archaeological Culture. In *Neolithic and Copper Age Between the Carpathians and the Aegean Sea: Chronologies and Technologies from the 6th to 4th Millennium BC*, edited by S. Hansen, P. Raczky, A. Anders, and A. Reingruber, pp. 157–217. Dr. Rudolf Habelt, Bonn.

Bray, D. 2005 *Social Space and Governance in Urban China: The Danwei System from Origins to Reform*. Stanford University Press, Stanford, California.

Brett Hill, J., J. J. Clark, W. H. Doelle, and P. D. Lyons 2004 Prehistoric Demography in the Southwest: Migration, Coalescence, and Hohokam Population Decline. *American Antiquity* 69(4):689–716.

Bronk Ramsey, C. 2008 Radiocarbon Dating: Revolutions in Understanding. *Archaeometry* 50(2):249–275.

Bronk Ramsey, C. 2009 Dealing with Outliers and Offsets in Radiocarbon Dating. *Radiocarbon* 51(3):1023–1045.

Brown, D. L., and J. M. Wardwell (editors) 1980 *New Directions in Urban–Rural Migration: The Population Turnaround in Rural America*. Academic Press, New York.

Browning, H. L. 1971 Migrant Selectivity and the Growth of Large Cities in Developing Societies. In *Rapid Population Growth: Consequences and Policy Implications*, pp. 273–314. National Academy of Sciences, Office of the Foreign Secretary, Johns Hopkins Press, Baltimore.

Brughmans, T. 2010 Connecting the Dots: Towards Archaeological Network Analysis. *Oxford Journal of Archaeology* 29(3):277–303.

Buckley, B. M., K. J. Anchukaitis, D. Penny, R. Fletcher, E. R. Cook, M. Sano, L. C. Nam, A. Wichienkeeo, T. T. Minh, and T. M. Hong 2010 Climate as a Contributing Factor in the Demise of Angkor, Cambodia. *Proceedings of the National Academy of Sciences* 107(15):6748–6752.

Butzer, K. W. 2008 Other Perspectives on Urbanism: Beyond Disciplinary Boundaries. In *The Ancient City: New Perspectives on Urbanism in the Old and New World*, edited by J. Marcus and J. A. Sabloff, pp. 77–92. School for Advanced Research, Santa Fe, New Mexico.

Capello, R., and P. Nijkamp (editors) 2004 *Urban Dynamics and Growth: Advances in Urban Economics*. Contributions to Economic Analysis 266. Elsevier, Oxford.

Carballo, D. M. (editor) 2013 *Cooperation and Collective Action: Archaeological Perspectives*. University of Colorado Press, Boulder.

Carballo, D. M., and B. Fortenberry 2015 Bridging Prehistory and History in the Archaeology of Cities. *Journal of Field Archaeology* 40(5):542–559.

Carballo, D. M., P. Roscoe, and G. M. Feinman 2014 Cooperation and Collective Action in the Cultural Evolution of Complex Societies. *Journal of Archaeological Method and Theory* 21(1):98–133.

Carneiro, R. L. 1967 On the Relationship Between Size of Population and Complexity of Social Organization. *Southwestern Journal of Anthropology* 23(3):234–243.

Carr, C., and J. E. Neitzel (editors) 1995 *Style, Society, and Person: Archaeological and Ethnological Perspectives.* Plenum Press, New York.

Cesaretti, R., J. Lobo, L. M. A. Bettencourt, S. Ortman, and M. E. Smith 2015 Population–Area Relationship in Medieval European Cities. *SFI Working Paper* 2015-10-036. Santa Fe Institute, Santa Fe, New Mexico.

Chapman, J., M. Y. Videiko, D. Hale, B. Gaydarska, N. Burdo, K. Rassmann, C. Mischka, J. Müller, A. Korvin-Piotrovskiy, and V. Kruts 2014 The Second Phase of the Trypillia Mega-Site Methodological Revolution: A New Research Agenda. *European Journal of Archaeology* 17(3):369–406.

Chase, A. F., D. Z. Chase, J. F. Weishampel, J. B. Drake, R. L. Shrestha, K. C. Slatton, J. J. Awe, and W. E. Carter 2011 Airborne LiDAR, Archaeology, and the Ancient Maya Landscape at Caracol, Belize. *Journal of Archaeological Science* 38(2):387–398.

Childe, V. G. 1950 The Urban Revolution. *Town Planning Review* 21:3–17.

Christaller, W. 1933 *Die zentralen Orte in Süddeutschland.* Gustav Fischer, Jena.

Clark, G., and H. Martinsson-Wallin 2007 Monumental Architecture in West Polynesia: Origins, Chiefs and Archaeological Approaches. *Archaeology in Oceania* 42:28–40.

Colantonio, A., and T. Dixon 2011 *Urban Regeneration and Social Sustainability: Best Practice from European Cities.* Wiley-Blackwell, Chichester.

Contreras, D. A., and J. Meadows 2014 Summed Radiocarbon Calibrations as a Population Proxy: A Critical Evaluation Using a Realistic Simulation Approach. *Journal of Archaeological Science* 52:591–608.

Cowgill, G. L. 2004 Origins and Development of Urbanism: Archaeological Perspectives. *Annual Review of Anthropology* 33:525–549.

Crane, D., N. Kawashima, and K. Kawasaki (editors) 2016 *Global Culture: Media, Arts, Policy, and Globalization.* 2nd ed. Routledge, New York.

Creekmore III, A. T., and K. D. Fisher (editors) 2014 *Making Ancient Cities: Space and Place in Early Urban Societies.* Cambridge University Press, New York.

Crissman, L. W. 1976 Specific Central Place Models for an Evolving System of Market Towns on the Changhua Plain, Taiwan. In *Regional Analysis*, Vol. I, edited by C. A. Smith, pp. 183–218. Academic Press, New York.

Cronon, W. 1991 *Nature's Metropolis: Chicago and the Great West.* W. W. Norton, New York.

Cutting, M. 2003 The Use of Spatial Analysis to Study Prehistoric Settlement Architecture. *Oxford Journal of Archaeology* 22(1):1–21.

Davies, T., H. Fry, A. G. Wilson, A. Palmisano, M. Altaweel, and K. Radner 2014 Application of an Entropy Maximizing and Dynamics Model for Understanding Settlement Structure: The Khabur Triangle in the Middle Bronze and Iron Ages. *Journal of Archaeological Science* 43:141–154.

Diachenko, A., and E. B. W. Zubrow 2015 Stabilization Points in Carrying Capacity: Population Growth and Migrations. *Journal of Neolithic Archaeology* 17:1–15.

Demarest, A. 2013 The Collapse of the Classic Maya Kingdoms of the Southwestern Petén: Implications for the End of Classic Maya Civilization. In *Millenary Maya Societies: Past Crises and Resilience*, edited by M.-C. Arnauld and A. Breton, pp. 22–48. Electronic document: www.mesoweb.com/publications/MMS/2_Demarest.pdf.

Dennehy, T. J., B. W. Stanley, and M. E. Smith 2016 Social Inequality and Access to Services in Premodern Cities. In *Archaeology of the Human Experience*, edited by M. Hegmon, pp. 143–160. Archeological Papers of the American Anthropological Association 27. American Anthropological Association, Washington, D.C.

de Souza Briggs, X. 2004 Civilization in Color: The Multicultural City in Three Millennia. *City and Community* 3:311–342.

Donati, J. C., and A. Sarris 2016 Geophysical Survey in Greece: Recent Developments, Discoveries, and Future Prospects. *Archaeological Reports* 62:63–76.

Drake B. L., W. H. Wills, M. I. Hamilton, and W. Dorshow 2014 Strontium Isotopes and the Reconstruction of the Chaco Regional System: Evaluating Uncertainty with Bayesian Mixing Models. *PLOS ONE* 9(5):e95580.

Drennan, R. D., C. A. Berrey, and C. E. Peterson 2015 *Regional Settlement Demography in Archaeology*. Eliot Werner, Clinton Corners, New York.

Drennan, R. D., and C. E. Peterson 2004 Comparing Archaeological Settlement Systems with Rank-Size Graphs: A Measure of Shape and Statistical Confidence. *Journal of Archaeological Science* 31(5):533–549.

Drennan, R. D., and C. E. Peterson 2012 Challenges for Comparative Study of Early Complex Societies. In *The Comparative Archaeology of Complex Societies*, edited by M. E. Smith, pp. 62–87. Cambridge University Press, Cambridge.

Duffy, P. R. 2015 Site Size Hierarchy in Middle-Range Societies. *Journal of Anthropological Archaeology* 37:85–99.

Dunbar, R. I. M. 2011 Constraints on the Evolution of Social Institutions and Their Implications for Information Flow. *Journal of Institutional Economics* 7(3):345–371.

Düring, B. S. 2013 The Anatomy of a Prehistoric Community: Reconsidering Çatalhöyük. In *From Prehistoric Villages to Cities: Settlement Aggregation and Community Transformation*, edited by J. Birch, pp. 23–43. Routledge, New York.

Earle, T. 1997 *How Chiefs Come to Power: The Political Economy in Prehistory*. Stanford University Press, Stanford, California.

Ehrenreich, R. M., C. L. Crumley, and J. E. Levy (editors) 1995 *Heterarchy and the Analysis of Complex Societies*. Archaeological Papers of the American Anthropological Association No. 6(1). Washington, D.C.

Evans, D., and R. Fletcher 2015 The Landscape of Angkor Wat Redefined. *Antiquity* 89(348): 1402–1419.

Falconer, S. E., and S. H. Savage 1995 Heartlands and Hinterlands: Alternative Trajectories of Early Urbanization in Mesopotamia and the Southern Levant. *American Antiquity* 69(1):37–58.

Fargher, L. F., V. Y. Heredia Espinoza, and R. E. Blanton 2011a Alternative Pathways to Power in Late Postclassic Highland Mesoamerica. *Journal of Anthropological Archaeology* 30(3):306–326.

Fargher, L. F., R. E. Blanton, V. Y. Heredia Espinoza, J. Millhauser, N. Xiuhtecutli, and L. Overholtzer 2011b Tlaxcallan: The Archaeology of an Ancient Republic in the New World. *Antiquity* 85(327):172–186.

Faulseit, R. K. (editor) 2016 *Beyond Collapse: Archaeological Perspectives on Resilience, Revitalization, and Transformation in Complex Societies*. Occasional Paper 42. Center for Archaeological Investigations, Southern Illinois University, Carbondale.

Feinman, G. M. 2011 Size, Complexity, and Organizational Variation: A Comparative Approach. *Cross-Cultural Research* 45(1):37–58.

Feinman, G. M. 2012 Comparative Frames for the Diachronic Analysis of Complex Societies: Next Steps. In *The Comparative Archaeology of Complex Societies*, edited by M. E. Smith, pp. 21–43. Cambridge University Press, Cambridge.

Feinman, G. M. 2013 The Emergence of Social Complexity: Why More than Population Size Matters. In *Cooperation and Collective Action: Archaeological Perspectives*, edited by D. M. Carballo, pp. 35–56. University of Colorado Press, Boulder.

Feinman, G. M., and J. Neitzel 1984 Too Many Types: An Overview of Sedentary Prestate Societies in the Americas. *Advances in Archaeological Method and Theory* 7:39–102.

Feinman, G. M., and T. D. Price 2010 Social Inequality and the Evolution of Human Social Organization. In *Pathways to Power: New Perspectives on the Emergence of Social Inequality*, edited by T. D. Price and G. M. Feinman, pp. 1–14. Springer, New York.

Fernández-Götz, M., and D. Krausse (editors) 2016 *Eurasia at the Dawn of History: Urbanization and Social Change*. Cambridge University Press, New York.

Fisher, K. D. 2009 Placing Social Interaction: An Integrative Approach to Analyzing Past Built Environments. *Journal of Anthropological Archaeology* 28(4):439–457.

Fisher C. T., J. C. Fernández-Diaz, A. S. Cohen, O. Neil Cruz, A. M. Gonzáles, and S. J. Leisz 2016 Identifying Ancient Settlement Patterns through LiDAR in the Mosquitia Region of Honduras. *PLOS ONE* 11(8):e0159890.

Fletcher, R. 1981 Space and Community Behaviour: A Discussion of the Form and Function of Spatial Order in Settlements. In *Universals of Human Thought*, edited by B. B. Lloyd and J. Gay, pp. 71–110. Cambridge University Press, Cambridge.

Fletcher, R. 1995 *The Limits of Settlement Growth: A Theoretical Outline*. Cambridge University Press, Cambridge.

Fox, R. G. 1977 *Urban Anthropology: Cities in Their Cultural Settings*. Prentice-Hall, Englewood Cliffs, New Jersey.

Fried, M. 1967 *The Evolution of Political Society: An Essay in Political Anthropology*. Random House, New York.

Gaspar, J., and E. L. Glaeser 1998 Information Technology and the Future of Cities. *Journal of Urban Economics* 43(1):136–156.

Gavrilets, S., D. G. Anderson, and P. Turchin 2010 Cycling in the Complexity of Early Societies. *Cliodynamics* 1(1):58–80.

Gearing, F. 1958 The Structural Poses of 18th Century Cherokee Villages. *American Anthropologist* 60(6):1148–1157.

Glaeser, E. 2011 *Triumph of the City: How Our Greatest Invention Makes Us Richer, Smarter, Greener, Healthier, and Happier*. Penguin Press, London.

Golitko, M., J. Meierhoff, G. M. Feinman, and P. R. Williams 2012 Complexities of Collapse: The Evidence of Maya Obsidian as Revealed by Social Network Graphical Analysis. *Antiquity* 86(332):507–523.

Goodchild, H. 2006 Modelling Roman Demography and Urban Dependency in Central Italy. In *TRAC 2005: Proceedings of the Fifteenth Annual Theoretical Roman Archaeology Conference*, edited by B. Croxford, H. Goodchild, J. Lucas, and N. Ray, pp. 42–56. Oxbow Books, Oxford.

Gottdiener, M., and L. Budd 2005 *Key Concepts in Urban Studies*. Sage, London.

Griffin, A. F. 2011 Emergence of Fusion/Fission Cycling and Self-Organized Criticality from a Simulation Model of Early Complex Polities. *Journal of Archaeological Science* 38:873–883.

Hansen, M. H. (editor) 2000 *A Comparative Study of Thirty City-State Cultures: An Investigation*. Historisk-filosofiske Skrifter 21. Kongelige Danske Videnskabernes Selskab, Copenhagen.

Hansen, M. H. (editor) 2002 *A Comparative Study of Six City-State Cultures: An Investigation Conducted by the Copenhagen Polis Centre*. Historisk-filosofiske Skrifter 27. Kongelige Danske Videnskabernes Selskab, Copenhagen.

Hansen, M. H. 2008 Analyzing Cities. In *The Ancient City: New Perspectives on Urbanism in the Old and New World*, edited by J. Marcus and J. A. Sabloff, pp. 67–76. School for Advanced Research, Santa Fe, New Mexico.

Hayden, B. 2001 Richman, Poorman, Beggarman, Chief: The Dynamics of Social Inequality. In *Archaeology at the Millennium: A Sourcebook*, edited by G. M. Feinman and T. D. Price, pp. 231–272. Kluwer Academic/Plenum Press, New York.

Hegmon, M. 1992 Archaeological Research on Style. *Annual Review of Anthropology* 21:517–536.

Hillier, B. 2008 Space and Spatiality: What the Built Environment Needs from Social Theory. *Building Research and Information* 36:216–230.

Hillier, B., and J. Hanson 1984 *The Social Logic of Space*. Cambridge University Press, Cambridge.

Hodder, I. 1982 *Symbols in Action: Ethnoarchaeological Studies of Material Culture*. Cambridge University Press, Cambridge.

Hodder, I. 2006 *The Leopard's Tale: Revealing the Mysteries of Çatalhöyük*. Thames and Hudson, New York.

Hodder, I. 2011 Çatalhöyük: A Prehistoric Settlement on the Konya Plain. In *The Oxford Handbook of Ancient Anatolia*, edited by S. R. Steadman and G. McMahon, pp. 934–949. Oxford University Press, Oxford.

Hoggarth, J. A., S. F. M. Breitenbach, B. J. Culleton, C. E. Ebert, M. A. Masson, and D. J. Kennett 2016 The Political Collapse of Chichén Itzá in Climatic and Cultural Context. *Global and Planetary Change* 138:25–42.

Hohenberg, P. M., and L. H. Lees 1985 *The Making of Urban Europe, 1000–1950*. Harvard University Press, Cambridge, Massachusetts.

Hutson, S. R., D. R. Hixson, A. Magnoni, D. Mazeau, and B. Dahlin 2008 Site and Community at Chunchucmil and Ancient Maya Urban Centers. *Journal of Field Archaeology* 33(1):19–40.

Isbell, W. H. 2000 What We Should be Studying: The "Imagined Community" and the "Natural Community." In *The Archaeology of Communities: A New World Perspective*, edited by M. A. Canuto and J. Yaeger, pp. 243–266. Routledge, New York.

Jacobs, J. 1969 *The Economy of Cities*. Random House, New York.

Jennings, J. 2016 *Killing Civilization: A Reassessment of Early Urbanism and Its Consequences*. University of New Mexico Press, Albuquerque.

Jennings, J., and T. Earle 2016 Urbanization, State Formation, and Cooperation: A Reappraisal. *Current Anthropology* 57(4):474–493.

Johnson, G. A. 1975 Locational Analysis and the Investigation of Uruk Local Exchange Systems. In *Ancient Civilization and Trade*, edited by J. A. Sabloff and C. C. Lamberg-Karlovsky, pp. 285–339. University of New Mexico Press, Albuquerque.

Johnson, G. A. 1982 Organizational Structure and Scalar Stress. In *Theory and Explanation in Archaeology: The Southampton Conference*, edited by C. Renfrew, M. J. Rowlands, and B. A. Segraves, pp. 389–421. Academic Press, New York.

Johnson, G. A. 1987 The Changing Organization of Uruk Administration on the Susiana Plain. In *The Archaeology of Western Iran*, edited by F. Hole, pp. 107–139. Smithsonian Institution Press, Washington, D.C.

Kantner, J., and R. Hobgood 2016 A GIS-Based Viewshed Analysis of Chacoan Tower Kivas in the US Southwest: Were They for Seeing or to Be Seen? *Antiquity* 90(353):1302–1317.

Kantner, J., and K. W. Kintigh 2006 The Chaco World. In *The Archaeology of Chaco Canyon: An Eleventh-Century Pueblo Regional Center*, edited by S. H. Lekson, pp. 153–188. School of American Research Press, Santa Fe, New Mexico.

Keenan, J. 2016 Dubai Wants to Be "World's Happiest City." Report Says It Has a Long Way to Go. *The Guardian*, 16 March. Electronic document: https://www.theguardian.com/cities/2016/mar/16/world-happiest-city-dubai-happiness-index-report.

Keith, K. 2003 The Spatial Patterning of Everyday Life in Old Babylonian Neighborhoods. In *The Social Construction of Ancient Cities*, edited by M. L. Smith, pp. 56–80. Smithsonian Institution Press, Washington, D.C.

Kelly, J. E. 1991 Cahokia and Its Role as a Gateway Center in Interregional Exchange. In *Cahokia and the Hinterlands: Middle Mississippian Cultures of the Midwest*, edited by T. E. Emerson and R. B. Lewis, pp. 61–80. University of Illinois Press, Urbana.

Kelly, J. E., and J. A. Brown 2014 Cahokia: The Processes and Principles of the Creation of an Early Mississippian City. In *Making Ancient Cities: Space and Place in Early Urban Societies*, edited by A. T. Creekmore III and K. D. Fisher, pp. 292–336. Cambridge University Press, New York.

Kent, S. (editor) 1990 *Domestic Architecture and the Use of Space: An Interdisciplinary Cross-Cultural Study*. Cambridge University Press, Cambridge.

Kenyon, K. M. 1981 *Excavations at Jericho: The Architecture and Stratigraphy of the Tell*. Vol. 3. British School of Archaeology in Jerusalem, London.

Knappett, C. (editor) 2013 *Network Analysis in Archaeology: New Approaches to Regional Interaction*. Oxford University Press, Oxford.

Knappett, C., R. Rivers, and T. Evans 2011 The Theran Eruption and Minoan Palatial Collapse: New Interpretations Gained from Modelling the Maritime Network. *Antiquity* 85(329):1008–1023.

Kosiba, S., and A. M. Bauer 2013 Mapping the Political Landscape: Toward a GIS Analysis of Environmental and Social Difference. *Journal of Archaeological Method and Theory* 20(1):61–101.

Kosse, K. 2001 Some Regularities in Human Group Formation and the Evolution of Societal Complexity. *Complexity* 6(1):60–64.

Kostof, S. 1991 *The City Shaped: Urban Patterns and Meanings through History*. Little Brown, Boston.

Kowalewski, S. A. 2006 Coalescent Societies. In *Light on the Path: The Anthropology and History of the Southeastern Indians*, edited by T. J. Pluckhahn and R. Ethridge, pp. 94–122. The University of Alabama Press, Tuscaloosa.

Kowalewski, S. A. 2008 Regional Settlement Pattern Studies. *Journal of Archaeological Research* 16(3):225–285.

Kristiansen, K., and T. B. Larsson 2005 *The Rise of Bronze Age Society: Travels, Transmissions and Transformations*. Cambridge University Press, New York.

Kuijt, I. 2002 Near Eastern Neolithic Research: Directions and Trends. In *Life in Neolithic Farming Communities: Social Organization, Identity, and Differentiation*, edited by I. Kuijt, pp. 311–322. Springer, New York.

Kuijt, I., and B. Finlayson 2009 Evidence for Food Storage and Predomestication Granaries 11,000 Years Ago in the Jordan Valley. *Proceedings of the National Academy of Sciences* 106(27):10966–10970.

Laurence, R. 2007 *Roman Pompeii: Space and Society.* Routledge, New York.

Lawrence, D. L., and S. M. Low 1990 The Built Environment and Spatial Form. *Annual Review of Anthropology* 19:453–505.

Leach, E. 1954 *Political Systems of Highland Burma: A Study of Kachin Social Structure.* G. Bell and Sons, London.

Lekson, S. H. 1985 Largest Settlement Size and the Interpretation of Socio-Political Complexity at Chaco Canyon, New Mexico. *Haliksʼi* 4:68–75.

Leonard, R. D., and H. E. Reed 1993 Population Aggregation in the Prehistoric American Southwest: A Selectionist Model. *American Antiquity* 58(4):648–661.

Lipe, W. D., M. D. Varien, and R. H. Wilshusen 1999 *Colorado Prehistory: A Context for Southern Colorado Drainage Basin.* Colorado Council of Professional Archaeologists, Denver.

Liu, L. 2004 *The Chinese Neolithic: Trajectories to Early States.* Cambridge University Press, Cambridge.

Lynch, K. 1981 *A Theory of Good City Form.* MIT Press, Cambridge, Massachusetts.

MacSweeney, N. 2004 Social Complexity and Population: A Study in the Early Bronze Age Aegean. *Papers from the Institute of Archaeology* 15:82–89.

Manzanilla, L. R. 1997 Early Urban Societies: Challenges and Perspectives. In *Emergence and Change in Early Urban Societies*, edited by L. Manzanilla, pp. 3–39. Plenum Press, New York.

Manzanilla, L. R. 2017 *Multiethnicity and Migration at Teopancazco: Investigations of a Teotihuacan Neighborhood Center.* University Press of Florida, Gainesville.

Marcus, J. 1998 The Peaks and Valleys of Ancient States: An Extension of the Dynamic Model. In *Archaic States*, edited by G. M. Feinman and J. Marcus, pp. 59–94. School of American Research, Santa Fe, New Mexico.

Marcus, J. 2000 Toward an Archaeology of Community. In *The Archaeology of Communities: A New World Perspective*, edited by M. A. Canuto and J. Yaeger, pp. 231–242. Routledge, New York.

Martín, A. J., and M. M. Herrera 2014 Networks of Interaction and Functional Interdependence in Societies across the Intermediate Area. *Journal of Anthropological Archaeology* 36:60–71.

McFarlane, C. 2010 The Comparative City: Knowledge, Learning, Urbanism. *International Journal of Urban and Regional Research* 34(4):725–742.

McIntosh, R. J. 1991 Early Urban Clusters in China and Africa: The Arbitration of Social Ambiguity. *Journal of Field Archaeology* 18(2):199–212.

McIntosh, R. J. 2005 *Ancient Middle Niger: Urbanism and the Self-Organizing Landscape.* Cambridge University Press, Cambridge.

McIntosh, R. J., and S. K. McIntosh 2003 Early Urban Configurations on the Middle Niger: Clustered Cities and Landscapes of Power. In *The Social Construction of Ancient Cities*, edited by M. L. Smith, pp. 103–120. Smithsonian Institution Press, Washington, D.C.

Mitchell, W. 1988 The Defeat of Hierarchy: Gambling as Exchange in a Sepik Society. *American Ethnologist* 15(4):638–657.

Moore, J. D. 1996 *Architecture and Power in the Ancient Andes: The Archaeology of Public Buildings.* Cambridge University Press, Cambridge.

Morgan, L. H. 1877 *Ancient Society, or Researches in the Lines of Human Progress from Savagery through Barbarism to Civilization.* Henry Holt, New York.

Morris, C. 2008 Links in the Chain of Inka Cities: Communication, Alliance, and the Cultural Production of Status, Value, and Power. In *The Ancient City: New Perspectives on Urbanism in the Old and New World*, edited by J. Marcus and J. A. Sabloff, pp. 299–319. School for Advanced Research, Santa Fe, New Mexico.

Morton, S. G., M. M. Peuramaki-Brown, P. C. Dawson, and J. D. Seibert 2014 Peopling the Past: Interpreting Models for Pedestrian Movement in Ancient Civic-Ceremonial Centres. In *Mapping Spatial Relations, Their Perceptions and Dynamics: The City Today and in the Past*, edited by S. Rau and E. Schönherr, pp. 25–44. Springer, New York.

Müller, J. 2012 Tells, Fire, and Copper as Social Technologies. In *Tells: Social and Environmental Space*, Vol. 3, edited by R. Hofmann, F.-K. Moetz, and J. Müller, pp. 47–52. Universitätsforschungen zur prähistorischen Archäologie 207. Dr. Rudolf Habelt, Bonn.

Müller, J. 2016 From the Neolithic to the Iron Age—Demography and Social Agglomeration: The Development of Centralized Control? In *Eurasia at the Dawn of History: Urbanization and Social Change*, edited by M. Fernández-Götz and D. Krausse, pp. 106–126. Cambridge University Press, New York and Cambridge.

Müller, J., K. Rassmann, and M. Videiko (editors) 2016 *Trypillia Mega-Sites and European Prehistory: 4100–3400 BCE*. Themes in Contemporary Archaeology 2. Routledge, London.

Mulligan, G. F., M. D. Partridge, and J. I. Carruthers 2012 Central Place Theory and Its Reemergence in Regional Science. *The Annals of Regional Science* 48(2):405–431.

Mumford, L. 1961 *The City in History*. Harcourt, Brace, and World, New York.

Mundy, B. E. 2015 *The Death of Aztec Tenochtitlan, the Life of Mexico City*. University of Texas Press, Austin.

Musterd, S., and W. Ostendorf (editors) 1998 *Urban Segregation and the Welfare State: Inequality and Exclusion in Western Cities*. Routledge, Abingdon.

National Intelligence Council of the United States 2017 *Global Trends: The Paradox of Progress*. Electronic document: https://www.dni.gov/index.php/global-trends-home.

Neitzel, J. E., and T. Earle 2014 Dual-Tier Approach to Societal Evolution and Types. *Journal of Anthropological Archaeology* 36:181–195.

Newman, P. 2006 The Environmental Impact of Cities. *Environment and Urbanization* 18(2): 275–295.

Nichols, D. L., and T. H. Charlton (editors) 1997 *The Archaeology of City States: Cross-Cultural Approaches*. Smithsonian Institution Press, Washington, D.C.

Nijman, J. 2007 Introduction—Comparative Urbanism. *Urban Geography* 28(1):1–6.

Nishimura, Y. 2014 North Mesopotamian Urban Neighborhoods at Titriş Höyük in the Third Millennium BC. In *Making Ancient Cities: Space and Place in Early Urban Societies*, edited by A. T. Creekmore III and K. D. Fisher, pp. 74–100. Cambridge University Press, New York.

O'Connor, A., C. Tilly, and L. Bobo (editors) 2001 *Urban Inequality: Evidence from Four Cities*. Russell Sage Foundation, New York.

Ohlrau, R. 2015 Trypillian Mega-Sites: Geomagnetic Survey and Socio-Architectural Perspectives. *Journal of Neolithic Archaeology* 17:17–99.

Oosthuizen, S. 2013 Beyond Hierarchy: The Archaeology of Collective Governance. *World Archaeology* 45(5):714–729.

Ortman, S. G., A. H. F. Cabaniss, J. O. Sturm, and L. M. A. Bettencourt 2014 The Pre-History of Urban Scaling. *PLOS ONE* 9(2):e87902.

Ortman, S. G., and G. D. Coffey 2015 Universal Scaling: Evidence from Village-Level Societies. *SFI Working Paper* 2015-10-044. Santa Fe Institute, Santa Fe, New Mexico.

Ortman, S. G., K. E. Davis, J. Lobo, M. E. Smith, L. M. A. Bettencourt, and A. Cabaniss 2016 Settlement Scaling and Economic Change in the Central Andes. *Journal of Archaeological Science* 73:94–106.

Orum, A. M., and X. Chen 2003 *The World of Cities: Places in Comparative and Historical Perspective*. Blackwell, Oxford.

Osborne, J. F. (editor) 2014 *Approaching Monumentality in Archaeology*. IEMA Proceedings Volume 3. State University of New York, Albany.

O'Shea, J. M. 1989 Pawnee Archaeology. *Central Plains Archaeology* 1(1):49–107.

Paliou, E., U. Lieberwirth, and S. Polla (editors) 2014 *Spatial Analysis and Social Spaces: Interdisciplinary Approaches to the Interpretation of Prehistoric and Historic Built Environments*. De Gruyter, Berlin.

Palmisano, A., and M. Altaweel 2015 Landscapes of Interaction and Conflict in the Middle Bronze Age: From the Open Plain of the Khabur Triangle to the Mountainous Inland of Central Anatolia. *Journal of Archaeological Science: Report* 3:216–236.

Papadopoulos, N., A. Sarris, M.-J. Yi, and J.-H. Kim 2009 Urban Archaeological Investigations Using Surface 3D Ground Penetrating Radar and Electrical Resistivity Tomography Methods. *Exploration Geophysics* 40(1):56–68.

Papagrigorakis, M. J., C. Yapijakis, P. N. Synodinos, and E. Baziotopoulou-Valavani 2006 DNA Examination of Ancient Dental Pulp Incriminates Typhoid Fever as a Probable Cause of the Plague of Athens. *International Journal of Infectious Diseases* 10(3):206–214.

Park, R. E. 1925 The City: Suggestions for the Investigation of Human Behavior in the Urban Environment. In *The City*, edited by R. E. Park, E. W. Burgess, and R. D. McKenzie, pp. 1–46. The University of Chicago Press, Chicago.

Parker Pearson, M., and C. Richards 1994 Architecture and Order: Spatial Representation and Archaeology. In *Architecture and Order: Approaches to Social Space*, edited by M. Parker Pearson and C. Richards, pp. 34–66. Routledge, London.

Parkinson, W. A. 2002 Integration, Interaction, and Tribal "Cycling": The Transition to the Copper Age on the Great Hungarian Plain. In *The Archaeology of Tribal Societies*, edited by W. A. Parkinson, pp. 391–438. Archaeological Series 15. International Monographs in Prehistory, Ann Arbor, Michigan.

Parkinson, W. A. 2006 *The Social Organization of Early Copper Age Tribes on the Great Hungarian Plain*. BAR International Series 1573. Archaeopress, London.

Paynter, R. W., and R. H. McGuire 1991 The Archaeology of Inequality: Material Culture, Domination, and Resistance. In *The Archaeology of Inequality*, edited by R. McGuire and R. Paynter, pp. 1–27. Blackwell, Oxford.

Paz-Arellano, P., A. Tejero-Andrade, and D. Argote-Espino 2016 2D-ERT Survey for the Identification of Archaeological and Historical Structures beneath the Plaza of Santo Domingo, Mexico City, Mexico. *Archaeological Prospection*, doi: 10.1002/arp.1560.

Perring, D. 1991a *Roman London: The Archaeology of London*. Routledge, Abingdon.

Perring, D. 1991b Spatial Organization and Social Change in Roman Towns. In *City and Country in the Ancient World*, edited by J. Rich and A. Wallace-Hadrill, pp. 273–293. Routledge, London and New York.

Peterson, C. E., and R. D. Drennan 2012 Patterned Variation in Regional Trajectories of Community Growth. In *The Comparative Archaeology of Complex Societies*, edited by M. E. Smith, pp. 88–137. Cambridge University Press, New York.

Portugali, J. 1984 Location Theory in Geography and Archaeology. *Geography Research Forum* 7:43–60.

Possehl, G. L. 1997 The Transformation of the Indus Civilization. *Journal of World Prehistory* 11(4):425–472.

Price, T. D., L. E. Wright, and C. White 2007 Victims of Sacrifice: Isotopic Evidence for Place of Origin. In *New Perspectives on Human Sacrifice and Ritual Body Treatments in Ancient Maya Society*, edited by V. Tiesler and A. Cucina, pp. 263–292. Springer, New York.

Raczky, P. 2015 Tells and Settlements in Southeast Europe. In *The Oxford Handbook of Neolithic Europe*, edited by C. Fowler, J. Harding, and D. Hofmann, pp. 235–254. Oxford University Press, Oxford.

Rapoport, A. 1977 *Human Aspects of Urban Form: Towards a Man–Environment Approach to Urban Form and Design*. Urban and Regional Planning Series 15. Pergamon Press, Oxford and New York.

Rapoport, A. 1982 *The Meaning of the Built Environment: A Nonverbal Communication Approach*. Sage, Beverly Hills, California.

Rapoport, A. 1990 Systems of Activities and Systems of Settings. In *Domestic Architecture and the Use of Space: An Interdisciplinary Cross-Cultural Study*, edited by S. Kent, pp. 9–20. Cambridge University Press, Cambridge.

Rapoport, A. 1994 Spatial Organization and the Built Environment. In *Companion Encyclopedia of Anthropology: Humanity, Culture, and Social Life*, edited by T. Ingold, pp. 460–502. Routledge, London.

Rautman, A. E. 2013 Social Integration and the Built Environment of Aggregated Communities in the North American Puebloan Southwest. In *From Prehistoric Villages to Cities: Settlement Aggregation and Community Transformation*, edited by J. Birch, pp. 111–133. Routledge, New York.

Read, D. W., and S. A. LeBlanc 2003 Population Growth, Carrying Capacity, and Conflict. *Current Anthropology* 44(1):272–300.

Redfield, R., and M. B. Singer 1954 The Cultural Role of Cities. *Economic Development and Cultural Change* 3(1):53–73.

Renfrew, C. 2008 The City through Time and Space: Transformations of Centrality. In *The Ancient City: New Perspectives on Urbanism in the Old and New World*, edited by J. Marcus and J. A. Sabloff, pp. 29–51. School for Advanced Research, Santa Fe, New Mexico.

Riebe, D. J. 2016 *Interaction and Socio-Cultural Boundaries during the Late Neolithic on the Great Hungarian Plain*. PhD dissertation, Department of Anthropology, University of Illinois at Chicago, Chicago.

Roberts, S. G. B. 2010 Constraints on Social Networks. In *Social Brain, Distributed Mind*, edited by R. I. M. Dunbar, C. Gamble, and J. A. J. Gowlett, pp. 115–134. Oxford University Press, Oxford.

Robinson, J. 2005 Urban Geography: World Cities, or a World of Cities. *Progress in Human Geography* 29(6):757–765.

Robinson, J. 2015 Comparative Urbanism: New Geographies and Cultures of Theorizing the Urban. *International Journal of Urban and Regional Research* 41(1):187–199.

Rodning, C. B. 2002 Reconstructing the Coalescence of Cherokee Communities in Southern Appalachia. In *The Transformation of the Southeastern Indians, 1540–1760*, edited by R. Ethridge and C. Hudson, pp. 155–175. University Press of Mississippi, Jackson.

Roscoe, P. B. 1993 Practice and Political Centralization: A New Approach to Political Evolution. *Current Anthropology* 34(2):111–140.

Rosenstock, E. 2012 Environmental Factors in Tell Formation: An Archaeometric Attempt. In *Tells: Social and Environmental Space*, edited by R. Hofmann, F.-K. Moetz, and J. Müller, pp. 33–45. Universitätsforschungen zur prähistorischen Archäologie 207. Dr. Rudolf Habelt, Bonn.

Saunders, P. 1981 *Social Theory and the Urban Question*. Holmes and Meier, New York.

Savage, S. H., and S. E. Falconer 2003 Spatial and Statistical Inference of Late Bronze Age Polities in the Southern Levant. *Bulletin of the American Schools of Oriental Research* 330:31–45.

Scargill, D. I. 1979 *The Form of Cities*. Bell and Hyman, London.

Schiller, N. G., and A. Çağlar 2009 Towards a Comparative Theory of Locality in Migration Studies: Migrant Incorporation and City Scale. *Journal of Ethnic and Migration Studies* 35(1):177–202.

Schortman, E. M., P. A. Urban, and M. Ausec 2001 Politics with Style: Identity Formation in Prehispanic Southeastern Mesoamerica. *American Anthropologist* 103(2):312–330.

Schwartz, G. M., and J. J. Nichols (editors) 2006 *After Collapse: The Regeneration of Complex Societies*. The University of Arizona Press, Tucson.

Service, E. R. 1962 *Primitive Social Organization*. Random House, New York.

Shapiro, J. S. 2005 *A Space Syntax Analysis of Arroyo Hondo Pueblo, New Mexico: Community Formation in the Northern Rio Grande*. School of American Research Press, Santa Fe, New Mexico.

Simmel, G. 1903 Soziologie des Raumes. *Jahrbuch für Gesetzgebung, Verwaltung und Volkswirtschaft im Deutschen Reich* 27:27–71.

Simmons, A. H., I. Kohler-Rollefson, G. O. Rollefson, R. Mandel, and Z. Kafafi 1988 'Ain Ghazal: A Major Neolithic Settlement in Central Jordan. *Science* 240(4848):35–39.

Smith, M. E. 1979 The Aztec Marketing System and Settlement Pattern in the Valley of Mexico: A Central Place Analysis. *American Antiquity* 44(1):110–125.

Smith, M. E. 2007 Form and Meaning in the Earliest Cities: A New Approach to Ancient Urban Planning. *Journal of Planning History* 6(1):3–47.

Smith, M. E. 2010 Sprawl, Squatters, and Sustainable Cities: Can Archaeological Data Shed Light on Modern Urban Issues? *Cambridge Archaeological Journal* 20(2):229–253.

Smith, M. E. 2011a Empirical Urban Theory for Archaeologists. *Journal of Archaeological Method and Theory* 18(3):167–192.

Smith, M. E. 2011b Classic Maya Settlement Clusters as Urban Neighborhoods: A Comparative Perspective on Low-Density Urbanism. *Journal de la société des américanistes* 97(1):51–73.

Smith, M. E. 2014 Peasant Mobility, Local Migration, and Premodern Urbanization. *World Archaeology* 46(4):516–533.

Smith, M. E. 2016 How Can Archaeologists Identify Early Cities? Definitions, Types, and Attributes. In *Eurasia at the Dawn of History: Urbanization and Social Change*, edited by M. Fernández-Götz and D. Krausse, pp. 153–168. Cambridge University Press, New York and Cambridge.

Smith, M. E., B. L. Stark, W. C. Chuang, T. J. Dennehy, S. L. Harlan, A. Kamp-Whittaker, B. W. Stanley, and A. M. York 2016 Comparative Methods for Premodern Cities: Coding for Governance and Class Mobility. *Cross-Cultural Research* 50(5):415–451.

Smith, M. L. 2003a Introduction: The Social Construction of Ancient Cities. In *The Social Construction of Ancient Cities*, edited by M. L. Smith, pp. 1–36. Smithsonian Institution Press, Washington, D.C.

Smith, M. L. (editor) 2003b *The Social Construction of Ancient Cities*. Smithsonian Institution Press, Washington, D.C.

Spencer, C. S. 1990 On the Tempo and Mode of State Formation: Neoevolutionism Reconsidered. *Journal of Anthropological Archaeology* 9(1):1–30.

Stambaugh, J. E. 1988 *The Ancient Roman City*. Johns Hopkins University Press, Baltimore, Maryland.

Stanley, B. W., T. J. Dennehy, M. E. Smith, B. L. Stark, A. M. York, G. L. Cowgill, J. Novic, and J. Ek 2015 Service Access in Premodern Cities: An Exploratory Comparison of Spatial Equity. *Journal of Urban History* 41(1):1–24.

Stark, M., D. Evans, C. Rachna, H. Piphal, and A. Carter 2015 Residential Patterning in Angkor Wat. *Antiquity* 89(348):1439–1455.

Stone, E. C. 1997 City States and Their Centers: The Mesopotamian Example. In *The Archaeology of City States: Cross-Cultural Approaches*, edited by D. L. Nichols and T. H. Charlton, pp. 15–26. Smithsonian Institution Press, Washington, D.C.

Storey, G. R. 1992 *Preindustrial Urban Demography: The Ancient Roman Evidence*. PhD dissertation, Department of Anthropology, Pennsylvania State University, University Park.

Storey, G. R. (editor) 2006a *Urbanism in the Preindustrial World: Cross-Cultural Approaches*. The University of Alabama Press, Tuscaloosa.

Storey, G. R. 2006b Introduction: Urban Demography of the Past. In *Urbanism in the Preindustrial World: Cross-Cultural Approaches*, edited by G. R. Storey, pp. 1–26. The University of Alabama Press, Tuscaloosa.

Tainter, J. 1988 *The Collapse of Complex Societies*. Cambridge University Press, Cambridge.

Tasić, N., D. Srejović, and B. Stojanović 1990 *Vinča: Centre of the Neolithic Culture of the Danubian Region*. Centre for Archaeological Research, Faculty of Philosophy, Belgrade.

Taylor, P. J., and B. Derudder 2016 *World City Network: A Global Urban Analysis*. 2nd ed. Routledge, New York.

Taylor, P. J., M. Hoyler, and R. Verbruggen 2010 External Urban Relational Process: Introducing Central Flow Theory to Complement Central Place Theory. *Urban Studies* 47(13):2803–2018.

Tilly, C. 1974 Do Communities Act? In *The Community: Approaches and Applications*, edited by M. P. Effrat, pp. 209–240. Free Press, New York.

Tonkiss, F. 2013 *Cities by Design: The Social Life of Urban Form*. Polity Press, Cambridge.

Trigger, B. G. 1972 Determinants of Urban Growth in Pre-Industrial Society. In *Man, Settlement, and Urbanism*, edited by P. J. Ucko, R. Tringham, and G. W. Dimbleby, pp. 575–599. Duckworth, London.

Trigger, B. G. 1990 Monumental Architecture: A Thermodynamic Explanation of Symbolic Behaviour. *World Archaeology* 22:119–132.

Trigger, B. G. 2003 *Understanding Early Civilizations: A Comparative Study*. Cambridge University Press, Cambridge.

Trigger, B. G. 2008 Early Cities. In *The Ancient City: New Perspectives on Urbanism in the Old and New World*, edited by J. Marcus and J. A. Sabloff, pp. 53–66. School for Advanced Research, Santa Fe, New Mexico.

Tsetskhladze, G. R. (editor) 2006 *Greek Colonisation: An Account of Greek Colonies and Other Settlements Overseas*. Mnemosyne, Bibliotheca Classica Batava Supplementum 193. Brill, Leiden and Boston.

Tsokas, G. N., P. I. Tsourlos, G. Vargemezis, and M. Novack 2008 Non-Destructive Electrical Resistivity Tomography for Indoor Investigation: The Case of Kapnikarea Church in Athens. *Archaeological Prospection* 15(1):47–61.

Ur, J. 2010 Cycles of Civilization in Northern Mesopotamia, 4400–2000 BC. *Journal of Archaeological Research* 18(4):387–431.

Ur, J. A. 2014 Households and the Emergence of Cities in Ancient Mesopotamia. *Cambridge Archaeological Journal* 24(2):249–268.

Varien, M. D., and R. H. Wilshusen (editors) 2002 *Seeking the Center Place: Archaeology and Ancient Communities in the Mesa Verde Region*. University of Utah Press, Salt Lake City.

Vis, B. N. 2014 Mapping Socio-Spatial Relations in the Urban Built Environment through Time: Describing the Socio-Spatial Significance of Inhabiting Urban Form. In *Mapping Spatial Relations, Their Perceptions and Dynamics: The City Today and in the Past*, edited by S. Rau and E. Schönherr, pp. 45–93. Springer, New York.

Walanus, A. 2009 Systematic Bias of Radiocarbon Method. *Radiocarbon* 51(2):433–436.

Wang, Z., F. Zhang, and F. Wu 2015 Intergroup Neighbouring in Urban China: Implications for the Social Integration of Migrants. *Urban Studies* 53(4):651–668.

Ward, K. 2008 *Comparative Urbanisms: Past Work and Future Agendas*. Imagining Urban Futures Programme, Working Paper 5. The University of Manchester, Manchester.

Weiss, H. (editor) 1986 *The Origins of Cities in Dry-Farming Syria and Mesopotamia in the Third Millennium BC*. Four Quarters, Guilford.

Wengrow, D. 2015 *Cities before the State in Early Eurasia*. Goody Lecture 2015. Max Planck Institute for Social Anthropology, Department "Resilience and Transformation in Eurasia," IMPRESS, Halle/Saale.

Wheatley, P. 1972 The Concept of Urbanism. In *Man, Settlement, and Urbanism*, edited by P. J. Ucko, R. Tringham, and G. W. Dimbleby, pp. 601–637. Duckworth, London.

White, C., M. Spence, F. J. Longstaffe, E. Rattray, and R. Storey 2009 The Teotihuacan Dream: An Isotopic Study of Economic Organization and Immigration. *Ontario Archaeology* 85–88: 279–297.

Whitelaw, T. 2001 From Sites to Communities: Defining the Human Dimensions of Minoan Urbanisation. In *Urbanism in the Aegean Bronze Age*, edited by K. Branigan, pp. 15–37. Sheffield Academic Press, Sheffield.

Wilkinson, T. J., G. Philip, J. Bradbury, R. Dunford, D. Donoghue, N. Galiatsatos, D. Lawrence, A. Ricci, and S. L. Smith 2014 Contextualizing Early Urbanization: Settlement Cores, Early States and Agro-Pastoral Strategies in the Fertile Crescent during the Fourth and Third Millennia BC. *Journal of World Prehistory* 27(1):43–109.

Wilshusen, R. H., and S. Ortman 1999 Rethinking the Pueblo I Period in the Northern Southwest: Aggregation, Migration, and Cultural Diversity. *Kiva* 64(3):369–399.

Wilson, A. G. 1970 *Entropy in Urban and Regional Modelling*. Pion, London.

Wilson, A. G. 2012 Geographic Modeling for Archaeology and History: Two Case Studies. *Advances in Complex Systems* 15(1–2), doi: 10.1142/S0219525911003384.

Wirth, L. 1938 Urbanism as a Way of Life. *American Journal of Sociology* 44(1):1–24.

Yaeger, J., and M. A. Canuto 2000 Introducing an Archaeology of Communities. In *The Archaeology of Communities: A New World Perspective*, edited by M. A. Canuto and J. Yaeger, pp. 1–15. Routledge, New York.

Yasuda, Y., T. Fujiki, H. Nasu, M. Kato, Y. Morita, Y. Mori, M. Kanehara, S. Toyama, A. Yano, M. Okuno, H. Jiejun, and S. Ishihara 2004 Environmental Archaeology at the Chengtoushan Site, Hunan Province, China, and Implications for Environmental Change and the Rise and Fall of the Yangtze River Civilization. *Quaternary International* 123–125:149–158.

York, A., M. E. Smith, B. Stanley, B. L. Stark, J. Novic, S. L. Harlan, G. L. Cowgill, and C. Boone 2011 Ethnic and Class-Based Clustering through the Ages: A Transdisciplinary Approach to Urban Social Patterns. *Urban Studies* 48(11):2399–2415.

Zeng, R., and P. M. Greenfield 2015 Cultural Evolution over the Last 40 years in China: Using the Google Ngram Viewer to Study Implications of Social and Political Change for Cultural Values. *International Journal of Psychology* 50(1):47–55.

CHAPTER TWO

Energized Crowding and the Generative Role of Settlement Aggregation and Urbanization

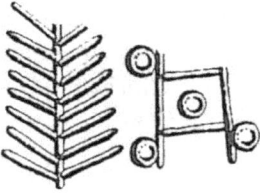

Michael E. Smith

Abstract   *I describe a new approach to understanding processes of village aggregation and urbanization in the past. The key concept—energized crowding—refers to the social effects of large numbers of social interactions that take place within settlements. Demographic processes of population growth and settlement nucleation (aggregation and urbanization) lead to increased energized crowding, which, in turn, generates a variety of social outcomes. I discuss those outcomes under three headings: scalar stress, community formation, and economic growth. In this model, aggregation and urbanization are crucial processes that lead—by way of energized crowding—to many documented social outputs in both contemporary and past settlement systems. Because this is a new approach for archaeology, conceptual tools for understanding these processes must be borrowed from other social sciences. In particular, recent research on settlement scaling provides empirical and theoretical support for the notion that aggregation and urbanization were of fundamental importance in generating social change in the past.*

Population aggregation—the concentration of formerly dispersed people into villages, towns, and cities—is one of the most consequential processes in the history of human society. When people come together in a settlement, the number and level of interactions among individuals increase exponentially, and these interactions have generative power. That is, they bring about a variety of social changes, both positive and negative. Research by sociologists and anthropologists has tended to focus on the negative consequences of urbanization—increased levels of stress, crime, poverty, and alienation (Redfield 1941; Wirth 1938). Research by economists and geographers, on the other hand, emphasize the positive consequences of aggregation. The acceleration of face-to-face social interaction in larger and denser settlements stimulates knowledge transfer, technological innovation, and economic growth (Duranton and Puga 2004, 2014). One well-documented finding for contemporary cities is that as cities grow larger, their per capita productivity increases—individuals are more productive in larger cities (Bettencourt 2013; Pumain 2012).

These positive and negative consequences of aggregation and urbanization are two sides of the same coin. Whether talking about the aggregation of small early farming groups into villages (e.g., Birch, Gaydarska, and Ryan this volume) or the processes of rural-to-urban migration that lead to urbanization in the developing world today, the results are similar. Increased numbers of people living in close contact activate a process that architectural historian Spiro Kostof called *energized crowding*: "Cities are places where a certain energized crowding of people takes place. This has nothing to do with absolute size or with absolute numbers; it has to do with settlement density" (1991:37). While research suggests that the magnitude of the social effects of energized crowding does, in fact, depend on both density and absolute population size (e.g., Bettencourt 2013; Fletcher 1995), Kostof's concept helps us understand processes of aggregation and urbanization.

In this paper, I argue that settlement aggregation and urbanization have been fundamental processes in structuring and generating change in human settlements in the past and present. Energized crowding is the pathway that connects these processes to their social consequences. It lies at a key causal nexus between demographic processes and social outcomes. I review a variety of empirical findings and theoretical perspectives that describe the role of energized crowding. In some scholarly traditions—for example, urban economics and the social reactors model of settlement scaling—face-to-face interaction is an explicit component of current models. In others—such as sociology and anthropology—such interactions are implicit, but important in theory and research.

CITIES, POPULATION, AND ENERGIZED CROWDING: THE POWER OF FACE-TO-FACE INTERACTIONS

I propose a basic causal model to portray the generative roles of population growth and aggregation (Figure 2.1). This model is supported by a wide variety of theoretical and conceptual approaches in the social sciences. There is not space to explore all of these here, so I list the relevant approaches in Table 2.1. My model contains two types of demographic process that create increased face-to-face contacts or energized crowding: population growth (which I separate into population growth per se and increases in population density) and population concentration (divided here into village aggregation and urbanization). Energized crowding, in turn, generates a variety of social outcomes that I organize under three headings: scalar stress, community formation, and economic growth. This classification is somewhat arbitrary since the demographic drivers and social outcomes are all closely interrelated.

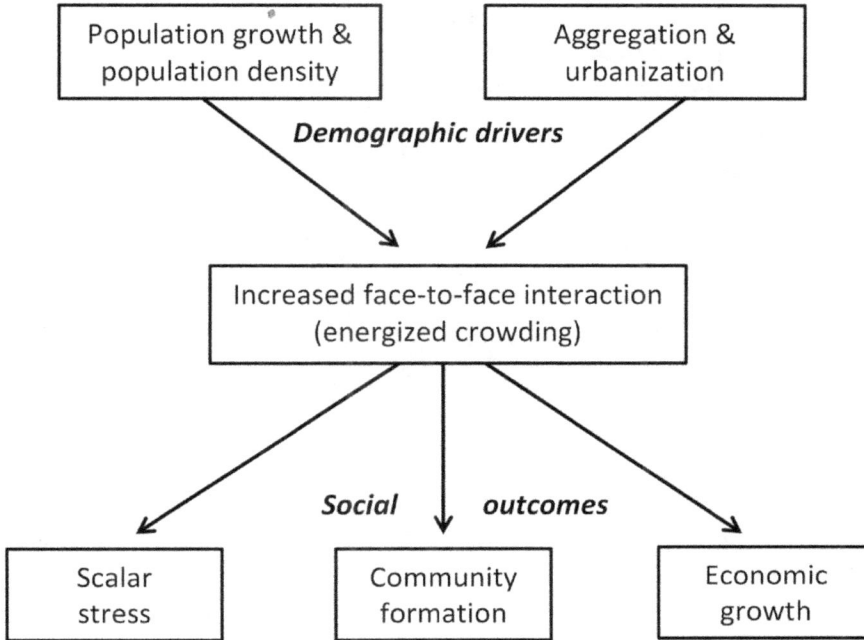

FIGURE 2.1 Drivers and outcomes of energized crowding.

POPULATION SIZE AND DENSITY

The notion that population growth, population size, and population density generate effects in cities resonates with a long tradition of research on cultural evolution in anthropology and archaeology. The role of population growth in generating cultural evolution was discussed by sociocultural anthropologists in the 1950s and 1960s (Carneiro 1962; Naroll 1956), and then it was taken up by archaeologists. After debates about the role of population pressure in generating various social changes in the past (Spooner 1972), archaeological consensus settled on the notion that while group size is correlated with sociopolitical complexity (Feinman 2011; Johnson and Earle 2000), population pressure is rarely the sole driver of cultural change and evolution. But in the more limited domain of agricultural intensification, Netting (1993) fleshed out Boserup's (1965) model and demonstrated the role of population growth in generating agricultural and social changes.

A parallel line of analysis outside of anthropology led to the development of demographic-structural theory by sociologist Jack Goldstone (1991, 2002). This approach, later elaborated by Turchin and Nefedov (2009), examines the joint roles of demographic variables and macrosociological variables in generating change in human institutions. Most of the research I review below—on the role of energized crowding in generating scalar stress, community formation, and economic growth—is based, explicitly or implicitly,

Table 2.1
Theoretical Approaches to the Effects of Population Growth and Aggregation

Outcome	Theoretical Approach
Population growth leads to:	
Cultural evolution	Archaeological cultural evolution
Agricultural intensification	Boserup/Netting
Institutional change	Demographic structural theory
Economic growth	Urban economics
Community formation	Sociology; political economy
Scalar stress	Cognitive cultural evolution
Increased population density leads to:	
Scalar stress	Settlement growth theory
Negative social outcomes	Urban sociology; environmental psychology
Economic growth	Urban economics
Village aggregation leads to:	
Scalar stress	Settlement growth theory
Community formation	Settlement growth theory
Urbanization leads to:	
Negative social outcomes	Urban sociology; public health
Community formation	Urban sociology; neighborhood theory
Agglomeration economies & growth	Urban economics; economic geography

on the notion that population growth is a cause of energized crowding. The fact that these outcomes are reported in a variety of disciplines—archaeology and anthropology, urban economics, political science, sociology, and cognitive cultural evolution (Table 2.1)—points to their widespread validity and applicability.

Whereas population growth leads to a variety of social changes at the societal or regional level, the effects of increased population density are felt primarily at the level of the settlement or community. As discussed below, there has been extensive archaeological research on the connection between population density and scalar stress (for major studies, see Adler and Wilshusen 1990; Birch 2013; Fletcher 1995; Jennings 2016), which I group together under the label "settlement growth theory" (Table 2.1).

Village Aggregation and Urbanization

Research on the generative effects of village aggregation has been carried out almost exclusively by archaeologists employing settlement growth theory. Scalar stress, as discussed below, can lead to a variety of outcomes, one of which is the development of institutions and facilities that promote community formation. This is a major theme of research in the U.S. Southwest, where integrative facilities, such as kivas, promote community formation (Adler and Wilshusen 1990; Schachner 2010; see also Ryan as well as the related work of Birch and Fernández-Götz in this volume).

The role of urbanization in creating negative social outcomes—from crime and poverty to physical and mental health problems—has long been a major theme of social science research (Kornhauser 1978; Nisbet 1966; Wirth 1938). Within urban sociology and neighborhood theory (e.g., Chaskin 1997; Sampson 2012; Smith et al. 2015), discussions of the positive effects of urbanization have focused on community formation, whereas urban economics and economic geography have emphasized economic growth and agglomeration effects as positive outcomes. Recent suggestions by archaeologists that urbanization may have preceded state formation (Jennings 2016; Wengrow 2015) provide intriguing empirical—if not yet theoretical—support for the causal role of urbanization in social change. Further support for that role comes from new research in settlement scaling, reviewed below.

COMMUNICATION, ENERGIZED CROWDING, AND CITIES

An increasingly popular perspective in the social sciences and history sees the primary purpose of cities as promoting social interaction and communication among residents. Some of the earliest expressions of this view were given by urban planners: "Cities were evolved primarily for the facilitation of human communication" (Meier 1962), and "more than anything else, the city is a communication network" (Lynch 1981:334). The implications for aggregation were elaborated by social historian Charles Tilly:

> H.A. Innis, his followers Marshall McLuhan, Richard Meier and Allan Pred have all argued, in their own ways, that where communications were both costly and crucial to the enterprises men were carrying on, men have agglomerated in towns and cities. The agglomeration is a response to high distance-cost. But, as these authors have usually pointed out, the relationship is reciprocal. The high premium placed on efficient communications stimulates urbanites to invent new media which will carry large volumes of information far and fast at low cost (1974:226).

Social interaction and communication among closely spaced residents create the "energized crowding" noted by Kostof. Historian Fernand Braudel expresses similar ideas: "Towns are like electric transformers. They increase tension, accelerate the rhythm of exchange and constantly recharge human life" (1981:479). In a study of contemporary urban economics, geographers Michael Storper and Anthony Venables (2004) refer to this characteristic of cities as "buzz." In this paper, I use the phrase "energized crowding" to refer to the various dynamic aspects of face-to-face social interaction in human settlements. In a related formulation, Lynch (1981:187–203) argued that the purpose of cities was to give their residents access—access to other people, to certain activities, to material resources, to places, and access to information.

The concept of energized crowding contributes greatly to explanations for many of the consequences of early aggregation and urbanization around the world. Before proceeding, though, I should note that this line of thought is a radical departure from traditional archaeological models of early cities and complex societies. Until quite recently, most archaeological accounts of early states assumed that all past rulers were powerful and despotic, and were willing and able to control many aspects of peoples' lives, whether through economic or ideological domination (for critiques of this approach outside of archaeology, see du Gay 2012; Mann 1986:526–527). Within archaeology, the primary challenge to this statist approach has been Blanton and Fargher's (2008) identification of both collective and autocratic rule in premodern polities. They show that the Classical Greeks (see Ault this volume) were not the only ancient society to create a collective form of government. Outside of archaeology, the prominence of generative, or bottom-up, social processes—often called self-organization or spontaneous order—has been recognized for many decades (Cronk and Leech 2013; Epstein 1999; Hakim 2007; Hayek 1967; Jacobs 1961; Mitchell 2009; Ward 1973). Indeed, most of the theoretical approaches listed in Table 2.1 emphasize the power of generative forces instead of top-down, centralized, decision making. When archaeologists abandon their obsession with statist models of all-powerful rulers, our understanding of many past social phenomena will advance more rapidly.

In their article titled "Buzz: Face-to-Face Contact and the Urban Economy," Storper and Venables (2004) list four broad functions of face-to-face contact in cities (Table 2.2). While their treatment focuses exclusively on contemporary capitalist urban economies, these basic functions of face-to-face interaction apply equally well to cities and towns before the modern era. For example, Storper and Venables point out that

TABLE 2.2
MAJOR PROPERTIES OF FACE-TO-FACE INTERACTION
(AFTER STORPER AND VENABLES 2004:354)

Function	Advantages of Face-to-Face Interaction
Communication technology	High frequency Rapid feedback Visual and body language cues
Trust and incentives in relationships	Detection of lying Co-presence is a commitment
Screening and socializing	Acquisition of shared values
Rush and motivation	Performance and display

face-to-face interaction as a communication technology is especially important "when much of the information to be transmitted cannot be codified" (2004:353), a condition prevailing in most premodern economies. Its role in establishing trust is a fundamental part of cooperation theory (Hechter 1987), and this insight is now being applied by archaeologists (Carballo 2013). One way that social interactions are affected by the built environment is through viewshed: who can see what (and whom) from where (see Kaiser this volume).

From a comparative perspective, the powerful role of face-to-face interaction in structuring urban societies and generating change is one of the major continuities between contemporary and ancient cities. The following quotations, from urban economist Edward Glaeser, apply equally well to ancient settlements and to the contemporary cities about which Glaeser writes, "The central theme of this book is that cities magnify humanity's strengths. Our social species' greatest talent is the ability to learn from each other, and we learn more deeply and thoroughly when we're face-to-face" (2011:250), and, "Cities enable the collaboration that makes humanity shine most brightly. Because humans learn so much from other humans, we learn more when there are more people around us" (2011:247). I now turn to the question of how energized crowding generates a variety of social outcomes in cities and other settlements (Figure 2.1).

THE EFFECTS OF ENERGIZED CROWDING

ENERGIZED CROWDING GENERATES SCALAR STRESS

Scalar stress is a term first used by archaeologist Gregory Johnson (1978, 1982) to describe the increase in intragroup conflict that happens as the size of the social group increases; ethnographer Roy Rappaport (1968:116) had earlier used the term *irritation coefficient* to describe the predictable growth in disputes as population density increased among tribal villagers in highland New Guinea. The number of potential social interactions of each individual increases exponentially with the size of the interacting social group. As certain thresholds are reached, conflict and psychological stress can increase dramatically (Hopstock et al. 1979; Kennedy and Adolphs 2011). Scalar stress is the negative face of energized crowding.

I broaden the concept of scalar stress here and use it as a label for the many negative effects of growth in population and population density identified by social scientists. More than a century ago, Simmel observed, "Every quantitative extension of a group requires certain qualitative modifications and adjustments" (1898:834). Since then, numerous social scientists have discussed the negative implications of large, dense urban populations. To begin, scalar stress has negative social effects at the individual level. It can lead to more transitory urban social relations and urban anomie (Mayhew and Levinger 1977), as well as psychological stress (Evans 2001). It also produces larger structural effects, such as poverty, crime, delinquency, and public health problems (O'Brien 2009; Spruill 2010). In the field of cognitive cultural evolution, scalar stress is posited as occurring above key population thresholds, such as Dunbar's number (Dunbar 2011), at which point it causes a variety of sociocultural changes (Coward and Dunbar 2014). This cognitive approach, however, has been criticized by sociologists and anthropologists (de Ruiter et al. 2011; Wellman 2012).

Archaeologists have discussed scalar stress primarily in terms of early village aggregation and growing early urban populations. A consensus view has developed that identifies the following processes as major outcomes of scalar stress in ancient times: village fission, specialization in roles, the development of social hierarchies, and increased group-integrating ritual activity (Alberti 2014; Bandy 2004; Fletcher 1995:ch. 4; Jennings 2016:ch. 4). Architecturally, scalar stress was reduced in early communities by enclosure of spaces and the spatial specialization of activities in the built environment (Fletcher 1995:ch. 6; Kent 1990), as well as by the development of integrative architectural features that promoted cohesion through group ritual (Adler and Wilshusen 1990; see also Birch 2013). Several chapters in the present volume (e.g., Birch, Harrison and Bilgen, Kelly, and Sastre and Currás) examine these themes.

The large volume of research by social scientists and archaeologists on scalar stress—conceived broadly—clearly shows its generative role in creating changes in human societies and behavior. Most authors are careful to emphasize that the negative effects of population are generated not just by the number of people but by the number of social interactions. This, in turn, is a function of both population size and density. In other words, the culprit is not just the number of people but the number of potential interactions. It is through these increased social interactions that energized crowding generates scalar stress. But energized crowding also has socially beneficial or positive outcomes, particularly community formation and economic growth.

ENERGIZED CROWDING DRIVES COMMUNITY FORMATION

Communities are primary sites of social interaction; indeed, a classic anthropological definition of community is "the maximal group of persons who normally reside together in face-to-face association" (Murdock 1949:79). In sociological theory going back to Emile Durkheim, energized crowding—intensive social interaction—is seen as the primary force that generates communities (Figure 2.2).[1] This line of thinking continues today both among archaeologists working on settlement aggregation (see Birch, Fernández-Götz, Osborne, and Ryan this volume) and in studies of community formation from a political economy perspective. For example, economists Sam Bowles and Herbert Gintis define community as follows:

> By community we mean a group of people who interact directly, frequently and in multifaceted ways. People who work together are usually communities in this sense, as are some neighbourhoods, groups of friends, professional and business networks, gangs, and sports leagues. The list suggests that *connection, not affection,* is the defining characteristic of a community. Whether one is born into a community or one entered by choice, there are normally significant costs to moving from one to another (2002:F420; emphasis added).

Basis for Interaction:	Frequency of Interaction:	Type of Social Group:

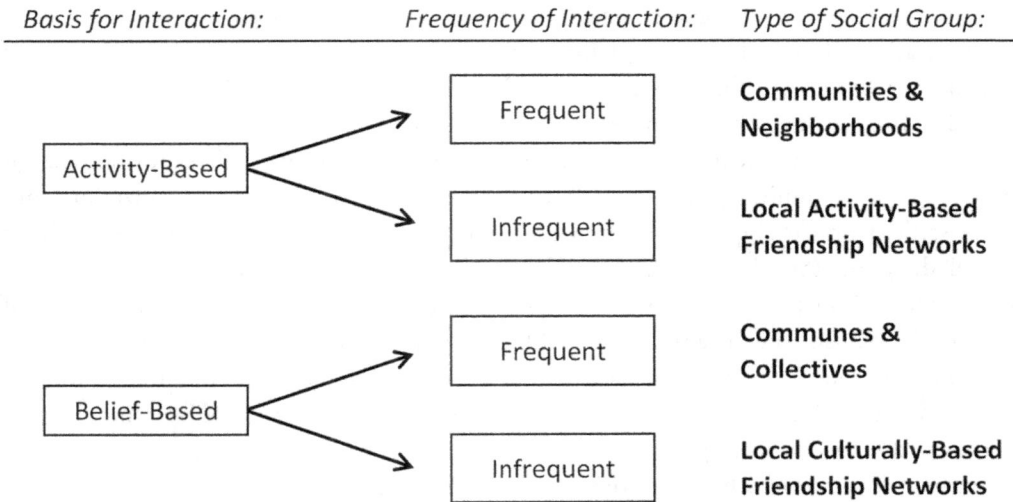

FIGURE 2.2. Social interaction and community formation (redrawn based on Brint 2001:10).

Urban planners see social interactions—with friends, neighbors, and other residents—not only as forces that generate community but as the force that creates successful cities and towns. This is because social interaction—particularly in or near neighborhood physical facilities, such as parks, playgrounds, and pedestrian-friendly streets—is a key dimension of social cohesion in cities (Jacobs 1961; Smith 1975). Stable neighborhoods facilitate social interaction, which promotes social cohesion or integration (Brower 2011).

The establishment and formation of successful communities have a variety of positive social effects. In the words of Bowles and Gintis:

> [C]ommunities solve problems that might otherwise appear as classic market failures or state failures: namely, insufficient provision of local public goods such as neighborhood amenities, the absence of insurance and other risk-sharing opportunities even when these would be mutually beneficial, exclusion of the poor from credit markets, and excessive and ineffective monitoring of work effort. Communities can sometimes do what governments and markets fail to do because their members, but not outsiders, have crucial information about other members' behaviours, capacities, and needs. Members use this information to uphold norms (2002:F422–F423).

The ability of communities to act—effectively and with positive outcomes—lies at the heart of the work of political economist Elinor Ostrom (1990, 2005). One of her basic arguments parallels precisely the conclusions of Bowles and Gintis: local communities can manage common-pool resources more successfully and sustainably than either states (government ownership) or markets (privatization). For Ostrom, one of the key attributes that allows communities to be successful is the prominence of face-to-face communication, which promotes trust, reputation, and reciprocity.

A major spatial outcome of community formation in growing cities and towns is the generation of spatial clusters of interaction, or neighborhoods. Most likely because of scalar stress, in the form of limits—whether cognitive or social—on the numbers of social interactions people can readily handle, neighborhoods have become universal traits of cities, from the past to the present (Smith 2010). Where authorities design settlements, they almost always include some form of neighborhood organization, and where settlements develop from bottom-up social processes, neighborhoods form without central direction (Smith et al. 2015). The creation of neighborhoods and other social communities is shaped by the built environment, a relationship stressed by advocates of the New Urbanism. For example, Talen (2000) proposes a causal chain that runs from the built environment, through social factors, to social interaction and the formation of communities (Figure 2.3). Energized crowding does not exert its effects in a spatial vacuum—the specific configuration of buildings and spaces plays an important role in generating its outcomes, both positive and negative. This feature provides one avenue by which archaeologists can study energized crowding.

ENERGIZED CROWDING LEADS TO ECONOMIC AND URBAN GROWTH

Urban agglomeration refers to the spatial concentration of economic activities in cities. Agglomeration effects are major causes of economic growth in cities today, and much work in urban economics and economic geography is devoted to understanding how these processes operate (Fujita et al. 1999; Glaeser 2008; Storper 2013). Energized crowding is viewed by economists as a basic component of urban agglomeration. In their discussion of "buzz," or energized crowding, Storper and Venables conclude, "We speculate that there is a superadditivity in these effects [the effects listed in Table 2.2 above], generating increasing returns for the people and the activities involved" (2004:365). These effects of social interactions on growth have been called a "social multiplier" (Glaeser et al. 2003; see also Helsley and Zenou 2014). Did such effects operate in past settlements? The answer is yes, but only if we define the concept of agglomeration more broadly, a task that has barely begun (Scott and Storper 2015).

Duranton and Puga (2004) explore what they call the "microfoundations" of agglomeration economies. These are divided into three broad categories: (1) *sharing*

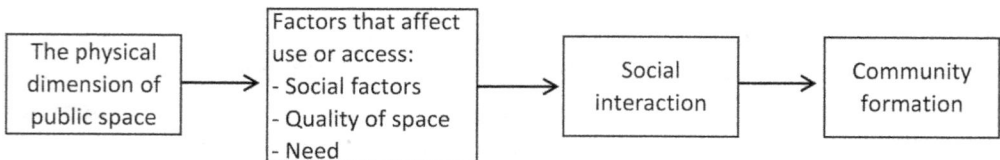

FIGURE 2.3. The built environment and community formation (redrawn based on Talen 2000:348).

refers to linkages among local production facilities, labor pools, markets, and public goods; (2) *matching* describes the way people and jobs pair up more efficiently in agglomerated economies; and (3) *learning* refers to the flows of knowledge and information within cities. Their discussion of agglomeration economies—like most work by economists and economic geographers—is clearly tailored to the capitalist economy, and to contemporary urban and national systems of governance. But these basic forces that generate agglomeration or concentration of activity in cities can be generalized to fit premodern cities.

The first step in broadening the applicability of the concept of agglomeration is to acknowledge that in many or most premodern cities political and religious institutions were more important than economic institutions for the operation and growth of cities. Scott and Storper suggest that early cities experienced agglomeration effects in "activities such as political administration, ceremonial and religious pursuits, craft production, and market trading" (2015:4). Following the scheme of Duranton and Puga (2014), the following activities can be suggested as components of premodern agglomeration:

1. Sharing. Many of the shared goods and places of agglomeration can be interpreted as club goods or toll goods. That is, they have low rivalry (use by one person does not compromise use by others), but moderate to high excludability (some people can be prevented from access). In past settlements, such goods included public facilities, such as marketplaces, temples, and formal open spaces. For urban residents, these were public goods, available to all (that is, they had low rivalry and low excludability), but from a societywide or a regional perspective, these facilities were urban club goods—they were limited to the people who resided in, or visited, the city. These were places that brought people together in settings that promoted social interaction, allowing goods and ideas to be shared (for discussion of club goods and public goods, see Ostrom 2007 or Cronk and Leech 2013).

2. Matching. This feature of agglomeration economies, which emphasizes firms and wage labor, seems less relevant to cities and settlements before the modern era.

3. Learning. Learning and knowledge transfers lie at the heart of modern agglomeration economies and urban growth (Glaeser et al. 2003; Ioaniddes 2012). Information about goods, prices, and opportunities "spills over" among urbanites, leading to economic and urban growth. In the past, we should expect similar processes for information about goods and prices, although the effects were almost certainly much weaker prior to the Industrial Revolution. But particularly in political capitals, information about taxes, warfare, corvée labor, crops, and ceremonies would have been exchanged in settlements, allowing agents from farmers to nobles to modify their

activity. In some cases, such learning contributed to urban growth. In this way, energized crowding in settlements stimulated growth and expansion, not only in the economy but in the political and religious realms also.

In agrarian societies with dispersed populations, one mechanism that promoted sharing and learning was the periodic movement of people into and out of nucleated settlements. Farmers came into town to attend a market or participate in a ceremony, and these activities promoted sharing and learning to a greater extent than might be expected for dispersed populations.

Perhaps the strongest evidence for the claim that energized crowding led to the growth of settlements in the ancient world comes from research in settlement scaling, to which I now turn.

SETTLEMENT SCALING AND GENERATIVE PROCESSES

The conceptual approaches reviewed above furnish a background for current models of settlement scaling in past and contemporary urban systems. Settlement scaling is part of a new perspective, arising from both empirical studies and theoretical considerations, developed at the intersection of a number of disciplines. The scaling of contemporary cities—"urban scaling"—was the first realm to develop. Urban scaling work shows how contemporary cities share certain predictable quantitative properties. A number of quantitative urban variables (surface area, amount of infrastructure, and a broad series of both positive and negative social outcomes) scale with population in a predictable manner (Bettencourt 2013; Pumain 2012; West 2017; Youn et al. 2016).

"Settlement scaling" is a broadened perspective that extends the domain of scaling research in two ways. First, consideration is given to urban systems prior to the modern era, using both historical and archaeological data. Recent studies show that the same quantitative patterns identified for contemporary urban systems also hold for city systems in early times (Cesaretti et al. 2015; Ortman et al. 2014, 2016). Second, nonurban or village settlement systems have now been included in the domain of settlement scaling, with the remarkable result that these same quantitative patterns also hold for village-level settlement systems (Ortman and Coffey 2017). These two sets of results provide strong empirical support for the generative role of aggregation and urbanization in creating changes in human society. In this section, I review very briefly the empirical and conceptual aspects of current research in settlement scaling (see also Raczky this volume).

CONTEMPORARY URBAN SYSTEMS

The existence of regularities in the sizes of cities within a given urban system has been recognized for many decades. City size in many systems conforms to a power law distribution (a distribution with many more small values and fewer high values than the normal distribution) known as Zipf's law or the rank-size rule. In these systems, the second-largest city has half the population as the largest city, the third-largest has one-third the population, and so on (Mitchell 2009:ch. 17). Archaeologists have used Zipf's law to investigate ancient settlement systems, under the label of "rank-size analysis" (Drennan and Peterson 2004; Johnson 1981; Smith 2005); most of these studies have focused on deviations from the rank-size rule, such as urban primacy (the label for settings where the largest settlement is larger than predicted by the model).

Research on urban scaling extended this search for power law regularities in city size by using city population to predict a series of quantitative urban variables (Bettencourt et al. 2007, 2010; Pumain et al. 2006). Empirical studies of contemporary city size identified some striking regularities in these data. These regularities are not about outcomes for individual cities, but rather they pertain to observable patterns of a distribution within an urban system. The quantitative patterns of greatest interest are expressed by a parameter called ß, which is the exponent of the power law. There are three classes of relationship between urban variables and city population: (1) linear scaling in which ß is equal to 1; the quantity in question increases at the same rate as population; (2) sublinear scaling in which ß is less than one; the quantity increases at a lower rate than population; and (3) superlinear scaling in which ß is greater than one; the output increases at a greater rate than population.

Several quantitative urban measures exhibit sublinear scaling with highly regular quantitative expressions. The area of a city, for example, increases with population with a ß of close to two-thirds (0.67). This means that the per capita area decreases with city size; larger cities are denser than smaller cities. Similarly, the total length of urban infrastructure (roads, cables, etc.) also increases with population with a ß of two-thirds. This makes sense—if city A is twice as large as city B, it does not need twice the amount of roads since some of the increased traffic can use the existing roads. The remarkable thing about these relationships is their regularity across urban systems (Bettencourt 2013).

More surprising than sublinear scaling are cases of superlinear scaling. A wide range of measures of social output—from income, wealth, and innovation to crime and poverty rates—exhibit superlinear scaling with city population. In other words, larger cities on average not only have more wealth or crime than smaller cities but they have larger per capita rates of these measures than smaller cities. This finding fits with long-standing social science research, reviewed above, showing that urbanization and urban growth have both positive and negative outcomes. Figure 2.4 shows data for superlinear scaling among contemporary U.S. cities compared with pre-Spanish settlements in the Mantaro region of the Andes; these data are from Bettencourt (2013) and Ortman and his colleagues (2016). Power law distributions are often graphed using a logarithmic transformation which produces a linear pattern (whose slope is ß) amenable to analysis with standard linear least-squares regression analysis. In Figure 2.4, the black lines mark a ß of 1.0 which would indicate linear scaling. The dotted lines show the prediction from theory for superlinear scaling (ß of 1.17), and the gray lines are the best fit lines (A: ß of 1.13; B: ß of 1.14).

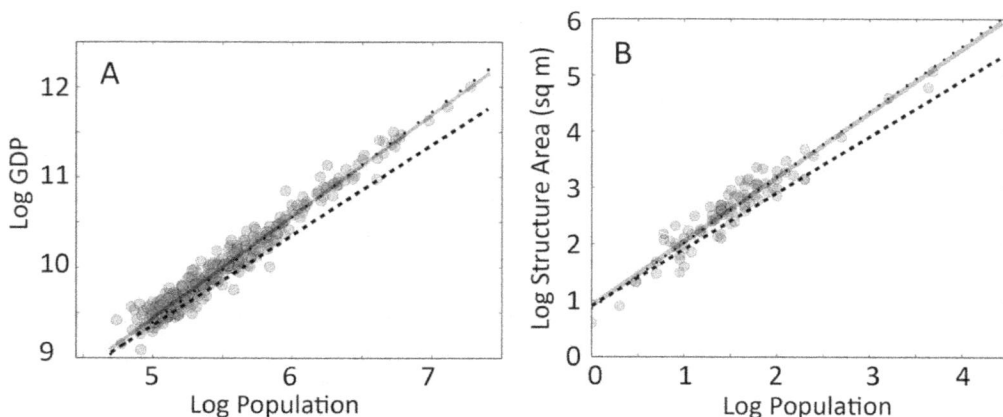

FIGURE 2.4. Superlinear scaling of economic output with population in modern and ancient settlement systems. A) GDP (Gross Domestic Product) in U.S. cities (Bettencourt 2013), B) structure area in prehispanic Andean settlements (Ortman et al. 2016). For both graphs, the dashed line shows the linear plot, the gray line is the best fit to the data, and the dotted line shows the predicted slope.

THE SOCIAL REACTORS MODEL

The data on sublinear and superlinear scaling in contemporary cities accumulated during the early 2000s. In 2013, Bettencourt published a quantitative model that predicts the empirical findings from a small number of variables. His model is based on the number of people in a settlement, the distance they can travel, the probabilities they will encounter other people, and the average output or productivity of each person. This is a network model in which the built environment acts to promote or hinder movement and interaction. The quantitative expression of these variables (for the formulae, see Bettencourt 2013) produces ideal or theoretical findings that predict quantitatively how urban measures should scale with city population. In fact, the empirical data match the predictions rather closely. In Bettencourt's words, "These results also suggest that, despite their apparent complexity, cities may actually be quite simple: Their average global properties may be set by just a few key parameters" (2013:1438).

Bettencourt calls his model the "social reactors model" of urban dynamics. Superlinear scaling indicates that the actions of individuals in cities yield per capita outputs greater than would be predicted by linear scaling alone. Cities are social reactors, and the bigger they are the greater the per capita output. This model can be seen as a kind of microfoundation for the notion, discussed above, that energized crowding generates changes in human settlements. Or, looked at from another perspective, the model of energized crowding provides a broad social science framework for Bettencourt's quantitative model of urban scaling.

EXPANSION OF THE FRAMEWORK TO PREMODERN SETTLEMENT SYSTEMS

Once the empirical findings of scaling regularities within systems of modern cities and the behavioral mechanisms of the social reactors model were established, an obvious question was whether this approach would also yield fruitful results for cities before the modern era. The basic assumptions of the social reactors model do not depend on contemporary economic institutions (the capitalist economy, wage labor, a monetary economy), and there is no obvious a priori reason why they should not hold for early or non-Western settlement systems. The next task was therefore to gather data to test the scaling models for past urban systems.

Ortman assembled the first set of archaeological data to evaluate scaling models in the distant past. He showed that both site area and wealth (using house size as a proxy for wealth) in the Aztec period Basin of Mexico scales with site population with the same scaling exponent as predicted by Bettencourt's theory and as found empirically for contemporary cities (Ortman et al. 2014, 2015). Given these initially promising results, the Social Reactors Project was formed in 2014 by Luís Bettencourt, Jose Lobo, Scott Ortman, and myself in order to explore the scaling models and other quantitative urban expressions in ancient and non-Western societies (see http://www.colorado.edu/socialreactors/). Our results to date have confirmed the presence of similar scaling regularities in a number of early urban systems, including city area in Medieval Europe (Cesaretti et al. 2015) and wealth in the Inca-period Andes (Ortman et al. 2016). Figure 2.4B shows the scaling of wealth against population for the latter region, resulting in a ß identical to that reported for contemporary economic output.

Recent research has now extended these findings to the settlement systems of small-scale farming groups that do not qualify as "urban" in most senses of that term. Two separate village settlement systems in prehistoric North America exhibit superlinear scaling of wealth and population (Ortman and Coffey 2017), and a number of twentieth-century peasant settlement systems in Mesoamerica and the Near East show the predicted sublinear scaling of area with population (Cesaretti 2016). A study of formal public plazas in ancient Mesoamerican settlements shows consistent sublinear scaling of plaza size with city population, but with values of ß that match neither prior empirical patterns nor theoretical predictions (Ossa et al. 2017). These new studies are summarized in Table 2.3; the close match between observed archaeological values for ß and the predicted values is striking.

DISCUSSION

The settlement scaling research reviewed above has two immediate implications for the analysis of settlement aggregation and urbanization in the past. First, the fact that village settlement systems exhibit the same scaling regularities as contemporary and premodern urban systems implies that processes of village aggregation and urbanization are expressions of the same or similar underlying social dynamics. As settlements—whether

Table 2.3
Quantitative Scaling Regularities in Premodern Settlement Systems

Variable	Scaling Coefficient	Examples	Societal Type	Citation
Area	*2/3 (0.67)*	*Predicted value*		*Bettencourt 2013*
	0.57 to 0.75	Contemporary cities		Bettencourt 2013
	0.58 to 0.74	14th-century Europe	A	Cesaretti et al. 2015
	0.73	Basin of Mexico, Aztec period	A	Ortman et al. 2014
	0.66, 0.70	Late Horizon Andes	A	Ortman et al. 2016
	0.66	Mesa Verde region	V	Ortman and Coffey 2017
	0.67	Middle Missouri region	V	Ortman and Coffey 2017
	0.62 to 0.91	20th-century peasant systems	P	Cesaretti 2016
	0.65	Imperial Roman cities	A	Hanson and Ortman 2017
Wealth	*7/6 (1.17)*	*Predicted value*		*Bettencourt 2013*
	1.10 to 1.22	Contemporary cities		Bettencourt 2013
	1.18	Basin of Mexico	A	Ortman et al. 2015
	1.14	Late Horizon Andes	A	Ortman et al. 2016
	1.17	Mesa Verde region	V	Ortman and Coffey 2017
	1.19	Middle Missouri region	V	Ortman and Coffey 2017
Plaza area	0.40, 0.61	Contemporary cities		no studies
		Mesoamerica	A	Ossa et al. 2017

Key to societal types: A: agrarian state, V: village system, P: peasant component of nation-state.

villages or cities—grow through immigration (and natural increase), they generate outputs with similar quantitative expressions. Second, the social reactors theory—which postulates energized crowding as the basic process that generates growth and quantitative regularities among systems—explains the observed patterns of aggregation and urbanization as the outcome of the increased social interactions created by those demographic processes.

These findings require a number of changes in the way that archaeologists think about past settlement dynamics and urbanization. First, these results challenge the traditional, strong separation of concepts of urban and nonurban. Past emphases on the concepts of city and urbanism, and their rigorous definition, have hindered scholarly understanding of fundamental human settlement processes. Archaeologists and others have long devoted attention to partitioning settlements into the categories of urban and nonurban. The urban category carries greater prestige, leading archaeologists working on early sites to distort definitions of urbanism so that their sites will qualify (e.g., Heckenberger 2009), or to propose definitions of special types of city (e.g., low-density agrarian city) that permit their sites to enter into the rarified realm of the urban (Fletcher 2009). Definitions are useful tools—particularly for comparative analysis (Smith 2016)—but they can also impede our understanding.

This has been the case in the realm of demography and settlement size. Because the study of villages and village aggregation has been carried out independently from research on cities and urbanization, scholars have been slow to recognize the many similarities between these two domains. The common elements are the demographic and spatial attributes of individuals who move into and among settlements, and who interact socially within settlements. These processes of movement and interaction generate social and economic effects, and it is starting to become clear that these processes occur in many kinds of settlements—from villages to cities, and in the ancient and modern worlds. Indeed, the chapters in this volume provide numerous examples of these processes.

The second change needed in archaeological approaches to settlement dynamics and urbanization is an expanded investigation of the quantitative relationships between demographic and social variables in ancient settlement systems (see Table 2.3). We need to examine these patterns in a larger number of contexts in order to explore their boundaries and limits. Just how extensive or universal are these patterns? Do they apply in some situations but not others?

Third, the identification of energized crowding as a key causal nexus in explaining a variety of social outcomes requires archaeologists to look beyond anthropology and archaeology for the conceptual tools to understand settlement changes in the past. Energized crowding—a process based on the increased social interactions that come from population growth and aggregation—is a phenomenon that has been poorly explored in the disciplines of anthropology and archaeology. Other fields have better models and theories in this area, and archaeologists need to take advantage of them in order to explain the regular (and important) empirical patterns we identify in past settlement systems. Our data, in turn, has a crucial role of play in the explanation of processes of demography, urbanization, and social change—not only in the deep past but in the world today.

ACKNOWLEDGMENTS

I thank Attila Gyucha for organizing the conference that led to the present volume, and Peter Biehl and the Institute for European and Mediterranean Archaeology at the University at Buffalo for hosting an excellent scholarly event. I thank the members of the Social Reactors Project—Luís Bettencourt, Jose Lobo, and Scott Ortman, as well as students and postdocs—for discussions and interactions that have created enough "energized scientific crowding" to generate real empirical and conceptual advances. Jose Lobo provided comments on an earlier draft that challenged me to think harder about some difficult issues.

NOTE

1.   A common approach to communities in archaeology diverges from social science consensus in emphasizing idealist and social constructionist models that posit shared meanings about identity as the main factor that creates communities (Canuto and Yaeger 2000). For a critique of this approach and how it serves to isolate archaeology from the social sciences, see Smith (2018).

REFERENCES CITED

Adler, M. A., and R. H. Wilshusen 1990 Large-Scale Integrative Facilities in Tribal Societies: Cross-Cultural and Southwestern US Examples. *World Archaeology* 22(2):133–146.

Alberti, G. 2014 Modeling Group Size and Scalar Stress by Logistic Regression from an Archaeological Perspective. *PLOS ONE* 9(3):e91510.

Bandy, M. S. 2004 Fissioning, Scalar Stress, and Social Evolution in Early Village Societies. *American Anthropologist* 106(2):322–333.

Bettencourt, L. M. A. 2013 The Origins of Scaling in Cities. *Science* 340(6139):1438–1441.

Bettencourt, L. M. A., J. Lobo, D. Helbing, C. Kühnert, and G. B. West 2007 Growth, Innovation, Scaling, and the Pace of Life in Cities. *Proceedings of the National Academy of Sciences* 104(17):7301–7306.

Bettencourt, L. M. A., J. Lobo, D. Strumsky, and G. B. West 2010 Urban Scaling and Its Deviations: Revealing the Structure of Wealth, Innovation and Crime across Cities. *PLoS ONE* 5(11):1–9.

Birch, J. (editor) 2013 *From Prehistoric Villages to Cities: Settlement Aggregation and Community Transformation*. Routledge, New York.

Blanton, R. E., and L. F. Fargher 2008 *Collective Action in the Formation of Pre-Modern States*. Springer, New York.

Boserup, E. 1965 *The Conditions of Agricultural Growth: The Economics of Agrarian Change under Population Pressure*. Aldine, Chicago.

Bowles, S., and H. Gintis 2002 Social Capital and Community Governance. *The Economic Journal* 112(483):F419–F436.

Braudel, F. 1981 *The Structures of Everyday Life*. Translated by S. Reynolds. Civilization and Capitalism, 15th–18th Century, Vol. I. Harper and Row, New York.

Brint, S. 2001 Gemeinschaft Revisited: A Critique and Reconstruction of the Community Concept. *Sociological Theory* 19(1):1–23.

Brower, S. N. 2011 *Neighbors and Neighborhoods: Elements of Successful Community Design*. APA Planners Press, Chicago.

Canuto, M. A., and J. Yaeger (editors) 2000 *The Archaeology of Communities: A New World Perspective*. Routledge, New York.

Carballo, D. M. 2013 Labor Collectives and Group Cooperation in Prehispanic Central Mexico. In *Cooperation and Collective Action: Archaeological Perspectives*, edited by D. M. Carballo, pp. 243–274. University Press of Colorado, Boulder.

Carneiro, R. L. 1962 Scale Analysis as an Instrument for the Study of Cultural Evolution. *Southwestern Journal of Anthropology* 18(2):149–169.

Cesaretti, R. 2016 *Regional Settlement Demography: Integrating Controlled Analogues into Archaeological Population Modeling*. Master's paper. School of Human Evolution and Social Change, Arizona State University, Tempe.

Cesaretti, R., J. Lobo, L. M. A. Bettencourt, S. Ortman, and M. E. Smith 2015 Population–Area Relationship in Medieval European Cities. *SFI Working Paper* 2015-10-036. Santa Fe Institute, Santa Fe, New Mexico.

Chaskin, R. J. 1997 Perspectives on Neighborhood and Community: A Review of the Literature. *Social Service Review* 71(4):521–547.

Coward, F., and R. I. M. Dunbar 2014 Communities on the Edge of Civilization. In *Lucy to Language: The Benchmark Papers*, edited by R. I. M. Dunbar, C. Gamble, and J. A. J. Gowlett, pp. 380–408. Oxford University Press, New York.

Cronk, L., and B. L. Leech 2013 *Meeting at Grand Central: Understanding the Social and Evolutionary Roots of Cooperation*. Princeton University Press, Princeton, New Jersey.

de Ruiter, J., G. Weston, and S. M. Lyon 2011 Dunbar's Number: Group Size and Brain Physiology in Humans Reexamined. *American Anthropologist* 113(4):557–568.

Drennan, R. D., and C. E. Peterson 2004 Comparing Archaeological Settlement Systems with Rank-Size Graphs: A Measure of Shape and Statistical Confidence. *Journal of Archaeological Science* 31(5):533–549.

du Gay, P. 2012 Leviathan Calling: Some Notes on Sociological Anti-Statism and Its Consequences. *Journal of Sociology* 48(4):397–409.

Dunbar, R. I. M. 2011 Constraints on the Evolution of Social Institutions and Their Implications for Information Flow. *Journal of Institutional Economics* 7(3):345–371.

Duranton, G., and D. Puga 2004 Micro-Foundation of Urban Agglomeration Economies. In *Handbook of Regional and Urban Economics*, Vol. 4, edited by J. Vernon Henderson and J.-F. Thisse, pp. 2064–2117. Elsevier, Amsterdam.

Duranton, G., and D. Puga 2014 The Growth of Cities. In *Handbook of Economic Growth*, Vol. 2B, edited by P. Aghion and S. N. Durlauf, pp. 781–863. Elsevier, Amsterdam.

Epstein, J. M. 1999 Agent-Based Computational Models and Generative Social Science. *Complexity* 4(5):41–60.

Evans, G. W. 2001 Crowding and Other Environmental Stressors. In *International Encyclopedia of the Social and Behavioral Sciences*, edited by N. J. Smelser and P. B. Baltes, pp. 3018–3022. Elsevier, New York.

Feinman, G. M. 2011 Size, Complexity, and Organizational Variation: A Comparative Approach. *Cross-Cultural Research* 45(1):37–58.

Fletcher, R. 1995 *The Limits of Settlement Growth: A Theoretical Outline*. Cambridge University Press, Cambridge.

Fletcher, R. 2009 Low-Density, Agrarian-Based Urbanism: A Comparative View. *Insights* 2(4):2–19.

Fujita, M., P. Krugman, and A. J. Venables 1999 *The Spatial Economy: Cities, Regions, and International Trade*. MIT Press, Cambridge, Massachusetts.

Glaeser, E. L. 2008 *Cities, Agglomeration, and Spatial Equilibrium*. Oxford University Press, New York.

Glaeser, E. 2011 *Triumph of the City: How Our Greatest Invention Makes Us Richer, Smarter, Greener, Healthier, and Happier*. Penguin Press, New York.

Glaeser, E. L., B. I. Sacerdote, and J. A. Scheinkman 2003 The Social Multiplier. *Journal of the European Economic Association* 1:345–353.

Goldstone, J. A. 1991 *Revolution and Rebellion in the Early Modern World*. University of California Press, Berkeley.

Goldstone, J. A. 2002 Efflorescences and Economic Growth in World History: Rethinking the Rise of the West and the British Industrial Revolution. *Journal of World History* 13(2):323–389.

Hakim, B. S. 2007 Generative Processes for Revitalizing Historic Towns or Heritage Districts. *Urban Design International* 12(2):87–99.

Hanson, J. W., and S. G. Ortman 2017 A Systematic Method for Estimating the Populations of Greek and Roman Settlements. *Journal of Roman Archaeology* 30:301–324.

Hayek, F. A. 1967 The Results of Human Action but not of Human Design. In *Studies in Philosophy, Politics, and Economics*, edited by F. A. Hayek, pp. 96–105. University of Chicago Press, Chicago.

Hechter, M. 1987 *Principles of Group Solidarity*. University of California Press, Berkeley.

Heckenberger, M. J. 2009 Lost Cities of the Amazon: The Amazon Tropical Forest Is not as Wild as It Looks. *Scientific American* 301(4):64–71.

Helsley, R. W., and Y. Zenou 2014 Social Networks and Interactions in Cities. *Journal of Economic Theory* 150:426–466.

Hopstock, P. J., J. R. Aiello, and A. Baum 1979 Residential Crowding Research. In *Residential Crowding and Design*, edited by J. R. Aiello and A. Baum, pp. 9–21. Plenum, New York.

Ioaniddes, Y. 2012 *From Neighborhoods to Nations: The Economics of Social Interactions*. Princeton University Press, Princeton, New Jersey.

Jacobs, J. 1961 *The Death and Life of Great American Cities*. Random House, New York.

Jennings, J. 2016 *Killing Civilization: A Reassessment of Early Urbanism and Its Consequences*. University of New Mexico Press, Albuquerque.

Johnson, A. W., and T. K. Earle 2000 *The Evolution of Human Societies: From Foraging Group to Agrarian State*. 2nd ed. Stanford University Press, Stanford, California.

Johnson, G. A. 1978 Information Sources and the Development of Decision-Making Organizations. In *Social Archaeology: Beyond Subsistence and Dating*, edited by C. L. Redman, pp. 87–112. Academic Press, New York.

Johnson, G. A. 1981 Monitoring Complex System Integration and Boundary Phenomena with Settlement Size Data. In *Archaeological Approaches to the Study of Complexity*, edited by S. van der Leeuw, pp. 144–189. Universiteit van Amsterdam, Amsterdam.

Johnson, G. A. 1982 Organizational Structure and Scalar Stress. In *Theory and Explanation in Archaeology: The Southampton Conference*, edited by C. Renfrew, M. J. Rowlands, and B. A. Segraves, pp. 389–421. Academic Press, New York.

Kennedy, D. P., and R. Adolphs 2011 Social Neuroscience: Stress and the City. *Nature* 474:452–453.

Kent, S. 1990 A Cross-Cultural Study of Segmentation, Architecture, and the Use of Space. In *Domestic Architecture and the Use of Space: An Interdisciplinary Cross-Cultural Study*, edited by S. Kent, pp. 127–152. Cambridge University Press, New York.

Kornhauser, R. 1978 *The Social Sources of Delinquency Theory: An Appraisal of Analytical Models*. University of Chicago Press, Chicago.

Kostof, S. 1991 *The City Shaped: Urban Patterns and Meanings through History*. Bulfinch Press, Boston.

Lynch, K. 1981 *A Theory of Good City Form*. MIT Press, Cambridge, Massachusetts.

Mann, M. 1986 *The Sources of Social Power. Volume 1: A History of Power from the Beginning to A.D. 1760*. Cambridge University Press, New York.

Mayhew, B. H., and R. L. Levinger 1977 Size and the Density of Interaction in Human Aggregates. *American Journal of Sociology* 82(1):86–110.

Meier, R. L. 1962 *A Communications Theory of Urban Growth*. MIT Press, Cambridge, Massachusetts.

Mitchell, M. 2009 *Complexity: A Guided Tour*. Oxford University Press, New York.

Murdock, G. P. 1949 *Social Structure*. Free Press, New York.

Naroll, R. 1956 A Preliminary Index of Social Development. *American Anthropologist* 58(4):687–715.

Netting, R. McC. 1993 *Smallholders, Householders: Farm Families and the Ecology of Intensive Sustainable Agriculture*. Stanford University Press, Stanford, California.

Nisbet, R. A. 1966 *The Sociological Tradition*. Basic Books, New York.

O'Brien, D. T. 2009 Sociality in the City: Using Biological Principles to Explore the Relationship Between High Population Density and Social Behavior. In *Advances in Sociology Research*, Vol. 8, edited by J. A. Jaworski, pp. 1–14. Nova Science, Hauppauge, New York.

Ortman, S. G., A. H. F. Cabaniss, J. O. Sturm, and L. M. A. Bettencourt 2014 The Pre-History of Urban Scaling. *PLOS ONE* 9(2):e87902.

Ortman, S. G., A. H. F. Cabaniss, J. O. Sturm, and L. M. A. Bettencourt 2015 Settlement Scaling and Increasing Returns in an Ancient Society. *Science Advances* 1(1):e1400066.

Ortman, S. G., and G. D. Coffey 2017 Settlement Scaling in Middle-Range Societies. *American Antiquity* 82(4):662–682.

Ortman, S. G., K. E. Davis, J. Lobo, M. E. Smith, L. M. A. Bettencourt, and A. Cabaniss 2016 Settlement Scaling and Economic Change in the Central Andes. *Journal of Archaeological Science* 73:94–106.

Ossa, A., M. E. Smith, and J. Lobo 2017 The Size of Plazas in Mesoamerican Cities and Towns: A Quantitative Analysis. *Latin American Antiquity* 28(4):457–475.

Ostrom, E. 1990 *Governing the Commons: The Evolution of Institutions for Collective Action*. Cambridge University Press, New York.

Ostrom, E. 2005 *Understanding Institutional Diversity*. Princeton University Press, Princeton, New Jersey.

Ostrom, E. 2007 Collective Action Theory. In *The Oxford Handbook of Comparative Politics*, edited by C. Boix and S. C. Stokes, pp. 186–208. Oxford University Press, New York.

Pumain, D. 2012 The Evolution of City Systems, Between History and Dynamics. *International Journal of Environmental Creation* 12(1):1–12.

Pumain, D., F. Paulus, C. Vacchiani-Marcuzzo, and J. Lobo 2006 An Evolutionary Theory for Interpreting Urban Scaling Laws. *Cybergeo*: Article 343. Electronic document: http://cybergeo.revues.org/2519?lang=en.

Rappaport, R. A. 1968 *Pigs for the Ancestors: Ritual in the Ecology of New Guinea People*. Yale University Press, New Haven, Connecticut.

Redfield, R. 1941 *The Folk Culture of Yucatan*. University of Chicago Press, Chicago.

Sampson, R. J. 2012 *Great American City: Chicago and the Enduring Neighborhood Effect*. University of Chicago Press, Chicago.

Schachner, G. 2010 Corporate Group Formation and Differentiation in Early Puebloan Villages of the American Southwest. *American Antiquity* 75(3):473–496.

Scott, A. J., and M. Storper 2015 The Nature of Cities: The Scope and Limits of Urban Theory. *International Journal of Urban and Regional Research* 39(1):1–15.

Simmel, G. 1898 The Persistence of Social Groups II. *American Journal of Sociology* 3:829–836.

Smith, M. E. 2005 City Size in Late Postclassic Mesoamerica. *Journal of Urban History* 31(4): 403–434.

Smith, M. E. 2010 The Archaeological Study of Neighborhoods and Districts in Ancient Cities. *Journal of Anthropological Archaeology* 29(2):137–154.

Smith, M. E. 2016 How Can Archaeologists Identify Early Cities? Definitions, Types, and Attributes. In *Eurasia at the Dawn of History: Urbanization and Social Change*, edited by M. Fernández-Götz and D. Krausse, pp. 153–168. Cambridge University Press, New York and Cambridge.

Smith, M. E. 2018 Quality of Life and Prosperity in Ancient Households and Communities. In *The Oxford Handbook of Historical Ecology and Applied Archaeology*, edited by C. Isendahl and D. Stump, pp. 486–505. Oxford University Press, New York.

Smith, M. E., A. Engquist, C. Carvajal, K. Johnston-Zimmerman, M. Algara, Y. Kuznetsov, B. Gilliland, and A. Young 2015 Neighborhood Formation in Semi-Urban Settlements. *Journal of Urbanism* 8(2):173–198.

Smith, R. A. 1975 Measuring Neighborhood Cohesion: A Review and Some Suggestions. *Human Ecology* 3(3):143–160.

Spooner, B. (editor) 1972 *Population Growth: Anthropological Implications*. MIT Press, Cambridge, Massachusetts.

Spruill, T. M. 2010 Chronic Psychosocial Stress and Hypertension. *Current Hypertension Reports* 12(1):10–16.

Storper, M. 2013 *Keys to the City: How Economics, Institutions, Social Interactions, and Politics Shape Development*. Princeton University Press, Princeton, New Jersey.

Storper, M., and A. J. Venables 2004 Buzz: Face-to-Face Contact and the Urban Economy. *Journal of Economic Geography* 4(4):351–370.

Talen, E. 2000 Measuring the Public Realm: A Preliminary Assessment of the Link Between Public Space and Sense of Community. *Journal of Architectural and Planning Research* 17(4):344–360.

Tilly, C. 1974 Do Communities Act? In *The Community: Approaches and Applications*, edited by M. P. Effrat, pp. 209–240. Free Press, New York.

Turchin, P., and S. A. Nefedov 2009 *Secular Cycles*. Princeton University Press, Princeton, New Jersey.

Ward, C. 1973 The Theory of Spontaneous Order. In *Anarchy in Action*, pp. 31–39. George Allen and Unwin, London.

Wellman, B. 2012 Commentary: Is Dunbar's Number Up? *British Journal of Psychology* 103(2): 174–176.

Wengrow, D. 2015 *Cities before the State in Early Eurasia*. Goody Lecture 2015. Max Planck Institute for Social Anthropology, Department "Resilience and Transformation in Eurasia." IMPRESS, Halle/Saale.

West, G. 2017 *Scale: The Universal Laws of Growth, Innovation, Sustainability, and the Pace of Life in Organisms, Cities, Economies, and Companies*. Penguin Press, New York.

Wirth, L. 1938 Urbanism as a Way of Life. *American Journal of Sociology* 44(1):1–24.

Youn, H., L. M. A. Bettencourt, J. Lobo, D. Strumsky, H. Samaniego, and G. B. West 2016 Scaling and Universality in Urban Economic Diversification. *Journal of The Royal Society Interface* 13(114):20150937.

SECTION I

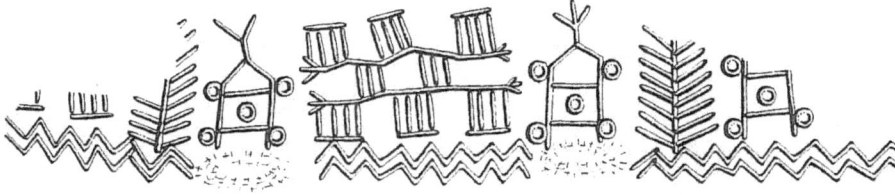

Coming Together: Origins and Processes

"... the nearest run thing ..."

The Genesis and Collapse of a Bronze Age Polity in the Maros Valley of Southeastern Europe

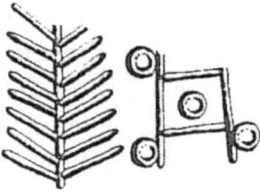

John M. O'Shea and Amy Nicodemus

Abstract   *Around 2000 B.C., the settlements of the Maros culture reached their widest extent across southeastern Hungary, western Romania, and northern Serbia. It was at this time that the Bronze Age site of Pecica Șanțul Mare was established. Over the next 500 years, Pecica rapidly became the preeminent Bronze Age center in the region, controlling the distribution of metals and domestic horses throughout the Carpathian Basin, and then with equal rapidity collapsed and was abandoned. Renewed research at Pecica Șanțul Mare affords a fine-grained view of the interplay of factors that led to the genesis and collapse of this important Bronze Age polity and allows regional patterns of growth, aggregation, and dispersal to be linked to specific social processes and elite strategies at this critical center. Pecica provides a valuable case in which a complex polity does not transition into a stable state-like organization. Its example may mirror developments in other contemporary Bronze Age societies in the eastern Carpathian Basin, and may provide important clues for why primary states failed to develop in temperate Europe.*

THE PROBLEM WITH POPULATION

Cities and urbanism are often linked with the origins of the state, and jointly with the traditional concept of civilization. Yet, from the perspective of temperate Europe, none of these concepts really resonate. Outside of the Classical world, both urban centers and state-level organizations are introduced only secondarily. Why such social forms do not develop in temperate Europe is itself an interesting question. The region certainly sees cycles of population aggregation and dispersal, long-distance trade, and technological innovation, but—outside of the Classical world—nothing approaching urbanism or a primary state. Complicating the investigation is the absence of literacy and both the historical narratives and basic economic records, which provide such insight into the formation of bureaucratic centers in the Aegean and Near East. In prehistoric (nonliterate) contexts, when states do arise—as in the Valley of Oaxaca in Mexico (Marcus and Flannery 1996; Spencer and Redmond 2004)—prehistorians can often reconstruct the key developments from the material evidence. But when cities and states do not emerge, explanations prove much harder to come by.

Absent literacy and the other trappings of civilization, prehistoric archaeologists have typically followed two approaches for the investigation of complexity. The first is typological, where the presence of complexity is asserted given the appearance of some key trait or set of traits, such as monumental construction, "rich graves," or imported "luxury" goods. These are then embedded in narratives that often invoke the seen and the unseen in equal proportions to account for complexity. Such approaches are rightly seen as static and nonexplanatory.

The second is to focus on population aggregation as a more dynamic indicator of increasing social and economic complexity. The emphasis on large and permanent aggregations rests ultimately on a posited causal relationship between population size and social complexity, of which the development of cities and urban centers is often cited as a special case. It is argued that integrative and hierarchical social structures *must* emerge to manage the greater demands for social control and information processing necessitated by an increasing density of local and regional populations. In essence, if growth or aggregation of population is observed, the emergence of integrative structures can be assumed (Carneiro 1967; MacSweeney 2004; Ortman 2013). While such approaches can accommodate the interaction of multiple social and economic factors and provide a basis for cross-cultural comparison, the causal engine remains the size and density of the population (see Gyucha and Smith this volume).

Arguments for population as a prime mover or causal agent have been around for a long time and periodically appear and disappear as the agent of choice (Boserup 1965; Carneiro 1967; Cohen 1979; Naroll 1956). There is no need to rehash that history here. The question of how to estimate population size, however, continues to perplex. Even contemporary observers viewing living populations have difficulties estimating population size, as anyone who has worked with historical population estimates will appreciate.

Archaeology has long struggled with how to estimate past population size and dynamics. In virtually all cases, these efforts require a series of normative assumptions, which inevitably homogenize the variation in the past we seek to investigate. One common approach is to apply cross-cultural values for floor space usage (Duffy 2014; Kramer 1982; LeBlanc 1971; Naroll 1962). In other cases, archaeologists have focused on their own raw data, equating numbers of carbon dates (Johnson and Brook 2011; Peros et al. 2010; Rick 1987; Shennan and Edinborough 2007; Shennan et al. 2013; Timpson et al. 2014) or the size of sherd scatters/site area (Brumfiel 1976; Parsons

1972; Postgate 1994; Schreiber and Kintigh 1996; Steponaitis 1981) with the number of people inhabiting the locality. These estimates require numerous additional assumptions about archaeological recovery, depositional processes, and unverifiable assertions about the interrelationship between all of these factors. In certain limited cases, such as the stone-constructed settlements at Lepenski Vir, sophisticated Bayesian modeling has been combined with paleodemographic evidence to estimate the size of the local populations (Porčić 2016). But even here, uncertainty regarding cultural practices—such as the portion of the population actually buried at the site and the seasonal organization of the settlement—make the estimates little more than speculative points within a very broad range of potential values.

In many instances, it is possible to make relative statements about population size and density even if precise numbers cannot be attached. An early example of this approach can be found in Sanders's (1976) population models, based on surface surveys in the Valley of Mexico. Similar estimates have been based on the changing number of occupied houses in Middle Neolithic sites (Dubouloz 2008) and Trypillia megasites (Müller et al. 2016; see also Gaydarska this volume). In both instances, the assessments are buttressed by a large number of high-precision radiocarbon dates. In these cases, a likely range of population estimates can be offered, making certain assumptions about the use life of houses, the housing of domestic animals, and the packing of people within structures. But even without precise estimates, the archaeologist can at least argue that there are more houses occupied at the site at one time than another, or that there is not significant change.

Similar relative arguments are commonly made based on the number of discovered sites within a region. In these cases, it is argued that many of the uncertainties associated with settlement organization, archaeological visibility, and the like are controlled by looking only at sites deriving from a particular cultural group and comparing internal changes within (e.g., Duffy 2014). This may be a reasonable assumption, but if one is looking for evidence of social change, this might be the precise instance when such assumptions should *not* be made.

An increase in the number of houses, in the surface area of settlements, or of the number of sites in a region are all meaningful observations, but none of these lead us unambiguously back to an estimate of population size, density, or organization. The point is not so much to criticize attempts to estimate population, but rather to suggest that a value that is so difficult for archaeology to estimate probably should not be the variable that we use to anchor our investigations of complexity.

A focus on aggregation provides a means to avoid placing absolute numbers on the size and density of past populations and, instead, directs attention to qualitative changes in the way population, or its supposed archaeological surrogates, are distributed and organized (for a similar approach, see Birch and Ryan this volume). This is not unreasonable, although it again must invoke the entire range of assumptions about past human behavior and archaeological formation processes described above. In the end, it is simply a proxy for population size, and continues to be invoked as the causal mechanism for change.

But what if we treat aggregation as a result rather than a cause and, instead, monitor change in the social and economic processes that were occurring contemporary with the apparent growth or reorganization of population? Such an archaeological approach is necessarily multiscalar, linking regional-scale changes in settlement distribution with nearby changes within the locality of the center, and microscaled changes in the spatial, economic, and social organization visible within the center itself. When accompanied by high-precision dating, this approach can produce a detailed and dynamic description of change that links variation observed at these different scales and indicates those factors which seem most closely involved as factors causing and maintaining the observed social changes. It has the additional virtue of focusing attention on a range of variables that can actually be quite successfully monitored in the archaeological record.

In the remainder of this paper, we will briefly describe a complex Bronze Age center from the eastern Carpathian Basin which exhibits a convergence of population aggregation with a series of internal restructurings that often herald the transformation of chiefly centers into protostates. However, in this case, the transformations led not to the establishment of a stable and more complex polity, but instead resulted in the collapse of the system and the abandonment of the center.

PECICA ŞANŢUL MARE AND THE MAROS CULTURE

The Maros group was one of a series of cultural entities that crystalized during the Early Bronze Age in the eastern Carpathian Basin, around 2500 B.C. The core region of the Maros group can be thought of as a triangle connecting the confluence of the Tisza and Maros rivers at Szeged in Hungary to the point at which the Maros enters the foothills of the Carpathian Mountains near Lipova, at a distance of 120 kilometers in Romania, and the point south along the Tisza about halfway, roughly 75 kilometers, between the confluence with the Maros and the confluence with the Danube, near Bečej in Serbia. The distance from Bečej back to Lipova is 135 kilometers (Figure 3.1). This constitutes an area of roughly 4,000 square kilometers within which the bulk of Maros settlements and cemeteries are found. Of course, the area described is not uniform or equally suited for settlement or subsistence activities.

The settlements of the Maros group span two distinct regional settings, which had a major impact on site location and distribution. The Lower Maros near the confluence of the Tisza and Maros rivers was—prior to canalization in the nineteenth century—a wet and flood-prone environment. Maros settlements within this region tend to be relatively small and to be concentrated on the limited areas of higher ground within the marsh zone, or on the fringes of marshes, particularly to the south and east (Girić 1984; O'Shea 1996). In this, the Bronze Age settlement pattern is quite similar to the nineteenth century A.D. settlements within the same region (see Third Military Mapping Survey of Austria–Hungary [1910] Sheet 38–46). While a number of Maros hamlet settlements are known, few have been excavated and none have been excavated in their entirety or have been radiocarbon dated. While common in the Lower Maros, hamlets are rare in the Middle Maros region.

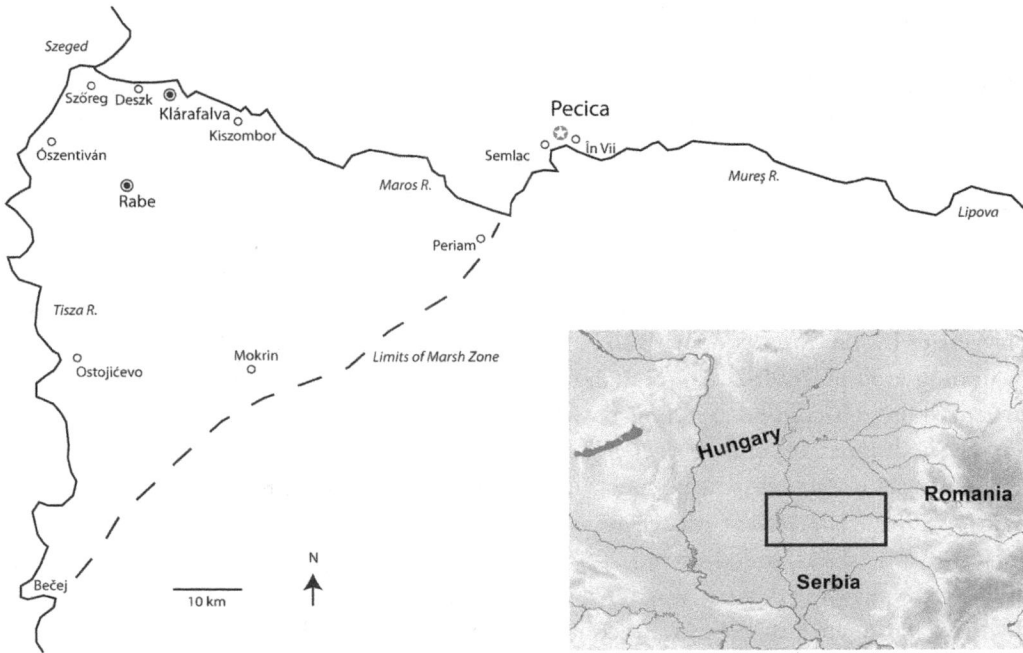

FIGURE 3.1. The Tisza–Maros confluence region and distribution of major Maros group settlements and cemeteries. The modern towns of Szeged in Hungary, Lipova in Romania, and Bečej in Serbia are indicated for reference. The approximate area of regular precanalization flooding is represented by a dashed line.

Hamlets are comprised of a small number of houses, and do not appear to have encircling ditches (e.g., Banner 1929; Girić 1987). Based on the study of the archaeological register of Csongrád County, they may also occur much closer together than the 6 kilometers separation normally observed for the Maros tells, although here the absence of precise dating must raise obvious questions about the contemporaneity of these settlements. Hamlets tend to cluster on raised landforms, which would have afforded some protection from seasonal flooding, as in the vicinity of Szőreg or Ószentiván (now Tiszasziget). The clusters also appear to be anchored by larger or smaller inhumation cemeteries into which the dead from surrounding communities were interred (O'Shea 1996). This use of cemeteries and death rituals as a social and spatial integrative medium is not observed among the Middle Maros tell settlements.

Settlement in the Middle Maros region is quite different. Here settlement tends to be located on high ground, often at the edge of the floodplain. The sites tend to be larger and more long lived, producing substantial tell deposits (Gogâltan et al. 2014), and typically are surrounded by encircling defensive ditches. The Middle Maros tells exhibit a tendency for regular spacing and rarely occur closer than 5 to 6 kilometers to one another. While regional survey only has been conducted on a small portion of the total area, smaller settlements of the kind seen on the Lower Maros are uncommon, as is any evidence for cemeteries.

The tell settlements contain a small, raised center, typically in the range of 0.5 to 1.2 hectares in area, commonly surrounded by multiple encircling ditches (Table 3.1). Habitation structures are found both in the central core and within the surrounding ditches. As few of the tell settlements have been extensively excavated, much remains unknown about settlement within, and potentially beyond, the ditch system or about the motivation for creation of the ditch works. What is known about off-tell occupation comes from the sites of Pecica Şanţul Mare in Romania and Kiszombor Új Élet Tsz. in Hungary.

Kiszombor Új Élet Tsz. is the earliest dated Maros settlement and much of its history is known due to the construction of a series of long silage trenches in the core of the site by the local cooperative (L. Horváth 1982). The initial Maros occupation— beginning around 2600 B.C.—contained a small, raised citadel (in an area subsequently destroyed by agricultural buildings) with additional habitation structures, storage pits, and ovens located beyond the central area. It seems likely that the citadel had a small encircling ditch, but subsequent construction has made it difficult to establish its existence with certainty. The earliest off-tell houses were not surrounded by a ditch, although an enclosing ditch was added about 200 years after the occupation began. Later, before 2000 B.C., this initial ditch was filled in and Maros houses were built over the top of it. There is evidence to suggest a second ditch was constructed, but it did not enclose a substantially larger area since the shape of the landform and surrounding wetland ulti- mately constrained the size of the settlement. At Kiszombor Új Élet Tsz., the multiple ditches do appear to reflect growth in the settlement over time.

The second instance where there is solid, datable evidence associated with encircling ditches is at Pecica Şanţul Mare itself. The Bronze Age settlement at Pecica began with the occupation of the central tell area around 1950 B.C. There may have been a ditch enclosing this initial occupation, but if so, its traces were destroyed by the subsequent

TABLE 3.1
AREA OF PRINCIPAL MAROS TELL SETTLEMENTS

Site	Center	Inner Ditch	Outer Ditch
Early Phase Tells			
Kiszombor Új Élet Tsz.	1.2	5.8	6.5
Periam Movila Şantului	1.2	4.8	6.8
Semlac Livada lui Onea	1.1	4.0	6.4
Pecica În Vii	0.6	4.7	
Late Phase Tells			
Pecica Şanţul Mare	1.0	5.7	20.8
Klárafalva Hajdova	1.2	2.8	
Rabe Anka Siget	1.2	5.3	15.1
Munar Dealul Lupului	1.0	5.9	13.1

Values derive from measurements on satellite imagery, and are reported in hectares. The site of Munar Dealul Lupului is likely not a Maros affiliated tell, but appears to be a contemporary Middle Bronze Age tell, and is located directly opposite Pecica on the south edge of the Maros floodplain.

construction of the "great ditch." About 50 years after the site was founded, the great ditch was constructed as part of the overall definition of the community plan at Pecica. Yet, no evidence of Bronze Age settlement dating to this time period is found beyond the great ditch. At the peak of Pecica's florescence, around 1820 B.C., the first occupation in the area surrounding the central tell is observed. It is likely that this was the time when the additional ditches were constructed, most likely as a rapid sequence of construction episodes.

Taking this reconstruction and the one from Kiszombor Új Élet Tsz. together, it is probably safe to assume that successively larger enclosures reflect population growth at all of the Maros tells. Such a pattern of construction in response to growth is not unique, and is assumed in other portions of the Carpathian Basin Bronze Age sites as well as elsewhere (e.g., Gogâltan et al. 2014; Steadman 2000; see also Birch and Raczky this volume).

The Pecica case is somewhat anomalous in the apparent absence of off-tell settlement prior to ditch construction—a characteristic that it shares with Klárafalva Hajdova. At both these sites, it appears that neighboring sites and not off-tell settlement were the source of community labor, although for quite different reasons.

Settlement Expansion, Aggregation, and Dispersal in the Maros Region

While it is not possible to independently estimate the numbers of people occupying the Maros region, it is possible to trace the pattern of settlement change that occurs during the span of the Maros group in the Early and Middle Bronze Ages. From their earliest appearance at Kiszombor Új Élet Tsz., the settlements of the Maros group appear to increase in number and in regional distribution, peaking around 2000 B.C.

After about 1850 B.C., the majority of settlements in both the Lower and Middle Maros region are abandoned, as are most of the inhumation cemeteries. As this happens, the site of Pecica Şanţul Mare grows in size and area occupied. Aside from Pecica, only the tell settlements at Klárafalva Hajdova and Rabe Anka Siget continue to be occupied (Grčki-Stanimirov and Stanimirov-Grčki 1998; F. Horváth 1982; Reizner 1891). In the Lower Maros, a few hamlets in the confluence area and around Deszk show evidence of continued occupation and cemetery use (Foltiny 1941a, 1941b). Interestingly, farther south along the Tisza, the Maros cemetery at Ostojićevo and its associated settlements also continue to be used (Girić 1987), arguing for continuous settlement in this region.

From around 1680 B.C., Pecica experiences a sharp decline in settlement density, and by 1545 B.C., it is entirely abandoned. It is followed soon after by the abandonment of Klárafalva Hajdova and Rabe Anka Siget, along with the remaining Maros hamlets and settlements in the Tisza–Maros region.

So while we cannot directly address the question of population size, the Maros group does exhibit a clear trajectory of settlement growth and expansion, followed by aggregation and then a relatively abrupt dispersal. The significance and potential causes for this trajectory can be found in the sequence of change and restructuring that is observed at the Pecica tell during this time period.

THE RISE AND FALL OF PECICA ŞANŢUL MARE

Pecica Şanţul Mare ("Great Ditch") is one of the most prominent Bronze Age tells in the Carpathian Basin, and one of the earliest investigated (Crişan 1978; Dömötör 1901; Dörner 1978; Hügel et al. 2012; Roska 1912, 1914). Pecica—and the nearby contemporary tell at Periam—provided the basis for Childe's Perjámos culture in his *The Danube in Prehistory* (1929), and has remained the focus for understanding the regional chronology, metallurgy, and material culture.

The Pecica tell is located on a high bluff line, which forms the northern boundary of the Maros floodplain, and was positioned advantageously to exploit the flow of raw ores or metalwork from the rich western Romanian metal sources in the Apuseni Mountains. Early excavations at the site by Roska (1912, 1914) produced quantities of stone molds, which confirmed the site's importance in the regional metalwork exchange networks. Renewed excavations at Pecica, since 2005, have established an absolute chronology for the site and have revealed much about the founding and role of the settlement within the Maros group (Nicodemus et al. 2015; O'Shea et al. 2005, 2006, 2011).

To understand the development at Pecica and its relationship with the regional changes in Maros settlement, it will be necessary to examine a series of social, economic, and organizational variables and to monitor how they changed relative to the observed shifts in regional Maros settlement. An overview of these transformations is presented in Figure 3.2 and Table 3.2.

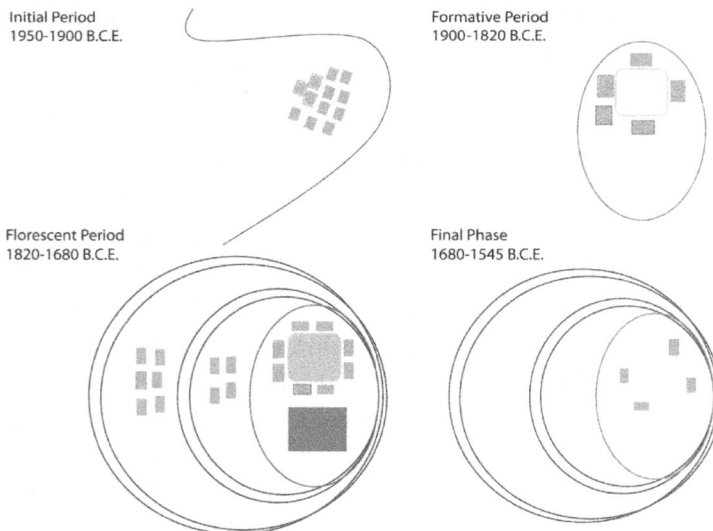

FIGURE 3.2. The evolution of Pecica Şanţul Mare. Light gray rectangles represent houses. The open gray square in the Formative Period represents the central plaza. The closed gray square in the Florescent Period represents the central platform, while the dark gray square marks the location of intensive metallurgical activity. The oval rings around the site area represent the ditch systems which encircle the settlement.

TABLE 3.2
CHRONOLOGY OF PECICA ŞANŢUL MARE

Culture/ Group	Site Period	Date	Major Developments	Economic Foci
Árpádian		A.D. 1000–1100		
Dacian		300–100 B.C.		
Maros	Final	1680–1545 B.C.	Off-tell settlement abandoned, decline in occupation intensity, house built over top of central platform	Generalized subsistence
Maros	Florescent	1820–1680 B.C.	Central platform constructed, construction of exterior ditches, off-tell occupation	Peak metal production, peak horse production, display storage and feasting
Maros	Formative	1900–1820 B.C.	Construction of "great ditch," establishment of central site plan, construction of central plaza	Intense metal production, beginning of horse rearing, craft production of elite regalia
Maros	Initial	1950–1900 B.C.	Site leveled, erection of ritual structure	Intensive ore smelting and production, craft production incorporating exotic materials
Hunyadihalom		3935–3800 B.C.		

Table refers to radiocarbon dates only. Previous studies place the Medieval Age occupation through the twelfth and thirteenth centuries A.D., and the Iron Age settlement through the first century A.D. (Hügel et al. 2012).

THE INITIAL PERIOD: 1950–1900 B.C.

It has already been noted that Bronze Age Pecica was established during the period when Maros settlements reached their maximum geographical extent and number. Pecica was founded *de novo* just after 2000 B.C. The site was located midway between two apparently preexisting Maros tell settlements, Semlac Livada lui Onea and potentially Pecica În Vii, at a distance of 2.5 kilometers from them, and on top of a Middle Copper Age Hunyadihalom culture settlement that had been abandoned almost two millennia previously (Nicodemus et al. 2015; Roman 1971). The Copper Age occupation was leveled and one of the initial Bronze Age structures exhibited many unusual features of potential ritual significance. Built into the floor of one of the houses were a series of perforated pig mandibles, along with a series of broken and unfinished stone axes. The house itself had an unusual circular structure, added to the normal, rectangular Maros house form, and on the floor of the house was found a series of feet from pots or figurines some of which were zoomorphic.

The other houses placed at the site were relatively light structures and were tightly packed together. There is no evidence for a central plan to the settlement, nor is there evidence that any defensive works were constructed during this initial phase. The entire settlement appears to have been confined to the core tell area.

Very rapidly after the initial occupation—perhaps a generation or less—the original habitation structures, including the ritual building, were intentionally burned (compare to Raczky this volume) and replaced by more substantial houses with wood planking and, in some cases, second stories. Substantial midden deposits formed around the base of these larger houses, along with many fired areas and ash dumps.

The principal economic activity evident on the site was metalworking, with a particular emphasis on the processing of raw ores. In addition to metalworking, there was also diverse craft production. This included manufacture of composite ornaments, which figure prominently in Maros elite display, such as the beaded sashes and head ornaments that mark hereditary social positions in Maros funerary treatment (O'Shea 1996). These items incorporated locally worked elements, such as pierced animal teeth, and beads made from imported, unworked raw materials, such as *Columbella* shell and amber. These finds demonstrate that the inhabitants were already well integrated into extraregional exchange networks. Further, the range and scale of high-value goods production far exceeds that seen at other Maros settlements, underscoring Pecica's prominence in local and regional economies. It is clear that the site was founded in a single, deliberate event and that the inhabitants hit the ground running.

THE FORMATIVE PERIOD: 1900–1820 B.C.

By 1900 B.C., roughly 50 years after its initial establishment, a major reorganization of the settlement is observed. House orientation shifts to correspond with the orientation of the tell, reflecting the construction of the great ditch, which effectively isolated the tell from the surrounding area. A central open plaza area also was created, which served as a focal point for community activities (see also Birch, Kelly, and Raczky this volume). One very large house with wood planking and a second story was constructed adjacent to this plaza. Other houses show a gradual evolution away from the traditional, thick clay Maros house floors to thinner floors with wood-lined wall trenches. Metallurgical activities and composite ornament manufacture continue unabated. These specialized, high-value crafts also continue to be made in spatially discrete areas of the site.

The neighboring tells—which preceded Pecica's foundation—may now be operating as subsidiary settlements, providing labor and subsistence goods. Differences in crop production between communities are apparent (Oas 2010); compared to the nearby tell of Semlac Livada Lui Onea, Pecica's inhabitants utilize much more barley, which may relate to the production of alcoholic beverages and feasting (Nicodemus et al. 2015). At this same time, the production of horses also begins to intensify.

THE FLORESCENT PERIOD: 1820–1680 B.C.

The Florescent Period sees the peak of cultural developments at the Pecica settlement. While the overall plan of the settlement remains the same, the large open plaza is replaced by a central platform which is bounded by elite residences on one side and storehouses on at least one of the other sides. This platform, constructed of sediments burned at industrial temperatures, measures up to 1 meter in thickness. The sheer scale of this construction— both in terms of its mass and invested resources (fuel, labor, and so on)—suggests that it should be viewed a rare example of monumental public architecture in the Carpathian Basin Bronze Age. This feature is unique to Pecica.[1] All of this construction occurs in the northern portion of the tell, while the southern portion is given over to intensive metal production. During this time, the outer encircling ditches are constructed and, importantly, extensive settlement is observed off-tell in the peripheral areas for the first time.

Evidence for economic activity on the tell also speaks to shifting foci. Metallurgy is being intensively pursued on the southern portion of the tell, but now the emphasis is on casting rather than the primary smelting of ores. This suggests that primary smelting is occurring elsewhere, with ingots arriving at Pecica for use in casting. In addition, finished metal objects—especially personal adornments—become far more frequent at the site and appear to replace the role of composite ornaments. While local manufacture of shell beads and polished teeth diminishes, there is a strong upswing in antler working, occurring at intensities unmatched for this period in the Carpathian Basin (Nicodemus and Lemke 2016).

At this time, horse rearing becomes perhaps the most important concern for the local elites. The number of horses peaks during this time period, with the highest proportion of horse remains known from any Middle Bronze Age site in the Carpathian Basin (Nicodemus 2013). The age and sex distribution of the horses reflect a strong emphasis on stock breeding and also suggest that efforts were being made to control the spread of breeding animals. Horses also become a focus of public display and ritual, with the conspicuous consumption of prime, reproductive-age mares in feasts on the central platform (Nicodemus 2018). These events were commemorated via ritualized deposition of feasting remains, including brazier fragments and meat-rich bones from horses and other high-value animals, some of which appear to have supported large poles. This new focus on horses is likely related to the adoption of chariotry technology—a series of model four-spoked chariot wheels from Florescent Period contexts provides the earliest securely dated evidence for chariots west of the Carpathians.

There is also a dramatic shift in the livestock management from generalized herding in the preceding periods—including an emphasis on secondary products—to practices that focus on the production of high-value meats which are mobilized by elites living on-tell. The contemporary population living off-tell has little access to such quality meats, nor possesses significant numbers of prestige storage vessels, underscoring substantial wealth and status differences between these two groups.

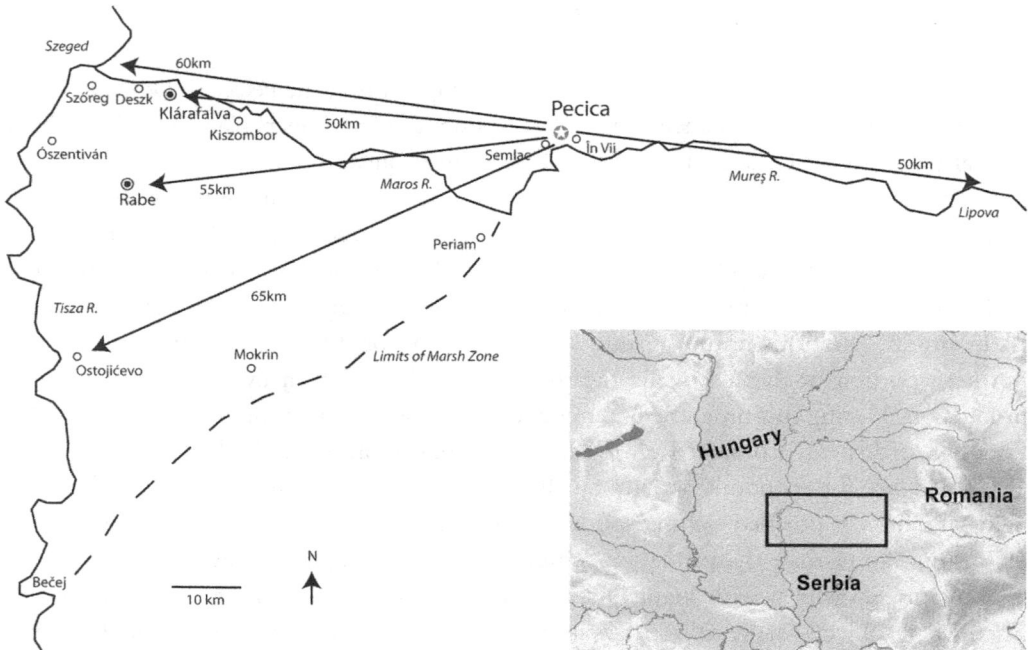

FIGURE 3.3. The Tisza–Maros confluence region during the Florescent Period at Pecica Şanţul Mare. Arrows indicate distances to major Late Maros settlements and to other strategic locations.

Concurrent with these changes at the Pecica tell, most other Maros settlements are abandoned, including those closest to Pecica that previously functioned as subsidiaries. Survey has not located any new Maros settlements in the area and it is tempting to view the sudden occupation of the large outer ditch areas at the Pecica as an influx of people from these other settlements in a process of synoecism.

As noted previously, the exceptions to tell abandonment are at Klárafalva Hajdova and Rabe Anka Siget. During this period, Pecica is a hub with spokes of roughly equal length connecting it to the other major tell sites (Figure 3.3). This regularity of spacing among the late Maros tells and the unequal densities of exotic trade ceramics and other imported goods have already been used to argue for a potential hierarchical relationship between Pecica and these two tells, sites that may have served as secondary centers (O'Shea 2013).

FINAL PHASE: 1680–1545 B.C.

After a relatively short-lived florescence, things go rapidly downhill at Pecica. The central site plan is abandoned, with only a few houses present on the tell, and these are built over the top of the central platform. At the same time, the settlement off the main tell is entirely abandoned. The intensive metalworking and horse rearing both collapse, as does the production of high-value craft goods and other items made on imported raw materials. The subsistence evidence indicates a return to a more generalized subsistence economy. After 1545 B.C., the site is entirely abandoned and is not reoccupied until the Iron Age.

Regionally, this is the time when the remaining Maros settlements and cemeteries also are abandoned. During the initial stages of Pecica's decline, one of its potential secondary centers, Klárafalva Hajdova, experiences its peak in metal production. Yet, with a bit of a lag, this site also experiences a similar or possibly even more abrupt abandonment. On a broader scale, most of the Middle Bronze Age polities of the eastern Carpathian Basin also collapse at this time.

DISCUSSION

If we look at the Pecica trajectory from a broad perspective, we can make several observations concerning the relationship between apparent population growth and aggregation, and the emergence and subsequent collapse of the Pecica polity. Pecica was a relatively new settlement, founded some 600 years after the first appearance of the Maros group, and was established at the time of maximum settlement expansion. Prior to this time, there were already numerous fortified tell settlements in the Middle Maros as well as unfortified tells and open sites, and, on the Lower Maros, large inhumation cemeteries. From these cemeteries, we know that in the Lower Maros the communities were organized as a confederacy of autonomous villages, with shared social markers and hereditary offices but no vertical political integration (O'Shea 1996).

Pecica was established close to and in between two existing Bronze Age settlements—indeed, it was placed too close, being a mere 2.5 kilometers from either. It is also clear that from the beginning Pecica was not an ordinary Maros settlement, nor was it simply a subsidiary location for the conduct of metal smelting. The elaborate site leveling that preceded construction, the production of elite regalia, and the erection of an unusual ritual structure with special offerings built into its floor all speak to its extraordinary status. It is hard to escape the impression that Pecica was founded as a special site with ritual sanction (for a similar situation, see Fernández-Götz this volume), for oversight of metal and craft production, and that it was rapidly transformed into the principal residence of an emergent elite. Yet, even as this happened, the actual population inhabiting the location was small. And it seems to have retained this modest size even as major public works were undertaken creating the great ditch and central settlement plan. It is only at its peak that the inhabited area of the Pecica site suddenly expanded, and this expansion coincided with the abandonment of most of the other Maros tells and settlements in the region. It is also at this time that elaborate public rituals come to the fore and that additional public architecture was constructed.

Changes in the direct elite control of the economy are also instructive (Table 3.3). From its inception, metallurgy was a major preoccupation of the Pecica elite. Yet, over time, the focus of this activity shifted from the primary processing of ores—which presumably also involved the active acquisition of metal ores—to an emphasis on the casting of bronze weapons and ornaments using metal that had been processed elsewhere and transported to Pecica.

The second category of elite-controlled activity was the production of craft goods. The items manufactured of bone and antler included both ornaments and tools, yet the most interesting category of materials is the composite ornaments. These items were comprised of multiple elements that were either themselves exotic imports, such as amber, marine shell, and faience, or required considerable fine finishing, such as the pierced and polished animal teeth. These ornaments are buried with the dead in the cemeteries of the Lower Maros, and many—including the beaded sashes and head ornaments—were employed as markers for hereditary offices (O'Shea 1996). The fact that these items of regalia performed an important symbolic function, and that they were regularly interred with the dead, implies an ongoing and perhaps dependent connection between the villages of the Lower Maros and Pecica. Yet, during the Florescent Period, the elites no longer maintained direct oversight of regalia production, shifting instead to the manufacture of elaborate metal goods and horse breeding. At this same time, the use of elite regalia in the funerary display of the Lower Maros cemeteries strikingly diminished.

Once large-scale horse rearing entered the picture, it remained under the firm control of the Pecica elite. Not only were horses scarce in the off-tell areas, they were similarly rare at other Maros settlements, including Klárafalva Hajdova (Nicodemus 2013). Horses would potentially have been a game changer for the Pecica elite since they provided not only a commodity to be exchanged and displayed but also a mobility multiplier for transportation and warfare. The monopoly on horses, and likely the attendant chariotry technology, was jealously maintained as long as the elites themselves controlled the Pecica tell. Yet, in the final phase of occupation, horse remains are as scarce on the tell as they

TABLE 3.3
DIRECT ELITE CONTROL OF THE ECONOMY THROUGH TIME
AT BRONZE AGE PECICA ŞANŢUL MARE

Economic Activity	Initial	Formative	Florescent	Final
Metal production—smelting	XXX	XX		
Metal production—casting	XXX	XXX	XXXX	
Elite regalia—composite ornaments	XXX	XXX		
Horse rearing		X	XXXX	
Fine ware ceramics				
Subsistence production				

Number of X's reflects strength of elite control.

are elsewhere. Indeed, the explosion of horse breeding, chariotry, and metal production—largely weaponry, as attested by the molds (Gogâltan 1999)—at Pecica's peak strongly suggests that it was not only a center for social, ritual, and economic activities but also for martial power during its zenith.

Finally, Table 3.3 highlights an additional feature of elite control of the economy at Pecica, namely, that fine ware ceramics and primary subsistence production do not appear to have ever figured in the elite economy, despite the prominence of fine ware ceramics as regional markers of identity. While the absence of ceramic workshops at the site is unambiguous, it might be argued that absent written records we would not expect to see overt evidence of elite control of basic subsistence production on the tell.

One line of evidence that may suggest some elite oversight of the subsistence economy is the occurrence of large storage vessels, which increase in number over time, along with the appearance of what is termed display storage, being large, burnished liquid containers that may be associated with alcoholic beverage production. This latter type of vessel is not found in the off-tell area. These—coupled with the appearance of specialized storage buildings—argue for the elite's interest in the productive economy, but they fall well short of the expectation for large-scale food redistribution. It seems likely that the storage represented on the tell relates more to elite usages, such as feasting and possibly for provisioning the immediate workforce on the tell.

The contrast in diet between the outer settlement and the main tell also indicates that the specialization in subsistence production—which may have occurred between neighboring settlements—is now full blown within the greater Pecica settlement itself, with the tell-dwelling elite being provisioned with high quality/value meats and grain from the surrounding community.

While the restructuring that occurs during the formation of the Pecica polity is clear, the causes and processes for its collapse are less obvious. There is no evidence for catastrophic destruction or burning at the end of the Florescent Period, nor overt signs of warfare or violence. Based on extensive aeolian deposits dated at this period, Sherwood and her colleagues (2013) have argued for a major episode of drought up and down the Maros, which may have been exacerbated by the extensive deforestation of the region produced by centuries of intensive metalworking. While environmental degradation may have been a contributing factor, the large-scale collapse of economic and social institutions suggests a more complex series of events at play, including the inability to maintain Pecica's centrality in regional trade networks. It is not clear where the elites or the people of the Maros group went once the system collapsed. Most likely they blended into the initial Late Bronze Age complexes that briefly appear and then disappear up and down the river.

So, the aggregation event that is documented at Pecica and in the Maros region generally does correspond to, and is an element in, the development of the Pecica polity. In terms of causality, however, population aggregation appears to be an effect rather than a cause. While the Maros population of the region does appear to grow from the time of initial appearance, this growth is not uniform, nor is the tendency toward aggregation universal. In the Lower Maros region, the only evidence for increase is the modest intrinsic growth suggested by paleodemographic reconstructions from the cemeteries (O'Shea 1996). On the Middle Maros, growth is suggested at each of the major tells. Yet, given the span of time represented by the tells and the near absence of smaller satellite settlements, it is likely that the rate of increase was similarly modest, and did not involve major recruitment of population from outside. Certainly, at Pecica itself most of the major restructuring occurred prior to the aggregation of population at the center, although the peak of development and population density do co-occur.

So, why did population coalesce at Pecica? It is clear that from the beginning the elites were able to mobilize labor on a substantial scale—to level and initially construct the site and later to construct the great ditch—all before there was any population aggregation at Pecica. It might be argued that the configuration of settlement during Pecica's Formative Period—with Semlac Livada lui Onea and potentially Pecica În Vii acting as subsidiary settlements—may have operated as a megasite that enjoyed the benefits of local labor and control, without incurring the costs associated with a large, nucleated settlement. Such an arrangement would also have had benefits in terms of access to arable land and graze. But if this was the case, why abandon the subsidiary settlements and aggregate at Pecica?

There is no evidence for destruction or violence associated with the abandonment of the neighboring sites, which might have necessitated a movement to Pecica. Pecica's continued ties to Klárafalva Hajdova and Rabe Anka Siget, and trade in metals and horses to points beyond, would similarly argue against military necessity. Instead, it seems most plausible that the pull to Pecica reflected an effort to solidify control over economic activities and to minimize the potential for political or economic competition from nearby centers. Yet, this political and social centralization ultimately failed and the system collapsed. While a range of environmental and social factors may have contributed, it is worth noting that similar collapses characterized most of the cultures of the eastern Carpathian Basin at this time.

We hope this brief example has demonstrated that—even in the absence of written records—archaeology can provide a highly detailed and dynamic account of the organizational and economic restructuring associated with the emergence and collapse of complex social forms. Rather than guessing at population numbers and arguing for structural changes that "must have occurred," archaeologists can describe in often great detail what actually did occur. In this sense, the archaeological case is not interpreted relative to the theory *du jour*, but rather provides an account of events that did occur, which can be compared and contrasted with similar trajectories derived from other archaeological, ethnographic, or historical cases, for use in the process of theory building.

ACKNOWLEDGMENTS

Excavations at Pecica Şanţul Mare was supported by the National Science Foundation, award numbers: BCS 0512162, 0620147, 1039380, and 1264315. We gratefully acknowledge the institutional support received from our colleagues at the Arad County Museum in Arad and the Museum of the Banat in Timişoara, and particularly our steady friend and advisor Dr. Peter Hügel. We also gratefully acknowledge the support of the village of Semlac, successive crews of Romanian and American undergraduate and graduate students, and most particularly of Carmen Ciolacu, who welcomed us as family in her home and at her table.

NOTE

1. Several other large tells in the region do have evidence for central plazas, but no platform constructions have been identified elsewhere to date.

REFERENCES CITED

Banner, J. 1929 Az ószentiváni bronzkori telep és temető. *Dolgozatok Szeged* 5(1–2):52–78.

Boserup, E. 1965 *The Conditions of Agricultural Growth: The Economics of Agrarian Change under Population Pressure.* George Allen and Unwin, London.

Brumfiel, E. M. 1976 Regional Growth in the Eastern Valley of Mexico: A Test of the "Population Pressure" Hypothesis. In *The Early Mesoamerican Village*, edited by K. V. Flannery, pp. 234–249. Academic Press, New York.

Carneiro, R. 1967 On the Relationship Between Size of Population and Complexity of Social Organization. *Southwestern Journal of Anthropology* 23(3):234–243.

Cohen, M. N. 1979 *The Food Crisis in Prehistory: Overpopulation and the Origins of Agriculture.* Yale University Press, New Haven, Connecticut.

Crişan, I. H. (editor) 1978 *Ziridava: Săpăturile de la "Şanţul Mare" din anii 1960, 1961, 1962, 1964.* Comitetul de Cultură şi Educaţie Socialistă al judeţului Arad, Arad.

Dömötör, L. 1901 Római korbeli edények a pécskai Nagy-sáncban. *Archaeologiai Értesítő* 21:327–335.

Dörner, E. 1978 Istoricul cercetărilor. In *Ziridava: Săpăturile de la "Şanţul Mare" din anii 1960, 1961, 1962, 1964*, edited by I. H. Crişan, pp. 16–22. Comitetul de Cultură şi Educaţie Socialistă al judeţului Arad, Arad.

Dubouloz, J. 2008 Impacts of the Neolithic Demographic Transition on Linear Pottery Culture Settlement. In *The Neolithic Demographic Transition and Its Consequences*, edited by J.-P. Bocquet-Appel and O. Bar-Yosef, pp. 207–235. Springer, Dordrecht.

Duffy, P. 2014 *Complexity and Autonomy in Bronze Age Europe: Assessing Cultural Developments in Eastern Hungary.* Prehistoric Research in the Körös Region 1. Archaeolingua, Budapest.

Foltiny, I. 1941a A szőregi bronzkori temető. *Dolgozatok Szeged* 17:1–89.

Foltiny, I. 1941b Koraréz és bronzkori temető Deszken. *Folia Archaeologica* 3–4:69–98.

Girić, M. 1984 Die Maros (Moriš, Mures)-Kultur. In *Kulturen der Frühbronzezeit des Karpatenbeckens und Nordbalkans*, edited by N. Tasić, pp. 33–58. Posebna Izdanja 22. Balkanološki Institut SANU, Beograd.

Girić, M. 1987 Naselja Moriške kulture. *Rad Vojvodanskih Muzeja* 30:71–83.

Gogâltan, F. 1999 *Bronzul timputiu şi mijlociu în Banatul românesc şi pe cursul inferior al Mureşulu. I: Cronologia şi descoperirile de metal.* Orizonturi Universitare, Timişoara.

Gogâltan, F., C. Cordoş, and A. Ignat (editors) 2014 *Bronze Age Tell, Tell-Like, and Mound-Like Settlements on the Eastern Frontier of the Carpathian Basin: History of Research.* Mega, Cluj-Napoca.

Grčki-Stanimirov, S., and S. Stanimirov-Grčki 1998 Nalazi sa Naselja iz Bronzanog Doba Anka Siget u Delti Moraša (Okolina Novog Kneževca). *Glasnik muzeja Banata* 8:18–28.

Horváth, F. 1982 Contributions to the Early and Middle Bronze Age of the Southern Alföld. *A Móra Ferenc Múzeum Évkönyve* 83(1):55–71.

Horváth, L. 1982 Kora bronzkori település Kiszomboron. *A Móra Ferenc Múzeum Évkönyve* 83(1):73–94.

Hügel, P., G. P. Hurezan, F. Mărginean, and V. Sava 2012 One and a Half Century of Archaeology on the Lower Mureş. *Ziridava* 26(1):7–34.

Johnson, C. N., and B. W. Brook 2011 Reconstructing the Dynamics of Ancient Human Populations from Radiocarbon Dates: 10 000 Years of Population Growth in Australia. *Proceedings of the Royal Society B* 278:3748–3754.

Kramer, C. 1982 *Village Ethnoarchaeology: Rural Iran in Archaeological Perspective.* Academic Press, New York.

LeBlanc, S. 1971 An Addition to Naroll's Suggested Floor Area and Settlement Population Relationship. *American Antiquity* 36(2):210–211.

MacSweeney, N. 2004 Social Complexity and Population: A Study in the Early Bronze Age Aegean. *Papers from the Institute of Archaeology* 15:82–89.

Marcus, J., and K. Flannery 1996 *Zapotec Civilization: How Urban Society Evolved in Mexico's Oaxaca Valley.* Thames and Hudson, New York.

Müller, J., K. Rassman, and M. Videiko (editors) 2016 *Trypillia Mega-Sites and European Prehistory 4100–3400 BCE.* Themes in Contemporary Archaeology 2. Routledge, London.

Naroll, R. 1956 A Preliminary Index of Social Development. *American Anthropologist* 58(4):687–715.

Naroll, R. 1962 Floor Area and Settlement Population. *American Antiquity* 27(4):587–589.

Nicodemus, A. 2013 Political Economy and Animal Production: A View from the Maros Region. Paper presented at the 19th Annual Meeting of the European Association of Archaeologists, Plzen.

Nicodemus, A. 2018 Food, Status, and Power: Animal Production and Consumption Practices during the Carpathian Basin Bronze Age. In *Social Dimensions of Food in the Prehistoric Balkans*, edited by M. Ivanova, B. Athanassov, V. Petrova, D. Takorova, and P. Stockhammer, pp. 248–262. Oxbow Books, Oxford.

Nicodemus, A., and A. Lemke 2016 Specialized Bone Working in the Bronze Age? The Organization of Production at Pecica-Şanţul Mare, Romania. *Cuadernos del Instituto Nacional de Antropologia y Pensamiento Latinoamericano, Series Especiales* 3(2): *Global Patterns in the Exploitation of Animal Based Raw Materials: Technical and Socio-Cultural Issues*, pp. 103–120.

Nicodemus, A., L. Motta, and J. O'Shea 2015 Archaeological Investigations at Pecica "Şanţul Mare" 2013–2014. *Ziridava* 29:105–118.

Oas, S. 2010 *Maros Macrobotanicals: An Archaeobotanical Analysis of Bronze Age Agriculture in the Maros Site of Semlac "Şanţul Mic."* Honors thesis, Department of Anthropology, University of Michigan, Ann Arbor.

Ortman, S. 2013 Introduction: Cahokia in a Global Context. In *Social Complexity at Cahokia*, edited by P. Peregrine, S. Ortman, and E. Rupley, pp. 4–9. SFI Working Paper 2014-03-004. Santa Fe Institute, Santa Fe, New Mexico.

O'Shea, J. 1996 *Villagers of the Maros: A Portrait of an Early Bronze Age Society.* Plenum Press, New York.

O'Shea, J. 2013 Reading Regional Identities in the Carpathian Basin Bronze Age: You Can't Judge a Book by Its Cover. Paper presented at the 19th Annual Meeting of the European Association of Archaeologists, Plzen.

O'Shea, J., A. W. Barker, L. Motta, and A. Szentmiklosi 2011 Archaeological Investigations at Pecica "Şanţul Mare" 2006–2009. *Analele Banatului* 18:67–74.

O'Shea, J., A. W. Barker, A. Nicodemus, S. Sherwood, and A. Szentmiklosi 2006 Archaeological Investigations at Pecica Şanţul Mare: The 2006 Campaign. *Analele Banatului* 14:211–228.

O'Shea, J., A. W. Barker, S. Sherwood, and A. Szentmiklosi 2005 New Archaeological Investigations at Pecica Şanţul Mare. *Analele Banatului* 12–13:81–109.

Parsons, J. R. 1972 Archaeological Settlement Patterns. *Annual Review of Anthropology* 1:127–150.

Peros, M. C., S. E. Munoz, K. Gajewski, and A. E. Viau 2010 Prehistoric Demography of North America Inferred from Radiocarbon Data. *Journal of Archaeological Science* 37(3): 656–664.

Porčić, M. 2016 The Approximate Bayesian Computation Approach to Reconstructing Population Dynamics and Size from Settlement Data: Demography of the Mesolithic–Neolithic Transition at Lepenski Vir. *Archaeological and Anthropological Sciences* 8(1):169–186.

Postgate, N. 1994 How Many Sumerians per Hectare?—Probing the Anatomy of an Early City. *Cambridge Archaeological Journal* 4(1):47–65.

Reizner, J. 1891 Rábéi ásatások. *Archaeologiai Értesítő* 11:206–210.

Rick, J. W. 1987 Dates as Data: An Examination of the Peruvian Preceramic Radiocarbon Record. *American Antiquity* 52(1):55–73.

Roman, P. 1971 Strukturänderungen des Endäneolithikums im Donau-Karpatenraum. *Dacia* 15:31–136.

Roska, M. 1912 Ásatás a pécska-szemlaki határban levő Nagy Sáczon. *Dolgozatok az Erdélyi Múzeum érem- és régiségtárából* 3:1–73.

Roska, M. 1914 Ásatás a perjámosi Sánczhalmon. *Múzeumi és Könyvtári Értesítő* 8:73–104.

Sanders, W. T. 1976 Settlement and Population History of the Basin of Mexico. In *Studies in Pre-Hispanic Ecology and Society*, edited by E. R. Wolf, pp. 69–100. University of New Mexico Press, Albuquerque.

Schreiber, K. J., and K. W. Kintigh 1996 A Test of the Relationship Between Site Size and Population. *American Antiquity* 61(3):573–579.

Shennan, S., S. S. Downey, A. Timpson, K. Edinborough, S. Colledge, T. Kerig, K. Manning, and M. G. Thomas 2013 Regional Population Collapse Followed Initial Agriculture Booms in Mid-Holocene Europe. *Nature Communications* (DOI: 10.1038/ncomms3486):1–8.

Shennan, S., and K. Edinborough 2007 Prehistoric Population History: From the Late Glacial to the Late Neolithic in Central and Northern Europe. *Journal of Archaeological Science* 34(8):1339–1345.

Sherwood, S., J. D. Windingstad, A. W. Barker, J. O'Shea, and W. C. Sherwood 2013 Evidence for Holocene Aeolian Activity at the Close of the Middle Bronze Age in the Eastern Carpathian Basin: Geoarchaeological Results from the Mureş River Valley, Romania. *Geoarchaeology* 28:131–146.

Spencer, C. S., and E. M. Redmond 2004 Primary State Formation in Mesoamerica. *Annual Review of Anthropology* 33:173–199.

Steadman, S. 2000 Spatial Patterning and Social Complexity on Prehistoric Anatolian *Tell* Sites: Models for Mounds. *Journal of Anthropological Archaeology* 19(2):164–199.

Steponaitis, V. 1981 Settlement Hierarchies and Political Complexity in Non-Market Societies: The Formative Period in the Valley of Mexico. *American Anthropologist* 83(2):320–363.

Timpson, A., S. Colledge, E. Crema, K. Edinborough, T. Kerig, K. Manning, M. G. Thomas, and S. Shennan 2014 Reconstructing Regional Population Fluctuations in the European Neolithic Using Radiocarbon Dates: A New Case-Study Using an Improved Method. *Journal of Archaeological Science* 52:549–557.

CHAPTER FOUR

Coming Together in the Iron Age

Population Aggregation and Urban Dynamics in Temperate Europe

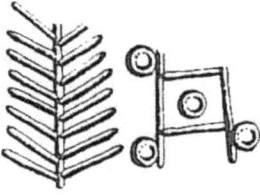

Manuel Fernández-Götz

Abstract   *Iron Age urbanization processes in temperate Europe were a nonlinear phenomenon which included changing and dynamic cycles of centralization and decentralization. Recent research has demonstrated that the first urban centers developed as early as the sixth and fifth centuries B.C. in an area stretching from Central France to Bohemia. However, this so-called Fürstensitze or "princely seats" constituted an ephemeral phenomenon that was followed by a period of decentralization that some authors have linked with the "Celtic migrations" recorded in Classical sources. A new period of centralization started in the late third century B.C. The appearance of open agglomerations was the prelude for the development of large fortified centers—the Late Iron Age oppida of the second and first centuries B.C. This paper will summarize the new evidence for the different stages of Iron Age urbanism, discussing the social dynamics that lie behind the emergence, abandonment, and reemergence of major agglomerations in temperate Europe during the first millennium B.C.*

EARLY URBANISM IN TEMPERATE EUROPE: THE *FÜRSTENSITZE*

The Iron Age (ca. 800–20 B.C.) was a period of profound changes in temperate Europe, with the appearance of a number of features—such as cities, writing, and coinage—that still deeply shape our modern world (Fernández-Götz and Krause 2016; Haselgrove et al. 2018; Wells 2011). The interactions with the Mediterranean Basin were intense and adopted different mechanisms, including trade, migration, and finally military conquest by the Roman Empire. While the use of the term *city* has controversially been debated, in this paper, I propose a context-dependent definition that recognizes the high levels of variation that often exist between and within different urban traditions: "a numerically significant aggregation of people permanently living together in a settlement which fulfils central place functions for a wider territory" (cf. Fernández-Götz and Krausse 2013:480).

Most scholars traditionally agreed that the first urban centers of Central-Western Europe developed in the second and first centuries B.C. (Collis 1984; Guichard et al. 2000; Wells 1984). They are referred to as *oppida,* after the Roman nomenclature used by Julius Caesar during his military campaigns in Gaul. Following this line of interpretation, the first cities would have appeared at the dawn of the Roman conquest, at least partially as a result of the growing influence of this Mediterranean civilization. However, advances in archaeological research have profoundly changed this picture over the last two decades, to the point that we can now assert that there was a much earlier, first wave of urbanization that preceded the *oppida* by more than four centuries (Fernández-Götz et al. 2014; Krausse et al. 2016; Sievers and Schönfelder 2012). This first period of centralization led to the development of the so-called Early Iron Age *Fürstensitze,* or "princely seats," of the sixth and fifth centuries B.C. (Brun and Chaume 2013; Fernández-Götz and Krausse 2013). They stretch from Central France in the west to Bohemia in the east (Figure 4.1), and thus have a much more restricted distribution area than the later

FIGURE 4.1. Main central places of the seventh to fifth centuries B.C. north of the Alps, and selected sites in Mediterranean Europe (after Fernández-Götz and Ralston 2017).

oppida. Among their main characteristics are the existence of a fortified settlement on a hilltop, or *acropolis,* the presence of Mediterranean imports (mostly Greek and Etruscan), and the clustering of large tumuli (*Fürstengräber*) in the surroundings. The latter served as last resting place for members of the sociopolitical elite and their relatives or retinues, manifesting an increasingly hierarchical social structure (Krausse 2006; Steffen 2012; Verger 2015).

Although known since the excavations of the 1950s at the Heuneburg hilltop plateau and in the environs of Mont Lassois, for a long time the *Fürstensitze* were thought to have covered only a few hectares—an idea that needs to be revised in light of new data. Thanks to large-scale excavation projects, systematic surveys, and the use of remote sensing techniques—such as aerial photography and LIDAR images—the corpus of the *Fürstensitze* has significantly increased since the early 1990s, and so has the extent of many of these sites (Krausse 2008a, 2010).

This change is best exemplified by the Heuneburg on the Upper Danube—the most intensively investigated central place of Early Iron Age Europe (Fernández-Götz 2014a; Krausse et al. 2016). The site has attracted international attention since the 1950s when a Mediterranean-inspired mudbrick wall and southern objects, such as high-quality Attic pottery, were discovered. Systematic settlement excavations over several decades have uncovered a detailed stratigraphy on the 3 hectares of the hilltop plateau, with 14 building and 10 fortification phases dating to the Late Hallstatt period (ca. 620–450 B.C.).

For a long time, it was thought that the settlement at the Heuneburg was mainly confined to this hilltop plateau. However, new investigations in the last 20 years have radically changed this picture. In fact, between the end of the seventh and the middle of the sixth century B.C., this *acropolis* was only the most visible component of a large agglomeration—recent fieldwork demonstrates the existence of a heavily fortified lower town and an enormous outer settlement of around 100 hectares (Kurz 2010). The latter was subdivided by an extensive system of banks and ditches, which, in turn, enclosed dense groups of farmsteads that were demarcated by rectangular palisades (Figure 4.2). It is tempting to interpret the subdivision of the outer settlement into quarters or neighborhoods as evidence for the existence of different kinship groups which joined during a process of synoecism that underpinned the creation of the agglomeration (for similar processes of *synoikismos* in the Greek world, see Ault this volume).

The new discoveries have radically changed our traditional image of the Heuneburg: instead of a small hillfort of only a few hectares, recent results now suggest an enormous settlement of 100 hectares with an estimated population of around 5,000 inhabitants in the first half of the sixth century B.C. (Fernández-Götz and Krausse 2013; Krausse et al. 2016). Moreover, the Heuneburg was also an important center of production, distribution, and innovation, in which skilled craftsmen produced ceramics, brooches, textiles, and jewelry. There are good reasons for believing that particular artifact types widely distributed at the site were actually created at the Heuneburg (for example, red-and-white colored vessels with a high neck). The settlement is also significant from

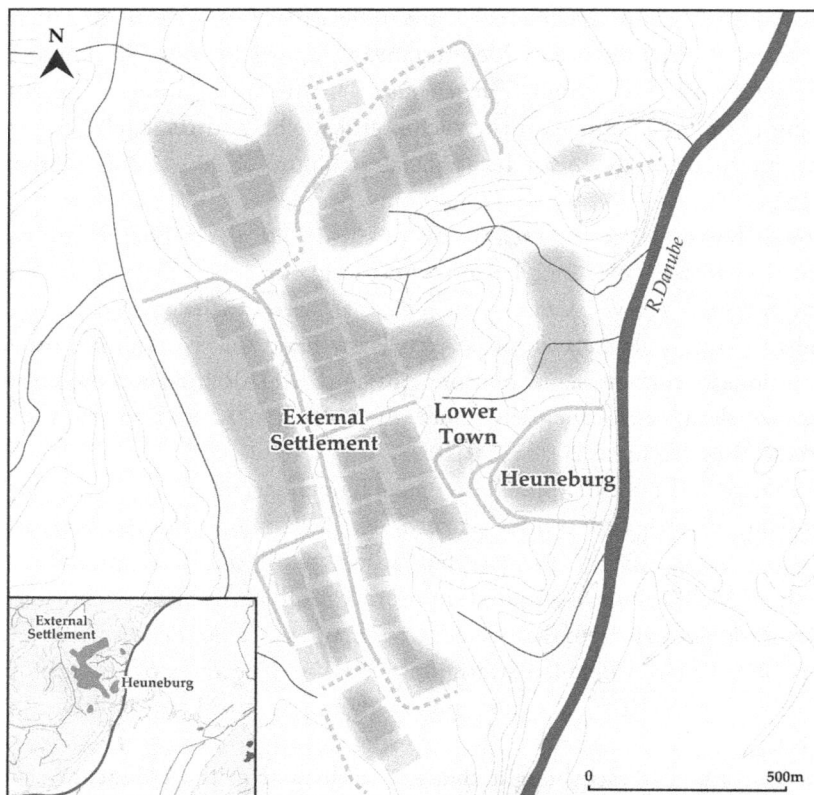

FIGURE 4.2. Heuneburg. Plan of the 100-hectare agglomeration during the mudbrick wall phase (after Fernández-Götz and Ralston 2017).

an archaeozoological point of view—stable isotope analysis shows that during the mudbrick wall period, with its highly concentrated population, a significant proportion of the animals were transported over a distance of 50–60 kilometers (Schatz and Stephan 2008).

However, this development was interrupted by a major reconfiguration related to a devastating fire that occurred around 540/530 B.C. After this traumatic event, the mudbrick fortification was replaced by a traditional timber-and-earth construction, the internal layout of the hilltop plateau was radically changed, and the greater part of the external settlement was abandoned. These major changes suggest that a violent conflict followed by significant population decline was the most likely cause. It is unclear whether this conflict arose through external attack or a struggle between internal factions. Settlement activity continued on the hilltop plateau and within the lower town for a few more generations; interestingly, most of the Mediterranean imports belong to this postdestruction period. A further conflagration finally ended the Iron Age occupation around the middle of the fifth century B.C.

Whereas the Heuneburg seems to have been the most extensive and powerful settlement north of the Alps during a large part of the sixth century B.C., in the following century it was Bourges in Central France that apparently surpassed all other centers (Ralston 2007, 2010). Until a few years ago, this site was best known for the Late Iron Age *oppidum* mentioned in Roman written sources. In the first century B.C., Bourges was indeed the town of *Avaricum*—the capital of the tribe of the Bituriges, which was besieged and captured by Julius Caesar during his Gallic Wars.

The fact that Bourges has been continuously settled even to the present day means that we have only a patchy picture of the internal structure of the Iron Age settlement and its peripheral areas. In spite of these difficulties, work carried out in recent years has produced important information on the Early Iron Age occupation (Augier et al. 2007, 2012; Milcent 2007). In the fifth century B.C., an enormous settlement with several foci stretched around the promontory on which the cathedral stands today. The entire agglomeration complex covered several hundred hectares, although the density of settlement was relatively low in some areas (Figure 4.3). Similar to the Heuneburg, Bourges

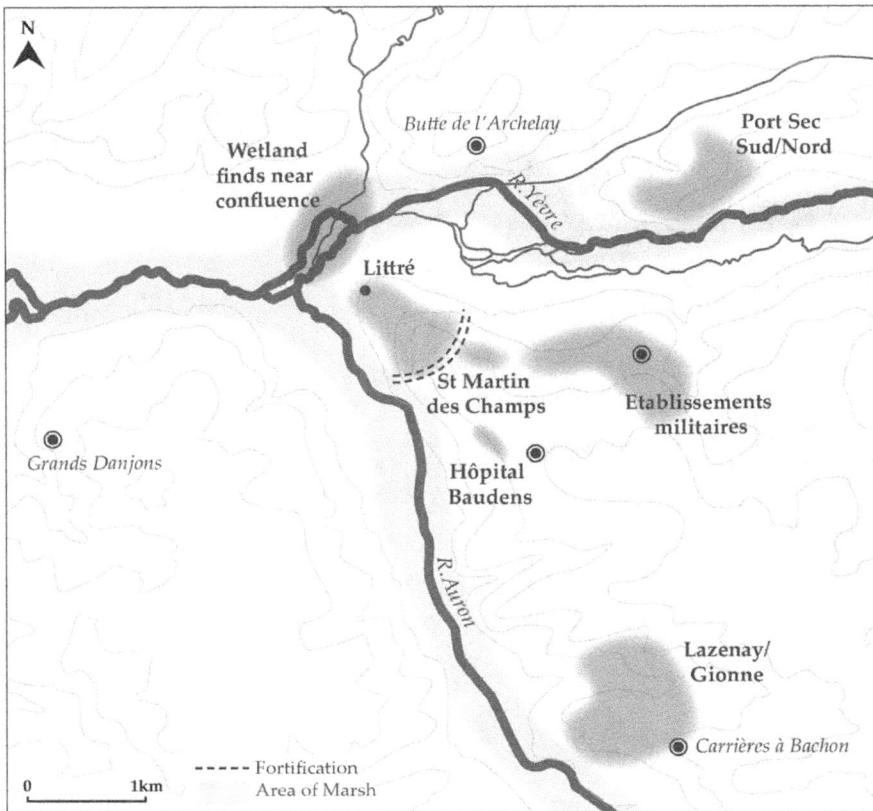

FIGURE 4.3. Bourges. Plan of the agglomeration and its surroundings in the fifth century B.C. (after Milcent 2014, modified by the author).

was a combination of an *acropolis,* suburbs, and rich elite burials in the surroundings. Both major settlements fit well within the definition of "low-density urbanism" as developed by Fletcher (2009, 2012).

Apart from the Heuneburg and Bourges, we can add several further examples of powerful Early Iron Age centers, such as Mont Lassois, Hohenasperg, Glauberg, Ipf-bei-Bopfingen, Ehrenbürg bei Forchheim, Závist, and Vladař (Biel and Krausse 2005; Krausse 2008a, 2010; Krausse et al. 2016:ch. 7). Monumental fortifications, profane, sacral, and funerary architecture, as well as workshop areas and Mediterranean imports highlight their manifold functions. Imposing fortification systems with banks, ditches, walls, and gates—such as those found at the Heuneburg and Mont Lassois—emphasize the defensive and highly symbolic significance of these sites (Figure 4.4). Craft and technical as well as economic and mercantile functions are reflected by the presence of imported goods, as well as workshops for specialized craftsmen and areas dedicated specifically to crafts production. Although sanctuaries are more difficult to identify, excavations have revealed several temples on the *acropolis* of Závist (Drda and Rybová 2008) as well as installations connected with ancestor worship at sites such as the Glauberg, with its 350 meters long processional way (Baitinger and Pinsker 2002), and Mont Lassois, with the enclosure at Les Herbues near the grave of the Princess of Vix (Chaume and Mordant 2011; Chaume et al. 2012).

FIGURE 4.4. Large ditch at the south foot of Wall 3 at Mont Lassois (after Chaume et al. 2012).

Among other things, the rich elite burials in the environs of central places (e.g., Hohmichele, Gießübel-Talhau, Hochdorf, Grafenbühl, Kleinaspergle, Sainte-Colombe, Vix) are indicative of the political and administrative significance of these settlements (Krausse 2006). Members of the elite included both men and women, with some exceptional new discoveries, such as the sumptuous graves of Bettelbühl tumulus 4 or Lavau (Dubuis et al. 2015; Krausse and Ebinger-Rist 2016). Rich burials for children—for example, at Bettelbühl and Bourges—indicate the establishment of hereditary principles based on social rank and status at this time.

Despite the disparity and heterogeneity of the sites classified as *Fürstensitze,* most may have represented focal settings for tribal polities that might have maintained relations similar to those proposed in the "peer polity interaction" model (Renfrew and Cherry 1986). This may also be indicated by their nearly regular spatial distribution which suggests that they were at the top of settlement hierarchies (see Figure 4.1). There is a great deal of evidence that from the late seventh to the late fifth centuries B.C., numerous local and regional groups north of the Alps were integrated into larger collective entities. With regard to the social typologies that have been defined by authors such as Johnson and Earle (2000), the communities that developed around centers of power, such as the Heuneburg or Bourges, can best be placed as transitional between complex chiefdoms and early states (Fernández-Götz and Krausse 2013; Ralston 2010).

Even if the genesis of the *Fürstensitze* cannot be understood completely independently from the simultaneous processes of urbanization in the Mediterranean (Osborne and Cunliffe 2005; see also Ault this volume), indigenous factors might have been heavily responsible for the foundation of these early centers of power. Rich burials of the eighth and seventh centuries B.C., such as Gomadingen or Frankfurt-Stadtwald, bear witness to the fact that the increase in social hierarchy and the development of powerful local elites had begun several generations before the arrival of the Greek colonists in southern France and the foundation of *Massalia* (Marseille) around 600 B.C. (Fernández-Götz and Arnold 2017). Trade with the Mediterranean was not the main cause for cultural change, but rather a consequence of demographic growth and increasing internal inequalities. Power and status would have depended mainly on land and animal ownership (Gosden 1985), and the control of local resources and production. This would include the protoindustrial level of production of goods, such as iron, recently documented in the Black Forest of Germany (Gassmann and Wieland 2015).

TIMES OF TURMOIL: TOWARD DECENTRALIZATION

The rise of the *Fürstensitze* can be regarded as the crystallization of the first urbanization processes north of the Alps, similar to those observed in other regions across Eurasia (Fernández-Götz and Krausse 2016). However, and in contrast to centralization processes observed in many areas of the Mediterranean Basin (Garcia 2013), their development in Central Europe was a short-lived phenomenon that differed in time and duration from site to site. In general terms, this short-lived wave of centralization and urbanization was followed by a phase where decentralization characterized the settlement record (Krausse 2008b). In other words, there was no continual evolutionary development on a European scale from simple to larger and more complex forms of settlements during the Iron Age, but rather multilayered, changing, and dynamic cycles of centralization and decentralization (Fernández-Götz 2014b; Salač 2012).

Where excavation has been taken farthest, it is clear that within the overall duration of the *Fürstensitze,* most seem to have been at their height for a rather brief span. The Heuneburg was finally abandoned around the middle of the fifth century B.C., more or less contemporaneously with comparable settlements, such as Mont Lassois. At around this time, a number of other central places became more significant, such as Bad Dürkheim and Glauberg (Krausse 2008b). These centers were able to maintain their importance for an additional generation or two, but they too were finally abandoned no later than the early fourth century B.C. Soon after 400 B.C., nearly all of the *Fürstensitze* had been abandoned.

These major settlements and their hinterlands can thus be envisaged as rather short-lived, unstable, ephemeral polities (Fernández-Götz and Ralston 2017). Nonetheless, they represent a significant stage in the cultural and political development of later prehistoric Europe, albeit one which was not immediately consolidated, but which rather gave way to subsequent collapse. During the fourth and early third centuries B.C., we see a return to more decentralized settlement patterns and a reduction of social inequalities, without any major agglomerations and with a reduction of social inequalities. This is precisely the period of the so-called Celtic migrations, during which numerous central European populations migrated toward Italy and the Balkans (Tomaschitz 2002).

Little is known about the reasons for these structural displacements and changes in the landscape of power. However, we can assume that the transformations did not always take a peaceful course and those episodes of social unrest may have played a role (Demoule 1999; Pauli 1985). For example, the heads that were forcibly broken off the two statues from the enclosure of Les Herbues at Mont Lassois are evidence for violent conflicts toward the end of the Hallstatt period, in the mid-fifth century B.C. A broadly similar situation can also be seen at the Glauberg, where three of the four monumental anthropomorphic stone sculptures were intentionally destroyed. A catastrophic fire that almost completely destroyed the fortification and the internal buildings at the end of Period I sealed the fate of the Heuneburg. The fact that the destruction level had a relative abundance of finds militates against the idea that the abandonment of the site was planned (Fernández-Götz 2017).

The factors responsible for the decline of the *Fürstensitze* might have been varied, and therefore monocausal explanations are insufficient. Nevertheless, there are indications that one of the catalysts was climate change—analysis of cores from the Greenland icecap indicates that as early as the first half of the fifth century B.C. temperatures dropped throughout the entire Northern Hemisphere, followed by a rapid climatic decline around 400 B.C. This process was linked to a reduction of solar activity, and appears to have occurred relatively abruptly (Maise 1998; Sirocko 2009). Although the cooler climate did not make the areas of settlement in southern Germany or eastern France uninhabitable, it could have resulted in bad harvests—particularly in the relatively unfavorable regions of the highlands that had only been occupied for a few generations—and this would have resulted in famine and/or migration.

At the macroperspective level, the main climatic phases of the first millennium B.C. do indeed correspond with the most important stages of the processes of centralization and decentralization north of the Alps (Figure 4.5). Thus, the processes of centralization that gave rise to the development of the Early Iron Age *Fürstensitze* and the Late Iron Age *oppida* took place predominantly in warmer periods, while the migrations of the fourth century B.C. occurred during a colder phase. Of course, this apparently clear general picture becomes more complicated when specific regions are considered. For example,

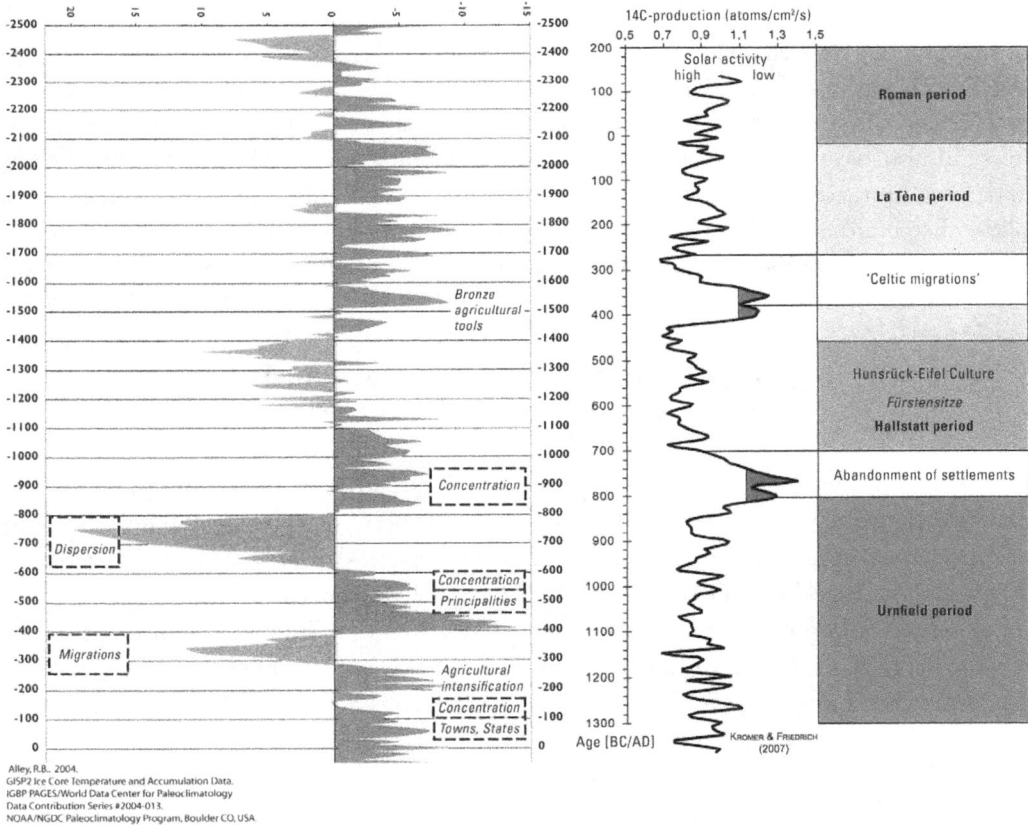

Alley, R.B., 2004.
GISP2 Ice Core Temperature and Accumulation Data.
IGBP PAGES/World Data Center for Paleoclimatology
Data Contribution Series #2004-013.
NOAA/NGDC Paleoclimatology Program, Boulder CO, USA.

FIGURE 4.5. Left: evolution of solar activity between ca. 2500 B.C. and the beginning of the Common Era, with cold periods marked in light gray and warmer periods in dark gray (after Brun and Ruby 2008). Right: evolution of solar activity between ca. 1300 B.C. and A.D. 100 (after Pare et al. 2009).

while the abandonment of Bourges and the decline in population in the Champagne at the beginning of the fourth century B.C. appears to coincide fairly closely with climate changes—which probably prompted a considerable part of the population to migrate—the environmental indicators do not explain so clearly why some *Fürstensitze,* such as Heuneburg or Mont Lassois, already had been abandoned around the middle of the fifth century B.C., while others, such as Hohenasperg or Glauberg, continued to function during the second half of the same century.

An explanatory model that should be considered—and which is perhaps complementary to the climate change model—concerns the role of migration as a mechanism for regulating power relationships (Demoule 2006). The emigration of a part of the population can indeed be a response to increased scalar stress generated by "energized crowding" (for a discussion of the concept, see Smith this volume), and a means of reducing social inequalities. As a series of historical and ethnological studies demonstrate (Godelier 2010; Testart 2005), during the course of history numerous societies have employed various strategies in order to counter the development of state organizations, something that is well reflected in the expression "societies against the state" used by the French anthropologist Pierre Clastres (1989). The fission of part of the group is a mechanism often used in this process, and in the case of temperate European societies, it could also have served as a reaction to the increasing social inequalities of the sixth and fifth centuries B.C. Although many aspects are still not fully understood, it is likely that internal conflicts against the ruling elites and episodes of intertribal warfare triggered by environmental pressures are among the reasons that explain the decline of the *Fürstensitze.*

URBANIZATION IN THE LATE IRON AGE: OPEN AGGLOMERATIONS AND *OPPIDA*

In the area immediately north of the Alps, a new trend toward centralization can be observed between the late third and the first centuries B.C., leading to the development of large, open agglomerations and more than 150 fortified *oppida* (Collis 1984; Fichtl 2005, 2012a; Rieckhoff and Fichtl 2011; Woolf 1993). The Latin term *oppidum* (plural *oppida*) has become a sort of *terminus technicus* used by Iron Age archaeologists to refer to large, Late Iron Age, fortified settlements with an area of at least 10 hectares. The temperate European *oppida* developed mostly between the late second and the first centuries B.C. in an area stretching from Atlantic France and southern Britain in the west to Hungary in the east (Figure 4.6). It is probably no coincidence that a number of these *oppida* were established on the same sites as earlier *Fürstensitze,* for example in Bourges (*Avaricum*) or in Závist. Topographical advantages but also social memory probably played a role in this reuse. On the other hand, other central places, such as the Heuneburg, remained uninhabited in the landscape.

Traditionally, Late Iron Age centralization processes have been identified with the fortified *oppida* (Collis 1984; Wells 1984). This picture, however, has become much more

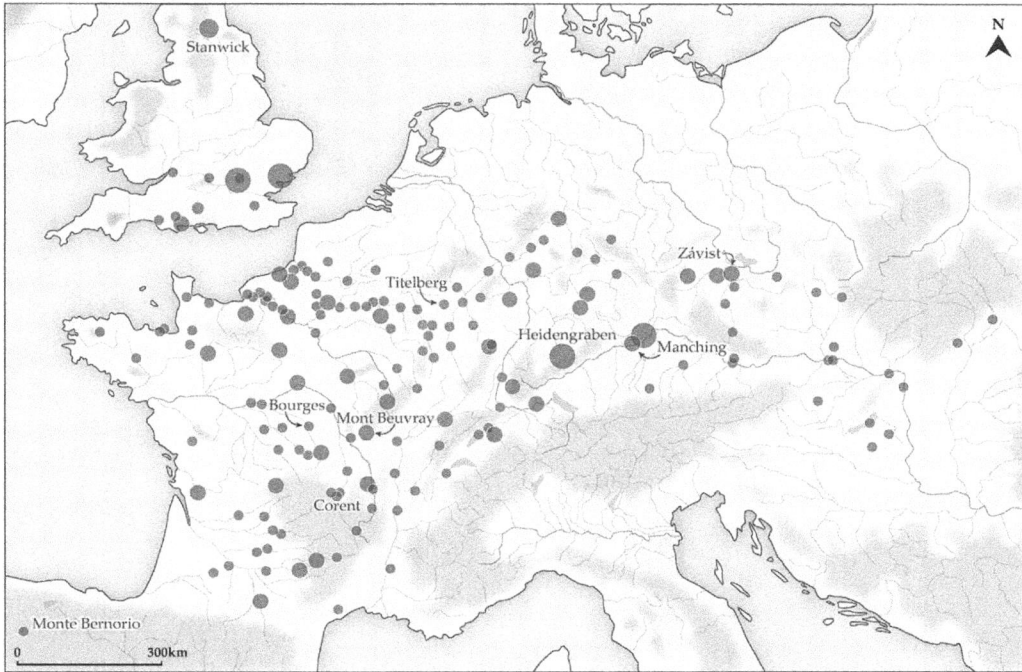

Figure 4.6. Distribution of Late Iron Age continental *oppida* (drawn by the author based on data from http://www.oppida.org/, with additions).

complex in recent decades with the discovery and large-scale investigation of numerous open agglomerations, many of which have yielded evidence of significant economic activities in the form of trade and craft production (Fichtl 2013; Kaenel 2006; Moore and Ponroy 2014; Moore et al. 2013). The size of these open settlements may be considerable, with some examples reaching several dozens or even more than 100 hectares (Figure 4.7). Equally important is their early chronology, since some of these unfortified sites can be traced back to the early second or even to the third century B.C. This has important consequences for our understanding of Late Iron Age centralization processes.

From France to Hungary, in many regions the concentration of the population and economic activities began already in the third century B.C., and thus, a long time before the foundation of the *oppida*. Thanks to examples such as Aulnat and Levroux in Gaul, Berching-Pollanten in Bavaria, Lovosice in Bohemia, Němčice in Moravia, or Sajópetri in Hungary (Collis et al. 2000; Fichtl 2013; Salač 2009), the former idea that industrial and trading activities of any importance were concentrated exclusively in the *oppida* can be discarded. Some of the open agglomerations of the third to first centuries B.C.—that preceded or coexisted with the *oppida*—were large production and distribution centers that performed economic functions at least equivalent to those of the most prominent

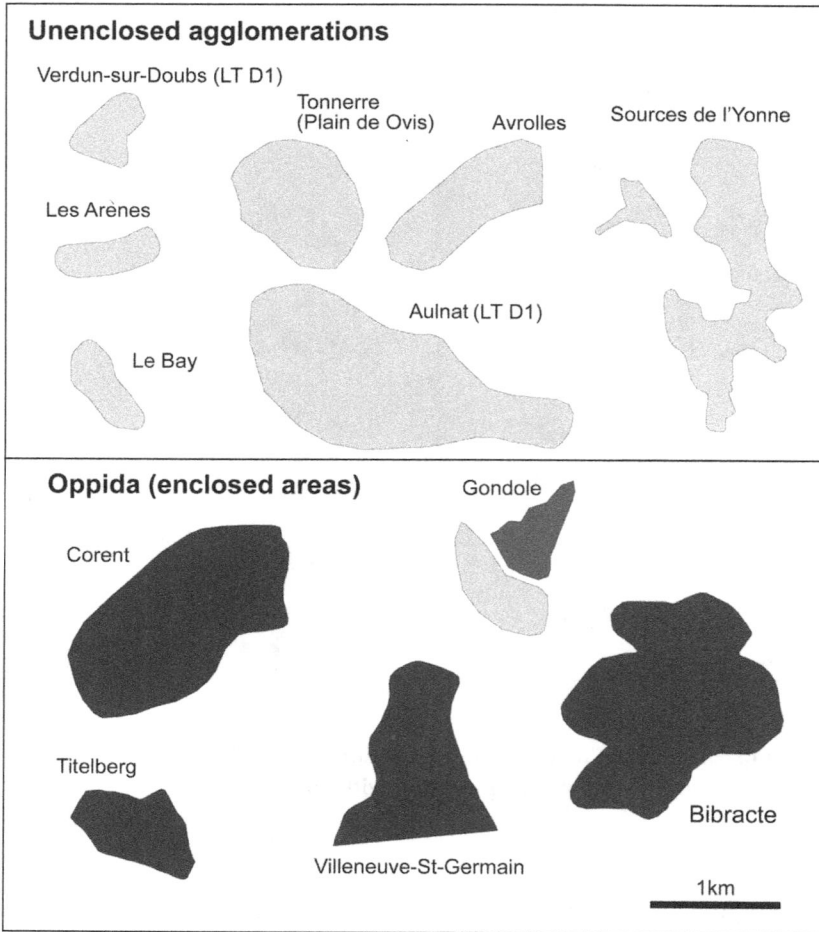

Figure 4.7. Size comparison between selected examples of unenclosed agglomerations and fortified *oppida* in Gaul (after Moore et al. 2013).

fortified settlements (Augstein 2006; Salač 2009). These functions are indicated by coin minting, imports originating in distant regions, large-scale metal production, manufacturing of glass objects, and so on.

On occasion, the number of finds recovered at these open settlements rivals or even exceeds those yielded from the *oppida*. It is well demonstrated by the following examples provided by Salač (2009, 2012). Although it has not yet been excavated, at the open site of Němčice, some 518 glass bracelets have been found, nearly as many as in the intensely excavated *oppidum* of Manching (620), and many more than in other important *oppida*, such as Stradonice (143) or Závist (4). Also, in the unfortified settlement of Roseldorf, some 1,500 coins have been found, clearly surpassing the recovered numbers at such important fortified sites like Staré Hradisko (91) or Závist (16). Another interesting example is the open site of Berching-Pollanten in southern Germany, where the range of objects found is not very different from that discovered in the nearby and contemporaneous *oppidum* of Manching—it includes, among other finds, iron tools, fine pottery, glass bracelets, coins, keys, scales, and hundreds of brooches (Schäfer 2010). Apparently, the same craft activities were carried out in Berching-Pollanten and Manching during the second century B.C.

The latter example also illustrates the complexity and diversity of settlement trajectories. While some large, open sites were abandoned at the time of the foundation of the *oppida* (e.g., the relocation of the open settlement of Levroux, located on the plain, to a nearby hill; see Buchsenschutz et al. 2000), many others continued to exist, and we also know cases, such as Manching, in which an open agglomeration was fortified at a later stage of its occupation (Sievers 2007; Wendling 2013) (Figure 4.8). Other

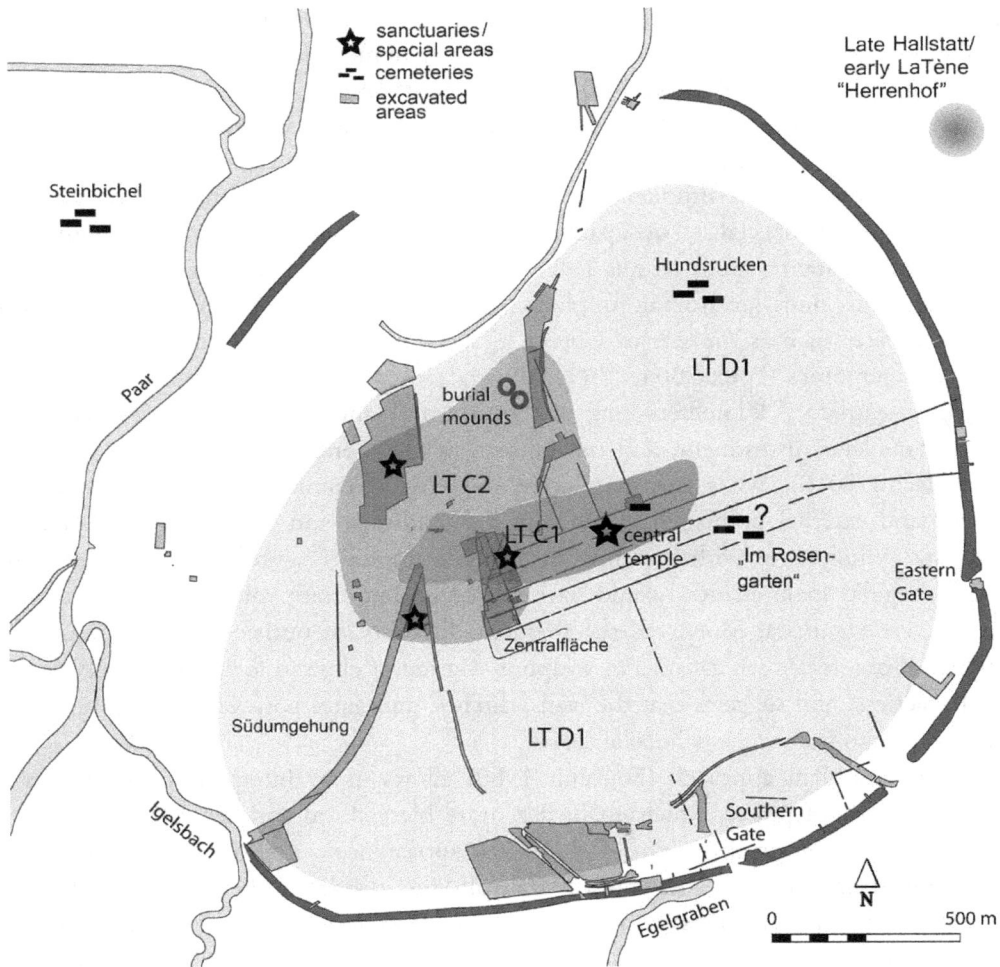

FIGURE 4.8. Manching. Archaeological features and sites within the area enclosed by or adjacent to the rampart of the later *oppidum*. Settlement expansion is indicated by different shades of gray (after Wendling and Winger 2014).

open agglomerations, on the contrary, started at a relatively late stage in the immediate vicinity of an already existing *oppidum,* such as Sources de l'Yonne near *Bibracte.* Taking a step further, it is worth considering the possibility that both the fortified settlement on the Mont Beuvray and the open agglomeration of Sources de l'Yonne were part of a single center, and could be regarded as part of the same "Bibracte complex" (Moore et al. 2013). Broader interpretations also have been proposed for the three *oppida* of the Arverni in the basin of Clermont-Ferrand (Corent, Gondole, *Gergovia*), which could represent an overlay of population clusters within a large, strongly urbanized area that spread over more than 2,500 hectares (Poux 2014). Instead of a single, fortified urban center, this example indicates a multipolar town pattern, raising completely new research questions and perspectives. What is clear is that the traditional view to prioritize enclosed sites may limit our interpretation regarding the nature of broader social change—open agglomerations and larger population clusters need to be better considered when discussing the origins and characteristics of urban development in Late Iron Age temperate Europe (Haselgrove and Guichard 2013; Moore and Ponroy 2014).

The above considerations, however, should not make us underestimate the significance of the imposing fortification works of the *oppida,* nor the economic importance of these sites. Some *oppida*—although not all—were indeed important centers of craft activities and trade, with specialized occupation, large-scale production of goods, and numerous imports from distant regions (Collis 1984; Fichtl 2005; Meylan et al. 2002). Among the most numerous finds are Roman amphorae, which demonstrate the mass consumption of wine at sites such as *Bibracte* or Corent in the framework of political assemblies and religious ceremonies (Poux 2004, 2011). On the other hand, the monumental walls of the *oppida*—up to 7 kilometers long in the case of Manching and *Bibracte*—represent a significant labor investment, and can be seen as the expression of a major communal effort (Fichtl 2010). Walls and gates were emblems of community identity, acting as internal and external points of reference in the landscape and in society—investing in them was synonymous with investing in symbolic capital (Figure 4.9). Their erection, but also regular maintenance, would have played an important role in the construction of collective identities. Moreover, the frequent discovery of burials, animal bones, and deposits of objects—such as coins or weapons—inside or close to fortifications testifies to ritual practices, and suggests that the walls, ditches, and gates possessed a legal, political, and sacred significance (von Nicolai 2014).

A Foucauldian approach (Foucault 1980) allows us to interpret the *oppida* as a new technology of power, which enabled a more hierarchical and centralizing ideology to be articulated. From this point of view, their appearance can also be seen as a way of reinforcing social cohesion and political control—the *oppida* are the expression of more unequal societies and, at the same time, contributed to the construction of those inequalities (Fernández-Götz 2014c; Rieckhoff 2014). Their internal structure usually indicates previous planning and a manifestation of the principles of social order that governed communities, including the overall proliferation of linear structures. In most cases, their foundation was a deliberate response to a political decision, one that in Gaul must have been initiated by the aristocracy (Buchsenschutz and Ralston 2012).

FIGURE 4.9. *Bibracte*-Mont Beuvray. Reconstruction of the impressive *murus gallicus* of the Porte du Rebout (after Rieckhoff 2014).

Recent research also has led to the identification of a great deal of communal spaces used for political and cultic activities within the *oppida*. Public spaces and sanctuaries have been discovered, and at least partly excavated, in sites such as Titelberg, Martberg, Wallendorf, Corent, *Bibracte*, and Manching, to give just a few examples (Fernández-Götz 2014c, 2014d; Fichtl 2012b). A particularly striking case is that of the Titelberg *oppidum* in Luxembourg, with its so-called public space, where assemblies, fairs, and religious ceremonies were held. This was a large area covering 10 hectares to the east of the *oppidum*, surrounded by a ditch and a mudbrick wall built on a stone base (Metzler et al. 2006, 2016) (Figure 4.10). The fill of the ditch contained numerous animal bones, fibulae, spearheads, miniature weapons, coins, and fragments of human skulls. These finds demonstrate that cult practices took place here and indicate that the ditch was not only a physical but also to a large extent a symbolic boundary as it separated the sacred space from the profane. Voting installations of the first half of the first century B.C. provide evidence for political decision making, and the enormous number of documented animal bones points toward the existence of large-scale feasting at Titelberg.

The assemblies, rituals, and ceremonies held at the *oppida* would have been key elements in fostering social cohesion, self-awareness, and shared identity (Fernández-Götz and Roymans 2015; Gerritsen and Roymans 2006). Written sources and an increasing amount of archaeological evidence demonstrate the importance of popular assemblies as fundamental mechanisms of collective governance in Late Iron Age Gaul (for discussions on collective action, see Blanton and Fargher 2008). These political institutions were to

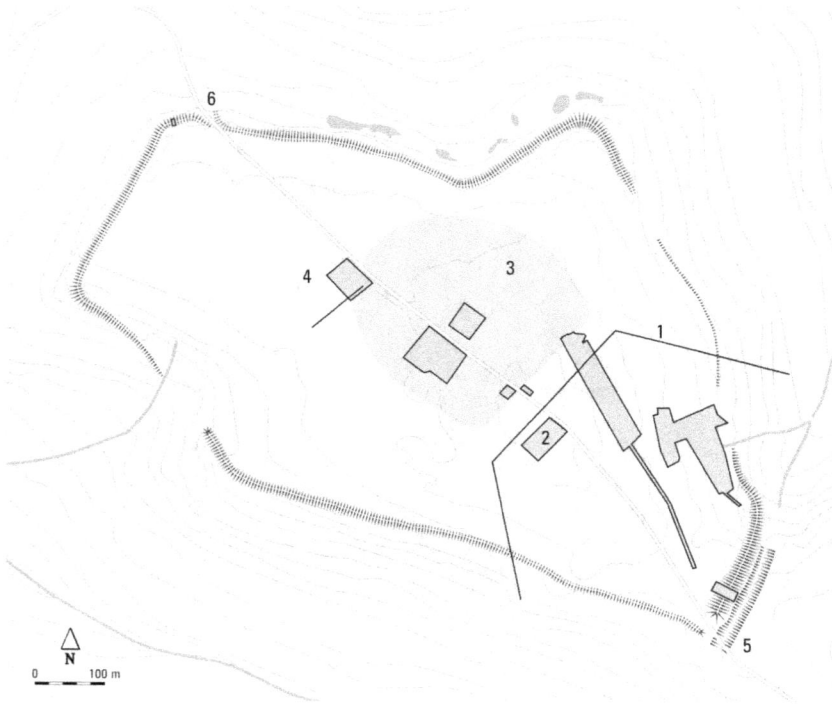

FIGURE 4.10. Plan of the Titelberg *oppidum*: (1) cultic ditch that marks the boundary of the public space, (2) excavated area of the monumental center, (3) concentration of the La Tène habitat, (4) possible Roman military establishment, (5) east gate, (6) west gate (after Metzler et al. 2006, redrawn by the author).

a certain extent instrumentalized by members of the elite through the clientage system, but they also limited the agency of the aristocratic classes and redistributed social power (Fernández-Götz 2013; González-Ruibal 2012). The number of people that lived permanently in the *oppida* would have been less important than the function of these centers as objects of identification for larger groups generating collective identities and serving as nuclei of aggregation, and points of reference for the rural populations.

These discoveries also have profound implications for the question of the origin of the *oppida*. Several examples at these sites prove the existence of places for cult activities and/or assemblies that preceded population concentration or even fortification. Thus, many Late Iron Age *oppida* may have had their origin at locations for ritual gatherings (Fernández-Götz 2014b:ch. 6; Metzler et al. 2006). In other words, they developed on particular sites precisely because those places had a sacred significance, and had already been frequented on a more or less regular basis from before the second and first centuries B.C. In a context of demographic growth, increased production, and the flourishing of contacts with the Mediterranean world, religion must have been the principal cohesive force through which the integration of communities into broader sociopolitical groupings was structured. Examples such as Manching, *Bibracte*, Gournay, Corent, or Titelberg show that, in many cases, the use of a place for cultic purposes and holding assemblies would have been the cause, and not the consequence, of the development of *oppida* at these sites. Although there would have been exceptions to this model, the recognition that in several cases open assembly spaces developed early and other urban functions occurred later has important implications for our understanding of centralization processes and the dynamics of collective aggregation.

A final question that deserves to be considered is what conditions led to the emergence of major urban settlements and some state entities in temperate Europe after the stage of decentralization that characterized the period of the "Celtic migrations." Although there could never have been a single motive, it can be ventured that with the conquest of northern Italy and later southern Gaul by Rome it was more difficult to export internal conflicts using the formula of migration. What is more, in some areas, there were probably "reflux" movements, especially of mercenaries who returned not only with new experiences but also social tensions. A combination of factors—including progressive demographic growth, an upsurge in demand by the Mediterranean world, and the introduction of new techniques that allowed agricultural and industrial output to be increased—would have led to a rise in "social density" and increased hierarchy. The result was the development of more unequal societies and the integration of communities on a larger scale—a process that in some cases brought about the emergence of early states, such as those of the Aedui, Arverni, or Helvetii (for the concept of early states, see Claessen and Skalník 1978; Yoffee 2005). They were characterized by not only urban settlements but also marked social inequalities, use of fiduciary coins, tax regulations, and, in some cases, even written population census (Brun and Ruby 2008; Collis 2014; Fernández-Götz 2014b:ch. 3).

Retrospective and Prospective: Iron Age Urbanization as a Nonlinear Phenomenon

As discussed above, the first millennium B.C. saw the emergence of the first urban centers in Central Europe. This was an extremely significant development with profound historical implications. However, some qualifications are required in order to fully understand these processes:

1. Early cities were crucial elements during the Iron Age, but they remained the exception rather than the rule in temperate Europe. The immense majority of the population continued to live in rural farmsteads and hamlets, and there are many regions in which urban sites never developed. We have to acknowledge the existence of a dynamic and multilayered

reality, with a high degree of synchronic and diachronic variability. In addition to hierarchically organized societies—such as those described for the *Fürstensitze*—there were other communities in which the structures of power were less clearly defined, and which present evidence for a more heterarchical and decentralized social landscape (Hill 2006).

2. The terms *Fürstensitze* and *oppida* cover a heterogeneous reality. Neither of them represents a uniform group of settlements, but rather they were centers of power that often varied enormously in regard to when they were established, their inner area and architecture, as well as the manner in which they functioned as central places. While settlements such as the Heuneburg, Bourges, Manching, Corent, or *Bibracte* can certainly be classified as urban on the basis of several criteria—such as evidence of a preconceived plan, population of several thousand inhabitants, co-occurrence of diverse population and activities—other *Fürstensitze* (e.g., Glauberg) or *oppida* (e.g., Mont Vully, Zarten/*Tarodunum*, Finsterlohr) seem to have been enormous assembly places or refuge sites rather than cities. Therefore, we can maintain that while all *Fürstensitze* and *oppida* were complex central places, only some of them should be classified as cities from a comparative urban perspective (Smith 2016; for a contextual definition of city, see also Fernández-Götz and Krausse 2013).

3. From a long-term perspective, a trend toward increasing inequality and centralization can be observed during late prehistory, but this was neither a teleological nor linear process. Instead, it included cycles of regression, crisis, reduced hierarchy, and demographic decrease, as exemplified in the disappearance of the *Fürstensitze*.

Overall, the most important factors that seem to drive social transformations in Iron Age Central Europe are demography and climate change, to which external influences by other cultures should be added—the latter appear to have had a more profound impact toward the end of the period, with Rome's gradual territorial and economic expansion. Demographic growth in temperate Europe, in most cases favored by climatically warmer periods, would have increased pressure on resources and generated an increase in "social density," that is, the frequency of communication and interactions between individuals and groups. This, in turn, would have triggered social hierarchization and processes of settlement nucleation (aggregation and urbanization), which reached their peak at the time of the *Fürstensitze* and the *oppida*. But at the same time, principles of a moral economy would have been in operation that were designed to limit the concentration of power in the hands of certain individuals or families (Fernández-Götz 2014b; González-Ruibal 2012; see also Sastre and Currás this volume). It is against this framework of dialectical tensions between political economies—that develop inequalities and hierarchies—*versus* moral economies—that emphasize collective values and isonomy—in which Iron Age centralization and urbanization processes need to be understood.

REFERENCES CITED

Augier, L., O. Buchsenschutz, R. Durand, A. Filippini, D. Germinet, M. Levéry, P. Maçon, B. Pescher, I. Ralston, M. Salin, and J. Troadec 2012 *Un complexe princier de l'âge du Fer: Le quartier artisanal de Port Sec sud à Bourges (Cher)*. Revue Archéologique Centre France Supplément 41. Bituriga, Tours and Bourges.

Augier, L., O. Buchsenschutz, and I. Ralston (editors) 2007 *Un complexe princier de l'âge du Fer: L'habitat du promontoire de Bourges (Cher) (VIe–IVe s. av. J.-C.)*. Revue Archéologique Centre France Supplément 32. Bituriga, Bourges and Tours.

Augstein, M. 2006 Handel und Handwerk: Überlegungen zur wirtschaftlichen Grundlage offener Siedlungen der Mittel- und Spätlatènezeit. In *Grundlegungen: Beiträge zur europäischen und afrikanischen Archäologie für Manfred K. H. Eggert*, edited by H.-P. Wotzka, pp. 595–606. A. Francke, Tübingen.

Baitinger, H., and B. Pinsker (editors) 2002 *Das Rätsel der Kelten vom Glauberg: Glaube—Mythos—Wirklichkeit*. Konrad Theiss, Stuttgart.

Biel, J., and D. Krausse (editors) 2005 *Frühkeltische Fürstensitze: Älteste Städte und Herrschaftszentren nördlich der Alpen?* Archäologische Informationen aus Baden-Württemberg 51. Regierungspräsidium Stuttgart Landesamt für Denkmalpflege, Esslingen.

Blanton, R. E., and L. F. Fargher 2008 *Collective Action in the Formation of Pre-Modern States*. Springer, New York.

Brun, P., and B. Chaume 2013 Une éphémère tentative d'urbanisation en Europe centre-occidentale durant les VIe et Ve siècles av. J.C.? *Bulletin de la Société Préhistorique Française* 110(2):319–349.

Brun, P., and P. Ruby 2008 *L'âge du Fer en France: Premières villes, premiers États celtiques*. La Découverte, Paris.

Buchsenschutz, O., A. Colin, G. Firmin, B. Fischer, J.-P. Guillaumet, S. Krausz, M. Levéry, P. Marinval, L. Orellana, and A. Pierret 2000 *Le village celtique des Arènes à Levroux. Synthèses.* 19ème supplément à la Revue Archéologique du Centre de la France. Levroux 5. FERAC—ADEL, Levroux.

Buchsenschutz, O., and I. Ralston 2012 Urbanisation et aristocratie celtiques. In *Die Frage der Protourbanisation in der Eisenzeit—La question de la proto-urbanisation à l'âge du Fer*, edited by S. Sievers and M. Schönfelder, pp. 347–364. Dr. Rudolf Habelt, Bonn.

Chaume, B., and C. Mordant (editors) 2011 *Le complexe aristocratique de Vix: Nouvelles recherches sur l'habitat, le système de fortification et l'environnement du Mont Lassois*. PU Dijon, Dijon.

Chaume, B., N. Nieszery, and W. Reinhard 2012 Der Mont Lassois—ein frühkeltischer Fürstensitz im Burgund. In *Die Welt der Kelten: Zentren der Macht—Kostbarkeiten der Kunst*, pp. 132–138. Jan Thorbecke, Ostfildern.

Claessen, H. J. M., and P. Skalník (editors) 1978 *The Early State*. Mouton, The Hague.

Clastres, P. 1989 *Society Against the State: Essays in Political Anthropology*. Zone Books, New York.

Collis, J. 1984 *Oppida: Earliest Towns North of the Alps*. Sheffield University Press, Sheffield.

Collis, J. 2014 Urbanisation in Temperate Europe in the Iron Age: Mediterranean Influence or Indigenous? In *Paths to Complexity: Centralisation and Urbanisation in Iron Age Europe*, edited by M. Fernández-Götz, H. Wendling, and K. Winger, pp. 15–23. Oxbow Books, Oxford.

Collis, J., S. Krausz, and V. Guichard 2000 Les villages ouverts en Gaule centrale aux IIe et Ier siècles av. J.-C. In *Les processus d'urbanisation à l'âge du Fer—Eisenzeitliche Urbanisationsprozesse*, edited by V. Guichard, S. Sievers, and O. H. Urban, pp. 73–82. Collection Bibracte 4. Centre archéologique européen, Glux-en-Glenne.

Demoule, J.-P. 1999 La société contre les princes. In *Les princes de la protohistoire et l'émergence de l'État*, edited by P. Ruby, pp. 125–134. Centre Jean Bérard and École française de Rome, Naples and Rome.

Demoule, J.-P. 2006 Migrations et théories migratoires aux époques préhistoriques et protohistoriques. In *Celtes et Gaulois, l'Archéologie face à l'Histoire. 2: La Préhistoire des Celtes*, edited by D. Vitali, pp. 17–28. Collection Bibracte 12/2. Centre archéologique européen, Glux-en-Glenne.

Drda, P., and A. Rybová 2008 *Akropole na hradišti Závist v 6.–4. stol. př. Kr. Akropolis von Závist im 6.–4. Jh. v. Chr.* Památky archeologické—Supplementum 19. Archeologický ústav Akademie věd České republiky, Praha.

Dubuis, B., D. Josset, E. Millet, and C. Villenave 2015 La tombe princière du Ve siècle avant notre ère de Lavau "ZAC du Moutot" (Aube). *Bulletin de la Société Préhistorique Française* 112(2):371–374.

Fernández-Götz, M. 2013 Politik, Religion und Jahrmärkte: Zur Rolle der Volksversammlungen im eisenzeitlichen und frühmittelalterlichen Europa. In *Interpretierte Eisenzeiten 5: Fallstudien, Methoden, Theorie*, edited by R. Karl and J. Leskovar, pp. 71–82. Studien zur Kulturgeschichte von Oberösterreich 37. Oberösterreichisches Landesmuseum, Linz.

Fernández-Götz, M. 2014a Understanding the Heuneburg: A Biographical Approach. In *Paths to Complexity: Centralisation and Urbanisation in Iron Age Europe*, edited by M. Fernández-Götz, H. Wendling, and K. Winger, pp. 24–34. Oxbow Books, Oxford.

Fernández-Götz, M. 2014b *Identity and Power: The Transformation of Iron Age Societies in Northeast Gaul.* Amsterdam Archaeological Studies 21. Amsterdam University Press, Amsterdam.

Fernández-Götz, M. 2014c Reassessing the Oppida: The Role of Power and Religion. *Oxford Journal of Archaeology* 33(4):379–394.

Fernández-Götz, M. 2014d Central Places and the Construction of Collective Identities in the Middle Rhine–Moselle region. In *Fingerprinting the Iron Age: Approaches to Identity in the European Iron Age. Integrating South-Eastern Europe into the Debate*, edited by C. Popa and S. Stoddart, pp. 175–186. Oxbow Books, Oxford.

Fernández-Götz, M. 2017 Contested Power: Iron Age Societies Against the State? In *Rebellion and Inequality in Archaeology*, edited by S. Hansen and J. Müller, pp. 271–287. Dr. Rudolf Habelt, Bonn.

Fernández-Götz, M., and B. Arnold 2017 Elites before the *Fürstensitze*: Hallstatt C Sumptuous Graves Between Main and Danube. In *Connecting Elites and Regions: Perspectives on Contacts, Relations and Differentiation during the Early Iron Age Hallstatt C Period in Northwest and Central Europe*, edited by R. Schumann and S. van der Vaart-Verschoof, pp. 183–199. Sidestone Press, Leiden.

Fernández-Götz, M., and D. Krausse 2013 Rethinking Early Iron Age Urbanisation in Central Europe: The Heuneburg Site and Its Archaeological Environment. *Antiquity* 87(336):473–487.

Fernández-Götz, M., and D. Krausse (editors) 2016 *Eurasia at the Dawn of History: Urbanization and Social Change.* Cambridge University Press, New York and Cambridge.

Fernández-Götz, M., and I. Ralston 2017 The Complexity and Fragility of Early Iron Age Urbanism in West-Central Temperate Europe. *Journal of World Prehistory* 30(3):259–279.

Fernández-Götz, M., and N. Roymans 2015 The Politics of Identity: Late Iron Age Sanctuaries in the Rhineland. *Journal of the North Atlantic* 8:18–32.

Fernández-Götz, M., H. Wendling, and K. Winger (editors) 2014 *Paths to Complexity: Centralisation and Urbanisation in Iron Age Europe.* Oxbow Books, Oxford.

Fichtl, S. 2005 *La ville celtique: Les Oppida de 150 av. J.-C. à 15 ap. J.-C.* Errance, Paris.

Fichtl, S. 2012a *Les premières villes de Gaule: Le temps des Oppida.* Archéologie Nouvelle, Lacapelle-Marival.

Fichtl, S. 2012b Places publiques et lieux de rassemblement à la fin de l'âge du Fer dans le monde celtique. In *Le forum en Gaule et dans les régions voisines*, edited by A. Bouet, pp. 41–53. Ausonius, Bordeaux.

Fichtl, S. 2013 Les agglomérations gauloises de la fin de l'âge du Fer en Europe celtique (IIIe–Ier siècles av. J.-C.). In *L'habitat en Europe celtique et en Méditerranée préclassique: Domaines urbains*, edited by D. Garcia, pp. 19–43. Errance, Arles.

Fichtl, S. (editor) 2010 *Murus celticus: architecture et fonctions des remparts de l'âge du Fer.* Collection Bibracte 19. Centre archéologique européen, Glux-en-Glenne.

Fletcher, R. 2009 Low-Density, Agrarian-Based Urbanism: A Comparative View. *Insights* 2(4):2–19.

Fletcher, R. 2012 Low-Density, Agrarian-Based Urbanism: Scale, Power, and Ecology. In *The Comparative Archaeology of Complex Societies*, edited by M. E. Smith, pp. 285–320. Cambridge University Press, New York.

Foucault, M. 1980 *Power/Knowledge: Selected Interviews and Other Writings.* Pantheon, New York.

Garcia, D. (editor) 2013 *L'habitat en Europe celtique et en Méditerranée préclassique: Domaines urbains.* Errance, Arles.

Gassmann, G., and G. Wieland 2015 Early Celtic Iron Production at Neuenbürg in the Northern Black Forest (Southern Germany). In *Persistent Economic Ways of Living: Production, Distribution, and Consumption in Late Prehistory and Early History*, edited by A. Danielisova and M. Fernández-Götz, pp. 91–99. Archaeolingua, Budapest.

Gerritsen, F., and N. Roymans 2006 Central Places and the Construction of Tribal Identities. The Case of the Late Iron Age Lower Rhine Region. In *Celtes et Gaulois, l'Archéologie face à l'Histoire. 4: Les mutations de la fin de l'âge du Fer*, edited by C. Haselgrove, pp. 251–266. Collection Bibracte 12/4. Centre archéologique européen, Glux-en-Glenne.

Godelier, M. 2010 *Les tribus dans l'Histoire et face aux États.* CNRS, Paris.

González-Ruibal, A. 2012 The Politics of Identity: Ethnicity and the Economy of Power in Iron Age Northern Iberia. In *Landscape, Ethnicity, and Identity in the Archaic Mediterranean Area*, edited by G. Cifani and S. Stoddart, pp. 245–266. Oxbow Books, Oxford.

Gosden, C. 1985 Gifts and Kin in Early Iron Age Europe. *Man* 20:475–493.

Guichard, V., S. Sievers, and O. H. Urban (editors) 2000 *Les processus d'urbanisation à l'âge du Fer—Eisenzeitliche Urbanisationsprozesse.* Collection Bibracte 4. Centre archéologique européen, Glux-en-Glenne.

Haselgrove, C., and V. Guichard 2013 Les Gaulois sont-ils dans la plaine? Reflections on Settlement Patterns in Gaul in the 1st Century BC. In *L'Âge du Fer en Europe: Mélanges*

Offerts à Olivier Buchsenschutz, edited by S. Krausz, A. Colin, K. Gruel, I. Ralston, and T. Dechezleprêtre, pp. 317–328. Ausonius, Paris.

Haselgrove, C., K. Rebay-Salisbury, and P. S. Wells (editors) 2018 *The Oxford Handbook of the European Iron Age.* Oxford University Press, Oxford.

Hill, J. D. 2006 Are We Any Closer to Understanding How Later Iron Age Societies Worked (or Did not Work)? In *Celtes et Gaulois, l'Archéologie face à l'Histoire. 4: Les mutations de la fin de l'âge du Fer*, edited by C. Haselgrove, pp. 169–179. Collection Bibracte 12/4. Centre archéologique européen, Glux-en-Glenne.

Johnson, A. W., and T. K. Earle 2000 *The Evolution of Human Societies: From Foraging Group to Agrarian State.* 2nd ed. Stanford University Press, Stanford, California.

Kaenel, G. 2006 Agglomérations et *oppida* de la fin de l'âge du Fer. Une vision synthétique. In *Celtes et Gaulois, l'Archéologie face à l'Histoire. 4: Les mutations de la fin de l'âge du Fer*, edited by C. Haselgrove, pp. 17–39. Collection Bibracte 12/4. Centre archéologique européen, Glux-en-Glenne.

Krausse, D. 2006 Prunkgräber der nordwestalpinen Späthallstattkultur. Neue Fragestellungen und Untersuchungen zu ihrer sozialhistorischen Deutung. In *Herrschaft—Tod—Bestattung: Zu den vor- und frühgeschichtlichen Prunkgräbern als archäologisch-historische Quelle*, edited by C. von Carnap-Bornheim, D. Krausse, and A. Wesse, pp. 61–80. Dr. Rudolf Habelt, Bonn.

Krausse, D. 2008b Etappen der Zentralisierung nördlich der Alpen: Hypothesen, Modelle, Folgerungen. In *Frühe Zentralisierungs- und Urbanisierungsprozesse: Zur Genese und Entwicklung frühkeltischer Fürstensitze und ihres territorialen Umlandes*, edited by D. Krausse, pp. 435–450. Forschungen und Berichte zur Vor- und Frühgeschichte in Baden-Württemberg 101. Konrad Theiss, Stuttgart.

Krausse, D. (editor) 2008a *Frühe Zentralisierungs- und Urbanisierungsprozesse: Zur Genese und Entwicklung frühkeltischer Fürstensitze und ihres territorialen Umlandes.* Forschungen und Berichte zur Vor- und Frühgeschichte in Baden-Württemberg 101. Konrad Theiss, Stuttgart.

Krausse, D. (editor) 2010 *„Fürstensitze" und Zentralorte der frühen Kelten.* 2 vols. Forschungen und Berichte zur Vor- und Frühgeschichte in Baden-Württemberg 120. Konrad Theiss, Stuttgart.

Krausse, D., and N. Ebinger-Rist 2016 The Princess' Grave from Bettelbühl. In *The Heuneburg and the Early Iron Age Princely Seats: First Towns North of the Alps*, pp. 132–134. Archaeolingua, Budapest.

Krausse, D., M. Fernández-Götz, L. Hansen, and I. Kretschmer 2016 *The Heuneburg and the Early Iron Age Princely Seats: First Towns North of the Alps.* Archaeolingua, Budapest.

Kurz, S. 2010 Zur Genese und Entwicklung der Heuneburg in der späten Hallstattzeit. In *„Fürstensitze" und Zentralorte der frühen Kelten*, edited by D. Krausse, pp. 239–256. Forschungen und Berichte zur Vor- und Frühgeschichte in Baden-Württemberg 120. Konrad Theiss, Stuttgart.

Maise, C. 1998 Archäoklimatologie—Vom Einfluss nacheiszeitlicher Klimavariabilität in der Ur- und Frühgeschichte. *Jahrbuch der Schweizerischen Gesellschaft für Ur- und Frühgeschichte* 81:197–235.

Metzler, J., P. Méniel, and C. Gaeng 2006 Oppida et espaces publics. In *Celtes et Gaulois, l'Archéologie face à l'Histoire. 4: Les mutations de la fin de l'âge du Fer*, edited by C. Haselgrove, pp. 201–224. Collection Bibracte 12/4. Centre archéologique européen, Glux-en-Glenne.

Metzler, J., C. Gaeng, and P. Méniel 2016 *L'espace public du Titelberg.* Dossiers d'archéologie du Musée National d'Histoire et d'Art 17. Centre National de Recherche Archéologique, Luxembourg.

Meylan, F., F. Perrin, and M. Schönfelder 2002 L'artisanat dans les *oppida* d'Europe tempérée: un état de la question. In *Les artisans dans la ville antique*, edited by J.-C. Béal and J.-C. Goyon, pp. 77–99. Université Lumière-Lyon 2, Lyon.

Milcent, P.-Y. 2014 Hallstatt Urban Experience before the Celtic Oppida in Central and Eastern Gaul. Two Case-Studies: Bourges and Vix. In *Paths to Complexity: Centralisation and Urbanisation in Iron Age Europe*, edited by M. Fernández-Götz, H. Wendling, and K. Winger, pp. 35–51. Oxbow Books, Oxford.

Milcent, P.-Y. (editor) 2007 *Bourges-Avaricum: un centre proto-urbain celtique du Ve s. av. J.-C.* Bituriga, Bourges.

Moore, T., A. Braun, J. Creighton, L. Cripps, P. Haupt, I. Klenner, P. Nouvel, C. Ponroy, and M. Schönfelder 2013 Oppida, Agglomerations, and Suburbia: The Bibracte Environs and New Perspectives on Late Iron Age Urbanism in Central-Eastern France. *European Journal of Archaeology* 16(3):491–517.

Moore, T., and C. Ponroy 2014 What's in a Wall? Considerations on the Role of Open Settlements in Late La Tène Gaul. In *Paths to Complexity: Centralisation and Urbanisation in Iron Age Europe*, edited by M. Fernández-Götz, H. Wendling, and K. Winger, pp. 140–155. Oxbow Books, Oxford.

Osborne, R., and B. Cunliffe (editors) 2005 *Mediterranean Urbanization 800–600 BC.* Oxford University Press, Oxford.

Pare, C., M. Egg, H. Nortmann, and F. Sirocko 2009 Änderung der Sonnenaktivität am Beginn der Hallstattzeit. In *Wetter, Klima, Menschheitsentwicklung: Von der Eiszeit bis ins 21. Jahrhundert*, edited by F. Sirocko, pp. 134–138. Konrad Theiss, Stuttgart.

Pauli, L. 1985 Early Celtic Society: Two Centuries of Wealth and Turmoil in Central Europe. In *Settlement and Society: Aspects of West European Prehistory in the First Millennium BC*, edited by T. C. Champion and J. V. S. Megaw, pp. 23–43. Leicester University Press, Leicester.

Poux, M. 2004 *L'âge du vin: Rites de boisson, festins et libations en Gaule indépendante.* Monique Mergoil, Montagnac.

Poux, M. 2014 Enlarging Oppida: Multipolar Town Patterns in Late Iron Age Gaul. In *Paths to Complexity: Centralisation and Urbanisation in Iron Age Europe*, edited by M. Fernández-Götz, H. Wendling, and K. Winger, pp. 156–166. Oxbow Books, Oxford.

Poux, M. (editor) 2011 *Corent: Voyage au coeur d'une ville gauloise.* Errance, Paris.

Ralston, I. 2007 Bourges in the Earlier Iron Age: An Interim View. In *Communities and Connections: Essays in Honour of Barry Cunliffe*, edited by C. Gosden, H. Hamerow, P. de Jersey, and G. Lock, pp. 217–239. Oxford University Press, Oxford.

Ralston, I. 2010 Fragile States in Mid-First Millennium B.C. Temperate Western Europe? The View from Bourges. *Social Evolution & History* 9(2):70–92.

Renfrew, C., and J. F. Cherry (editors) 1986 *Peer Polity Interaction and Socio-Political Change.* Cambridge University Press, Cambridge.

Rieckhoff, S. 2014 Space, Architecture, and Identity in Gaul in the 2nd/1st Centuries BC. In *Paths to Complexity: Centralisation and Urbanisation in Iron Age Europe*, edited by M. Fernández-Götz, H. Wendling, and K. Winger, pp. 101–110. Oxbow Books, Oxford.

Rieckhoff, S., and S. Fichtl 2011 *Keltenstädte aus der Luft.* Konrad Theiss, Stuttgart.

Salač, V. 2009 Zur Interpretation der Oppida in Böhmen und in Mitteleuropa. In *Interpretierte Eisenzeiten 3: Fallstudien, Methoden, Theorie*, edited by R. Karl and J. Leskovar, pp. 237–252. Studien zur Kulturgeschichte von Oberösterreich 18. Oberösterreichisches Landesmuseum, Linz.

Salač, V. 2012 Les Oppida et les processus d'urbanisation en Europe central. In *Die Frage der Protourbanisation in der Eisenzeit—La question de la proto-urbanisation à l'âge du Fer*, edited by S. Sievers and M. Schönfelder, pp. 319–345. Dr. Rudolf Habelt, Bonn.

Schäfer, A. 2010 *Berching-Pollanten II: Die Kleinfunde der jüngerlatènezeitlichen Siedlung Berching-Pollanten, Lkr. Neumarkt i.d. Oberpfalz*. Marie Leidorf, Rahden/Westf.

Schatz, K., and E. Stephan 2008 Archäozoologie frühkeltischer Faunenfunde. In *Frühe Zentralisierungs- und Urbanisierungsprozesse: Zur Genese und Entwicklung frühkeltischer Fürstensitze und ihres territorialen Umlandes*, edited by D. Krausse, pp. 349–366. Forschungen und Berichte zur Vor- und Frühgeschichte in Baden-Württemberg 101. Konrad Theiss, Stuttgart.

Sievers, S. 2007 *Manching: Die Keltenstadt*. Konrad Theiss, Stuttgart.

Sievers, S., and M. Schönfelder (editors) 2012 *Die Frage der Protourbanisation in der Eisenzeit—La question de la proto-urbanisation à l'âge du Fer*. Dr. Rudolf Habelt, Bonn.

Sirocko, F. (editor) 2009 *Wetter, Klima, Menschheitsentwicklung: Von der Eiszeit bis ins 21. Jahrhundert*. Konrad Theiss, Stuttgart.

Smith, M. E. 2016 How Can Archaeologists Identify Early Cities? Definitions, Types, and Attributes. In *Eurasia at the Dawn of History: Urbanization and Social Change*, edited by M. Fernández-Götz and D. Krausse, pp. 153–168. Cambridge University Press, New York and Cambridge.

Steffen, C. 2012 *Gesellschaftswandel während der älteren Eisenzeit*. Konrad Theiss, Stuttgart.

Testart, A. 2005 *Eléments de classification des sociétés*. Errance, Paris.

Tomaschitz, K. 2002 *Die Wanderungen der Kelten in der antiken literarischen Überlieferung*. Mitteilungen der Prähistorischen Kommission 47. Österreichische Akademie der Wissenschaften, Vienna.

Verger, S. 2015 L'Âge du Fer ancien: l'Europe moyenne avant les Celtes historiques (800–400). In *L'Europe celtique à l'âge du Fer (VIIIe–Ier siècle)*, edited by O. Buchsenschutz, pp. 75–176. PUF, Paris.

von Nicolai, C. 2014 Symbolic Meanings of Iron Age Hillfort Defences in Continental Europe. In *Paths to Complexity: Centralisation and Urbanisation in Iron Age Europe*, edited by M. Fernández-Götz, H. Wendling, and K. Winger, pp. 111–121. Oxbow Books, Oxford.

Wells, P. S. 1984 *Farms, Villages and Cities: Commerce and Urban Origins in Late Prehistoric Europe*. Cornell University Press, Ithaca, New York.

Wells, P. S. 2011 The Iron Age. In *European Prehistory: A Survey*, edited by S. Milisauskas, pp. 405–460. 2nd ed. Springer, New York.

Wendling, H. 2013 Manching Reconsidered: New Perspectives on Settlement Dynamics and Urbanization in Iron Age Central Europe. *European Journal of Archaeology* 16(3):459–490.

Wendling, H., and K. Winger 2014 Aspects of Iron Age Urbanity and Urbanism at Manching. In *Paths to Complexity: Centralisation and Urbanisation in Iron Age Europe*, edited by M. Fernández-Götz, H. Wendling, and K. Winger, pp. 132–139. Oxbow Books, Oxford.

Woolf, G. 1993 Rethinking the Oppida. *Oxford Journal of Archaeology* 12(2):223–234.

Yoffee, N. 2005 *Myths of the Archaic State: Evolution of the Earliest Cities, States and Civilizations*. Cambridge University Press, Cambridge.

CHAPTER FIVE

Contextualizing Aggregation and Nucleation as Demographic Processes Leading to Cahokia's Emergence as an Incipient Urban Center

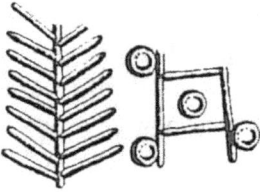

John E. Kelly

Abstract *For nearly 50 years, the large Mississippian complex, Cahokia, has been viewed as North America's only precolumbian city. Kelly and Brown (2014) have argued that Cahokia and its satellites represent the beginnings of the urban process in eastern North America. Our recent discussion has focused on Cahokia's unique cosmological configuration of four quadrilateral plazas centered on a large, 30 meters high earthen platform mound. This built environment encompasses a landscape of more than 150 hectares, and is at the heart of a ritual city covering nearly 15 square kilometers rooted in the site's Emergent Mississippian community. This paper focuses on the demographic and social processes leading to urbanism in the Central Mississippi River valley traceable back some three to four centuries earlier as populations initially aggregated into small villages. Within a century, the process of nucleating into much larger communities eventually resulted in much larger, urban settlements. Especially important to our understanding of this process are the social and cosmological mechanisms employed in the organization at the most fundamental level of settlement as they were the building blocks involved in integrating more people into larger spaces that resulted in the urban center of Cahokia and other towns in the American Bottom portion of the Central Mississippi River valley.*

Today, nearly one-half of the world's population resides in cities. The genesis of urbanism began to take root more than 5,000 years ago in Mesopotamia, eventually spreading to some extent out from this original urban nucleus. It also occurred independently—without any clear external stimulus—in other areas of the globe, such as in the Lower Nile River and the Yellow River valleys at least 4,000 years ago. In sub-Saharan Africa, urbanism took root in a number of places, such as the highlands of Ethiopia, the Niger River valley of West Africa, and Southeast Africa between 1,000 and 2,000 years ago. In the New World, early urbanism has been documented in the Andes and adjacent coastal areas of South America as well as across the Yucatan and highland areas of Mesoamerica over 2,000 years ago.

The last place in which this process began to independently emerge was eastern North America 1,000 years ago. Kelly and Brown (2014) have argued that this urban development—with its beginnings at Cahokia and the American Bottom at the onset of the second millennium A.D.—was truncated within five centuries when Europeans encountered the incipient urban polities of indigenous peoples. Thus, urbanism was only beginning to take root resulting—with the exception of Cahokia—in small towns often under 1,000 residents. The primary goal of this paper is to examine how this process unfolded, and to explore the role of aggregation in the centuries prior to Cahokia.

CAHOKIA AS AN URBAN CENTER

The idea that the Early Mississippian mound center of Cahokia was indeed a city can be traced back to more than 40 years ago, when a number of archaeologists (Fowler 1975; O'Brien 1972a) and anthropologists (Pfeiffer 1973, 1974) began to characterize Cahokia as urban or as a metropolis (see Young and Fowler 2000). To a large degree, this realization can be attributed to the highway salvage excavations at Cahokia beginning in 1960 (Fowler 1997). Although professional excavations at the site extend back to the 1920s and occurred occasionally afterward, continuous investigations at Cahokia—following the revelations of the site's complexity based on highway salvage work—have been maintained through additional research projects for more than a half-century. A more complete understanding of Cahokia's character as an urban center came about as a result of a second wave of salvage excavations beginning in the mid-1970s when a large highway mitigation undertaking—known as the FAI-270 project—was initiated in the area outside the settlement (Bareis and Porter 1984). The published results of this and more recent projects have provided the basis for establishing the historic context for the emergence of Cahokia, and for addressing the role of settlement aggregation and nucleation in this process discussed in this paper.

NATURAL AND CULTURAL SETTING OF CAHOKIA

Cahokia is located in the American Bottom, a 120 kilometers long and 10 to 20 kilometers wide segment of the Central Mississippi River valley, between the Kaskaskia and Missouri rivers (Figure 5.1). Its maximum width of 20 kilometers across from St. Louis is where Cahokia was centrally placed within the floodplain. The Ozark Highlands, including the St. Francois Mountains, are to the west of the valley, and the prairies of the Illinois Till Plain are to the east.

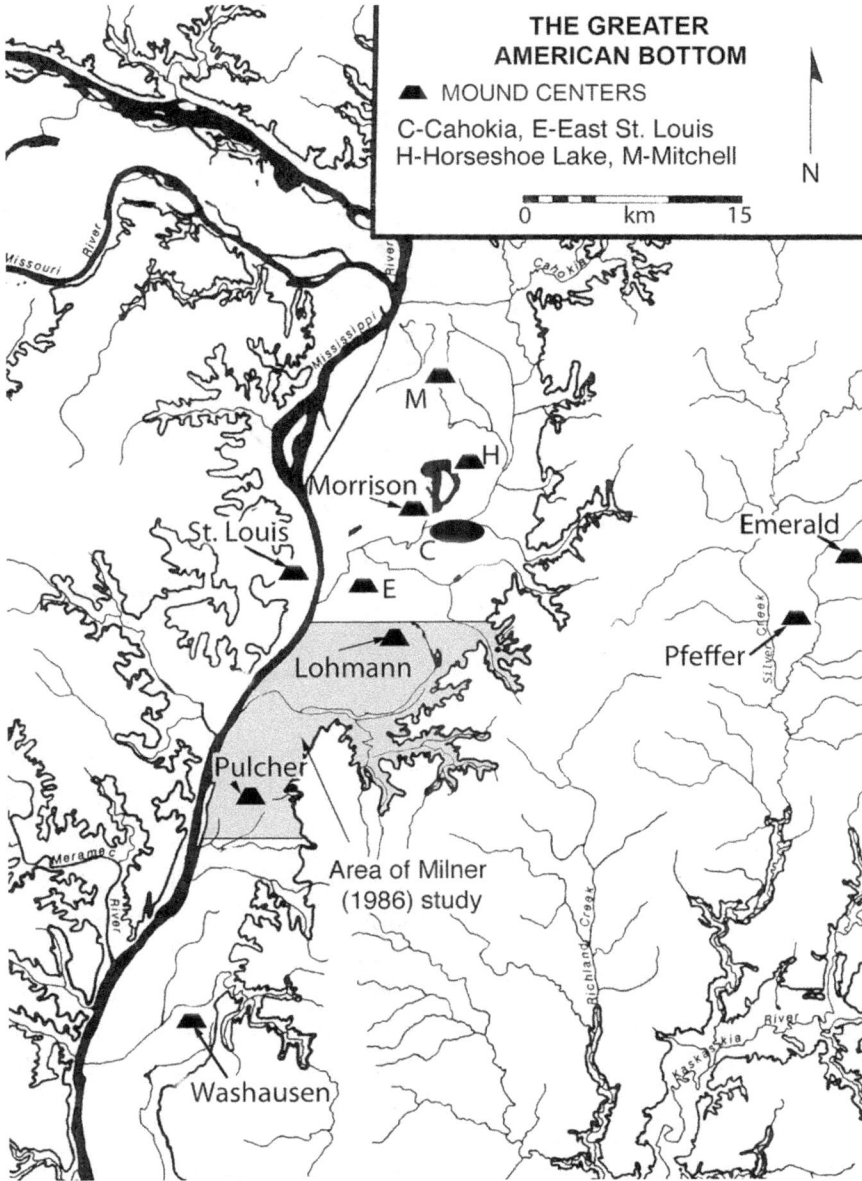

FIGURE 5.1. Distribution of Mississippian mound centers, with Milner's (1986) study area.

Given Cahokia's impressive size of nearly 15 square kilometers, we do not fully grasp its physical scale and, more importantly, the striking way in which the landscape has been culturally shaped and spatially differentiated with its overall design as an urban center. Of significance are the quadripartite configuration of the site's epicenter and its

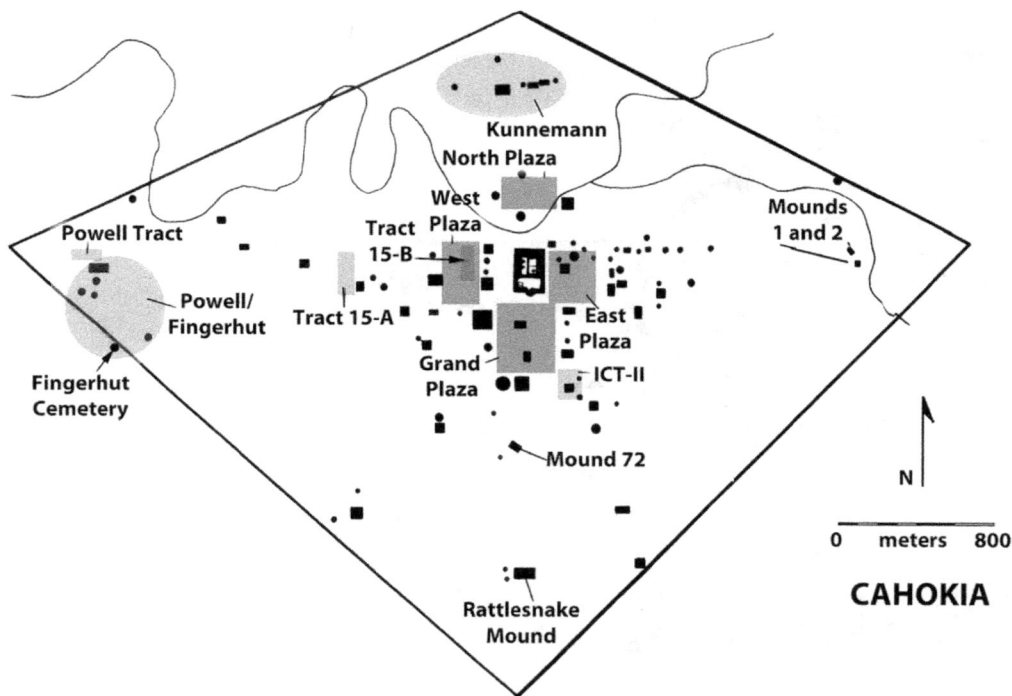

FIGURE 5.2. The plan of Cahokia.

link to its indigenous cosmology (Kelly 1996) (Figure 5.2). The surrounding region within a 50-kilometer radius of Cahokia represents a landscape of numerous Mississippian settlements. Communities in this area ranged in size from the many, smaller farmsteads (Emerson 1997; Mehrer 1995; Milner et al. 1984; Yerkes 1987) up to the larger satellite towns of East St. Louis, Pulcher, Mitchell, St. Louis, and Emerald (see Figure 5.1). Certainly, Cahokia was the ritual center of this urban polity, attracting pilgrims (Kelly and Brown 2012) and new immigrants (Alt 2006; Slater et al. 2014), with each of the smaller towns servicing their immediate surrounding area (see Kelly 1995:96–100).

In what way can we now address the rapid process of nucleation within this urban setting? An enormous amount of energy by some researchers has been expended on external sources to account for what resulted in Cahokia. In turn, anything indigenous to the region and their contribution has been rapidly and purposefully diminished. Nevertheless, given the various observations by numerous scholars since the 1940s, there is no question of the role that the indigenous pre-Mississippian populations have played in Cahokia's creation. This does not exclude the contributions of external actors and ideas in this process, and certainly by the 1970s researchers, such as Hall (1975) and Vogel (1975), already had discussed the evidence for this.

AGGREGATION AND NUCLEATION

As a prelude to settlement nucleation and urbanism, one of the initial and important steps is delineating demographic processes, such as aggregation. Birch (2013) has prepared an excellent cross-cultural treatise on settlement aggregation, in which she examines the history of theory building in the study of prestate communities, the importance of their fluid nature, and the different ways aggregation figures into the way communities may arise. For purposes here, I have differentiated between aggregation and nucleation. Conceptually, my use of distinguishing these processes here differs a bit from Rautman's (2013:116), where nucleation in the Southwest occurs within the context of aggregation. In the case of nucleated settlements in the American Bottom, the primary differences between aggregation and nucleation are in the demographic scale and the presence of a focal point in the overall configuration of the community. In general, the difference in scale occurred horizontally and vertically, which are visible and, in turn, reflect differences in the degree of social differentiation along both axes. Aggregation in the context here is viewed as a simple concentration of people in permanent settlements on the landscape. Nucleation is a much more complex form of aggregation both in terms of settlement size and the differences evident in the way the population is distributed in a much larger space. In general, both processes can be related to population growth, density, and the manner in which communities occupy and shape the natural landscape. Both aggregation and nucleation can take place without an increase in population within a given larger region. In the case of the American Bottom, there is evidence for population growth that can be linked to biological, social, and technological changes.

Before discussing the evidence for demographic growth in the American Bottom, an examination of subsistence changes underwriting this process is warranted (Table 5.1). The process of plant domestication emerged independently in the mid-continent of the Eastern Woodlands (Smith 1998), and is known as the Eastern Agricultural Complex (EAC). This included fleshy fruits, such as gourds and squashes, followed by the oily seeds of sunflower and marshelder, culminating in a suite of starchy seeds of early spring grasses, mayflower, and little barley, and the fall crops of chenopodium and erect knotweed. This complex of domesticated plants coalesced some 2,000 years ago, when Middle Woodland female farmers throughout the mid-continent were actively involved in the cultivation of all of these crops to varying degrees (Watson and Kennedy 1991).

We know very little regarding the amount of land needed for these domesticated crops. While we can assume that large plots were not needed, Mueller (2017) proposed that ancient farmers focused on the subtle differences in topography in order to avoid the risks of flooding or drought. Another aspect of cultivation relates to arable lands, which in the case of the various cultigens is not well understood. Once harvested and processed, seeds could be stored for later use. Presumably, the household was the primary social and economic unit employed in planting and harvesting, which was a labor-intensive process that required a coordinated effort to be successful.

TABLE 5.1

CHRONOLOGY OF AGGREGATION, NUCLEATION, AND URBANIZATION
WITHIN THE AMERICAN BOTTOM BY CULTURAL PERIOD AND PHASE

A.D.	Culture	North	South	Characteristics
	Mississippian	Stirling	Stirling	Urbanization of a highly differentiated landscape of towns, villages, nodal communities, and farmsteads
		Lohman	Lindhorst	
1050				
	Emergent Mississippian	Edelhardt	Lindeman	Beginnings of small villages nucleating into larger (more than 1 ha) villages and towns
		Merrell	George Reeves	
		Loyd	Range	Continuation of small villages within aggregated clusters. Villages as cosmograms. Introduction of maize to EAC
		Collinsville	Dohack	
850				
	Florescent Late Woodland	Sponemann	Patrick	Aggregation in the form of small (less than 0.5 ha) villages within aggregated clusters
		Patrick	Patrick	Focus on crops of the Eastern Agricultural Complex (EAC)
650				

In studying the production of ceramic vessels throughout the Woodland sequence in the Midwest, Braun (1983, 1985) documented two major technological changes between the Middle Woodland and Late Woodland. One was a thinning of vessel walls and the second was a shift from the flat-bottomed Early and Middle Woodland vessels to the subconoidal jars of the Late Woodland. These modifications in ceramic technology were intricately entangled with the starchy seeds being harvested and their preparation for cooking and subsequent consumption. In addition to being parched in large, open bowls and pans, the seeds could be prepared as gruel in subconoidal jars. The latter cuisine could be fed easily to infants allowing them to be weaned at a young age. It was proposed by Buikstra, Konigsberg, and Burlington (1986:539–540) that such behavior allowed for a decreased birthing interval, thus resulting in increased fertility. This allows for additional births that, in turn, may result in an increase in population.

If Buikstra and her colleagues' model for population growth is viable, then we can examine the actual evidence from excavated contexts. Milner's (1986) calculation of Mississippian population density within a segment of the American Bottom also can be applied to the various pre-Mississippian occupations. His study included a 15-kilometer-long segment of the floodplain south of Cahokia, from the single-mound

Lohmann site to an area just south of the larger, multimound Pulcher site (see Figure 5.1). These two nucleated Mississippian towns were excluded from his research, and he focused on the spatially discrete, yet widely dispersed farmsteads that had been uncovered by extensive highway excavations within his study area. These farmsteads, covering 400 years of occupation within the region, all produced domestic structures, thus providing a means of estimating population density. Milner considered the excavated area, habitable land, number of structures, structure longevity, and household size in his calculations. Since Milner's efforts, several other excavations (e.g., Fortier 2014) have taken place within his study area. No attempt, however, has been made to update Milner's study with these new datasets since much of it remains unpublished.

In order to determine the population density of pre-Mississippian complexes, I first applied Milner's methodology and the aforementioned five variables in 1992, and I use it also in this paper. The total excavation area for both Milner's and the current study is 31.33 hectares. The percentage of inhabitable land above 125.00 meters above mean sea level within the excavated area is 74.9. The total number of structures for the six archaeological phases, from the earliest Late Woodland Mund phase to the latest Emergent Mississippian phases, is 461. Although it is difficult to accurately estimate structure longevity, it was assumed—as Milner did—to vary from three to five years, and in some instances as long as 10 years. This longevity, in part, was supported by Pauketat's (1989) subsequent study on Mississippian household occupation span. Household size also is highly variable. In examining the extant literature, Milner decided that Cook's (1972) model was the most appropriate for his purposes to calculate household populations. This was based on ethnographic data from California, where 25 square feet (2.32 square meters) per person for the first six individuals and 100 square feet for each additional individual was employed. None of the domestic structures for the pre-Mississippian would have exceeded the space (i.e., 13 square meters) needed for more than six individuals. The major difference between Milner's study of the population of Mississippian farmsteads and the present study focusing on the much larger size of pre-Mississippian occupations is that the latter is represented by multihousehold villages.

The following sections focus on a discussion of the evidence for aggregation beginning with the Late Woodland settlements, and then an examination of the shift from aggregation to nucleation during the nearly two centuries of the Emergent Mississippian (see Table 5.1). This helps us better understand the underlying role of demography in conjunction with social changes that result in the process of urbanization at Cahokia at the end of the Emergent Mississippian. Much of the data used in this paper was derived from the large, multicomponent Range site. The highway salvage excavations at the 10-hectare Range site resulted in the delineation of over 5,000 features that included more than 600 domestic structures representing 25 separate occupational episodes, beginning with the Late Woodland and extending into the Early Mississippian period (Kelly 1990a). Although this site has provided much of the data, other sites also are an integral part of this study.

LATE WOODLAND SETTLEMENT AGGREGATION

In general, the Patrick phase (A.D. 650–850) is one of the several phases delineated by researchers to cover the nearly five centuries of Late Woodland (A.D. 350–850) occupation, after the more elaborate manifestation known as Middle Woodland (A.D. 250–350). The Patrick phase ceramic assemblages are quite similar stylistically to those coeval Late Woodland complexes that extend as far north as the Central Illinois River valley, and cover much of southern Illinois and west into the eastern Ozarks. This suggests a shared identity among presumably exogamous patrilocal communities. Holley (2000) has referred to this episode—along with the Sponemann phase (A.D. 800–850)—as the Florescent Late Woodland, which highlights the significance of this epoch (Figure 5.3; see also Table 5.1).

In addition to technological changes in ceramics, the introduction of the bow and arrow in this period was not only important in hunting large mammals, such as deer, but also as a weapon used in settling conflicts that may have been precipitated by the establishment of male hunting territories away from settlements. Besides its versatility and portability (Shott 1993), Holley (2000:154) suggests that the adoption of the bow and arrow also allowed for year-round hunting outside the prime fall/winter period when deer congregated. The drop in the number of projectile points from the Florescent Late Woodland into the later complexes, as noted by Holley (2000:159), occurs in conjunction with other changes that may be related to overhunting in the uplands, especially given the demands precipitated by a growing population. Kelly (2007:476–477, Figure 19.2) also noted a decline in the frequency of arrow points from the Late Woodland into the late Emergent Mississippian George Reeves phase (A.D. 950–1000), and proposed that the increase in population density in the American Bottom may have been related to an increased reliance on maize, a decrease in hunting territories as the population increased with smaller settlement catchments, and hence, access to fewer large mammals.

Presumably, having populations focusing on landscapes with readily available resources related to food production and procurement was important, and within a few decades people aggregated at some of these favorable loci. The archaeological record of these sites predominantly includes raw materials, such as chert and other lithics, from nearby sources (Fortier 2014; Kelly et al. 1987). In contrast, exotic materials obtained through exchange or direct procurement were not a major part of the communities' material inventory.

When compared with the widely dispersed occupations of the earlier portion of the Late Woodland sequence, such as the Mund (Fortier et al. 1983) and Cunningham (Meinkoth et al. 2003) sites, the subsequent Florescent Late Woodland aggregation appears to have taken place quite quickly with an expansion out into the floodplain away from bluff base and upland occupation areas as the population increased (see Table 5.1). The bluff base settlements located on alluvial fans adjacent to a tributary entering the Mississippi River floodplain were a holdover from an older pattern of the Middle Woodland (Kelly 2002a). The aggregation during the Florescent Late Woodland was not only advantageous with regard to the available labor needed in harvesting seed crops but it may have had a collective advantage in terms of protection from outside attacks.

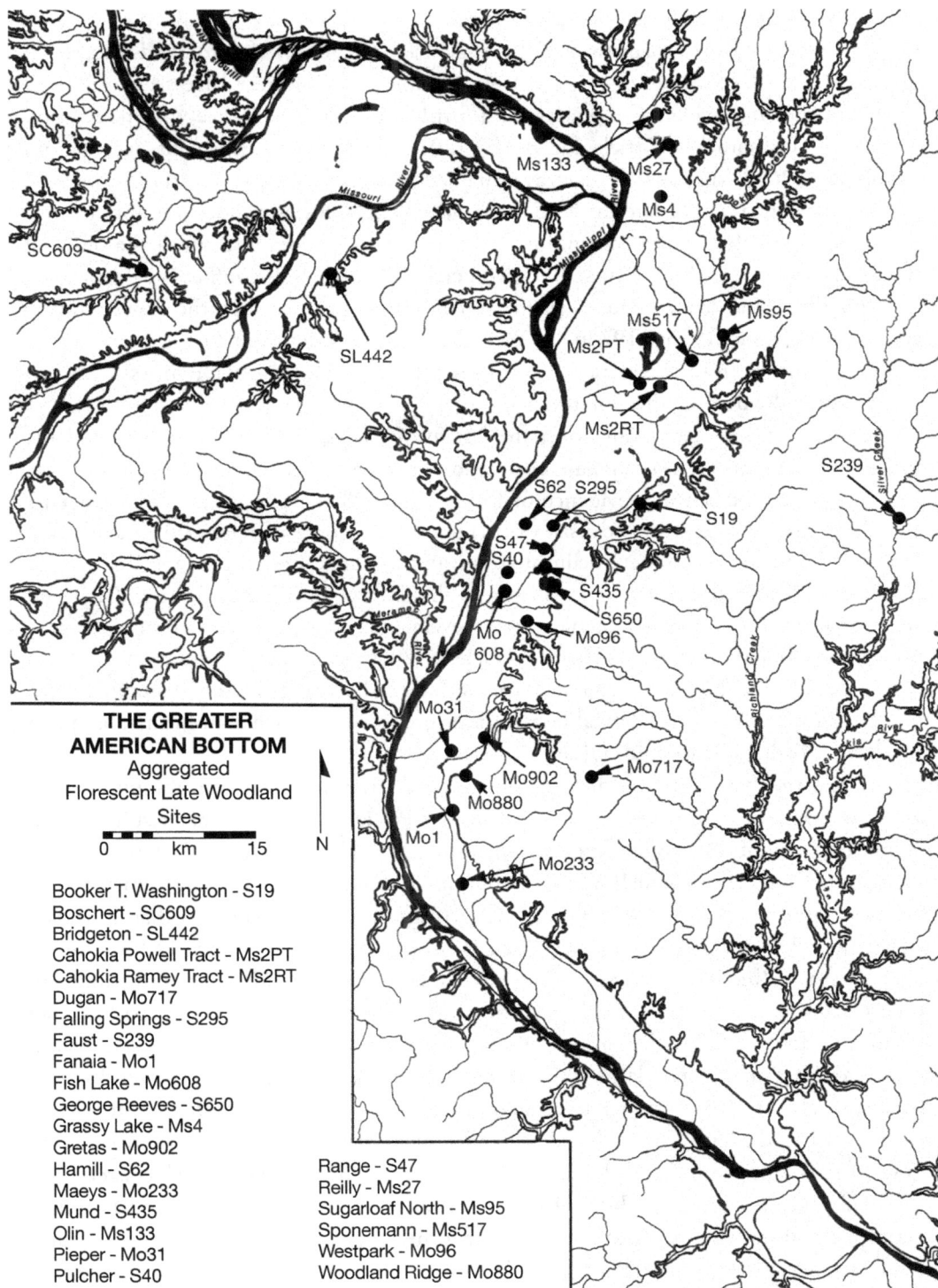

THE GREATER AMERICAN BOTTOM
Aggregated Florescent Late Woodland Sites

0 ——— km ——— 15   N

Booker T. Washington - S19
Boschert - SC609
Bridgeton - SL442
Cahokia Powell Tract - Ms2PT
Cahokia Ramey Tract - Ms2RT
Dugan - Mo717
Falling Springs - S295
Faust - S239
Fanaia - Mo1
Fish Lake - Mo608
George Reeves - S650
Grassy Lake - Ms4
Gretas - Mo902
Hamill - S62
Maeys - Mo233
Mund - S435
Olin - Ms133
Pieper - Mo31
Pulcher - S40

Range - S47
Reilly - Ms27
Sugarloaf North - Ms95
Sponemann - Ms517
Westpark - Mo96
Woodland Ridge - Mo880

FIGURE 5.3. Distribution of Florescent Late Woodland aggregated sites in the American Bottom.

In our original research design for the mitigation of the Late Woodland and subsequent Emergent Mississippian sites (Kelly et al. 1984a, 1984b), we proposed—based on Carneiro's (1970) earlier work—that if we were able to delineate village-size communities, we would find evidence of warfare and fortifications in accordance with population increase. In his summary article for Birch's (2013) volume on settlement aggregation, Kowalewski (2013) discusses warfare as a major factor leading to aggregation in prestate societies. Evidence for warfare in the Eastern Woodlands, however, does not appear until the beginning of the second millennium A.D., and is not widespread until the onset of the thirteenth century A.D. (Krus 2016; Milner 1999). Although conflict is evident from Late Woodland mortuary contexts to the north of the study area in the Lower Illinois River valley (Perino 1973a, 1973b, 1973c), there is no evidence of fortifications in the American Bottom from this period, and violent deaths were presumably ones related to episodes of individual conflict or revenge.

On the basis of excavations over the last five decades, the Late Woodland and the subsequent Emergent Mississippian occupations are characterized by a variety of site sizes and types, without any evidence of fortifications. When present at Florescent Late Woodland sites, the structures consist of small, ca. 4–6 square meters, rectilinear houses. Portions of several villages were delineated during the Range site excavations (Kelly et al. 1987), as well as more amorphous villages at the sites of Fish Lake (Fortier 2014) and Faust (Holley 2000). Smaller hamlets with several structures also have been excavated in other areas of the region (Fortier and Jackson 2000; Harl 1995; Holley 2000; Kelly 1990b, 2002b; Koldehof and Golley 2006), and are indicative of loosely structured communities in that there is no definable pattern of organization, such as seen in subsequent Emergent Mississippian communities.

While the Patrick phase sites in the American Bottom are quite ubiquitous, one interesting pattern is the close presence of nearby Patrick phase sites that result in what we can best describe as large, aggregated clusters (see Table 5.1). These clusters represent a relatively large area in which a village composed of multiple households emerges (for a similar pattern, see Ryan this volume). The village occupies an area less than a hectare within the large area of the cluster, which is several hectares in extent. Delineation of the cluster as defined here represents use of its area over an extended period of time—in some instances, it may be several centuries, while in other instances, it may be less than a century. Holley (2000) first noted this pattern in the Central Silver Creek drainage, in an area that underwent large-scale surveys and subsequent excavations, resulting in the identification of the Faust site complex, an example of an aggregated cluster. More recent work at the Fish Lake site has expanded the excavated Patrick phase occupation (Fortier 2014), such that it helps us to better understand the aggregated clusters. For the floodplain and adjacent bluffs of the American Bottom, these Late Woodland clusters are at a distance of 2–5 kilometers from other aggregated clusters and, thus, they stand in marked contrast to earlier Late Woodland sites. Occasionally, there are smaller contemporary sites dispersed between the larger clusters. Although a significant part of the American Bottom—especially east of the Mississippi River—has been subjected to pedestrian surveys and some extensive excavations (Harl 1995; Harn 1971; Holley 2000;

Jackson 1979; Kelly et al. 1979; Linder et al. 1978; Munson 1971; Pauketat et al. 1998; Woods 1986), there are still gaps in the coverage area. Thus, at this point, we have a settlement pattern model that needs to be updated as new data come forth.

Presumably, these Late Woodland clusters represent the location of communities in the form of small, unstructured villages that are relocating within these cluster areas over time, that is, for a number of generations before the eventual abandonment of the aggregated cluster (for a comparable pattern, see Birch this volume). In some instances, such as the Range, Westpark, and George Reeves sites, these aggregated clusters persist into the initial Emergent Mississippian. In many respects, this pattern is indicative of the overall aggregation of perhaps 50–100 people within a village that thrives for a number of years before it is relocated within the larger cluster area.

The aggregate cluster around the Range site also extends south to include the Missouri Pacific No. 2 (Harn 1971) and Schlemmer (Berres 1984; Szuter 1979) sites. One fully defined settlement, P-5, within the Range site aggregate consists of a small community square or plaza, with clusters of structures distributed around this communal space (Kelly 1990a; Kelly et al. 1987) (Figure 5.4). Village P-5 is one of several such Late Woodland

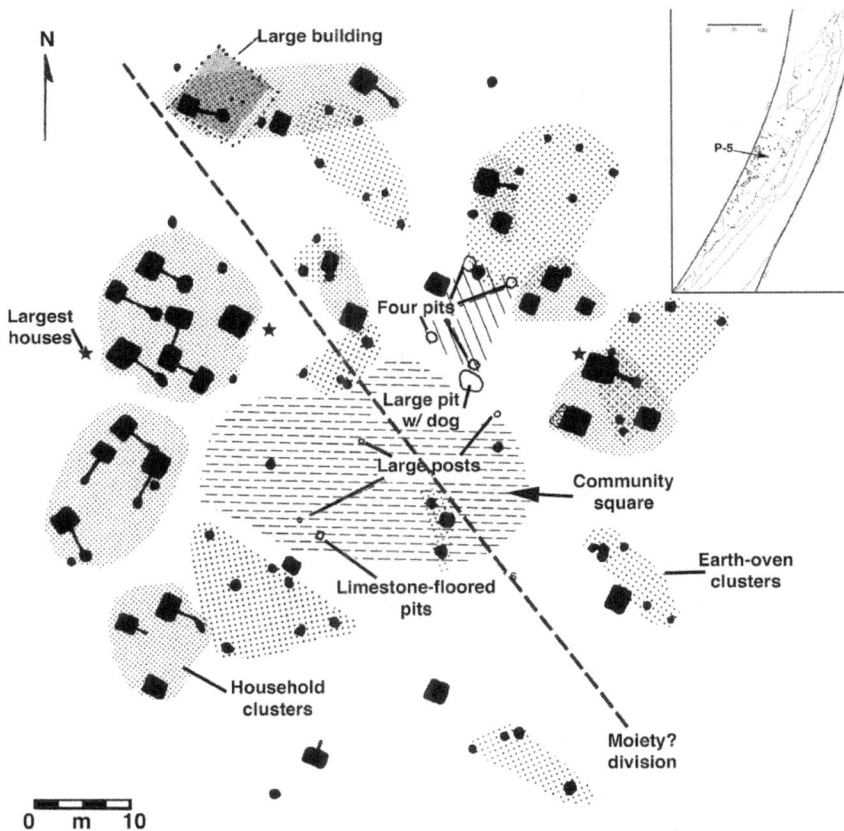

FIGURE 5.4. The community organization of the Late Woodland Patrick phase village P-5 at the Range site.

villages that occupy a much larger area of the Range site. Additional Late Woodland aggregation loci to date include the large area that coincides with the later Pulcher mound group just north of the Fish Lake complex (Fortier 2014), the Woodland Ridge (Koldehof 2002), and the Dugan Airfield complexes in the uplands to the east (Koldehof and Galloy 2006), as well as the Faust complex within the Silver Creek drainage (Holley 2000) (see Figure 5.3). Other possible clusters may be present in two areas of the Cahokia site, and also are interspersed among the larger aggregates; these latter are groups of smaller extractive and household sites that are spatially and temporally restricted.

As mentioned earlier, there is a significant increase in population density for the Patrick phase in the area south of Cahokia—using structure longevity of five years, the population density is 18.7 people per square kilometer in this area (Figure 5.5). This is a marked increase from 3.13 people per square kilometer since the earlier Late Woodland Mund phase (A.D. 550–650). However, the known number of structures for the Mund phase is undoubtedly underrepresented.

The basic social unit of the Late Woodland period is the household, and in the case of the Range site village P-5, there are seven house clusters presumably reflective of extended households (see Figure 5.4). These extended households become important in the labor-intensive activities associated with harvesting of agricultural crops during late spring and early fall. The largest household cluster (No. 3) has six structures, two of which are the largest houses in the village (Kelly et al. 1987). While researchers have yet to resolve why there are two house forms—keyhole-shaped and simple rectilinear

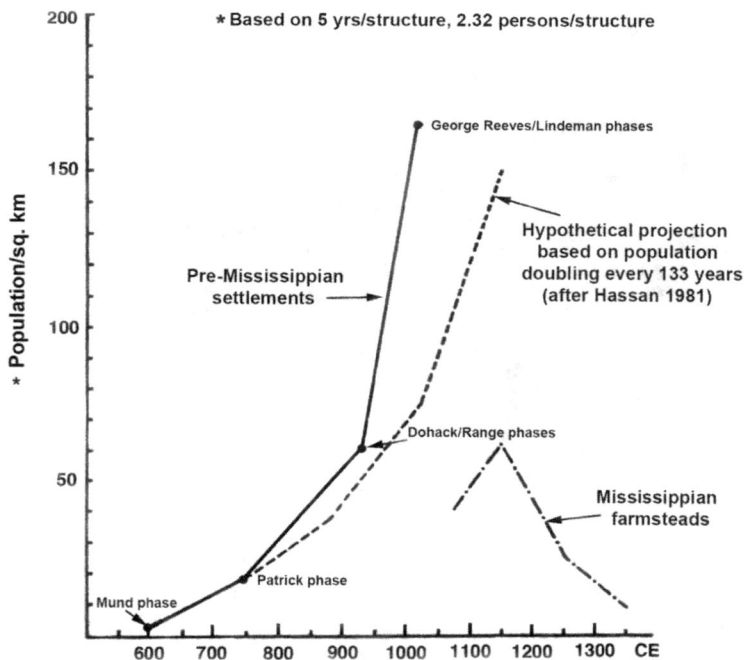

FIGURE 5.5. Population density for pre-Mississippian and Mississippian sites.

ones—their distribution is such that there appears to be a division within the village that may represent a moiety. In the southwestern part of village P-5, there are 16 structures, 75 percent of which are keyhole-shaped, while the northeastern segment has 15 structures, with the majority, 73 percent, being rectilinear in shape. This may represent the beginning of larger corporate groups, such as clans, in Late Woodland settlements that are intrinsic to tribes in the American Midwest historically (e.g., Bailey 1995). The significance of corporate groups is in the way in which reciprocal relations are developed and, in turn, help establish balance within communities, and also between communities.

At the core of village P-5 at the Range site was the community square. This central area included numerous pit features, and a number of large posts also were present; however, they were not centrally placed. One set of quadripartite pits with limestone slab–lined floors was placed along the northeastern edge of this community square. Between this arrangement and the square was a large storage facility with the skeleton of a female dog at the bottom—the dog had been placed on the floor with smaller puppies in the birth canal, suggesting she may have been in the process of giving birth at the time she may have been ritually sacrificed. Undoubtedly, these were ritual elements within this Late Woodland community that were in a peripheral location along the community square margins. Likewise, a large building also was positioned on the northwestern margins of the community as a separate facility.

The importance of ritual in the organization of space at Late Woodland sites also can be seen in the widespread distribution of small clay and stone pipes presumably associated with tobacco or other related plants. At the Fish Lake site, Fortier (2014) documented pipes within one of the large buildings in one of the villages that constituted the site. In general, pipes are quite ubiquitous as are the small discoidals, employed in the ritual game of *chunk-ge* historically (Culin 1907). Both are harbingers of similar items that continue to be present into the later Mississippian occupations in the region. Unlike their later counterparts, it appears that there is a more recreational or casual use of the pipes, although they are more likely to be present at larger village sites. The animistic nature of Late Woodland societies, again, foreshadows the Emergent Mississippian and Mississippian belief systems, however, without the stronger ritual institutions and positions that are so integral to the descendant societies.

THE EMERGENT MISSISSIPPIAN AND THE SHIFT
FROM AGGREGATION TO NUCLEATION

The concept of Emergent Mississippian (A.D. 850–1050) as a taxonomic unit between Late Woodland and Mississippian was defined as part of the abovementioned FAI-270 project chronology in part to replace the term Late Bluff, an American Bottom derivative of Jersey Bluff (Kelly et al. 1984b) (see Table 5.1). Originally defined on the basis of pottery associated with Late Woodland sites in the Lower Illinois River valley, Wray (1952:159) characterized it "as a blend of Late Woodland and Mississippian traits." Amateurs collecting at Cahokia in the 1940s and 1950s recognized "a type of Bluff culture . . . related to the Titterington [*sic*] Bluff Culture" (Perino 1950:15). During the extensive highway excavations at Cahokia and surveys of the surrounding area in the early 1960s, American Bottom researchers used the terms Early and Late Bluff (Harn 1971; Munson 1971; Vogel 1975; Wittry and Vogel 1962). The former is primarily the equivalent of the Late Woodland Patrick phase and the latter coincides with the Emergent Mississippian in the current terminology. In contrast to the Early Bluff, Late Bluff ceramics—present in the large, rectangular, single–post house basins and pits—were prevalent at the three major highway salvage excavations at Cahokia, including Powell Tract (O'Brien 1972b), and Tracts 15-A and 15-B (Vogel 1975; Wittry and Vogel 1962) (see Figure 5.2).

It is clear that we can define at least two separate ceramic traditions within the Emergent Mississippian period of the American Bottom: Late Bluff and Pulcher (Kelly 1990b). Differences between these two traditions are evident in the selection of certain techniques of production, such as tempering, the frequency and type of surface treatments, as well as frequency and type of decorative modes. The ceramics for both traditions can easily be distinguished from earlier Late Woodland—Patrick and Sponemann phases—assemblages. The Late Bluff tradition is restricted to the northern part of the region, including the Lower Missouri River valley, and is an extension of the Jersey Bluff tradition to the north in the Lower Illinois River valley, southward into the American Bottom. The Pulcher tradition is restricted primarily to the area south of Prairie du Pont Creek (Kelly 1993, 2002b), and is related to similar assemblages in the northeastern Ozark Plateau to the west, especially along the Lower Meramec River drainage (Reeder 2000). In addition to changes in material culture, another major transformation during the Emergent Mississippian period was the adoption of maize as part of the array of domesticated plants already present in the Late Woodland (Fritz and Lopinot 2007).

Why suddenly do we see such differences in the archaeological record of the American Bottom? At the end of the Late Woodland period, the cultural landscape is beginning to rapidly change. In the northern part of the American Bottom—especially north of Cahokia—an amalgamation or hybridization of Patrick phase material culture occurs in conjunction with Late Woodland complexes to the north of the American Bottom along the Mississippi River. This mixture of two distinct ceramic assemblages has been defined as the Sponemann phase (Fortier 2015a, 2015b), and is part of Holley's (2000) Florescent Late Woodland.

More than a decade ago, it was proposed (Kelly 2000, 2002a) that there was a brief abandonment of the northern portion of the American Bottom at the end of the Late Woodland, during the ninth century A.D., and that within a short period of time Jersey Bluff populations began to expand southward into the area. In part, this perspective was generated by the lack of continuity between the Sponemann and the early Late Bluff ceramic assemblages. In general, there seemed to be a paucity of the earlier Late Bluff sites. Three major creeks—Wood River, Indian Creek, and Cahokia Creek—flow southward from the Illinois Till Plain to the north into the American Bottom. These drainages are the conduits that allowed populations from the Lower Illinois River valley to readily move southward into the American Bottom, particularly during the early Emergent Mississippian of the late ninth and early tenth centuries A.D. Presumably, this was a gradual process of these communities expanding along these drainages over time.

To the south, the northern extent of the Pulcher ceramic tradition is primarily defined by the Prairie du Pont Creek. The creek enters the Mississippi River floodplain and abandoned Mississippi River meanders known as Goose Lake and Grand Marais (Figure 5.6). The topographically much lower meander, Goose Lake, would have been subject to changes in hydrology, resulting in this area being an extensive aquatic landscape of lakes and marshes. While it would not have limited contact and interaction between

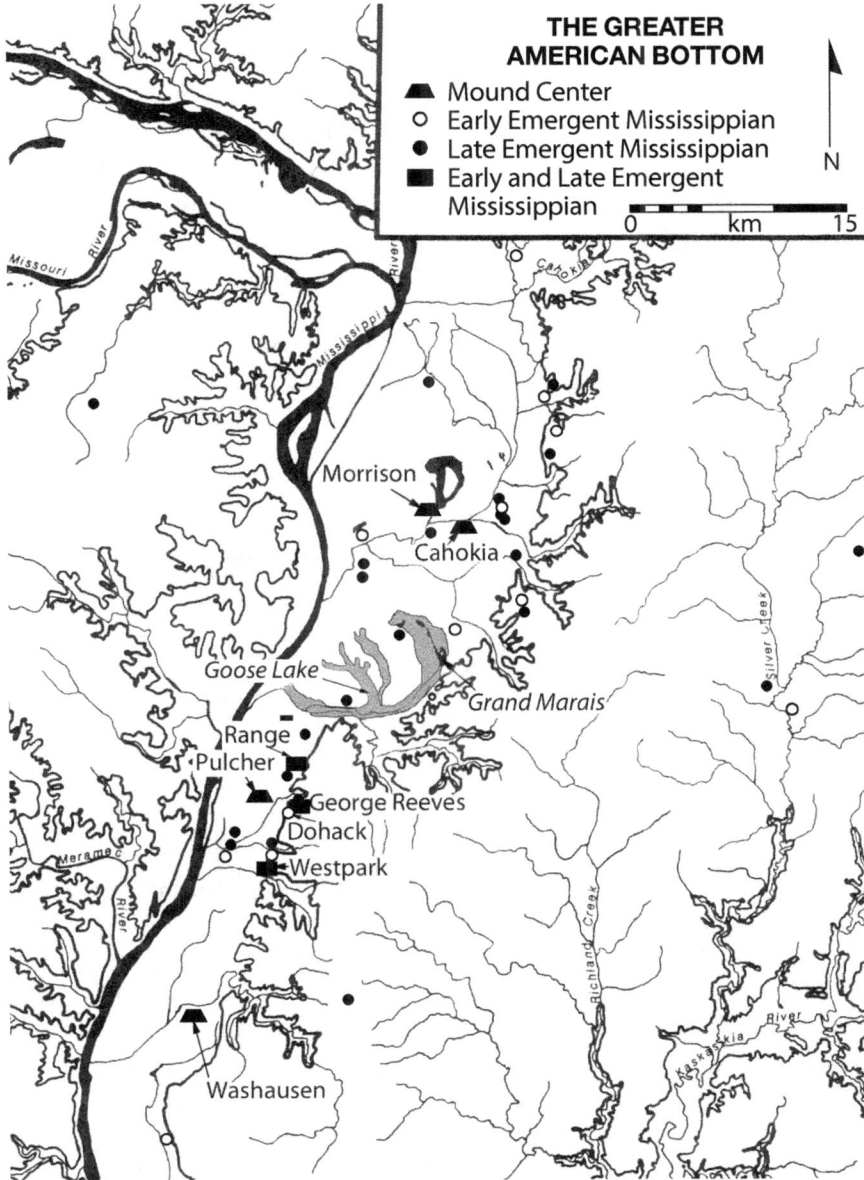

FIGURE 5.6. Distribution of Emergent Mississippian sites in the American Bottom.

populations in the area north of Goose Lake and the area to the south of it, it would have restricted the amount of inhabitable land. In other words, the spatial and, in turn, the social distance between communities was increased. Presumably, this is one of the factors contributing to the distinct differences in material culture between the northern and central parts of the American Bottom throughout the Emergent Mississippian and into the Early Mississippian periods.

While materials from pedestrian surveys provided important insights into the distribution of sites related to the Late Bluff and Pulcher traditions, it is clearly the extensive excavations that have resulted in substantial details on community size and organization (Kelly 1990b). The initial part of the Emergent Mississippian—toward the end of the ninth and beginning of the tenth centuries A.D.—is characterized by a number of changes in community organization and a significant increase in population density starting from the Late Woodland (see Figure 5.5). Based on extensive excavations at a number of sites related to highway and other rescue and salvage excavations, this density increased from the abovementioned approximately 19 people per square kilometers to 60 people per square kilometer in the Milner study area of the American Bottom. This tripling of the population density may relate to the number of people entering the Mississippi River floodplain from the interior uplands that were being abandoned at the end of the Late Woodland period. Most of our settlement data is derived from sites that are part of the Pulcher ceramic tradition in the central part of the American Bottom region. At this point, it is simply a lack of comparable level of data for the Late Bluff tradition to the north that limits our understanding on a broader scale.

Settlement Aggregation during the Early Emergent Mississippian

For the Emergent Mississippian occupation of the Range site, we have a sequence of communities characterized by clearly defined community plans (Figure 5.7). Other nearby contemporary sites—including Westpark, Dohack, and George Reeves—have also produced distinctive settlement plans (Kelly 1990b). As with the aforementioned Late Woodland community of P-5 at the Range site, these small, early Emergent Mississippian villages consist of small structures distributed around a small central plaza (Kelly 1990a; Kelly et al. 1990). At the Range site, the center of each small community square or plaza is marked by one of three distinctive sets of features consisting of a central pole, a central pole with a quadripartite set of rectangular pits, or a larger central structure. The early Emergent Mississippian communities defined at the other nearby sites also have one of these central features. While there are hints of these types of central features already in Patrick phase villages (Fortier 2014; Holley 2000; Kelly et al. 1987), the small plazas of the early Emergent Mississippian communities become symbolically charged with elements linked to the fundamental principles of their cosmology (see Kelly 1996). These plazas become a focal point of community integration and interaction—important to each community, in much the same way the large plazas were for later Mississippian towns (Lewis and Stout 1998).

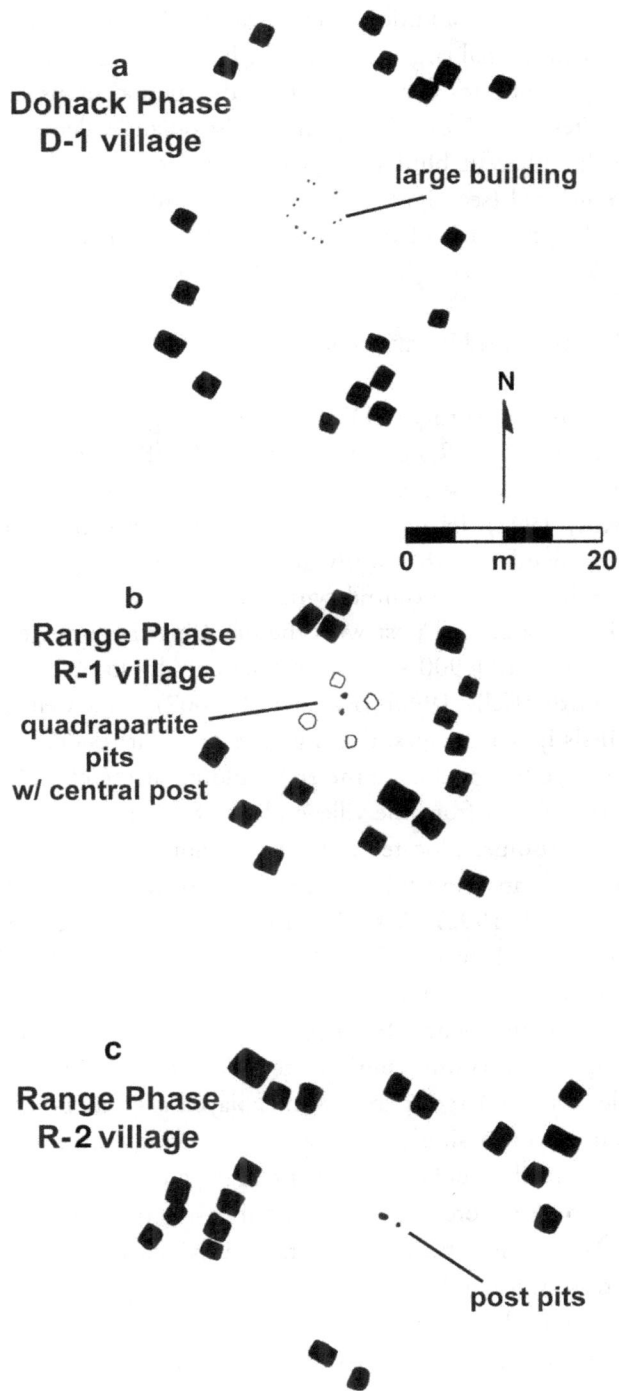

a
Dohack Phase
D-1 village

large building

N

0   m   20

b
Range Phase
R-1 village

quadrapartite
pits
w/ central post

c
Range Phase
R-2 village

post pits

FIGURE 5.7. Community organization types for the early Emergent Mississippian villages at the Range site.

Although there have been additional investigations in the American Bottom, especially to the north, no additional large communities have undergone extensive excavations. Some level of clustering of sites occurred during this period as well. However, unlike the Late Woodland sites, most early Emergent Mississippian settlements are restricted to the floodplain and the adjacent bluff tops, with no evidence that the interior portions of the uplands were utilized (see Figure 5.6). Exceptions to this rule are those Late Bluff tradition sites located along some of the major streams within the uplands to the north (Jackson 1979; Linder et al. 1978; Munson 1971; Woods 1986).

LATE EMERGENT MISSISSIPPIAN NUCLEATION

By the middle to late tenth century A.D., the small village populations were nucleated into larger villages, such as the Range site (Kelly 1990a; Kelly et al. 2007) (see Figure 5.6 and Table 5.1). These new settlements covered approximately 1 hectare, with more than 200 people (Kelly 1992). In addition, other, smaller settlement categories occurred in the region, such as hamlets with linearly aligned houses (Kelly 1990b). The plans of the nucleated villages integrate the central symbolic elements of the earlier communities (i.e., a large central post, a central post with the quadripartite arrangement of pits, or a large structure) into large, 400–900 square meters, centrally located, quadrilateral plazas and attendant courtyards (Kelly 1990b; Kelly et al. 2007). As a well-established feature of late Emergent Mississippian villages, the largest rectangular residences fronted on these plazas, with another large (ca. 36 square meters) building at the end of the earliest plaza. However, mounds were absent from the village plans of this period, with two exceptions. One exception, the Morrison site located immediately northwest of Cahokia, has two low (< 1 meter) mounds with an intervening plaza some 70 meters in length (Betzenhauser et al. 2015; Pauketat et al. 1998). A similar arrangement is evident at the Washausen site some 30 kilometers south of Cahokia (Barrier and Horsley 2014). Both settlements date to the initial decades of the eleventh century A.D.

The houses in the Emergent Mississippian villages were dispersed around small courtyards. While these courtyards continue to relate to specific corporate or family groups and their identity, the larger plazas, again, played a symbolic and integrative role within each community (for a similar phenomenon with kivas, see Ryan this volume). The site clusters that served to define settlement aggregation—beginning in the seventh century A.D. and lasting for more than three centuries—appear to have been replaced by single, large, nucleated communities which were maintained for nearly a century, beginning in the late tenth century and continuing into the early part of the eleventh century A.D. These were not static but rather dynamic nodes in the landscape subject to rapid changes, particularly in regard to their spatial configuration. Late Emergent Mississippian communities—similar to those at the Range site in the area surrounding Cahokia—were those whose populations began to nucleate into Cahokia. It is also assumed that a similar nucleation took place in the area near Pulcher.

THE EMERGENT MISSISSIPPIAN NUCLEATION AND THE ONSET OF CAHOKIA AS A CITY

The question is how do the marked differences in settlement size and function across the landscape come about in the American Bottom by the Emergent Mississippian period? The nucleation expressed at Cahokia and the other, contemporary, nearby large towns and villages consisted of approximately 37,000–50,000 people by the twelfth century A.D., and a resident population of upward of 15,000 people at Cahokia itself by the end of the eleventh century A.D. (Milner 1986, 1998; Pauketat and Lopinot 1997) (see Table 5.1). Thus, understanding the demographic evidence in conjunction with the processes that resulted in large, nucleated towns and the city of Cahokia is critical to the discussion on settlement aggregation.

In the 1960s and 1970s, Vogel (1975), Hall (1975), and Porter (1969) entertained the idea of outsiders contributing to Cahokia's emergence. They did not elucidate whether this was a result of migration and/or whether new ideas were being simply introduced in this process. During the last decade, Pauketat (2003) and Alt (2006) have argued that there was evidence of migration into the American Bottom from at least two areas to the south—one was centered at the mouth of the Ohio River and the other was upriver in the area of the confluence of the Wabash River with the Ohio. Most of the evidence of migration to Cahokia points to the uplands to the east, and is part of Pauketat's (2003) loosely defined Richland complex.

Although Yankeetown incised ceramics from the Wabash/Ohio region are ubiquitous, the shell-tempered Varney Red Filmed ceramics from sites within a 100-kilometer radius of the Ohio River's confluence with the Mississippi River are not only ubiquitous but in a few instances quite frequent within existing late Emergent Mississippian and Early Mississippian assemblages in the American Bottom (Kelly 1991). While the idea that pots are equal to people is a bit tenuous, I thought that Pauketat and Alt were correct in the idea that people were being physically integrated into Cahokian society relatively early in the site's history. This may in part explain the seemingly exponential increase in population during the early part of the eleventh century A.D. that I had documented (Kelly 1992:Figure 3).

More recently Slater, Hedman, and Emerson (2014) have documented evidence of migration based on the outcomes from the strontium analysis of human remains from Mississippian mortuary contexts at Cahokia. This has provided support of Alt's and Pauketat's original position. Slater and his colleagues' study is an important first step toward understanding the role of migration in Cahokia's emergence, florescence, and dissolution. Unfortunately, we have few mortuary samples from Emergent Mississippian context that could help us understand the role of migration at this early time in Cahokia's history. If nonlocals were probably migrating to Cahokia during the late Emergent Mississippian, historically, we know that outsiders were readily adopted into other indigenous societies and there were rituals, as discussed by Hall (1997, 2006), to address the issues associated with people being incorporated into their new society as fictive kin within existing corporate groups.

As noted above, by the onset of the tenth century A.D., Cahokia was underway with a massive nucleation of people into the central part of the site. The late Emergent Mississippian settlement at Cahokia extends at least 1.7 kilometers along the natural levee of an abandoned meander (see Figure 5.2). The population for this 17 to 34 hectares could have been between 3,400 and 6,800 people if settlement was continuous and the density corresponds to the 1-hectare George Reeves phase village at the Range site (Kelly 1990a; Kelly et al. 2007) (Figure 5.8), which had a population of approximately 200 people. As opposed,

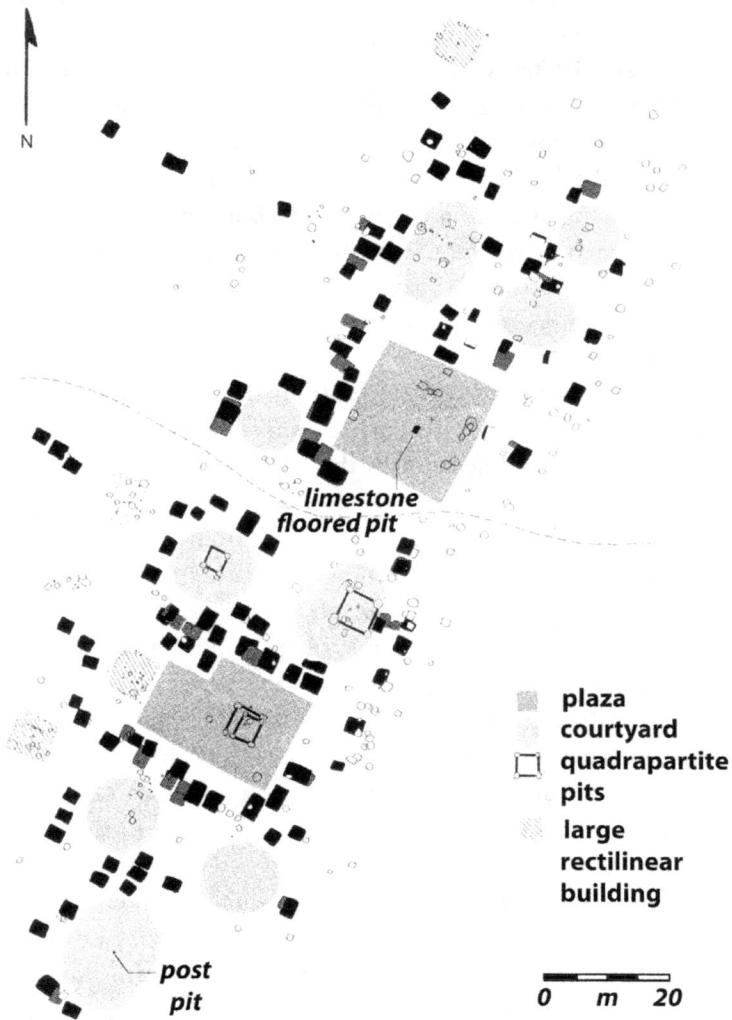

FIGURE 5.8. The community organization of the late Emergent Mississippian George Reeves phase village at the Range site.

Pauketat and Lopinot (1997) suggest a rather small population of 1,000 to 3,000 for pre–"Big Bang" Cahokia, that is, the Emergent Mississippian period just before the site's rapid expansion and transformation around A.D. 1050. Dalan and her colleagues (2003:Figure 20) propose an extensive—greater than 4 square kilometers—Emergent Mississippian occupation from the eastern margins of the site to its western end, concentrated along the natural levee containing the Canteen and Cahokia creeks confluence to the north. Present evidence for this foundational settlement, however, lacks monumental architecture and a clearly defined epicenter, and may conform to the "urban cluster" configuration described by McIntosh (1991) for West Africa and the Neolithic of Northeast China. However, there is some evidence that the creation of the four plazas occurred prior to the "Mississippianization" of Cahokia that has been highlighted as the "Big Bang." In fact, we might call plaza creation as "setting the stage." These spaces at Cahokia were designed to accommodate large numbers of people and, thus, provide in part what Renfrew (2001) and others refer to as "places of high devotion." Plazas delimited by small mounds and other special buildings were integral to the activities and performances occurring within them.

As to why Cahokia was selected and why A.D. 1000 was the point in time this occurred, we can only point to a number of possible juxtapositions. For example, Cahokia as a place is uniquely situated along a stretch of landscape upon which one could easily travel from near the banks of the Mississippi River along the natural levees of Horseshoe Lake and Edelhardt Lake meanders. One or two sloughs or swales may have been present and Canteen Creek needed to be crossed near the bluffs. Just east of Cahokia were some of the most productive agricultural soils. If these fields were controlled by women and their respective kin groups, then the potential exists for amassing surplus (Brown and Kelly 2015) and the creation of wealth and social ranking within corporate groups. This allows for the ability to host feasts important in the performance of rituals (Kelly 2001; Pauketat et al. 2002) and also for the distribution of resources and goods as part of an economic system embedded in what is a ritualized economy.

The timing of this rather large nucleation of people, even if only a few thousand, may be related to perhaps the largest supernova, a celestial event that occurred in A.D. 1006 (Stephenson and Green 2002). The timing in early May on the southern horizon with a brightness only exceeded by the moon and sun lasted three years, and must have caught people's attention and, thus, had a strong effect on the population at some level. If not this, then perhaps the creation of a place that could accommodate large numbers of people might represent a way of scheduling important annual ceremonies that in the past would have been held at the various large, nucleated villages. Perhaps having a central location was the solution and it played the most important role in the nucleation of smaller communities to Cahokia and eventually a major pilgrim site drawing in people from other regions (Kelly and Brown 2012; for similar potential processes in prehistoric Europe, see Fernández-Götz and Gaydarska this volume).

It is important to note that most of the other Mississippian mound centers have evidence of a late Emergent Mississippian nucleated community at the beginning of their occupation. These include the Pulcher and Washausen centers located within the

Pulcher tradition and the centers at East St. Louis, Lohmann, Mitchell/Fill, Horseshoe Lake, and Emerald (see Figure 5.1). In the end, the massive nucleation at Cahokia is the byproduct of the initial aggregation of Late Woodland populations throughout the American Bottom some four to five centuries before Cahokia, which were, in fact, present at a number of locations within the site, but do not exhibit continuity with the later, Emergent Mississippian/Mississippian city of Cahokia.

CONCLUSION

The evidence of aggregation beginning during the Late Woodland in the American Bottom can be tied to a noticeable increase in population density over the four centuries from the initial Late Woodland Mund phase, through the late Emergent Mississippian, and into the Early Mississippian (see Figure 5.5 and Table 5.1). Initially, when aggregation is present during the Late Woodland and the early Emergent Mississippian, the increase in density follows that of a normal growth curve (Hassan 1981). The accelerated increase in density can be attributed to a number of factors. First, of course, is the focus on a single site, Range; this will undoubtedly change as the sample is expanded. Second, the continued increase in density at the beginning of the Emergent Mississippian can be attributed to an influx of population onto the floodplain from the interior uplands. By the end of the Emergent Mississippian, we may see the beginnings of immigration taking place before the onset of Mississippian. This sets the stage for the massive changes that begin to occur by the middle of the eleventh century A.D., called the "Big Bang" by Pauketat (1993), with the urbanization of the American Bottom landscape.

The aggregation of Late Woodland peoples into what I, following Holley (2000), have called "aggregated clusters" is certainly an important stage in a process that resulted within several centuries in the organization of settlements into much larger, nucleated villages, eventually culminating in eastern North America's first city, Cahokia. The extent to which aggregation followed a similar path elsewhere has yet to be fully documented. We should not assume that aggregation will culminate in a city, or that cities or that the process of urbanization is simply a product of aggregation. There are multiple roads that lead to urbanization, and this is one example that will undergo scrutiny in the years to come.

ACKNOWLEDGMENTS

I would like to thank Dr. Attila Gyucha for the invitation to participate in the 9th IEMA Conference. It was a pleasure to meet and interact with the various participants from various parts of the globe and share our insights about ancient population aggregation and urbanization. I am also greatly indebted to Attila for the various suggestions and assistance with my chapter that greatly enhanced the final product. The author also extends special thanks to Drs. Lucretia Kelly, Jim Brown, and Natalie Mueller for their input on the chapter. While it is not possible to thank all those that have been involved in American Bottom archaeology for the last four decades, their efforts and insights are, hopefully, included within the chapter. Finally, various institutions, including the Illinois Department of Transportation, University of Illinois Urbana-Champaign, Southern Illinois University at Edwardsville, and Washington University, are gratefully appreciated for their support.

REFERENCES CITED

Alt, S. M. 2006 The Power of Diversity: The Roles of Migration and Hybridity in Cultural Change. In *Leadership and Polity in Mississippian Society*, edited by B. M. Butler and P. D. Welch, pp. 289–308. Occasional Paper 33. Center for Archaeological Investigations, Southern Illinois University, Carbondale.

Bailey, G. A. 1995 *The Osage and the Invisible World: From the Works of Francis La Flesche.* Civilization of the American Indian 217. University of Oklahoma Press, Norman.

Bareis, C. J., and J. W. Porter (editors) 1984 *American Bottom Archaeology: A Summary of the FAI-270 Project Contribution to the Culture History of the Mississippi Valley.* University of Illinois Press, Urbana.

Barrier, C. R., and T. J. Horsley 2014 Shifting Communities: Demographic Profiles of Early Village Population Growth and Decline in the Central American Bottom. *American Antiquity* 79(2):295–313.

Berres, T. E. 1984 *A Formal Analysis of Ceramic Vessels from the Schlemmer Site (11-S-382): A Late Woodland/Mississippian Occupation in St. Clair County, Illinois.* Master's thesis, Department of Anthropology, University of Illinois Urbana-Champaign, Urbana-Champaign.

Betzenhauser, A., T. R. Pauketat, E. W. Malouchos, N. H. Lopinot, and D. Marovitch 2015 The Morrison Site: Evidence for Terminal Late Woodland Mound Construction in the American Bottom. *Illinois Archaeology* 27:6–32.

Birch, J. 2013 Between Villages and Cities: Settlement Aggregation in Cross-Cultural Perspective. In *From Prehistoric Villages to Cities: Settlement Aggregation and Community Transformation*, edited by J. Birch, pp. 1–22. Routledge, New York.

Braun, D. P. 1983 Pots as Tools. In *Archaeological Hammers and Theories*, edited by J. A. Moore and A. S. Keene, pp. 107–134. Academic Press, New York.

Braun, D. P. 1985 Ceramic Decorative Diversity and Illinois Woodland Regional Integration. In *Decoding Prehistoric Ceramics*, edited by B. A. Nelson, pp. 128–153. Southern Illinois University Press, Carbondale and Edwardsville.

Brown, J. A., and J. E. Kelly 2015 Surplus Labor, Ceremonial Feasting, and Social Inequality: A Study in Social Process. In *Surplus: The Politics of Production and the Strategies of Everyday Life*, edited by C. T. Morehart and K. De Lucia, pp. 221–244. University Press of Colorado, Boulder.

Buikstra, J. E., L. W. Konigsberg, and J. Burlington 1986 Fertility and the Development of Agriculture in the Prehistoric Midwest. *American Antiquity* 51(3):528–546.

Carneiro, R. L. 1970 A Theory for the Origin of the State. *Science* 169(3947):733–738.

Cook, S. F. 1972 *Prehistoric Demography.* Addison-Wesley Modular Publications, Module 16. Addison-Wesley, New York.

Culin, S. 1907 *Games of the North American Indians.* Twenty-fourth Annual Report of the Bureau of American Ethnology. Smithsonian Institution, Washington, D.C.

Dalan, R. A., G. R. Holley, W. I. Woods, H. W. Watters Jr., and J. A. Koepke 2003 *Envisioning Cahokia: A Landscape Perspective*. Northern Illinois University Press, DeKalb.

Emerson, T. E. 1997 *Cahokia and the Archaeology of Power*. The University of Alabama Press, Tuscaloosa.

Fortier, A. C. 2015a *A Late Woodland Procurement and Ceremonial Complex at the Reilley and Husted Sites in the Northern American Bottom*. Illinois State Archaeological Survey Research Report 32. Illinois State Archaeological Survey, Champaign.

Fortier, A. C. (editor) 2014 *Late Woodland Communities in the American Bottom: The Fish Lake Site*. Illinois State Archaeological Survey Research Report 28. Illinois State Archaeological Survey, Champaign.

Fortier, A. C. (editor) 2015b *A Multicomponent Late Woodland Complex at the Vasey Site in the Northern American Bottom Uplands*. Illinois State Archaeological Survey Research Report 37. Illinois State Archaeological Survey, Champaign.

Fortier, A. C., and D. K. Jackson 2000 The Formation of a Late Woodland Heartland in the American Bottom, Illinois cal A.D. 650–900. In *Late Woodland Societies: Tradition and Transformation across the Midcontinent*, edited by T. E. Emerson, D. L. McElrath, and A. C. Fortier, pp. 123–147. University of Nebraska Press, Lincoln.

Fortier, A. C., F. A. Finney, and R. B. Lacampagne 1983 *The Mund Site (11-S-435)*. American Bottom Archaeology, FAI-270 Site Reports 5. University of Illinois Press, Urbana.

Fowler, M. L. 1975 A Pre-Columbian Urban Center on the Mississippi. *Scientific American* 233:92–101.

Fowler, M. L. 1997 *The Cahokia Atlas: A Historical Atlas of Cahokia Archaeology, Revised Edition*. Studies in Archaeology 2. University of Illinois at Urbana-Champaign, Urbana-Champaign.

Fritz, G. J., and N. H. Lopinot 2007 Native Crops at Early Cahokia: Comparing Domestic and Ceremonial Contexts. In *People, Plants, and Animals: Archaeological Studies of Human-Environment Interactions in the Midcontinent: Essays in Honor of Leonard W. Blake*, edited by R. E. Warren, pp. 90–111. Illinois Archaeology 15–16. Illinois Archaeological Survey, Kampsville.

Hall, R. L. 1975 Chronology and Phases at Cahokia. In *Perspectives in Cahokia Archaeology*, edited by J. A. Brown, pp. 15–31. Illinois Archaeological Survey Bulletin 10. University of Illinois Press, Urbana.

Hall, R. L. 1997 *An Archaeology of the Soul: North American Indian Belief and Ritual*. University of Illinois Press, Urbana.

Hall, R. L. 2006 Exploring the Big Bang at Cahokia. In *A Pre-Columbian World*, edited by J. Quilter and M. Miller, pp. 187–229. Dumbarton Oaks, Washington, D.C.

Harl, J. L. 1995 *Master Plan for the Management of Archaeological Resources within St. Louis City and County*. Research Report 51. Archaeological Research Center of St. Louis Inc., St. Louis, Missouri.

Harn, A. D. 1971 An Archaeological Survey of the American Bottoms in Madison and St. Clair Counties, Illinois. In *Archaeological Surveys of the American Bottoms and Adjacent Bluffs, Illinois*, edited by P. J. Munson and A. D. Harn, pp. 19–39. Illinois State Museum Reports of Investigations 21. Illinois State Museum, Springfield.

Hassan, F. A. 1981 *Demographic Archaeology*. Academic Press, New York.

Holley, G. R. 2000 Late Woodland on the Edge of the Looking Glass Prairie: A Scott Joint-Use Archaeological Perspective. In *Late Woodland Societies: Tradition and Transformation across the*

Midcontinent, edited by T. E. Emerson, D. L. McElrath, and A. C. Fortier, pp. 149–162. University of Nebraska Press, Lincoln.

Jackson, D. 1979 An Archaeological Survey of the Wood River Basin, Madison County, Illinois. Manuscript on file, Illinois Department of Transportation, Springfield.

Kelly, J. E. 1990a The Range Site Community Patterns and the Mississippian Emergence. In *The Mississippian Emergence*, edited by B. D. Smith, pp. 67–112. The University of Alabama Press, Tuscaloosa.

Kelly, J. E. 1990b The Emergence of Mississippian Culture in the American Bottom Region. In *The Mississippian Emergence*, edited by B. D. Smith, pp. 113–152. The University of Alabama Press, Tuscaloosa.

Kelly, J. E. 1991 The Evidence for Prehistoric Exchange and Its Implications for the Development of Cahokia. In *New Perspectives on Cahokia: Views from the Periphery*, edited by J. B. Stoltman, pp. 65–92. Monographs in World Archaeology 2. Prehistory Press, Madison, Wisconsin.

Kelly, J. E. 1992 The Impact of Maize on the Development of Nucleated Settlements: An American Bottom Example. In *Late Prehistoric Agriculture: Observations from the Midwest*, edited by W. I. Woods, pp. 167–197. Studies in Illinois Archaeology 8. Illinois Historic Preservation Agency, Springfield.

Kelly, J. E. 1993 The Pulcher Site: An Archaeological and Historical Overview. In *Highways to the Past: Essays on Illinois Archaeology in Honor of Charles J. Bareis*, edited by T. E. Emerson, A. C. Fortier, and D. L. McElrath, pp. 433–451. Illinois Archaeology 5(1–2). Illinois Archaeological Survey, Kampsville.

Kelly, J. E. 1995 *The Fingers and Curtiss Steinberg Road Sites: Two Stirling Phase Mississippian Farmsteads in the Goose Lake Locality*. Illinois Transportation Archaeological Research Program, Transportation Archaeological Research Reports 1. University of Illinois at Urbana-Champaign, Urbana-Champaign.

Kelly, J. E. 1996 Redefining Cahokia: Principles and Elements of Community Organization. In *The Ancient Skies and Sky Watchers of Cahokia: Woodhenges, Eclipses, and Cahokian Cosmology*, edited by M. L. Fowler, pp. 97–119. The Wisconsin Archeologist 77(3–4). Wisconsin Archaeological Society, Milwaukee.

Kelly, J. E. 2000 The Nature and Context of Emergent Mississippian Cultural Dynamics in the Greater American Bottom. In *Late Woodland Societies: Tradition and Transformation across the Midcontinent*, edited by T. E. Emerson, D. L. McElrath, and A. C. Fortier, pp. 163–178. University of Nebraska Press, Lincoln.

Kelly, J. E. 2002a Woodland Period Archaeology in the American Bottom. In *The Woodland Southeast*, edited by D. G. Anderson and R. C. Mainfort, pp. 134–161. The University of Alabama Press, Tuscaloosa.

Kelly, J. E. 2002b The Pulcher Tradition and the Ritualization of Cahokia: A Perspective from Cahokia's Southern Neighbor. In *Frontiers, Peripheries, and Backwaters: Social Formations at the Edges of the Mississippian World*, edited by A. King and M. Myers, pp. 136–148. Southeastern Archaeology 21(2). Southeastern Archaeological Conference, Maney.

Kelly, J. E. 2007 An Interpretation of the Lindeman Phase Occupation of the Range Site. In *The Range Site 4: Emergent Mississippian George Reeves and Lindeman Phase Occupations*, edited by J. E. Kelly, S. J. Ozuk, and J. A. Williams, pp. 469–489. Illinois Transportation Archaeological Research Program, Transportation Archaeological Research Reports 18. University of Illinois at Urbana-Champaign, Urbana-Champaign.

Kelly, J. E., and J. A. Brown 2012 In Search of Cosmic Power: Contextualizing Spiritual Journeys Between Cahokia and the St. Francois Mountains. In *Archaeology of Spiritualities*, edited by K. Rountree, C. Morris, and A. A. D. Peatfield, pp. 107–129. Springer, New York.

Kelly, J. E., and J. A. Brown 2014 Cahokia: The Processes and Principles of the Creation of an Early Mississippian City. In *Making Ancient Cities: Space and Place in Early Urban Societies*, edited by A. T. Creekmore and K. D. Fisher, pp. 292–336. Cambridge University Press, New York.

Kelly, J. E., F. A. Finney, D. L. McElrath, and S. J. Ozuk 1984a Late Woodland Period. In *American Bottom Archaeology: A Summary of the FAI 270 Project Contribution to the Culture History of the Mississippi Valley*, edited by C. J. Bareis and J. W. Porter, pp. 104–127. University of Illinois Press, Urbana.

Kelly, J. E., A. C. Fortier, S. J. Ozuk, and J. A. Williams 1987 *The Range Site: Archaic through Late Woodland Occupations*. American Bottom Archaeology, FAI-270 Site Reports 16. University of Illinois Press, Urbana.

Kelly, J. E., J. R. Linder, and T. J. Cartmell 1979 *The Archaeological Intensive Survey of the FAI-270 Alignment in the American Bottom Region of Southern Illinois*. Illinois Transportation Archaeology Scientific Reports 1. Illinois Department of Transportation, Springfield.

Kelly, J. E., S. J. Ozuk, D. K. Jackson, D. L. McElrath, F. A. Finney, and D. Esarey 1984b Emergent Mississippian Period. In *American Bottom Archaeology: A Summary of the FAI-270 Project Contribution to the Culture History of the Mississippi Valley*, edited by C. J. Bareis and J. W. Porter, pp. 128–157. University of Illinois Press, Urbana.

Kelly, J. E., S. J. Ozuk, and J. A. Williams 1990 *The Range Site 2 (11-S-47): The Emergent Mississippian Dohack and Range Phase Occupations*. American Bottom Archaeology, FAI-270 Site Reports 20. University of Illinois Press, Urbana and Chicago.

Kelly, J. E., S. J. Ozuk, and J. A. Williams 2007 *The Range Site: The Emergent Mississippian, George Reeves and Lindeman Phase Components*. Illinois Transportation Archaeological Research Program, Transportation Archaeological Research Reports 18. University of Illinois at Urbana-Champaign, Urbana-Champaign.

Kelly, L. S. 2001 A Case of Ritual Feasting at the Cahokia Site. In *Feasts: Archaeological and Ethnographic Perspectives on Food, Politics, and Power*, edited by M. Dietler and B. Hayden, pp. 334–367. Smithsonian Institution Press, Washington, D.C.

Koldehof, B. 2002 *The Woodland Ridge Site and Late Woodland Land Use in the Southern American Bottom*. Illinois Transportation Archaeological Research Program, Transportation Archaeological Research Reports 15. University of Illinois at Urbana-Champaign, Urbana-Champaign.

Koldehof, B., and J. M. Galloy 2006 *Late Woodland Frontiers: Patrick Phase Settlement along the Kaskaskia Trail, Monroe County, Illinois*. Illinois Transportation Archaeological Research Program, Transportation Archaeological Research Reports 23. University of Illinois at Urbana-Champaign, Urbana-Champaign.

Kowalewski, S. A. 2013 The Work of Making Community. In *From Prehistoric Villages to Cities: Settlement Aggregation and Community Transformation*, edited by J. Birch, pp. 201–218. Routledge, New York.

Krus, A. M. 2016 The Timing of Precolumbian Militarization in the U. S. Midwest and Southeast. *American Antiquity* 81(2):375–388.

Lewis, R. B., and C. Stout (editors) 1998 *Mississippian Towns and Sacred Spaces: Searching for an Architectural Grammar*. The University of Alabama Press, Tuscaloosa.

Linder, J. R., T. J. Cartmell, and J. E. Kelly 1978 *Preliminary Archaeological Reconnaissance of the Segments under Study for FAP 413 in Madison County, Illinois.* 2 vols. Illinois Department of Transportation, District 8, Fairview Heights.

McIntosh, R. J. 1991 Early Urban Clusters in China and Africa: The Arbitration of Social Ambiguity. *Journal of Field Archaeology* 18(2):199–212.

Mehrer, M. W. 1995 *Cahokia's Countryside: Household Archaeology, Settlement Patterns, and Social Power.* Northern Illinois University Press, DeKalb.

Meinkoth, M. C., K. Hedmon, and D. L. McElrath 2003 *The Cunningham Site: An Early Late Woodland Occupation in the American Bottom.* Illinois Transportation Archaeological Research Program, Transportation Archaeological Research Reports 9. University of Illinois at Urbana-Champaign, Urbana-Champaign.

Milner, G. R. 1986 Mississippian Period Population Density in a Segment of the Central Mississippi River Valley. *American Antiquity* 51(2):227–238.

Milner, G. R. 1998 *The Cahokia Chiefdom: The Archaeology of a Mississippian Society.* Smithsonian Institution Press, Washington, D.C.

Milner, G. R. 1999 Warfare in Prehistoric and Early Historic Eastern North America. *Journal of Archaeological Research* 7(2):105–151.

Milner, G. R., T. E. Emerson, M. W. Mehrer, J. A. Williams, and D. Esarey 1984 Mississippian and Oneota Period. In *American Bottom Archaeology: A Summary of the FAI-270 Project Contribution to the Culture History of the Mississippi Valley*, edited by C. J. Bareis and J. W. Porter, pp. 158–186. University of Illinois Press, Urbana.

Mueller, N. G. 2017 *Seeds as Artifacts: The Domestication of Erect Knotweed in Eastern North America.* PhD dissertation, Department of Anthropology, Washington University, St. Louis, Missouri.

Munson, P. J. 1971 An Archaeological Survey of the Wood River Terrace and Adjacent Bottoms and Bluffs in Madison County, Illinois. In *Archaeological Surveys of the American Bottoms and Adjacent Bluffs, Illinois*, edited by P. J. Munson and A. D. Harn, pp. 3–17. Illinois State Museum Reports of Investigations 21. Illinois State Museum, Springfield.

O'Brien, P. J. 1972a Urbanism, Cahokia, and Middle Mississippian. *Archaeology* 25(3):189–197.

O'Brien, P. J. 1972b *A Formal Analysis of Cahokia Ceramics from the Powell Tract.* Illinois Archaeological Survey Monograph 3. Illinois Archaeological Survey, Urbana.

Pauketat, T. R. 1989 Monitoring Mississippian Homestead Occupation Span and Economy Using Ceramic Refuse. *American Antiquity* 54(2):288–310.

Pauketat, T. R. 1993 Big Bang in the Bottom: Political Consolidation and Mississippianism at Cahokia. Paper presented at the 58th Annual Meeting of the Society for American Archaeology, St. Louis.

Pauketat, T. R. 2003 Resettled Farmers and the Making of a Mississippian Polity. *American Antiquity* 68(1):39–66.

Pauketat, T. R., L. S. Kelly, G. J. Fritz, N. H. Lopinot, S. Elias, and E. Hargrave 2002 The Residues of Feasting and Public Ritual at Early Cahokia. *American Antiquity* 67(2):257–279.

Pauketat, T. R., and N. Lopinot 1997 Cahokian Population Dynamics. In *Cahokia: Domination and Ideology in the Mississippian World*, edited by T. R. Pauketat and T. E. Emerson, pp. 103–123. University of Nebraska Press, Lincoln.

Pauketat, T. R., M. A. Rees, and S. L. Pauketat 1998 *An Archaeological Survey of the Horseshoe Lake Park, Madison County, Illinois.* Illinois State Museum Reports of Investigations 55. Illinois State Museum, Springfield.

Perino, G. 1950 Three Cultures at Cahokia. In *Cahokia Brought to Life: An Artifactual Story of America's Great Monument*, edited by R. E. Grimm, pp. 15–16. Greater St. Louis Archaeological Society, St. Louis.

Perino, G. 1973a The Koster Mounds, Greene County, Illinois. In *Late Woodland Site Archaeology in Illinois I: Investigations in South-Central Illinois*, edited by J. A. Brown, pp. 141–210. Illinois Archaeological Survey Bulletin 9. Illinois Archaeological Survey, Urbana.

Perino, G. 1973b The Late Woodland Component at the Pete Klunk Site, Calhoun County, Illinois. In *Late Woodland Site Archaeology in Illinois I: Investigations in South-Central Illinois*, edited by J. A. Brown, pp. 58–89. Illinois Archaeological Survey Bulletin 9. Illinois Archaeological Survey, Urbana.

Perino, G. 1973c The Late Woodland Component at the Schild Sites, Greene County, Illinois. In *Late Woodland Site Archaeology in Illinois I: Investigations in South-Central Illinois*, edited by J. A. Brown, pp. 90–140. Illinois Archaeological Survey Bulletin 9. Illinois Archaeological Survey, Urbana.

Pfeiffer, J. 1973 Indian City on the Mississippi. *1974 Nature/Science Annual*. Time-Life Books, New York.

Pfeiffer, J. 1974 America's First City. *Horizon* 16(2):58–63.

Porter, J. W. 1969 The Mitchell Site and Prehistoric Exchange Systems at Cahokia: AD 1000 ±300. In *Explorations into Cahokia Archaeology*, edited by M. L. Fowler, pp. 137–164. Illinois Archaeological Survey Bulletin 7. Illinois Archaeological Survey, Urbana.

Rautman, A. E. 2013 Social Integration and the Built Environment of Aggregated Communities in the North American Puebloan Southwest. In *From Prehistoric Villages to Cities: Settlement Aggregation and Community Transformation*, edited by J. Birch, pp. 111–133. Routledge, New York.

Reeder, R. L. 2000 The Maramec Spring Phase. In *Late Woodland Societies: Tradition and Transformation across the Midcontinent*, edited by T. E. Emerson, D. L. McElrath, and A. C. Fortier, pp. 187–210. University of Nebraska Press, Lincoln.

Renfrew, C. 2001 Production and Consumption in a Sacred Economy: The Material Correlates of High Devotional Expression at Chaco Canyon. *American Antiquity* 66(1):14–25.

Shott, M. J. 1993 Spears, Darts, and Arrows: Late Woodland Hunting Techniques in the Upper Ohio Valley. *American Antiquity* 58(3):425–443.

Slater, P. A., K. M. Hedman, and T. E. Emerson 2014 Immigrants at the Mississippian Polity of Cahokia: Strontium Isotope Evidence for Population Movement. *Journal of Archaeological Science* 44:117–127.

Smith, B. D. 1998 *The Emergence of Agriculture*. Scientific American Library, New York.

Stephenson, F. R., and D. A. Green 2002 *Historical Supernovae and Their Remnants*. International Series on Astronomy and Astrophysics 5. Oxford University Press, Oxford.

Szuter, C. R. 1979 *The Schlemmer Site: A Late Woodland–Mississippian Site in the American Bottom*. Master's thesis, Department of Anthropology, Loyola University, Chicago.

Vogel, J. O. 1975 Trends in Cahokia Ceramics: Preliminary Study of the Collections from Tracts 15A and 15B. In *Perspectives in Cahokia Archaeology*, edited by J. A. Brown, pp. 32–125. Illinois Archaeological Survey Bulletin 10. Illinois Archaeological Survey, Urbana.

Watson, P. J., and M. C. Kennedy 1991 The Development of Horticulture in the Eastern Woodlands of North America: Women's Role. In *Engendering Archaeology: Women and Prehistory*, edited by J. M. Gero and M. W. Conkey, pp. 255–275. Blackwell, Oxford.

Wittry, W. L., and J. O. Vogel 1962 Illinois State Museum Projects: October 1961 to June 1962. In *First Annual Report: American Bottoms Archaeology, July 1, 1961–June 30, 1962*, edited by M. L. Fowler, pp. 14–30. Illinois Archaeological Survey, Urbana.

Woods, W. I. 1986 *Prehistoric Settlement and Subsistence in the Upper Cahokia Creek Drainage*. PhD dissertation, Department of Geography, University of Wisconsin-Milwaukee, Milwaukee.

Wray, D. E. 1952 Archaeology of the Illinois Valley: 1950. In *Archaeology of Eastern United States*, edited by J. B. Griffin, pp. 152–164. University of Chicago Press, Chicago.

Yerkes, R. W. 1987 *Prehistoric Life on the Mississippi Floodplain: Stone Tool Use, Settlement Organization, and Subsistence Practices at the Labras Lake Site, Illinois*. University of Chicago Press, Chicago.

Young, B. W., and M. L. Fowler 2000 *Cahokia: The Great Native American Metropolis*. University of Illinois Press, Urbana.

CHAPTER SIX

Why Athens?

Population Aggregation in Attica in the Early Iron Age

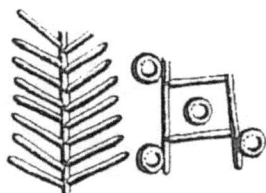

Robin Osborne

Abstract *This paper asks how population aggregation, urbanization, and state formation relate to each other in Early Iron Age Attica. Scholars have long noted and debated the sudden appearance of new population nucleations in Attica and the coincident rapid increase in numbers of burials across Attica and in Athens itself in the eighth century B.C. Past discussion has focused on state formation and has paid much more attention to the increased number of burials—as indicators of a higher proportion of the population claiming the right to burial in an archaeologically visible manner—than to settlement patterns. This paper looks instead at the pattern of settlement and at the probable movement of population between Athens and the rest of Attica, and asks what changing settlement priorities and the development of a distinctly urban community indicate about social and economic networks as well as political priorities.*

INTRODUCTION

How and why did Athens emerge as the dominant settlement in the southeastern peninsula of the Greek mainland, the territory known as Attica? To answer that question we have at our disposal some literary traditions from centuries later and the archaeological evidence of settlement history built up from essentially chance finds, with no systematic survey work in any key area. Yet, although this archaeological evidence is low-grade, by putting the emphasis on patterns of settlement and differential occupation of different settlement basins, sufficiently marked changes emerge at least to suggest what the crucial questions are, if not definitively to answer those questions. The concentration of settlement in and around Athens itself in the eighth century B.C. proves the single most marked change from the settlement pattern of the tenth and ninth centuries B.C. and raises the question of whether it was not a consequence of a change of economic, social, and political priorities. Certainly, what happened in the eighth century had long-term political and sociocultural consequences—consequences that stem, I suggest, from the energized crowding and superlinear aspects of aggregation, for which Smith argues in this volume.

THE LITERARY EVIDENCE AND THE QUESTION OF SYNOECISM

The Homeric "Catalogue of Ships" already treats all inhabitants of Athens as Athenians (*Iliad* 2.546–556), although it is uncertain what period of history, if any, is reflected in that catalogue. According to a myth-history forged in the fifth century B.C., the Athenians had always lived in Attica, they were "autochthonous," born from the earth itself. But fifth-century Athenian writers, and plausibly also the sixth-century Athenians who celebrated the festival of the *Synoikia* (literally, "Living Together"; Parker 1996:12, Note 9), also believed that the Athenians had not always been politically united. There had been, they believed, a process of synoecism which they associated with Theseus (Thucydides 2.15). This synoecism was taken by Thucydides to have been political, not material, that is, a matter of agreeing to have a single decision-making structure not of physical relocation. What Theseus did, on this story, was to create the political and residential arrangements that prevailed in Thucydides's own day, when the residents in the Attica of his day were scattered in more than 100 villages across the territory of Attica, but decisions affecting all of them were taken in one place—Athens itself (Traill 1975, 1986). Later authors had a more detailed story in which Athens had once been inhabited in 12 "cities," enumerated by Philochoros (*FGH* 328 F94 = Strabo 9.1.20 C 397) as Kekropia, Tetrapolis, Epakria, Dekeleia, Eleusis, Aphidna, Thorikos, Brauron, Kytheros, Sphettos, and Kephisia (which makes 11, so that scholars have suggested that Tetrakomoi has dropped out by haplography). But there is nothing in Strabo's quotation from Philochoros that indicates whether what he says was based on tradition or evidence—scholars have generally believed it was based on neither but constructed as a story deliberately parallel to that of the 12 Ionian cities.

Scholars have generally taken the crucial issue in relation to the synoecism of Attica to be when it occurred and how complete it was—sometimes using, or perhaps abusing, literary evidence to argue that Eleusis, at least, was politically independent until at least the seventh century B.C. (for earlier discussions, see Hornblower 1991:259–264; van Gelder 1991). But it is unclear whether this issue can be settled, or rather, how one settles this issue depends upon what particular assumptions one imports about the relationship of political independence to residential choices, and it is not clear how the circularity of this can be avoided. While we would dearly like to know whether changing settlement patterns brought about synoecism or were a result of synoecism—that is, whether Athens became dominant because those previously resident elsewhere in Attica had chosen to move there, or whether those previously resident elsewhere in Attica had chosen to move to Athens because it had become politically dominant—our literary accounts do not answer that question. In the end, we must inevitably interpret those literary accounts in the light of archaeology, and we will do so more effectively if we start not from questions thrown up by the literary texts but from questions thrown up by archaeology.

ARCHAEOLOGY AND SETTLEMENT IN ATTICA IN THE TENTH AND NINTH CENTURIES B.C.

What can we deduce from the archaeological evidence for the particular forms of population aggregation in Attica about urbanization and state formation? What are the implications of the particular settlement patterns for the (un)changing ways in which residents of Attica interacted with each other over time, and how did the functions of individual settlements relate to the functions of the settlement network as a whole?

Since we have a rather well-dated ceramic sequence of distinctive Athenian pottery from the eleventh century onward, the settlement history of Early Iron Age Attica is relatively clear.[1] Some 14 sites have occupation during the later eleventh or tenth century (Figure 6.1), 14 sites (10 of those sites and four others) during the ninth century (Figure

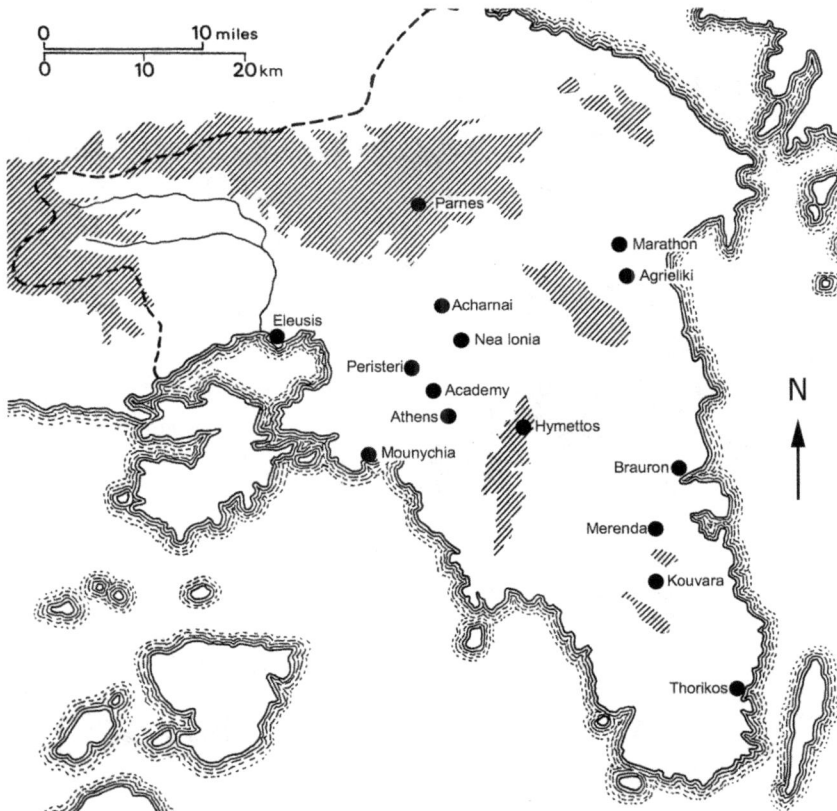

FIGURE 6.1. Sites in Attica with archaeological evidence from 1025–900 B.C. (after D'Onofrio 1995).

6.2), but 53 sites have occupation during the eighth century (Figure 6.3), and some 57 sites during the seventh century (Figure 6.4). Material dated to no more precisely than Geometric (i.e., either ninth or eighth century) may mask a less abrupt change—another 15 sites additional to those known to have been occupied in the ninth or eighth centuries can be dated only by pottery defined as Geometric (and eight sites known to be occupied in the eighth century also have Geometric pottery of possible ninth-century date). But the picture given by the clearly datable evidence is unlikely to be seriously misleading: settlement takes off in Attica after 800 B.C., perhaps multiplying by a factor of more than three.

To make sense of this expansion in the number of locations showing signs of human occupation, we need to look more closely at the changing pattern of occupation. In terms of space, the 14 tenth-century sites include three sites north of Athens (Academy, Nea Ionia, and Peristeri), and Mounychia Hill in Peiraieus, but otherwise consist of two mountaintop sites (Parnes and Hymettos), two sites in the plain of Marathon (Agrieliki

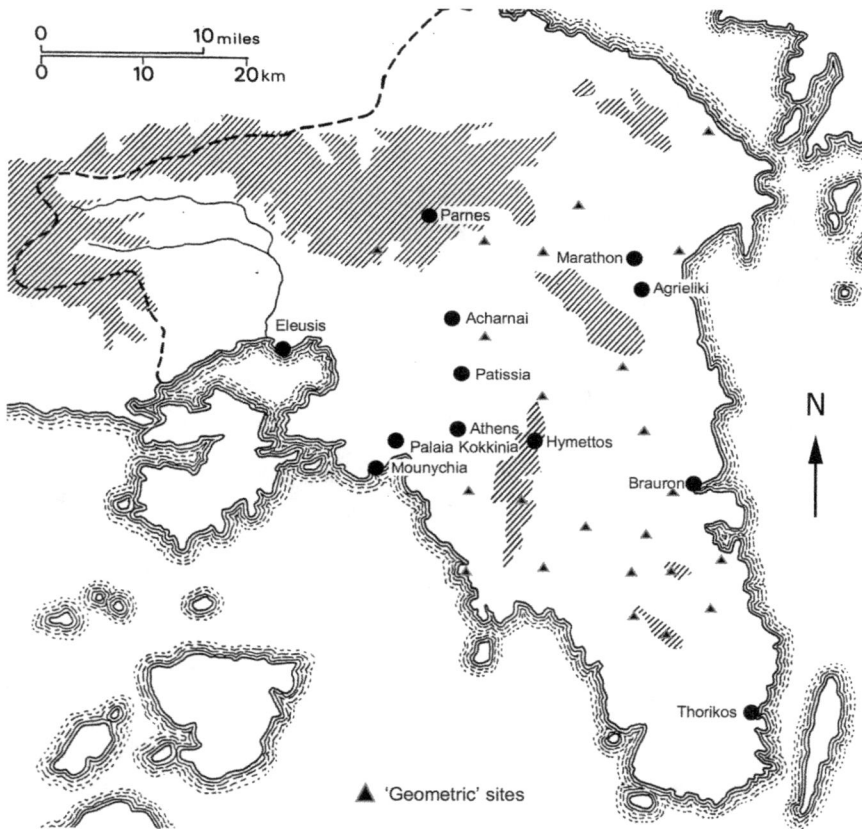

FIGURE 6.2. Sites in Attica with archaeological evidence from 900–800 B.C. (after D'Onofrio 1995).

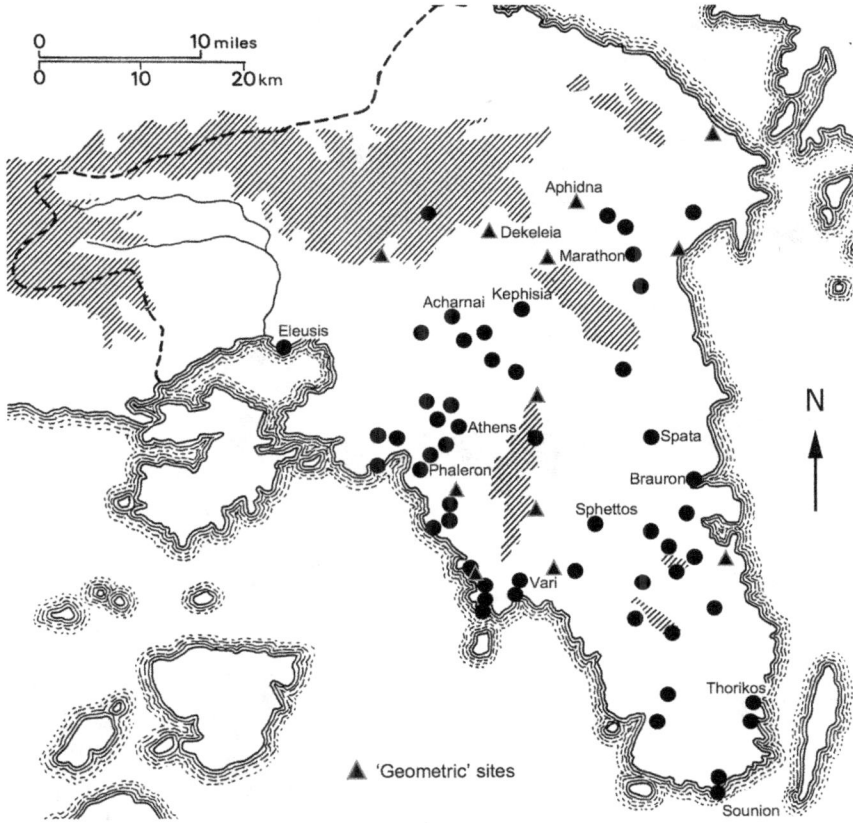

FIGURE 6.3. Sites in Attica with archaeological evidence from 800–700 B.C. (after D'Onofrio 1995).

and Marathon), three sites south of the Mesogaia (Merenda, Kouvara, and Brauron), and Eleusis and Acharnai (Menidi). No human presence can certainly be dated to the tenth or ninth centuries along the whole western coast of Attica, south of Mounychia Hill. Apart from the area around Athens itself and the northern part of the plain of Athens at Acharnai, it is the plain of Marathon, the southeast of the Mesogaia, and the harbor settlements of Thorikos and Eleusis alone that are occupied, with cult attention devoted to gods on various mountaintops.

The eighth century saw settlement thicken across the whole plain of Athens and extend all down the west coast of Attica to Sounion (Theodoropoulou-Polychroniadis 2015). Eleusis remained rather isolated and in general the least settlement development occurred in the north of Attica. Settlement seems to have avoided the larger plains outside the plain of Athens, particularly the Thriasian Plain and the Mesogaia, except for a small group of graves at Kolioukrep (Spata), and it also avoided the low hills from the Mesogaia, southwest to the west coast (Philadelpheus 1920–1921). Although some particular places

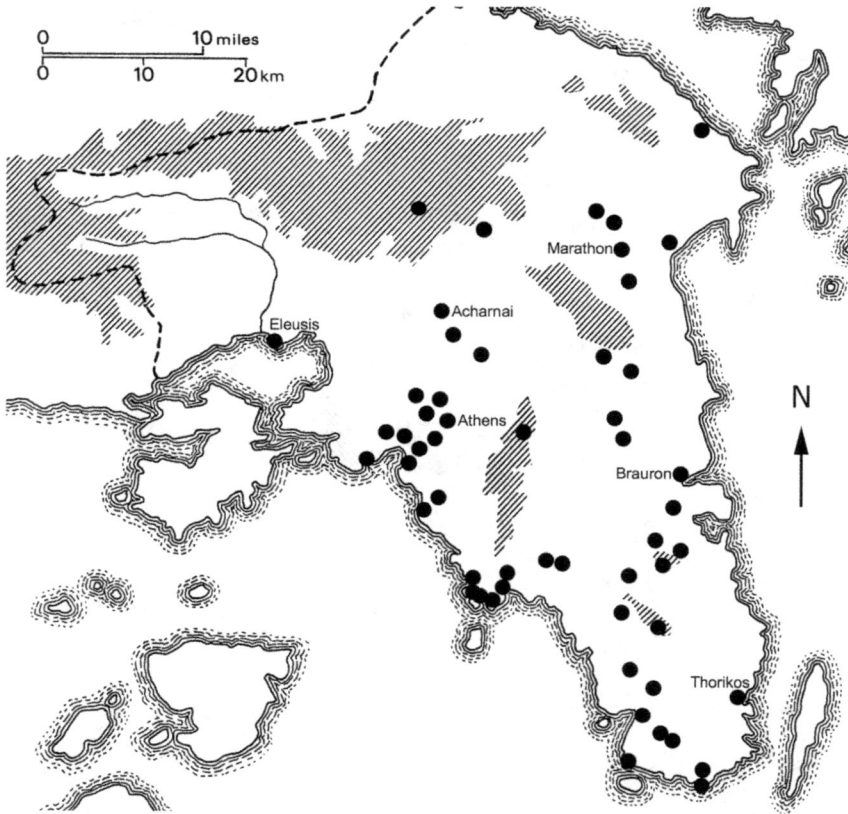

FIGURE 6.4. Sites in Attica with archaeological evidence from 700–600 B.C. (after D'Onofrio 1995).

show signs of occupation in the seventh but not the eighth century and some in the eighth but not the seventh, there is no change of general pattern between the eighth and seventh centuries. However, it is notable that several of the sites added to the map in the seventh century are sites with cult activity rather than human residential settlement.

In the light of later developments, at least, the pattern of tenth- and ninth-century settlement in Attica seems to focus on a small number of settlements in locations made prime by the natural resources to which their location gave them access, and which enabled them to supply their natural needs. Acharnai commands a large plain and the foothill environment of Parnes and stands at the crossroads of both east–west and north–south communication routes (e.g., the pass via Phyle). Athens itself dominates a large plain, with strong communication routes in all directions, including—if we take the sanctuary on Mounychia Hill as a sign of this—access to the sea. Marathon commands a fertile plain and access routes to the north, south, and west, as well as having a shore-line suitable for beaching ships. Eleusis provides a safe haven for boats and commands a broad plain and important land routes west and north. Thorikos has a harbor, access to mineral resources, and a small, fertile plain. Brauron lies in a fertile estuary, with access to wider agricultural lands inland and adequate shelter for boats.

The settlements also provide for their own supernatural needs. Eleusis, Brauron, and Athens itself have their own sanctuaries from as early as we can trace any occupation, Marathon links with the cult place on Agrieliki above, and Thorikos certainly develops significant cult activity, though the date at which cult activity began is not clear. None of these centers needs to rely on any other particular settlement in Attica for resources of any kind, though no doubt local crisis might cause them to seek help from one or another of their Attic neighbors. Whether they were in fact independent or not, these are sites that could operate independently—or to put it another way, these are sites for which it is as or more important to form a network with other sites outside Attica as to form a network with other sites within Attica.

These primary sites in tenth- and ninth-century Attica are placed so as to communicate as easily with the world outside as with other settlements in Attica. Inland Acharnai might seem an exception, but in fact it was extremely well placed for land communications north through the Phyle Gorge, as Aristophanes's story in *Acharnians* about the Acharnians suffering raids from Boiotia illustrates. The implication of this placement is surely that being part of a wider network is crucial. We might imagine that that wider network was crucial in order to supply deficiencies in the event, for example, of crop failure, frequent in an area climatically marginal for arable agriculture, but the development of both Eleusis and Thorikos as significant cult centers for Demeter—centers explicitly mentioned in the *Homeric Hymn to Demeter*—and of Brauron as a cult center not only for Artemis but for Iphigenia—where Iphigenia becomes strongly linked to other parts of the Greek world—suggests that we should think of a wider network of opportunity, not just a wider network of security. The contrast with the Argolid site of Kalamianos, discussed by Pullen in this volume, which perished when the palatial center at Mycenae perished, is marked.

As Ault (this volume) also points out, de Polignac (1995) argued that we should consider sanctuaries on the edge of territories as marking borders, and scholars have debated, in particular, whether the sanctuary of Eleusis should be thought of in these terms. But the pattern we observe in tenth- and ninth-century Attica suggests that we might think instead of these sanctuaries on the edge as inviting interaction—as the Eleusinian Mysteries did by opening themselves up to all Greeks. We have perhaps too readily thought of a world where drawing a border and defending that border is what matters and where immigrants represent a threat. We might rather think of a world in which settlements are greedy for contact with a wider world and where immigrants constitute a welcome sign that the wider world has noticed you. In this world, the arrival of outsiders who wish to settle is to be encouraged—as the possible basis for future networking—rather than resisted. Malthusian fears of overpopulation have been too often foisted onto the ancient world, when all the evidence is that the general Greek belief was that more people simply resulted in more prosperity (Gallo 1980).

Archaeology and Settlement in Attica
in the Eighth Century B.C.

How are we to understand the apparently dramatic change in settlement of Attica in the eighth century? One pattern to be observed is that settlement fills out around each of the sites prominent earlier—around Athens itself, Eleusis, Acharnai, Brauron, Marathon, and Thorikos—but that this is most dramatically true of Athens. We can see a cluster in the upper plain of Athens south of Acharnai, to the north of the Marathon Plain, in the southern Mesogaia, and south and west of Thorikos. In the case of Athens itself, the whole lower plain of Athens down to modern Vari at the southern tip of Hymettos fills up—and in general fills up with sites not serving religious functions.

It is also notable that whereas many of the sanctuary sites of the tenth century were coastal (Eleusis, Mounychia, Thorikos, Brauron), the additional sanctuary sites of the eighth century are almost all inland—the only exception being the sanctuaries on the promontory at Sounion. That is, whereas one might reckon the sanctuaries of the ninth century to offer themselves to a world outside Attica, these new manifestations of cult activity seem to serve only Attic communities, primarily filling out the earlier pattern of peak sanctuaries by adding lower peaks, although in some cases we might wonder about regional boundary functions too. D'Onofrio went as far as to suggest that "the people who lived in the nucleated villages or isolated dwellings which contributed to the dense settlement or the countryside as early as the 8th century BC, found a sense of unity around the sacred mountaintop sites in their own districts" (1997:77).

The most significant feature of the eighth-century pattern is that what happens with regard to Athens is on a quite different scale from what happens with regard to other communities in Attica. Compared with the modest expansion seen around Acharnai, Brauron, Marathon, or Thorikos, let alone with the absence of any expansion around Eleusis—"the population is concentrated at Eleusis, while no scattered dwellings or villages are known nearby" (D'Onofrio 1997:72)—the number of additional settlements around and to the south of Athens itself is of a different order of magnitude. So we must ask, Why Athens?

To answer that we need to look a bit more closely at what is happening. Two features of Athens's exceptionalism need to be stressed. The first is that what happens around Athens cannot be explained by internally generated growth—the increase is simply too great for that to be plausible. We must be dealing with a population that is growing because people are coming from elsewhere to settle at Athens. Athens's growth is therefore a sign that it was proving attractive in this period as it had not in earlier periods, and the rate of growth shows indeed that it was proving more attractive than anywhere else. It is indeed a feature of "energized crowding," as described by Smith in this volume, that the greater opportunities that it brings attract yet further people who then, in turn, increase the energies displayed.

The debate about how to interpret the increased number of graves recovered from later eighth-century—as opposed to ninth- or earlier eighth-century—Athens has focused on the possibility that the population was growing by natural increase (Snodgrass 1980, and persistently repeated by others since, despite Morris's demonstration that this would not account for the pattern once child and adult grave numbers were plotted separately), or the community was enlarging the range and proportion of afforded visible burial (Morris 1987:87–155; see also Alexandridou 2016:353–355). By contrast, the spread of settlements seems likely to be a product neither of natural increase nor of settlement becoming more visible (Morris 1987:156–158). There must be incomers involved here, whether those incomers come from other Attica communities or from outside Attica altogether.

The second implication is that whatever the attractions of Athens were, they could be enjoyed at a distance—in this case, the energizing occurred without the crowding needing to be particularly dense. That is, the spread of settlement implies that one did not have to be in Athens itself continuously to enjoy, and to contribute to, the advantages of association with the community. D'Onofrio asked "whether the *asty* was not slowly attracting inhabitants from its neighboring areas," noting possible thinning of settlement toward Acharnai, and she responded that "[o]n the contrary, a well-ordered row of demes was still flourishing towards the Phaleron, along the course of the River Kephisos . . . with a remarkable settlement concentration towards the coast" (1997:68). The more we think that all the settlements in the southern part of the plain of Athens were capitalizing on links with Athens, the more we must think that those links needed to be physically effected only on a weekly or monthly basis, not on a daily basis. Athens was attractive not because it was a source of daily needs but because it could offer services required intermittently or occasionally—and one might think of access to the gods, access to military might, access to a social subgroup of viable size, or access to luxury goods.

None of this is to deny that Athens itself—that is settlement within the area later surrounded by the Themistoklean Wall—grew and that for some people the goods of the town were accessed daily. Certainly, we have a great deal more evidence from later eighth-century Athens than from earlier periods. But however much urban density increased, suburban and periurban density increased also. What happened within the town of Athens must be seen in relation to what went on around it.

That Athens's unusual attractions might be enjoyed at a distance implies that those attractions were not exclusively the attractions of employment or the attractions of setting up as a trader. Athens's position was in fact not at all prime if what one wanted to do was to prioritize relations with a wider Greek world—Thorikos or indeed Eleusis could do that better. Either of those places might have been the Lefkandi, or at least the Oropos, of Attica. Athens's position was actually prime if, and only if, what mattered primarily was accessing Attica. It is local land communication not distant communication and not communication by sea that Athens is best placed to maximize. It is hard to think that the primacy of Athens was not politically driven.

Accessing Attica had precisely the reverse advantages to accessing a wider world. One way of thinking about this is to think about settlements as belonging to networks (e.g., Knappett 2011; Malkin 2011). The advantage of the wider world was that one could access one place on one occasion and for one purpose, another on another occasion for another purpose—one element of the strength of weak ties. One aspect of this is the possibility of arriving, acquiring what one wanted, and disappearing never to appear again, which is a behavior that stories in the *Odyssey* explore in relation to the Phoenicians. By contrast, the advantages of accessing Attica were that the ties could be strong: links formed for one purpose might (have to) be accessed for quite different purposes. The farms that were sources of (particular) foodstuffs also might be the sources of manpower for military activity, or of mourners for a grand funeral. The skein of links that might be formed with neighboring communities enabled the embedding of any particular set of relationships, whether economic, familial, ritual, military, or political, in a wider set of relationships.

The reason for gravitating to Athens was that if the other communities and residents of Athens decided to work cooperatively, then Athens would necessarily be the center of the hub. The potential that the energies of a significant proportion of residents of Attica would be pooled in Athens itself led to the pooling of energies in Athens. The greater the degree to which communities in Attica decided to work together, the more dominant Athens became, and the denser the skein of links that the members of the cooperating communities enjoyed. The funerary archaeology of the eighth century, as described by Morris (1987), is marked by a greater inclusion of subadults in the visible burial record, reduction in the variability in grave goods, and the development of an elite cemetery in Athens. This elite cemetery uniquely featured grave markers consisting of specially made monumental pots. Inclusion and standardization are clear signs that the possibilities of cooperation were being explored across the community. But even the development of a distinct elite cemetery, although in one sense marking a refusal by some to cooperate, was possible only through cooperation within the elite. The advantages of cooperation were both the advantages of inclusion and the advantages of using the multiple ties created to distinguish oneself from others. Athens, becoming the dominant settlement at the center of a wider web, had capital advantages. Granovetter's (1973) classic lesson about the strength of weak ties is pertinent here.

One of the primary indications that the changing pattern of settlement may cor-relate with state formation—that is, the functional discrimination between roles (whose physical correlates are discussed by Ault in this volume)—may be in the manner of gender discrimination. Some gender distinction in burials is apparent from the Proto-Geometric period onward, particularly in the types of metal goods found in graves and in the shape of the pot used as an ash urn. But gender distinction becomes writ large in the Late Geometric period when the distinction in pot shape is carried into the outsized Late Geometric pots that mark the burials, and when these outsized pots show scenes of the laying out of the corpse, which distinguish men from women. Thirty-five such scenes show a male corpse, four a female corpse (Ahlberg 1971a:32–33; Boardman 1988:173). What is more, Houby-Nielsen (1991:358–359; see also Alexandridou 2016:353, 355) has argued that all Proto-Attic burials with offering trenches, and all Proto-Attic primary cremations without offering trenches, were male and that the decline in visible burials in seventh-century Attica should be attributed, at least in part, to the exclusion of women from visible burial. Just how deep-seated this gender division was is shown by the ongoing discrepancy until the Classical period between the monumental marking of male and female graves (Osborne 1997). This makes it unlikely that the changed pattern in burial did not correspond to a changed pattern in life and to the emergence of prominent male roles that did not depend directly on position within a family. Tradition ascribed the earliest Athenian archons to the early seventh century.

All of this leaves effectively unanswered the question of why the residents of Attica originally decided that cooperation was the way forward. We have no trace of pressure from outside forcing the various settlements of Attica together, unless in the iconography of sea battle on some Late Geometric pots, which there is no reason to explain with reference to life rather than myth. As far as we can see, those who gravitated to Athens, or its immediate environs, jumped without being pushed. We should entertain the possibility, at least, that what made them jump was their growing numbers and growing inequality (see Morris 1987:145–146). Once a community grows to greater than a certain size then the self-interested cohesion of the small group becomes lost and competition within the group encourages the seeking of ties outside; this is the centrifugal force that may balance the centripetal force of energized crowding. It is in this context that the multipurpose strong ties offered by being at the center of the network of Attic communities become more valuable than single-purpose weak ties with a wider world. Both the emergence of a distinct elite, seen in the emergence of the Dipylon cemetery at Athens, and the emergence of the Acropolis as *the* cult center for Attica (Scholl 2006:42–44, 76–81, 127) may be not merely a consequence of Athens growth but part of the motivation that brought about that growth.

The settlement pattern of Attica does not show us when the communities started working together, but it does show that that process was underway by the start of the eighth century—the essentially stable pattern of occupation from the end of the eighth to the end of the seventh century strongly suggests that the process of communities working together was completed before the end of the eighth century.

CONCLUSION: WHY ATHENS MATTERS

If my analysis has correctly identified why Athens became dominant in Attica, then it raises some interesting further issues. The story I have told is essentially one of eighth-century residents and would-be residents of Attica gaming—acting on the basis of calculations about what others might do and trying to ensure that others' decisions did not leave them weak. The game they were playing was not, however, prioritizing high risk with high profits. To settle in the lower plain of Athens was to settle for an agricultural life; not necessarily a life as a subsistence farmer, but certainly life as a farmer. Basing oneself at Thorikos or Eleusis would offer some potentially far more lucrative resources for exploitation—but with much lower security. The images of many-oared ships that proliferate on the outsize burial markers of the Late Geometric period show something of both the promise of what could be achieved by cooperation and the threats in the face of which cooperation might be needed (Ahlberg 1971b).

This game is a game with different priorities than the priorities apparent in settlement decisions in the tenth and ninth centuries. In the eighth century, the Athenians were turning inward, whereas previously they had turned outward. Archaeologists have long noted that whereas Attic Proto-Geometric and Middle Geometric pottery is found relatively widely distributed outside Attica, Late Geometric and Proto-Attic Athenian pottery is found almost only in Attica. The settlement preferences confirm this turn inward. Whereas much of the tenth-century settlement pattern looks set to ensure that Attic communities do not become isolated, the eighth-century pattern is unconcerned about isolation from the wider world. Wherever the people who lived in late eighth-century Attica came from, their very numbers gave them security. Threats to that security would arguably now also be generated internally, not externally—but that is the next episode of this story.

We are no closer to being able to put a date on the synoecism of Attica, but we can certainly say that by the end of the eighth century such synoecism was inevitable. Athens's dominance was by 700 B.C. such that if it came to a power struggle within Attica, Athens was bound to win. More than this, we can see that the changing game between the ninth and eighth centuries cannot have been politically innocent. That is, whether we think that Athens became dominant because of some decision taken by the discrete communities of ninth-century Attica to cooperate, or whether we think that the change of game was a consequence of a lot of individual decisions that Athens was the place with potential, the effective decision to play an inward-looking rather than an outward-looking game was a decision about who it was that one wanted to work most closely with and rely on most heavily. At the end of the day, it was that decision, and not any formal synoecism, that decisively determined the future of Attica, and of Greece.

The material on which I have based my case is not of high quality, and the methods that I have employed are traditional and unsophisticated. But the conclusion has significant implications. Methodologically, it emphasizes the importance not just of overall settlement density but of spatial patterning. In terms of our understanding of Attica, and of the dramatic changes visible in the eighth century, it makes clear that Morris was correct on the one hand to see in the increased numbers of burials profound social change, and on the other to deny that that change was a product simply of population increase fueled by increased fertility. The differential filling up of the plains around different earlier nodes of settlement cannot be explained by differential local human fertility. The tenth- and ninth-century priority on establishing contacts outside Attica is an important background to the eighth-century change. It is a double irony that the policy of inserting themselves into a wider world pursued by Attic settlements in the tenth and ninth centuries enabled the inward-looking policy of the eighth century, and that our study of the settlement pattern of Attica ends up by suggesting that we will understand what is happening around Athens only if we can insert those changes into the story of a wider Greek world.

ACKNOWLEDGMENTS

I am grateful to Attila Gyucha for the invitation to take part in the stimulating 9th IEMA Conference in Buffalo and for comments on my paper, and to all the participants for their friendly engagement.

NOTE

1.   For the pottery, the classic discussion is Coldstream (1968), updated in Coldstream (2008). For settlement, I use as a database the material collected by D'Onofrio (1995), updating and correcting Osborne (1989) and Morris (1987). A slightly less complete collection of material is discussed by Mersch (1996; see also Mersch 1997). A region-by-region discussion of the data is found in D'Onofrio (1997).

REFERENCES CITED

Ahlberg, G. 1971a *Prothesis and Ekphora in Greek Geometric Art*. Studies in Mediterranean Archaeology 32. Paul Åströms, Göteborg.

Ahlberg, G. 1971b *Fighting on Land and Sea in Greek Geometric Art*. Swedish Institute of Classical Studies at Athens, Stockholm.

Alexandridou, A. 2016 Funerary Variability in Late Eighth-Century B.C.E. Attica (Late Geometric II). *American Journal of Archaeology* 120(3):333–360.

Boardman, J. 1988 Sex Discrimination in Grave Vases. *AION* 10:171–178.

Coldstream, J. N. 1968 *Greek Geometric Pottery: A Survey of Ten Local Styles and Their Chronology*. Methuen, London.

Coldstream, J. N. 2008 *Greek Geometric Pottery: A Survey of Ten Local Styles and Their Chronology*. 2nd ed. Bristol Phoenix Press, Exeter.

de Polignac, F. 1995 *Cults, Territory, and the Origins of the Greek City-State*. The University of Chicago Press, Chicago.

D'Onofrio, A. M. 1995 Santuari "rurali" e dinamiche insediative in Attica tra il Protogeometrico e l'Orientalizzante (1050–600 A.C.). *Annali di Archeologia e Storia Antica Nuova Serie* 2:57–88.

D'Onofrio, A. M. 1997 The 7th Century BC in Attica: The Basis of Political Organization. In *Urbanization in the Mediterranean in the 9th to 6th Centuries BC*, edited by H. Damgaard Andersen, H. W. Horsnaes, S. Houby-Nielsen, and A. Rathje, pp. 63–88. Acta Hyperborea 7. Museum Tusculanum Press, Copenhagen.

Gallo, L. 1980 Popolosità e scarsità di popolazione: contributo allo studio di un topos. *Annali della Scuola Normale Superiore di Pisa Ser. III* 10:403–412.

Granovetter, M. S. 1973 The Strength of Weak Ties. *American Journal of Sociology* 78(6): 1360–1380.

Hornblower, S. 1991 *A Commentary on Thucydides. Volume I: Books I–III*. Clarendon Press, Oxford.

Houby-Nielsen, S. 1991 Interaction Between Chieftains and Citizens? 7th Century B.C. Burial Customs in Athens. In *Ancient Portraiture: Image and Message*, edited by T. Fischer-Hansen, J. Lund, M. Nielsen, and A. Rathje, pp. 343–374. Acta Hyperborea 4. Museum Tusculanum Press, Copenhagen.

Knappett, C. 2011 *An Archaeology of Interaction: Network Perspectives on Material Culture and Society*. Oxford University Press, Oxford.

Malkin, I. 2011 *A Small Greek World: Networks in the Ancient Mediterranean*. Oxford University Press, Oxford.

Mersch, A. 1996 *Studien zur Siedlungsgeschichte Attikas von 950 bis 400 v. Chr.* Peter Lang, Frankfurt.

Mersch, A. 1997 Urbanization in the Attic Countryside from the Late 8th Century to the 6th Century BC. In *Urbanization in the Mediterranean in the 9th to 6th Centuries BC*, edited by H. Damgaard Andersen, H. W. Horsnaes, S. Houby-Nielsen, and A. Rathje, pp. 45–62. Acta Hyperborea 7. Museum Tusculanum Press, Copenhagen.

Morris, I. M. 1987 *Burial and Ancient Society: The Rise of the Greek City-State*. Cambridge University Press, Cambridge.

Osborne, R. 1989 A Crisis in Archaeological History? The Seventh Century B.C. in Attica. *The Annual of the British School at Athens* 84:297–322.

Osborne, R. 1997 Law, the Democratic Citizen, and the Representation of Women in Classical Athens. *Past and Present* 155:3–33.

Parker, R. C. T. 1996 *Athenian Religion: A History*. Clarendon Press, Oxford.

Philadelpheus, A. 1920–21 Άνασκαφὴ παρὰ τὸ χωρίον Σπατα. *Arkhaiologikon Deltion* 6:131–138.

Scholl, A. 2006 ΑΝΑΘΗΜΑΤΑ ΤΩΝ ΑΡΧΑΙΩΝ: Die Akropolisvotive aus dem 8. bis frühen 6. Jahrhundert v. Chr. und die Staatswerdung Athens. *Jahrbuch des Deutschen Archäologischen Instituts* 121:1–173.

Snodgrass, A. M. 1980 *Archaic Greece: The Age of Experiment*. J. M. Dent, London.

Theodoropoulou-Polychroniadis, Z. 2015 *Sounion Revisited: The Sanctuaries of Poseidon and Athena at Sounion in Attica*. Archaeopress, Oxford.

Traill, J. S. 1975 *The Political Organization of Attica: A Study of the Demes, Trittyes, and Phylai, and Their Representation in the Athenian Council*. Hesperia Supplement 14. American School of Classical Studies, Princeton, New Jersey.

Traill, J. S. 1986 *Demos and Trittys: Epigraphical and Topographical Studies in the Organization of Attica*. Athenians, Victoria College, Toronto.

van Gelder, K. 1991 The Iron-Age Hiatus in Attica and the *Synoikismos* of Theseus. *Mediterranean Archaeology* 4:55–64.

CHAPTER SEVEN

Synoikismos

Formation and Form of Ancient Greek Cities

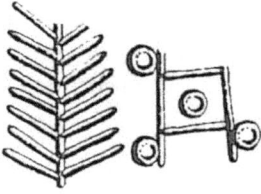

Bradley A. Ault

Abstract *Following the Late Bronze Age "collapse" of Mycenaean civilization (ca. 1200 B.C.), the formative Greek states and the palace centers that spawned them had vanished. What emerged in their wake over the course of the following centuries was the city-state or polis, a system with a remarkably different pedigree. Bottom-up formations rather than top-down creations, established by people and populations, rather than implemented by aristocratic monarchies. As many as 1,500 such city-states existed in the Greek world, some 600 in the Aegean homeland and perhaps another 900 in colonial settings abroad. That is how successful this system proved to be. This paper will explore not only the mechanisms of Greek city-state formation but also the character of its urban core, and especially how this organization reflected its sociocultural profile.*

INTRODUCTION

If we look beyond the palaces of the Bronze Age Aegean world—those of Minoan Crete in the Middle Bronze Age and of the Mycenaean mainland in the Late Bronze Age—we would see an already well-developed urbanized landscape, dotted with villages and even recognizable cities (see especially Branigan 2001; see also Pullen this volume). This is documented by the findings of archaeological surface surveys and occasionally, too, of excavations. The "progress" of archaeology is such, however, that the focus—with notable exceptions—has remained on the palaces, which were themselves centers of urban developments (see more recently Driessen 2009; French 2009; Schoep 2009). Bronze Age towns and cities in Greek lands are a fact, and one need only cite examples such as Late

Bronze Age Ayia Irini on Kea or Phylakopi on Melos, both of which existed as island communities beyond and to a certain degree independently of the palace centers, which ultimately controlled them (Barber 1987). And it is this which makes their abandonment at the end of the Bronze Age (ca. 1200–1100 B.C.) all the more profound. For not only do the palaces and palace systems vanish in flames but also the urban centers and satellite settlements, which supported them, subsequently decline as well.

Equally remarkable, if rather less sudden, is the new beginning that followed. For the Greeks really did hit the "reset" button. Emerging in the eighth century B.C., after 300 years of what was formerly known as the Greek "Dark Age" (1100–800 B.C.; see for example Desborough 1972; Snodgrass 1971)—but in light of more recent reappraisal is less judgmentally termed the "Early Iron Age" (Bintliff 2012:209–233)—Greece and the Aegean are home to a recovery and transformation that lead to the reconstitution of an urban way of life. But one that had a very different profile from that of the Bronze Age, ultimately inherited from and indebted to, as it were, Near Eastern prototypes. This new system is that of the Greek city-state, known as the *polis* (Hansen 2006; Mitchell and Rhodes 1997; Morris 1987, 1991; Nichols and Charlton 1997; Sakellariou 1989). The *polis*, rather laboriously rendered in German as *Stadtstaat*, is the symbiotic pairing of an urban center (the *asty*) with its territorial hinterland (the *chora*), which may comprise subsidiary settlements as well.

It has been estimated that as many as 1,500 *poleis* existed in the ancient Greek world. Six hundred have been accounted for in the Aegean homeland, plus another 400 abroad in colonial settings, while several hundred more were founded in the Hellenistic East in the wake of Alexander the Great's conquests (Hansen 2006:18). Never exceeding more than 1,000 *poleis* at any one time, most were small, with territories averaging 400 square kilometers and populations of 2,000–3,000 out of a total population of the Greek-speaking world estimated between 7.5 and 10 million in the fourth century B.C. (Hansen 2006:82). Of these 1,500 *poleis*, only about 10 percent have been explored archaeologically (see Hansen 2006:100), while a mere 3.5 percent have literary sources which do much more than mention them by name (see Bintliff 2012:259). The Greeks had by far the most prolific of the 37 historically documented city-state cultures (Hansen 2006:17–23). Theirs was also the most long-lived, spanning more than a millennium—between the eighth century B.C. and the sixth century A.D. (Hansen 2006:48–50). In what follows, I will, admittedly, generalize detail and simplify nuance, but by so doing I hope to distill some of the most salient features of Greek urbanism.

THE FORMATION OF GREEK CITIES

Singing the praises of the *polis*, Aristotle—writing in the fourth century B.C.—says "Man is by nature an animal intended to live in a *polis*. . . . The man who is isolated—who is unable to share in the benefits of political association, or has no need to share because he is already self-sufficient—is no part of the *polis*, and must, therefore, be either a beast or a god" (*Politics* 1253a, translated by E. Barker). He charts the evolution of the *polis* from a time when people lived in villages (*komai*), and were organized into tribes (*ethne*) under the rule of a king (*basileus*) "as an individual family is ruled by its head" (*Politics* 1253b; see Coldstream 1984:8). And just as each village was formed by the union of individual households (or was a "colony" made from households), in time, villages came together in partnership to form a *polis* "for their own common good" and to achieve "complete self-sufficiency" (Coldstream 1984:8). And so here is the *synoikismos* of my title, and indeed, from the title of this collection as a whole: a "coming together," literally of *oikoi* or "households," to form communities. It is worth pointing out the degree to which Aristotle's model prefigured that of Elman Service's in the 1950s for the development of societal complexity (Service 1975).

The extent of the "collapse," which attended the end of the Bronze Age, is characterized by three major features: the depopulation of Greek landscapes by some estimates as much as two-thirds; the severing of foreign contacts which had hitherto supplied Greece with copper and tin, the raw materials of bronze; and a loss of elevated arts from monumental architecture to literacy (Bintliff [2012:210] terms this a "deskilling"). When these elements return, and return they do, all are accompanied by innovation. Population densities increased, gradually at first, but perhaps tripling during the eighth century B.C. For this reason—and others noted in what follows—the eighth century is known as the "Greek Renaissance" (see Hägg 1983). Foreign exchange is reinitiated, eventually on a grand scale, bringing with it not only copper and tin once more but iron and iron-working technology (probably diffused from Cyprus; presciently, the main source of copper since the Bronze Age). The new medium of iron—already present as a trickle since 1100 B.C.—which marks the onset of the Greek Iron Age, becomes a flood over the course of subsequent centuries as Greece "reskills." Again, by the eighth century, we see a conscious return to monumental architecture marked initially by the building of inherently functional and sensible fortification walls, but soon extending to symbolic architecture with the rise of the so-called *hecatompedon,* the 100-foot-long temple. Literacy is reborn too, with Greeks living and working abroad alongside Phoenicians adopting that alphabet to their own language and for their own uses.

But, and especially for our purposes here, the eighth century B.C. is also witness to the birth of the *polis* and its attendant feature—genuine urbanism. As with population growth, foreign contacts, and technological innovation, however, neither the *polis* nor urbanism appeared without precedent. Numerous Early Iron Age communities can be pointed to as providing examples of experiments in urbanism, as proto-, nascent, or "failed" *poleis*. Depending on how widely we choose to cast our chronological net, some of the more prominent examples of these include Emborio on Chios, Karphi on Crete, Lefkandi on Euboea, Nichoria in Messenia, Scala Oropos in Boeotia, and Zagora on Andros (see Lang 1996).

I think we can best approach and gain an appreciation for the dynamics of *polis* formation and its urban manifestations through a sort of multivariate analysis

(Figure 7.1). This is not a one-size-fits-all model, but most examples share at least some of these common features. And while it is a causal model, it is not a monocausal one. Nor is it unidirectional, but rather systems-based and interactive. The baseline constant to this modeling is the geographical diversity coupled with a high degree of fragmentation of the Greek landscape: composed alternately of mountains and plains, an indented and undulating coastline, islands, and a lack of interior waterways, but with each area's relative ease of access to the interconnectivity of the sea. Such varied topography provides for many areas suitable to individual populations settling and developing control of discrete regions or territories within them. And so the landscapes of Aegean Greece ultimately encouraged the development of the *polis* (Grove and Rackham 2001; Horden and Purcell 2000; Rackham 1990).

Turning to human agency, we begin with demography. The dramatic decline and resurgence of populations at the end of the Bronze Age and in the Early Iron Age has already been noted. Mapped through the density of settlements recorded by intensive

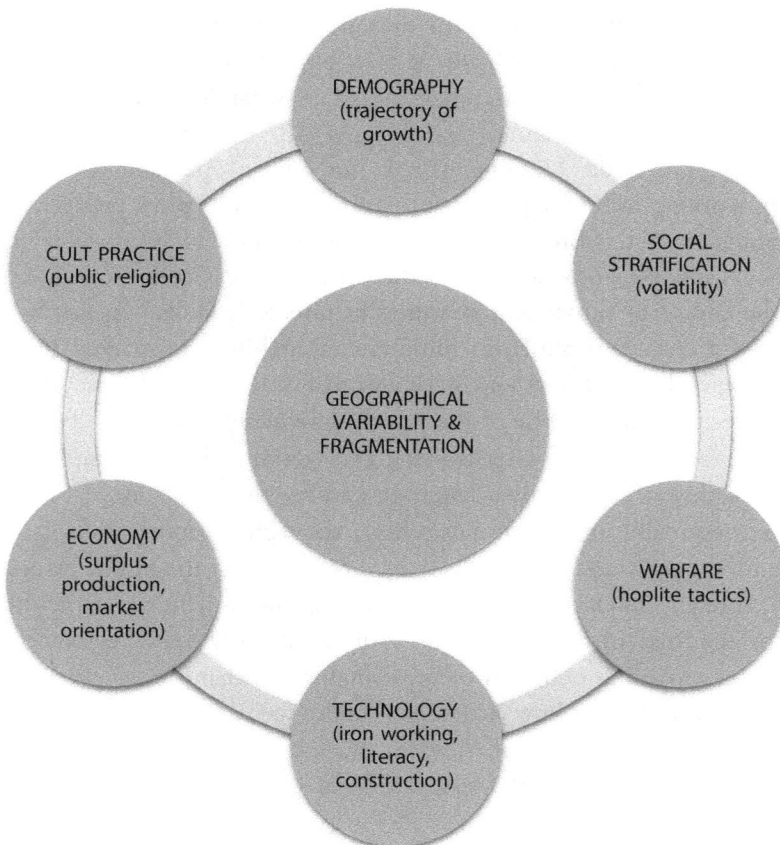

FIGURE 7.1. Systems-based model of the primary variables in *polis* formation.

surface survey and numbers of graves excavated that date to the period in question, the astonishing upswing in the eighth century B.C. of both settlements and cemeteries has been linked to the establishment of the *polis*. But more than that (as explored by Osborne, this volume), to the social revolution that was part and parcel of *polis* formation (for the original argument see Snodgrass 1977, 1980). By the eighth century, the low-level aristocracy of Early Iron Age "chieftains" (*basileis*) or "big men" (collectively known as the *agathoi*) was forced to integrate more fully with a substratum of the population (*kakoi*) who could either support or oppose them. This is the so-called middling class of yeoman farmers (Morris 1987).[1] And why else was this partnership necessary? To claim and defend territory. For the farmers whose lands were at stake were also the fighters.

In Greece, the social upheaval of the eighth century B.C. is not only linked to the rise of the *polis* but to the development of a tactical order known as "hoplite warfare," in which the infantry is comprised of soldiers whose first line of defense was a formation of shields (*hopla*) and spears locked together in a controlled phalanx. Side-by-side warfare in a face-to-face society whereby a whole new social class is empowered in a way it was not previously. This makes for a veritable "hoplite revolution," and translates into a measure of equality, of citizenship, and citizen rights gained and defended, which were to characterize *polis* organization (see especially Hanson 1991; Rich and Shipley 1996; van Wees 2004).

Technology played no small role in this. With the advent of iron—a cheaper, stronger, and more accessible metal than bronze (hence, a "democratic metal")—more individuals could afford to arm themselves, and thereby sway the balance of power. But the technical achievements, which defined the Iron Age, were not limited to metallurgical ones alone. For population growth, limitations of natural resources at home and the need for the raw materials of land and metals led Greeks to begin venturing abroad in some numbers during the eighth century B.C. Not only did they establish trading posts in Syria, Egypt, and Italy but these were soon followed by actual colonies, emanating particularly from land-poor regions of the homeland (Boardman 1999; see also Descoeudres 1990; Pugliese Carratelli 1996; Tsestkhladze and De Angelis 1994). Writing was surely developed in these contexts in order to facilitate commerce and to record rules of conduct (in spite of some arguments to the contrary: e.g., Powell 1991). Hence, we see the earliest surviving Greek law-codes dating to soon after this period (e.g., the Dreros code, 650–600 B.C.), followed shortly thereafter in the sixth century by coinage itself, inspired by Near Eastern, specifically Lydian, prototypes (Whitley 2001:128–133, 188–194).

Therefore, an economic motivation is discernable as well, albeit one that has been present throughout this modeling. It used to be thought that the Greeks, particularly during this period, operated at the level of subsistence-based production, or were characterized by what is known as a "primitive economy." However, the sustained growth and development documented in the foregoing underscores a more "modernist" interpretation of the ancient economy, whereby the Greeks always aimed for the production and acquisition of surplus commodities that were oriented toward market-level distribution, and hence generating a profit no matter how small (for the "primitivist" versus "modernist" debate, see Bresson 2016; Harris et al. 2015).

All of these trends and characteristics find an outlet in the institution of public cult practice. Taking the premise of "religion as social glue," which provides a spiritual rallying point for populations, it is worth noting that sanctuaries are among the first to reap the benefits of a return to monumentality. This is nowhere more evident than in the rise of the 100-foot temple, the *hecatompedon,* noted previously. The grandiose residence of the king (a *megaron,* literally "great hall") was transformed into the house of the god(-ess) (Mazarakis Ainian 1997; see also Hellmann 2006:36–43 for the theory of the *megaron,* and 69–70 for the *hecatompedon*). And the establishment of sanctuaries not only in urban centers but in their extraurban and rural periphery are taken as territorial markers, as boundaries physically drawn not just by their placement but during collective visitation at public festivals accompanied by communal processions (de Polignac 1995).

So these are the "ingredients" which contribute to the "recipe" of *polis* and urban formation in Greece—geographical, demographic, social, military, technological, economic, and religious ones.[2]

THE FORM OF GREEK CITIES

But what of the form of the *asty* or city itself? Once again, I propose a simple modeling based on interpenetrating spheres of activity (Figure 7.2).[3] The Greek city, like other urban formations, is composed of defensive, sacred, civic, economic, private, and arterial

FIGURE 7.2. Modeling the interrelated spheres of *polis* activity.

or connective space. And so I will treat these in turn. Virtually all Greek cities were sited so as to incorporate naturally defensive elements of the landscape into their position. Early cities, in particular, often included a steep outcropping eminence, known as the *acropolis* or "high city." Initially, the *acropolis* might also be the preferred location for a ruler's residence, and could be provided with its own fortification system. But with the rise of "popular government," the need for common defense meant that entire settlements required a surrounding enceinte of fortifications (Adam 1982; Frederiksen 2011; Hellmann 2010:293–374; Lawrence 1979; McNicoll 1997; Winter 1971; Wycherley 1962:36–49).[4] City walls were a marker of *polis* sovereignty; much like the coinage, many would come to issue from the sixth century on. And speaking of money—as was the case for military expenditures generally (Bintliff 2012:267, citing van Wees 2000)—they are by far the single most costly undertaking of city construction. The more impressive the walls, the more powerful the *polis*.

Ranking alongside defensive space in preeminence is the sacred realm. Developing from humble beginnings as open-air shrines, for the only requirement for sanctuaries is an altar at which to perform sacrifice, a free-standing building set aside for the "house of the god" develops as the temple, the practical function of which is to contain a cult image and dedications made to propitiate the deity. The earliest temples are little differentiated from private dwellings. However, it is worth underscoring again that they are ultimately derivatives in the plan of the kingly hall of Mycenaean rulers, the *megaron* already noted (Hellmann 2006:36–43; Mazarakis Ainian 1997). In an admitted element of circularity, the *megaron* itself is nothing more than the monumentalization of the basic house plan. But in time too, the temple itself is monumentalized, standardized, and petrified. Elements reflecting its original construction in perishable materials—from wooden columns to elements of roofing superstructure—are translated into the permanence of stone. And while the Greeks had a multitude of deities to worship and to whom they dedicated temples, two above all are associated with the city and its territory, especially in their formative phases: Athena in her guise as Athena Polias presided from the *acropolis* as protector of the city, while Hera, as nurturer, or Hera Kourotrophos, marked the extraurban territory not only to keep it safe but to ensure its fertility (de Polignac 1995).[5]

Greek cities combined their primary civic and economic zones into a common space, alongside the presence of sacred elements as well. This is an open area reserved within the surrounding urban development, known as the *agora* (Hellmann 2010:239–292; Hoepfner and Lehman 2006; Hölscher 1999:29–45; Kenzler 1999; Kolb 1981; Martin 1951; Wycherley 1962:50–86), taking its name from the verb *agorazein*, "to buy, sell, or go to market."[6] The *agora* likely developed as a central place within the city—perhaps at the foot of its *acropolis*—for public assembly, and so like the simplest of sanctuaries, required very little by way of dedicated architecture. Such gatherings should be taken to include military ones as this unencumbered area would have been ideal for mustering, exercising, and training the citizen army. The *agora* was a multifunctional space, home not only to political gatherings but market stalls and other temporary structures designed to accommodate performances ranging from theatral to athletic. In time, increasingly specialized and monumentalized architecture came to demarcate the *agora,* especially around its periphery, which was increasingly bounded and well defined by public buildings. These include the *stoa,* a multipurpose hall offering shelter and shade, laid out as a rectangular structure closed on three sides, but open on the one long side which faced onto the *agora.* The *bouleuterion* was an assembly hall for council meetings (*boule*), while the *prytaneion* served the rotating members of the *prytany* who oversaw day-to-day city business. Law courts, city archives, and offices of public officials were located here. The area also served as a locus for the dissemination of news not only by the speeches delivered and debates held there but by word-of-mouth among those who frequented the place, and by offering venues for the posting of decrees. The *agora* was the town square where the *polis* met itself.[7]

But the urban fabric of the Greek city—like cities generally—was comprised primarily of private rather than public space. The housing and housing tracts of citizens tell us a great deal about social organization (for a selection of more recent studies, see Ault 2016; Ault and Nevett 2005; Hoepfner 1999; Hoepfner and Schwandner 1994; Jameson 1990a, 1990b; Nevett 1999, 2010, 2012). Indeed, they are a microcosm of the *polis* itself. For example, what we find in Greek cities is that citizen housing tends to be of approximately the same size. So, for example, the average dimensions of the courtyard-centered houses characteristic of the Classical period, during the fifth and fourth centuries B.C., are approximately 15 x 15 meters. When laid out contiguously in rows—two houses deep and intersected by streets and avenues at right angles—these insular blocks come to characterize what is known as orthogonal or regular city planning (Castagnoli 1971). As such, given their ordered division, they reflect the form of "popular government" with varying degrees of democratic implementation that we tend to associate with the Greeks (Bintliff 2010; Westgate 2007). They offered an immediate and total transition from urban bustle to (relative) tranquil domesticity. But even these urban dwellers made a daily passage to work their agricultural holdings which lay in the *chora,* beyond the walled confines of the *asty* proper.

Hence, the importance of arterial or connective space—the streets and avenues for pedestrian, quadrupedal, and wheeled traffic—which provided entry and egress through city gates and linked up various areas from neighborhoods to markets and to temples. The location of such apertures in the surrounding walls tended to be situated along major extramural thoroughfares, and hence, determined the orientation or at least influenced the hierarchy of roads that lay within the city.[8] At least one major city gate usually gave way to a wider avenue that led directly to the *agora,* and similarly may have marked an important route for public processions, a "sacred way" (Hölscher 1999, 2012). Finally, as Pullen reminds us in this volume, ports and harbors also make a critical contribution to the city's connective tissue.

CONCLUSION

Bintliff (2010) has recently made the case for considering the *polis* as a sociobiological entity, reflecting and demonstrating in its physical organization principles of eusociality. In its preurban form, the Greek city as a village or *Dorfstadt* was small-scale, ranging up to perhaps 200 inhabitants. At this level, horizontal organization was the prime means for unifying and controlling it (one graded according to status based on power, wealth, and age). When growth surpassed 200 and groups were subject to the variables of *polis* formation discussed previously (see Figure 7.1), these measures become insufficient, and need to be balanced against vertically distributed ones which act as a leveling mechanism. The outcome of this verticality is reflected in the form of the *polis* (see Figure 7.2) which is itself a response to the stimulus variables. As unpopular as a Darwinian approach to human behavior is in some corners (Terrenato and Haggis 2011), when tempered with the acknowledged variability of cultural context and custom, it appears quite meaningful as an explanatory device.

One of the many beauties of Classical archaeology is the wealth of evidence offered for considering the past, from abundant textual sources to impressive material remains. Urbanism is a prime example of this. At the same time, this "embarrassment of riches" has not infrequently led to the neglect of genuinely important areas, which continue to be ripe for study (for appraisals on the history and state of Greek archaeology within the broader spectrum of Classical archaeology, see Haggis and Antonaccio 2015; Morris 1994; Nevett 2017; Snodgrass 2012; Whitley 2001:3–59). I believe that we have much to gain from turning our attention to the Greek city. And I hope here to have shared some of what we know, what we have yet to learn, and how these contribute to our understanding of urban processes in general.

ACKNOWLEDGMENTS

I am most grateful to Attila Gyucha for the invitation to participate in the 9th IEMA Conference which hosted the original presentation of this work, and for his efforts in bringing the whole to fruition in the form of publication, as well as to the other contributors who took part and provided such a stimulating weekend environment for considering the archaeology of urbanism.

NOTES

1. Morris refines the observations of Snodgrass, making the upsurge in population less dramatic, but its social implications all the more profound.
2. Compare the approaches of Fernández-Götz and Smith in this volume, as well as those collected in Terrenato and Haggis (2011).
3. The modeling of urban space is taken up by many. In addition to providing an excellent cross-cultural introduction to "the ancient city," see Marcus and Sabloff (2008) for several such models. From the same collection, equally astute essays applicable to the present paper, in particular, are those of Hansen (2008) and Renfrew (2008). Overarching treatments of the Greek city, or including the Greek city, not cited further below, include Gates (2011), Greco and Torelli (1983), Martin (1974), Owens (1991), and Ward-Perkins (1974).
4. It is worth noting the observations of Aristotle again who states that "[a]n *acropolis* is suitable to oligarchies and monarchies; a level plain suits the character of democracy" (*Politics* 1330b, translated by E. Barker).

5. Myriad studies are devoted to Greek temples and sanctuaries, which also feature prominently in handbooks of Greek art, architecture, and archaeology (see also the relevant sections in Bintliff 2012 and Hellmann 2006). Specialized collections include those of Alcock and Osborne (1996) and Marinatos and Hägg (1995).
6. The most completely studied *agora* is that of Athens which has its own extensive bibliography, but is effectively summarized in Camp (1992).
7. See also the quote from Aristotle's *Politics*, cited above, which surely refers to a "level plain" for communal congregation and interaction. Relevant considerations of public architecture and civic space, in addition to those in works already cited, include Coulton (1976) (for the *stoa*), Hansen and Fischer-Hansen (1994), Hölscher (2012), McDonald (1943), and Miller (1978) (for the *prytaneion*). For dissemination of information within the city, see Lewis (1996).
8. *Necropoleis* for "formal burial," literally "cities of the dead," might also be located along these main extramural roads. I have excluded them from further consideration here, concentrating instead on "cities of the living." See also Snodgrass (2009) and Osborne (this volume) for considerations of their contribution to the study of Greek urbanism.

REFERENCES CITED

Adam, J.-P. 1982 *L'architecture militaire grecque*. Picard, Paris.

Alcock, S. E., and R. Osborne (editors) 1996 *Placing the Gods: Sanctuaries and Sacred Space in Ancient Greece*. Clarendon Press, Oxford.

Ault, B. A. 2016 Greek Domestic Architecture. In *A Companion to Science, Technology, and Medicine in Ancient Greek and Rome*, edited by G. L. Irby, pp. 656–671. Wiley-Blackwell, Hoboken, New Jersey.

Ault, B. A., and L. C. Nevett (editors) 2005 *Ancient Greek Houses and Households: Chronological, Regional, and Social Diversity*. University of Pennsylvania Press, Philadelphia.

Barber, R. L. N. 1987 *The Cyclades in the Bronze Age*. University of Iowa Press, Iowa City.

Bintliff, J. 2010 Classical Greek Urbanism: A Social Darwinian View. In *Valuing Others in Classical Antiquity*, edited by R. M. Rosen and I. Sluiter, pp. 15–41. Mnemosyne Supplements 323. Brill, Leiden.

Bintliff, J. 2012 *The Complete Archaeology of Greece: From Hunter-Gatherers to the 20th Century A.D.* Wiley-Blackwell, Malden, Massachusetts.

Boardman, J. 1999 *The Greeks Overseas: Their Early Colonies and Trade*. 4th ed. Thames and Hudson, London.

Branigan, K. (editor) 2001 *Urbanism in the Aegean Bronze Age*. Sheffield Academic Press, Sheffield.

Bresson, A. 2016 *The Making of the Ancient Greek Economy: Institutions, Markets, and Growth in the City-States*. Princeton University Press, Princeton, New Jersey.

Camp, J. M. 1992 *The Athenian Agora: Excavation in the Heart of Classical Athens*. Thames and Hudson, London.

Castagnoli, F. 1971 *Orthogonal Town Planning in Antiquity*. MIT Press, Cambridge, Massachusetts.

Coldstream, J. N. 1984 *The Formation of the Greek Polis: Aristotle and Archaeology*. Westdeutscher, Opladen.

Coulton, J. J. 1976 *The Architectural Development of the Greek Stoa*. Oxford University Press, Oxford.

de Polignac, F. 1995 *Cults, Territory, and the Origins of the Greek City-State*. The University of Chicago Press, Chicago.

Desborough, V. R. d'A. 1972 *The Greek Dark Ages*. Palgrave Macmillan, London.

Descoeudres, J.-P. (editor) 1990 *Greek Colonists and Native Populations*. Clarendon Press, Oxford.

Driessen, J. 2009 Daidalos' Designs and Ariadne's Threads: Minoan Towns as Places of Interaction. In *Inside the City in the Greek World: Studies of Urbanism from the Bronze Age to the Hellenistic Period*, edited by S. Owen and L. Preston, pp. 41–54. Oxbow Books, Oxford.

Frederiksen, R. 2011 *Greek City Walls of the Archaic Period, 900–489 BC*. Oxford University Press, Oxford.

French, E. 2009 Town Planning in Palatial Mycenae. In *Inside the City in the Greek World: Studies of Urbanism from the Bronze Age to the Hellenistic Period*, edited by S. Owen and L. Preston, pp. 55–61. Oxbow Books, Oxford.

Gates, C. 2011 *Ancient Cities: The Archaeology of Urban Life in the Ancient Near East and Egypt, Greece, and Rome*. 2nd ed. Routledge, London.

Greco, E., and M. Torelli 1983 *Storia dell'urbanistica: il mondo greco*. Laterza, Rome.

Grove, A. T., and O. Rackham 2001 *The Nature of Mediterranean Europe: An Ecological History*. Yale University Press, New Haven, Connecticut.

Hägg, R. (editor) 1983 *The Greek Renaissance of the Eighth Century B.C.* Acta Instituti Atheniensis Regni Sueciae 30. Swedish Institute of Classical Studies at Athens, Stockholm.

Haggis, D. C., and C. Antonaccio (editors) 2015 *Classical Archaeology in Context: Theory and Practice in Excavation in the Greek World*. De Gruyter, Berlin.

Hansen, M. H. 2006 *Polis: An Introduction to the Ancient Greek City-State*. Oxford University Press, Oxford.

Hansen, M. H. 2008 Analyzing Cities. In *The Ancient City: New Perspectives on Urbanism in the Old and New World*, edited by J. Marcus and J. A. Sabloff, pp. 67–76. School for Advanced Research Press, Santa Fe, New Mexico.

Hansen, M. H., and T. Fischer-Hansen 1994 Monumental Political Architecture in Archaic and Classical Greek Poleis: Evidence and Historical Significance. In *From Political Architecture to Stephanus Byzantius: Sources for the Ancient Greek Polis*, edited by D. Whitehead, pp. 23–90. Papers from the Copenhagen Polis Centre 1. Historia Einzelschriften 87. Steiner, Stuttgart.

Hanson, V. D. (editor) 1991 *Hoplites: The Classical Greek Battle Experience*. Routledge, London.

Harris, E. M., D. M. Lewis, and M. Woolmer (editors) 2015 *The Ancient Greek Economy: Markets, Households, and City-States*. Cambridge University Press, Cambridge.

Hellmann, M.-C. 2006 *L'architecture grecque, 2. Architecture religieuse et funéraire*. Picard, Paris.

Hellmann, M.-C. 2010 *L'architecture grecque, 3. Habitat, urbanisme et fortifications*. Picard, Paris.

Hoepfner, W. 1999 Die Epoche der Griechen. In *Geschichte des Wohnens. Band I: 5000 v.Chr.—500 n.Chr. Vorgeschichte—Frühgeschichte—Antike*, edited by W. Hoepfner, pp. 123–607. Deutsche Verlags-Anstalt, Stuttgart.

Hoepfner, W., and L. Lehmann (editors) 2006 *Die Griechische Agora*. Philipp von Zabern, Mainz am Rhein.

Hoepfner, W., and E.-L. Schwandner 1994 *Haus und Stadt im Klassischen Griechenland*. 2nd ed. Deutscher Kunstverlag, Munich.

Hölscher, T. 1999 *Öffentliche Räume frühen griechischen Städten*. Schriften der Philosophisch-historischen Klasse der Heidelberger Akademie der Wissenschaften 7. Universitätsverlag C. Winter, Heidelberg.

Hölscher, T. 2012 Urban Spaces and Central Places: The Greek World. In *Classical Archaeology*, edited by S. E. Alcock and R. Osborne, pp. 170–186. Wiley-Blackwell, Malden, Massachusetts.

Horden, P., and N. Purcell 2000 *The Corrupting Sea: A Study of Mediterranean History*. Wiley-Blackwell, Oxford.

Jameson, M. H. 1990a Domestic Space in the Greek City-State. In *Domestic Architecture and the Use of Space: An Interdisciplinary Cross-Cultural Study*, edited by S. Kent, pp. 92–113. Cambridge University Press, Cambridge.

Jameson, M. H. 1990b Private Space and the Greek City. In *The Greek City: From Homer to Alexander*, edited by O. Murray and S. Price, pp. 171–195. Clarendon Press, Oxford.

Kenzler, U. 1999 *Studien zur Entwicklung und Struktur der griechischen Agora in archäischer und klassischer Zeit*. Peter Lang, Frankfurt am Main.

Kolb, F. 1981 *Agora und Theater: Volks- und Festversammlung*. Gebrüder Mann, Berlin.

Lang, F. 1996 *Archäische Siedlungen in Griechenland: Struktur und Entwicklung*. Akademie, Berlin.

Lawrence, A. W. 1979 *Greek Aims in Fortification*. Oxford University Press, Oxford.

Lewis, S. 1996 *News and Society in the Greek Polis*. University of North Carolina Press, Chapel Hill.

Marcus, J., and J. A. Sabloff 2008 Introduction. In *The Ancient City: New Perspectives on Urbanism in the Old and New World*, pp. 3–26. School for Advanced Research Press, Santa Fe, New Mexico.

Marinatos, N., and R. Hägg (editors) 1995 *Greek Sanctuaries: New Approaches*. Routledge, London.

Martin, R. 1951 *Recherches sur l'Agora grecque: Études d'histoire et d'architecture urbaines*. Bibliothèques des l'Ecole française d'Athènes et de Rome 174. De Boccard, Paris.

Martin, R. 1974 *L'urbanisme dans la Grèce antique*. 2nd ed. Picard, Paris.

Mazarakis Ainian, A. 1997 *From Rulers' Dwellings to Temples: Architecture, Religion and Society in Early Iron Age Greece (1100–800 B.C.)*. Studies in Mediterranean Archaeology 121. Paul Åströms, Jonsered.

McDonald, W. A. 1943 *The Political Meeting Places of the Greeks*. Johns Hopkins University Press, Baltimore.

McNicoll, A. W. 1997 *Hellenistic Fortifications from the Aegean to the Euphrates*. Oxford University Press, Oxford.

Miller, S. G. 1978 *The Prytaneion: Its Function and Architectural Form*. University of California Press, Berkeley.

Mitchell, L. G., and P. J. Rhodes (editors) 1997 *The Development of the Polis in Archaic Greece*. Routledge, New York.

Morris, I. 1987 *Burial and Ancient Society: The Rise of the Greek City-State*. Cambridge University Press, Cambridge.

Morris, I. 1991 The Early Polis as City and State. In *City and Country in the Ancient World*, edited by J. Rich and A. Wallace-Hadrill, pp. 24–57. Routledge, London.

Morris, I. 1994 Archaeologies of Greece. In *Classical Greece: Ancient Histories and Modern Archaeologies*, edited by I. Morris, pp. 8–47. Cambridge University Press, Cambridge.

Nevett, L. C. 1999 *House and Society in the Ancient Greek World*. Cambridge University Press, Cambridge.

Nevett, L. C. 2010 *Domestic Space in Classical Antiquity*. Cambridge University Press, Cambridge.

Nevett, L. C. 2012 Housing and Households in Ancient Greece. In *Classical Archaeology*, edited by S. E. Alcock and R. Osborne, pp. 208–227. Wiley-Blackwell, Malden, Massachusetts.

Nevett, L. C. (editor) 2017 *Theoretical Approaches to the Archaeology of Ancient Greece: Manipulating Material Culture*. University of Michigan Press, Ann Arbor.

Nichols, D. L., and T. H. Charlton (editors) 1997 *The Archaeology of City-States: Cross-Cultural Approaches*. Smithsonian Institution Press, Washington, D.C.

Owens, E. J. 1991 *The City in the Greek and Roman World.* Routledge, London.

Powell, B. B. 1991 *Homer and the Origin of the Greek Alphabet.* Cambridge University Press, Cambridge.

Pugliese Carratelli, D. (editor) 1996 *The Greek World: Art and Civilization in Magna Graecia and Sicily.* Rizzoli, Milan.

Rackham, O. 1990 Ancient Landscapes. In *The Greek City: From Homer to Alexander,* edited by O. Murray and S. Price, pp. 85–111. Clarendon Press, Oxford.

Renfrew, C. 2008 The City through Time and Space: Transformations of Centrality. In *The Ancient City: New Perspectives on Urbanism in the Old and New World,* edited by J. Marcus and J. A. Sabloff, pp. 29–51. School for Advanced Research Press, Santa Fe, New Mexico.

Rich, J., and G. Shipley (editors) 1993 *War and Society in the Greek World.* Routledge, New York.

Sakellariou, M. B. 1989 *The Polis State: Definition and Origin.* Meletemata 4. Diffusion De Boccard, Athens.

Schoep, I. 2009 Social and Political Aspects of Urbanism in Middle Minoan I–II Crete: Towards a Regional Approach. In *Inside the City in the Greek World: Studies of Urbanism from the Bronze Age to the Hellenistic Period,* edited by S. Owen and L. Preston, pp. 27–40. Oxbow Books, Oxford.

Service, E. R. 1975 *Origins of the State and Civilization: The Process of Cultural Evolution.* W. W. Norton, New York.

Snodgrass, A. M. 1971 *The Dark Age of Greece: An Archaeological Survey of the Eleventh to Eighth Centuries B.C.* Edinburgh University Press, Edinburgh.

Snodgrass, A. M. 1977 *Archaeology and the Rise of the Greek State: An Inaugural Lecture.* Cambridge University Press, Cambridge.

Snodgrass, A. M. 1980 *Archaic Greece: The Age of Experiment.* Dent, London.

Snodgrass, A. M. 2009 The Classical Greek Cemetery: A Barometer of Citizenship? In *Inside the City in the Greek World: Studies of Urbanism from the Bronze Age to the Hellenistic Period,* edited by S. Owen and L. Preston, pp. 99–107. Oxbow Books, Oxford.

Snodgrass, A. M. 2012 What Is Classical Archaeology? Greek Archaeology. In *Classical Archaeology,* edited by S. E. Alcock and R. Osborne, pp. 13–29. Wiley-Blackwell, Malden, Massachusetts.

Terrenato, N., and D. C. Haggis (editors) 2011 *State Formation in Italy and Greece: Questioning the Neoevolutionist Paradigm.* Oxbow Books, Oxford.

Tsestkhladze, G. R., and F. De Angelis (editors) 1994 *The Archaeology of Greek Colonisation: Essays Dedicated to Sir John Boardman.* Monograph 40. Oxford University School of Archaeology, Oxford.

van Wees, H. 2000 The City at War. In *Classical Greece,* edited by R. Osborne, pp. 80–110. Oxford University Press, Oxford.

van Wees, H. 2004 *Greek Warfare: Myths and Realities.* Duckworth, London.

Ward-Perkins, J. B. 1974 *Cities of Ancient Greece and Italy: Planning in Classical Antiquity.* George Braziller, New York.

Westgate, R. 2007 The Greek House and the Ideology of Citizenship. *World Archaeology* 39(2):229–245.

Whitley, J. 2001 *The Archaeology of Ancient Greece.* Cambridge University Press, Cambridge.

Winter, F. E. 1971 *Greek Fortifications.* University of Toronto Press, Toronto.

Wycherley, R. E. 1962 *How the Greeks Built Cities: The Relationship of Architecture and Town Planning to Everyday Life in Ancient Greece.* W. W. Norton, New York.

Pathways to Sustainability:
Challenges and Resolutions

CHAPTER EIGHT

Trypillia Megasites

The First Cities in Europe?

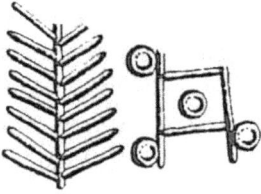

Bisserka Gaydarska

Abstract   *Little known until recently, the largest sites so far discovered in fourth millennium B.C. Europe, the Trypillian megasites of Ukraine, have enjoyed an upsurge of research interest during the past decade. Despite their impressive size of up to 320 hectares, traditionally they have been viewed as overgrown villages, and only a handful of Ukrainian archaeologists have posited a protourban development. Such views were based on aerial photographs, first-generation Russian geophysics, and limited excavations. The recent involvement of two international teams—an Anglo-Ukrainian and a German-Ukrainian—in the field investigation of the Trypillia phenomenon has invigorated the debate about the characteristics of these sites, their emergence and sustainability, and their place in global settlement trajectories. This paper offers a brief assessment of the outcome of the two international projects that included high-precision geophysics, AMS dating, sediment coring, intensive systematic fieldwalking, and selective excavations. These outcomes have resulted in an alternative to the long-held view that these sites are "giant," permanently occupied Neolithic settlements. The discussion is framed by the social, economic, and environmental implications sites of such size may have, all pointing to a socioeconomic system usually associated with urban formations.*

INTRODUCTION

The Trypillia[1] megasites, with their extraordinarily large size, are ideal candidates for a volume entitled *Coming Together: Comparative Approaches to Population Aggregation and Early Urbanization.* They are located in the modern country of Ukraine, and are more broadly known as a part of the vast prehistoric network—traditionally termed as "archaeological culture"—called Cucuteni-Trypillia (Mantu et al. 1997; Videiko 2004). This remarkably long-lived network (4800 to 2800 B.C.) occurred in an area of more than 250,000 square kilometers (Figure 8.1), and the current number of known Trypillia sites is arguably ca. 5,000.

A typical characteristic of Cucuteni-Trypillia is the overwhelming predominance of settlement contexts, with formal burials being more frequent toward the tail end of this network (Topal and Tserna 2010). Another common feature is the preponderance of clay-based material culture—wattle-and-daub houses, exquisite pottery, and more than 20,000 known figurines, dwarfing the number of other materials, perishable and durable alike. The third distinctive element, the regular appearance of sites larger than 100 hectares, is the topic of the current paper. Although at present their distribution is known only from the territory of Ukraine, there is no agreement about their internal spread, with some scholars arguing for a wide distribution with the area between the Buh (Bug) and Dnipro (Dniepr) rivers being a core region, while other see this interfluve as the only "real" area of the distribution of megasites. The abandonment of the Cucuteni-Trypillia settlements is marked by house burning, resulting in a series of piles of burnt rubble, popularly known as *ploshchadki*.[2] The vigorous debate about the reasons underpinning such a practice is currently overwhelmingly in favor of deliberate ritual burning (Kruts 2003).

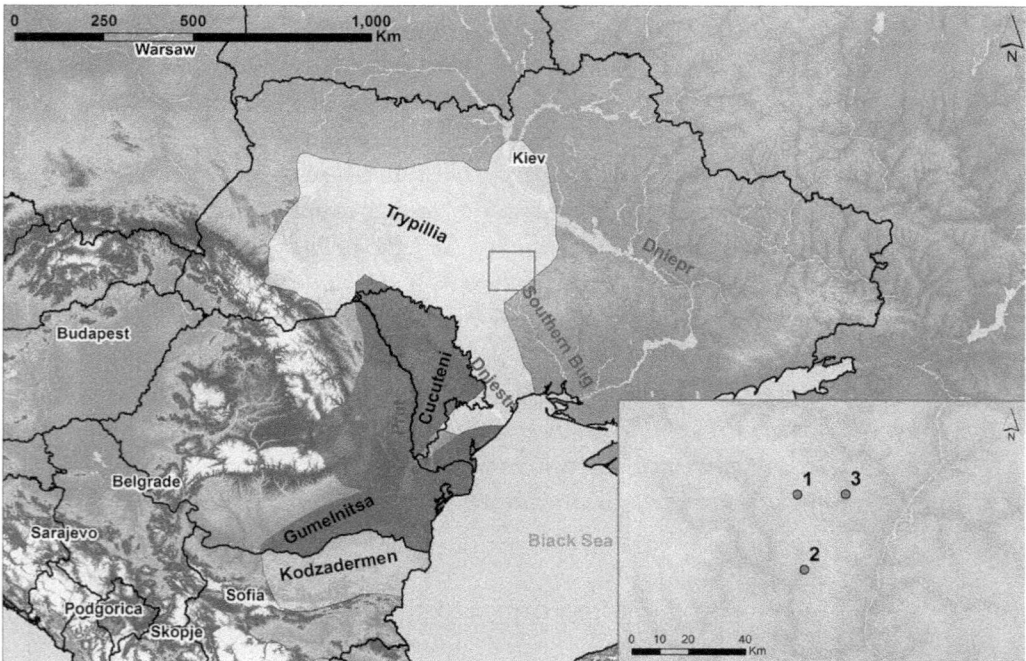

FIGURE 8.1. Location of the Cucuteni-Trypillia network, and location of sites mentioned in the text: (1) Talianky, (2) Nebelivka, (3) Maidanetske.

This paper is very much a work in progress, drafting the research agenda for years to come, rather than the final word on the large Trypillia settlements. It starts by setting the scene with a selective history of research, and a brief account of the most recent advances in Trypillia investigations. The succeeding discussion is organized around the underlying themes of the volume (see the introductory chapter by Gyucha), followed by some concluding thoughts on whether we can see the megasites as hitherto unrecognized urban formations.[3]

A Selected History of Research

Traditionally called "settlement-giants" (Korvin-Piotrovskiy 2003), the Trypillia megasites have remained largely unknown to the wider archaeological community owing to geopolitical arrangements and linguistic barriers. Until very recently, Western scholarship had a limited access to the ever-increasing knowledge about these sites, mainly through the work of a few interested parties (Anthony 2007; Childe 1945; Fletcher 1995; Kohl 2002) and the occasional "outing" of local archaeologists (e.g., Videiko 1996). In contrast, multiple aspects of the megasites have been hotly debated, initially in the U.S.S.R., then in Ukraine, in the last 25 years—from the number of stories of Trypillia houses (Korvin-Piotrovskiy et al. 2012), through the reasons for the emergence and demise of the megasites (Diachenko 2010; Kruts 1989; Manzura 2005; Videiko 2002; Zbenovich 1990), to the nature of these sites as settlement-giants (Korvin-Piotrovskiy 2003) or protourban centers (Shmaglij 2001). Shifting paradigms in Western archaeological practice had very little effect on these internal discussions, and the basic premises put forward some 40–50 years ago largely remain the same.

In a nutshell, there is no common agreement as to the reasons leading up to such massive aggregation of people, but the most popular explanations include internal or external conflict, migration, and population pressure (Diachenko and Menotti 2017). Interestingly, the same reasons are suggested for the abandonment of these sites, with the addition of resource depletion (Anthony 2013). Despite the various opinions about the origin of the large Trypillia sites, all Ukrainian archaeologists agree that it was underpinned by migration processes, which are inferred on the basis of changes in pottery style seen and proliferated as internal periodization (Diachenko 2016a; Ryzhov 2012; Videiko 2002). Details and particularities may vary, but the core framework of migration and relative chronology based on pottery has never been questioned, thus ignoring the possibility of the unfolding of other social processes and largely disregarding the reliability of absolute dating (see Gaydarska 2015). The alleged "genetic" ties claimed between pottery shapes and decorations (Ryzhov 2012), and from there between different sites, form the basis for formal modeling (Diachenko and Menotti 2012:Figures 3 and 5). In human terms, this means that the same core population, with some outside influx, was abandoning their settlements after 50–80 years of occupation and was settling at new places and starting to produce similar, but not the same, pottery as before on the new sites.

Although concerning abandonment the hypotheses for conflicts and resource exhaustion have largely been discredited due to the lack of evidence (Gaydarska and Chapman 2016), the suggested alternatives remain either unsupported (Videiko 2013) or are still gathering pace (Diachenko 2016b). The former alternative rests on a perfectly legitimate approach of putting these sites in an overall European perspective, but it is difficult to understand how—as the latter approach suggests—progress can be made toward explaining the demise of these sites with arguments drawn from a range of incompatible approaches borrowed from Karl Marx, Elman Service, and Vere Gordon Childe. Diachenko's (2016b) perspective also relates to a wider European context, referring to a much more solid—if contested—theoretical model (Earle and Kristiansen 2010), and seeing the abandonment of these huge sites as a part of transformation processes extending across Europe in the fourth millennium B.C. when the emerging, dispersed political economies would have been incompatible with such massive agricultural entities.

NEW INVESTIGATIONS

In the last 10 years, the megasites have enjoyed a lively research interest underpinned by a very strong international component. It started as revisiting, updating, and summarizing already known data (e.g., Diachenko 2010; Menotti and Korvin-Piotrovskiy 2012; Rassamakin and Menotti 2011), followed by two international field projects, a German-Ukrainian and a British-Ukrainian. Both teams embarked on the ambitious task of performing high-precision magnetometry on these vast sites. The British-Ukrainian team has completed a geophysical plan of an entire megasite, Nebelivka (Chapman et al. 2014a), while the German-Ukrainian team has produced three partial plans of sites over 100 hectares (Talianky, Maidanetske, and Dobrovody in Ukraine), an almost complete plan of a site under 100 hectares (Petreni in Moldova), and a complete plan of a "small," 26-hectare site (Apolianka in Ukraine) (Rassmann et al. 2014), with their work still ongoing. Both teams have been involved in excavation and sampling for AMS dates (Millard et al. 2019; Müller et al. 2016a), while the British-Ukrainian team also conducted intensive systematic fieldwalking (Nebbia 2016), pollen coring (Albert et al. 2019), and experimental house building and burning (Johnston et al. 2019).

The new geophysical plans brought a lot of clarity, and were justifiably called the "second phase of methodological revolution" (Chapman et al. 2014b). Despite the reluctance to accept such a description (Diachenko and Menotti 2017), the fact remains that the old and the new plans are incomparable in terms of precision and accuracy, and it is only with the new plans that various types of features could be identified (compare Figures 8.2 and 8.3). Nine new elements were registered by recent magnetometry surveys: perimeter ditches, tracks, paleochannels, unburnt houses, household clusters (neighborhoods), pit clusters, bounded unbuilt spaces, larger ensembles of houses (quarters), and buildings much larger than "normal" houses (assembly houses). A tenth novel group of features, pottery kilns, has been claimed at Nebelivka, Maidanetske, and Talianky (Korvin-Piotrovskiy et al. 2016). Each of these newly identified elements deserves proper

FIGURE 8.2. Old geophysical plan of Maidanetske (after Shmaglij 2001).

FIGURE 8.3. New geophysical plan of Maidanetske (after Rassmann et al. 2014).

assessment that cannot be offered here owing to word limits. However, highlighting a few points will be beneficial for the discussion further below.

The excavations of the perimeter ditch in Nebelivka revealed that it was relatively narrow (1.5 meters wide) and shallow (maximum depth of 1.2 meters), with no traces of associated palisade or other constructions. These characteristics, together with the interrupted layout at several places, suggest a more symbolic connotation of delineating space rather than a defensive structure. The perimeter ditch may also have been related to stock control.

The spatial patterning of the assembly houses shows that they are predominantly flanking the main house circuits, and are oriented at 90 degrees to these circuits. Their geophysical signal is very different from that of the regular *ploshchadka* (Figure 8.4), and the visual "emptiness" of these features, caused by the lack of burnt daub in the inner part of the structures, is confirmed by test excavations of two assembly houses at Nebelivka, which yielded structural daub (i.e., in situ platforms) and very little else (Figure 8.5). The size, location, and physical appearance of these structures make them very different from the mass of burnt structures, and prompts the notion that the assembly houses were the key integrating structures in the assemblages of houses, provisionally called the "quarters." Since assembly houses were unrecognized in the old geophysical plans, their role in the overall formation of the settlements could not be considered.

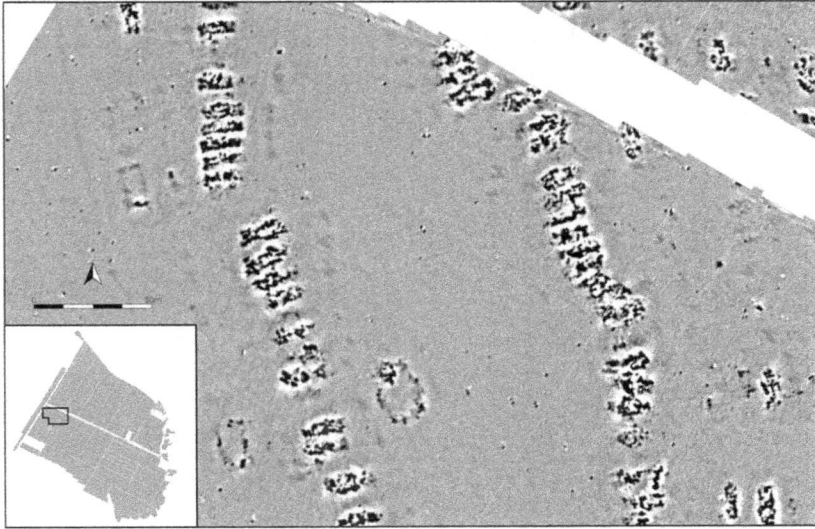

FIGURE 8.4. Location of the perimeter ditch and a pair of assembly houses at Nebelivka.

FIGURE 8.5. Structural "daub-platform" in test pit 27/3 (assembly house).

The current hypothesis for the formation of the megasites, either in two (Rassamakin and Menotti 2011) or four stages (Videiko 2013), is riddled with contradictions stemming from overreliance on relative chronology, very few radiocarbon dates, and imposing an overall spatial and chronological pattern from relatively small, and hence nonrepresentative set of evidence (Gaydarska and Chapman 2016). Until these contradictions are addressed, a plausible alternative is a polyfocal emergence of quarters each centered around its own assembly house (Chapman 2016).

The quarters consist of a varied number of smaller house clusters most readily associated with the sociospatial concept of "neighborhood" (Smith 2010). Fourteen quarters and more than 160 neighborhoods were identified at Nebelivka on the basis of topographic characteristics (e.g., paleochannels) and the position and orientation of houses (Figures 8.6 and 8.7). The suggested division is made by visual inspection, but more

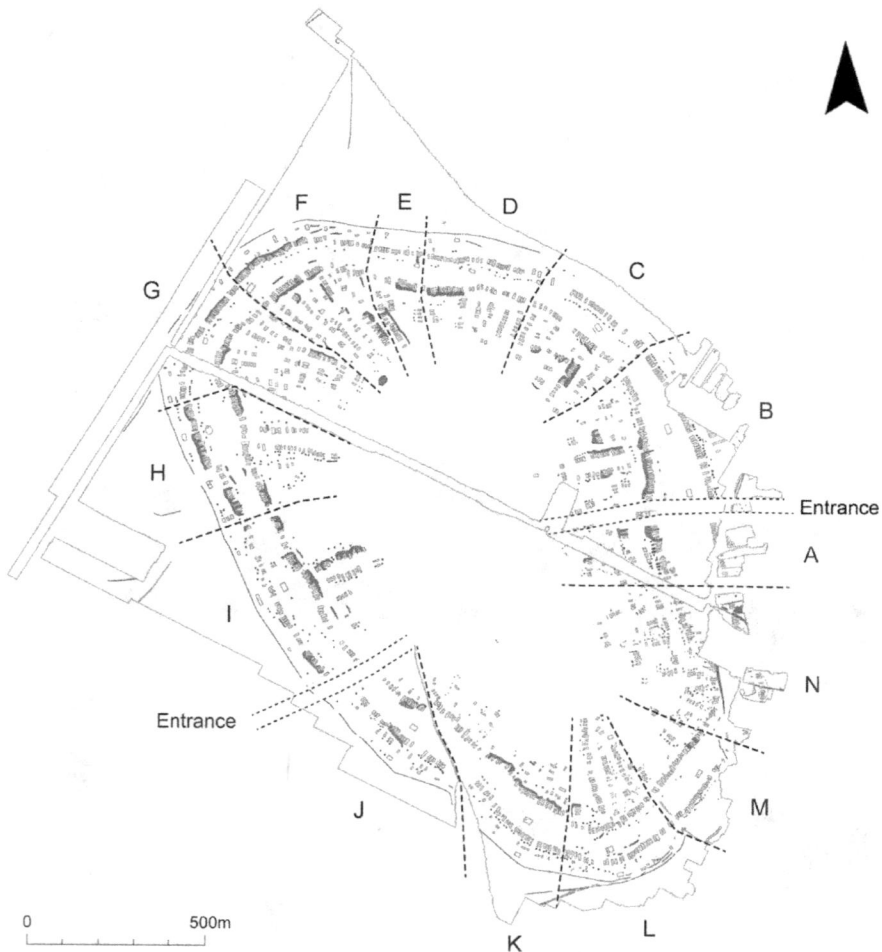

FIGURE 8.6. The complete interpretative geophysical plan for the Nebelivka megasite, with putative division into quarters.

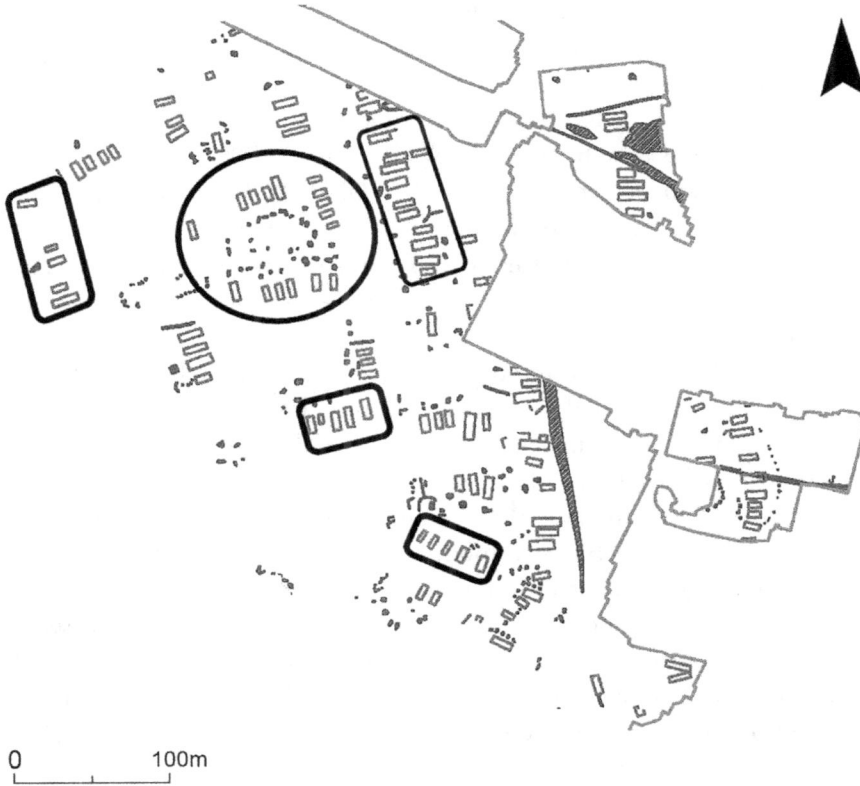

Figure 8.7. Quarter N with some of its neighborhoods at Nebelivka.

formal spatial modeling and cluster analysis are to be performed in the near future. This will bring more accuracy and precision to the microlevel spatial patterning without changing the general impression of an overall planned design differentiated by an abundance of local variability.

One of the most contested issues relating to the megasites is the number of their inhabitants. While contemporaneity of most, if not all, structures is presumed, it is only in the last 5 to 10 years that attempts have been made to substantiate such claims with radiocarbon dates (for the state of absolute chronology of Cucuteni-Trypillia, see Diachenko 2016b; Lazarovici 2010; Müller et al. 2016a; Rassamakin 2012; Rassamakin and Menotti 2011). At present, only two megasites have more than 10 AMS dates collected according to modern sampling strategies and lab protocols. The site of Maidanetske has a total of 36 AMS dates of which 14 have secure associations with the Trypillia occupation, only seven of them from houses. On this basis, the German-Ukrainian team has asserted that all of the estimated 2,970 houses at Maidanetske were occupied contemporaneously, with all settlement features in use ca. 3700 B.C. (Müller and Videiko 2016:91). Although sampling houses in a line that crosses all the seven circuits at this site is a valid strategy, it only gives the temporal relationship along that line and, by extension, may include the neighboring area and reveal the building sequence within a quarter. Ultimately, however, the lack of radiocarbon dates has not stopped speculations about the population number of the megasites in general and Maidanetske in particular. Contributors to the most recent volume on Trypillia megasites cannot agree on the number of inhabitants, and the following figures have been put forward: 8,750–31,700 (Ohlrau et al. 2016:208, Table 1), 14,000 (Rassmann et al. 2016:44), 7,500–25,000 (Müller et al. 2016a:133), and 15,000 (Kirleis and Dal Corso 2016:195). In any case, these figures are much lower than the 46,000 people suggested earlier by Rassmann and his colleagues (2014). It is important to note, however, that in Europe during the fifteenth century A.D. there were only 18 cities with a population exceeding 40,000 (de Vries 1984:Table 3.4).

More than 80 AMS dates are available for the site of Nebelivka (Millard et al. 2019). They are relatively evenly spread across the entire site—covering key features such as houses from both circuits, radial streets, assembly houses, and pits—and show a period of occupation between ca. 3970 and 3770 B.C. Unfortunately, the dates fall at a problematic part of the calibration curve, and hence 64 out of 74 measurements are statistically indistinguishable. Bayesian modeling suggests a weak overall tendency of the outer circuit being slightly later than the inner circuit. The British-Ukrainian team is currently working on a methodology to overcome these shortcomings, and sees the possibility of all structures to have been occupied at the same time for a period of 150 years as highly unlikely. The number of people in Nebelivka depended on the socioeconomic model adopted by its inhabitants. Permanent, all-year-round occupation at all megasites has so far been assumed rather than proven.

The first intensive systematic fieldwalking in Ukraine was conducted in a 5-kilometer radius around the Nebelivka megasite. Almost half of this area was surveyed depending on the availability of crop-free fields, and a single Trypillia sherd was found among numerous later scatters and finds (Nebbia 2016). That prompted to extend the survey area up to 20 kilometers from the site, yet fieldwalking focused only on specific regions with anomalies identified on satellite images. Only one new site was discovered 20 kilometers from the megasite that, according to its pottery characteristics, was occupied after the abandonment of Nebelivka. The closest contemporary site is Orlovets, some 7 kilometers to the southwest of Nebelivka; however, this site is known only from the literature, and has not been resurveyed (Nebbia 2016). The results of the field survey suggest that there was no immediate hinterland around the megasite, or in other words, the contemporarily occupied landscape should be sought well beyond the settled agricultural limit of 5 kilometers, and must be looked for in a much larger survey area.

Three pollen cores have been taken from the vicinity of Nebelivka, but only the closest one (Core 1B, 250 meters from the edge of the site) was analyzed further. It revealed very low cereal production—the maximum amount of cereal pollen was 4.8 percent, and the minimum was 1.8 percent in the samples—at the time of the occupation of the site, with peaks appearing before and after (Albert et al. 2019). Another unsuspected result was the low to moderate incidence of deforestation, making it difficult to account for the amount of trees needed for the construction of ca. 1,500 houses, the day-to-day fuel needs, and the massive quantities required for the successful burning down of more than 1,000 structures (see below). A final mismatch between the environmental data and the so far unsupported, but also unchallenged, narrative of Trypillia lifeways is the lack of a major fire event that would correspond to the final conflagration and abandonment of the site. As with cereal production, massive fire signals are present before and after the occupation of Nebelivka (Albert et al. 2019).

Last but not least, important lessons were learned from the house building and burning experiment (Johnston et al. 2019). While the 214 eight-hour people days needed to build two approximately half-sized houses (footprint of 3 x 4 meters)—one one-story and one two-story—should be scaled up due to use of modern tools and already felled construction timber, our experience has shown that building a Trypillia house was more an extended household project rather than a small nuclear family affair. The biggest lesson of all was that the amount of wood needed for the successful burning of a house (to produce a *ploshchadka*) is almost 10 times the amount needed to build it (Johnston et al. 2019). The absence of major deforestation and burning episodes in the pollen core makes it very unlikely that many houses were burned during the same abandonment event.

What Factors and Integrative Processes Brought Large Populations Together?

The only formal modeling of the demographic pattern underlying the formation of megasites (in contrast to the good tradition demonstrated by Kelly in this volume) is a complex combination of variable datasets and methods, such as pottery typochronology, the gravity model, geophysical plans with different resolution, the frequency of one- or two-story houses, the number of burnt/unburnt houses, and so on (Diachenko 2016a). According to this model, there is an abnormally high population growth immediately preceding the emergence of megasites in the Buh–Dnipro Interfluve. Since this demographic boom is matched by a significant change in ceramic style, it is explained by migration (Diachenko 2016a:187). There are two fundamental problems with this model. The first is the abovementioned unquestioned equivalence of pots (pottery phases) to people, and the second is the irreconcilable disparity of the data (e.g., the different resolution of the geophysical plans, despite Diachenko's attempt to mitigate it). Even if we accept Diachenko's model, suggesting population pressure and migration as a probable cause for the appearance of megasites, it does not explain the reasons behind the alleged demographic growth and people's mobility.

It is indeed tempting to refer the emergence of such large settlement formations to existing historical examples, where polycentric and dispersed settlement patterns converged into one large center (e.g., Birch and Williamson 2013; Scarre 2013), which is the underlying logic of Diachenko's model. For the Trypillia case, that would require a difficult shift in fieldwork agenda moving from the currently favored unit of investigation—

the *ploshchadka*—to more targeted intrasite, intersite, regional, and interregional surveys (for best practice, see Raczky this volume) that are now the exception rather than the rule. In the current state of research, I can offer only some more general observations.

The megasites are unique agglomerations in European prehistory. The ancestral settlement pattern—if we accept the Balkan roots of the Cucuteni-Trypillia network—is very different (Chapman 2019; see also Raczky this volume). It is also very important to underline that the great majority of Cucuteni-Trypillia sites consist of many small settlements and a restricted percentage of middle-range sizes (Videiko 2013). The ratio of small, middle, and large sites in particular settlement networks depends on the sources used and the size definitions, but a ratio of 75:20:5 is an acceptable approximation (for rank-size rule, see Smith this volume). The longevity of the megasites—that currently occurs over a period of 500–700 years and features in all Trypillia phases (defined based on pottery typology) apart from the very first and very last—is an argument against external and internal threats. Otherwise, these communities would have been involved in constant conflicts—a scenario currently unsupported by the evidence. In that sense, it is perhaps more helpful to think of more positive reasons for people coming together rather than defense and warfare.

The most obvious candidates are exchange of goods, meeting friends and relatives, finding marriage partners, renegotiating the social order, and performing rituals and ceremonies (for a similar set of practices, see Fernández-Götz and Kelly this volume). There is a tendency in archaeology for such activities to be acknowledged as meaningful factors only if they are institutionalized and materialized, for example, through markets or temples (Pyburn 2008). While the structuring role of the latter should not be underestimated, it also should not be essentialized, allowing for people to gather, gossip, worship, and trade in a more informal and spontaneous manner. Such gatherings must have taken place in the Cucuteni-Trypillia network, as is evident from the widely shared material culture. It is possible that, at the turn of the fifth millennium B.C., the space for these communal happenings started to be formalized, initially perhaps for practical reasons and convenience, and later for the increased place value derived from recurrent ancestral visits. Such places may have been visited sporadically at first, as may have been the case in Nebelivka, but becoming more and more permanent as this settlement form becomes established. The catchment area of these settlements—that is, the distance at which the megasites stand out as statistical outliers compared to the vicinity of smaller sites—is currently estimated at ca. 100 kilometers (Nebbia 2016). That reconciles the apparent lack of contemporary occupation around Nebelivka with its possible role of a central place (for the specific meaning of central place, see Chapman 2017; Gaydarska 2017).

WHAT KIND OF SOCIAL PRACTICES AND ORGANIZATIONS FACILITATED THE DEVELOPMENT AND SUSTAINABILITY OF THESE SITES?

Paradoxically, the long-debated link between massive aggregation of people and increasing social complexity has never been seriously explored for Trypillia societies, although it has been acknowledged by both local and Western scholarship (e.g., Ellis 1984; Masson 1990). A further local twist is the tension between the small-scale agricultural practices characteristic of the Neolithic communities—and therefore assumed to be the subsistence base of the megasites—and the massive scale of logistical operations required at these sites. There are currently two approaches trying to mitigate this tension. The first one is breaking down the socioeconomic space to smaller, more manageable units. Kruts (1989) has suggested a kin-based aggregation that is echoed by Chapman's (2016) polyfocal model of settlement formation pivoting around assembly houses. The latter is implicated also in Müller and his colleagues' (2016a) claim for suprahousehold social organization. While this approach certainly distributes responsibilities and maintenance issues across the site and offers ways to cope with scalar stress, it still needs to address the challenge of what was the "social glue" that kept these variable entities together.

The second approach is speculating about seasonal agglomerations or cyclic pilgrimages carried out during many or most months of the year. One working hypothesis sees these large congregations as seasonal events, whereby participants bring their own supplies. Alternatively, small core populations may have occupied these sites on a permanent basis, maintaining them for either a constant stream of small group visits or less frequent stays involving much larger groups of people. Such a pattern would account for the negligible human impact caused by the megasites, which is otherwise difficult to explain.

There is yet a third possibility that may reconcile the environmental with the settlement data. Specifically, an economic system of tribute underpinned by social heterarchy, whereby distributed and regularly shifting authority assured the smooth supply of goods and services from a wider area in the megasite-centered networks. A heterarchical model could account for the social cohesion formalized, symbolized, and maintained by the creation and proliferation of these remarkable sites.

These three possibilities would be underlined by very different modes of operation, although certain social practices (e.g., structured deposition or house burning) would have been germane to all three types of occupation. Until a coherent model—well supported by all lines of evidence—is presented, any discussion about the social practices and organizations that facilitated the development and sustainability of these sites will be highly speculative and misleading. Paradoxically, the only approach favored so far (e.g., Chapman 2016; Kruts 1989; Müller et al. 2016b) fails to answer these questions as it addresses the *how* (e.g., kin-based), but not the *why*. The other two approaches are not only heretical in terms of the local archaeological tradition but they advocate forms of social relations hitherto unexplored and/or unknown in the evidential data of the prehistory of East Europe (for a positive rejuvenation of old models and new data, see Fernández-Götz this volume). This, however, should not be a reason for their rejection before serious consideration.

In all three hypotheses, the megasites were emerging forms of aggregation and, as such, resilience (of old traditions) as well as support (for the new form) would have characterized their initial existence. The overall size[4] and density of structures[5]—both gradually increasing with time—may reflect rising recognition of the importance of places for large gatherings, where more and more people committed to the advantages and disadvantages of living together in huge numbers, relative to the "norm." Such commitments would have had a different form if the sites had been seasonally or permanently occupied, or if resource procurement had been local as opposed to traded or brought in. In a recent article, Chapman (2017) has demonstrated how the same set of evidence—and by extension social practices—can be used for two diametrically opposed interpretations. Thus, in the current state of research, what is more important for the Trypillia megasites is a concrete suggestion for the overarching social formation, without, of course, losing sight of the social practices underpinning this formation.

LONG-TERM SOCIOCULTURAL INFLUENCE OF POPULATION AGGREGATION

If longevity is in any way informative about preferences and choices that people have made in the past, then the long-lasting recurrence of sites more than 100 times larger than the average settlement form is a clear indication of the importance of these sites. Fifteen to twenty generations of Trypillia people would have either known of or participated in the creation and maintenance of what were ultimately large gathering places. Whatever the function of these places, they were sought out and highly appreciated, as is evident from their perpetual appearance. The megasites became a monumental part of the *habitus* of Trypillia people.

Such claim puts the question of their disappearance in a very different light from the current, predominantly external causations, such as conflicts or resource depletion. The Trypillia network continued for some 200 years or so after the abandonment of the last megasites. Interestingly, this is also the period when formal burial grounds started to feature more prominently (Topal and Tserna 2010). Another factor that may have some bearing on the shift away from megasites that has been much overlooked is that there were regions in the Trypillia area—predominantly in modern Romania—in which such a settlement form was never known. In other words, there were communities that were never convinced of, or even were actively rejecting, the rationale behind the formation of megasites—a sentiment that may have become more common in the dynamically changing world of the late fourth millennium B.C.

In practical terms, if the megasites had been permanently occupied, their abandonment would have resulted in population dispersal, but far less so if they had been visited seasonally. Neither scenario has been explored so far. In terms of social cohesion, however, this settlement form had outlived its usefulness. Perhaps it is not a coincidence that the latest stages of the Cucuteni-Trypillia network are characterized by the greatest diversity of material culture, usually identified as subvariants and groups; currently, nine such entities are claimed for the Late Trypillia communities (Topal and Tserna 2010). The millennia-held worldviews underpinned by the proliferation of broadly similar material culture (Chapman and Gaydarska 2018) were challenged, leading to the gradual abandonment of the megasites in favor of a very different way of life. This area of the forest steppe remained under less permanent occupation for centuries to come.

The lack of a legacy for the megasites formed the perception of these sites for a very long time as an isolated, though important, episode of decentralized, nonhierarchical human aggregation. It is about time that these assumed, rather than argued, characteristics are teased out and, whatever the outcome, they need to be discussed in the local Trypillia context, but also in terms of their implications for global settlement trajectories.

There are at least two issues here that need further exploration. The first one feeds into the old debate about the inevitability of tiers and hierarchy in structures of power that—despite some strong voices questioning this premise (e.g., Crumley 1995; Kienlin 2010)—is still very much the dominant assertion in archaeology (Thurston 2010). Thus, if complex societies are always stratified and, by implication, egalitarian communities are anything but complex, it raises the question: Exactly what are they? Space prevents us from a deeper deconstruction of the increasing unhelpfulness of the term *complex society* (but see Moore 2017), and its equation to hierarchical structure of power (see Souvatzi 2007; Thurston 2010). Suffice it to ask the question: How would nearly 1,500 houses be built, 1,000 pits and a 5.8 kilometers long ditch dug forming an overall consistent plan with multiple internal variability without control, consensus, and negotiation. And consequently, how can we claim that such social relations were pertinent to only stratified societies?

Alternatively, we need to address the second issue, namely, that Trypillia societies were ranked, but that such differentiation is not materialized. The problem here is not that Trypillia communities could have been stratified, but how to identify this social order in the archaeological record. Decades of excavations at Talianky and Maidanetske have revealed little differences between find assemblages in burnt structures, there are very few formal burials to be representative of the entire network, and monumentality remains bitterly debated—that is to say, at first sight, the conventional factors for recognition of social differentiation have been exhausted even if other criteria exist.

One such is the creation of assembly houses much larger than usual domestic dwellings. The only so far fully excavated one is probably the largest fourth-millennium structure in Europe—hence the term *megastructure* (Chapman et al. 2014c)—yielded far fewer artifacts than we anticipated. Yet, three types of finds stand out: a gold hair ornament, 20 clay tokens/counters, and a set of 21 miniature vessels. These finds—in combination with the very unusual size and spatial layout of the megastructure—may be informative for the architectural and artifactual arrangements facilitating a space for negotiation and/or public meetings and/or ceremonies and worship. There are 21 other assembly houses in Nebelivka that may have held similar roles.

Another feature to consider in this regard is the empty space in the middle of the site. Whatever activities took place in this space, the houses of the first circuit would always have had more direct access (e.g., to goods and services) or direct exposure (e.g., to noise, bad smells), in comparison to the houses of the second circuit. Control of access and movement has social dimensions (see Harrison and Bilgen this volume), as well as the spatial variability on the level of neighborhoods and quarters.

Yet, a third possibility is the ratio of burnt and unburnt structures that stands at 2:1 in Nebelivka. Hundreds of years of experience have assured that if the aim of a fire was complete burning down of a house, it was achieved in a spectacular manner (Johnston et al. 2019). Why, then, were almost one-third of the houses in Nebelivka not burnt in the same way? Was it because there were not that many helpers from the community to collect the necessary fuel, or was it because these households were not allowed to have a spectacle of such intensity?

These are just a few of the many avenues along which the search for social differentiation can be performed. The fact that the megasites did not have a lasting legacy should not prevent us from exploring those avenues.

Are the Megasites a Hitherto Unrecognized Urban Form?

Looking at the plan in Figure 8.6, an obvious tension appears between the large, ordered, possibly preplanned space and the environmental data showing low to moderate human impact, on one hand, and between the megasites and the presumed Neolithic character—which in this part of the world means small, sedentary, egalitarian, farming communities—of the Cucuteni-Trypillia society on the other hand. Since this tension came to light as a result of the new investigations, such as high-precision geophysics and pollen coring, a reference to preceding arguments in the settlement-giants versus prototowns debate is not really profitable.

Starting with the first tension, we need to raise the possibility of subsistence strategies and woodland management that would have produced less impact on the environment. The longevity of this settlement form suggests that any experience gathered during the construction, habitation, and abandonment of earlier megasites may have been fed into the planning and organization of later megasites. One possibility is less permanent occupation, another one is a socioeconomic system whereby procurement of cereal-based food and wood is outsourced. Neither of these two possibilities has ever been explored due to the second tension mentioned above—that is, the presumed Neolithic organization of these communities. This issue taps into a much larger debate of evolutionary development, where stages of human development have regularly been matched by appropriate sets of socioeconomic practices and corresponding settlement patterns (Childe 1950; Kristiansen and Earle 2015; Service 1962). Space prevents us from a full engagement in this debate here; suffice to point the very obvious fact that setting the Trypillia megasites within the "Neolithic package" (Chapman 2019) has hindered their unbiased critical assessment.

I have argued elsewhere that *urban* is an unhelpful term and in its narrow evolutionary understanding will never accommodate the Trypillia megasites (Gaydarska 2016, 2017). A relational approach, however, would make them stand out in comparison to both contemporary and preceding settlements in the region as well as in the global development of settlement trajectories. In that sense, there is no evidence to suggest that they operated, or indeed were perceived, as any other contemporary site, only bigger. On the contrary, the scale of operation at these vast sites made them distinctively different among the sea of smaller sites. Whether social practices toward aggregation at this scale were operationalized once or twice a year for a relatively short time or were more permanent but underpinned by an extended procurement network remains to be explored. In either case, the socioeconomic organization and the accompanying settlement pattern had hitherto been unprecedented not only locally but across prehistoric Europe as well. They would have required very different day-to-day practices as compared to the average Neolithic settlement. The overall planning and maintenance of the megasites also would have been incomparable with similar activities on small-scale sites. As such, anyone trying to argue that these sites are overgrown examples of otherwise typical Neolithic lifeways will need appropriate arguments that are currently lacking in the discussions of the nature of the megasites.

What is more likely is that we are faced with an emerging and then persisting settlement form trying to accommodate tradition and innovation. Modern scholars have overwhelmingly paid attention to the tradition (seen as proliferation of similar material culture) and repeatedly underplayed the role of innovation (e.g., formalization of the gathering of large numbers of people or employment of flexible subsistence strategies), not least because the megasites did not survive and evolve in what we now called "first cities." As a result, we are only now in a position to start compiling data to substantiate the claim that these sites may qualify as Europe's first cities. Such a claim is based on the abovementioned relational difference of these sites, a difference that from the Bronze Age onward is readily associated with urban life (Rothman 2001). In other words, social organization that addresses scalar stress for large numbers of people—caused by logistics, supply, waste management, and other matters—is known almost entirely from urban centers, and is spatially negotiated by the nested units of neighborhoods and quarters (Smith 2003).

CONCLUSIONS

The Trypillia megasites are the largest settlements in fourth-millennium B.C. Europe. They are continuously seen as the exceptions that prove the rule as far as global settlement development is concerned (e.g., Liverani 2013:171). Coupled with the obvious methodological difficulty of how to study effectively units of such size, it has resulted in the complacent view that, apart from extent, there is nothing out of the ordinary about these sites. And although size matters (Cowgill 2004), in this instance, it has been trivialized to dry—and in some cases inflated—demographic figures with little appreciation of the economic consequences (e.g., Kruts 1989; Ohlrau et al. 2016), but none whatsoever of the social implications of gatherings of such magnitude.

The internationalization of Trypillia studies in the last decade has confirmed some long-held insights—for example, the concentric spatial organization of the megasites—while it has also challenged a series of assumptions stemming from the unquestioned premise of rotational migration—for example, the exaggerated scale of human impact on available resources. As a result of the new investigations, a tipping point has been reached (Chapman 2016) that made untenable the free reign of claims for tens of thousands of people (up to 46,000) living together in a basically Neolithic way.

Three alternatives have been suggested for further exploration in regard to the emergence and social roles of the Trypillia megasites: (1) seasonal occupation characterized by forms of social practices (e.g., house burning, pit digging), which already had been important on smaller, permanent sites, but whose roles were transformed by scalar processes on megasites, as well as other practices confined to megasites (e.g., restocking diminishing goods, finding a marriage partner); (2) pilgrimage sites visited cyclically by large number of people or constantly by small groups of people, where at stake was the successful renegotiation of the Trypillia world order; and (3) permanent occupation introducing a novel social network relationship, that of a tribute system underpinned by a distributed heterarchical form of authority. In the traditional concept of urbanism (Childe 1950; Ucko et al. 1972), the activities that took place in scenarios (1) and (2) would be very similar to those usually associated with the urban settlement form, such as exchange of goods and services, craft production, and renegotiation of social order. However, following this trait list would trap us in an evolutionary essentialism, and very soon will ensure that Trypillia megasites fall short of the necessary criteria.

An alternative approach—better fit to embrace the variety of evidence—is a relational framework that credits equal importance for local contexts as well as for global trends. In this framework, different categories of sites coemerge in relation to each other (Gaydarska 2016, 2017), and what we now call "urban" can only make sense not in absolute terms but against a backdrop of preceding and contemporary settlements. Thus, Trypillia megasites were the first European cities because they were massive and long-lasting projects markedly different from anything known till then and standing out from a mass of smaller sites, whose success was predicated on multifaceted cohesive power.

ACKNOWLEDGMENTS

I would like to thank Attila Gyucha for his invitation to participate in the 9th IEMA Conference, to Peter Biehl for the imaginative and diverse postconference activities, and of course to my fellow participants for the inspirational and stimulating talks and discussions. I am also grateful to John Chapman and Marco Nebbia for the support and endless discussions of the issues raised above. Also, I thank Yvonne Beadnell, Marco Nebbia, Joe Roe, and the Archaeological Services Durham University for their help in the illustrations of this chapter.

NOTES

1.   The wider-known name Tripolye is the Russian equivalent of the Ukrainian name Trypillia.
2.   A common feature in Russian and Ukrainian literature is the discussion of *ploshchadka* rather than house. The fact that the former is the physical remains and the latter is its social counterpart remains, to my knowledge, unrecognized.
3.   The final manuscript of this chapter was submitted on June 28, 2016.
4.   Although the largest megasite of Talianky (320 hectares) is not the latest in the sequence, the trend is toward size increase (Diachenko 2016b).
5.   Only two megasites—Nebelivka and Talianky—fall outside of this trajectory (Diachenko 2016b).

REFERENCES CITED

Albert, B., J. Innes, K. Kremenetskiy, A. Millard, B. Gaydarska, M. Nebbia, and J. Chapman
2019 What Was the Ecological Impact of a Trypillia Mega-Site Occupation? Multi-Proxy Palaeo-Environmental Investigations at Nebelivka, Ukraine. Submitted to *Vegetation History and Archaeobotany.*

Anthony, D. W. 2007 *The Horse, the Wheel, and the Language: How Bronze Age Riders from the Eurasian Steppes Shaped the Modern World.* Princeton University Press, Princeton, New Jersey.

Anthony, D. W. 2013 Review of *The Tripolye Culture Giant-Settlements in Ukraine: Formation, Development and Decline*, edited by F. Menotti and A. Korvin-Piotrovskiy. *Antiquity* 87(338):1233–1235.

Birch, J., and R. F. Williamson 2013 Organizational Complexity in Ancestral Wendat Communities. In *From Prehistoric Villages to Cities: Settlement Aggregation and Community Transformation*, edited by J. Birch, pp. 153–178. Routledge, New York.

Chapman, J. 2016 Can We Reconcile Seasonal Dwelling with Urban Settlements? A Close Look at the Trypillia Megasite of Nebelivka. Paper presented at the conference entitled "First Cities"—An Exploration of Early Cities in Europe and Asia, Durham.

Chapman, J. 2017 The Standard Model, the Maximalists, and the Minimalists: New Interpretations of Trypillia Megasites. *Journal of World Prehistory* 30(3):221–237.

Chapman, J. 2019 *Forging Identities in Balkan Prehistory: Dividuals, Individual and Communities 7000–3000 BC.* Cambridge University Press, Cambridge. In press.

Chapman, J., and B. Gaydarska 2018 The Cucuteni—Trypillia 'Big Other'—Reflections on the Making of Millennial Cultural Traditions. In *Between History and Archaeology: Papers in Honour of Jacek Lech*, edited by D. H. Werra and M. Woźny, pp. 267–277. Archaeopress, Oxford.

Chapman, J., M. Videiko, B. Gaydarska, N. Burdo, D. Hale, R. Villis, N. Swann, N. Thomas, P. Edwards, A. Blair, A. Hayes, M. Nebbia, and V. Rud 2014a The Planning of the Earliest European Proto-Towns: A New Geophysical Plan of the Trypillia Mega-Site of Nebelivka, Kirovograd Domain, Ukraine. *Antiquity Gallery.* Electronic document: http://antiquity.ac.uk.ezphost.dur.ac.uk/projgall/chapman339/.

Chapman, J., M. Videiko, D. Hale, B. Gaydarska, N. Burdo, K. Rassmann, C. Mischka, J. Müller, A. Korvin-Piotrovskiy, and V. Kruts 2014b The Second Phase of the Trypillia Mega-Site Methodological Revolution: A New Research Agenda. *European Journal of Archaeology* 17(3):369–406.

Chapman, J., M. Videiko, B. Gaydarska, N. Burdo, and D. Hale 2014c Architectural Differentiation on a Trypillia Mega-Site: Preliminary Report on the Excavation of a Mega-Structure at Nebelivka, Ukraine. *Journal of Neolithic Archaeology* 16:135–157.

Childe, V. G. 1945 Tripil's'ka Kultura. *Antiquity* 19(76):203–206.

Childe, V. G. 1950 The Urban Revolution. *The Town Planning Review* 21(1):3–17.

Cowgill, G. 2004 Origins and Development of Urbanism: Archaeological Perspectives. *Annual Review of Anthropology* 33:525–549.

Crumley, C. L. 1995 Heterarchy and the Analysis of Complex Societies. In *Heterarchy and the Analysis of Complex Societies*, edited by C. L. Crumley and J. E. Levy, pp. 1–5. Archaeological Papers of the American Anthropological Association 6. American Anthropological Association, Washington, D.C.

de Vries, J. 1984 *European Urbanization 1500–1800.* Routledge, London.

Diachenko, A. 2010 Evstaticheskie kolebaniya urovnya Chernogo morya i dinamika razvitiya naseleniya Kukuten-Tripolskoj obshchnosti. *Stratum plus* 2:37–48.

Diachenko, A. 2016a Demography Reloaded. In *Trypillia Mega-Sites and European Prehistory 4100–3400 BCE*, edited by J. Müller, K. Rassmann, and M. Videiko, pp. 181–194. Themes in Contemporary Archaeology 2. Routledge, London.

Diachenko, A. 2016b Small Is Beautiful: A Democratic Perspective? In *Trypillia Mega-Sites and European Prehistory 4100–3400 BCE*, edited by J. Müller, K. Rassmann, and M. Videiko, pp. 269–280. Themes in Contemporary Archaeology 2. Routledge, London.

Diachenko, A., and F. Menotti 2012 The Gravity Model: Monitoring the Formation and Development of the Tripolye Culture Giant-Settlements in Ukraine. *Journal of Archaeological Science* 39(4):2810–2817.

Diachenko, A., and F. Menotti 2017 Proto-Cities or Non-Proto-Cities: On the Nature of Cucuteni–Trypillia Mega-Sites. *Journal of World Prehistory* 30(3):207–219.

Earle, T., and K. Kristiansen 2010 Organizing Bronze Age Societies: Concluding Thoughts. In *Organizing Bronze Age Societies: The Mediterranean, Central Europe, and Scandinavia Compared*, edited by T. Earle and K. Kristiansen, pp. 218–256. Cambridge University Press, Cambridge.

Ellis, L. 1984 *The Cucuteni-Tripolye Culture: A Study of Technology and Origins of Complex Society*. BAR International Series 217. British Archaeological Reports, Oxford.

Fletcher, R. 1995 *The Limits of Settlement Growth: A Theoretical Outline*. Cambridge University Press, Cambridge.

Gaydarska, B. 2015 Poseleniya-giganti ili proto-goroda: oshibochnoe protivopostavlenie. In *The Cucuteni-Tripolye Cultural Complex and Its Neighbours: Essays in Memory of Volodymyr Kruts*, edited by A. Diachenko, F. Menotti, S. Ryzhov, K. Bunyatyan, and S. Kadrow, pp. 35–56. Astrolabe, Lviv.

Gaydarska, B. 2016 The City Is Dead! Long Live the City! *Norwegian Archaeological Review* 49(1): 40–57.

Gaydarska, B. 2017 Introduction: European Prehistory and Urban Studies. *Journal of World Prehistory* 30(2):1–12.

Gaydarska, B., and J. Chapman 2016 Nine Questions for Trypillia Megasites Research. In *Professor Boris Borisov—Friends and Students. Studia in honorem professoris Borisi Borisov*, edited by B. Borisov, pp. 179–197. Veliko Turnovo University St. Cyril and St. Methodius and Bulgarian Archaeology 2. IVIS, Veliko Turnovo.

Johnston, S., V. Litkevych, A. Diachenko, B. Gaydarska, P. Voke, M. Nebbia, and J. Chapman 2019 The Nebelivka Experimental House Construction and House-Burning, 2014–2015. In *Alternative Approaches to House Studies*, edited by M. Spasić. Belgrade City Museum, Belgrade. In press.

Kienlin, T. 2010 *Traditions and Transformations: Approaches to Eneolithic (Copper Age) and Bronze Age Metalworking and Society in Eastern Central Europe and the Carpathian Basin*. BAR International Series 2184. Archaeopress, Oxford.

Kirleis, W., and M. Dal Corso 2016 Trypillian Subsistence Economy: Animal and Plant Exploitation. In *Trypillia Mega-Sites and European Prehistory 4100–3400 BCE*, edited by J. Müller, K. Rassmann, and M. Videiko, pp. 196–206. Themes in Contemporary Archaeology 2. Routledge, London.

Kohl, P. 2002 Archaeological Transformations: Crossing the Pastoral/Agricultural Bridge. *Iranica Antiqua* 37:151–190.

Korvin-Piotrovskiy, A. G. 2003 Teoreticheskie problemy issledovanij poselinij-gigantov. In *Tripolian Settlements-Giants: The International Symposium Materials*, edited by V. A. Kruts, A. G. Korvin-Piotrovskiy, and S. M. Ryzhov, pp. 5–7. Korvin Press, Kiev.

Korvin-Piotrovskiy, A. G., V. Chabaniuk, and L. Shatilo 2012 Tripolian House Construction: Conceptions and Experiments. In *The Tripolye Culture Giant-Settlements in Ukraine: Formation, Development and Decline*, edited by F. Menotti and A. G. Korvin-Piotrovskiy, pp. 210–229. Oxbow Books, Oxford.

Korvin-Piotrovskiy, A., R. Hofmann, K. Rassmann, M. Videiko, and L. Brandtstätter 2016 Pottery Kilns in Trypillian Settlements: Tracing the Division of Labour and the Social Organization of Copper Age Communities. In *Trypillia Mega-Sites and European Prehistory 4100–3400 BCE*, edited by J. Müller, K. Rassmann, and M. Videiko, pp. 221–252. Themes in Contemporary Archaeology 2. Routledge, London.

Kristiansen, K., and T. Earle 2015 Neolithic versus Bronze Age Formations: A Political Economy Approach. In *Paradigm Found: Archaeological Theory—Present, Past, and Future. Essays in Honour of Evžen Neustupný*, edited by K. Kristiansen, L. Šmejda, and J. Turek, pp. 234–247. Oxbow Books, Oxford and Philadelphia.

Kruts, V. A. 1989 K istorii naseleniya tripolskoj kultury v mezhdurechye Yuzhnogo Buga i Dnepra. In *Pervobytnaya Archeologiya: Materialy i Issledovaniya*, edited by S. S. Berezanskaya, pp. 117–132. Naukova Dumka, Kyiv.

Kruts, V. A. 2003 Tripolskie ploshchadki—rezultat ritualnogo sozhzheniya domov. In *Tripolian Settlements-Giants: The International Symposium Materials*, edited by V. A. Kruts, A. G. Korvin-Piotrovskiy, and S. M. Ryzhov, pp. 74–76. Korvin Press, Kiev.

Lazarovici, C.-M. 2010 New Data Regarding the Chronology of the Precucuteni, Cucuteni, and Horodiştea-Erbiceni Cultures. In *PANTHA REI: Studies on the Chronology and Cultural Development of South-Eastern and Central Europe in Earlier Prehistory Presented to Juraj Pavúk on the Occasion of His 75th Birthday*, edited by J. Šuteková, P. Pavúk, P. Kálabková, and B. Kovár, pp. 71–94. Studia Archaeologica et Mediaevalia 11. Comenius University, Bratislava.

Liverani, M. 2013 Power and Citizenship. In *The Oxford Handbook of Cities in World History*, edited by P. Clark, pp. 164–180. Oxford University Press, Oxford.

Mantu, C.-M., Gh. Dumitroaia, and A. Tsaravopoulos (editors) 1997 *Cucuteni: The Last Great Chalcolithic Civilization of Europe*. Athena, Thessaloniki.

Manzura, I. V. 2005 Severnoe Prichernomorje v eneolite i nachale bronzovogo veka. *Stratum plus* 2:63–85.

Masson, V. M. 1990 Tripolskoe obshchestvo i ego sotsialno-ekonomicheskie charakteristiki. In *Rannezemledelcheskie poseleniya-giganty tripolskoj kultury na Ukraine: Tezisy dokladov pervogo polevogo seminara*, edited by V. G. Zbenovich, pp. 8–10. Institute of Archaeology of the AS of the USSR, Talianki.

Menotti, F., and A. Korvin-Piotrovskiy (editors) 2012 *The Tripolye Culture Giant-Settlements in Ukraine: Formation, Development and Decline*. Oxbow Books, Oxford.

Millard, A., J. Chapman, M. Nebbia, and B. Gaydarska 2019 Dating Nebelivka: Too Many Houses, Too Little Time. In *Early Urbanism in Europe: The Case of the Trypillia Mega-Sites*, edited by B. Gaydarska. In press.

Moore, T. 2017 Alternatives to Urbanism? Reconsidering *Oppida* and the Urban Question in Late Iron Age Europe. *Journal of World Prehistory* 30(3):281–300.

Müller, J., R. Hofmann, L. Brandtstätter, R. Ohlrau, and M. Videiko 2016a Chronology and Demography: How Many People Lived in a Mega-Site? In *Trypillia Mega-Sites and European*

Prehistory 4100–3400 BCE, edited by J. Müller, K. Rassmann, and M. Videiko, pp. 133–170. Themes in Contemporary Archaeology 2. Routledge, London.

Müller, J., R. Hofmann, and R. Ohlrau 2016b From Domestic Households to Mega-Structures: Proto-Urbanism? In *Trypillia Mega-Sites and European Prehistory 4100–3400 BCE*, edited by J. Müller, K. Rassmann, and M. Videiko, pp. 253–268. Themes in Contemporary Archaeology 2. Routledge, London.

Müller, J., and M. Videiko 2016 Maidanetske: New Facts of a Mega-Site. In *Trypillia Mega-Sites and European Prehistory 4100–3400 BCE*, edited by J. Müller, K. Rassmann, and M. Videiko, pp. 71–94. Themes in Contemporary Archaeology 2. Routledge, London.

Nebbia, M. 2016 *Early Cities or Mega-Villages? Settlements Dynamics in the Trypillia Culture, Ukraine*. PhD dissertation, Department of Archaeology, Durham University, Durham.

Ohlrau, R., M. Dal Corso, W. Kirleis, and J. Müller 2016 Living on the Edge? Carrying Capacities of Trypillian Settlements in the Buh-Dnipro Interfluve. In *Trypillia Mega-Sites and European Prehistory 4100–3400 BCE*, edited by J. Müller, K. Rassmann, and M. Videiko, pp. 207–220. Themes in Contemporary Archaeology 2. Routledge, London.

Pyburn, K. A. 2008 Pomp and Circumstance before Belize: Ancient Maya Commerce and the New River Conurbation. In *The Ancient City: New Perspectives on Urbanism in the Old and New World*, edited by J. Marcus and J. A. Sabloff, pp. 247–272. School for Advanced Research Press, Santa Fe, New Mexico.

Rassamakin, Yu. 2012 Absolute Chronology of Ukrainian Tripolian Settlements. In *The Tripolye Culture Giant-Settlements in Ukraine: Formation, Development and Decline*, edited by F. Menotti and A. Korvin-Piotrovskiy, pp. 19–69. Oxbow Books, Oxford.

Rassamakin, Yu., and F. Menotti 2011 Chronological Development of the Tripolye Culture Giant-Settlement of Talianki (Ukraine): 14C Dating vs. Pottery Typology. *Radiocarbon* 53(4):645–657.

Rassmann, K., A. Korvin-Piotrovskiy, M. Videiko, and J. Müller 2016 The New Challenge for Site Plans and Geophysics: Revealing the Settlement Structure of Giant Settlements by Means of Geomagnetic Survey. In *Trypillia Mega-Sites and European Prehistory 4100–3400 BCE*, edited by J. Müller, K. Rassmann, and M. Videiko, pp. 29–54. Themes in Contemporary Archaeology 2. Routledge, London.

Rassmann, K., R. Ohlrau, R. Hofmann, C. Mischka, N. Burdo, M. Videiko, and J. Müller 2014 High Precision Tripolye Settlement Plans, Demographic Estimations, and Settlement Organization. *Journal of Neolithic Archaeology* 16:97–134.

Rothman, M. S. (editor) 2001 *Uruk Mesopotamia and Its Neighbors: Cross-Cultural Interactions in the Era of State Formation*. School for Advanced Research Press, Santa Fe, New Mexico.

Ryzhov, S. 2012 Relative Chronology of the Giant-Settlement Period BII–CI. In *The Tripolye Culture Giant-Settlements in Ukraine: Formation, Development and Decline*, edited by F. Menotti and A. Korvin-Piotrovskiy, pp. 79–115. Oxbow Books, Oxford.

Scarre, C. 2013 Social Stratification and the State in Prehistoric Europe: The Wider Perspective. In *The Prehistory of Iberia: Debating Early Social Stratification and the State*, edited by M. Cruz Berrocal, L. García Sanjuán, and A. Gilman, pp. 381–405. Routledge, London.

Service, E. 1962 *Primitive Social Organization: An Evolutionary Perspective*. Random House, New York.

Shmaglij, N. M. 2001 *Veliki Trypil'ski poselenia i problema rannih form urbanizatsii*. Kyiv.

Smith, M. E. 2010 The Archaeological Study of Neighborhoods and Districts in Ancient Cities. *Journal of Anthropological Archaeology* 29(2):137–154.

Smith, M. L. (editor) 2003 *The Social Construction of Ancient Cities*. Smithsonian Books, Washington, D.C.

Souvatzi, S. 2007 Social Complexity Is not the Same as Hierarchy. In *Socialising Complexity: Structure, Interaction, and Power in Archaeological Discourse*, edited by S. Kohring and S. Wynne-Jones, pp. 37–59. Oxbow Books, Oxford.

Thurston, T. 2010 Bitter Arrows and Generous Gifts: What Was a "King" in the European Iron Age? In *Pathways to Power: New Perspectives on the Emergence of Social Inequality*, edited by T. D. Price and G. M. Feinman, pp. 193–254. Springer, New York.

Topal, D. A., and S. V. Tserna 2010 A Cemetery and Settlements of the Late Tripolye Culture near the Village of Cunicea (Floreşti District, Republic of Moldova). *Stratum plus* 2:281–298.

Ucko, P. J., R. Tringham, and G. W. Dimbleby (editors) 1972 *Man, Settlement, and Urbanism*. Duckworth, Cambridge.

Videiko, M. Yu. 1996 Die Großsiedlungen der Tripol'e-Kultur in der Ukraine. *Eurasia Antiqua* 1:45–80.

Videiko, M. Yu. 2002 *Trypilski protomista: Istoriya doslidzen*. Akademperiodyka, Kyiv.

Videiko, M. Yu. 2004 *Entsiklopediya Tripil'skoi tsivilizatsii*. Ukrpoligrafmedia, Kyiv.

Videiko, M. Yu. 2013 *Kompleksnoe izuchenie krupnykh poselenij Tripolskoj kultury V–IV tys. do n.e.* Lambert Academic, Saarbrücken.

Zbenovich, V. G. 1990 K probleme krupnyh tripolskih poselenij. In *Rannezemledelcheskie poseleniya-giganty tripolskoj kultury na Ukraine: Tezisy dokladov pervogo polevogo seminara*, edited by V. G. Zbenovich, pp. 10–12. Institute of Archaeology of the AS of the USSR, Talianki.

CHAPTER NINE

Emergent Urbanism

Trade, Settlement, and Society at Seyitömer Höyük in Early Bronze Age Western Anatolia

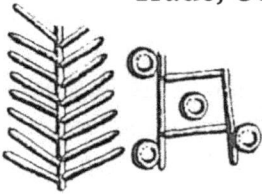

Laura K. Harrison and A. Nejat Bilgen

Abstract *The Early Bronze Age III period (EBIII, ca. 2300–2000 B.C.) witnesses urbanization in western Anatolia and societal collapse in the Aegean. Archaeological studies of these processes often operate at the regional and macroregional scales, and do not address the impact of these changes on social relations at the local scale. Seyitömer Höyük is an EBIII urban settlement that is located in the inland western Anatolia region, at a crossroad between the Aegean and Syro-Cilicia. It maintained trade relationships with both regions in EBIII, and managed to sustain itself amid shifting regional trajectories of urbanization and disintegration. This chapter investigates social interaction among individuals and communities at Seyitömer Höyük at the local scale, with an integrative analysis of the built environment that incorporates observations from space syntax analysis and nonverbal communication. This perspective demonstrates that local actors used vernacular architecture to create contexts for various types of public and private occasions. The deliberate attempts to shape movement and interaction in space created a reciprocal relationship between human actors and the built environment, and promoted the maintenance of community integrity during a period of upheaval in western Anatolia.*

INTRODUCTION

The relationship between urbanization and long-distance trade in Early Bronze Age III (EBIII, ca. 2300–2000 B.C.) western Anatolia and the Aegean is poorly understood, although both factors are tightly intertwined. In the Aegean EBIII, maritime trade routes fall out of use, settlements are abandoned, and deurbanization takes hold (Kouka 2013; Rutter 1983, 1984). Western Anatolia, on the other hand, continues to experience urbanization and population growth during the same period, and expands its role in interregional trade by engaging with societies in the Aegean and Syro-Cilicia, in Southeast Anatolia (Fidan et al. 2015; Mellink 1986:151).

Our understanding of urbanization in this context is based primarily on surveys carried out at the regional scale that gloss over local details. Often, these studies investigate processes of population nucleation through settlement size analyses (e.g., Çevik 2007), or focus on the development and spread of iconic architectural styles using functional and typological approaches (e.g., Shaw 1987; Warner 1979, 1994; Werner 1993). These studies are useful in establishing a general understanding of trajectories of urbanization and dispersal as well as summarizing typical architectural characteristics. They do not, however, adequately address specific ways in which the built environment of urban settlements impacts socialization among institutions, elites, and nonelites, or how these interactions engender conflict or promote the maintenance of community integrity at the local scale.

In this chapter, we address the recursive relationship between architecture and power at the EBIII settlement of Seyitömer Höyük located in inland western Anatolia (Figure 9.1). In addition to its role as a crossroad of trade and exchange, Seyitömer Höyük is

FIGURE 9.1. Map of the eastern Mediterranean, with regions and sites mentioned in the text.

important because it managed to sustain itself during a period of shifting trade alliances and volatile regional trajectories of urbanization and collapse that lasted from approximately 2250 to 2150 B.C. (Harrison 2017). We suggest that interplay between individualizing and communal activities strengthened horizontal bonds among social groups and, at the same time, spurred an increase in hierarchical sociopolitical organization. Interplay between these top-down and bottom-up social relations fostered a complex web of social interdependency that promoted the maintenance of community integrity. From this perspective, architecture can be seen an embodiment of social relations that contains a wide range of nonverbal cues created through human agency. These nonverbal cues, which include moveable artifacts, architecture, and spatial layout, impact the formality of social interaction in public and private spaces. In certain spaces, architecture is mobilized as an instrument of hierarchical power, and in others, it becomes an integrative medium of community building. Below, we investigate these issues with an integrative approach adapted from Fisher (2009, 2013), which combines quantitative observations about architecture with quantitative observations about movement and interaction in space.

Urbanization in EBIII Western Anatolia and the Aegean

Settlement Patterns

The trajectories of sociopolitical development in the Early Bronze Age Aegean and western Anatolia diverge in EBIII (Figure 9.2). The Aegean, which reaches its apex of sociopolitical complexity in EBIIb, subsequently falls into a period of decline around 2200 B.C. (Forsén 1992:204–220; Renfrew 1972:533–534; Wiener 2013:584–585). A wave of destructions leaves prosperous EBII regional centers abandoned and in ruins—most notably at Lerna, where the House of the Tiles was destroyed violently (Caskey 1960; Wiencke 1989). Site hierarchies fall apart, leading to population dispersal in mainland Greece and nucleation in the Cyclades (Forsén 1992:257–258). This cultural collapse is accompanied by a decline in population, which lasts throughout EBIII (Peltenburg 2000).

In western Anatolia, a movement toward urbanization begins in the Late Chalcolithic and EBI, crystallizes in EBII, and lasts into the EBIII period (Figure 9.2), as a tendency toward fewer and larger settlements continues (Çevik 2007; Cultraro 2007; Fidan et al. 2015:74). By 2500 B.C., identifiable characteristics of early urban settlements arise—tightly packed rowhouses are arranged around a central open space and surrounded by a fortification wall (Efe 2003; Erkanal 2011; Korfmann 1983). Korfmann (1983) initially identified this type as the *"Anatolisches Siedlungsschema,"* or the "Anatolian Settlement Model," the best examples of which are found at Demircihöyük, Küllüoba, and Troy (Efe 2003; Korfmann 1983). This phenomenon, which Bachhuber (2015) refers to as the ascendance of citadels, is accompanied by a homogenization of material culture and a rise in competitive emulation. Dedeoğlu (2008:593–594) and others (Efe 2007:55; Erkanal 2011) have argued that nucleation in larger centers from EBII onward is due to changing internal dynamics. Bachhuber's recent work goes into greater detail by suggesting that the EBI–II villages of Anatolia did not directly evolve into EBIII citadels,

B.C.	Seyitömer	Troy	Demircihöyük	Küllüoba	Beyçesultan	Poliochni	Thermi	Aegina	Lerna	Aegean
1900	V-A	V								
2000	V-A									
2100	V-B	IV								
2200	V-B	III		IID-E	XII				IIID	Kastri-Lefkandi I
2300	V-C	IId-h		IIIA		Yellow		III		
2400	V-C	IIc		IIIB						
2500	V-C	IIb	Hiatus	IIIC	Hiatus			II		
2600		IIa	Q	IV-A		Red			IIIC	
2700		Id		IV-B	XIIIa		IV			
2800			O-P	IV-C	XIIIb-c					
2900			N-M		XIV					
3000										

FIGURE 9.2. Early Bronze Age chronology of Seyitömer Höyük and surrounding regions.

but rather that villages were slowly abandoned as people nucleated in larger centers. This may have been fueled by participation in large-scale communal building projects—an integrative factor also discussed by Kelly in this volume. Bachhuber also suggests that the rise of citadels in western Anatolia was accompanied by ideological transformation, as the ancestral worldview of EBI–II society was replaced in EBIII by a new type of elite ideology characterized by wealth sacrifice, cremation, and feasting in monumental citadels (Bachhuber 2015:107, 128–129). The ascension of the citadel thus represents a shift in the "social logic" of EB III settlements, with a new emphasis on architecture as an expression of elite identity in both public and private contexts.

The architectural remains of EBIII Seyitömer Höyük Phase B consist of approximately 30 megaron-type rowhouse buildings that share party walls, and are linked together with a simple street system (Figure 9.3). All of the buildings are part of a single, integrated

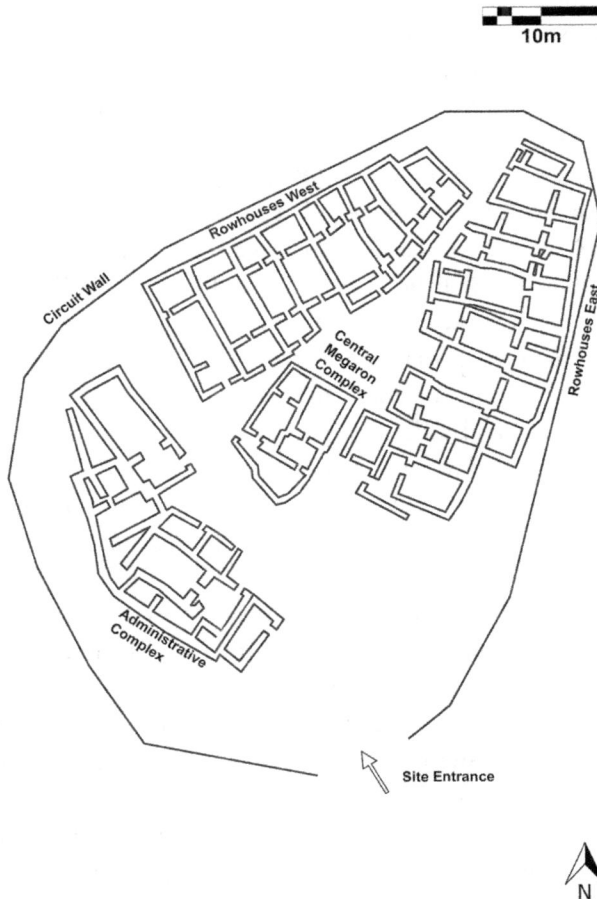

FIGURE 9.3. Plan of Seyitömer Höyük Phase B settlement.

settlement. The nonelite residential buildings—which are found in the Rowhouses East and Rowhouses West areas of the site—are arranged into semiorthogonal blocks and their rooms abut each other at right angles. These buildings share party walls, and are built according to a tripartite megaron-type plan, resulting in a rowhouse layout. Planning is evident in the consistent orientation, plan, and dimensions of residential buildings, as well as in the decision to construct a freestanding, religious building at the center of the settlement, and to locate an administrative complex at the highest topographical point on the mound (Bilgen 2011; Bilgen and Bilgen 2015; Harrison 2016). To a large extent, the archaeological remains of this settlement are consistent with broader patterns of urbanization in western Anatolia during the EBIII period.

TRADE RELATIONS

The divergent trajectories of western Anatolia and the Aegean in EBIII are evident in changes in interregional trade routes as well. In EBIIb, an influx of Anatolian material culture—known as Kastri/Lefkandi I—expands westward into the Aegean and eventually mixes with local pottery styles (Broodbank 2000:309–319; Pullen 2013; Renfrew 1972:172–174; Rutter 1979; Sotirakopoulou 1993). This coincides with an increase in the number of tin-bronze artifacts throughout the eastern Mediterranean (Şahoğlu 2005:340–344; Wiener 2013:586; Yener 2000:88–98; Yener and Vandiver 1993). In the Cyclades, the appearance of Kastri/Lefkandi I pottery has been taken as evidence for a westward migration from Anatolia that disrupted local traditions and contributed to the disappearance of Early Helladic II settlements (Caskey 1960). However, it has been argued that the presence of Anatolian-style pottery in the Aegean is the result of import or imitation rather than an actual movement of people (Broodbank 2000:309–319). By the end of EBIII, Aegean societies enter into a period of decline characterized by abandonment of key sites and a drop in population (Rahmstorf 2015:149–150; Wiener 2013:586). These changes may be a response to a climatic disturbance around 2200 B.C. (Forsén 1992:258), which is documented in ice cores and pollen records, and is considered a significant factor in societal collapse throughout the eastern Mediterranean world (Manning 1997; Staubwasser and Weiss 2006).

During the late EBIII period, the communities of inland western Anatolia shift their focus from pursuing long-distance trade with coastal regions to the west, and begin to more intensively engage in exchange with neighbors in Syro-Cilicia, to the southeast (Efe 2007; Şahoğlu 2005). A greater degree of Near Eastern influence is seen in the material culture of inland western Anatolia at this time, which suggests a more intensive exploitation of an overland trade route that traverses Central Anatolia (Efe 2007; Fidan et al. 2015:79). A key impetus for this development was an elite desire to obtain exotic trade goods. By the beginning of the Middle Bronze Age, cultural connections between the Aegean and Central Anatolia disintegrate, and each region develops more or less independently—a situation that continues relatively unchanged throughout the second millennium B.C. (Fidan et al. 2015:75).

Material culture from Phase B at Seyitömer Höyük indicates that the site was involved in trade with both the Aegean and Syro-Cilician regions at this time, and suggests it played a role in mediating indirect exchange between these areas. The coexistence of materials from both regions at the site also demonstrates that the shift from pursuing trade relations with the Aegean to Syro-Cilicia was not exclusive or immediate. Between 2009 and 2012, excavations at Seyitömer Höyük produced several *depas amphikypellon* cups, a two-handled vessel type associated with ritual drinking (Bilgen 2011; Bilgen and Kuru 2015). This artifact type is considered a marker of trade with Troy, and indicates communication between Seyitömer and the northwestern Aegean coastal region. The large number of these *depas* cups found at Seyitömer—a total of 13 objects—indicate that this contact was relatively commonplace in the EBIII period (Bilgen and Kuru 2015:2). Further evidence for contact with the Aegean world is found in the presence of an *askos* vessel of Aegean type recovered from Room 20d, a Phase B storeroom at the site (Efe and Ilasli 1997:603; Harrison 2016:452, 519). In addition, a ritual vessel deposit in the Central Megaron Complex of Phase B contains three anthropomorphic *rhyta*, whose closest stylistic parallel is the "hedgehog" vessel from the cemetery at Chalandriani on the Aegean island of Syros (Broodbank 2000:216, Figure 64). Thus, there is considerable evidence for regular contact between the Aegean and Seyitömer Höyük during the EBIII period. This data agrees with the proposed EBIII "Great Caravan Route," which stretched from the Kütahya/Eskişehir regions of inland western Anatolia to the Aegean coast (Efe 2007). In the early EBIII period, this route fed into Aegean maritime routes at coastal sites—such as Troy, Thermi, Liman Tepe, and Poliochni—and these routes were instrumental in bringing the Kastri/Lefkandi I wares westward from Anatolia to the Aegean (Kouka 2013:577; Rahmstorf 2006). The finds associated with the Aegean world from Seyitömer Höyük Phase B, therefore, fit into a broader context of overland trade that links the inland western Anatolian region with the Aegean coast in the EBIII period (Efe 2007; Fidan et al. 2015; Şahoğlu 2005).

Alongside the evidence for contact between Seyitömer Höyük and the Aegean is material culture that points to Seyitömer Höyük's trade relations with distant areas in Syro-Cilicia, during Phase B (Efe and Türkteki 2011:232; Fidan et al. 2015:81). In this respect, one of the most important finds from this site is a group of 10 cylinder seals found within a *pithos* inside a Phase B elite residence within an administrative building (Harrison 2017). In addition to being the largest group of EBIII cylinder seals found in western Anatolia, this assemblage is important because it bears stylistic ties to Akkadian types that date to approximately 2200 B.C. (Bilgen 2011:552, Resim 761; Bilgen and Bilgen 2015:163; Harrison 2016:412–415). As the foregoing discussion illustrates, the final centuries of the third millennium B.C.—the EBIII period—in inland western Anatolia were a period of urbanization that also witnessed the apex and eventual disintegration of Aegean trade relations as well as a strengthening of ties with Syro-Cilician societies. In the following section, we discuss a new framework for studying urbanism at this time in western Anatolia at the local scale. Our analysis contextualizes Seyitömer Höyük as a crossroad located at the intersection of the Aegean and Syro-Cilician worlds, and investigates how interplay between individualizing and commensal activities fostered community integrity during a period of upheaval. In doing so, we engage with concepts of space and place (Low and Lawrence-Zuniga 2003).

Urbanism as a Sociospatial Process

Past studies of urbanism in western Anatolia have successfully documented the functional, technological, economic, and stylistic attributes of canonical buildings—like the *megaron* (Werner 1993)—and settlement types—such as the *Anatolisches Siedlungsschema* (Korfmann 1983)—associated with urbanism, but they fail to articulate the specific nature of the underlying social processes responsible for their emergence and subsequent transformations. Consequently, we are left to speculate about the mutually constituting relationship between urban spatial arrangement and the integrative social mechanisms that foster urban development.

This chapter applies a modified version of Fisher's (2009) approach—which is tailored to the archaeological remains of Seyitömer Höyük Phase B—in order to better understand urban development as a sociospatial process. Our integrative approach considers architecture to be a distinctive type of material culture—a medium through which social actors communicate, manipulate, and express various social roles. This interdisciplinary approach emphasizes social action in the analysis of architecture and power, and it reveals specific ways in which human actors responded in a local context to the surrounding trajectories of sociopolitical development and decline in the third millennium B.C.

Movement and Interaction in Space: Axial and Convex Analysis

The integrative approach presented here incorporates observations from (1) environmental psychology, which examines ways in which fixed features and semifixed features in the built environment communicate nonverbal messages that influence human behavior (Rapoport 1982); (2) the field of architecture, which uses the graph-based method of space syntax to measure patterns of movement and encounter in buildings and settlements (i.e., Hillier and Hanson 1984); and (3) structuralist theories, which stress that buildings are a unique kind of material culture that play an active role in social production and reproduction rather than being a passive backdrop to social dramas (Moore 1996; Parker Pearson and Richards 1994).

Space Syntax Analysis

Space syntax analysis is a graph-based method that measures patterns of movement and interaction in urban environments and displays them graphically (Hillier and Hanson 1984). It considers each settlement to be a unique spatial system, and operates on the premise that the spatial arrangement of buildings and settlements impacts human social interaction within and around those spaces. In space syntax, the relationships between interior convex spaces and linear paths of movement are represented as nodes and lines, and their spatial relationships are analyzed according to mathematical measures of closeness, centrality, and integration. When considered in concert with anthropological concepts of social inequality, privacy, and power relations, these measures can offer insight into social interaction in the past (Hillier and Hanson 1984) (Table 9.1).

TABLE 9.1
SPACE SYNTAX MEASURES AND THEIR SOCIAL SIGNIFICANCE
(ADAPTED FROM HILLIER AND HANSON 1984)

Measure		Formula	Significance
RA	Relative Asymmetry	The Relative Asymmetry (RA) describes the integration of a node by a value between (or equal to) 0 and 1, where a low value describes high integration. RA is calculated by the formula $RA = 2*(MD-1)/(k-2)$.	Global measure of integration that reveals the relative accessibility of spaces; highlighting likely patterns of social interaction, such as differential access for visitors and inhabitants, or the interfacing of different social groups.
i	Integration	A parameter that (contrary to RA) describes integration by a high number when a node is highly integrated is the "integration value" (i). The integration value is found by inverting the RA, $I = 1/RA$.	Global measure that is the inverse of RA. Reveals how well-integrated or segregated a particular space is to the entire spatial system. Integrated spaces promote movement and encounter, segregated spaces restrict and control movement.
C	Control	The Control Values (CV) are found by letting each node give the total value of 1 equally distributed to its connected nodes. The Control Value of node n, CV(n), is the total value received by node n during this operation.	Local measure that expresses the influence a particular space has in controlling movement between its neighbors. Reveals unequal power relations as expressed in space.
MD	Mean Depth	Mean Depth for a node n is the average depth (or average shortest distance) from node n to all the other nodes. If k is the total number of nodes in the system, then $MD(n) = TD(n)/(k-1)$.	Local measure that reveals the total number of spaces, on average, that one must pass through to travel from any space in the system to the outside. Measures the privacy and exclusivity of a particular space with relation to the entire spatial system.
TD(n)	Total Depth	Total Depth of a node n, TD(n), is the total of the shortest distances from node n to the other nodes in the system.	Global measure that captures the depth of a particular space in relation to the other spaces in the system; measures the *closeness* of spaces to each other.

There are two primary categories of space syntax analysis: convex analysis and axial analysis (Hillier and Hanson 1984). Convex analysis focuses on modeling movement through building interiors—convex spaces are represented as nodes, and paths of movement from one space to another are represented as lines (Hillier and Hanson 1984). The various combinations of nodes and lines together create a spatial network, and can be analyzed with the program DepthMap, which measures network centrality. The most valuable measures in convex analysis are integration and control. Integration measures the degree to which a space is public and accessible. Integrated spaces encourage informal social interactions and chance encounters, whereas segregated spaces discourage casual interaction and send a message of privacy and exclusivity. The control value determines the amount of influence a particular space has over movement of people between two adjacent spaces. Spaces with a high degree of control are often associated with processes of social mediation and negotiation, while spaces with a low degree of control are often very segregated, private spaces.

Axial analysis measures pedestrian routes through a settlement by modeling all possible pedestrian routes from a chosen point and calculating the number of times these routes intersect with each other (Hillier and Hanson 1984). DepthMap quantifies these patterns of movement and circulation through space by generating measures of centrality, closeness, and connectivity for every possible pedestrian path, and displays them graphically. Axial graphs also succinctly express the length and direction of pedestrian routes through public and private spaces. The most valuable measures of axial analysis are choice, integration, and line length. The measure of choice quantifies the centrality of a particular route, and expresses the congestion of a particular pedestrian path. Similarly, integration measures the likelihood of chance social encounters and the distribution of a population within a given urban setting, such as a street. Finally, line length measures the visible continuity of straight axial sight lines in an urban environment.

Together, these measures reveal that vernacular architecture and settlement layout are the outcomes of a complex decision-making process. These decisions represent deliberate attempts to control movement and interaction, and are therefore integral to social production. Kaiser (this volume) approaches his analysis of the built environment of Pompeii from a similar perspective by using micro-viewshed analysis to shed light on public visibility as a mechanism for the advancement of social and economic goals in urban environments. His kinetic-visual approach, like the integrative approach used here, supports the concept that architecture is a socially mediated tool that is used strategically by different groups to advance their goals within a particular cultural context.

THE BUILT ENVIRONMENT AS A MEDIUM OF NONVERBAL COMMUNICATION

NONVERBAL COMMUNICATION

In addition to investigating how the topological spatial arrangement of an urban settlement impacts movement and interaction, the integrative approach presented here also investigates ways in which the formal properties of the built environment nonverbally encourage or discourage certain behaviors. Rapoport (1982) first articulated the concept that the built environment is a medium of nonverbal communication. According to Rapoport (1990:18), the built environment is made up of certain "systems of settings" that consist of a combination of fixed, semifixed, and nonfixed features which affect the "systems of activities" that occur within specific spaces (see also Keith 2003). The built environment provides cues that structure human behavior, essentially communicating the concept of "who does what, where, when, including or excluding whom?" (Rapoport 1990:9).

Archaeologists typically evaluate only fixed features—permanent architectural features, such as walls and floors—and semifixed elements—furnishings and portable artifacts—because nonfixed features—like language, clothing, and accessories—do not survive in the archaeological record. As pointed out by Ryan (this volume), the fixed features of architectural environments can be used to communicate messages about individual and group identity. Particularly relevant to the themes of this volume, Ryan also notes that conventionalism in the fixed features of vernacular architecture can aid in social cohesion by supporting public, integrative activities that bond communities together, especially during periods of turmoil. The analytical approach carried out here incorporates a similar line of thinking in making observations about the built environment. Data about the wall construction technique, fixed features, and semifixed features are used to categorize spaces in the built environment as special function buildings, elite residences, and non-elite residences. These observations also are used to infer group membership, and assess the degree to which the archaeological remains represent individualizing and/or collective decision making. For a more complete discussion of this methodology, including a broader set of room function categories, see Harrison (2016). To access a comprehensive open archive of the raw data used in the analysis, see Harrison (2017).

WALL CONSTRUCTION

The physical characteristics of walls have a significant impact on people's perception of their environment, and are instrumental in communicating meaning about a building's purpose, the status of its inhabitants, and the type of interactions that it is meant to host. In addition, the choice of a wall construction technique is deeply embedded within a context of available resources, time and building expertise, as well as broader cultural preferences and patterns. Hence, a wall construction technique is deeply intertwined with the "middle-level" expression of status, power, and identity (Rapoport 1988, 1990; Smith 2007, 2010). Each type of wall represents a combination of a particular set of formal building techniques that encompasses wall construction material, coursing, cross-section or bonding technique, dry or wet masonry, and surface dressing.

FIXED FEATURES

Fixed features are permanent elements of settings—such as buildings, floors, and walls—that are important in creating social settings and structuring environment–behavior relationships. Fixed features affect the way that people behave in space by guiding or encouraging them to elicit certain behavioral responses, while limiting and restricting other responses (Rapoport 1990:13). The fixed features identified in Seyitömer Höyük Phase B are benches, platforms, ash compartments, utilitarian hearths, formal hearths, kilns, clay-mixing areas, formal pottery production areas, and permanent storage facilities (Harrison 2016:172–179).

SEMIFIXED FEATURES

Semifixed features are furnishings or moveable objects associated with a particular space, such as furniture, curtains, plants, and so on (Kent 1990, 1991). Like fixed features, semifixed features communicate a message of appropriate behavior in space by serving as cues that encourage certain kinds of conduct (Rapoport 1982:187; 1990). In archaeological contexts, semifixed features encompass everything from ecofacts, to small, portable artifacts, to large artifacts (such as *pithoi*), which are more difficult to move and may be used as territorial markers or to partition a space (Fisher 2009:446). The categories of semifixed features present in Seyitömer Höyük Phase B are ritual/symbolic deposit, imported object, luxury object, bureaucratic object, and industrial debris.

THE FORMALITY OF SOCIAL INTERACTION: APPLICATION OF THE INTEGRATIVE APPROACH

When considered together, particular combinations of space syntax values, fixed features, and semifixed features of the built environment create settings that encourage certain types of social interactions which range on a continuum from gatherings to public/inclusive occasions and to private/exclusive occasions (Table 9.2; see also Fisher 2013:169–172). These settings are important places for the negotiation of social roles, the establishment of community bonds, and the expression of power relations.

Gatherings are informal encounters that involve unfocused or unsustained actions. They often occur in spaces of movement, such as streets or courtyards, in which there is a high potential for chance encounters. Public/inclusive occasions are sustained social interactions that occur within a well-defined spatial context. They are more formalized than casual gatherings, and often take place in large, architecturally elaborate and relatively integrated spaces. Public/inclusive occasions tend to occur in highly convex (square) spaces, which support continued social interactions rather than directional movement forward. Private/exclusive occasions tend to involve a more exclusive group of participants than public/inclusive occasions. They can occur in rooms of any size, and involve formal, sustained meetings between individuals or people with a high degree of social status. These occasions encourage private discussions between leaders and smaller groups of powerful individuals, rather than the active negotiation of power relations among large groups.

TABLE 9.2
FORMALITY OF SOCIAL INTERACTION IN PHASE B AT SEYITÖMER HÖYÜK
(ADAPTED FROM FISHER 2009:448, TABLE 2)

Occasions	Space Syntax Values	Description of Social Interaction	Shape and Dimensions
Gatherings	Low Real Relative Asymmetry; Medium to High Control Value	Movement spaces; unfocused/ unsustained actions; high potential for chance social encounters.	Low convexity; may be a narrow space
Public/Inclusive Occasions	Low Real Relative Asymmetry; Medium to High Control Value	Formal, sustained, focused interaction; a well-defined spatial and temporal context; often located on direct axial path from outside if intended to include visitors; important fixed and semifixed features and elaborate architecture likely.	High convexity; large size (12 square meters or larger); may be a "node"
Private/Exclusive Occasions	Medium or High Real Relative Asymmetry; Low Control Value; High Depth Value	Formal, sustained, focused interactions; a well-defined spatial and temporal context; space is not easily accessible or well integrated; located away from a main axial route for privacy; important fixed and semifixed features and elaborate architecture likely.	Generally high convexity; size not important

Based on the theoretical and methodological premises of the preceding sections, we focus on two questions in the rest of the paper: (1) What are the key insights about the spatial dimensions of power and social organization drawn from an integrative mixed methods analysis of Seyitömer Höyük Phase B?, and (2) How do these patterns of interaction facilitate the maintenance of community integrity at the local scale?

CASE STUDY: URBANISM AS A SOCIAL PROCESS AT SEYITÖMER HÖYÜK

OVERVIEW OF PHASE B SETTLEMENT

The construction technique, spatial arrangement, and in situ archaeological remains at Seyitömer Höyük reveal the presence of four contiguous blocks of buildings—linked together with a simple street system—which are referred to as the Administrative Complex, the Central Megaron Complex, the Rowhouses West, and the Rowhouses East

(Harrison 2016) (Figure 9.3). There is a badly damaged area to the southeast of the site, which contains the ruins of what appear to be three to five additional rowhouse-style buildings which originally may have been part of the Rowhouses East section. These buildings are not included in the current analysis because their poor state of preservation makes it impossible to identify specific buildings or routes of access with any degree of certainty (architectural drawings of this damaged section are available in open access in Harrison 2017). Determining exactly how discounting these buildings from analysis may impact results is an exercise in speculation, but it is likely that the highest and lowest measures of global integration in the convex analysis would be affected. Removing these damaged buildings from analysis does not impact the location of the three busiest axial routes of movement.

Each of the four sections included in this analysis shares broad similarities in terms of undressed stone construction technique, the use of compressed soil floors, and the regular placement of utilitarian hearths in the center of large rectangular rooms within megaron-type residential buildings. Variations in the presence of ritual/symbolic deposits, luxury items and metal goods, pottery kilns, and the degree of architectural elaboration allow for the classification of certain buildings as elite residences, nonelite residences, administrative buildings, storage rooms, workshops, and special function buildings (Harrison 2016, 2017). Further functional variation is evident in many areas, including elite and nonelite storage practices and the organization of pottery production ranging from dedicated specialist workshops located within the Administrative Complex to pottery and textile activity areas located within mixed-use spaces in nonelite residences (Harrison 2016). These findings reveal a small society with a moderate degree of specialization and emergent social and political hierarchies. This is broadly consistent with developments at other Early Bronze Age settlements in inland western Anatolia, particularly Demircihöyük and Küllüoba, both of which have been classified as examples of the *Anatolisches Siedlungsschema* model of urbanism proposed by Korfmann (1983).

Debating whether Seyitömer Höyük should be considered an example of the *Anatolisches Siedlungsschema,* despite its lack of an open space at the center of the settlement, a defining characteristic of the model, is not the intent of this chapter. Rather, we consider how the local built environment of Seyitömer Höyük impacted the lives of inhabitants, and allowed the community to sustain itself amid regional sociopolitical upheavals. While room size/area calculations indicate that the settlement's population was less than 1,000, and therefore below urban population thresholds advocated by some archaeologists, the density of the settlement, its functional variation, and its uniqueness in the context of the surrounding region suggest a lifestyle qualitatively different than that of people who inhabited the rural countryside. Furthermore, the analyses offered here problematize the interaction between humans and the built environment that they inhabited, and are relevant regardless of the site's semantic classification as "urban" or "preurban." The analysis simply requires a well-preserved group of contiguous rooms with clearly established patterns of accessibility connecting them and a record of in situ features and deposits from within those rooms.

Application of the Integrative Approach

The Choice Axial Map (Figure 9.4) reveals the three busiest and most integrated pedestrian routes at Seyitömer Höyük in Phase B. Perhaps the most remarkable aspect of Axial Routes 1 and 2 in Phase B is that each leads directly to the entrance of a special function building. These special function buildings are both important spaces for public/inclusive occasions, and serve as the primary territories for local elites. They would have been central to the negotiation of power relations between elite and nonelite residents. The convergence of busy axial routes of movement with special function rooms likely

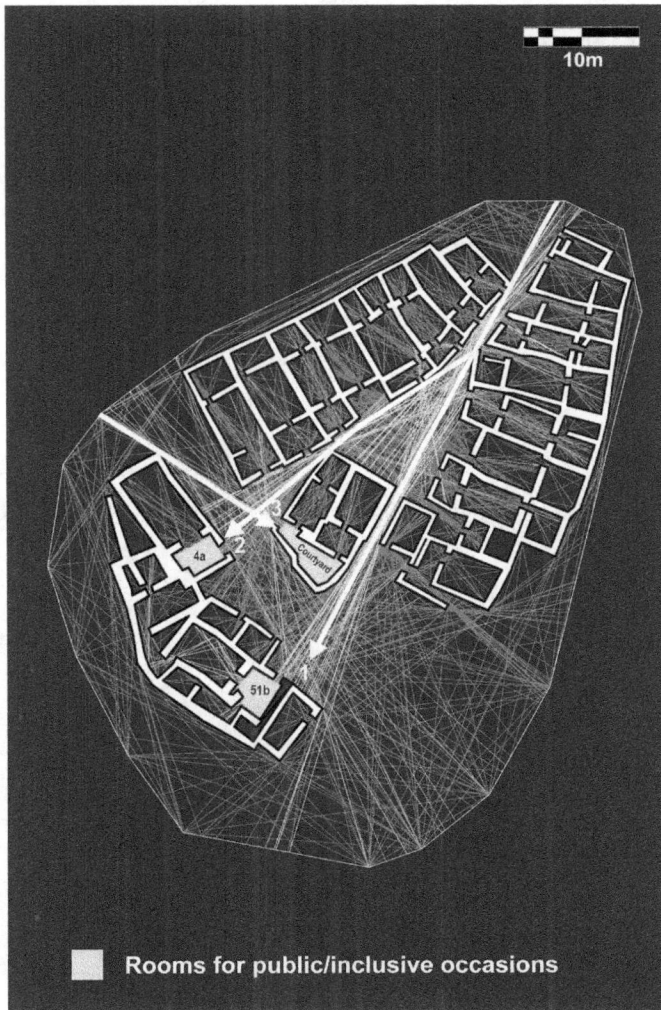

Figure 9.4. Choice Axial Map showing the three busiest and most integrated pedestrian routes in Phase B at Seyitömer Höyük.

represents a deliberate act of planning that supported the creation and maintenance of an elite ideology at Seyitömer Höyük.

Axial Route 3 leads to the courtyard of the Central Megaron Complex which is a space for informal gatherings (Figure 9.5). Entering this space is the first stage in a process of social filtering that involves passing through physical boundaries—such as stepped entrances and offset doorways—and waiting on benches in two designated areas before being admitted to enter the private/exclusive main room of the Central Megaron Complex (Harrison 2016:298, 307). In addition to having a high degree of centrality, the three main axial routes in Phase B are all highly integrated. This would have enhanced their ability to invite residents and visitors to participate in public/inclusive occasions in Room 51b and Room 4a and the gatherings in the courtyard in front of the Central Megaron Complex (see Figure 9.4). This concept of strategically mobilizing architecture and visibility to promote social advancement in some contexts, while shielding certain activities in others, calls to mind Kaiser's (this volume) findings from his micro-viewshed analysis of Pompeii.

A second conclusion drawn from the analysis is that there is an underlying spatial logic in the construction of nonelite houses in Phase B at Seyitömer Höyük, based on the rectangular megaron-type building as a solution for privacy in a densely populated settlement (Figure 9.6). In megaron-type buildings, the front room controls access to the main room. There is a recurring pattern in the integration values of the megaron-type buildings in Phase B that ranges in three distinct groups from highly integrated (front

FIGURE 9.5. Illustration of the Central Megaron Complex showing wall construction technique, use of exterior wall plaster, and freestanding location. Also note the stone bench in the courtyard, which would have been used during social gatherings (drawn by K. Donner).

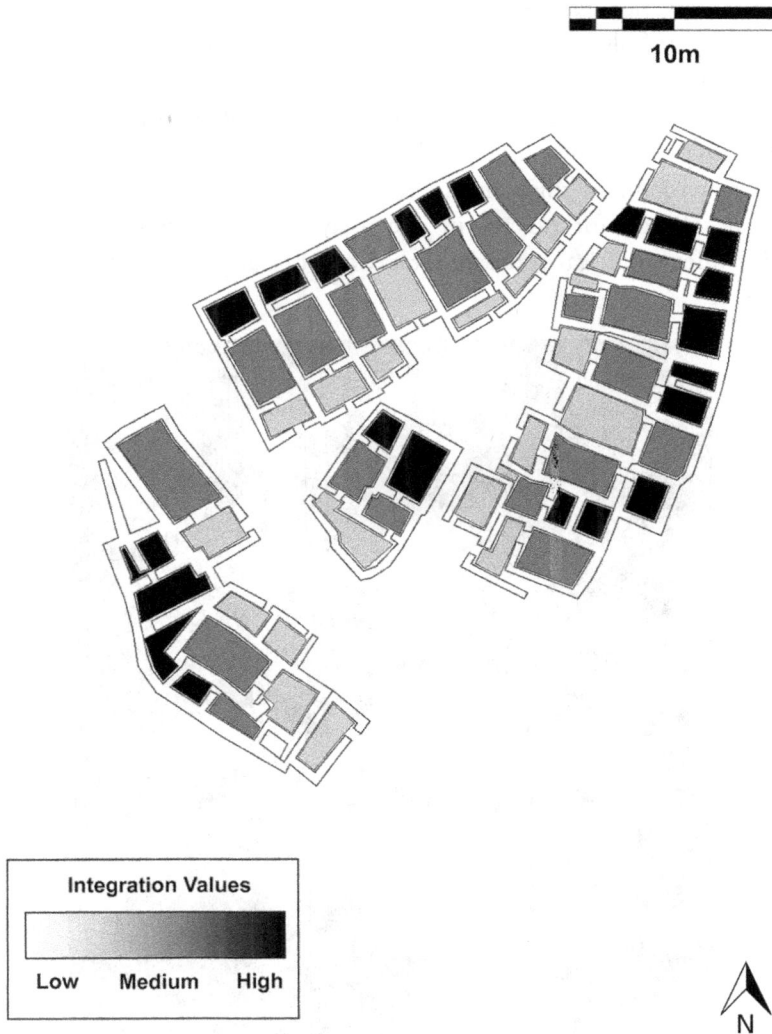

FIGURE 9.6. Integration of convex spaces in Phase B at Seyitömer Höyük showing recurring pattern of integration values in megaron-type buildings.

room), to semiintegrated (main room), and segregated (rear room). This pattern is particularly clear in the Phase B Rowhouses West and Rowhouses East. Space syntax analysis reveals this recurring overall pattern, while also drawing attention to nuanced differences between different spaces, a topic discussed in greater detail in Harrison (2016). This standardization of building form can be thought of as an expression of group membership, representative of a shared ideology, within the nonelite community. In her chapter in this volume, Ryan identifies a similar theme in exploring the role of architectural conventionalism in bolstering the public, integrative function of great houses and kivas during a period of population increase and sociopolitical change in the U.S. Southwest.

A third observation can be made on the basis of the Fewest Line Choice Axial Map analysis that reveals two primary patterns of movement within private spaces at Seyitömer Höyük. The first pattern is found in the nonelite residences and pottery workshops in the Rowhouses West and Rowhouses East sections of the site (Figure 9.7). These megaron-type buildings promote linear movement from the front room to the more private rear room. In this context, the widespread use of megaron-type buildings is a horizontal solution for privacy in a densely populated settlement, much as skyscrapers today offer a vertical solution for privacy in congested metropolitan areas. The

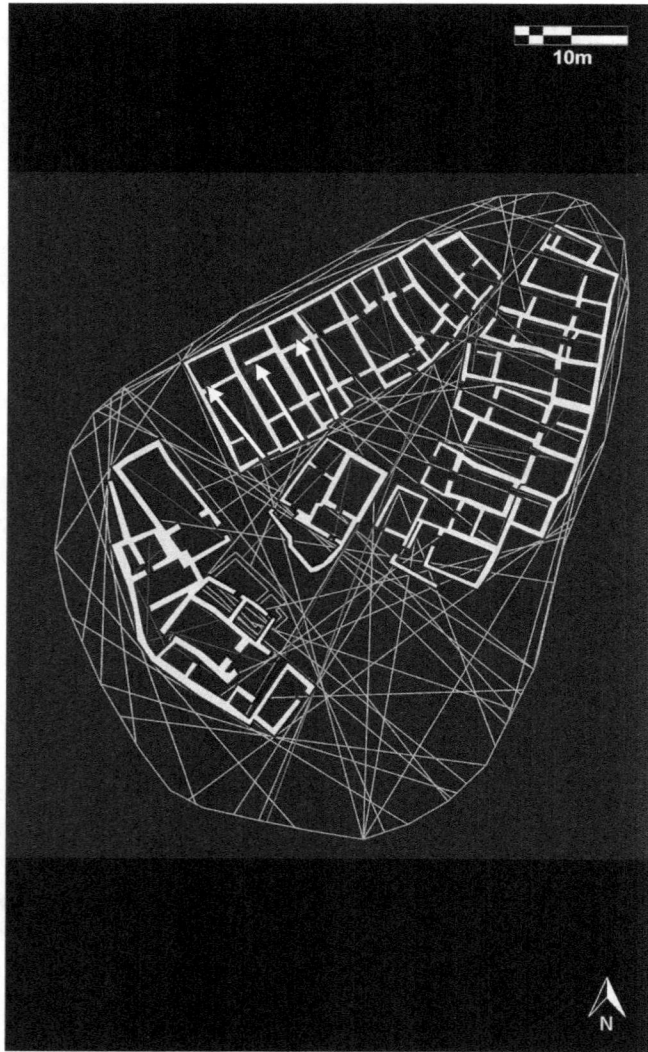

FIGURE 9.7. Fewest Line Choice Axial Map showing linear pattern of movement through nonelite megaron-type buildings in Phase B at Seyitömer Höyük.

consistency of this linear axial movement pattern throughout all rowhouse buildings is striking. It suggests a form of canonical communication in which individuals express their participation in a broader cultural tradition through a recurring pattern of internal spatial arrangement (Blanton 1994; Harrison 2016:274).

It is possible to discern a "rowhouse neighborhood" in Seyitömer Höyük Phase B, on the basis of spatial clustering and the use of shared party walls rather than separate or abutting walls. This architectural coordination creates a sense of continuity, which is a form quality of cities that facilitates the perception of a complex physical reality as one, interrelated entity (Lynch 1960:106). The continuity of the Rowhouses West is further reinforced through the use of uniform building materials (uncoursed rubble bonded together with a compound technique), orientation, dimensions, and the standard treatment of fixed features, particularly hearths. The regularity of the linear pattern of movement through interior spaces of these rowhouses further supports the identification of a well-defined vernacular architectural tradition and the existence of a neighborhood.

The Axial Graph in Figure 9.8 reveals a recurring pattern of movement in each special function building in Phase B at Seyitömer Höyük. Once visitors enter a building from the street, they are forced to change direction; in both special function rooms in the Administrative Complex, they must turn to the right, and in the Central Megaron Complex they must turn to the left. This layout increases the perception of distance and makes the space feel deeper with each turn. It represents an innovative solution to communicating exclusivity and increasing privacy in a settlement in which space is limited and where the expansion of physical distance is not a viable option for the expression of social difference. This suggests that in Phase B one of the primary ways that power is communicated nonverbally is by increasing the complexity of axial routes by requiring pedestrians to shift direction when entering special function rooms. Segmented pedestrian pathways are used only in private/exclusive and special function spaces, and they are never used in utilitarian buildings—such as nonelite residences, pottery workshops, or kitchens—in which linear patterns of movement are favored.

SOCIAL INTERACTION AND COMMUNITY IDENTITY

Multiple, overlapping communities inhabited the Phase B settlement at Seyitömer Höyük, two of which are elite communities and nonelite communities. Each of these communities is associated with socially constructed locales—the physical settings that generate community identity through the concentration of interaction (Giddens 1984; for a further discussion of additional community identities reflected in the built environment of Phase B, see Harrison 2016).

The private/exclusive occasions the elite community hosted in their elaborate residences involved formal, sustained interactions in elaborate spatial contexts, such as Room 51a and Room 4b (see Figure 9.4). The personalization of these elite spaces—with elaborate, thick, plastered walls—reflects a desire to create a highly "imageable" environment (Lynch 1960). The privacy of these occasions is underlined by the use of offset entrances

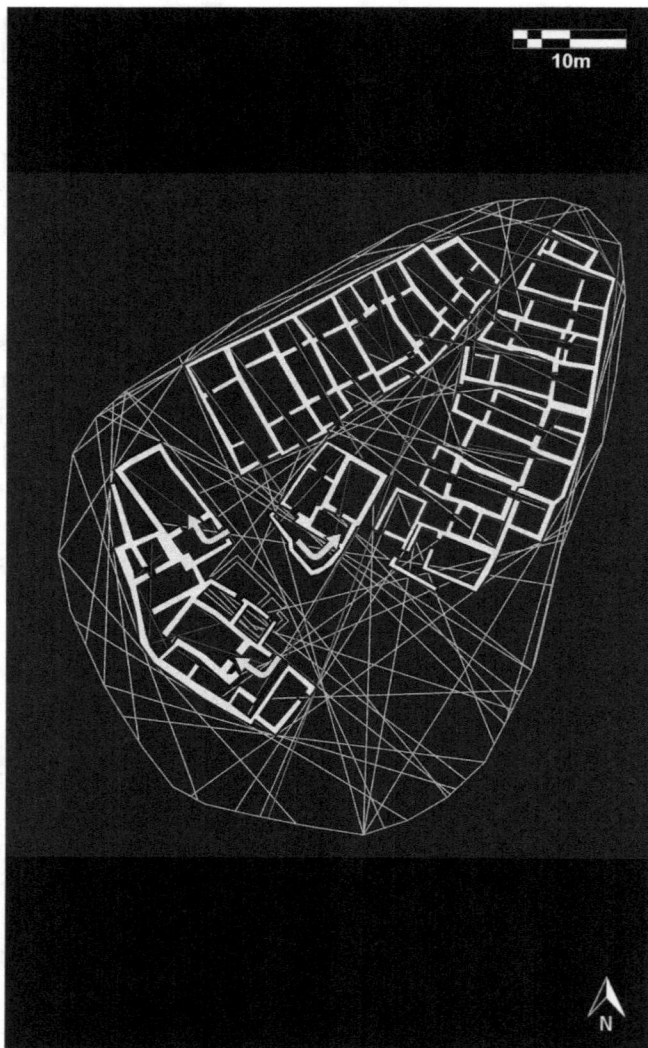

FIGURE 9.8. Fewest Line Choice Axial Map showing L-shaped routes of movement into spaces used for private/exclusive occasions in Phase B at Seyitömer Höyük.

that increase the physical and social distance between these elite locales and the public realm. In addition, the use of offset entrances in spaces used for private/exclusive occasions creates a social boundary that structures relationships between "us" and "them" (Mac Sweeney 2011:39–41). This relationship can be thought of as a "social rationale of community identity" (Mac Sweeney 2011:40) in which the community's identity is the result of combined social factors and a geographical identity.

The elite community also was involved in carrying out public/inclusive occasions, which included communal feasting. These occasions were hosted in well-integrated, public, and highly visible spaces, such as Room 51b, Room 4a, and the courtyard of the Central Megaron Complex (see Figure 9.4). Power relations here were expressed hierarchically because they involved interaction among vertically differentiated elite and nonelite communities. This can be thought of as a kind of indexical communication (Blanton 1994).

The nonelite community is defined by a shared treatment of physical elements. This encompasses the overall layout of nonelite building clusters in the Rowhouses West and Rowhouses East as well as their internal spatial arrangements and features. These buildings are the result of a vernacular architectural tradition, and use internal barriers and spatial clustering to establish territoriality and structure public/private interactions. As Rapoport (1977:334) notes, spatial clustering is a way of reducing the stress—inherent in city life—of encountering many stimuli and making visual, olfactory, and acoustic contact with many unknown people. This standard way of treating physical elements aids in the perception of a complex physical reality as a single, interconnected unit, and enhances the "predictability of the communicative environment" (Rapoport 1977:335). Therefore, it is essential in the production of community-level social bonds.

Thus, in Phase B at Seyitömer Höyük, architecture can be viewed as a unique form of material culture (Moore 1996). Its formal attributes contain symbolic cues that communicate messages of group-level identity nonverbally. Interplay between various groups—each of which expressed their identity vis-à-vis the built environment in distinctive ways—was critical to the maintenance of community integrity during the volatile EBIII period.

Conclusion

As the foregoing discussion illustrates, third-millennium B.C. western Anatolia is characterized by the emergence of a new kind of radial urban settlement form with tightly packed rowhouses inside of a circuit wall (Çevik 2007; Erkanal 1996:80; Fidan et al. 2015; Korfmann 1983). The emergence of these settlements coincides with the rise of a citadel elite, a nascent metals trade, an increase in economic complexity, and transformations in the sociopolitical organization of society (Bachhuber 2015). The archaeological remains from Seyitömer Höyük Phase B indicate that this site was a crossroad involved in long-distance trade relationships with societies in the Aegean and Syro-Cilicia during EBIII.

The built environment of Seyitömer Höyük embodies a complex web of decisions made in the pursuit of social and political goals. Control over movement is one of the most important channels through which power was expressed, as shown in the decision to locate important public/inclusive buildings at the termination of busy routes at the site. In addition, use of offset entrances to special function buildings communicates a clear shift from the public to the private realm, which increases the perception of spatial and social distance and expresses a message of social inequality that was integral to the establishment of an elite ideology. Nonelites also used megaron-type buildings, with internal spatial partitions, to establish boundaries between the public and private domains and communicate suprahousehold social bonds. This vernacular architectural tradition allowed nonelites to organize into corporate groups within an increasingly hierarchical society. Interplay between these individualizing and group-oriented goals fostered independency, which aided in the maintenance of community integrity during a volatile period.

While these insights address a diverse set of issues, the findings are complementary in the context of developing a richer picture of the built environment as a medium of nonverbal communication and an instrument of top-down and bottom-up power relations. In particular, the topological arrangement of space and its ability to impact patterns of movement and interaction are critical to the production of social identities. Likewise, community integrity is strengthened through integrative social occasions and gatherings as well as participation in vernacular architectural traditions. This perspective elucidates the multiple intersecting social roles encoded in architecture and spatial arrangement, and clearly contrasts with earlier, more traditional studies that consider urbanism to be a simple marker of sociopolitical complexity or a normative type in the process of cultural evolution.

ACKNOWLEDGMENTS

We would like to warmly thank Dr. Attila Gyucha for inviting us to participate in the 9th IEMA Conference, and for providing us with valuable comments and edits on an earlier draft of this paper. Thanks are also due to the National Science Foundation for supporting research into the absolute dating at Seyitömer Höyük (Award #1523389). Lively discussion and feedback at the conference improved this paper as well.

REFERENCES CITED

Bachhuber, C. 2015 *Citadel and Cemetery in Early Bronze Age Anatolia*. Monographs in Mediterranean Archaeology 13. Equinox, Sheffield.

Bilgen, A. N. 2011 *Seyitömer Höyük kazısı ön raporu, 2006–2010*. Dumlupınar Üniversitesi Fen-Edebiyat Fakültesi Arkeoloji Bölümü, Kütahya.

Bilgen, A. N., and Z. Bilgen 2015 Early Bronze Age III Settlement. In *Seyitömer Höyük kazısı ön raporu, 2013–2014*, edited by A. N. Bilgen, pp. 143–204. Dumlupınar Üniversitesi, Kütahya.

Bilgen, A. N., and A. Kuru 2015 A Group of Depas Amphikypellon from Seyitömer Mound. *Anadolu* 41:1–23.

Blanton, R. E. 1994 *Houses and Households: A Comparative Study*. Plenum Press, New York.

Broodbank, C. 2000 *An Island Archaeology of the Early Cyclades*. Cambridge University Press, Cambridge.

Caskey, J. L. 1960 The Early Helladic Period in the Argolid. *Hesperia* 29(3):285–303.

Çevik, Ö. 2007 The Emergence of Different Social Systems in Early Bronze Age Anatolia: Urbanisation versus Centralisation. *Anatolian Studies* 57:131–140.

Cultraro, M. 2007 Domestic Architecture and Public Space in Early Bronze Age Poliochni (Lemnos). In *Building Communities: House, Settlement and Society in the Aegean and Beyond*, edited by R. Westgate, N. Fisher, and J. Whitley, pp. 55–64. British School at Athens Studies 15. British School at Athens, Athens.

Dedeoğlu, F. 2008 Cultural Transformation and Settlement System of Southwestern Anatolia from Neolithic to LBA: A Case Study from Denizli/Çivril Plain. In *Proceedings of the 5th International Congress on the Archaeology of the Ancient Near East*, Vol. I., edited by J. M. Cordoba, M. Molist, M. C. Pérez, I. Rubio, and S. Martinez, pp. 587–601. UAM, Madrid.

Efe, T. 2003 Küllüoba and the Initial Stages of Urbanism in Western Anatolia. In *From Villages to Towns: Early Villages in the Near East. Studies Presented to Ufuk Esin*, edited by M. Özdoğan, H. Hauptmann, and N. Başgelen, pp. 265–282. Arkeoloji ve Sanat Yayinlari, Istanbul.

Efe, T. 2007 The Theories of the "Great Caravan Route" Between Cilicia and Troy: The Early Bronze Age III Period in Inland Western Anatolia. *Anatolian Studies* 57:47–64.

Efe, T., and A. Ilasli 1997 Pottery Links Between the Troad and Inland Northwestern Anatolia during the Trojan Second Settlement. In *He Poliochne kai he proime epoche tou Chalkou sto Voreio Aigaio*, edited by C. G. Doumas and V. La Rosa, pp. 596–609. Scuola Archeologica Italiana di Atene, Atene.

Efe, T., and M. Türkteki 2011 Inter-Regional Relations and Trade in the Early Bronze Age. In *Across: The Cyclades and Western Anatolia during the 3rd Millennium BC*, edited by V. Şahoğlu and P. Sotirakopoulou, pp. 232–233. Sabancı Üniversitesi, Sakıp Sabancı Müzesi, Istanbul.

Erkanal, H. 1996 Early Bronze Age Urbanization in the Coastal Region of Western Anatolia. In *Housing and Settlement in Anatolia: A Historical Perspective*, edited by Y. Sey, pp. 70–82. Tepe Architectural Culture Center, Istanbul.

Erkanal, H. 2011 Early Bronze Age Settlement Models and Domestic Architecture in the Coastal Region of Western Anatolia. In *Across: The Cyclades and Western Anatolia during the 3rd Millennium BC*, edited by V. Şahoğlu and P. Sotirakopoulou, pp. 130–135. Sabancı Üniversitesi, Sakıp Sabancı Müzesi, Istanbul.

Fidan, E., D. Sari, and M. Türkteki 2015 An Overview of the Western Anatolian Early Bronze Age. *European Journal of Archaeology* 18(1):60–89.

Fisher, K. D. 2009 Placing Social Interaction: An Integrative Approach to Analyzing Past Built Environments. *Journal of Anthropological Archaeology* 28(4):439–457.

Fisher, K. D. 2013 Investigating Monumental Social Space in Late Bronze Age Cyprus: An Integrative Approach. In *Spatial Analysis and Social Spaces: Interdisciplinary Approaches to the Interpretation of Prehistoric and Historic Built Environments*, edited by E. Paliou, U. Lieberwirth, and S. Polla, pp. 167–202. Topoi: Berlin Studies of the Ancient World 18. De Gruyter, Berlin and Boston.

Forsén, J. 1992 *The Twilight of the Early Helladics: A Study of the Disturbances in East-Central and Southern Greece toward the End of the Early Bronze Age*. Studies in Mediterranean Archaeology 116. Paul Åströms, Jonsered.

Giddens, A. 1984 *The Constitution of Society: Outline of the Theory of Structuration*. University of California, Berkeley.

Harrison, L. K. 2016 *Living Spaces: Urbanism as a Social Process at Seyitömer Höyük in Early Bronze Age Western Anatolia*. PhD dissertation, Department of Anthropology, State University of New York at Buffalo, Buffalo.

Harrison, L. K. (editor) 2017 *Architecture, Urbanism, and Radiocarbon Dating at Seyitömer Höyük, Turkey*. Electronic document: https://opencontext.org/projects/347286db-b6c6-4fd2-b3bd-b50316b0cb9f.

Hillier, B., and J. Hanson 1984 *The Social Logic of Space*. Cambridge University Press, Cambridge.

Keith, K. 2003 The Spatial Patterning of Everyday Life in Old Babylonian Neighborhoods. In *The Social Construction of Ancient Cities*, edited by M. L. Smith, pp. 56–80. Smithsonian Institution Press, Washington, D.C.

Kent, S. 1990 Activity Areas and Architecture: An Interdisciplinary View of the Relationship Between Use of Space and Domestic Built Environments. In *Domestic Architecture and the Use of Space: An Interdisciplinary Cross-Cultural Study*, edited by S. Kent, pp. 1–8. Cambridge University Press, Cambridge.

Kent, S. 1991 Partitioning Space: Cross-Cultural Factors Influencing Domestic Spatial Segmentation. *Environment and Behavior* 23(4):438–473.

Korfmann, M. 1983 *Demircihöyük 1: Architektur, Stratigraphie und Befunde*. Philipp Von Zabern, Mainz am Rhein.

Kouka, O. 2013 "Minding the Gap" Against the Gaps: The Early Bronze Age and the Transition to the Middle Bronze Age in the Northern and Eastern Aegean/Western Anatolia. *American Journal of Archaeology* 117(4):569–580.

Low, S. M., and D. Lawrence-Zuniga (editors) 2003 *The Anthropology of Space and Place: Locating Culture*. Blackwell, Malden, Massachusetts.

Lynch, K. 1960 *The Image of the City*. MIT Press, Cambridge, Massachusetts.

Mac Sweeney, N. 2011 *Community Identity and Archaeology: Dynamic Communities at Aphrodisias and Beycesultan*. University of Michigan Press, Ann Arbor, Michigan.

Manning, S. W. 1997 Cultural Change in the Aegean c. 2200 B.C. In *Third Millennium B.C. Climate Change and Old World Collapse*, edited by H. N. Dalfes, G. Kukla, and H. Weiss, pp. 149–172. NATO ASI Series I: Global Environment Change 49. Springer, Berlin and New York.

Mellaart, J. 1958 The End of the Early Bronze Age in Anatolia and the Aegean. *American Journal of Archaeology* 62(1):9–33.

Mellink, M. J. 1986 The Early Bronze Age in West Anatolia. In *The End of the Early Bronze Age in the Aegean*, edited by G. Cadogan and J. L. Caskey, pp. 139–152. Cincinnati Classical Studies New Series 6. Brill, Leiden.

Moore, J. D. 1996 *Architecture and Power in the Ancient Andes: The Archaeology of Public Buildings*. Cambridge University Press, Cambridge.

Parker Pearson, M., and C. Richards 1994 Architecture and Order: Spatial Representation and Archaeology. In *Architecture and Order: Approaches to Social Space*, edited by M. Parker Pearson and C. Richards, pp. 34–66. Routledge, London.

Peltenburg, E. 2000 From Nucleation to Dispersal: Late 3rd Millennium BC Settlement Pattern Transformations in the Near East and Aegean. In *La Djéziré et l'Euphrate syriens de la protohistoire à la fin du IIe millénaire av. J.-C.: Tendances dans l'interprétation historique des données nouvelles*, edited by O. Rouault and M. Wäfler, pp. 183–206. Subartu 7. Brepols, Turnhout.

Pullen, D. J. 2013 "Minding the Gap" Bridging the Gaps in Cultural Change Within the Early Bronze Age Aegean. *American Journal of Archaeology* 117(4):545–553.

Rahmstorf, L. 2015 The Aegean before and after c. 2200 BC Between Europe and Asia: Trade as a Prime Mover of Cultural Change. In *2200 BC—Ein Klimasturz als Ursache für den Zerfall der Alten Welt?—2200 BC—A Climatic Breakdown as a Cause for the Collapse of the Old World?*, edited by H. Meller, H. W. Arz, R. Jung, and R. Risch, pp. 149–180.

Tagungen des Landesmuseums für Vorgeschichte Halle 12/I. Landesamt für Denkmalpflege und Archäologie Sachsen-Anhalt, Landesmuseum für Vorgeschichte, Halle/Saale.

Rapoport, A. 1977 *Human Aspects of Urban Form: Towards a Man–Environment Approach to Urban Form and Design.* Urban and Regional Planning Series 15. Pergamon Press, Oxford and New York.

Rapoport, A. 1982 *The Meaning of the Built Environment: A Nonverbal Communication Approach.* Sage, Beverly Hills, California.

Rapoport, A. 1988 Levels of Meaning in the Built Environment. In *Cross-Cultural Perspectives in Nonverbal Communication*, edited by F. Poyatos, pp. 317–336. Hogrefe, Toronto.

Rapoport, A. 1990 Systems of Activities and Systems of Settings. In *Domestic Architecture and the Use of Space: An Interdisciplinary Cross-Cultural Study*, edited by S. Kent, pp. 9–20. Cambridge University Press, Cambridge.

Renfrew, C. 1972 *The Emergence of Civilization: The Cyclades and the Aegean in the Third Millennium B.C.* Metheun, London.

Rutter, J. B. 1979 *Ceramic Change in the Aegean Early Bronze Age: The Kastri Group, Lefkandi I, and Lerna IV: A Theory Concerning the Origin of Early Helladic III Ceramics.* Institute of Archaeology, University of California, Los Angeles.

Rutter, J. B. 1983 Some Observations on the Cyclades in the Later Third and Early Second Millennia. *American Journal of Archaeology* 87(1):69–76.

Rutter, J. B. 1984 The Early Cycladic III Gap: What It Is and How to Go About Filling It Without Making It Go Away. In *The Prehistoric Cyclades: Contributions to a Workshop on Cycladic Chronology*, edited by J. A. MacGillivray and R. L. N. Barber, pp. 95–107. Department of Classical Archaeology, University of Edinburgh, Edinburgh.

Şahoğlu, V. 2005 The Anatolian Trade Network and the Izmir Region during the Early Bronze Age. *Oxford Journal of Archaeology* 24(4):339–361.

Shaw, J. W. 1987 The Early Helladic II Corridor House: Development and Form. *American Journal of Archaeology* 91(1):59–79.

Smith, M. E. 2007 Form and Meaning in the Earliest Cities: A New Approach to Ancient Urban Planning. *Journal of Planning History* 6(1):3–47.

Smith, M. E. 2010 Empirical Urban Theory for Archaeologists. *Journal of Archaeological Method and Theory* 18(3):167–192.

Sotirakopoulou, P. 1993 The Chronology of the "Kastri Group" Reconsidered. *The Annual of the British School at Athens* 88:5–20.

Staubwasser, M., and H. Weiss 2006 Holocene Climate and Cultural Evolution in Late Prehistoric–Early Historic West Asia. *Quaternary Research* 66(3):372–387.

Warner, J. 1979 The Megaron and Apsidal House in Early Bronze Age Western Anatolia: New Evidence from Karataş. *American Journal of Archaeology* 83(2):133–147.

Warner, J. 1994 *Elmali-Karataş II: The Early Bronze Age Village of Karataş.* Bryn Mawr College, Bryn Mawr, Pennsylvania.

Werner, K. 1993 *The Megaron during the Aegean and Anatolian Bronze Age: A Study of Occurrence, Shape, Architectural Adaptation, and Function.* Studies in Mediterranean Archaeology 108. Paul Åströms, Jonsered.

Wiencke, M. H. 1989 Change in Early Helladic II. *American Journal of Archaeology* 93(4):495–509.

Wiener, M. H. 2013 "Minding the Gap" Gaps, Destructions, and Migrations in the Early Bronze Age Aegean: Causes and Consequences. *American Journal of Archaeology* 117(4):581–592.

Yener, K. A. 2000 *The Domestication of Metals: The Rise of Complex Metal Industries in Anatolia.* Culture and History of the Ancient Near East 4. Brill, Leiden and Boston.

Yener, K. A., and P. B. Vandiver 1993 Tin Processing at Göltepe: An Early Bronze Age Site in Anatolia. *American Journal of Archaeology* 97(2):207–238.

CHAPTER TEN

If You Build It, Will They Come? Will They Stay?

The Mycenaean Port Town of Kalamianos

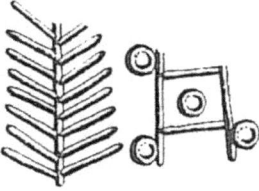

Daniel J. Pullen

Abstract *In this paper, I consider what organization, structure, and resources might be needed both for the establishment of an urban community in a region lacking such population agglomerations and for that urban community to thrive. Particular attention is paid to mechanisms for ensuring the self-sufficiency of the new settlement and its hinterland. I focus on the site of Kalamianos, dating to the Late Helladic IIIA2 to Late Helladic IIIB period (ca. 1330–1180 B.C.), a port town founded on the Saronic Gulf by the palatial center at Mycenae.*

INTRODUCTION

The theme of the 9th IEMA Conference and this volume provides me the opportunity to address the emergence and sustainability of urban settlements, that is, what organization, structure, and resources might be needed both for the establishment of an urban community in a region lacking such population agglomerations and for that urban community to thrive. In particular, I am interested in how an organizational elite could ensure the success of such an urban "imperial" settlement, in contrast to the more organic process of *synoikismos* (synoecism), the coming together of households to form communities as discussed by Ault, Osborne, Birch, and others in this volume. I focus on the site of Kalamianos, a port town founded near the end of the Late Helladic (LH) IIIA2 period, ca. 1390–1330 B.C., on Greece's Saronic Gulf, apparently as an outpost of the palatial center at Mycenae, and that ceased to exist when the palatial system was destroyed at the end of the LH IIIB period, ca. 1190/1180 B.C. Some questions to be addressed include:

- What role did the (palatial) elites play in the founding of this settlement?

- What arrangements were made for this settlement's self-sufficiency?

- What role did the (palatial) elites play in the daily maintenance of this settlement?

- How connected was the hinterland to the urban core at Kalamianos?

- Was the terraced area sufficient to supply the food needed for the urban settlement?

- What was the degree of centralized control over agricultural production and distribution in the Kalamianos region?

- Would Kalamianos have depended upon one of the palatial centers for provisioning of the inhabitants, in some system of rations or mobilization?

I first present a short overview of Kalamianos, including the evidence for elite involvement in the construction of the settlement, followed by a discussion of the relationship between the urban community and its hinterland, especially concerning agricultural self-sufficiency of Mycenaean Kalamianos. I conclude with a discussion of the role of Kalamianos in its "small world" of the Saronic, seeking to explain its *raison d'être* and demise. The establishment of Kalamianos provides a good case study for what one Late Bronze Age state thought were the necessary arrangements for a successful community.

KALAMIANOS: A MYCENAEAN PORT TOWN ON THE SARONIC GULF

From 2007 through 2010, the Saronic Harbors Archaeological Research Project (SHARP)—codirected by Thomas F. Tartaron (University of Pennsylvania) and me—conducted fieldwork to explore the harbor settlement at Kalamianos and its surrounding region in order to test a model of state competition and expansion (Pullen 2013a; Tartaron and Pullen 2013; Tartaron et al. 2011). Of particular interest for us was the expansion during the Late Bronze Age of the land-based power center of Mycenae into the Saronic Gulf, at a time of increasing competition among newly emerging economic centers in the Saronic that coincides with the demise of the long-dominant center of Kolonna on Aigina (Pullen and Tartaron 2007) (Figure 10.1). We suggest that the elites at Mycenae and other Argolid centers—whether palatial or not—optimized their opportunities for trade by exploiting ports on all three major bodies of water surrounding the Argolid/Corinthia, including the Saronic Gulf.

As we have shown elsewhere (Pullen 2013a; Tartaron et al. 2011), at Kalamianos, there was a small Early Bronze Age settlement adjacent to a small peninsula that provided shelter for two basins—a typical harbor situation favored by prehistoric Aegean societies, such as at Ayia Irini (Kea), Ayios Kosmas and Askitario (Attica), Manika (Euboia), and Kolonna (Aigina), among others (Shaw 1990:423). We have not found any ceramics

FIGURE 10.1. Kalamianos in the Northeast Peloponnese and Saronic Gulf.

dated to the Middle Bronze Age at the site, and there is only limited evidence for Early Mycenaean occupation. Underwater work in 2009 by Joseph Boyce of McMaster University and Despina Koutsoumba of the Enalion (Underwater Antiquities) Ephoreia— under the auspices of a Canadian Greek *synergasia* permit—has delineated the extent of the Mycenaean period harbor (Dao 2011; Tartaron et al. 2011:569–575). By the Palatial Mycenaean period, the relative sea level had risen sufficiently that the peninsula was now a shallow reef connecting an island to the mainland but still with two protected basins for anchoring ships (Dao 2011; Tartaron et al. 2011:571–575). At this time, in the ceramic period late LH IIIA or early LH IIIB, the settlement at Kalamianos underwent a rapid expansion into a walled urban settlement of more than 7 hectares, oriented toward the two harbor basins (Figure 10.2). If one lays the plan of Kalamianos over the topographical reconstruction of the Mycenaean period, one can see how the town of Kalamianos is clearly oriented to encompass the eastern basin, and perhaps part of the western basin (Figure 10.3). Interestingly, the scant evidence for the earlier periods is oriented mostly to the western basin or even the far western shore, not the eastern basin. There are ballast piles of unknown date in the western basin (and indeed to the west of the site), so at some period ships made use of the western basin. If there were harbor facilities, they have disappeared beneath the waves, but Shaw (1990) and others caution

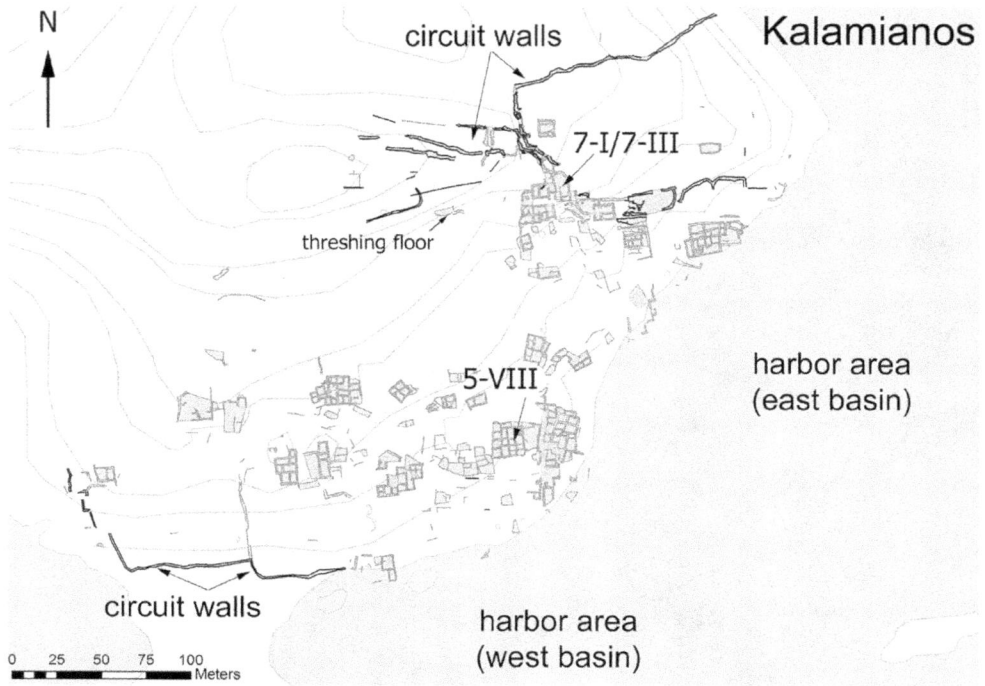

FIGURE 10.2. Circuit walls and buildings documented at Kalamianos.

us against expecting built harbor facilities in the Bronze Age (Pullen 2013a:246–248). With the collapse of the palaces at the end of LH IIIB, Kalamianos ceased to be occupied, perhaps exacerbated by local tectonic events that rendered the harbor unusable. In the currently accepted chronology for Mycenaean Greece, this would mean that the town of Kalamianos existed for at most 150 years.

The Kalamianos site is unusual in that the architectural foundations and lower walls of an entire Mycenaean town are exposed because of extensive loss of soil. Richard K. Dunn, one of the SHARP geologists, has estimated that up to ca. 0.5 meter of soil has been lost in some portions of the site (Tartaron et al. 2011:568–569). There is very little evidence for later occupation of the site, and most of what little disturbance of the remains there is can be attributed to recent agricultural activities and to the collecting of stones for a limekiln found on the site near the coast. We have not conducted any excavations, and all of our data have been collected solely through above ground techniques, ranging from high-resolution Differential GPS mapping to old-fashioned drawing of architecture with pencil and paper, from innovative collection strategies to traditional fieldwalking by survey teams (for field methods, see Tartaron et al. 2011:579–583, 604–607).

Our architectural documentation program has succeeded in generating a detailed plan of the enclosed Mycenaean (LH IIIA2 to LH IIIB) town (Figure 10.2). By the end of the 2010 field season, we had mapped about 50 buildings with 120 measurable

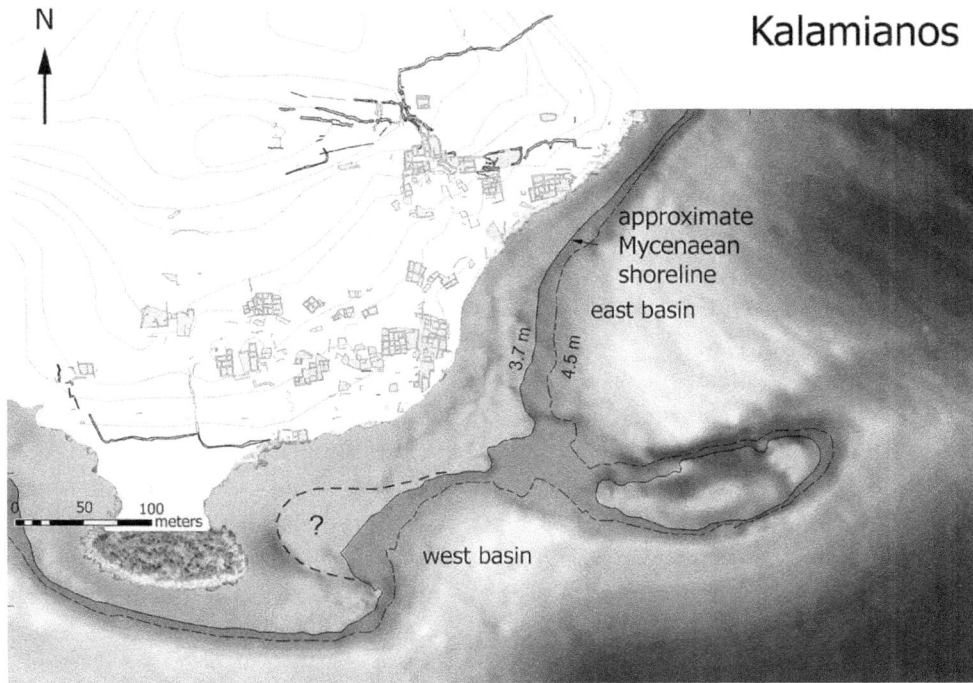

FIGURE 10.3. Kalamianos town plan and harbor reconstruction of Late Bronze Age date.

rooms, more than two dozen additional structures and features, and over 500 meters of the circuit walls at Kalamianos (Pullen 2015; Tartaron et al. 2011).

A recent analysis by Nagle (2015) using spatial analysis techniques of a few structures at Kalamianos suggests that at least one building, 5-VIII, was most likely used for workshops and storage, not domestic purposes; analysis of additional buildings using these techniques would undoubtedly suggest more (for another application of these techniques, see Harrison and Bilgen in this volume). Building 7-I/7-III, at 520 square meters, is one of the largest Late Helladic structures anywhere on the mainland that is not a palace—it has character-istics of a public structure in terms of its access as well as architectural features that have parallels with elite architecture at the Argive centers, such as the use of orthostate building blocks, column bases, and piers. Orthostates—large blocks whose thickness is much less than their width or height—are placed in conspicuous positions throughout the building, such as at the corners and at the north and south entrances; these are found rarely outside of palatial centers. A square pillar of three squared blocks—stacked on bedrock whose top was at the same level as cuttings in the bedrock at the north end of the space—would have supported the floor for one of the largest rooms recorded at Kalamianos. Large stones were used as antas and corner blocks, in itself not an unusual practice at Kalamianos, but in Building 7-I/7-III they form a grid pattern similar to the structural supports in elite LH IIIB architecture, such as the palace at Pylos (Pullen 2015:386–388).

INTERNAL ORGANIZATION OF KALAMIANOS

Because the builders exploited the exposed bedrock and bedrock fractures that run pre-dominately in an east–west direction for the foundations and the support of buildings, and often aligned their buildings to bedrock ridges, the overall plan of Kalamianos seems to be deceptively gridlike in organization. While an orthogonal grid is often thought to be the principal organizing schema for the planning of urban settlements from ancient times throughout the world, several scholars have demonstrated that many other types of plan-ning schemes are apparent in ancient societies (Creekmore 2010; Evans et al. 2007; Kostof 1991; Smith 2007). Nevertheless, there is evidence for the organization of Kalamianos in the association or alignment of one structure to another in a number of areas of the site—for instance, it is apparent that several walls in Buildings 7-I, 7-II, 7-III, and 7-X align with each other (see Figure 10.4). Many structures are placed without regard for the contours of the land, suggesting that maintaining the overall east–west orientation of the settlement was important. Two building types are repeated throughout the site: smaller, four-roomed buildings, roughly 10 meters on a side and usually set at a distance from other structures, and larger, multiroomed complexes—some of which seem to have the smaller,

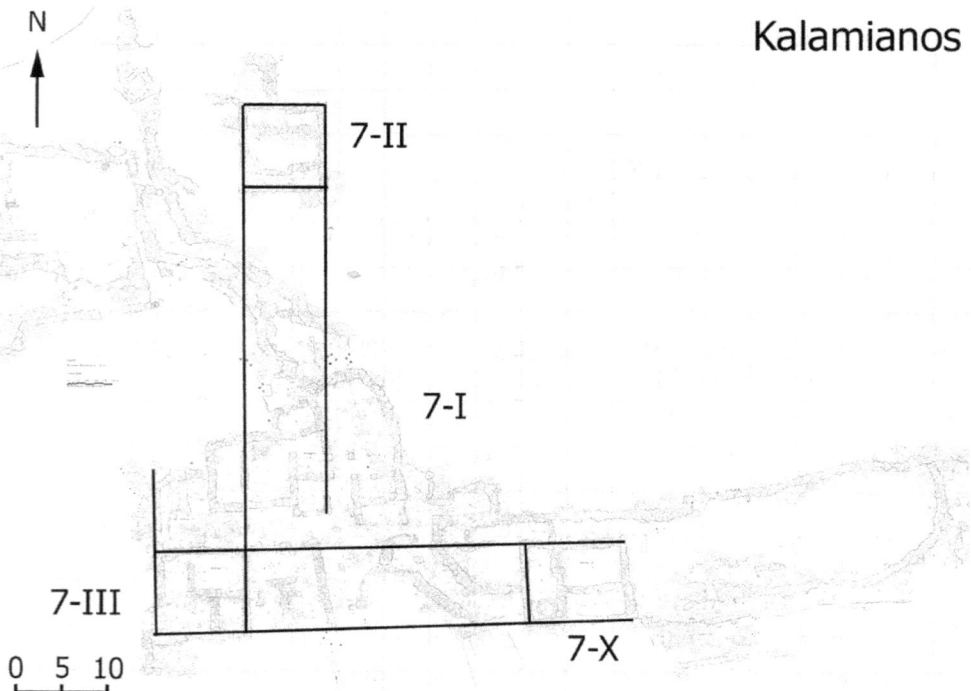

FIGURE 10.4. Alignment of walls among Buildings 7-I, 7-II, 7-III, and 7-X at Kalamianos.

10 x 10-meter unit as a core—that are often crowded together, separated by streets and paths. The smaller, 10 x 10-meter unit has not yet been identified at other Mycenaean sites (Darcque 2005), but few Mycenaean settlements have been explored sufficiently. Darcque (2005:323–326, Figure 100) lists only 141 buildings from all excavated Mycenaean sites— spanning the period from LH I through LH IIIC (i.e., several centuries more than the period represented by Kalamianos)—that are preserved well enough to provide dimensions. Those portions of Mycenaean settlements outside of citadel walls that have been explored seem to have been used continuously over many generations and, thus, would not have provided the same opportunity for the construction *ex novo* of a settlement.

The buildings at Kalamianos are found both in densely packed neighborhoods with no exterior space between adjacent structures as well as free standing with substantial space between nearby structures. This difference in the spacing of structures may be due in part to functions of the buildings or their location within the site. But some of the groupings of the architecture are apparently due to the proximity of water sources, in the form of fresh water being found in bedrock fractures (fissures) located along exposed fault lines. Some of these fractures have been enlarged through erosion, forming linear solution joints or fissures, which are the source of fresh water even today (Figure 10.5); several

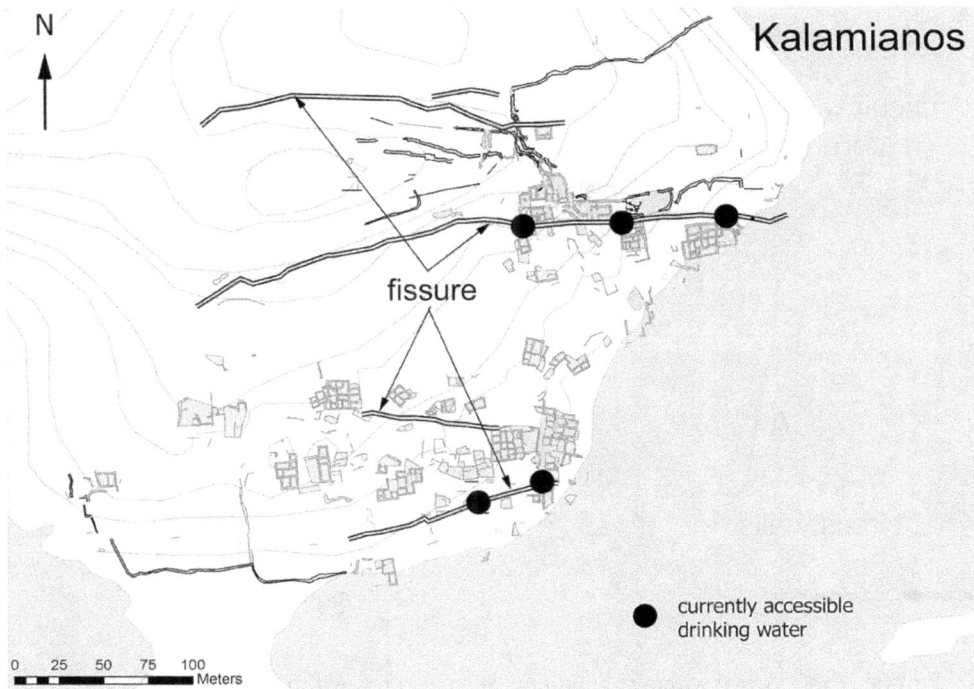

FIGURE 10.5. Bedrock fractures (fissures) and currently available water sources at Kalamianos.

of the fissures have artificially been widened or modified (Tartaron et al. 2011:566–567, Figure 8).

One of the most unusual aspects of the space enclosed by the circuit wall is how much of it is empty (Figure 10.6). Structures occupy less than one-half, approximately 3.5 hectares, of the total 7.2 hectares space within the circuit walls. We have counted as occupied land that lies within 20 meters of structures or land between structures separated by no more than 30 meters; we included areas of debris without defined walls as structural. Furthermore, terraces—many of which are most likely Mycenaean in construction—cover a significant portion of the "unoccupied" area of the enclosed town site, approximately 2 hectares (Kvapil 2012).

What is particularly striking about the pattern of structures versus terraces identified as Mycenaean within the circuit wall is how the majority of the terraces seem to be located within a distinct quadrant that measures over 160 meters east–west by 90 meters north–south, or 1.4 hectares (Figure 10.7). One explanation for the presence of

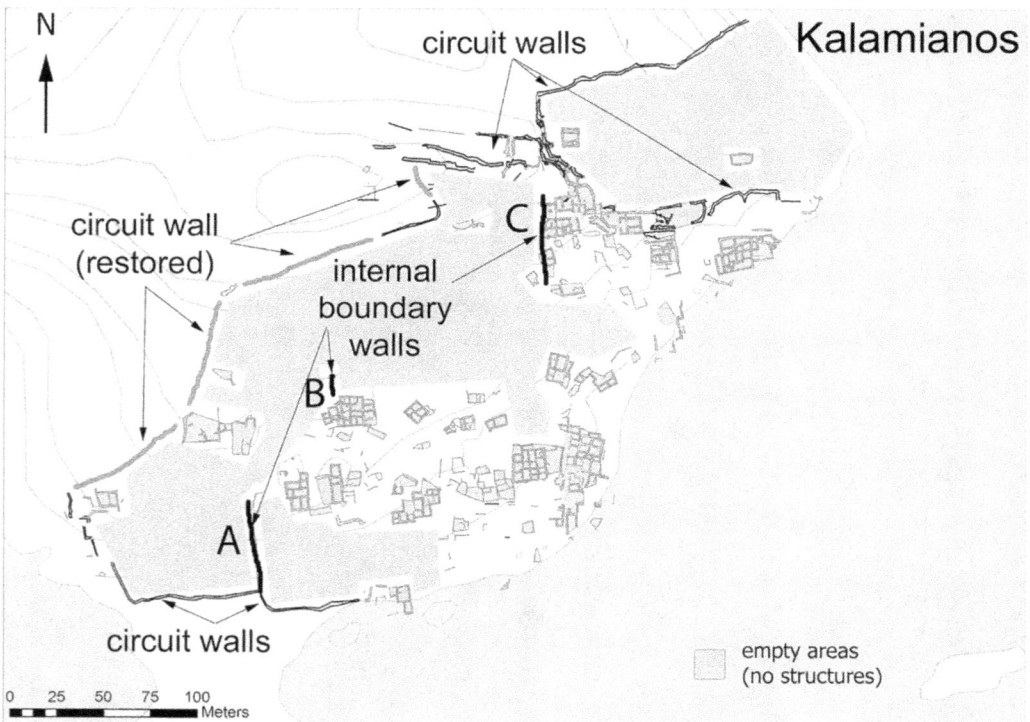

FIGURE 10.6. Areas without buildings or structures within the circuit walls at Kalamianos.

FIGURE 10.7. Quadrant of terraces within the circuit walls at Kalamianos.

terraces and no structures in this quadrant might be the apparent lack of readily available water in the fissures.

On one of the higher elevations within the circuit walls of Kalamianos along the northern edge of the terraced quadrant—with a view downslope over the terraces—we found a threshing floor of a semicircular shape, roughly 11 x 5 meters (Figure 10.8; for location, see Figure 10.2). The dating of this feature is admittedly circumstantial, but a Mycenaean date is the best suggestion given its location and masonry style. The masonry style of the retaining wall is consistent with the architecture of the buildings as well as with the style of terrace wall construction that Lynne Kvapil has identified as Mycenaean. As Kvapil (2012:233) points out, the later terraces at Kalamianos were used for olives and, thus, no threshing floor would have been needed. Early modern threshing floors tend to be located in close proximity to structures, such as houses or churches. If the Mycenaean date for the Kalamianos threshing floor is upheld, this would be a unique find for Late Bronze Age Greece.

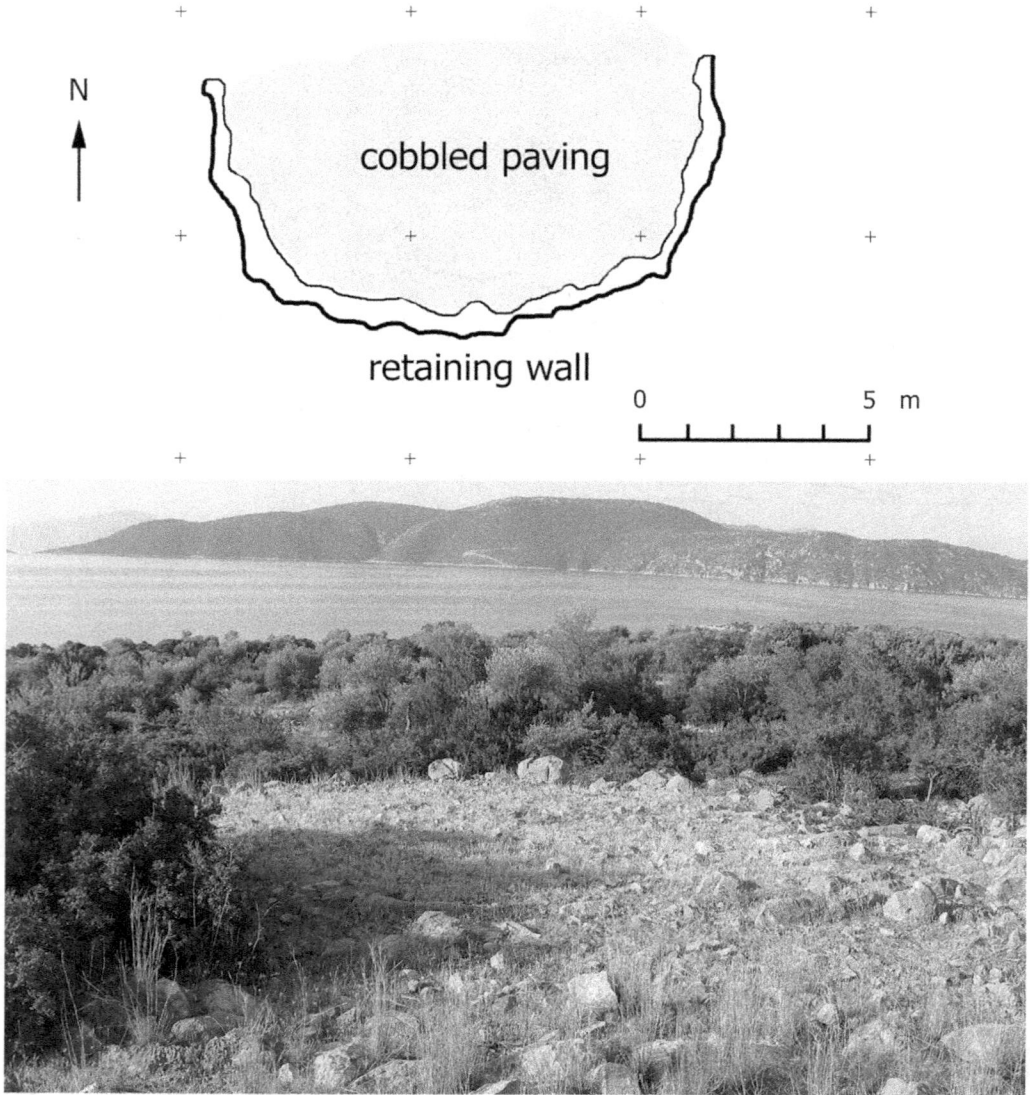

FIGURE 10.8. Threshing floor of possible Mycenaean date at Kalamianos. Plan (above) and view to south (below).

THE HINTERLANDS OF KALAMIANOS

In the hinterlands of Kalamianos, we documented one additional large Mycenaean site, Stiri at 1.4 hectares, and two small Late Bronze Age sites that controlled various points of access (Tartaron 2015; Tartaron et al. 2011) (Figure 10.9). The buildings at Stiri are different from those at Kalamianos in that they lack the monumentality of many of the

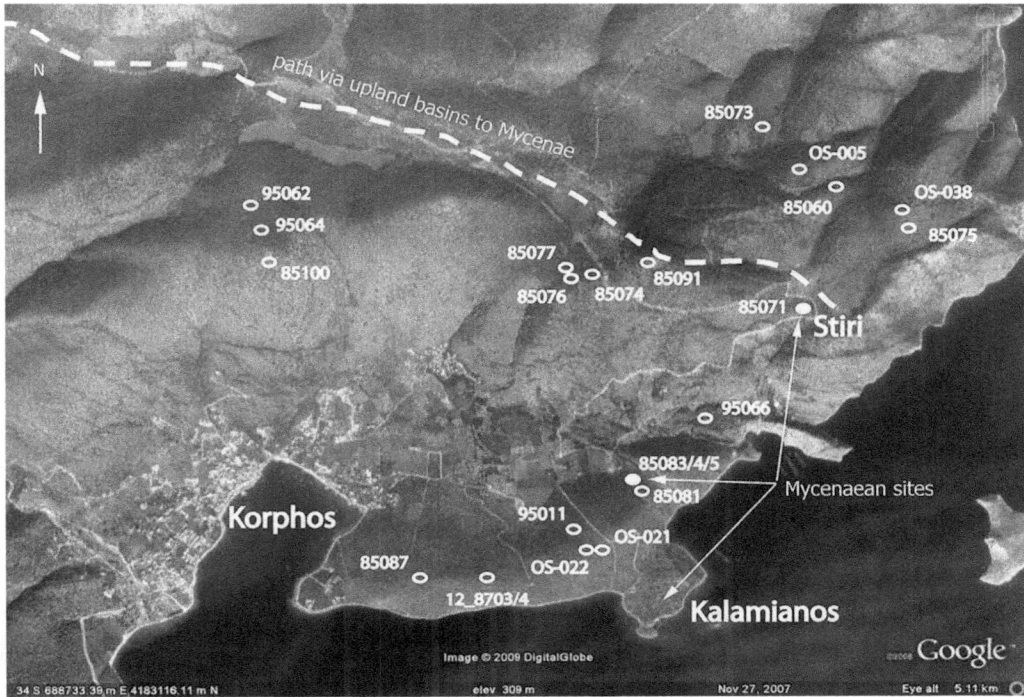

FIGURE 10.9. Activity areas of all periods, including those of Mycenaean date, identified in the hinterlands of Kalamianos through archaeological survey, with path via upland basins to Mycenae.

Kalamianos structures and they seem to be more sprawling. The settlement at Stiri is on the low hills that surround one of two *poljes,* or upland basins, that would have provided some agricultural land. Stiri lies at the eastern end of an overland route to Mycenae, about 50 kilometers (one long day's walk) to the west via a series of additional upland basins and valleys, which also could have been exploited without significant alterations of the landscape.

All around Kalamianos and Stiri are hundreds of agricultural terraces, many constructed in typical Mycenaean masonry style. Kvapil (2012) estimates that at least 15 hectares of land outside of the urban settlement of Kalamianos and the settlement at Stiri was covered with terraces in the Late Bronze Age—a substantial investment in labor; she estimates 105,000 workdays for their construction, probably a large overestimate. Within the walls of Kalamianos, the 2 hectares of terraces would have required an estimated 14,000 workdays to construct, a figure that Kvapil (2012:201–202) points out is similar to the estimate of Cavanagh and Mee (1999:100) for the construction of the Treasury of Atreus at Mycenae (but for different estimates, see Harper 2016). Thus, nearly 120,000 workdays might have been needed just to construct the agricultural terraces, according to Kvapil's estimates. If these terraces were built during the same period as the rapid expansion of Kalamianos, which seems highly likely, then the total construction effort of the 7.2 hectares large town, the circuit walls, buildings, and terrace walls, and at least 15 hectares of agricultural terraces outside of the circuit walls represents a tremendous investment of labor and capital in this region.

Mycenaean Planning and Settlement Founding

At this point, we can see that there is a large amount of capital and labor invested in the construction of Kalamianos town and its hinterland. Two questions now arise: first is to consider the extent to which this investment came from the palatial authorities at Mycenae; and second, once established, how much control over the daily maintenance of the population did the palatial authorities retain, or were people left to other mechanisms, such as markets or independent household self-sufficiency, in order to sustain themselves?

The architectural features of several of the buildings, especially Building 7-I/7-III, the repetition of the 10 x 10 meters core building plan, and the overall planning of the settlement—including the setting aside of a distinct sector for terraces within the circuit walls—are most likely due to palatial involvement. As noted above, we generally lack comparable data on Mycenaean settlements, therefore it is difficult to tell how much planning there is at sites other than Kalamianos. The site of Glas in Boeotia (Central Greece)—built in conjunction with the massive infrastructure to drain the Kopais Basin and, thus, create an immensely rich agricultural area—provides our sole comparable Mycenaean situation of the establishment of a new settlement (Iakovidis 2001). The buildings at Glas were erected at the beginning of LH IIIB1, and were continually occupied until destroyed in LH IIIB2, a time span similar to that of Kalamianos. It has been suggested that the draining of the Kopais and the founding of Glas was undertaken by the long-settled neighboring palace center of Orchomenos to the west (Iakovidis 2001:151–153). Thus, Glas could be considered an outpost founded by a palatial center (Orchomenos) in a situation similar to that at Kalamianos. The 20 hectares enclosed by the circuit walls at Glas have not been well explored by excavations, except for the central enclosure of ca. 5 hectares. Recent geophysical exploration by Christofilis Maggidis and his team has revealed a large number of possible structures outside of the central enclosure, some of them on the same alignments, but there has been no archaeological confirmation of the dates of these anomalies (Maggidis and Stamos 2016). The central enclosure, as published by Iakovidis (2001), has a series of extremely large structures—some measuring 130 meters in length—formally laid out in at least two subenclosures. Many of the structures seem to be devoted to large-scale storage of the agricultural produce from the now-drained Kopais, though the question of why some storerooms were decorated with frescoes remains unanswered. Architecturally, the structures in the central enclosure at Glas are quite different from those at Kalamianos. Until there is archaeological confirmation of the dates of the numerous structures outside of the central enclosure, we cannot make viable comparisons between them and those at Kalamianos.

The rareness of examples of newly founded settlements within Mycenaean Greece may well be a reflection of the already relatively dense settlement patterns on mainland Greece that have a long history stretching back into the Neolithic period (Pullen 2018). The draining of the Kopais Basin—in the case of Glas—and the need by Mycenae for a port on the Saronic Gulf—in the case of Kalamianos—would be two unusual circumstances that would have provided the opportunity for Mycenaean palatial elites to impose top-down urban planning. But the construction of Kalamianos or Glas was by no means out of the ordinary for the Mycenaean states. Large-scale infrastructure projects are a characteristic product of the Mycenaean states during this time period, including such projects as the draining of Lake Kopais, the construction of a dam near Tiryns to divert a river prone to flooding that town (Zangger 1994), the road systems around Mycenae and elsewhere (Jansen 2002; Morgan 1999:362–365, 437–447; Sjöberg 2004:144; Tartaron 2010:171–172), and the large number of fortified citadels and monumental buildings throughout the various Mycenaean kingdoms on mainland Greece.

MYCENAEAN MOBILIZATION, AGRICULTURAL SELF-SUFFICIENCY, AND KALAMIANOS

But it is the extent of palatial involvement in the provisioning of the construction workers, and whether that continued, that is of greater concern. The Linear B textual archives, best preserved at Pylos—and, thus, perhaps not pertinent to the situations in other regions, such as the Argolid with its multiple palace centers—document some mobilization of labor, transformation of exotic materials into finished goods, and, perhaps most impressively, the mobilization of huge quantities of foodstuffs for feasts. At the same time, the Linear B tablets are silent on large parts of the economy, such as ceramic and obsidian production. In the last decade or so, there has been a growing recognition of the variability among Aegean states and polities, and recognition of the importance of the nonpalatial components of the Mycenaean economy and society (Nakassis et al. 2011; Parkinson and Galaty 2007). Indeed, the growing consensus is that "most economic activity within the territories of the Mycenaean palaces took place outside the scrutiny of the Linear B bureaucracy. The same is very probably true even of transactions involving the palaces themselves" (Halstead 2007:72).

We can presume that the palatial centers had much to do with many of the large-scale infrastructure projects mentioned above, but the problem is that we do not know for certain as construction and building is one component of the economy that is not well documented in the preserved Linear B tablets. And we must keep in mind that there is a great variability among the various Mycenaean states and, thus, how one Mycenaean state operated may not reflect the ways other states operated. Nevertheless, one Linear B tablet at Pylos (PY An 35.1-3) records the assignments of wall-builders (*to-ko-do-mo*) in four towns (Duhoux 2008:296–298), some seemingly already in position (two men at Pylos and four men at Leuctron), whereas three men were to go to *me-te-to* (a town in the Hither Province) and three men to *sa-ma-ra*, one of the district capitals in the Further Province. In a reanalysis of Pylos tablet PY Fn 7 (a join of An 7 and Fn 1427), Nakassis (2013:275–279; 2015) argues that the two named individuals, *qa-ra₂* and *pa-ka*, are given large quantities of foodstuffs as payment for supplying (or provisions of) the unskilled labor of as many as 24 or more people for a building project that would last a month. The other personnel on the tablet are designated by their occupations, 20 wall-builders (*to-ko-do-mo*), five sawyers (*pi-ri-e-te-re*), and one all-builder (*pa-te-ko-to*) who is most likely the foreman or supervisor, and receive rations of at least wheat. In sum, then, this is a large work crew of multiple teams—about half of whom are skilled—for what must be a fairly substantial building project. I would suggest that we can extrapolate this evidence for wall-builders or masons in the Pylian kingdom to the manpower needed for the capital projects at Kalamianos as a distinct possibility. We can thus see substantial mobilization of labor under the auspices of the palace for various kinds of projects, including those related to building.

Oxen, in pairs or multiples of two, are recorded in the Linear B tablets from Knossos (e.g., KN Ce 59) as being given out for agricultural purposes by the palatial center (Palaima 2015:633–635). This indicates the interest of the palace (at least that at Knossos) in providing some of the "equipment" for agricultural production. Ox-tenders (*qo-u-ko-ro*) are recorded at Pylos and in conjunction with personnel involved in building projects (PY An 18 and PY An 852), suggesting some level of skill or responsibility, and on PY An 850 at least 18, but as many as 66, ox-tenders are listed in association with *ke-ke-me-na* land that Palaima (2015:626–628, 635) argues is "uninhabited" land in the process of being brought under cultivation. Thus, one could imagine a palatial authority sending oxen to Kalamianos for large-scale plowing of land, perhaps initially until the local residents could establish themselves, or for hauling large stones and other materials to worksites.

The palace at Pylos was able to mobilize large quantities of foodstuffs for feasts attended by many participants, sometimes on the order of thousands of people, but these seem to be periodic and not daily events (Bendall 2008; Nakassis 2012). Though more limited in variety of foods, the palace also distributed rations, as we see in conjunction with labor mobilization (Palaima [2015:617] prefers the term *food allotment* instead of *rations*). There is still uncertainty over the specifics of the measurement systems employed, but several lines of evidence point to a standard male worker ration of 1.2 liters of grain per day. A recent architectural production study by Harper (2016) suggests that the principal buildings at Kalamianos—but not including the circuit wall or terraces—would entail 158,079 person hours for construction, equivalent to 19,760 daily rations or 23,712 liters of grain for the project. Nakassis has estimated that the set of Linear B tablets at Pylos that deal with rations or payments in grain were equivalent to 55,000 daily rations. We do not know the length of time over which those 55,000 rations were disbursed, but it could be as short as a month (Nakassis 2010:134–136). As Harper (2016:311) concludes: "The volume of staple payments monitored by the palace at Pylos for perhaps a month well exceeds the equivalent daily rations that would be consumed during any of the architectural projects [at Kalamianos]; from the perspective of staple finance, architectural production may not have been especially burdensome."

Thus, based on the evidence from the Linear B tablets at Pylos, Kalamianos could have been provisioned by the palace at Mycenae, but this seems an unlikely scenario to have continued for the 100 to 150 years of existence of Kalamianos. Certainly, for the construction projects of the harbor town (at least those public portions) and the terraces in the hinterland, food allotments or provisions would need to have been mobilized and distributed, but from where these were mobilized is not known. The huge labor and capital investment in constructing the agricultural terraces indicates that a certain degree of agricultural self-sufficiency was part of the plan for the "colonization" of Kalamianos and its hinterland, at least after the establishment of the settlement.

Kalamianos is situated at the extreme limit of a one day's walk from Mycenae (50 kilometers), a distance greater than that generally thought to characterize the limits of a Late Bronze Age mainland polity (Pullen and Tartaron 2007:156–157), and we have little knowledge of Mycenaean settlement between Mycenae and Kalamianos. The mountainous interior of the Argolid/Corinthia east of Mycenae and the Berbati Valley is not well known archaeologically, though the presence of cyclopean fortifications at Vassa (modern Dimaina) west of Nea Epidavros (Hope Simpson and Dickinson 1979:Site A30) and the sanctuary on Mount Arachnaion (Psychogiou and Karatzikos 2015) hint that much more Mycenaean activity may well have been present in this area. Still, we lack an understanding of the political geography of the Late Bronze Age Argolid, such as the relationships among the various palatial and other fortified centers, and the extent of territorial control by the various centers, such as Mycenae, Midea, Tiryns, Asine, and others (Pullen 2013b:437–438; Pullen and Tartaron 2007). We do not know if a hierarchical settlement and political system of palace center, provinces, provincial centers, and other settlements—like those that characterize the Pylian kingdom—was operating at Mycenae and other sites in the Argolid. In contrast to Kalamianos, most of the other Mycenaean settlements in the Saronic Gulf lack the monumentality in their buildings, strengthening our suggestion of the ties between Kalamianos and Mycenae. Thus, while we posit that Mycenae itself was politically responsible for the establishment of the harbor town at Kalamianos, the provisioning of the construction projects of the circuit wall, town buildings, and the terraces may have taken place physically from one or more other—perhaps as yet unidentified—sites in the interior that may lie closer to Kalamianos, such as Vassa or somewhere near Angelokastro. Seaborne provisioning is possible from a port, such as the nearby Mycenaean town of Palaia Epidavros, undoubtedly one destination of the well-known Mycenaean road that runs across the several bridges in the Kazarma region.

Though 15 to 20 hectares of terraces documented throughout the study region represent a substantial investment in labor, the terraced land itself would be insufficient to supply a town of the size of Kalamianos. Using admittedly very gross estimates—and based on the identification of at least 50 structures (not all of them residential nor necessarily single-family occupied) and a standard five-person household—a guesstimate population of 250 people might require the harvest from at least ca. 75 hectares, based on minimal cereal production with some ox-plowed fields of 1,000 liters per hectare (Halstead [2014] provides much discussion of the ethnographic evidence; see especially p. 247–248). There are, however, other areas of arable land, such as the upland basins, that would not need terracing in order to be exploited, but the terraced land would be more accessible to the settlements.

Land close to a village is often exploited for gardens with more intensive husbandry practices (Halstead 2014:206–209), and this would perhaps include the terraces within the walls of Kalamianos, despite the presence of the threshing floor. Kvapil (2012:226–230) makes the suggestion that aromatics, herbs, or other nonsubsistence plants documented in the Linear B texts at Pylos were grown on these urban terraces. She argues that the large quantities of such aromatics supplied to the palace at Pylos for purposes of perfumed oil and cooking necessitated large-scale, dependable production of them. Some of the aromatics—such as cumin, coriander, safflower, and sesame—were domesticated by the Late Bronze Age, and would be good candidates for crops grown on the terraces within the Kalamianos circuit walls. Other aromatics and herbs were not domesticated and prefer moist environments (Kvapil 2012:227). The coastal region of Kalamianos would provide access to the many resources available in marshes (perhaps more extensive than in the present day), including some of the wild plants mentioned by Kvapil (Rothaus et al. 2003).

The suggestion of specialized agricultural production on the urban Kalamianos terraces is intriguing in that it may help explain not only why the palatial elite might have invested the capital and labor in constructing the terraces but also why a discrete area was set aside for agricultural production within the circuit walls of Kalamianos. One might expect gardens tended by individual households to be located adjacent to the houses, and many structures at Kalamianos do have open space around them, but the terraced quadrant for agricultural production could have been divided into smaller plots. Plots as small as ca. 120 square meters are recorded in the Linear B tablets (Palaima 2015:628–629), and it seems that one individual's landholdings could be dispersed in more than one locality. Given over to intensive cultivation practices, fertilized by manure of animals and watered by exploiting the fissures, small plots in the terraced quadrant of Kalamianos could have supplied substantial quantities of some of the specialized crops mentioned in the tablets, thus providing a return on some of the capital investment.

The evidence is strong, then, for a Mycenaean state to ensure that some degree of agricultural self-sufficiency was possible over the long term when founding an "imperial" outpost, such as the harbor town of Kalamianos. On the other hand, while feasible, the practicality of continued maintenance of the population at Kalamianos is doubtful. To more completely address this question of the self-sufficiency of the Kalamianos region, one could investigate the productive capacity of the entire Kalamianos region taking into account a variety of agricultural production strategies, including animal husbandry, establishing a better population estimate for Kalamianos and its satellite community of Stiri, and deriving more precise labor and time inputs for the construction projects of circuit walls, terraces, and structures, along with estimates of food allotments (whether through feasting or rations). Ryan (this volume) likewise calls for the examination of the "sustainable community," that is, the social network necessary to maintain a residential community.

KALAMIANOS AND THE ECONOMIC DYNAMICS OF THE SARONIC GULF "SMALL WORLD"

Why did the palatial authorities at Mycenae go to such lengths to establish Kalamianos and settle the region? For this, we need to examine the historical dynamics of the Saronic Gulf "small world" within the context of our newer understanding of Mycenaean political economies.

In our current understanding of the political and economic dynamics in the Saronic Gulf, Kolonna on Aigina—one of, if not the largest and most important settlements in Middle Bronze Age Greece outside of the palaces on Crete—ceased to be the dominant center in the Saronic by the beginning of LH IIIA, if not before. Kolonna no longer was the endpoint of maritime traffic into the Saronic (Gauss 2010). At the same time, several other sites around the Saronic emerged as important centers, including Megali Magoula near Poros (Konsolaki 2003), Kanakia on Salamis (Lolos 2012), Eleusis (Cosmopoulos 2014), Athens, and Kontopigado Alimos in Attica (Kaza-Papageorgiou 2011), though most of these sites were long-established and not new foundations like Kalamianos. Kalamianos was founded by the end of LH IIIA2 in order for the Argolid centers to participate in this multicentric economy of the Saronic Gulf. Palaia Epidavros, on the east end of the Mycenaean road from Nafplion, undoubtedly also prospered at this time. What sets Kalamianos apart from these other circum-Saronic centers is its foundation by, and close association with, Mycenae.

Attempts to assess the scale of long-distance exchange between the Aegean and the East Mediterranean regions generally reveal infrequent exchange events (Cline 2007; Parkinson 2010; Ward 2010), though the Uluburun shipwreck (Pulak 1998, 2001, 2008, 2010) often skews our perceptions. Little attempt has been made to assess the scale of medium-distance or short-distance exchange within the Aegean. The increasing number of petrographic and other, similar sourcing studies will provide much-needed data to address the issue of medium- and short-distance exchange in the Mycenaean period. Shelton (2010) and Thomas (2005) have each argued for large-scale production of ceramics at Mycenae by a few potters, such as the owner of the Petsas House. If one considers the scale of distribution systems needed to supply the population of a region with ceramics, market exchange provides a more reasonable mechanism than centralized palatial redistribution or mobilization (Hruby 2006:Note 74; Pullen 2013b:441–442; Stark and Garraty 2010:43–44; Thomas 2005:536–537; Whitelaw 2001:64–65).

There is a great need to consider the role of merchants and market exchange in Aegean societies and to move away from the old redistribution model of Polanyi (1968) and Finley (1973) that has dominated discussions of Aegean Bronze Age economies (Parkinson et al. 2013; see also Bennet and Halstead 2014). All too often Mycenaean political and economic organization is viewed through a monolithic, strictly hierarchical model of the Mycenaean state, as formulated by Kilian (1988:297, Figure 3), and based in large part on the Linear B tablets from Pylos (Nakassis 2010; Pullen 2013b). In that model, there is little room for any economic activity other than palatial redistribution nor is there allowance for any social or political organization other than familial, lineage, or royal hierarchies. As noted above, there has been a growing recognition of the variability among Aegean states and polities and recognition of the importance of the nonpalatial components of the Mycenaean economy and society (Nakassis et al. 2011; Parkinson and Galaty 2007). Nakassis's (2012, 2013) work on Pylian prosopography has demonstrated that individuals in the Linear B tablets can have multiple roles in activities related to palatial interests, some of them at the local level and others at the kingdom level. If we consider the large portion of sociopolitical and economic activities that are not of interest to the palace and, thus, not recorded in the Linear B archives, then those individuals with multiple roles to play would also have multiple loyalties, multiple allegiances—in short, they would be involved in multiple exchange relationships with people at many different levels of the political spectrum, from local to kingdom levels, both within and outside the interests of the palace. Many of those exchanges outside the sphere of palatial interests could take place in the context of market exchange, as I suggested in the recent *American Journal of Archaeology* forum on Aegean Bronze Age markets (Pullen 2013b).

I suggest that the establishment of the port town of Kalamianos was part of the infrastructure to facilitate exchange and markets. A characteristic of market systems in complex societies is the construction of facilities for exchange to take place or the establishment of ways to facilitate exchanges (Feinman and Garraty 2010; Stark and Garraty 2010). We lack the evidence for physical marketplaces, and here we must state that we do not think the courtyards of the palaces are suitable as marketplaces (see Nagle 2015). We have extensive evidence for roads in the Argolid, and it is clear that many of these roads are for local circulation, connecting rural agricultural areas with the urban centers (Jansen 2002; Morgan 1999:362–365, 437–447; Sjöberg 2004:144; Tartaron 2010:171–172). Markets in general facilitate the horizontal integration of many actors and, at the same time, provide opportunities for interaction among actors at different levels in a society. The roads provide the physical means for the horizontal integration of producers and consumers through market exchange. Local elites provide a means of vertical integration between the common households of the countryside and the palatial centers as these elites operate both at the local level and at the regional/palatial center level.

The establishment of Kalamianos allowed the elites at Mycenae specifically to tap into the burgeoning economic activity in the Saronic Gulf, connected with the wider Aegean and Crete to the south and also via the Isthmus of Corinth to the Corinthian Gulf, and expanding regions to the north and west. While Polanyi's (1963) concept of "port of trade" might at first be thought to be applicable to Kalamianos, problems with his overly strict definitions, erroneous interpretations of textual evidence from the eastern Mediterranean and ancient Near Eastern polities, and his refusal to recognize market forces in "precapitalist" societies (McGeough 2007:8–37; Monroe 2009:1–23) make his concept as explicitly defined difficult to utilize. Kelly's (1991; see also this volume) gateway model as applied to Cahokia provides some interesting points to consider in how Kalamianos might have operated within the larger state based at Mycenae, in particular, how the distinction between long-distance and local trade may not be especially pertinent. But perhaps more appropriate for Kalamianos would be to consider it as a newly established node in a dynamic network of exchange relationships in the Late Bronze Age Aegean.

But Kalamianos was perhaps not completely self-sufficient and too dependent upon its link with Mycenae, for when the palace system collapsed at the end of LH IIIB Kalamianos ceased to be occupied, unlike many of the other preexisting centers around the gulf. Local tectonic events may have exacerbated this demise, though geological events are notoriously difficult to pinpoint in archaeological chronology. We may perhaps have a historical reference to this sequence of events in Strabo's *Geographica* of the late first century B.C.: he describes the hitherto unlocated Homeric site of Eïones in Diomedes's coastal kingdom (*Iliad* 2.561), along either the Argolic or Saronic Gulf, as originally a small community, only to have the people from Mycenae come and transform it into a naval station. But, as Strabo (*Geographica* 8.6.13) continues, the harbor disappeared from view, and is no longer usable as a port. Indeed, today the usable harbor of the area is some 3 kilometers to the west at the small, modern village of Korphos, and the urban center of Kalamianos still stands abandoned.

ACKNOWLEDGMENTS

I would like to thank my good friend and colleague Attila Gyucha for the invitation to participate in the 9th IEMA Conference at the University at Buffalo. I would like to thank Dimitri Nakassis and Thomas Tartaron for their comments on my paper. The Saronic Harbors Archaeological Research Project operates under the auspices of the American School of Classical Studies at Athens with a permit granted by the Hellenic Ministry of Culture. I would like to thank Dr. Konstantinos Kissas and Panayiota Kasimis of the 37th Ephoreia of Prehistoric and Classical Antiquities, Dr. Dimitris Athanassoulis of the 25th Ephoreia of Byzantine Antiquities, the Ephoreia of Underwater Antiquities (Enalion), and the Institute for Geology and Mineral Exploration (IΓME) for their assistance with all parts of our research. Thanks are due to the former director of the American School, Jack Davis, for his help and advice. Funding for SHARP has come from the following agencies and institutions: Institute for Aegean Prehistory, U.S. National Science Foundation (BCS-08100960), Stavros S. Niarchos Foundation, Loeb Classical Library Foundation, Arete Foundation, Florida State University, and the University of Pennsylvania.

REFERENCES CITED

Bendall, L. M. 2008 How Much Makes a Feast? Amounts of Banqueting Foodstuffs in the Linear B Records of Pylos. In *Colloquium Romanum*, edited by A. Sacconi, M. Del Freo, L. Godart, and M. Negri, pp. 77–101. Pasiphae 1. Fabrizio Serra, Pisa.

Bennet, J., and P. Halstead 2014 O-no! Writing and Righting Redistribution. In *KE-RA-ME-JA: Studies Presented to Cynthia W. Shelmerdine*, edited by D. Nakassis, J. Gulizio, and S. A. James, pp. 271–282. INSTAP Academic Press, Philadelphia.

Cavanagh, W., and C. B. Mee 1999 Building the Treasury of Atreus. In *MELETEMATA: Studies in Aegean Archaeology Presented to Malcolm H. Wiener as He Enters His 65th Year*, edited by P. P. Betancourt, V. Karageorghis, R. Laffineur, and W.-D. Niemeier, pp. 93–102. Aegaeum 20. Université de Liège, Histoire de l'art et archéologie de la Grèce antique, Liège.

Cline, E. H. 2007 Rethinking Mycenaean International Trade with Egypt and the Near East. In *Rethinking Mycenaean Palaces II*, edited by M. L. Galaty and W. A. Parkinson, pp. 190–200. UCLA Cotsen Institute of Archaeology Monograph 60. UCLA Cotsen Institute of Archaeology, Los Angeles.

Cosmopoulos, M. B. 2014 *The Sanctuary of Demeter at Eleusis: The Bronze Age*. Archaeological Society at Athens Library 295. Archaeological Society at Athens, Athens.

Creekmore, A. 2010 The Structure of Upper Mesopotamian Cities: Insight from Fluxgate Gradiometer Survey at Kazane Höyök, Southeastern Turkey. *Archaeological Prospection* 17:73–88.

Dao, P. 2011 *Marine Geophysical and Geomorphic Survey of Submerged Bronze Age Shorelines and Anchorage Sites at Kalamianos (Korphos, Greece)*. Master's thesis, School of Geography and Earth Sciences, McMaster University, Hamilton.

Darcque, P. 2005 *L'Habitat mycénien: Formes et fonctions de l'espace bâti en Grèce continentale à la fin du IIe millénaire avant J.-C.* Bibliothèque des Écoles françaises d'Athènes et de Rome 319. École française d'Athènes, Paris.

Duhoux, Y. 2008 Mycenaean Anthology. In *A Companion to Linear B: Mycenaean Greek Texts and Their World*, Vol. I., edited by Y. Duhoux and A. Morpurgo Davies, pp. 243–393. Bibliothèque des Cahiers de l'Institut de Linguistique de Louvain 120. Peeters, Leuven.

Evans, D., C. Pottier, R. Fletcher, S. Hensley, I. Tapley, A. Milne, and M. Barbetti 2007 A Comprehensive Archaeological Map of the World's Largest Preindustrial Settlement Complex at Angkor, Cambodia. *Publications of the National Academy of Science* 104(36): 14277–14282.

Feinman, G. M., and C. P. Garraty 2010 Preindustrial Markets and Marketing: Archaeological Perspectives. *Annual Review of Anthropology* 39:167–191.

Finley, M. I. 1973 *The Ancient Economy*. Sather Classical Lectures 43. University of California Press, Berkeley.

Gauss, W. 2010 Aegina Kolonna. In *The Oxford Handbook of the Bronze Age Aegean*, edited by E. H. Cline, pp. 737–751. Oxford University Press, Oxford.

Halstead, P. 2007 Toward a Model of Mycenaean Palatial Mobilization. In *Rethinking Mycenaean Palaces II*, edited by M. L. Galaty and W. A. Parkinson, pp. 66–73. UCLA Cotsen Institute of Archaeology Monograph 60. UCLA Cotsen Institute of Archaeology, Los Angeles.

Halstead, P. 2014 *Two Oxen Ahead: Pre-Mechanized Farming in the Mediterranean*. Wiley-Blackwell, Chichester.

Harper, C. R. 2016 *Laboring with the Economies of Mycenaean Architecture: Theories, Methods, and Explorations of Mycenaean Architectural Production*. PhD dissertation, Department of Classics, Florida State University, Tallahassee.

Hope Simpson, R., and O. T. P. K. Dickinson 1979 *A Gazetteer of Aegean Civilization in the Bronze Age: The Mainland and the Islands*, Vol. I. Studies in Mediterranean Archaeology 52. Paul Åströms, Göteborg.

Hruby, J. A. 2006 *Feasting and Ceramics: A View from the Palace of Nestor at Pylos*. PhD dissertation, Department of Classics, University of Cincinnati, Cincinnati.

Iakovidis, S. E. 2001 *Gla and the Kopais in the 13th Century B.C.* Library of the Athens Archaeological Society 221. Athens Archaeological Society, Athens.

Jansen, A. G. 2002 *A Study of the Remains of Mycenaean Roads and Stations of Bronze-Age Greece*. Mellen Studies in Archaeology 1. Edwin Mellen Press, Lewiston, New York.

Kaza-Papageorgiou, K. 2011 Κοντοπήγαδο Αλίμου Αττικής. Οικισμός τών ΠΕ καί ΥΕ χρόνων καί ΥΕ εργαστηριακή εγκατάσταση. *Αρχαιολογική Εφημερίς* 150:197–274.

Kelly, J. E. 1991 Cahokia and Its Role as a Gateway Center in Interregional Exchange. In *Cahokia and the Hinterlands: Middle Mississippian Cultures of the Midwest*, edited by T. E. Emerson and R. B. Lewis, pp. 61–80. University of Illinois Press, Urbana.

Kilian, K. 1988 The Emergence of *Wanax* Ideology in the Mycenaean Palaces. *Oxford Journal of Archaeology* 7(3):291–302.

Konsolaki, E. 2003 Η μαγούλα στον Γαλατά της Τροιζηνίας: Ένα νέο ΜΕ-ΥΕ κέντρο στον Σαρωνικό. In *Αργοσαρωνικός: Πρακτικά 1ου Διεθνούς Συνεδρίου Ιστορίας καί Αρχαιολογίας του Αργοσαρωνικού, Πόρος, 26–29 Ιουνίου 1998*, edited by E. Konsolaki-Yiannopoulou, pp. 159–228. Demos Porou, Athens.

Kostof, S. 1991 *The City Shaped: Urban Patterns and Meanings through History*. Little Brown, Boston.

Kvapil, L. A. 2012 *The Agricultural Terraces of Korphos-Kalamianos: A Case Study of the Dynamic Relationship Between Land Use and Socio-Political Organization in Prehistoric Greece*. PhD dissertation, Department of Classics, University of Cincinnati, Cincinnati.

Lolos, G. 2012 Η πρωτεύουσα του Τελαμώνιου Αίαντος: Αρχαιολογία και Ιστορία. In *Σαλαμίς Ι: Συμβολή στην Αρχαιολογία του Σαρωνικού*, edited by G. Lolos, pp. 15–66. Δωδώνη 83. Πανεπιστήμιο Ιωαννίνων, Ioannina.

Maggidis, C., and A. Stamos 2016 Re-Interperting Glas and Mycenaean Political Geography in the Light of Recent Field Discoveries. Paper presented at the 117th Annual Meeting of the Archaeological Institute of America, San Francisco. Electronic document: http://glas-excavations.org/pdf%20documents/Glas%20Paper.pdf.

McGeough, K. M. 2007 *Exchange Relationships at Ugarit*. Ancient Near Eastern Studies Supplement 26. Peeters, Leuven.

Monroe, C. M. 2009 *Scales of Fate: Trade, Tradition, and Transformation in the Eastern Mediterranean ca. 1350–1175 BCE*. Alter Orient und Altes Testament 357. Ugarit, Münster.

Morgan, C. 1999 *Isthmia VIII: The Late Bronze Age Settlement and Early Iron Age Sanctuary*. American School of Classical Studies at Athens, Princeton, New Jersey.

Nagle, D. M. 2015 *Principles of Spatial and Social Organization in Mycenaean Architecture and Settlements*. PhD dissertation, Department of Classics, Florida State University, Tallahassee.

Nakassis, D. 2010 Reevaluating Staple and Wealth Finance at Mycenaean Pylos. In *Political Economies of the Aegean Bronze Age*, edited by D. J. Pullen, pp. 127–148. Oxbow Books, Oxford.

Nakassis, D. 2012 Prestige and Interest: Feasting and the King at Mycenaean Pylos. *Hesperia* 81(1):1–30.

Nakassis, D. 2013 *Individuals and Society in Mycenaean Pylos*. Mnemosyne Supplements History and Archaeology of Classical Antiquity 358. Brill, Leiden and Boston.

Nakassis, D. 2015 Labor and Individuals in Late Bronze Age Pylos. In *Labor in the Ancient World*, edited by P. Steinkeller and M. Hudson, pp. 583–615. International Scholars Conference on Ancient Near Eastern Economies 5. ISLET, Dresden.

Nakassis, D., W. A. Parkinson, and M. L. Galaty 2011 Redistributive Economies from a Theoretical and Cross-Cultural Perspective. In *Forum: Redistribution in Aegean Palatial Societies*, edited by M. L. Galaty, D. Nakassis, and W. A. Parkinson. *American Journal of Archaeology* 115(2):177–184.

Palaima, T. G. 2015 The Mycenaean Mobilization of Labor in Agriculture and Building Projects: Institutions, Individuals, Compensation, and Status in the Linear B Tablets I. In *Labor in the Ancient World*, edited by P. Steinkeller and M. Hudson, pp. 617–648. International Scholars Conference on Ancient Near Eastern Economies 5. ISLET, Dresden.

Parkinson, W. A. 2010 Beyond the Peer: Social Interaction and Political Evolution in the Bronze Age Aegean. In *Political Economies of the Aegean Bronze Age*, edited by D. J. Pullen, pp. 11–34. Oxbow Books, Oxford.

Parkinson, W. A., and M. L. Galaty 2007 Secondary States in Perspective: An Integrated Approach to State Formation in the Prehistoric Aegean. *American Anthropologist* 109(1):113–129.

Parkinson, W. A., D. Nakassis, and M. L. Galaty 2013 Introduction. In *Forum: Crafts, Specialists, and Markets in Mycenaean Greece*, edited by W. A. Parkinson, D. Nakassis, and M. L. Galaty. *American Journal of Archaeology* 117(3):413–422.

Polanyi, K. 1963 Ports of Trade in Early Societies. *Journal of Economic History* 23(1):30–45.

Polanyi, K. 1968 *Primitive, Archaic, and Modern Economies: Essays of Karl Polanyi*. Edited by G. Dalton. Beacon Press, Boston.

Psychogiou, O., and Y. Karatzikos 2015 Mycenaean Cult on Mount Arachnaion in the Argolid. In *Mycenaeans Up to Date: The Archaeology of the Northeastern Peloponnese—Current Concepts and New Directions*, edited by A.-L. Schallin and I. Tournavitou, pp. 261–276. Skrifter utgivna av Svenska Institutet i Athen 4°, 56. Swedish Institute in Athens, Stockholm.

Pulak, C. 1998 The Uluburun Shipwreck: An Overview. *International Journal of Nautical Archaeology* 27(3):188–224.

Pulak, C. 2001 The Cargo of the Uluburun Ship and Evidence for Trade with the Aegean and Beyond. In *Italy and Cyprus in Antiquity 1500–450 B.C.*, edited by L. Bonfante and V. Karageorghis, pp. 13–60. Cyprus Antiquities, Nicosia.

Pulak, C. 2008 The Uluburun Shipwreck and Late Bronze Age Trade. In *Beyond Babylon: Art, Trade, and Diplomacy in the Second Millennium B.C.*, edited by J. Aruz, K. Benzel, and J. M. Evans, pp. 288–385. The Metropolitan Museum of Art, New York.

Pulak, C. 2010 Uluburun Shipwreck. In *The Oxford Handbook of the Bronze Age Aegean*, edited by E. H. Cline, pp. 862–876. Oxford University Press, Oxford.

Pullen, D. J. 2013a The Life and Death of a Mycenaean Port Town: Kalamianos on the Saronic Gulf. *Journal of Maritime Archaeology* 8(2):245–262.

Pullen, D. J. 2013b Exchanging the Mycenaean Economy. In *Forum: Crafts, Specialists, and Markets in Mycenaean Greece*, edited by W. A. Parkinson, D. Nakassis, and M. L. Galaty. *American Journal of Archaeology* 117(3):437–445.

Pullen, D. J. 2015 How to Build a Mycenaean Town: The Architecture of Kalamianos. In *Mycenaeans Up to Date: The Archaeology of the Northeastern Peloponnese—Current Concepts and New Directions*, edited by A.-L. Schallin and I. Tournavitou, pp. 377–390. Skrifter utgivna av Svenska Institutet i Athen 4°, 56. Swedish Institute in Athens, Stockholm.

Pullen, D. J. 2018 Caves and the Landscape of Late Neolithic–Early Helladic I Greece: Comparing Excavation and Survey Data from the Peloponnese. In *Communities in Transition: The*

Circum-Aegean Area during the 5th and 4th Millennia BC, edited by S. Dietz, F. Mavridis, Ž. Tankosić, and T. Takaoğlu, pp. 314–322. Oxbow Books, Oxford.

Pullen, D. J., and T. F. Tartaron 2007 Where's the Palace? The Absence of State Formation in the Late Bronze Age Corinthia. In *Rethinking Mycenaean Palaces II*, edited by M. L. Galaty and W. A. Parkinson, pp. 146–158. UCLA Cotsen Institute of Archaeology Monograph 60. UCLA Cotsen Institute of Archaeology, Los Angeles.

Rothaus, R., E. Reinhardt, T. Tartaron, and J. Noller 2003 A Geoarchaeological Approach for Understanding Prehistoric Usage of the Coastline of the Eastern Korinthia. In *Metron: Measuring the Aegean Bronze Age*, edited by K. Foster and R. Laffineur, pp. 37–48. Aegaeum 24. Université de Liège, Histoire de l'art et archéologie de la Grèce antique, Liège.

Shaw, J. W. 1990 Bronze Age Aegean Harboursides. In *Thera and the Ancient World III*, Vol. I, edited by D. A. Hardy, C. G. Doumas, J. A. Sakellarakis, and P. M. Warren, pp. 420–436. The Thera Foundation, London.

Shelton, K. 2010 Citadel and Settlement: A Developing Economy at Mycenae, the Case of Petsas House. In *Political Economies of the Aegean Bronze Age*, edited by D. J. Pullen, pp. 184–204. Oxbow Books, Oxford.

Sjöberg, B. L. 2004 *Asine and the Argolid in the Late Helladic III Period: A Socio-Economic Study*. BAR International Series 1225. Archaeopress, Oxford.

Smith, M. E. 2007 Form and Meaning in the Earliest Cities: A New Approach to Ancient Urban Planning. *Journal of Planning History* 6(1):3–47.

Stark, B. L., and C. P. Garraty 2010 Detecting Marketplace Exchange in Archaeology: A Methodological Review. In *Archaeological Approaches to Market Exchange in Ancient Societies*, edited by C. P. Garraty and B. L. Stark, pp. 33–58. University of Colorado Press, Boulder.

Tartaron, T. F. 2010 Between and Beyond: Political Economy in Non-Palatial Mycenaean Worlds. In *Political Economies of the Aegean Bronze Age*, edited by D. J. Pullen, pp. 161–183. Oxbow Books, Oxford.

Tartaron, T. F. 2015 Late Bronze Age Architecture and Regional Dynamics at Korphos in the Corinthia. In *Mycenaeans Up to Date: The Archaeology of the Northeastern Peloponnese— Current Concepts and New Directions*, edited by A.-L. Schallin and I. Tournavitou, pp. 391–401. Skrifter utgivna av Svenska Institutet i Athen 4°, 56. Swedish Institute in Athens, Stockholm.

Tartaron, T. F., and D. J. Pullen 2013 The Saronic Harbors Archaeological Research Project (SHARP): Two Seasons at Mycenaean Kalamianos. In *The Corinthia and the Northeast Peloponnese: Topography and History from Prehistoric Times until the End of Antiquity*, edited by K. Kissas and W.-D. Niemeier, pp. 231–238. Athenaia 4. Hirmer, Munich.

Tartaron, T. F., D. J. Pullen, R. K. Dunn, L. Tzortzopoulou-Gregory, A. Dill, and J. I. Boyce 2011 The Saronic Harbors Archaeological Research Project (SHARP): Investigations at Mycenaean Kalamianos, 2007–2009. *Hesperia* 80(4):559–634.

Thomas, P. M. 2005 A Deposit of Late Helladic IIIB1 Pottery from Tsoungiza. *Hesperia* 74(4):451–573.

Ward, C. A. 2010 Seafaring in the Bronze Age Aegean: Evidence and Speculation. In *Political Economies of the Aegean Bronze Age*, edited by D. J. Pullen, pp. 149–160. Oxbow Books, Oxford.

Whitelaw, T. M. 2001 Reading Between the Tablets: Assessing Mycenaean Palatial Involvement in Ceramic Production and Consumption. In *Economy and Politics in the Mycenaean Palace States*, edited by S. Voutsaki and J. T. Killen, pp. 51–79. Cambridge Philological Society Supplement 27. Cambridge Philological Society, Cambridge.

Zangger, E. 1994 Landscape Changes around Tiryns during the Bronze Age. *American Journal of Archaeology* 98(2):189–212.

CHAPTER ELEVEN

Architectural Visibility as an Integrating Mechanism in Roman Urbanism

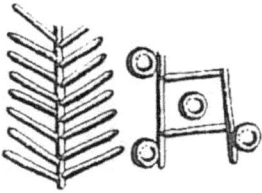

Micro-Viewshed Analysis at Pompeii

Alan Kaiser

Abstract   *Aggregated settlements need integrating mechanisms to hold the population together and keep the city viable. In Roman cities, integrative mechanisms also served to moderate tension between elite and nonelite—tension that sometimes erupted into violence. Among the integrative mechanisms was the opportunity for social, political, and economic advancement—an opportunity not so readily available in the countryside. A key tool for such advancement in Roman culture was public visibility of both an individual and architecture. This paper explores how the builders of four edifices at Pompeii manipulated views of the architecture in order to advance their own agendas. It also introduces modifications to traditional techniques of Geographic Information Systems viewshed analysis to better meet the needs of urban archaeologists.*

INTRODUCTION

In his introduction to this volume, Attila Gyucha quotes a CEO from Dubai worried that unhappy people will abandon a city. This CEO inadvertently touched on a major issue within the study of ancient agglomerated settlements—the agency of the individual in making and keeping such settlements viable. Cowgill has articulated this concern by arguing that "early cities did not simply 'happen' as consequences of technological, political, and economic innovations, but instead were actively and intentionally created" (2004:528). He suggests the key to finding how individual decisions add up collectively to create various aspects of urban society lies in improving "our ability to use the built environment to validly infer the social phenomena of which the built environment is both outcome and shaper" (2004:544).

This paper examines how four Pompeians from different classes and with different goals made choices about visibility when making their contribution to the built environment of the city. By understanding the nature of their decisions, we can begin to see how all were taking advantage of the opportunity presented by Roman cities for economic, social, and/or political advancement. Such opportunities helped to integrate these individuals into the city and created a safety valve that prevented them from leaving the city or turning to violence to get what they wanted, both of which happened in Roman cities. This paper also introduces some simple modifications to traditional Geographic Information Systems (GIS) viewshed analysis that overcome criticisms of the technique and make it more useful for analyzing data from urban sites.

THE ROLE OF VIEW IN THE INTEGRATION OF ROMAN AGGREGATED SETTLEMENTS

Roman civic officials must have shared the fear of the Dubai CEO mentioned above that urban residents might leave, because they actually did leave Rome on several occasions. Roman society was rigidly hierarchical, with the elite patricians holding more rights and privileges than the nonelite plebeians. Throughout the Republican period, the plebeians sought more economic, social, and political opportunities through either a process known as "secession," leaving the city *en masse* until their demands were met (Cornell 1995:256–258, 265–267), or through mob violence, which remained an endemic urban problem throughout Roman history (Maddox 1983).

If they are going to survive, all aggregated settlements need centripetal mechanisms to channel social tension into a positive and productive direction—a direction that avoids the centrifugal and debilitating extremes of secession or violence. In Roman cities, one of these centripetal mechanisms was social mobility. When an individual could seize an opportunity to improve his or her economic, social, or political situation that person became integrated into urban society, gaining a vested interest in keeping the city functioning rather than tearing it down through rioting or the abandonment of the city. We see this mechanism functioning successfully in Horace's *Epode* 4, where he describes an unnamed freedman proudly parading down one of Rome's busiest and most symbolically laden thoroughfares, the Via Sacra, wearing a toga, an outfit denied him by law when he was still a slave. This freedman earned a great deal of wealth after his manumission, and is happy to show everyone his elevation in economic and social position. Tension between elite and nonelite is still evident in the poem, however. Horace uses acerbic language to express the disgust he and his patrician readers felt at having to see this proud freedman wearing "their" clothing in public, but the tension has become a war of words rather than one of fists and swords. To the nonelite of Rome who saw this man and knew his story, he was a symbol of what they might one day become—he was a billboard for the benefits of urban life and working within the system.

Horace's freedman was not the only urbanite to use visibility to advance a personal agenda. Roman politicians were well aware of the prestige they could gain by being seen walking to the Roman Forum followed by a large crowd of supporters (Kaiser 2011:38, Note 236). Prostitutes wore distinctive outfits in the street to advertise their services (McGinn 1998:156–171), while beggars positioned themselves at city bridges so that those crossing would see them and, hopefully, give them a coin (Juv. 4.116–118, 5.4–9, and 14.134; Ov. *Ib.* 218). The manipulation of visibility went beyond personal appearance and extended to architecture as well. Cicero wanted to make his house highly visible to passersby, understanding that the exposure could benefit his political career (*Att.* 12.19; *Nat. D.* 2.141; *Dom.* 100 and 116). With a similar thought in mind, Publius Valerius Publicola built a house on Rome's Velian Hill; unfortunately, he went too far. His house overlooked, and was visible from, the Roman Forum—a move contemporaries interpreted as a bid for tyrannical power. To allay the fears of his critics, Publicola had to demolish his house and rebuild it in the least visible part of the city; a story that indicates the power of visibility (Plut. *Vit. Pub.* 10.2; Livy 2.7.9–12). The competition for pedestrians' eyes was fierce in Roman urban culture, but winning that competition, even for a few seconds, could bring significant benefits.

Archaeology can contribute to the study of view as an integrative social mechanism, and help us understand how that mechanism functioned within the built environment. Over the past generation, archaeologists working across the globe have come to recognize the active role architecture plays within a settlement. As Harrison and Bilgen state so succinctly in this volume, architecture is "a medium through which social actors communicate, manipulate, and express various social roles." Among Roman urban archaeologists, interest has grown in trying to identify how builders intended the view of their building to "communicate, manipulate, and express" their social aspirations, in addition to their roles. Unfortunately, a good methodology for conducting visibility studies has been slow to emerge. Diane Favro helped create a new method of investigating questions of architectural visibility and perception by pioneering a technique that can be called "imaginative viewshed" in her influential work *The Urban Image of Augustan Rome* (1996). Based on her extensive knowledge of the archaeological and literary evidence for construction in Rome during the reign of Augustus, she sought to show how the first emperor used architecture to reinforce his political messages by describing what an imaginary pedestrian would have seen journeying through the city. One problem with Favro's work is a lack of objective evidence; she shows a few plans, photographs, and reconstructions, but one must trust she has mastered the material—falsifying her work is a difficult task. In separate works, Laurence (2007) and Wallace-Hadrill (1995) have explored the issue of the visibility of brothels. Both argue, based on the literary evidence, that prostitution was shameful in the eyes of the elite. Using a plan of Pompeii, both point out that identified brothels are on side streets and, therefore, would have been invisible to the upper-class population of the city. DeFelice (2001:136–137) has scoffed at their argument, pointing out that prostitution is a highly mobile profession; prostitutes at Pompeii could have plied their trade on the main streets, as the literary evidence indicates they did at Rome. At the very least, a prostitute standing in front of one of the brothels on a Pompeian side street as an advertisement could have dramatically increased the visibility of that brothel, leaving

Laurence's and Wallace-Hadrill's contentions unproven. Ellis (2004:381–383) imagined the viewshed of 13 "bars," a term he uses for any business that sold drinks as well as ready-to-eat food, lining Pompeii's Via Stabiana north of the Stabian Gate. He believes the purpose of their location was to catch the attention of people entering Pompeii through the Stabian Gate, encouraging these hungry and thirsty travelers to refresh themselves once they caught sight of the beckoning establishments' counters. Ellis offers a plan of this section of the city, by which he suggests the viewshed is self-evident, but it does not, in fact, prove the bars' counters were visible from the Stabian Gate.

GIS programs avoid the pitfalls of the imaginative approach through objectivity and an inductive approach. GIS viewshed grew out of landscape archaeology and analyzes a digitized topographic map of the area of interest, allowing one to determine which parts of the plan a person could see from a chosen point (for examples from Roman contexts, see Eckardt 2009; Friedman 2008; Palet and Orengo 2011). Favro's reading of a photo or Ellis's of a plan are subjective interpretations which we can dispute—the thousands of calculations that produce a viewshed are an objective interpretation, one that we can check for accuracy. In addition, GIS viewshed analysis allows for an inductive investigation of the view of landscapes—one can run the viewshed and explore the resulting image. "Playing" with the data in this way can be a powerful exercise. Imaginative viewshed, as it has been used in Roman urban studies, is a deductive exercise involving the reading of the ancient Roman texts, forming a hypothesis about viewshed, and then looking for confirmation or falsification amid the physical evidence.

Despite these obvious advantages, there has been only one published GIS viewshed analysis of a Roman city (Kaiser 2003), even though the technique has been used to analyze rural landscapes from across the Roman world (e.g., Britain: Eckardt 2009; Spain: Palet and Orengo 2011; Jordan: Friedman 2008). Indeed, there has been resistance, and even antagonism, to the use of GIS viewshed to study Roman urban landscapes. Critics make some valid points. Coming from landscape archaeology, GIS viewshed is a big-picture tool concerned with visibility over a vast landscape or cityscape and so seems ill-suited to address the very local urban issues, such as those argued by Laurence, Wallace-Hadrill, DeFelice, and Ellis discussed above. The computer program also fails to consider the kinetic element of visibility in a city, something of which ancient Romans were fully aware as shopkeepers, politicians, and others sought to slow passage in order to get the full attention of passersby (Kaiser 2011:40; Laurence 2011:394–397). Indeed, the ancient poet Martial (7.61) complains of shopkeepers spreading their wares into the streets of Rome, slowing traffic in the hopes of turning a passerby into a customer. The interplay between movement and visibility forms the basis for much interaction within all aggregated settlements, leading to "energized crowding"—as Smith suggests in his intriguing chapter in this volume—that may be at the root of the very phenomenon of urbanism. Without considering movement, a GIS viewshed image lacks crucial contextual information. Finally, some modern scholars have complained that a computer-generated viewshed lacks clues to how one would have interacted with the environment using other senses (e.g., Betts 2011:119; Favro and Johanson 2010:15; Frieman and Gillings 2007:4–7). Porteus (1985:375) has summed up this criticism by mocking all types of "sheds," as "blandscapes," a joke repeated by Frieman and Gillings (2007:7) with specific reference to GIS viewsheds. Holleran (2011) has gone so far as to encourage urban scholars to utilize the older but better-trusted technique of imaginative viewshed analysis, abandoning GIS altogether.

We should not be so quick to dismiss GIS viewshed, however, as these shortcomings are not the fault of the technique but, instead, demonstrate a lack of imagination on the part of us, archaeologists. While a computer program will never be able to address all of the issues outlined above, we can deploy GIS viewshed in a much more creative way in order to adapt it to our needs in studying not just the ancient Roman urban environment but perhaps that of other cityscapes now lost to time. Below, I suggest some simple ways we can modify GIS viewshed analysis to make it a tool for answering current questions specific to Roman urbanism—and, in particular, the study of Pompeii—without losing the advantage of objectivity. Pompeii presents an unusual opportunity for urban spatial analysis thanks both to its extensive preservation and excavation (compare with Pullen and Ryan this volume). The central question addressed in the remainder of this chapter is whether four property owners at Pompeii (Figure 11.1) considered and manipulated views of their buildings either through the choice of their building's location or its decoration in order to advance their social, political, or economic agenda. This is a question a rebooted version of GIS viewshed can answer.

FIGURE 11.1. Aerial photo of central Pompeii, with buildings mentioned in the text.

GIS Viewshed 2.0: The View of a Bar

The easiest way to explain modifications to the traditional use of GIS viewshed analysis is through an example. As noted previously, Ellis was interested in explaining the location of bars along the Via Stabiana. The owners and operators of these bars were seeking customers, which guided their choice of location. Ellis argues that the placement of these bars indicates that the primary intended customers were travelers entering the city through the Stabian Gate, although issues with this assertion were noted above. GIS can help resolve these issues while also making it possible to explore the role of view in choosing a bar location and, ultimately, view as a tool for economic advancement.

Bar I.2.13 is one of a string of 13 that line the Via Stabiana north of the Stabian Gate mentioned by Ellis. To use GIS viewshed analysis on this building requires a rethinking of the global nature of the technique. In a crowded city such as Pompeii, people could have seen most buildings only from a short distance along the path of a street. Few buildings at Pompeii, or most other Roman cities, stood on a high enough elevation to be seen from a great distance. Therefore, micro-viewshed analysis is a better way to describe visibility within the very circumscribed area along the Via Stabiana from which pedestrians could have seen this particular bar. I selected 100 meters in both directions along the path of a street as the maximum extent of the urban micro-viewshed, using the very unscientific technique of walking down a street while paying attention to the maximum distance that I noticed and began to identify objects, buildings, and people. Higuchi (1983:9–12) argues that our perception of objects or people changes as we walk closer to them, moving through three different zones. To explain his idea using the Pompeian bar as an example, at first we have a long-distance view in which we are only peripherally aware of the bar; other elements of the environment closer to us capture most of our attention. Once we move closer into a middle-distance view, the bar moves further into our consciousness, perhaps reminding us we are hungry or thirsty. Entering the near-distance view, we begin to engage more of our senses, perhaps noting bar I.2.13 is busier than others nearby, then noting the laughter of patrons and catching the scent of the fare on offer (for a discussion of the perception of bar and shop sounds from the street, see Veitch 2017; for smell, see Derrick 2017). Following Higuchi's idea, we can break the 100 meters micro-viewshed into three equal zones: a short-distance view of 0–33 meters from the bar, a middle-distance of 33–66 meters, and a long-distance of 66–100 meters. By vectorizing the raster viewshed—in other words, tracing the finished viewshed image and laying the outline over an aerial photo of the neighborhood around the bar—it is possible to add a great deal of contextual information into the micro-viewshed analysis that is missing in a traditional GIS viewshed. An initial attempt to test the micro-viewshed of the counter in I.2.13 proved that it could only be seen from fairly close, so instead I assumed the owner placed a 1-meter-tall amphora on the sidewalk 1 meter in front of the counter to advertise, as we know shopkeepers in Rome did (Mart. 7.61). The resulting image, Figure 11.2, contains a great deal of information.

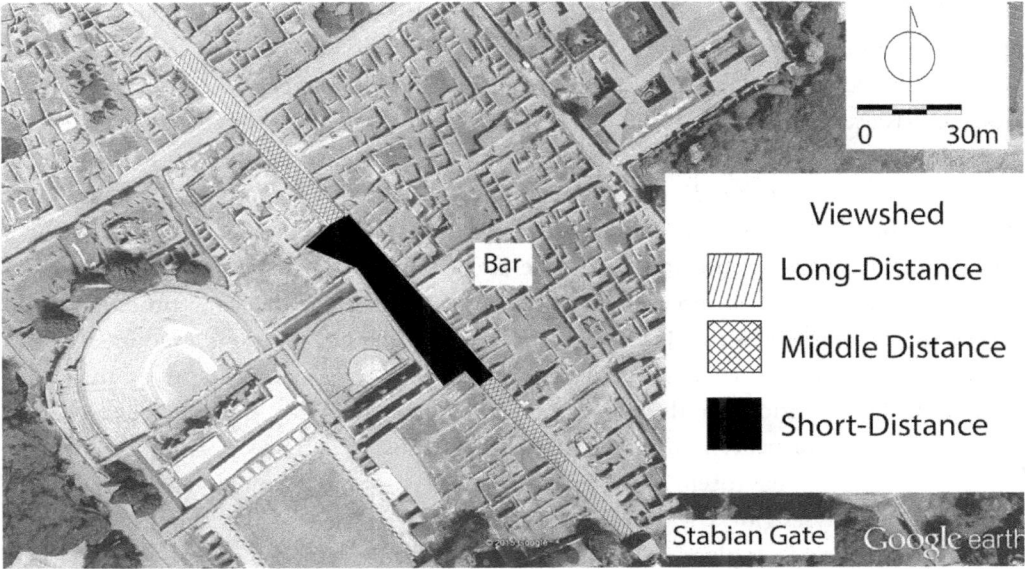

FIGURE 11.2. Micro-viewshed of bar I.2.13.

By sheer coincidence, the Stabian Gate is about 100 meters from bar I.2.13, the edge of the micro-viewshed analysis. The amphora would have been visible from the gate as well as 100 meters in the other direction, to the north. Nothing about its visibility privileges the view from the gate. More interesting than the bar's visual relationship with the gate is its visibility from the passages leading to the large and small theaters across the street from the bar. Theatergoers exiting these venues would have been within the short-distance view of the bar and, more importantly, coming from the west would have seen directly into the bar and the patrons enjoying the establishment's menu. If the owner considered the view in attracting customers when locating this bar, it seems far more likely he understood its power of drawing theatergoers rather than travelers from the gate. While theatrical performances did not happen every day, they must have occurred with enough frequency to comfortably support a bar like this. Supplying travelers with food and drink at times when the theaters were empty seems more like a supplementary way to gain income.

We can use Figure 11.2 to capture the kinetic half of the kinetic–visual experience by counting the number of doorways within the viewshed of the bar. Using the number of doorways as a proxy for the amount of traffic in that street has become one way of measuring the amount of activity as, presumably, people were coming and going through those doorways (Laurence 2007:102–116). Table 11.1 shows the number of doorways within the 200 meters micro-viewshed of bar I.2.13, which is very high when compared with the other three locations examined below. It is also well above the average number of doorways for a 200 meters stretch of street in Pompeii determined by dividing the total number of doorways in the city by the total length of all streets for an average number of doorways per meter, and then multiplying by the 200 meters street frontage of the viewshed (Kaiser 2011:63–64) (Table 11.1). We can also identify how the owners of the 57 buildings whose doorways are within the micro-viewshed used their structures (Table 11.2). The use of each building at Pompeii has been intensively studied for many years and numerous broad and specialized publications have discussed this subject, to which I have added my own observations at the site (Kaiser 2011:74–77). What is striking about Table 11.2 is the number of other bars one could see at the same time one could see I.2.13; the number is much higher than any of the other locations examined in this study—within the 33 meters short-distance view of the bar were no fewer than four other bars. Competition for the owner of bar I.2.13 was clearly quite fierce, especially from the moment a pedestrian first noticed it 100 meters away.

Of late, there has been a great deal of interest among Roman archaeologists in multisensory analyses (for a wide variety of examples, see Betts 2017). Figure 11.2 gives us the opportunity to explore the multisensory experience of walking past bar I.2.13 by determining what sounds and smells as well as sights would have emanated from this one bar in competition with its neighbors. Determining the multisensory experience of passing

TABLE 11.1
NUMBER OF DOORWAYS WITHIN THE MICRO-VIEWSHED OF EACH CASE-STUDY LOCATION

Case-Study Location	Doorways	Expected Number of Doorways	Total Length of Viewshed (m)
Bar I.2.13	57	30	200
Grand Lupanar	27	25	165
Temple of Fortuna Augusta	27	24	160
House of the Faun	54	30	200

TABLE 11.2
USES OF BUILDINGS WITHIN THE MICRO-VIEWSHED OF EACH CASE-STUDY LOCATION

Case-Study Location	Bars	Shops	Residences	Hospitia/ "Hotels"	Other
Bar I.2.13	13	28	6	2	8
Grand Lupanar	2	5	6	5	9
Temple of Fortuna Augusta	4	17	1	0	5
House of the Faun	5	29	13	0	7

this bar requires approaching it from what has been described as a "human scale" of the urban experience. Humans can recognize a face at a distance of about 21–25 meters; to comfortably speak with someone in the bar or smell the food being warmed at the counter one would have needed to have been within about 10 meters (Higuchi 1983:9–10). To taste a sample of the food or feel the cool of the marble counter one would have had to have been within an arm's length. The distance of 0–10 meters would seem to be a critical multisensory zone to the bar owner hoping to attract customers by engaging more of their senses. Within the 10 meters zone to the south of this bar is another entrance to this same bar, to the north is a bakery, and across the street to the west is the blank wall of the small theater. This bar was in an excellent multisensory location with little competition from neighbors. While the smell of fresh-baked bread may have competed with the smells of warm food from this bar, the two establishments sought different customers. The bar would have generated more sound than the bakery as customers chatted, perhaps loudly after a few drinks, and the sound bounced off the blank wall across the street. A bar owner could have leveraged several of the senses in this location to generate business.

Ellis (2004:81) argued that the analysis of visibility reveals a source of customers for this bar. The micro-viewshed analysis indicates that the person who chose I.2.13 as a location for a bar understood that the location's visibility could increase revenue, which was presumably the owner's goal. But it reveals more. The bar owner had studied this location, the traffic flow, the competition nearby, and the rhythm of the theater schedule. To be a successful entrepreneur, this bar owner had to learn about the city, and then invest in its built environment. This process integrated the bar owner into the urban culture of Pompeii. Below are three more case studies, where a micro-viewshed analysis reveals how others used architectural visibility to achieve their goals and, by so doing, become vested in Pompeian society.

THREE ADDITIONAL MICRO-VIEWSHED ANALYSES FROM POMPEII

A BROTHEL

In order to increase revenue, a well-chosen location allowed a bar owner to have the greatest possible visibility. As discussed above, Laurence and Wallace-Hadrill have argued the owners of brothels had the opposite desire, since prostitution was marked by shame. We cannot know for certain where prostitutes not affiliated with brothels may have plied their trade, but the architecture of brothels offers the opportunity to examine the micro-viewshed of prostitution. A number of brothels have been identified at Pompeii, the largest of which is Grand Lupanar (VII.12.18–19), whose identification is secure (DeFelice 2001:102–103). The brothel stands on a corner, and has an entrance onto two streets: the Vicolo del Lupanare, a north–south oriented street, and the Vicolo del Balcone Pensile which heads west from the brothel. To create the micro-viewshed, I assumed that a prostitute stood in front of each of the Grand Lupanar's doorways as a form of advertisement.

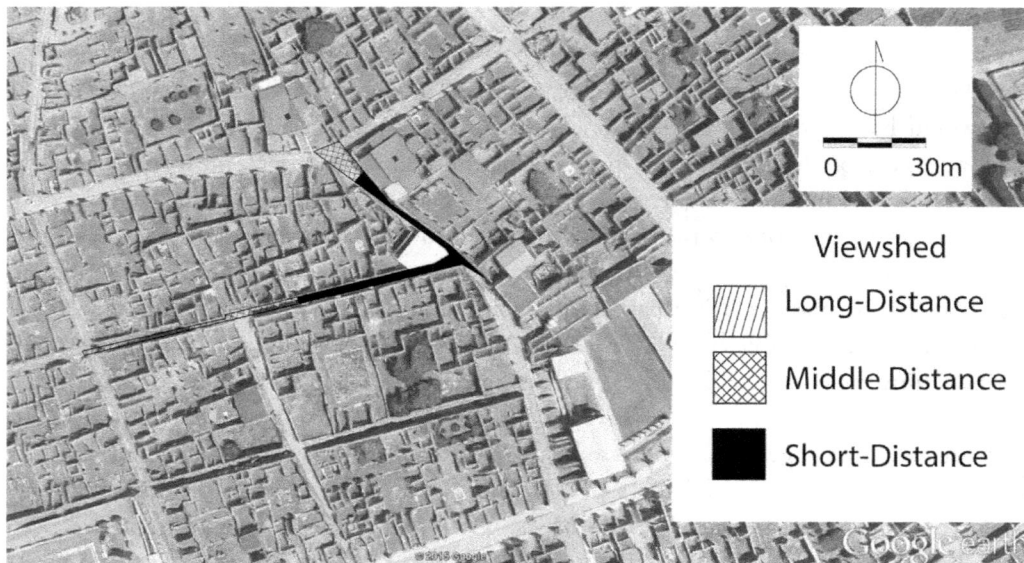

FIGURE 11.3. Micro-viewshed of the Grand Lupanar.

Figure 11.3 vindicates the position of Laurence and Wallace-Hadrill fairly power-fully—fewer people would have seen the prostitutes than the amphora in front of the bar, but it also suggests that the "right" people would have been made aware of the brothel's location. The curving of the streets limited the total viewshed to only 165 meters, not the full 200 meters of the bar, and the 27 doorways within the micro-viewshed are lower than the bar, while about average for a 165 meters stretch of a street at Pompeii (Table 11.1). The multisensory competition for attention was also much greater for the brothel than for the bar, with a malodorous laundry to the north, a noisy workshop to the east, a *hospitium* (or hotel) to the south, and a probable shop to the west. Despite its relatively lower visibility, the brothel's prostitutes were still highly visible to those who may have been their customer base. Doorways leading to five *hospitia* are within the micro-viewshed of the brothel (Table 11.2). Those who stayed at *hospitia* were usu-ally travelers from the nonelite class, such as sailors, itinerant merchants, or craftsmen (DeFelice 2001:23–27). Five is a high number to have within the brothel's viewshed; Pompeii has 33 identified *hospitia* and we should expect one at most in the 165 meters viewshed if they were distributed evenly across the city's streets. The unusual clustering of so many *hospitia* within the micro-viewshed of the Grand Lupanar may indicate a business strategy. Perhaps the central customer base for the brothel was not passersby on the street, but rather the visitors of the *hospitia,* an ever-changing group of men away from home and the prying eyes of friends, relatives, and neighbors.

Doorways leading to six residences are within the micro-viewshed of the brothel, a fairly typical number based on the evidence in Table 11.2. We can break down residences

TABLE 11.3

NUMBER OF DOORWAYS LEADING TO ELITE AND NONELITE RESIDENCES
VISIBLE WITHIN THE MICRO-VIEWSHED OF EACH CASE-STUDY LOCATION

Case-Study Location	Elite Residences	Nonelite Residences
Bar I.2.13	3	3
Grand Lupanar	1 (cellar entrance)	5
House of the Faun	7	6
Temple of Fortuna Augusta	0	1

into the categories of elite and nonelite based on factors such as building size, the existence and quality of decoration, and whether or not the building had an atrium, a requirement for an elite house according to the ancient architect Vitruvius (6.5.2–3; see also Kaiser 2011:76). The issue is relevant here as Laurence (2007:82–90) and Wallace-Hadrill (1995:51–55) argued that the elite wanted to shield their women and children from the corrosive moral effects of brothels. Only one of the six residences near the brothel can be considered an elite house, VII.1.40 (Table 11.3). Its main door is oriented toward a different street from the one that leads to the brothel, therefore people coming and going from the house would not have been within the brothel's viewshed. A side door, VII.1.43, opens onto the same street as the brothel, and is within the short-distance view of the brothel, but that door leads to a cellar. It is unlikely either the lady of the house or the children would have been using this door. The location of this brothel appears to have been very carefully chosen to create a compromise viewshed acceptable to elite moral norms without necessarily inhibiting the brothel owner's ability to make a profit. The micro-viewshed analysis suggests that—like the bar owner—the brothel owner used visibility in a carefully planned way to advance an economic agenda. The brothel owner clearly understood, and so must have been deeply integrated into, Pompeian culture.

THE TEMPLE OF FORTUNA AUGUSTA

The owners of the bar and brothel clearly chose their locations with visibility in mind for the purpose of economic advancement, but entrepreneurs were not the only people at Pompeii who understood the power of visibility to advance their agenda—freedmen did as well. Born slaves, some freedmen managed to acquire substantial resources after becoming free, and aspired to move their families up in social ranking. One way to do this was to participate in the imperial cult, a political-religious institution, whose priesthood—at least at Pompeii—consisted of freedmen and slaves. The Pompeian priests would make offerings to the goddess Fortuna for the health and safety of the living and dead emperors and their families. Sacrifices were always a public act—one stood in front of an altar that was outside of the temple and in view of both the deity's statue inside and of spectators outside. For someone trying to change his family's status, being able to publicly sacrifice something expensive—for instance, an ox—would offer a great opportunity to show his hearty support of the regime as well as his respect for the gods, crucial demonstrations for political and social mobility.

The Temple of Fortuna Augusta stood at the intersection of two important streets, the Via di Nola and the Via del Foro (Figure 11.4). According to an inscription, Marcus Tullius built this temple on his own land, dedicating it in 4 or 3 B.C., and leaving its care to a college of priests of the imperial cult. This temple is unusual in that the altar is on a platform that covers the sidewalk, and so stands almost directly on the street (Richardson 1988:202–206). Precinct walls or colonnades surround all the other temples and their altars at Pompeii; the lack of these features makes this temple unique. The obvious question is whether this was intentional in order to make sacrifices at this altar more visible than those at other temples, enabling wealthy freedmen to improve their social and political status.

Figure 11.5 demonstrates that the answer to this question is complicated. It shows from where a freedman standing at the altar in front of the Temple of Fortuna Augusta could have been seen and—given the discussion above—it appears to have been limited. Marcus Tullius did not choose this location in order for freedmen to be seen from far

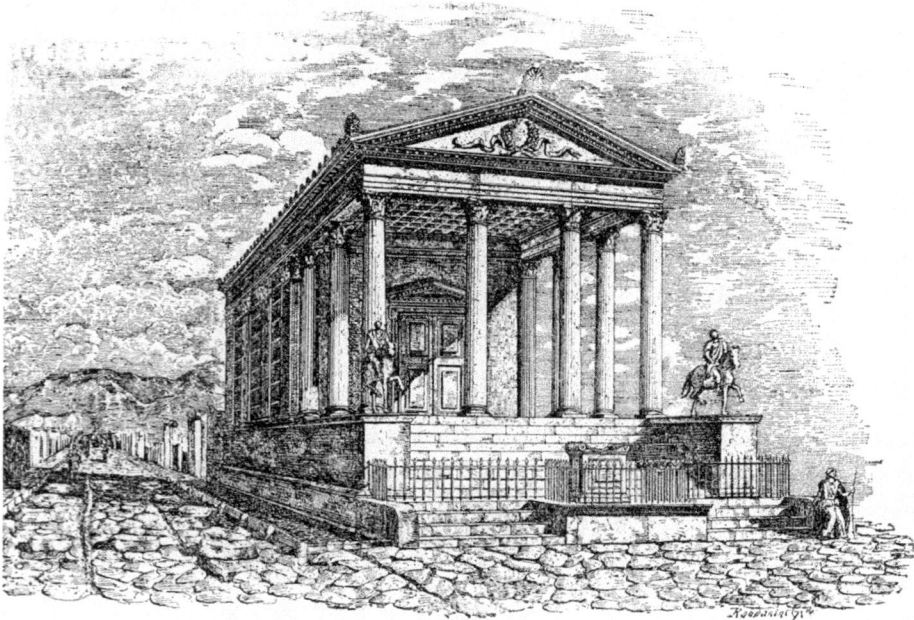

FIGURE 11.4. Reconstruction of the Temple of Fortuna Augusta (after Mau 1899:Figure 53).

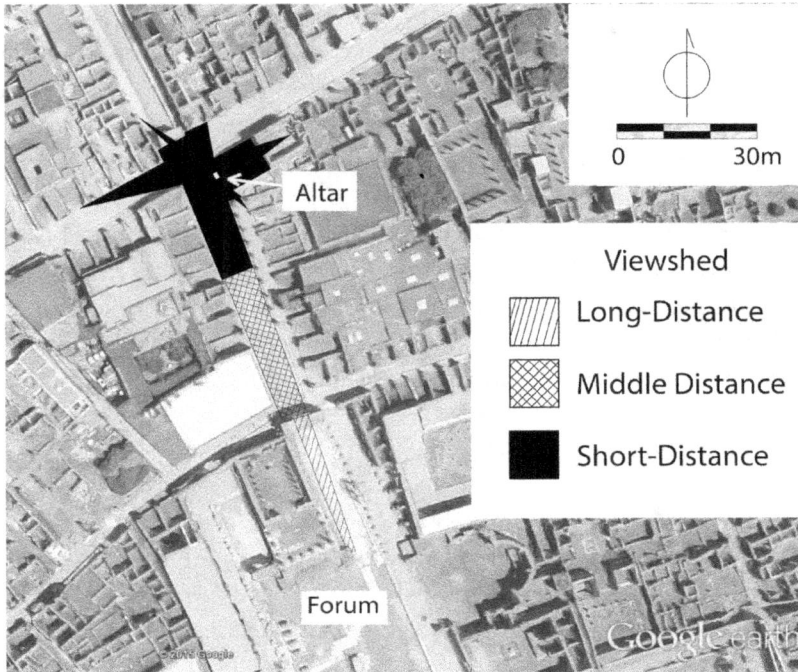

FIGURE 11.5. Micro-viewshed of the Temple of Fortuna Augusta.

away. The doorway count in Table 11.1 confirms that the person making a sacrifice would have been seen by as few passersby as would have seen the prostitutes standing in front of the brothel. It could be that the temple's location is opportunistic—Marcus Tullius just happened to own property at that corner and being seen making a sacrifice was not high on his list of considerations for locating the project. That does not mean this location lacked advantages, however, that helped the freedmen achieve their goals. A sacrifice was an unusual event and when it happened it was a spectacle. It was preceded by a procession as the person making the sacrifice walked to the temple with his toga drawn like a hood over his head. Servants with the offering—sometimes a live animal and a man to kill and butcher the animal—followed him as did a flautist, a servant with a fly whisk, as well as family and friends. We do not know the route such processions took at Pompeii, but it seems safe to assume from the close proximity of the temple to the forum, the political and social center of the city, that the procession passed through that location, allowing the freedman to parade in front of the town's elites, the very people whose ranks he hoped his children would join. People would surely have followed the procession in order to watch the show at the temple. The constricted space in Figure 11.5 would have meant those crowding in to watch the action at the altar and listen to the freedman's prayer would have blocked traffic temporarily on the Via di Nola and the Via del Foro, the former of which cart drivers used heavily, as deep ruts in the pavement indicate, and the latter of which gave access to the forum. The viewshed reaches into the forum; the elite who missed the procession and whose curiosity was piqued by the crowd could have stood in the northeastern part of the forum to see who was causing all the commotion. This is an ideal location for drawing views in the short distance and for a freedman to dominate a corner, and back up traffic, within view of the forum.

Visibility was a tool freedmen could use as well as the bar and brothel owners could. Having a path toward political and social advancement for themselves and their descendants must have made these men want to help Pompeii succeed and thrive. Knowing they could command attention—even if only briefly—by sacrificing at the Temple of Fortuna Augusta made them an integral part of the city's culture.

THE HOUSE OF THE FAUN

Elites were just as eager to draw attention to themselves as merchants and freedmen—in Roman society, getting people to notice them was essential for maintaining their social status and for successfully competing with their peers. Patricians were constantly trying to outdo one another by paying for plays and games during religious festivals, building or rebuilding parts of the urban infrastructure, and passing through the streets with a more impressive array of followers than anyone else. The view of the front door of the House of the Faun allowed the owner of this elite Pompeian property to remind people he was a force in the community, and to challenge his elite neighbors for the attention of passersby.

The House of the Faun is the largest house in Pompeii, and was famous from the time of its excavation nearly 200 years ago for its spectacular decorations, such as the delicate statue of a Faun. The main entrance to the house, facing the Via di Nola, is typical of elite homes in the city: it is quite high and imposing. Unfortunately, the top of the doorway was shorn off during the eruption of Mount Vesuvius, so we do not know how it was decorated, but since other elite homes had meter-high emblems above the door, it seems safe to assume this house had something similar.

Figure 11.6 shows the micro-viewshed of the emblem above the main door to the House of the Faun. Within the 200 meters viewshed of the house's entrance are 54 doorways, which indicates a large number of people would have had the opportunity to see it. This number is well above the average for a 200 meters stretch of street at Pompeii; only the view of the bar has more doorways (Table 11.1), and the doorway count for the House of the Faun is twice that of the Grand Lupanar and the Temple of Fortuna Augusta. Although many people would have seen the entrance to the House of the Faun, the owner may have had a more specific primary audience in mind when creating this ostentatious entry: fellow Pompeian elites. One would have had a view of the House of the Faun's entry decoration from seven elite houses, more than any of the other case-study locations. Of these, four were within the short-distance view, while the other three were in the medium view. These elite houses seem clustered within view of

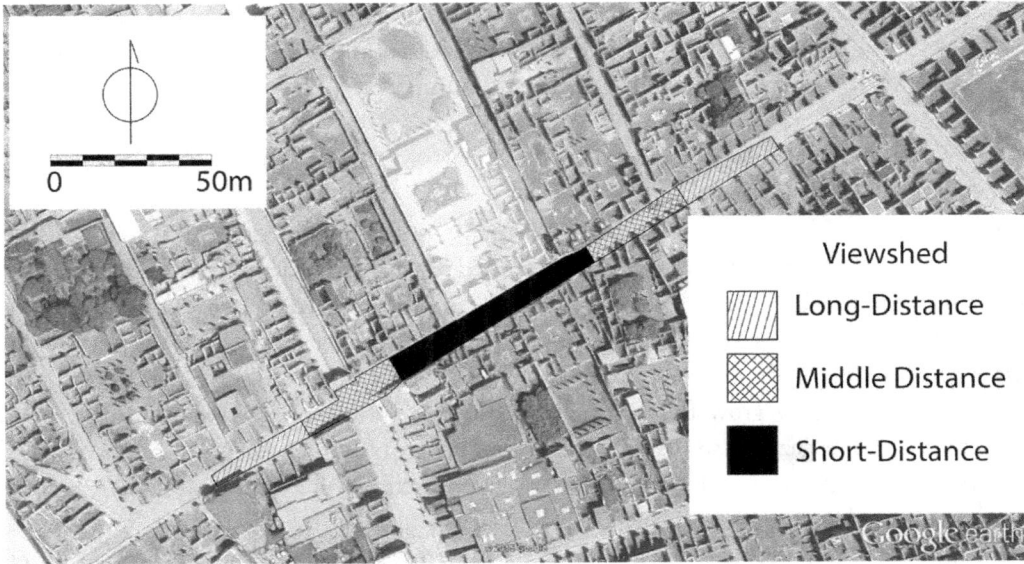

FIGURE 11.6. Micro-viewshed of the House of the Faun.

one another, allowing them to compete with showy entrances. Passersby could easily compare the entrances and decide which was the most eye-catching.

The multisensory experience of walking past the House of the Faun would have been very visually focused. There is no reason to think any particular smells or sounds would have come from this house; rather, the emblem alerted pedestrians that they were approaching a special house. Once they were near the front door, which was left open during the day, pedestrians knew they could peer in to see the decoration (contrast this visibility with the elite structures described by Harrison and Bilgen in this volume). Across the street was another elite house, a competitor for the pedestrians' visual attention. Flanking the entrance to the House of the Faun were two shops; it is not clear from surviving evidence what they were selling and which senses their products would have engaged. Regardless of how much noise or odor these shops may have generated, the owner of the House of the Faun may not have seen them as competitors for the attention of people passing by. The shops are built into the façade of the house—everyone could have seen that the owner of the House of the Faun owned these shops as well and, therefore, was wealthy. That thought must have been in the back of the mind of anyone who noticed these shops through whichever sense. In the long- and middle-distance view the emblem drew the pedestrians to the house, while in the short-distance view the open door and surrounding shops would have done the same.

Roman elites needed to feel as part of urban culture as the nonelites discussed above. The competition for social status was one integrative force for the elite of Pompeii. The micro-viewshed analysis demonstrates that the owner of the House of the Faun had as sophisticated an understanding of the power of architectural visibility to help him achieve his goals as the freedmen and the owners of the brothel and bar. Seeking status required the owner of the house have a stake in urban culture.

CONCLUSION

It was not inevitable that Roman urban settlements would remain viable, but mechanisms such as the opportunity for advancement helped integrate residents who then held the city together. The tools for achieving advancement were varied, but one of those tools was certainly the visibility of architecture. Pompeians had a sophisticated understanding of the power of the view of architecture to enhance their ability to sell goods and services, as well as to grow their social and political prestige. They were also aware of how to avoid the gaze of some in the community to hide their activities. The obvious question is whether others in other Roman cities used architectural visibility in a similar way. It is the hope of this author that others will take up and further develop the techniques of micro-viewshed analysis outlined in this chapter, and apply them to other Roman cities and beyond. Urban viewshed analysis is still in its infancy, but this study shows its enormous potential for addressing questions about what unified the residents of cities of the past.

ACKNOWLEDGMENTS

I would like to thank Attila Gyucha for inviting me to the 9th IEMA Conference. The conversations I had there with fellow archaeologists working in a variety of places and studying many different time periods were quite lively and informative. I enjoyed the opportunity to get out of the bubble of Classical archaeology for a little while and look at issues related to urbanism from many different points of view. I must also extend a debt of gratitude to the anonymous reviewers who kindly offered some very useful suggestions for improving this chapter.

REFERENCES CITED

Betts, E. 2011 Towards a Multisensory Experience of Movement in Rome. In *Rome, Ostia, Pompeii: Movement and Space*, edited by R. Laurence and D. J. Newsome, pp. 118–132. Oxford University Press, Oxford and New York.

Betts, E. (editor) 2017 *Senses of Empire: Multisensory Approaches to Roman Culture*. Routledge, New York.

Cornell, T. J. 1995 *The Beginnings of Rome*. Routledge, New York.

Cowgill, G. L. 2004 Origins and Development of Urbanism: Archaeological Perspectives. *Annual Review of Anthropology* 33:525–549.

DeFelice, J. 2001 *Roman Hospitality: The Professional Women of Pompeii*. Marco Polo Monographs 6. Shangri-La Publications, Warren Center, Pennsylvania.

Derrick, T. J. 2017 Sensory Archaeologies: A Vindolanda Smellscape. In *Senses of Empire: Multisensory Approaches to Roman Culture*, edited by E. Betts, pp. 71–85. Routledge, New York.

Eckardt, H. 2009 Roman Barrows and Their Landscape Context: A GIS Case Study at Bartlow, Cambridgeshire. *Britannia* 40:65–98.

Ellis, S. J. R. 2004 The Distribution of Bars at Pompeii: Archaeological, Spatial, and Viewshed Analyses. *Journal of Roman Archaeology* 17(1):371–384.

Favro, D. G. 1996 *The Urban Image of Augustan Rome*. Cambridge University Press, Cambridge.

Favro, D. G., and C. Johanson 2010 Death in Motion: Funeral Processions in the Roman Forum. *Journal of the Society of Architectural Historians* 69(1):12–37.

Friedman, H. 2008 Forced Labour, Mines, and Space: Exploring the Control of Mining Communities. In *TRAC 2008: Proceedings of the Eighteenth Annual Theoretical Roman Archaeology Conference*, edited by M. Driessen, S. Heeren, J. Hendriks, F. Kemmers, and R. Visser, pp. 1–12. Oxbow Books, Oxford.

Frieman, C., and M. Gillings 2007 Seeing Is Perceiving? *World Archaeology* 39(1):4–16.

Higuchi, T. 1983 *The Visual and Spatial Structure of Landscapes*. MIT Press, Cambridge, Massachusetts.

Holleran, C. 2011 The Street Life of Ancient Rome. In *Rome, Ostia, Pompeii: Movement and Space*, edited by R. Laurence and D. J. Newsome, pp. 245–261. Oxford University Press, Oxford and New York.

Kaiser, A. 2003 The Application of GIS Viewshed Analysis to Roman Urban Studies: The Case-Study of Empúries, Spain. *Internet Archaeology* 14. Electronic document: http://intarch.ac.uk/journal/issue14/kaiser_index.html.

Kaiser, A. 2011 *Roman Urban Street Networks*. Routledge, New York.

Laurence, R. 2007 *Roman Pompeii: Space and Society*. 2nd ed. Routledge, New York.

Laurence, R. 2011 Endpiece: From Movement to Mobility: Future Directions. In *Rome, Ostia, Pompeii: Movement and Space*, edited by R. Laurence and D. J. Newsome, pp. 386–401. Oxford University Press, Oxford and New York.

Maddox, G. 1983 The Economic Causes of the *Lex Hortensia*. *Latomus* 42(2):277–286.

Mau, A. 1899 *Pompeii, Its Life and Art*. Macmillan, London.

McGinn, T. 1998 *Prostitution, Sexuality, and the Law in Ancient Rome*. Oxford University Press, New York.

Palet, J. M., and H. A. Orengo 2011 The Roman Centuriated Landscape: Conception, Genesis, and Development as Inferred from the Ager Tarraconensis Case. *American Journal of Archaeology* 115(3):383–402.

Porteus, J. D. 1985 Smellscape. *Journal of Human Geography* 9(2):356–378.

Richardson, L. 1988 *Pompeii: An Architectural History*. The Johns Hopkins University Press, Baltimore.

Veitch, J. 2017 Soundscape of the Street: Architectural Acoustics in Ostia. In *Senses of Empire: Multisensory Approaches to Roman Culture*, edited by E. Betts, pp. 54–70. Routledge, New York.

Wallace-Hadrill, A. 1995 Public Honour and Private Shame: The Urban Texture of Pompeii. In *Urban Society in Roman Italy*, edited by T. Cornell and K. Lomas, pp. 39–62. St. Martin's Press, New York.

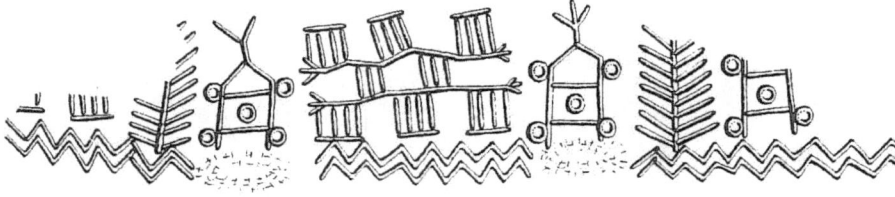

Transformative Effects:
Social, Political, and Cultural Change

Cross-Scale Settlement Morphologies and Social Formations in the Neolithic of the Great Hungarian Plain

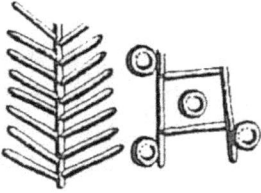

Pál Raczky

Abstract *This paper focuses on shifts in settlement configurations as they relate to the spatial and temporal aspects of socioeconomic transformations on the Great Hungarian Plain during the Neolithic (6000–4500 B.C.). The perspective applied here utilizes the findings of recent studies on urban scaling processes that have convincingly argued for similar mechanisms in the formation of agricultural villages and urban settings. The presented case studies incorporate multiple geographic scales and illustrate the long-term development of early farming settlements in the central and northern parts of the Great Hungarian Plain. The analysis reveals organizational principles that vary over time in relation to the interplay of the changing spatial and social modules of these settlements. The results highlight various interaction mechanisms and associated cycles of nucleation and dispersal, along with the emergence of polities of various types and scales.*

Introduction

With its two major rivers, the Danube and Tisza, the Carpathian Basin is a natural link with the eastern, southern, western, and northern parts of Europe (Bulla and Mendöl 1947, 1999; Pécsi and Sárfalvi 1964). This is eloquently illustrated by the fact that the northern boundary of neolithization from Anatolia and the Balkans extended to the central zone of the Carpathian Basin at the onset of the sixth millennium B.C. (Bánffy and Sümegi 2012:Figure 1; Bocquet-Appel et al. 2009:Figure 10.2; Guilaine 2000–2001:Figure 1; Kozłowski 2013:Figure 9; Quitta 1970:51–59)

(Figure 12.1). Likewise, the northernmost frontier of the Southeast European tell-type settlements was located in the northern part of the Great Hungarian Plain, in the eastern section of the Carpathian Basin (Anders et al. 2010:Figure 1; Chapman 1989, 1997; Gogâltan 2003; Kalicz 1970; Kalicz and Raczky 1987; Makkay 1982:104–164, Map 3; Raczky 1995:Figure 1; Sherratt 1982; Tompa 1937:47, 62).

This paper discusses the spatial and chronological dimensions of the Neolithic, and the related socioeconomic dynamics and internal transformations in the central and northern sections of the Great Hungarian Plain. The overall approach is adopted from a study that explores social aggregation and interaction through settlement pattern analysis in the Körös region of the Plain during the Late Neolithic and Bronze Age (Duffy et al. 2013). Based on spatial configurations over time, this multiscalar analysis suggested the existence of various types of polities of different scales and also shed light on the associated environmental factors and demographic processes (Neitzel and Earle 2014; Parkinson and Gyucha 2012:110–112). The broader approach taken here in part was inspired by studies demonstrating that the emergence of agricultural villages and cities can be viewed as the outcome of virtually identical processes as described in urban scaling models (Bettencourt 2013). A recent study summarizes the essence of settlement scaling theory: "Our results

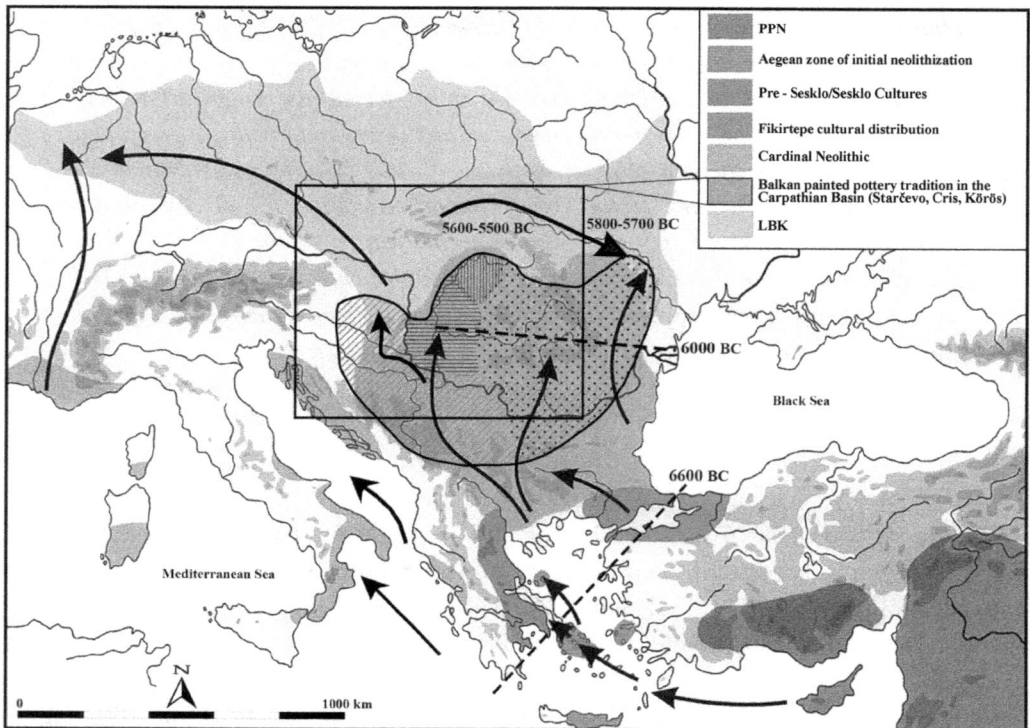

FIGURE 12.1. Major directions of the spread of Neolithic from the Near East to the Carpathian Basin (after Kozłowski 2013).

are of interest because they extend the scaling framework to small settlements set in a non-commercial economy and add support to the hypothesis that settlement scaling theory captures several fundamental properties of all human settlements regardless of time, place, culture, technology, or level of socio-economic development" (Ortman et al. 2016:104).

Regional differences in the archaeological research of the Great Hungarian Plain and the varying quality of data from the investigated sites restrict the extent to which a uniform methodological approach can be used to study Neolithic settlement trajectories. On the southern Plain, a solid foundation for further research has been provided by the Archaeological Topography of Hungary program (Ecsedy et al. 1982; Jankovich et al. 1989, 1998) and the Hungarian-American Körös Regional Archaeological Project (KRAP) through the incorporation of systematic surveys and analytical studies in an area of 3,800 square kilometers (e.g., Gyucha et al. 2010; Parkinson et al. 2010). In northern Hungary, the British-Hungarian Upper Tisza Project (UTP) was equally important; this program investigated three ecological zones in an area of ca. 3,000 square kilometers (e.g., Chapman and Laszlovszky 2010). The study region of this paper includes the central and northern portions of the Great Hungarian Plain, from the Tisza–Zagyva to the Tisza–Sajó confluences, located between the KRAP study area to the south and the UTP study area to the north. At a broader scale, this region coincides with the northern frontier of the Southeast European Neolithic cultural network (Figure 12.2).

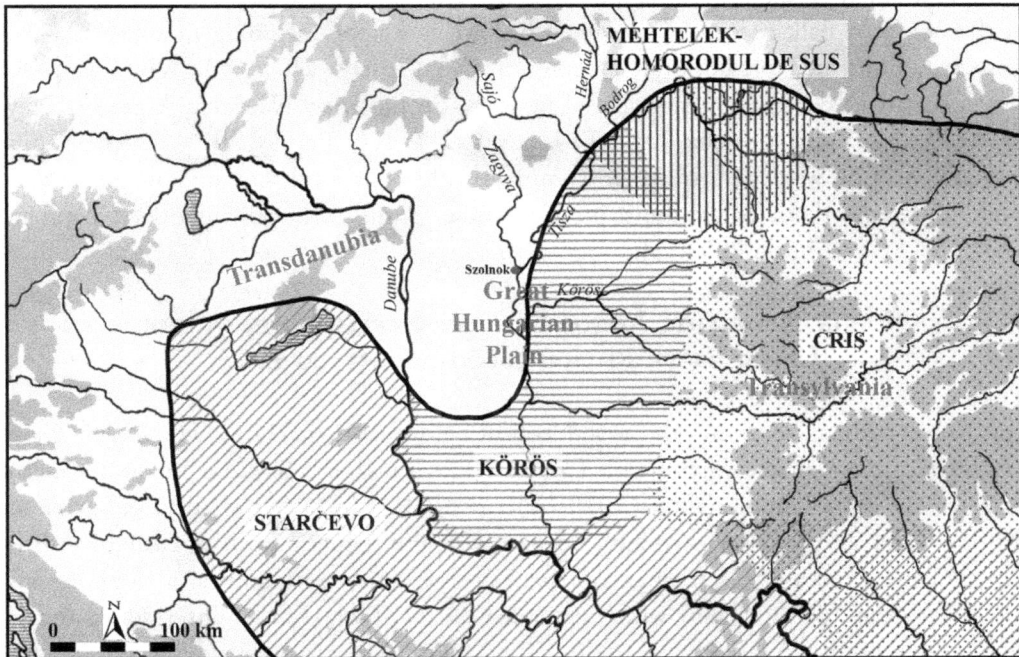

FIGURE 12.2. Distribution of the Early Neolithic Starčevo, Körös, and Criş groups as well as the Méhtelek–Homorodul de Sus-type assemblages in the Carpathian Basin.

THE ROLE OF THE CARPATHIAN BASIN IN THE
SPREAD OF THE AGROPASTORAL WAY OF LIFE IN EUROPE

The results of recent mathematical models and DNA studies to simulate the Neolithic transition in Europe correspond to earlier, archaeological narratives that argued for the primacy of demic diffusion in the spread of farming and stockbreeding from the Aegean through the Balkans to the Carpathian Basin during the seventh and sixth millennia B.C. (Bocquet-Appel et al. 2009; Fort 2015; Fort et al. 2015; Guilaine 2007:170–176; Kozłowski 2013:88–90; Lemmen 2015; Silva et al. 2014; Szécsényi-Nagy et al. 2015; Weninger et al. 2014; Zanotti et al. 2014:Figures 2–4). The central territories of the Great Hungarian Plain and Transdanubia are considered frontier zones between the northernmost representatives of the "First Temperate Neolithic Complex" in Southeast Europe—the Körös, Criş, and Starčevo (Kalicz 1990; Nandris 2007)—and the indigenous Mesolithic communities at the beginning of the sixth millennium B.C. (i.e., Central European Balkanic Agro-Ecological Barrier; for the definition and history of the term, see Bánffy and Sümegi 2012) (Figure 12.2).

During the Early Neolithic, the regions north of the Balkan Mountains were characterized by dispersed, ephemeral settlements. These sites represented various levels of social integration, from single houses and hamlets to small villages (Chapman 2008). The model of "elusive houses and shifting places of the Starčevo–Körös–Criş pottery complex" proposed by Borić (2008:122–124) expresses concisely the essence of this settlement configuration. It seems likely that the lack of Early Neolithic nucleated tell settlements in the northern Balkans can be explained by several factors, including mobility and the dispersed, multisited organization of communities (Rosenstock 2005). While the tells were permanent centers of transregional networks in the Early Neolithic Aegean (Bailey 1999; Parkinson and Gyucha 2012; Perlès 2001:174–180; Raczky 2015), intercommunity interactions were performed predominantly through local and microregional networks in the northern Balkans and the Carpathian Basin during this period (Chapman 1997:158–162; Whittle 2003:55).

EARLY NEOLITHIC KÖRÖS CULTURE SETTLEMENTS IN THE
UPPER TISZA REGION (6000–5600/5500 B.C.)

The Körös culture represents the first Neolithic groups on the Great Hungarian Plain that shared many characteristics with Criş in Transylvania and Starčevo in the northern Balkans and Transdanubia (Kalicz 2010) (Figure 12.2). Körös sites at the confluence of the Tisza and Zagyva rivers—roughly in line with the modern town of Szolnok—usually are considered as the settlements of pioneer Neolithic communities in the northern "marginal" zone of the Plain, which extended to the Tokaj Mountains (Domboróczki 2010a; Domboróczki and Raczky 2010). The Méhtelek-Homorodul de Sus-type assemblages represent a fuzzy, transitional zone between the Körös sites of the Plain and the Criş sites of Transylvania (Kalicz 2011:39–41, Figure 1).

Paleoenvironmental data from the Carpathian Basin suggest that the regional land-scape was characterized by a mosaic spatial patterning at the micro-, mezo-, and macroscales in the Early Neolithic (Sümegi 2004, 2012). The Körös farmers may have perceived the marshy landscape of the Upper Tisza region as a volatile and unpredictable environment, ill-suited to the subsistence strategies employed in the warmer and drier regions of the Bal-kans (Raczky et al. 2010). The difficulties that food production economies encountered in this landscape are reflected by the wide variety of fish, bird, and wild animal bones recovered from Körös sites.

Körös settlements on the Great Hungarian Plain typically stretch along watercourses, and their size ranges from 50 to 250 meters in width and 50 to 2,000 meters in length (Makkay 1982, 2007). The larger sites tend to have been surrounded by several smaller ones. An example of this configuration was observed at Szajol-Felsőföld, where the surface finds indicate a settlement covering 600 x 200 meters, around which seven small sites of ca. 150 x 50 meters in size were located (Figure 12.3). These eight Körös sites show an

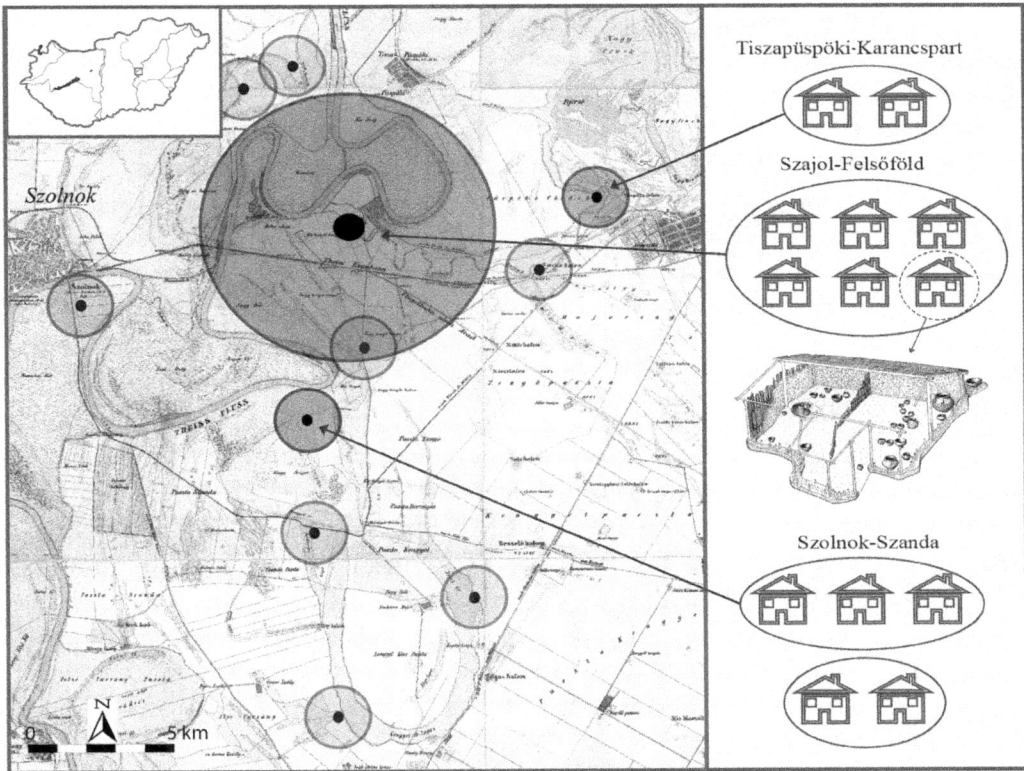

FIGURE 12.3. Distribution of the Körös culture settlements in the Middle Tisza region in a nineteenth-century map. The size of the dots is proportional to the estimated site areas. The circles of 1 and 5 kilometers in radius represent potential catchment areas. The excavated sites of Tiszapüspöki-Karancspart, Szajol-Felsőföld, and Szolnok-Szanda provide an insight into the spatial organization of Körös settlements.

average density of 0.124 sites per square kilometers over a 425 square kilometers large area, which corresponds to site densities recorded on the southern Great Hungarian Plain (Parkinson and Gyucha 2012:110–111, Table 2). The satellite sites near the large settlement of Szajol-Felsőföld were located within ca. 5 kilometers, about an hour's walk away along the edge of the catchment territory, while the estimated catchment area of these small sites was 1 kilometer in radius. These values correspond to the ones calculated for dry farming (Bintliff 2000:21–23; Jarman et al. 1982:168–179). This microregional spatial configuration may have been associated with seasonal occupation, with the local movement of social groups and a multisited community model in place. Additionally, discussing one of the satellite settlements at Tiszaszőlős-Domaháza on the northern Great Hungarian Plain, Domboróczki (2010a; see also Domboróczki et al. 2010) reconstructed clusters of larger "mother" and smaller "daughter" sites as a typical Körös settlement pattern on the Plain.

Regarding spatial organization, the Körös settlements at Szajol-Felsőföld, Tiszapüspöki-Karancspart, and Szolnok-Szanda—each located in the Szolnok microregion close to the assumed northern boundary of the Körös culture—had different layouts, from a dispersed to a more concentrated structure (Raczky 2012) (Figure 12.3). The surface distribution of burnt daub fragments and other finds suggested some 25 to 30 buildings arranged in two parallel rows spaced 25–50 meters apart at the extensive site of Szajol-Felsőföld. This spatial organization implies that farming was conducted in household-based garden plots, with each plot covering an area of 15–25 meters in radius, resembling the pattern documented at Ecsegfalva on the southern Plain (Whittle 2010a:193–194). A comparable house row system and linear space configuration were documented at the Endrőd 39 site of the Körös culture on the southern Great Hungarian Plain (Domboróczki 2010a:Figure 13). This implies that in addition to the stable basic social module of households, the linear arrangement of settlements manifests a higher level of integration (Hillier 2014).

Szajol-Felsőföld stands out from the other known Körös sites on the Plain as the maximum number of inhabitants might have been 125 to 150, a relatively high figure for Early Neolithic Southeast Europe. It suggests that this site represents a village-level agglomeration between 5790 and 5620 B.C. The question remains whether this large size indicates a permanent settlement of a larger community or a site that developed over a longer period of time through the seasonal integration of several smaller groups (Oross and Siklósi 2012:146–147).

A 7.5 x 4.5 meters, aboveground, postframed house with daub walls was uncovered at Szajol-Felsőföld (Raczky 2012:85–87, Figure 1). The two-room plan indicates that this building—as well as several others at Körös settlements, including Tiszajenő-Szárazérpart (Tringham 1971:Figure 14c–d) and Szolnok-Szanda (Kalicz and Raczky 1982:14–15, Tables 1–3)—may be regarded as the possible forerunners of the multiroomed, timber-framed longhouses of the Central European Linearbandkeramik (LBK) and the Alföld Linear Pottery (ALP) (Lenneis 2000:384, Figures 3 and 4; Meier-Arendt 1989:183–185, Figures 1–6).

Located 5.5 kilometers from Szajol-Felsőföld, a 150 x 50 meters large settlement was identified on an alluvial island at Szolnok-Szanda (Kalicz and Raczky 1982; Raczky 2012) (Figure 12.3). At this site, the houses formed closely-spaced blocks along a watercourse (Figure 12.4). Thus, in contrast to the linear arrangement at Szajol-Felsőföld, the Szolnok-Szanda settlement was featured by a patchwork-like layout. The striking difference between the spatial configurations of these two Körös settlements may reflect a stable or, conversely, an intermittently diverse fabric of social interactions.

The Szolnok-Szanda settlement was occupied in two major phases, 5840–5710 and 5610–5490 B.C. (Oross and Siklósi 2012:147, Figure 7), and were preceded by a

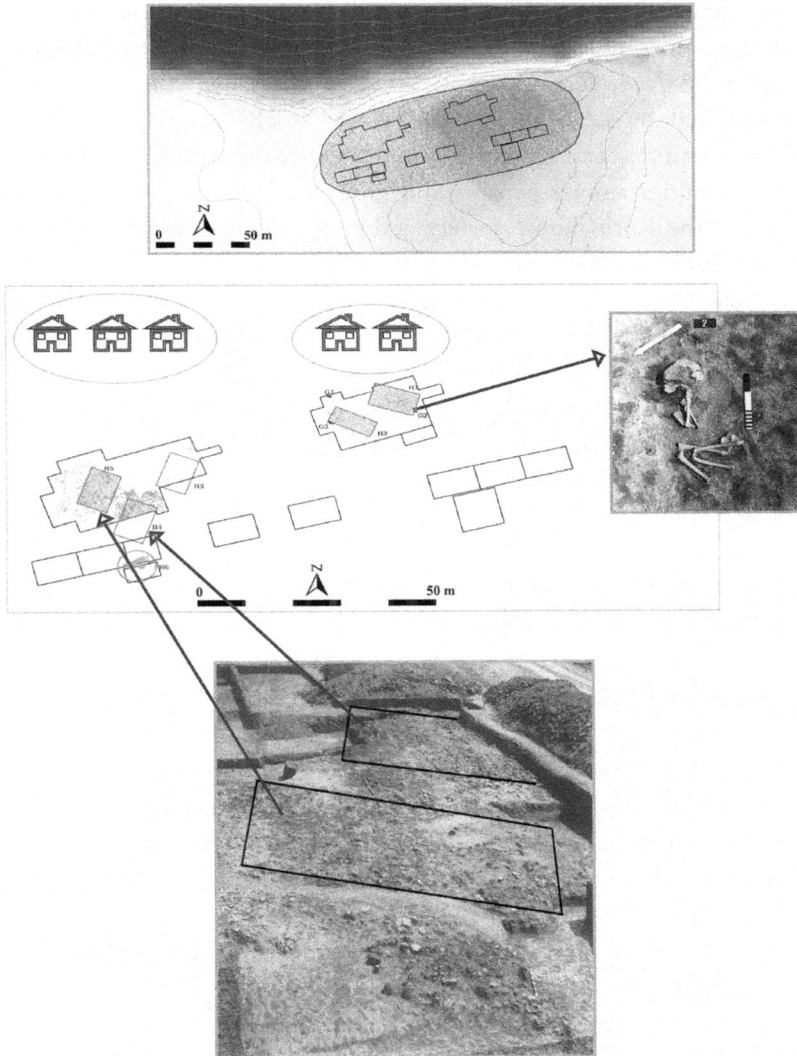

FIGURE 12.4. Szolnok-Szanda. A hamlet-like settlement of the Körös culture.

much more dispersed, initial occupation. The AMS dates indicate that Szajol-Felsőföld and Szolnok-Szanda were used contemporaneously (Oross and Siklósi 2012:Figures 6 and 7). The duration of the two main occupation phases at Szolnok-Szanda may have been 0–70 years and 60–170 years, respectively, which corresponds to the life span of Körös sites on the southern Great Hungarian Plain (Whittle 2010b). Szolnok-Szanda may have been occupied by 25–30 people in both phases. It would appear that small-scale Körös communities consisting of five to six households successively occupied the same sites, suggesting a shifting subsistence strategy (Bartosiewicz 2012; Chapman 2008).

This brief overview of the Early Neolithic Körös settlements in the Szolnok area of the central part of the Great Hungarian Plain indicates that early food production economies were practiced in a social configuration centered around the house. In Thomas's (2015) interpretation, physical buildings as social entities were active agents in house-holds, and the term *house societies* can be used in this sense. This concept, which was originally introduced by Lévi-Strauss (1982), was briefly summarized by Gillespie as follows: "Alliance and descend are cross-cutting relationships that give rise to conflicting tendencies and loyalties among persons and groups, all of which come together in the house" (2000:8). The Körös house society comprised of stable house communities with 5–6 individuals, and two more or less standardized aggregated settlement forms (with 25–30 individuals versus 125–130 individuals). Larger settlements scarcely occurred on the Plain during the Early Neolithic (Chapman 2008). In the aggregated sites, the spatial organization of multiple, small settlement blocks, like at Szolnok-Szanda, and linear configurations, like at Szajol-Felsőföld, are indicative of the development of higher-level social integration. In the former case, the "neighborhood" is characterized by a relatively dense spacing of buildings, while the latter is featured by a looser spatial distribution of structures.

MIDDLE NEOLITHIC ALFÖLD LINEAR POTTERY (ALP) SETTLEMENTS IN THE UPPER TISZA REGION (5600/5500–5100/5000 B.C.)

EARLY ALFÖLD LINEAR POTTERY (ALP I)

The expansion of the Körös population of the Great Hungarian Plain and the Criş population of northwestern Transylvania into the Upper Tisza region resulted in the convergence of two interregional networks in the foreland of the Carpathians around 5800 B.C. (Domboróczki and Raczky 2010; Raczky 1989:233–235, Figure 1; Sherratt 1997:277–279, Figure 11.5) (Figure 12.5). The adjacent mountains provided access to new lithic resources (Kaczanowska and Kozłowski 2008; Mester and Rácz 2010). The traditional sheep and goat husbandry declined, while cattle and pig grew increasingly dominant. Additionally, adaptation to local circumstances is reflected by the increasing importance of hunting, fowling, fishing, and gathering in subsistence strategies (Bartosiewicz 2012:199–203; Kovács et al. 2010:248–252). Along with other factors, these processes led to the emergence of new activities and new people–places–animals–

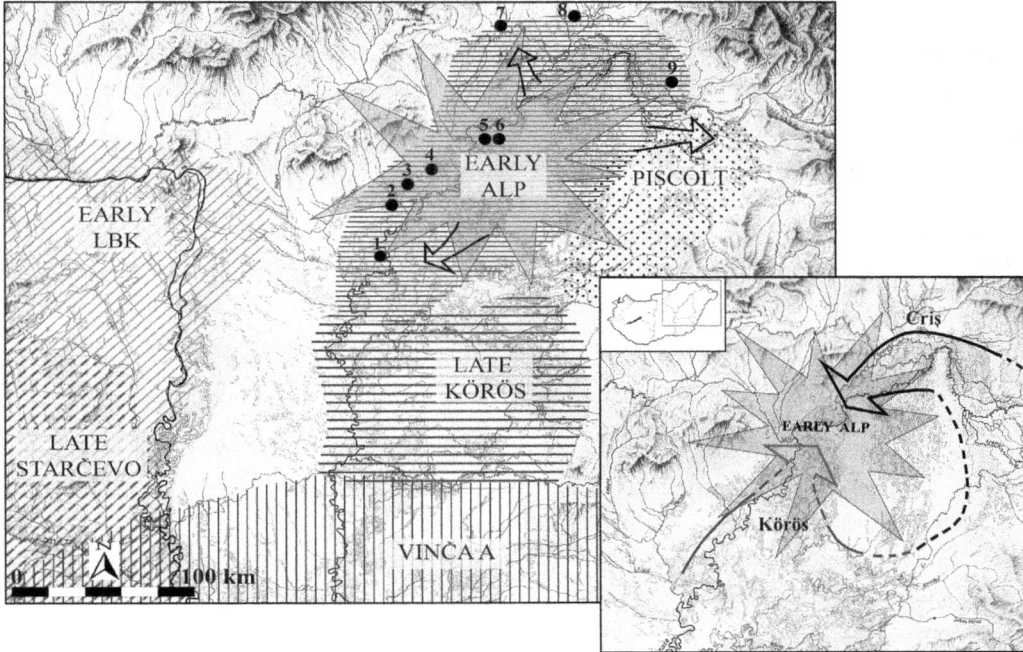

FIGURE 12.5. Cultural changes at the beginning of the Middle Neolithic, and major ALP sites in the Upper Tisza region and beyond: (1) Kőtelek-Huszársarok, (2) Füzesabony-Gubakút, (3) Mezőkövesd-Mocsolyás, (4) Bükkábrány-Bánya, Site VII, (5) Polgár-Ferenci-hát, (6) Polgár-Piócási-dűlő, (7) Košice-Červený Rak, (8) Moravany, (9) Zastavne-Mala Hora.

things interactions and, ultimately, brought about new internal and external networks among newly defined communities (Harris 2014:92). In addition, the material mediums of earlier symbolic communications underwent a similar transformation, and a completely new symbolic repertoire occurred (Raczky et al. 2010).

AMS dates indicate that the Early ALP material culture evolved between 5620 and 5470 B.C. (Domboróczki 2010a:140), suggesting a fairly rapid cultural change—that is to say, a swift reorganization of social networks in a relatively restricted geographic area. The Early ALP sites are located in the region where the Körös and Criş communities are thought to have regularly interacted (Kozłowski and Nowak 2010), creating multidirectional local formations (Figure 12.5). In fact, assemblages assigned to the formative ALP have been recovered from Kőtelek-Huszársarok in the Middle Tisza region to Košice-Červený Rak and Moravany in Slovakia, and Zastavne-Mala Hora in Ukraine, along the Tisza River and its tributaries (Kaczanowska and Kozłowski 2008:Figure 2; Kovács 2007:Figure 2; Kozłowski and Nowak 2010:Figure 1). The northern Early ALP groups also occupied certain zones in the mountains, along the tributaries of the Tisza River (Sajó, Hernád, and Bodrog rivers), that had not been colonized by Körös and Criş communities (Csengeri 2015:129–137). Around 5500/5400 B.C., these groups quickly spread southward to the Körös region, while farther to the south—between the Körös and Maros rivers—Early Neolithic Körös cultural traditions continued to persist for some time (Raczky 1989:234–236).

Extensive field surveys in the Füzesabony area of the northern Great Hungarian Plain revealed a complex pattern of evenly distributed, larger ALP villages ("mother" settlements), surrounded by smaller hamlets or single-house settlements (satellite or "daughter" settlements) (Figure 12.6). These clusters of larger and smaller sites developed along rivers, and they indicate complex settlement zones at the microregional scale (Domboróczki 2009:Figures 16 and 18; Whittle et al. 2013:64–65). While subsistence units associated with the larger Körös sites constituted 5 kilometers in radius (see above), the Early ALP settlement clusters may have had catchment areas of 1 kilometer in radius in which these communities were capable of pursuing sustainable subsistence strategies. It would appear that this settlement system illustrates the success of a creative, local-scale subsistence based on a broad range of food resources.

The extensive archaeological investigations at Füzesabony-Gubakút (Domboróczki 2009, 2010b) and Mezőkövesd-Mocsolyás (Kalicz and Koós 2014) provide excellent

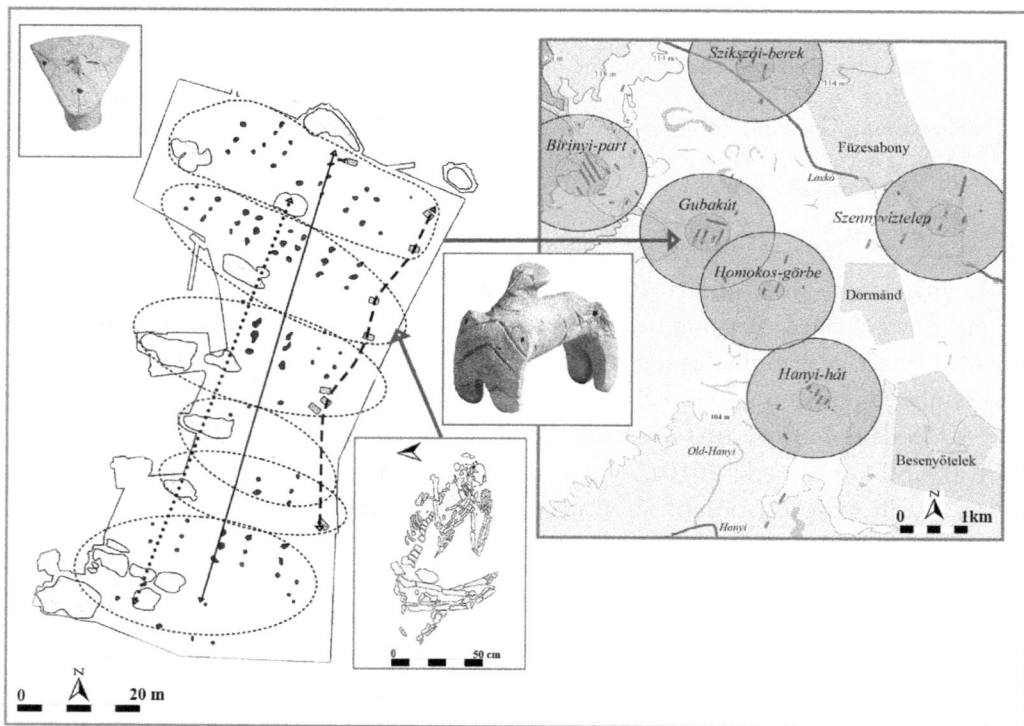

FIGURE 12.6. Füzesabony-Gubakút. An Early ALP settlement in the Middle Tisza region (after Domboróczki 2009).

opportunities to study ALP settlement organization. The excavation results indicate that a layout with buildings arranged in rows, which had occurred already in the Early Neolithic (e.g., Szajol-Felsőföld; see above), became the norm by the Early ALP period. The plan of the Füzesabony-Gubakút settlement demonstrates that aside from the parallel rows of postframed longhouses, the associated pits and burials also were organized linearly (Domboróczki 2009:91–103) (Figure 12.6). Some 12–14, simultaneously occupied houses—and a similar number of households—were present at this site, with a total of 60–70 occupants during the settlement's most developed phase (Domboróczki 2009:96–98, Table 2). The emergence of a complex spatial system—with a configuration of spatial modules including single houses, house rows, and "mother" and satellite settlements—dates between 5550 and 5200 B.C. The reconstruction of this system runs into difficulties because during these 350 years the various spatial modules developed their own trajectories that range from growth to stagnation and decline (Domboróczki 2009:96–97, Figures 7 and 17).

Ceramic refitting studies at Füzesabony-Gubakút indicate that multiple households jointly used the pits along the houses (Domboróczki 2009:91–97, Figure 5). This implies that certain activities were conducted not only at the household level but also in the framework of a wider integration through cooperating households in the settlement. A similarly sophisticated spatial organization was noted at the recently investigated Early ALP site at Bükkábrány-Bánya, Site VII (Faragó et al. 2015). The houses of this settlement display two parallel rows, with a 50 meters wide and 300 meters long, street-like zone lacking features. In association with the linear setting of houses, pits, and graves, three wells were located along the central axis of this vast community tract. The prominent location of the wells is reflected by the fact that they were visible from the entrance of each house, indicating the importance of visibility among the organizational principles (Hillier 2014; for the significance of visibility, see also Kaiser this volume). In this configuration, the immediate environment of the wells was one of the settlement's focal points where communal activities might have been conducted (Carballo et al. 2014).

Taken together, a three-tier sociospatial configuration may be conceptualized at Füzesabony-Gubakút, including households (1 household = 5 individuals), groups of cooperating households (3–4 households = 15–20 individuals), and the settlement community (12–14 households = 60–70 individuals). Additionally, in the Early ALP period, smaller, external social modules in the form of single households or cooperating households were linked to the internal system of the larger settlements. The combinations of many different types of activities, their community background, and the utilized spaces resulted in a rich spatial diversity, similarly to the Central European LBK (Kuna and Dreslerová 2007:154–156; Květina and Končelová 2013:5–6; Pavlů 2013).

In contrast to the Early Neolithic structures, the Middle Neolithic buildings were postframed longhouses in the Upper Tisza region. When compared to Körös culture houses, the most distinctive feature of the Early ALP buildings is the increase in their size (Raczky 2006). The observation that the 12–16 meters long and 5–6 meters wide buildings were divided into two or three rooms provided new perspectives to the social analysis of domestic space (Domboróczki 2009:78–80; Kalicz and Koós 2014:9–15; Whittle et al. 2013). The structural characteristics and the construction techniques of the ALP buildings on the Great Hungarian Plain share numerous similarities with the contemporaneous longhouses in Transdanubia and Central Europe (Bánffy 2013; Oross 2013).

Developed Alföld Linear Pottery Phases (ALP II–III and IV)

A system of small, densely occupied settlements occurred in several areas of the Upper Tisza region during the ALP II and III phases (ca. 5450–5250 B.C.), which was followed by a trend toward settlement aggregation during the ALP IV phase (ca. 5200–5050 B.C.) (Raczky and Anders 2009a). A similar development was noted in the Körös region of the southern Great Hungarian Plain (Parkinson and Gyucha 2012). During this period, regional ceramic stylistic variations occurred (Kalicz and Makkay 1977; Raczky and Anders 2009a, 2012), suggesting that the use of ceramics as social and spatiotemporal markers was highly complex (Strobel 1997). This period also marked a turning point in the sense that, in addition to internal social dynamics, broader, regional community interactions and supraregional contacts also influenced settlement development and the organization of space.

The best archaeological illustration of later Middle Neolithic settlement characteristics is provided by the systematic archaeological research of the Polgár Island on the northern Great Hungarian Plain (Sümegi et al. 2005). In this 67 square kilometers microregion, some 20 sites covering 1 to 5 hectares date to the ALP II–III phase, while the size of eight sites assigned to the ALP IV phase ranges between 5 to 10 hectares (Magyari et al. 2012:281–282; Raczky and Anders 2009a:38–43). Polgár-Ferenci-hát and Polgár-Piócási-dűlő best represent the latter period, and both sites had 20–40 houses and a population of 100 to 200 (Nagy et al. 2014; Raczky and Anders 2012; Whittle et al. 2013) (Figure 12.7).

The 18–20 x 5–6 meters large timberframed buildings next to one another recovered at Polgár-Piócási-dűlő indicate that—similarly to the preceding period—the linear arrangement of houses remained the norm (Nagy et al. 2014:Figures 2 and 7). The larger size of the houses may be explained in part by greater storage capacities and/or that these buildings accommodated larger social groups. Additionally, based on evidence from other European regions, a deliberate effort to monumentalize longhouses also must be considered (Hofmann 2013:41–45).

Polgár-Ferenci-hát illustrates the development of a complex settlement layout during the final phase of the ALP (Raczky and Anders 2009a:40–45, 2012:276–280; Whittle et al. 2013:78–88) (Figure 12.7). At this 4–5 hectares large aggregated site, dating to 5300 and 5100 B.C., the accumulation of vertical deposits enclosed by a ditch system was documented in the central area of the horizontal settlement. The enclosure may have generated and articulated new human attitudes to space, which gave rise to novel social and ritual activities, such as the deposition of fragmented storage vessels and burnt daub

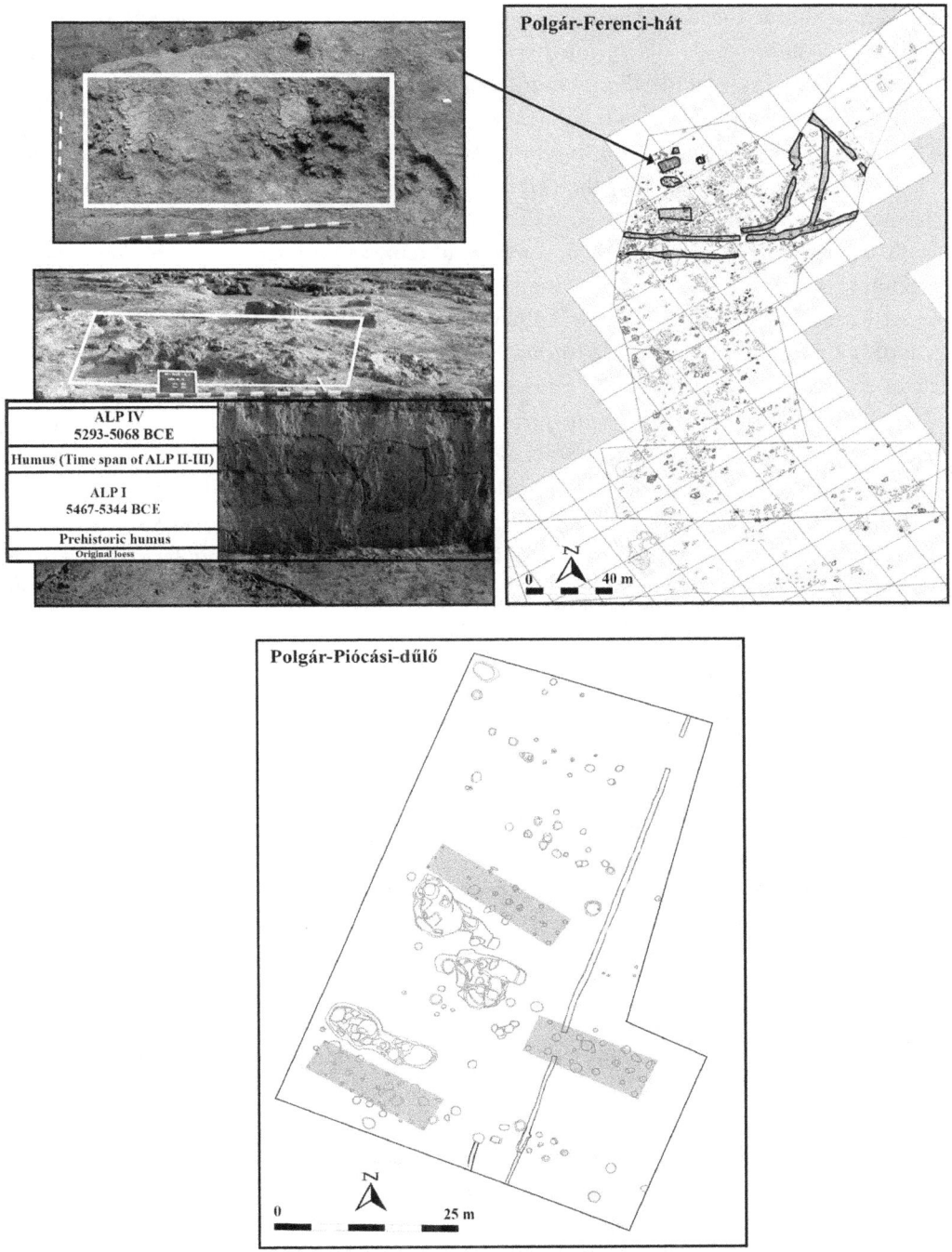

Labels within the figure:

Polgár-Ferenci-hát

ALP IV
5293-5068 BCE

Humus (Time span of ALP II-III)

ALP I
5467-5344 BCE

Prehistoric humus
Original loess

0   40 m
N

Polgár-Piócási-dűlő

0   25 m
N

FIGURE 12.7. Polgár-Ferenci-hát and Polgár-Piócási-dűlő. ALP IV nucleated villages on the Polgár Island.

remains as well as the use of grinding stones in symbolic contexts (Raczky and Anders 2012:278; Whittle et al. 2013). Furthermore, the enclosure divided the settlement into two main segments within which communal ritual activities followed different rules. A major difference between the two segments is that remains of burnt houses were identified in the central area, while unburnt buildings were found outside the enclosure. Compared to the two-dimensional scape of the external, single-layer settlement, the successive occupational levels within the enclosure reflect activities choreographed in three dimensions, which created the dimensions of a convergent representational space. In other words, communal actions generated horizontal and vertical axes to the spatial organization of the settlement and developed a new framework for identity formation. At the same time, in addition to the previous inside-to-outside integration, an outside-to-inside integration can be noted in the layout of the houses of Polgár-Ferenci-hát, which suggests that the principles of spatial organization overrode earlier traditions as well. The dual spatial organization of local-to-global and global-to-local, as described by Hillier and Hanson (1984:20–23), was manifested in the settlement layout at this site. The construction of a vertical "earth architecture" in the central segment and the creation of the enclosure system required community efforts and acted as a social mobilizing factor at a scale unprecedented during the preceding ALP periods. The new concept of space and time documented at Polgár-Ferenci-hát also can be noted at other Middle Neolithic settlements across the Tisza region from 5300 B.C. onward (Parkinson and Gyucha 2012:111–112; Sherratt 1982:19–23).

In sum, population aggregation occurred at ALP settlements toward the end of the Middle Neolithic. In addition to settlement features, the 113 burials organized in discrete clusters at Polgár-Ferenci-hát are clear indicators of this process. This shift may suggest that the occupants of the houses built next to each other were not bounded exclusively by kinship, and that the construction and expression of a new cultural identity—emerging from diverse origins—largely were dependent on local processes (Bernardini 2005:32–36). These social formations are perhaps best described as "house societies" or "coalescent societies" (Birch 2013:10–13; Borić 2007; see also Birch and Ryan this volume). In this system, the community of the entire settlement integrated their households and household groups into a higher organizational level, and this system generated regional and supraregional interactions due to the preexisting contacts of the various subgroups.

LATE NEOLITHIC SETTLEMENTS IN THE
UPPER TISZA REGION (5100/5000–4500/4400 B.C.)

The Late Neolithic on the Great Hungarian Plain is marked by the emergence of the Tisza–Herpály–Csőszhalom cultural complex (Chapman 1997; Gogâltan 2003; Horváth 2009; Link 2006; Makkay 1982; Raczky and Anders 2008; Whittle 1996:107–112). The tell sites of this complex represent the northernmost distribution of this settlement form in Europe. Scholars agree that these settlements occurred through a process of settlement and demographic aggregation, which partly derived from regional ALP processes (Chapman 1997:148–158; Makkay 1982:104–164; Parkinson and Gyucha 2012:110–113; Sherratt 1982:17–21). Recent magnetometry surveys have demonstrated that many of the Late Neolithic tells (with occupational deposits of 3 to 4 meters) and tell-like settlements (with deposits of 1 to 2.5 meters) on the Great Hungarian Plain were enclosed by ditch and palisade systems, and were surrounded by either a large, horizontal settlement or clusters of small hamlets, or both (e.g., Szeghalom-Kovácshalom: Gyucha et al. 2015; Polgár-Bosnyákdomb: Raczky and Anders 2009b; Uivar: Schier 2008; Bordoš: Medović et al. 2014).

A multiscalar approach implies that the spatial modules of activities in the Late Neolithic of the Plain were as follows: activity area, single-household settlement, hamlet, village, supersite complex (central place), and settlement cluster organized around a supersite complex at the microregional scale. These modules were incorporated into a higher unit at the regional and macroregional scales by the settlement blocks of the Tisza–Herpály–Csőszhalom complex (Müller 2009:96–97; Parkinson 2006:47–53). Activities and interactions in the microscale spatialities were conducted in a social organization that ranged from individuals and households to the settlement community and to the highest level of the polity. The Late Neolithic society of the Great Hungarian Plain is generally described as tribal or middle-range (Duffy 2014:23–55; Duffy et al. 2013; Parkinson 2002; Parkinson and Gyucha 2007). The cultural spatiality created by various interactions between social modules of different forms and scales served as the physical setting for the diverse dimensions of life.

POLGÁR-CSŐSZHALOM: A CASE STUDY FROM THE UPPER TISZA REGION

The Polgár-Csőszhalom site on the Polgár Island bears an outstanding importance regarding the study of cultural interrelations in the Late Neolithic of the Carpathian Basin (Kalicz and Raczky 1987:11–19; Müller 2010:250–251; Raczky 2015; Raczky et al. 1994). The site includes two macrostructural units: a tell settlement characteristic on the southern Great Hungarian Plain and a Transdanubian Lengyel-type enclosure system (Bertók and Gáti 2014:17–91; Pásztor et al. 2015). The structural unity of the tell and the surrounding multiditch enclosure system with four entrances manifests the multimodal unit of monumental display expressing community identity (Raczky 1995; Raczky and Anders 2008:35–40; Raczky et al. 1994; Sherratt 2005:143). Furholt and Müller (2011:16–25) pursued a similar line of reasoning when they argued that the Central European Neolithic enclosures and megalithic structures should be conceptualized as monuments and interpreted as temporal metaphors of cultural memory; these structures come under the heading of "external symbolic storage" in Anglo-Saxon scholarship (Renfrew 1998). The Cucuteni-Trypillia megasites in East Europe also may be interpreted as similar expressions of monumentality. These single-layer sites feature hundreds and thousands of houses and other settlement features arranged in concentric circles that formed integrative units (Chapman 2010:81–85, Figures 3–7; Chapman et al. 2014:1–5, Figures 1 and 3; Mischka 2010; Müller 2016; Müller and Rassmann 2016; Wengrow 2015; see also

Gaydarska this volume). One of the westernmost appearances of settlement features in a concentric arrangement in the Carpathian Basin during the Neolithic occurred at the Iclod site in Transylvania (Mischka 2012:154–158, Figures 5 and 6). Thus, we may say that tells (Tisza–Herpály–Csőszhalom), circular enclosures surrounding empty spaces (Lengyel), and horizontal settlements with concentric layouts (Cucuteni-Trypillia) embodied three different expressions of monumentality (Furholt and Müller 2011; Osborne 2014) in the Carpathian Basin during the Late Neolithic (Figure 12.8). Polgár-Csőszhalom lies at the interface of these three community practices, each of which appears—even if in a hybrid format—in the spatiality of this settlement (Stockhammer 2012).

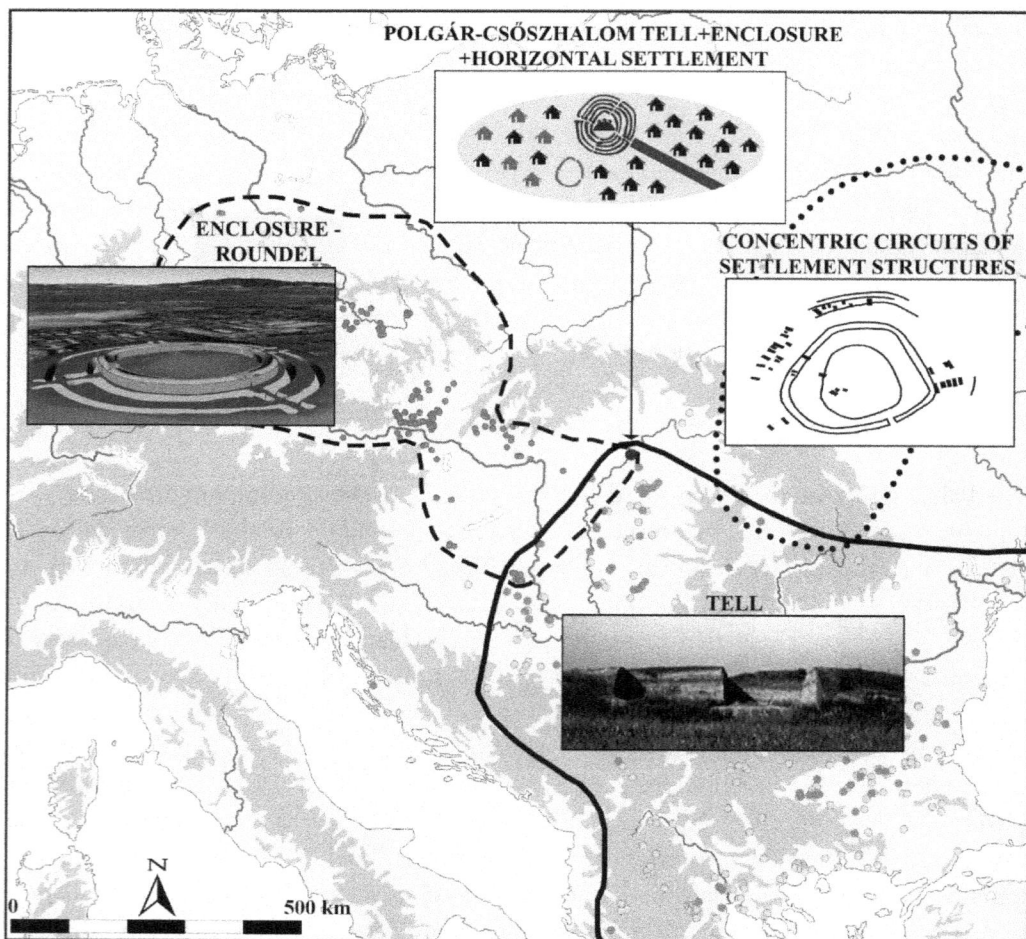

FIGURE 12.8. Spatial distribution of tell settlements in Southeast Europe, enclosures in Central Europe, and settlement features arranged in multiple concentric circles in Transylvania and in the Chalcolithic Cucuteni-Trypillia territory. Specific elements of these "macroarchitectures" are present in a synergetic set at Polgár-Csőszhalom.

Paleoecological studies have shown that the Late Neolithic settlement complex at Polgár-Csőszhalom was part of the socioecological setting of the Polgár Island, a reconfigured continuation of the preceding Middle Neolithic system. Polgár-Csőszhalom and the other 12 Late Neolithic settlements identified in this microregion—located in two concentric zones at a distance of 1–1.5 kilometers and 5 kilometers—can be interpreted as the outcome of a process of aggregation at the onset of the Late Neolithic (Figure 12.9). In terms of their size and spatial organization, the tell-like settlements at Polgár-Bosnyákdomb and Polgár-Kígyós-domb on the southwestern fringes of the Polgár Island constitute the next spatial module in the settlement cluster beyond the central settlement at Polgár-Csőszhalom. The additional 10 sites were small, farmstead-like settlements representing a lower integrative level in the microregional settlement system.

An approximately 400 x 100 meters section of the horizontal settlement was investigated in the eastern part of Polgár-Csőszhalom during salvage excavations (Raczky and

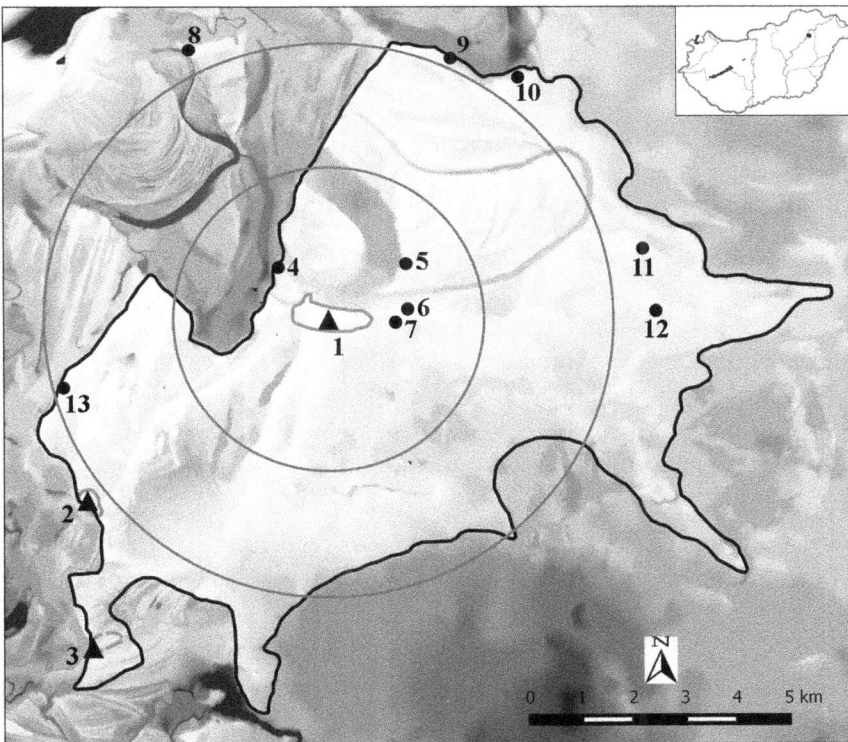

FIGURE 12.9. The Late Neolithic settlement network on the paleohydrological reconstruction of the Polgár Island: (1) Polgár-Csőszhalom (tell + nucleated supersite), (2) Polgár-Bosnyákdomb (tell-like mound + village), (3) Polgár-Kígyósdomb (tell-like mound + village), (4–13) horizontal, small satellite settlements (after Füzesi et al. 2016).

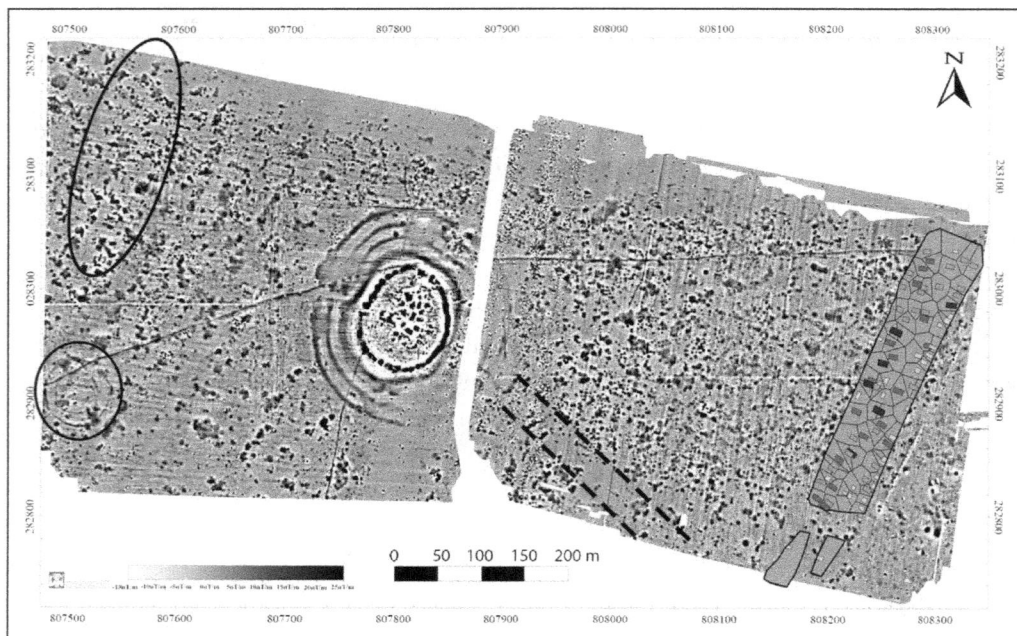

FIGURE 12.10. Polgár-Csőszhalom. Magnetometric plan of the settlement complex, with the excavated area of the horizontal settlement to the east as well as burnt structures and a double enclosure to the west (after Raczky et al. 2014).

Anders 2008, 2010; Raczky et al. 2011) (Figure 12.10). In addition to some 80 unburnt, timberframed houses, 68 wells, and 238 pits, a total of 124 burials were found in the immediate vicinity of the buildings. Recent magnetometry surveys provided a wealth of new information in regard to the settlement organization at Polgár-Csőszhalom (Füzesi et al. 2016; Raczky et al. 2014). The results indicate that the external settlement around the tell covered ca. 65 hectares, and show another enclosure composed of two ditches ca. 180 meters southwest of the tell. Burnt house structures were identified in the western section of the horizontal settlement. A minimum of 400 coeval houses can be extrapolated from the data of the excavated part of the horizontal settlement, suggesting 2,000–2,400 inhabitants at any given time at the site. This population estimate raises the question of whether the community of Polgár-Csőszhalom was permanently large throughout its development or whether this value can be attributed, at least in part, to the regular congregations of various groups from the microregion at the site for specific community events (for similar processes, see Fernández-Götz, Gaydarska, and Kelly this volume). Concerning the latter possibility, Polgár-Csőszhalom may be interpreted as a central place, as has been proposed for Vésztő-Mágor in the Körös region on the Great Hungarian Plain (Parkinson 2006:52), or as a megasite in the Upper Tisza region, similarly to the Trypillia megasites (Chapman and Gaydarska 2016; Müller 2016). As estimated for

Polgár-Csőszhalom, a population of 1,500–2,000 was calculated for the Late Neolithic tell settlement at Okolište in Bosnia, and that site is considered one of the central places in the Visoko Basin (Müller 2012:48–49).

It would seem that the tell and the associated enclosure system represent the highest level of integrative architecture—in this context, the tell was not simply a residential area but an arena for communal events with a unique choreography (Whittle 2013), while the horizontal settlement with domestic structures was the sphere for day-to-day activities (Raczky et al. 2014). The Polgár-Csőszhalom tell and its concentric enclosure evolved simultaneously during their development. As the tell expanded both horizontally and vertically, the circular ditches expanded as well, and this movement resulted in an increasing spatial complexity within the tell–enclosure system (Raczky et al. 2011). The excavations indicate that a two-story building was erected in the center of the tell at the beginning of its development (Raczky and Sebők 2014). This structure later was deliberately set on fire in order to manipulate the building's context and meaning. This, then, was the act that served as the ritual foundation of the tell–enclosure architecture, and reinforced psychological bonds and fusion as part of a dysphoric ritual (Whitehouse and Lanman 2014; for a similar event, see O'Shea and Nicodemus this volume). A number of superimposed burnt houses were uncovered at the core of the tell, around which the central axes of additional burnt houses were aligned to the center. This organization reflects entirely different organizational principles and attitudes to space from those of the external settlement where the houses were northwest to southeast in orientation (Raczky and Anders 2010).

The analysis of 31,268 animal bones excavated at the Polgár-Csőszhalom settlement complex yielded results that highlight the differences in the use of space on the enclosed tell and the external settlement. The bones from the tell demonstrate a clear dominance of wild animals, while the majority of animal remains from the horizontal settlement come from domesticates (Raczky and Anders 2008:44–45; Raczky et al. 2011:65–69). The massive concentration of animal bones suggests that major community events and ceremonies occurred on the tell. Based on the mass slaughter of animals, meat consumption and food sharing appear to have been a remarkably important part of these gatherings (Raczky et al. 2011:69–71). Caches or hoards of everyday and miniature artifacts vested with a special meaning, and objects with symbolic connotations also were exclusively recovered from the tell (Raczky and Anders 2008). The significance of the tell for the Late Neolithic community is suggested also by the fact that artifacts fashioned from copper and malachite were found in this area. Thus, specific materials and artifact types did not appear in the everyday domestic sphere of the horizontal settlement, instead, they occurred only in symbolic contexts as defined by the community. The lead isotope analysis of metal objects indicates that the copper was procured from deposits in modern Serbia and Bulgaria, further illustrating the far-reaching social interactions with Southeast European Late Neolithic and Aeneolithic communities (Siklósi et al. 2015:86–88). Moreover, the metal indicates that the community at Polgár-Csőszhalom was part of a supraregional network, and this broader embeddedness was reaffirmed periodically through symbolic actions at the tell (Chapman 2013:327–332). The assessment of the burials uncovered at Polgár-Csőszhalom revealed another distinctive feature between the tell and the horizontal settlement: predominantly male burials were found on the tell, while female burials constituted the majority of the graves excavated on the horizontal settlement (Anders and Nagy 2007; Raczky and Anders 2008:45–49). These data imply a clear gender differentiation in the interment of the dead.

The proposed structural organization of Polgár-Csőszhalom implies a unique interplay of spatial and social configurations at the settlement complex. In Figure 12.11, the tell, the enclosure, and the horizontal settlement appear on the left side. The northeastern entrance of the enclosure was aligned toward Mount Tokaj, and a wide road documented ca. 300 meters long led to the southeastern entrance. There were no burnt houses in the eastern part of the horizontal settlement, while burnt and unburnt structures were found to the west. A smaller, double enclosure was located southwest of the tell–enclosure system. The next structural level is represented by the spatial modules of the double enclosure, the western zone of the horizontal settlement, the tell–enclosure system, and the eastern zone of the horizontal settlement. The following structural level is the tell and the enclosure system. The lowermost structural level consists of the smaller settlement features (pits, burnt and unburnt houses, workshops, hearths, wells) and female and male burials (on the left and right side, respectively).

On the right side of Figure 12.11, the reconstructed system of the social modules of Polgár-Csőszhalom is displayed. The community of the settlement constitutes the highest level of integration, followed by the configurations and groupings of the basic modules, that is, the various households and individuals (Anders and Raczky 2013:Figure 1). The social modules were embedded in the physical context of the spatial modules through a wide range of interactions, thereby creating an intricate and dynamic mechanism at the Polgár-Csőszhalom settlement complex. This model suggests that the different spatial modules also determined the range of particular human activities along with their temporality (Salisbury 2012).

Based on 109 AMS dates, the isochronic correlation of the space/time model of the horizontal settlement and the enclosed tell at Polgár-Csőszhalom offers an outline regarding which features and spatial segments of the tell and the outer settlement were contemporaneous. The occupation of the settlement complex falls between 5105–4855 and 4500–4450 B.C. (Raczky et al. 2015:39–45). Our results indicate that the settlement organization retained its internal stability during these ca. 500 years—the tell–enclosure system, functioning as an institutional ritual regulatory mechanism, might have played a crucial role in this stability and ensured the economic prosperity of the horizontal settlement (Smith and Stewart 2011). Thus, as proposed by Marcus and Flannery (2004), a similar model of ritual and society coevolution can be assumed at Polgár-Csőszhalom.

Interestingly, a more intense occupation of Polgár-Bosnyákdomb in the southern part of the Polgár Island began during the final phase at Polgár-Csőszhalom (Raczky and Anders 2009b). This suggests population dispersal from the center to the fringes of the micoregion between 4500 and 4400 B.C., leading to the termination of the internal social

POLGÁR-CSŐSZHALOM

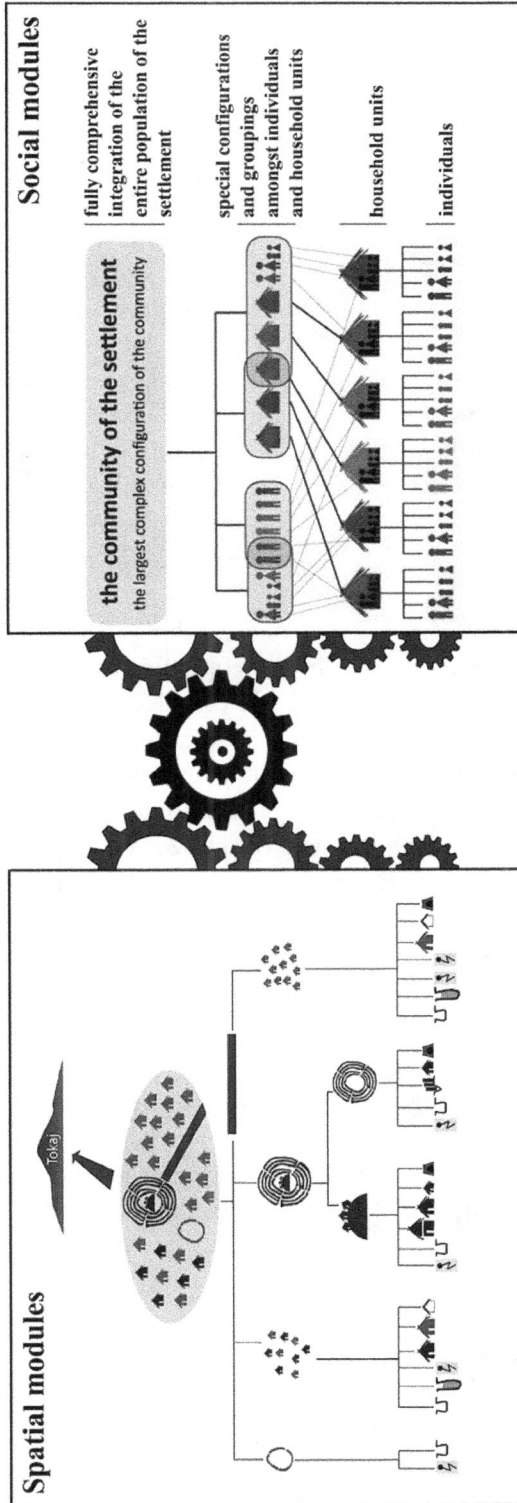

FIGURE 12.11. Polgár-Csőszhalom. A tentative model of the interplay of the spatial and social modules reconstructed at the site (after Anders and Raczky 2013) (for a detailed description of the model, see the text).

arena at Polgár-Csőszhalom. In a broader context, this dispersal process resulted in the disintegration of the Late Neolithic settlement network of the Polgár Island. A similar development occurred at the end of the Late Neolithic across the Great Hungarian Plain and in the neighboring regions (Borić 2015; Gyucha et al. 2014; Link 2006; Parkinson 2006).

Conclusion

A closer look at the diachronic changes in the spatial organization of settlements during the successive periods of European prehistory reveals cyclically recurrent trajectories from small, autonomous sites dispersed in the landscape to aggregated, hierarchically organized settlement patterns, indicating a spatial imprint of the dynamics of long-term cultural changes (Fowles 2002; Harding 2013; Peters and Zimmermann 2017; Zimmermann 2012; see also Fernández-Götz this volume). The continuously restructured configurations of space reflect structural changes in community organization. This cyclicality constituted transformations from simple face-to-face interactions to distant, complex community interactions.

The contextual quality of the single house—the basic spatial module from the Neolithic onward—and the household—the corresponding social unit—depends on their contexts. The uppermost organizational level of a complex system overrides the rules and conventions of the lower levels. Thus, house and household have different meanings in a small-scale and in a complex society (Lemke 2000). Another dimension can be added to the cyclical changes of the fusion and fission of communities (Duffy et al. 2013). During network analyses, social group evolution was quantified, yielding interesting patterns in community dynamics—large groups persist longer if their smaller units are capable of altering their memberships. The behavior of small groups illustrates the opposite strategy—the precondition of stability is that their composition remains unchanged (Palla et al. 2007; Watkins 2013:7–8). Thus, in order to ensure the sustainability of aggregated communities, the dynamics of internal cohesion need to be changed, many times repeatedly. The long-term success of the aggregation depends largely on altering strategies related to the community's changing size and internal dynamics (Carballo et al. 2014; see also Gyucha this volume).

Similarly to other regions of Europe, long-term cultural adaptations led to the emergence of a range of settlement forms and different levels of social modules on the Neolithic Great Hungarian Plain (Müller 2009; Salisbury et al. 2013). Single-household (farmstead) and hamlet-type settlement modules, with fairly rare larger, village-level agglomerations characterized the Körös and Criş communities of the Early Neolithic. The various interpretations of these settlements—seasonal residence, local movement, or multisited communities—reflect the diversity of adaptation strategies to the local environment and the different composition of social groups. Stable social units constituted groups of 5–6 to 25–30 individuals, while communities of 125–130 people were infrequent.

The settlement forms of the Middle Neolithic ALP range from single households and hamlets to large villages with houses arranged in linear rows—a system that conforms to a spatial development described as local-to-global (Hillier and Hanson 1984). This three-tier settlement organization implies processes of aggregation giving rise to the development of sites with 100–200 inhabitants. Another outcome of this multilevel adaptive process during the Middle Neolithic is a change in the structure of the house representing the lowermost structural level—the emergence of the multiroomed longhouse. The larger interior of these buildings transformed the spaces of social interactions. An additional global-to-local phenomenon on ALP settlements is the introduction of enclosures—the act of creating spatial boundaries for new identity groups. In addition to a horizontal division, the emergence of settlement spaces with vertical deposits is an equally important process that created a three-dimensional perception of the world within which various activities and interactions were performed. At the same time, the top-down transformations represented by enclosure systems and tells meshed with the bottom-up order—the outcomes of this process are reflected by the regionally nonformalized settlement layouts. The spatial clusters of smaller and larger ALP settlements constituted settlement zones along watercourses.

The spatial and social modules of the latest ALP settlements were deconstructed and a new configuration of the preceding spatial elements occurred at the local, microregional, and regional scales ca. 5100–5000 B.C., leading to the formation of the Late Neolithic Tisza–Herpály–Csőszhalom macroregional complex on the Great Hungarian Plain. The settlement organization differed from the ALP in that the macroarchitecture of tells and enclosures represented highly formalized spaces (Whittle 2013). An intriguing question is whether the tells were domestic spaces or whether they served as settings for special community events, such as feastings or ritual performances (Parkinson and Gyucha 2012; Sherratt 2005).

The settlement complex at Polgár-Csőszhalom can be conceptualized as a supersite on the northern Great Hungarian Plain. The burnt houses on the enclosed tell aligned toward its center and the houses of the external horizontal settlement with their northwest to southeast alignment reflect fundamentally different organizational principles. Additionally, the archaeological evidence confirms that the community events in these two spatial segments followed different choreographies. The more than 2,000 occupants of the settlement complex indicate a strong community nucleation, as well as a horizontally and vertically structured space, conforming to the diverse groupings and levels of community interactions. The formalized space of the tell–enclosure system represents a strongly ritual space. Twelve smaller sites on the Polgár Island, including two village-like and 10 single-household settlements, surrounded the central settlement of Polgár-Csőszhalom. Together, they formed a microregional settlement cluster, similarly to other parts of the Great Hungarian Plain during the Late Neolithic (Gyucha 2015; Makkay 1982). These clusters constituted socioecological units with tells as their centers which—in the absence of other formalized institutions—have been described as supraregional central places (Parzinger 1992), places of assembly (Whittle 2013), or centers of congregation (Renfrew 2013). It would appear that following a millennium-long initial Neolithic development on the Great Hungarian Plain, a novel, monumentalized expression of group identity evolved (Bradley 2012:139–146). The tell and enclosure system also contributed to formalizing the cosmology of the communities, characterized by recurrent constructional and deconstructional actions, and manifested a long-term life history in a broader time/space context.

ACKNOWLEDGMENTS

I would like to thank Peter Biehl and Attila Gyucha for the invitation to participate in the 9th IEMA Conference. Special thanks to Attila Gyucha for the scientific encouragement and critical comments on this paper. I would also like to acknowledge the help of Denissa Lonhardt with the illustrations.

REFERENCES CITED

Anders, A., Z. Czajlik, M. Csányi, N. Kalicz, E. Gy. Nagy, P. Raczky, and J. Tárnoki 2010 Archaeological Register of Tell Settlements in Hungary. *Archaeologiai Értesítő* 135:147–160.

Anders, A., and E. Nagy 2007 Late Neolithic Burial Rites at the Site of Polgár-Csőszhalom-dűlő. In *The Lengyel, Polgár and Related Cultures in the Middle/Late Neolithic in Central Europe*, edited by J. K. Kozłowski and P. Raczky, pp. 83–96. Polish Academy of Arts and Sciences, Kraków.

Anders, A., and P. Raczky 2013 Háztartások és települési egység viszonya Polgár-Csőszhalom késő neolitikus lelőhelyén [The Relation Between Households and Settlement Units at the Late Neolithic Settlement of Polgár-Csőszhalom]. *Ősrégészeti Levelek* 13:78–101.

Bailey, D. W. 1999 What Is a Tell? Spatial, Temporal, and Social Parameters. In *Making Places in the Prehistoric World*, edited by J. Brück and M. Goodman, pp. 94–111. UCL Press, London.

Bánffy, E. 2013 *The Early Neolithic in the Danube-Tisza Interfluve*. Archaeolingua Central European Series 7. BAR International Series 2584. Archaeopress, Oxford.

Bánffy, E., and P. Sümegi 2012 The Early Neolithic Agro-Ecological Barrier in the Carpathian Basin: A Zone for Interaction. In *Archaeological, Cultural and Linguistic Heritage: Festschrift for Erzsébet Jerem in Honour of Her 70th Birthday*, edited by P. Anreiter, E. Bánffy, L. Bartosiewicz, W. Meid, and C. Metzner-Nebelsick, pp. 57–69. Archaeolingua, Budapest.

Bartosiewicz, L. 2012 Mammalian Remains from Körös Culture Sites in Hungary. In *The First Neolithic Sites in Central/South-East European Transect. Volume III: The Körös Culture in Eastern Hungary*, edited by A. Anders and Zs. Siklósi, pp. 195–204. BAR International Series 2334. Archaeopress, Oxford.

Bernardini, W. 2005 Reconsidering Spatial and Temporal Aspects of Prehistoric Cultural Identity: A Case Study from the American Southwest. *American Antiquity* 70(1):31–54.

Bertók, G., and Cs. Gáti 2014 *Old Times—New Methods*. Archaeolingua, Budapest and Pécs.

Bettencourt, L. M. A. 2013 The Origins of Scaling in Cities. *Science* 340(6139):1438–1441.

Bintliff, J. L. 2000 Settlement and Territory: A Socio-Ecological Approach to the Evolution of Settlement Systems. In *Human Ecodynamics*, edited by G. Bailey, R. Charles, and N. Winter, pp. 21–30. Oxbow Books, Oxford.

Birch, J. 2013 Between Villages and Cities: Settlement Aggregation in Cross-Cultural Perspective. In *From Prehistoric Villages to Cities: Settlement Aggregation and Community Transformation*, edited by J. Birch, pp. 1–22. Routledge, New York.

Bocquet-Appel, J.-P., S. Naji, M. Vander Linden, and J. K. Kozłowski 2009 Detection of Diffusion and Contact Zones of Early Farming in Europe from the Space-Time Distribution of 14C Dates. *Journal of Archaeological Science* 36(3):807–820.

Borić, D. 2007 The House Between Grand Narratives and Microhistories: A House Society in the Balkans. In *The Durable House: House Society Models in Archaeology*, edited by R. A. Beck, Jr., pp. 97–129. Occasional Papers 35. Center for Archaeological Investigations, Southern Illinois University, Carbondale.

Borić, D. 2008 First Households and "House Societies" in European Prehistory. In *Prehistoric Europe: Theory and Practice*, edited by A. Jones, pp. 109–142. Wiley-Blackwell, Oxford.

Borić, D. 2015 Mortuary Practices, Bodies, and Persons in the Neolithic and Early–Middle Copper Age of South-East Europe. In *The Oxford Handbook of Neolithic Europe*, edited by C. Fowler, J. Harding, and D. Hofmann, pp. 927–957. Oxford University Press, Oxford.

Bradley, R. 2012 *The Idea of Order: The Circular Archetype in Prehistoric Europe.* Oxford University Press, Oxford.

Bulla, B., and T. Mendöl 1947 *A Kárpát-medence földrajza.* Egyetemi Nyomda, Budapest.

Bulla, B., and T. Mendöl 1999 *The Geography of the Carpathian Basin.* Lucidus, Budapest.

Carballo, D., P. Roscoe, and G. M. Feinman 2014 Cooperation and Collective Action in the Cultural Evolution of Complex Societies. *Journal of Archaeological Method and Theory* 21(1):98–133.

Chapman, J. 1989 The Early Balkan Village. In *Neolithic of Southeastern Europe and Its Near Eastern Connections*, edited by S. Bökönyi, pp. 33–53. Varia Archaeologica Hungarica 2. Institute of Archaeology of the Hungarian Academy of Sciences, Budapest.

Chapman, J. 1997 The Origins of Tells in Eastern Hungary. In *Neolithic Landscapes*, edited by P. Topping, pp. 139–164. Oxbow Books, Oxford.

Chapman, J. 2008 Meet the Ancestors: Settlement Histories in the Neolithic. In *Living Well Together? Settlement and Materiality in the Neolithic of South-East and Central Europe*, edited by D. Bailey, A. Whittle, and D. Hofmann, pp. 68–80. Oxbow Books, Oxford.

Chapman, J. 2010 Houses, Households, Villages, and Proto-Cities in Southeastern Europe. In *The Lost World of Old Europe: The Danube Valley, 5000–3500 BC*, edited by D. W. Anthony and J. Y. Chi, pp. 75–89. Princeton University Press, Princeton and Oxford.

Chapman, J. 2013 From Varna to Brittany via Csőszhalom: Was There a "Varna Effect"? In *Moments in Time: Papers Presented to Pál Raczky on His 60th Birthday*, edited by A. Anders, G. Kulcsár, G. Kalla, V. Kiss, and G. V. Szabó, pp. 323–335. Ősrégészeti Tanulmányok/ Prehistoric Studies 1. L'Harmattan, Budapest.

Chapman, J., and B. Gaydarska 2016 Low-Density Agrarian Cities: A Principle of the Past and the Present. In *Trypillia Mega-Sites and European Prehistory 4100–3400 BCE*, edited by J. Müller, K. Rassmann, and M. Videiko, pp. 289–299. Themes in Contemporary Archaeology 2. Routledge, London.

Chapman, J., and J. Laszlovszky 2010 Introduction to the Upper Tisza Project. In *The Upper Tisza Project: Studies in Hungarian Landscape Archaeology. Book 2: Settlement Patterns in the Bodrogköz Block*, edited by J. Chapman, M. Gillings, E. Magyari, R. Schiel, B. Gaydarska, and C. Bond, pp. 1–27. BAR International Series 2087. Archaeopress, Oxford.

Chapman, J., M. Videiko, D. Hale, B. Gaydarska, N. Burdo, K. Rassmann, C. Mischka, J. Müller, A. Korvin-Piotrovskiy, and V. Kruts 2014 The Second Phase of the Trypillia Mega-Site

Methodological Revolution: A New Research Agenda. *European Journal of Archaeology* 17(3):369–406.

Csengeri, P. 2015 Middle Neolithic Painted Pottery from Borsod-Abaúj-Zemplén County, North-Eastern Hungary. In *Neolithic Cultural Phenomena in the Upper Tisa Basin*, edited by C. Virag, pp. 127–160. Muzeului Sătmărean, Satu Mare.

Domboróczki, L. 2009 Settlement Structures of the Alföld Linear Pottery Culture (ALPC) in Heves County (North-Eastern Hungary): Development Models and Historical Reconstructions on Micro, Meso, and Macro Levels. In *Interactions Between Different Models of Neolithization North of the Central European Agro-Ecological Barrier*, edited by J. K. Kozłowski, pp. 75–127. Polish Academy of Arts and Sciences, Kraków.

Domboróczki, L. 2010a Report on the Excavation at Tiszaszőlős-Domaháza-Puszta and a New Model for the Spread of the Körös Culture. In *Neolithization of the Carpathian Basin: Northernmost Distribution of the Starčevo/Körös Culture*, edited by J. K. Kozłowski and P. Raczky, pp. 137–176. Polish Academy of Arts and Sciences, Institute of Archaeological Sciences of the Eötvös Loránd University, Kraków and Budapest.

Domboróczki, L. 2010b The Problem of the Neolithization in North-Eastern Hungary: Older Theories and New Perspectives. In *Die Neolithisierung Mitteleuropas—The Spread of the Neolithic to Central Europe*, edited by D. Gronenborn and J. Petrasch, pp. 175–187. Römisch-Germanischen Zentralmuseum Tagungen 4. Römisch-Germanischen Zentralmuseums, Mainz.

Domboróczki, L., M. Kaczanowska, and J. K. Kozłowski 2010 The Neolithic Settlement of Tiszaszőlős-Domaháza-Puszta and the Question of the Northern Spread of the Körös Culture. *Atti della Società Preistorica e Protostorica Friuli-Venezia* (Giulia 17):101–155.

Domboróczki, L., and P. Raczky 2010 Excavation at Ibrány-Nagyerdő and the Northernmost Distribution of the Körös Culture in Hungary. In *Neolithization of the Carpathian Basin: Northernmost Distribution of the Starčevo/Körös Culture*, edited by J. K. Kozłowski and P. Raczky, pp. 191–218. Polish Academy of Arts and Sciences, Institute of Archaeological Sciences of the Eötvös Loránd University, Kraków and Budapest.

Duffy, P. R. 2014 *Complexity and Autonomy in Bronze Age Europe: Assessing Cultural Developments in Eastern Hungary.* Prehistoric Research in the Körös Region 1. Archaeolingua, Budapest.

Duffy, P. R., W. A. Parkinson, A. Gyucha, and R. W. Yerkes 2013 Coming Together, Falling Apart: A Multiscalar Approach to Prehistoric Aggregation and Interaction on the Great Hungarian Plain. In *From Prehistoric Villages to Cities: Settlement Aggregation and Community Transformation*, edited by J. Birch, pp. 44–62. Routledge, New York.

Ecsedy, I., L. Kovács, B. Maráz, and I. Torma 1982 *Magyarország Régészeti Topográfiája 6. Békés Megye Régészeti Topográfiája: A szeghalmi járás (IV/1).* Akadémiai, Budapest.

Faragó, N., E. K. Tutkovics, and A. Kalli 2015 Előzetes jelentés Bükkábrány-Bánya VII. lelőhely pattintott kőeszköz anyagáról [Preliminary Report on the Chipped Stone Assemblage of Bükkábrány-Bánya VII]. *A Herman Ottó Múzeum Évkönyve* 54:25–37.

Fort, J. 2015 Demic and Cultural Diffusion Propagated the Neolithic Transition across Different Regions of Europe. *Journal of the Royal Society Interface* 12:20150166. Electronic document: http://dx.doi.org/10.1098/rsif.2015.0166.

Fort, J., E. R. Crema, and M. Madella 2015 Modeling Demic and Cultural Diffusion: An Introduction. *Human Biology* 87(3):141–149.

Fowles, S. M. 2002 From Social Type to Social Process: Placing "Tribe" in a Historical Framework. In *The Archaeology of Tribal Societies*, edited by W. A. Parkinson, pp. 13–33. Archaeological Series 15. International Monographs in Prehistory, Ann Arbor, Michigan.

Furholt, M., and J. Müller 2011 The Earliest Monuments in Europe—Architecture and Social Structures (5000–3000 BC). In *Megaliths and Identities: Early Monuments and Neolithic Societies from the Atlantic to the Baltic*, edited by M. Furholt, F. Lüth, and J. Müller, pp. 15–32. Frühe Monumentalität und soziale Differenzierung 1. Dr. Rudolf Habelt, Bonn.

Füzesi, A., G. Mesterházy, G. Serlegi, G. Márkus, and P. Raczky 2016 Polgár-Csőszhalom: Results of the New Multidisciplinary Investigations of a Late Neolithic Settlement in the Tisza Region. *Hungarian Archaeology* (2016 Autumn):1–13. Electronic document: http://files. archaeolingua.hu/2016O/Fuzesi_et_al_E16OSZ.pdf.

Gillespie, S. D. 2000 Beyond Kinship. An Introduction. In *Beyond Kinship: Social and Material Reproduction in House Societies*, edited by R. A. Joyce and S. D. Gillespie, pp. 1–21. University of Pennsylvania Press, Philadelphia.

Gogâltan, F. 2003 Die neolitische Tellsiedlungen im Karpatenbecken. Ein Überblick. In *Morgenrot der Kulturen: Frühe Etappen der Menschengeschichte in Mittel- und Südeuropa. Festschrift für Nándor Kalicz zu 75. Geburtstag*, edited by E. Jerem and P. Raczky, pp. 223–262. Archaeolingua, Budapest.

Guilaine, J. 2000–2001 La diffusion de l'agriculture en Europe: une hypothese arythmique. *Zephyrus* 53–54:267–272.

Guilaine, J. 2007 Die Ausbreitung der neolithischen Lebensweise im Mittelmeerraum. In *Vor 12.000 Jahren in Anatolien: Die älteste Monumente der Menschheit*, edited by C. Lichter, pp. 166–176. Badisches Landesmuseum, Konrad Theiss, Stuttgart.

Gyucha, A. 2015 *Prehistoric Village Social Dynamics: The Early Copper Age in the Körös Region*. Prehistoric Research in the Körös Region 2. Archaeolingua, Budapest.

Gyucha, A., W. A. Parkinson, and R. W. Yerkes 2010 A Multi-Scalar Approach to Settlement Pattern Analysis: The Transition from the Late Neolithic to the Early Copper Age on the Great Hungarian Plain. In *Reimagining Regional Analyses: The Archaeology of Spatial and Social Dynamics*, edited by T. Thurston and R. B. Salisbury, pp. 100–129. Cambridge Scholars Publishing, Cambridge.

Gyucha, A., W. A. Parkinson, and R. W. Yerkes 2014 The Transition from the Late Neolithic to the Early Copper Age: Multidisciplinary Investigations in the Körös Region of the Great Hungarian Plain. In *The Neolithic and Eneolithic in Southeast Europe: New Approaches to Dating and Cultural Dynamics in the 6th to 4th Millennium BC*, edited by W. Schier and F. Draşovean, pp. 273–296. Prähistorische Archäologie in Südosteuropa 28. Marie Leidorf, Rahden/Westf.

Gyucha, A., R. W. Yerkes, W. A. Parkinson, A. Sarris, N. Papadopoulos, P. R. Duffy, and R. B. Salisbury 2015 Settlement Nucleation in the Neolithic: A Preliminary Report of the Körös Regional Archaeological Project's Investigations at Szeghalom-Kovácshalom and Vésztő-Mágor. In *Neolithic and Copper Age Between the Carpathians and the Aegean Sea: Chronologies and Technologies from the 6th to the 4th Millennium BCE*, edited by S. Hansen, P. Raczky, A. Anders, and A. Reingruber, pp. 129–142. Archäologie in Eurasien 31. Dr. Rudolf Habelt, Bonn.

Harding, A. 2013 World Systems, Cores, and Peripheries in Prehistoric Europe. *European Journal of Archaeology* 16(3):378–400.

Harris, O. J. T. 2014 (Re)assembling Communities. *Journal of Archaeological Method and Theory* 21(1):76–97.

Hillier, B. 2014 Spatial Analysis and Cultural Information: The Need for Theory as well as Method in Space Syntax Analysis. In *Spatial Analysis and Social Spaces: Interdisciplinary Approaches to the Interpretation of Prehistoric and Historic Built Environments*, edited by E. Paliou, U. Lieberwirth, and S. Polla, pp. 19–48. De Gruyter, Boston.

Hillier, B., and J. Hanson 1984 *The Social Logic of Space*. Cambridge University Press, Cambridge.

Hofmann, D. 2013 Narrating the House: The Transformation of Longhouses in Early Neolithic Europe. In *Memory, Myth and Long-Term Landscape Inhabitation*, edited by A. M. Chadwick and C. D. Gibson, pp. 32–53. Celtic Studies Publications 17. Oxbow Books, Oxford.

Horváth, F. 2009 Comments on the Tells in the Carpathian Basin: Terminology, Classification and Formation. In *Ten Years After: The Neolithic of the Balkans, as Uncovered by the Last Decade of Research*, edited by F. Draşovean, D. L. Ciobotaru, and M. Maddison, pp. 159–166. Bibliotheca Historica et Archaeologica Banatica 49. Marineasa, Timişoara.

Jankovich, D., J. Makkay, and B. M. Szőke 1989 *Magyarország Régészeti Topográfiája 8. Békés Megye Régészeti Topográfiája: A szarvasi járás (IV/2)*. Akadémiai, Budapest.

Jankovich, B. D., P. Medgyesi, E. Nikolin, I. Szatmári, and I. Torma 1998 *Magyarország Régészeti Topográfiája 10. Békés Megye Régészeti Topográfiája: Békés és Békéscsaba környéke (IV/3)*. Akadémiai, Budapest.

Jarman, N. R., G. N. Bailey, and H. N. Jarman 1982 *Early European Agriculture: Its Foundation and Development*. Cambridge University Press, Cambridge.

Kaczanowska, M., and J. K. Kozłowski 2008 The Körös and the Early Eastern Linear Culture in the Northern Part of the Carpathian Basin: A View from the Perspective of Lithic Industries. In *Proceedings of the International Colloquium: The Carpathian Basin and Its Role in the Neolithisation of the Balkan Peninsula*, edited by S. A. Luca, pp. 9–39. Acta Terrae Septemcastrensis 7. Lucian Blaga University, Sibiu.

Kalicz, N. 1970 Chronologische und terminologische Probleme im Spätneolithikum des Theißgebietes. In *Neolithic of Southeastern Europe and Its Near Eastern Connections*, edited by S. Bökönyi, pp. 103–122. Varia Archaeologica Hungarica 2. Institute of Archaeology of the Hungarian Academy of Sciences, Budapest.

Kalicz, N. 1990 *Frühneolithische Siedlungsfunde aus Südwestungarn*. Inventaria Praehistorica Hungariae 4. Hungarian National Museum, Budapest.

Kalicz, N. 2010 An der Grenze "zweier Welten"—Transdanubien (Ungarn) im Frühneolithikum. In *Die Neolithisierung Mitteleuropas—The Spread of the Neolithic to Central Europe*, edited by D. Gronenborn and J. Petrasch, pp. 235–254. Römisch-Germanischen Zentralmuseum Tagungen 4. Römisch-Germanischen Zentralmuseums, Mainz.

Kalicz, N. 2011 *Méhtelek: The First Excavated Site of the Méhtelek Group of the Early Neolithic Körös Culture in the Carpathian Basin*. Archaeolingua Central European Series 6. BAR International Series 2321. Archaeopress, Oxford.

Kalicz, N., and J. Koós 2014 *Mezőkövesd-Mocsolyás: A neolitikus Szatmár-csoport (AVK I) települése és temetője a Kr. e. 6. évezred második feléből—Mezőkövesd-Mocsolyás: A Brief Overview of the Szatmár Group (ALBK 1) in the Light of the Excavations and the Assessment of the Site and Its Finds*. Borsod-Abaúj-Zemplén Megye Régészeti Emlékei 9. Herman Ottó Múzeum, Miskolc.

Kalicz, N., and J. Makkay 1977 *Die Linienbandkeramik in der Grossen Ungarischen Tiefebene.* Studia Archaeologica 7. Akadémiai, Budapest.

Kalicz, N., and P. Raczky 1982 Siedlung der Körös-Kultur in Szolnok Szanda. *Mitteilungen des Archäologischen Institutes der Ungarischen Academie der Wissenschaften* 10–11:13–24.

Kalicz, N., and P. Raczky 1987 The Late Neolithic of the Tisza Region. A Survey of Recent Archaeological Research. In *The Late Neolithic of the Tisza Region*, edited by L. Tálas and P. Raczky, pp. 11–30. Directorate of the Szolnok County Museums, Budapest and Szolnok.

Kovács, K. 2007 A tiszaszőlős-aszóparti középső neolitikus település legkorábbi időszakának vizsgálata a kronológiai és a kulturális kapcsolatok tükrében [The Earliest Occupation Period of the Middle Neolithic Settlement at Tiszaszőlős-Aszópart in the Light of Its Chronological and Cultural Connections]. *Ősrégészeti Levelek* 8–9:19–38.

Kovács, Zs. E., E. Gál, and L. Bartosiewicz 2010 Early Neolithic Animal Bones from Ibrány-Nagyerdő, Hungary. In *Neolithization of the Carpathian Basin: Northernmost Distribution of the Starčevo/Körös Culture*, edited by J. K. Kozłowski and P. Raczky, pp. 238–254. Polish Academy of Arts and Sciences, Institute of Archaeological Sciences of the Eötvös Loránd University, Kraków and Budapest.

Kozłowski, J. K. 2013 Man and Environment in Transitional Periods of Prehistory. In *Universitatis Ovetensis Magister: Estudios en homenaje*, edited by M. de la Rasilla Vives, pp. 79–93. Ménsula-Universidad de Oviedo, Oviedo.

Kozłowski, J. K., and M. Nowak 2010 From Körös/Criş to the Early Eastern Linear Complex: Multidirectional Transitions in the North-Eastern Fringe of the Carpathian Basin. In *Neolithization of the Carpathian Basin: Northernmost Distribution of the Starčevo/Körös Culture*, edited by J. K. Kozłowski and P. Raczky, pp. 65–90. Polish Academy of Arts and Sciences, Institute of Archaeological Sciences of the Eötvös Loránd University, Kraków and Budapest.

Kuna, M., and D. Dreslerová 2007 Landscape Archaeology and "Community Areas" in the Archaeology of Central Europe. In *Envisioning Landscape: Situations and Standpoints in Archaeology and Heritage*, edited by D. Hicks, L. McAtackney, and G. Fairclough, pp. 146–171. One World Archaeology Series 52. Left Coast Press, Walnut Creek, California.

Květina, P., and M. Končelová 2013 Neolithic LBK Intrasite Settlement Patterns: A Case Study from Bylany (Czech Republic). *Journal of Archaeology*: Article 581607. Electronic document: http://dx.doi.org/10.1155/2013/581607.

Lemke, J. Y. 2000 Opening Up Closure: Semiotics across Scales. In *Closure: Emergent Organizations and Their Dynamics*, edited by J. L. R. Chandler and G. van de Vijver, pp. 100–111. Annals of the New York Academy of Sciences 901. New York Academy of Science Press, New York.

Lemmen, C. 2015 Cultural and Demic Diffusion of First Farmers, Herders, and Their Innovations across Eurasia. *Documenta Praehistorica* 42:93–102.

Lenneis, E. 2000 Hausformen der mitteleuropäischen Linearbandkeramik und des balkanischen Frühneolithikums im Vergleich. In *Karanovo III: Beiträge zum Neolithikum in Südosteuropa*, edited by S. Hiller and V. Nikolov, pp. 383–388. Phoibos, Wien.

Lévi-Strauss, C. 1982 *The Way of the Mask.* University of Washington Press, Seattle.

Link, T. 2006 *Das Ende der neolithischen Tellsiedlungen: Ein kulturgeschichtliches Phänomen des 5. Jahrtausends v. Chr. im Karpatenbecken.* Universitätsforschungen zur prähistorischen Archäologie 134. Dr. Rudolf Habelt, Bonn.

Magyari, K. E., J. Chapman, A. S. Fairbairn, M. Francis, and M. de Guzman 2012 Neolithic Human Impact on the Landscapes of North-East Hungary Inferred from Pollen and Settlement Records. *Vegetation History and Archaeobotany* 21(4–5):279–302.

Makkay, J. 1982 *A magyarországi neolitikum kutatásának új eredményei: Az időrend és a népi azonosítás kérdései.* Akadémiai, Budapest.

Makkay, J. 2007 The Excavations of the Early Neolithic Sites of the Körös Culture in the Körös Valley. In *Hungary: The Final Report. Volume I: The Excavations: Stratigraphy, Structures, and Graves,* edited by E. Starnini and P. Biagi. Societá per la Prehistoria e Protohistoria della Regione Friuli-Venezia Giulia, Quaderno 11. Museo Civico di Storia Naturale, Trieste.

Marcus, J., and K. Flannery 2004 The Coevolution of Ritual and Society: New 14C Dates from Ancient Mexico. *Publications of the National Academy of Science* 52:18257–18261.

Medović, A., R. Hofmann, T. Stankovic-Pešterac, R. Dreibrodt, I. Medović, and R. Pešterac 2014 The Late Neolithic Settlement Mound Borđoš near Novi Bečej, Serbian Banat, in a Multiregional Context: Preliminary Results of Geophysical, Geoarchaeological, and Archaeological Research. *Rad Muzeja Vojvodine* 56:1–33.

Meier-Arendt, W. 1989 Überlegungen zur Herkunft des linienbandkeramischen Langhauses. In *Neolithic of Southeastern Europe and Its Near Eastern Connections,* edited by S. Bökönyi, pp. 183–189. Varia Archaeologica Hungarica 2. Institute of Archaeology of the Hungarian Academy of Sciences, Budapest.

Mester, Zs., and B. Rácz 2010 The Spread of the Körös Culture and the Raw Material Sources in the Northeastern Part of the Carpathian Basin: A Research Project. In *Neolithization of the Carpathian Basin: Northernmost Distribution of the Starčevo/Körös Culture,* edited by J. K. Kozłowski and P. Raczky, pp. 23–36. Polish Academy of Arts and Sciences, Institute of Archaeological Sciences of the Eötvös Loránd University, Kraków and Budapest.

Mischka, C. 2010 Beispiele für Ähnlichkeit und Diversität neolithischer und kupferzeilicher regionaler Siedlungsmuster in Rumänien anhand von geomagnetischen Prospektionen. In *Leben auf Tell als soziale Praxis,* edited by S. Hansen, pp. 71–84. Kolloquien zur Vor- und Frühgeschichte 14. Dr. Rudolf Habelt, Bonn.

Mischka, C. 2012 Late Neolithic Multiphased Settlements in Central and Southern Transylvania: A Geophysical Survey and Test Excavation. In *Tells: Social and Environmental Space,* edited by R. Hofmann, F.-K. Moetz, and J. Müller, pp. 153–166. Universitätsforschungen zur prähistorischen Archäologie 207. Dr. Rudolf Habelt, Bonn.

Müller, J. 2009 Materielle Kultur, Territorialität und Bedeutungsinhalte von Identitäten: die Wirkung verdichteter Kommunikationsräume. In *Kulturraum und Territorialität: Archäologische Theorien, Methoden und Fallbeispiele,* edited by D. Krausse and O. Nakoinz, pp. 95–105. Internationale Archäologie 13. Marie Leidorf, Rahden/Westf.

Müller, J. 2010 Dorfanlagen und Siedlungssysteme. Die europäische Perspektive: Südosteuropa und Mitteleuropa. In *Jungsteinzeit im Umbruch: Die „Michelsberger Kultur" und Mitteleuropa vor 6000 Jahren,* edited by C. Lichter, pp. 250–267. Badisches Landesmuzeum, Karlsruhe.

Müller, J. 2012 Tells, Fire, and Copper as Social Technologies. In *Tells: Social and Environmental Space,* edited by R. Hofmann, F.-K. Moetz, and J. Müller, pp. 47–52. Universitätsforschungen zur prähistorischen Archäologie 207. Dr. Rudolf Habelt, Bonn.

Müller, J. 2016 Demography and Social Agglomeration: Trypillia in a European Perspective. In *Trypillia Mega-Sites and European Prehistory 4100–3400 BCE,* edited by J. Müller, K. Rassmann, and M. Videiko, pp. 7–16. Themes in Contemporary Archaeology 2. Routledge, London.

Müller, J., and K. Rassmann 2016 Introduction. In *Trypillia Mega-Sites and European Prehistory 4100–3400 BCE*, edited by J. Müller, K. Rassmann, and M. Videiko, pp. 1–5. Themes in Contemporary Archaeology 2. Routledge, London.

Nagy, E. Gy., M. Kaczanowska, J. K. Kozłowski, M. Moskal-Del Hoyo, and M. Lityńska-Zając 2014 Evolution and Environment of the Eastern Linear Pottery Culture: A Case Study in the Site of Polgár-Piócási-dűlő. *Acta Archaeologica Academiae Scientiarum Hungaricae* 65:217–284.

Nandris, J. 2007 Adaptive Mediation in the FTN: The Nature and Role of the First Temperate European Neolithic. In *A Short Walk through the Balkans: The First Farmers of the Carpathian Basin and Adjacent Regions*, edited by M. Spataro and P. Biagi, pp. 11–23. Società per la Preistoria e Protostoria della Regione Friuli-Venezia Giulia, Quaderno 12. Museo Civico di Storia Naturale, Trieste.

Neitzel, J. E., and T. Earle 2014 Dual-Tier Approach to Societal Evolution and Types. *Journal of Anthropological Archaeology* 36:181–195.

Oross, K. 2013 Regional Traits in the LBK Architecture of Transdanubia. In *Moments in Time: Papers Presented to Pál Raczky on His 60th Birthday*, edited by A. Anders, G. Kulcsár, G. Kalla, V. Kiss, and V. G. Szabó, pp. 187–202. Ősrégészeti Tanulmányok/Prehistoric Studies 1. L'Harmattan, Budapest.

Oross, K., and Zs. Siklósi 2012 Relative and Absolute Chronology of the Early Neolithic in the Great Hungarian Plain. In *The First Neolithic Sites in Central/South-East European Transect. Volume III: The Körös Culture in Eastern Hungary*, edited by A. Anders and Zs. Siklósi, pp. 129–159. BAR International Series 2334. Archaeopress, Oxford.

Ortman, S. G., K. E. Davis, J. Lobo, M. E. Smith, L. M. A. Bettencourt, and A. Cabaniss 2016 Settlement Scaling and Economic Change in the Central Andes. *Journal of Archaeological Science* 73:94–106.

Osborne, J. F. 2014 Monuments and Monumentality. In *Approaching Monumentality in Archaeology*, edited by J. F. Osborne, pp. 1–19. State University of New York Press, Albany, New York.

Palla, G., A.-L. Barabási, and T. Vicsek 2007 Quantifying Social Group Evolution. *Nature* 446:664–667.

Parkinson, W. A. 2002 Integration, Interaction, and Tribal "Cycling": The Transition to the Copper Age on the Great Hungarian Plain. In *The Archaeology of Tribal Societies*, edited by W. A. Parkinson, pp. 391–438. Archaeological Series 15. International Monographs in Prehistory, Ann Arbor, Michigan.

Parkinson, W. A. 2006 *The Social Organization of Early Copper Age Tribes on the Great Hungarian Plain*. BAR International Series 1573. Archaeopress, Oxford.

Parkinson, W. A., and A. Gyucha 2007 A késő neolitikum–kora rézkor átmeneti időszakának társadalomszerkezeti változásai az Alföldön. Rekonstrukciós kísérlet. *Archaeologiai Értesítő* 132(1):37–81.

Parkinson, W. A., and A. Gyucha 2012 Tells in Perspective: Long-Term Patterns of Settlement Nucleation and Dispersal in Central and Southeast Europe. In *Tells: Social and Environmental Space*, edited by R. Hofmann, F.-K. Moetz, and J. Müller, pp. 105–116. Universitätsforschungen zur prähistorischen Archäologie 207. Dr. Rudolf Habelt, Bonn.

Parkinson, W. A., R. W. Yerkes, A. Gyucha, A. Sarris, M. Morris, and R. B. Salisbury 2010 Early Copper Age Settlements in the Körös Region of the Great Hungarian Plain. *Journal of Field Archaeology* 35(2):164–183.

Parzinger, H. 1992 Zentrale Orte—Siedelverband und Kultgemeinschaft im karpatenländischen Neo- und Äneolithikum. In *Hommage à Nikola Tasić à l'occasion de ses soixante ans*, edited by M. Garašanin and D. Srejović, pp. 221–230. Balcanica 23. Academie Serbe des Sciences et des Arts, Belgrade.

Pásztor, E., J. P. Barna, and G. Zotti 2015 Neolithic Circular Ditch Systems ("Rondels") in Central Europe. In *Handbook of Archaeoastronomy and Ethnoastronomy*, edited by C. L. N. Ruggles, pp. 1317–1326. Springer, New York.

Pavlů, I. 2013 The Role of Linear Pottery Houses in the Process of Neolithisation. *Documenta Praehistorica* 40:31–37.

Pécsi, M., and B. Sárfalvi 1964 *The Geography of Hungary*. Corvina, Budapest.

Perlès, C. 2001 *The Early Neolithic in Greece: The First Farming Communities in Europe*. Cambridge University Press, Cambridge.

Peters, R., and A. Zimmermann 2017 Resilience and Cyclicity: Towards a Macrohistory of the Central European Neolithic. *Quaternary International* 446:43–53.

Quitta, H. 1971 Der Balkan als Mittler zwischen Vorderem Orient und Europa. In *Evolution und Revolution im Alten Orient und in Europa: Das Neolithikum als historische Erscheinung*, edited by F. Schlette, pp. 38–63. Akademie, Berlin.

Raczky, P. 1989 Chronological Framework of the Early and Middle Neolithic in the Tisza Region. In *Neolithic of Southeastern Europe and Its Near Eastern Connections*, edited by S. Bökönyi, pp. 233–251. Varia Archaeologica Hungarica 2. Institute of Archaeology of the Hungarian Academy of Sciences, Budapest.

Raczky, P. 1995 Neolithic Settlement Patterns in the Tisza Region of Hungary. In *Settlement Patterns Between the Alps and the Black Sea 5th to 2nd Millennium B.C.*, edited by A. Aspes, pp. 77–86. Memorie del Museo Civico di Storia Naturale di Verona IIa/4. Museo Civico di Storia Naturale di Verona, Verona.

Raczky, P. 2006 House-Structures under Changes on the Great Hungarian Plain in Earlier Phases of the Neolithic. In *Homage to Milutin Garašanin*, edited by N. Tasić and C. Grozdanov, pp. 379–398. Serbian Academy of Sciences and Arts, Belgrade.

Raczky, P. 2012 Research on the Settlements of the Körös Culture in the Szolnok Area: The Excavations at Szajol-Felsőföld and Szolnok-Szanda. In *The First Neolithic Sites in Central/South-East European Transect. Volume III: The Körös Culture in Eastern Hungary*, edited by A. Anders and Zs. Siklósi, pp. 85–95. BAR International Series 2334. Archaeopress, Oxford.

Raczky, P. 2015 Settlements in South-East Europe. In *The Oxford Handbook of Neolithic Europe*, edited by C. Fowler, J. Harding, and D. Hofmann, pp. 235–253. Oxford University Press, Oxford.

Raczky, P., and A. Anders 2008 Late Neolithic Spatial Differentiation at Polgár-Csőszhalom, Eastern Hungary. In *Living Well Together? Settlement and Materiality in the Neolithic of South-East and Central Europe*, edited by D. Bailey, A. Whittle, and D. Hofmann, pp. 35–53. Oxbow Books, Oxford.

Raczky, P., and A. Anders 2009a Settlement History of the Middle Neolithic in the Polgár Micro-Region (The Development of the Alföld Linearband Pottery in the Upper Tisza Region, Hungary). In *Interactions Between Different Models of Neolithisation North of the Central European Agro-Ecological Barrier*, edited by J. K. Kozłowski, pp. 31–50. Prace Komisji Prehistorii Karpat PAU 5. Polish Academy of Arts and Sciences, Kraków.

Raczky, P., and A. Anders 2009b Régészeti kutatások egy késő neolitikus településen—Polgár-Bosnyákdomb [Archaeological Research at a Late Neolithic Settlement—Polgár-Bosnyákdomb]. *Archaeologiai Értesítő* 134:5–21.

Raczky, P., and A. Anders 2010 Activity Loci and Data for Spatial Division at a Late Neolithic Site-Complex (Polgár-Csőszhalom: A Case Study). In *Leben auf dem Tell als soziale Praxis*, edited by S. Hansen, pp. 143–163. Kolloquien zur Vor- und Frühgeschichte 14. Dr. Rudolf Habelt, Bonn.

Raczky, P., and A. Anders 2012 Neolithic Enclosures in Eastern Hungary and Their Survival into the Copper Age. In *Neolithische Kreisgrabenanlagen in Europa—Neolithic Circular Enclosures in Europe,* edited by F. Bertemes, P. F. Biehl, and H. Meller, pp. 271–309. Tagungen des Landesmuseums für Vorgeschichte Halle 8. Landesamt für Denkmalpflege und Archäologie Sachsen-Anhalt, Landesmuseum für Vorgeschichte, Halle/Saale.

Raczky, P., A. Anders, and L. Bartosiewicz 2011 The Enclosure System of Polgár-Csőszhalom and Its Interpretation. In *Sozialarchäologische Perspektiven: Gesellschaftlicher Wandel 5000–1500 v. Chr. zwischen Atlantik und Kaukasus,* edited by S. Hansen and J. Müller, pp. 57–79. Archäologie in Eurasien 24. Philipp von Zabern, Darmstadt.

Raczky, P., A. Anders, N. Faragó, and G. Márkus 2014 Short Report on the 2014 Excavations at Polgár-Csőszhalom. *Dissertationes Archaeologicae Ser. III.* 2:363–375.

Raczky, P., A. Anders, K. Sebők, P. Csippán, and Zs. Tóth 2015 The Times of Polgár-Csőszhalom: Chronologies of Human Activities on the Polgár-Csőszhalom Horizontal Settlement. In *Neolithic and Copper Age Between the Carpathians and the Aegean Sea: Chronologies and Technologies from the 6th to the 4th Millennium BCE,* edited by S. Hansen, P. Raczky, A. Anders, and A. Reingruber, pp. 21–48. Archäologie in Eurasien 31. Dr. Rudolf Habelt, Bonn.

Raczky, P., W. Meier-Arendt, K. Kurucz, Zs. Hajdú, and Á. Szikora 1994 Polgár-Csőszhalom: A Late Neolithic Settlement in the Upper Tisza Region and Its Cultural Connections (Preliminary Report). *Jósa András Múzeum Évkönyve* 36:231–240.

Raczky, P., and K. Sebők 2014 The Outset of Polgár-Csőszhalom Tell and the Archaeological Context of a Special Central Building. In *In Honorem Gheorghe Lazarovici: Interdisciplinaritate în Arheologie,* edited by S. Forţiu and A. Cîntar, pp. 51–100. Arheovest II/1. JATEPress, Szeged.

Raczky, P., P. Sümegi, L. Bartosiewicz, E. Gál, M. Kaczanowska, J. K. Kozłowski, and A. Anders 2010 Ecological Barrier versus Mental Marginal Zone? Problems of the Northernmost Körös Culture Settlements in the Great Hungarian Plain. In *Die Neolithisierung Mitteleuropas—The Spread of the Neolithic to Central Europe,* edited by D. Gronenborn and J. Petrasch, pp. 147–173. Römisch-Germanisches Zentralmuseum Tagungen 4. Römisch-Germanischen Zentralmuseums, Mainz.

Renfrew, C. 1998 Mind and Matter: Cognitive Archaeology and External Symbolic Storage. In *Cognition and Material Culture: The Archaeology of Symbolic Storage*, edited by C. Renfrew and C. Scarre, pp. 1–6. McDonald Institute for Archaeological Research, Cambridge.

Renfrew, C. 2013 Centres of Congregation. *Neo-Lithics* 2/13:30–34.

Rosenstock, E. 2005 Höyük, Toumba and Mogila: A Settlement Form in Anatolia and the Balkans and Its Ecological Determination 6500–5500 BC. In *How Did Farming Reach Europe? Anatolian–European Relations from the Second Half of the 7th through the First Half of the 6th Millennium cal BC,* edited by C. Lichter, pp. 221–237. BYZAS 2. Ege Yayınları, Istanbul.

Salisbury, R. B. 2012 Place and Identity: Networks of Neolithic Communities in Central Europe. *Documenta Praehistorica* 39:203–213.

Salisbury, R. B., G. Bácsmegi, and P. Sümegi 2013 Preliminary Environmental Historical Results to Reconstruct Prehistoric Human–Environmental Interactions in Eastern Hungary. *Central European Journal of Geosciences* 5(3):331–343.

Schier, W. 2008 Uivar: A Late Neolithic–Early Eneolithic Fortified Tell Site in Western Romania. In *Living Well Together? Settlement and Materiality in the Neolithic of South-East and Central Europe,* edited by D. W. Bailey, A. Whittle, and D. Hofmann, pp. 54–67. Oxbow Books, Oxford.

Sherratt, A. 1982 Mobile Resources: Settlement and Exchange in Early Agricultural Europe. In *Ranking, Resource, and Exchange: Aspects of the Archaeology of Early European Society,* edited by C. Renfrew and S. Shennan, pp. 13–26. Cambridge University Press, Cambridge.

Sherratt, A. 1997 *Economy and Society in Prehistoric Europe: Changing Perspectives.* Edinburgh University Press, Edinburgh.

Sherratt, A. 2005 Settling the Neolithic: A Digestif. In *(un)settling the Neolithic,* edited by D. Bailey, A. Whittle, and V. Cummings, pp. 140–145. Oxbow Books, Oxford.

Siklósi, Zs., M. Prange, N. Kalicz, and P. Raczky 2015 New Data on the Provenance of Early Copper Finds from the Great Hungarian Plain. In *Neolithic and Copper Age Between the Carpathians and the Aegean Sea: Chronologies and Technologies from the 6th to the 4th Millennium BCE,* edited by S. Hansen, P. Raczky, A. Anders, and A. Reingruber, pp. 57–92. Archäologie in Eurasien 31. Dr. Rudolf Habelt, Bonn.

Silva, F., J. Steele, K. Gibbs, and P. Jordan 2014 Modeling Spatial Innovation Diffusion from Radiocarbon Dates and Regression Residuals: The Case Study of Early Old World Pottery. In *Proceedings of the Radiocarbon and Archaeology 7th International Symposium,* edited by M. Van Strydonck, P. Crombé, and G. De Mulder, pp. 723–732. Radiocarbon 56(2). University of Arizona, Tucson.

Smith, A. C. T., and B. Stewart 2011 Organizational Rituals: Features, Functions and Mechanisms. *International Journal of Management Reviews* 13(2):113–133.

Stockhammer, P. W. 2012 Conceptualizing Cultural Hybridization in Archaeology. In *Conceptualizing Cultural Hybridization: A Transdisciplinary Approach,* edited by P. W. Stockhammer, pp. 43–58. Springer, Heidelberg.

Strobel, M. 1997 Ein Beitrag zur Gliederung der östlichen Linienbandkeramik. Versuch einer Merkmalanalyse. In *Saarbrücker Studien und Materialien zur Altertumskunde 4/5,* edited by J. Lichardus and F. Stein, pp. 9–98. Dr. Rudolf Habelt, Bonn.

Sümegi, P. 2004 Findings of Geoarchaeological and Environmental Historical Investigations at the Körös Site of Tiszapüspöki-Karancspart-Háromág. *Antaeus* 27:307–342.

Sümegi, P. 2012 The Environmental Background of the Körös Culture. In *The First Neolithic Sites in Central/South-East European Transect. Volume III: The Körös Culture in Eastern Hungary,* edited by A. Anders and Zs. Siklósi, pp. 39–47. BAR International Series 2334. Archaeopress, Oxford.

Sümegi, P., B. Csökmei, and G. Persaits 2005 The Evolution of Polgár Island. A Loess-Covered Lag Surface and Its Influences on the Subsistence of Settling Human Cultural Groups. In *Environmental Historical Studies from the Late Tertiary and Quaternary of Hungary,* edited by L. Hum, S. Gulyás, and P. Sümegi, pp. 141–163. University of Szeged, Szeged.

Szécsényi-Nagy, A., G. Brandt, W. Haak, V. Keerl, J. Jakucs, S. Möller-Rieker, K. Köhler, B. G. Mende, K. Oross, T. Marton, A. Osztás, V. Kiss, M. Fecher, Gy. Pálfi, E. Molnár,

K. Sebők, A. Czene, T. Paluch, M. Šlaus, M. Novak, N. Pećina-Šlaus, B. Ősz, V. Voicsek, K. Somogyi, G. Tóth, B. Kromer, E. Bánffy, and K. W. Alt 2015 Tracing the Genetic Origin of Europe's First Farmers Reveals Insights into Their Social Organization. *Proceedings of the Royal Society* B 282:20150339. Electronic document: 10.1098/rspb.2015.0339.

Thomas, J. 2015 What Do We Mean By "Neolithic Societies"? In *The Oxford Handbook of Neolithic Europe*, edited by C. Fowler, J. Harding, and D. Hofmann, pp. 1073–1091. Oxford University Press, Oxford.

Tompa, F. 1937 25 Jahre Urgeschichtsforschung in Ungarn 1912–1936. *Bericht der Römisch-Germanischen Kommission* 24–25:27–127.

Tringham, R. 1971 *Hunters, Fishers, and Farmers of Eastern Europe, 6000–3000 BC.* Routledge, London.

Watkins, T. 2013 Neolithisation Needs Evolution, as Evolution Needs Neolithisation. *Neo-Lithics* 2/13:5–10.

Wengrow, D. 2015 *Cities before the State in Early Eurasia.* Goody Lecture 2015. Max Planck Institute for Social Anthropology, Department "Resilience and Transformation in Eurasia," IMPRESS, Halle/Saale.

Weninger, B., L. Clare, F. Gerritsen, B. Horejs, R. Krauss, J. Linstädter, R. Özbal, and E. J. Rohling 2014 Neolithisation of the Aegean and Southeast Europe during the 6600–6000 cal BC Period of Rapid Climate Change. *Documenta Praehistorica* 41:1–31.

Whitehouse, H., and J. A. Lanman 2014 The Ties That Bind Us: Ritual, Fusion, and Identification. *Current Anthropology* 55(6):674–695.

Whittle, A. 1996 *Europe in the Neolithic: The Creation of New Worlds.* Cambridge University Press, Cambridge.

Whittle, A. 2003 *The Archaeology of People: Dimensions of Neolithic Life.* Routledge, London and New York.

Whittle, A. 2010a The Körös Culture of the Great Hungarian Plain: Implications of a Recent Research Project at Ecsegfalva, Co. Békés. In *Die Neolithisierung Mitteleuropas—The Spread of the Neolithic to Central Europe*, edited by D. Gronenborn and J. Petrasch, pp. 189–210. Römisch-Germanisches Zentralmuseum Tagungen 4. Römisch-Germanischen Zentralmuseums, Mainz.

Whittle, A. 2010b The Long and Winding Road: Reflections on Sixth-Millennium Process. In *Neolithization of the Carpathian Basin: Northernmost Distribution of the Starčevo/Körös Culture*, edited by J. K. Kozłowski and P. Raczky, pp. 91–102. Polish Academy of Arts and Sciences, Institute of Archaeological Sciences of the Eötvös Loránd University, Kraków and Budapest.

Whittle, A. 2013 Enclosures in the Making: Knowledge, Creativity, and Temporality. In *Moments in Time: Papers Presented to Pál Raczky on His 60th Birthday*, edited by A. Anders, G. Kulcsár, G. Kalla, V. Kiss, and G. V. Szabó, pp. 457–466. Ősrégészeti Tanulmányok/ Prehistoric Studies 1. L'Harmattan, Budapest.

Whittle, A., A. Anders, R. A. Bentley, P. Bickle, L. Cramp, L. Domboróczki, L. Fibiger, J. Hamilton, R. Hedges, N. Kalicz, Zs. E. Kovács, T. Marton, K. Oross, I. Pap, and P. Raczky 2013 Hungary. In *The First Farmers in Central Europe: Diversity in LBK Lifeways*, edited by P. Bickle and A. Whittle, pp. 49–97. Oxbow Books, Oxford.

Zanotti, A., R. Moussa, and J.-P. Bocquet-Appel 2014 Towards Modeling a Multi-Agent System for Balkan Neolithic Spread. Poster presented at the Centre national de la recherche scientifique

UPR2147, Paris, France. Electronic document: https://www.academia.edu/8238043/Towards_Modeling_a_Multi-Agent_System_for_Balkan_Neolithic_Spread.

Zimmermann, A. 2012 Cultural Cycles in Central Europe during the Holocene. *Quaternary International* 274:251–258.

CHAPTER THIRTEEN

Aggregation and Dispersal

Rural Landscapes of the Northwestern Iberian Peninsula from the Iron Age to the Early Roman Empire

Inés Sastre and Brais Currás

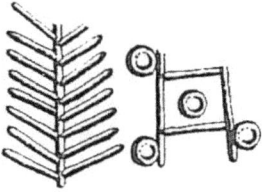

Abstract *We present a long-term settlement development trajectory in which intercultural contact, namely, the Roman expansion, is the touchstone for understanding aggregation processes. In the northwestern Iberian Peninsula, Iron Age societies from the ninth/eighth to the second century B.C. are characterized by castros—small, fortified, politically independent and economically self-sufficient settlements. This situation only changed around the second century B.C., when Rome appears as a transformative power just beyond the region. Hence, the final phase of the Iron Age brings a sharp change in the archaeological record of the southern coastal regions, including a novel trend toward population concentration in larger castros. After Augustus's conquest, a new profound change was imposed, marked by the construction of a provincial system based on civitates whose capitals do not resemble classic models of monumental urbanism, as they are eminently rural in nature.*

The European Iron Age is currently undergoing a debate regarding forms of social organization (e.g., Moore and Armada 2011). The deactivation of universal aristocratic paradigms rooted in purported Celtic systems and the increase in regional studies have revealed much greater variability than previously considered (Arnold and Blair Gibson 1995; Bueno et al. 2010; Gwilt and Haselgrove 1997). Meanwhile, the concept of "Romanization" has been critically reviewed and homogenizing interpretations also have been rejected (Mattingly 1997). In this context, the northwestern Iberian Peninsula is of enormous interest (Figure 13.1), and the combination of regional studies and theoretical approaches has produced alternative insights into the Iron Age and provincial societies.

FIGURE 13.1. Map of the northwestern Iberian Peninsula, with sites mentioned in the text.

The interpretations of the long-term social development from the ninth/eighth century B.C. to the first century A.D. normally minimize the impact of the initial stages of Roman domination, preferring to interpret the changes as an endogenous development of Iron Age communities, with the involvement of Phoenician traders (González-Ruibal 2004). We, however, argue for a transformation process in which Roman imperial expansion is the touchstone for understanding the genesis of settlement aggregation—a process indicating a radical change in social relations, dramatically disrupting pre-Roman social dynamics. Our conclusions are based on solid evidence of landscape archaeology analysis in two regions: on the one hand, the Bierzo, León (Fernández-Posse and Sánchez-Palencia 1998), and on the other, the Baixo Miño River basin (Currás 2014). Although the former area has always been considered as tangential to the processes at hand, the latter is undoubtedly central to the traditionally named Castro culture. As other studies prove (Carballo 2001; Lemos 1993), the conclusions presented here can be applied to the whole northwestern Iberian Peninsula.

Dispersion: Segmentary Communities during the Iron Age

Between the ninth/eighth and second centuries B.C., landscapes in Northwest Iberia were characterized by fortified settlements, so-called *castros*. The *castro* is a small, peasant village, located in a prominent position in the landscape. They are clearly confined within a perimeter, and often include built structures, such as enclosure walls, which mark the group's identity and make these settlements visible in their territory. During the Iron Age, *castros* are the only known form of settlement in the study area (Fernández-Posse and Sánchez-Palencia 1998; Parcero and Criado 2013). The social landscape of this period is a rural world constituted by a large number of small villages dotting the region—the absolute antithesis of urban centralized systems.

We have called these *castro* communities "segmentary agrarian" (Sastre 2012); however, we do not propose to return to the "segmentary lineage" concept of Fortes and Evans-Pritchard (1940). Our model is rooted in Durkheim's (1893) original concept of "segmentarity," which has received renewed attention in recent times (Albergoni 2003; Dresch 1986; Sigrist 2004). One key point is the structural definition of segmentation, based on the principles of complementary opposition, fusion, and fission of equivalent aggregates or segments. These segments may reflect several forms of social relations—not only kinship or lineage—and the sociopolitical system is characterized by the absence of centralized power above the segments. Social relations in Iron Age *castros* are articulated in equivalent segments structured at two levels: households and settlements. The relationship between segments is based on complementary opposition—they build their identity by confronting others that are exactly the same, but they also need interaction to guarantee the reproduction of the system. We have identified the segmentary principles in both the territorial and domestic spheres, which are discussed below.

Segmentary Landscape

The *castro*'s landscape is a network of communities that express their independence to, and against, their neighbors (Carballo 2001; Currás 2014; Esparza 2009; Lemos 1993; Orejas 1996). This opposition of equivalent social groups underpins all sociopolitical relations in their specific areas. Territorial organizations are formed by monotonously replicating equivalent corporate units—with no hierarchical relations between them—

which are always in opposition, always equidistant, and arranged in a spatial continuum (Figure 13.2).

The key factors of these settlement patterns are those related to access to farming resources necessary for establishing a peasant community. In this system, there is no evidence of specialized production and redistribution centers. *Castros* were economically self-sufficient, with a complex agricultural system and a notable development of iron metallurgy on the local scale (Fernández-Posse et al. 1993). Their catchment areas provided all the necessary natural resources, including clay, stone, and iron (Fernández-Posse and Sánchez-Palencia 1998).

The inhabited area of these *castros* is roughly 1 hectare, with a mean population of 150–200 people. A "settlement-growth discipline" is evident (Sastre 2008)—that is, settlements always were kept under a certain demographic limit, a maximum of about 200 inhabitants, a critical threshold in the process of social complexity that many scholars have emphasized (Bintliff 1999:533; Feinman 2011; Fletcher 1995:89). As a result, Iron Age *castros* never increased in size over the boundary imposed by their enclosures, as opposed to the later era of Roman domination (see below). Population growth would very

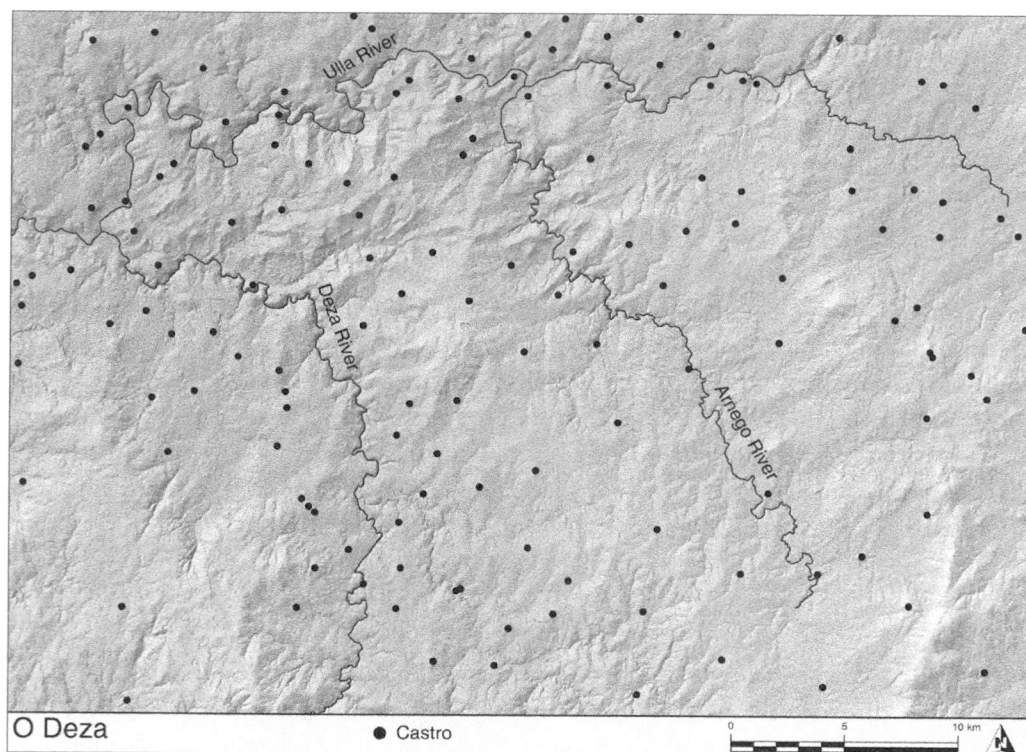

FIGURE 13.2. Segmentary landscape in the O Deza region (Pontevedra) (after Carballo 2001).

probably be resolved by fission: some families would move to found a new settlement at a similar location in the landscape, with similar productive conditions.

The *castro* represented the liminal level within the Iron Age political structure and constituted the reference point for intercommunity relations. There was no significantly higher level of integration beyond the village within the regional settlement organization. The projection and visibility of *castros* over the landscape show a splitting landscape with *castros* facing each other. It is this game between likeness and opposition, without power centers or territorial hierarchies, that gives meaning to the segmentary society.

SEGMENTARY SETTLEMENTS

Within the settlements, nonhierarchical relations also are evident. The *castro* is a collection of households, all similar in shape and size (Figure 13.3), sometimes with empty spaces of variable size in the center of the settlement, which may be explained through communal terms. The archaeological record of households—and self-sufficiency as referred above— allows us to discuss the "underproduction discipline," in line with peasant economic mentalities (Vicent 1991). The term refers to control over surplus production—households had the technological capability for generating more products, but intensification of production was subordinated to cultural rules. As a study of food storages at the *castros* suggests, these features were associated with domestic units and remained extremely stable over the course of time—they did not become larger or change in shape, thus, intensification was carefully avoided (Fernández-Posse and Sánchez-Palencia 1998). This indicates that the households acted as centrifugal forces controlling the means and scale of production in accordance with principles that aimed to stabilize production rather than intensify it. But it was the community as a whole that held the power structure: households were not dispersed, as in other European Iron Age landscapes, but actually gathered in *castros,* which often had a conspicuous walled enclosure and shared a key activity, metallurgy. The results of a study of *castros* in León indicate that a specific metallurgical unit existed in each settlement, with a specialized household that operated full-time, supplying tools to the other, agrarian households (Fernández-Posse and Sánchez-Palencia 1993). This implies an obvious functional division, which does not overcome the village level of organization of production. Settlement dispersal at the regional level and the separation of households within the *castros* staved off power concentration and territorial hierarchies, and permitted the maintenance of strong local-scale relationships based on face-to-face contact. This allowed people to keep social control in communal hands— Iron Age *castros* represent the success of resistance to exploitation and hierarchization (Sastre 2008). A productive system avoiding surplus production, exclusive communal identities, and strategies of intercommunity relationships conditioned by complementary opposition would form a part of this success. As a result, rural societies with long-term stability—but marked by structural conflicts—developed. These conflicts occurred both within communities due to the centrifugal forces of domestic units, and between them due to the complementary opposition between *castros*. Therefore, conflicts had important

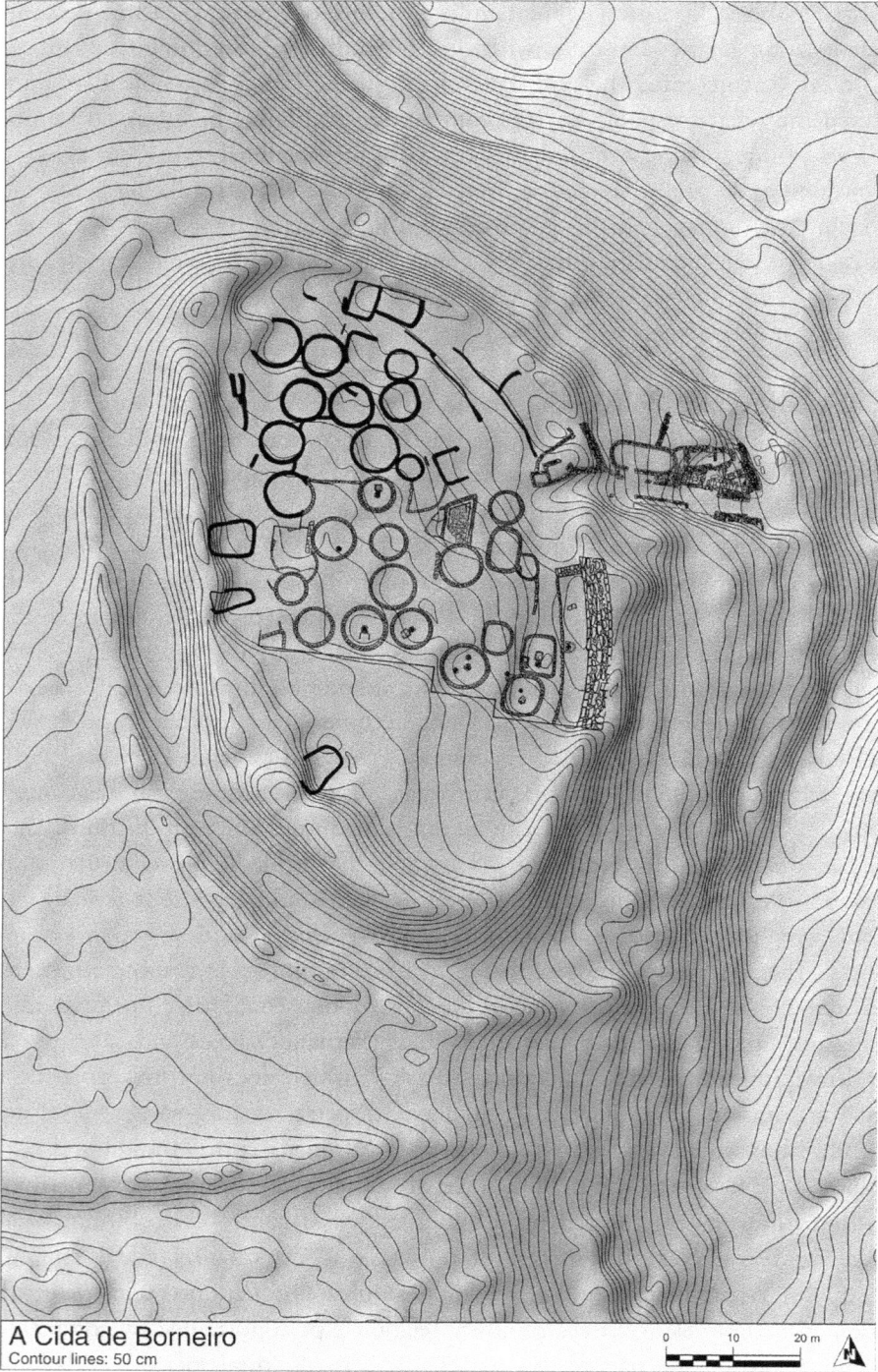

A Cidá de Borneiro
Contour lines: 50 cm

0   10   20 m

FIGURE 13.3. The *castro* of Borneiro (Cabana de Bergantiños, A Coruña) (after Romero Masiá 1985 and López González et al. 2007).

social consequences through fragmenting space and making resistance against hierarchical tendencies possible.

AGGREGATION AND SETTLEMENT CONCENTRATION DURING THE LATE IRON AGE AND THE LATE REPUBLIC—THE ARRIVAL OF ROME

The sociopolitical landscape changes dramatically in the southern and coastal regions of Northwest Iberia around the second century B.C. The archaeological record represents a clear break from the Iron Age patterns, with population concentrations and the disappearance of segmentary territorial principles. Most scholars consider it as an endogenous process, the result of an internal development, which began already in the fifth century B.C. According to this scenario, after the Early Iron Age, small *castros* "against the State" (in Clastres's [1974] term), a process of change—including the development of productive forces and the intensification of warfare—is thought to have started giving place to Germanic chiefdoms (Parcero 2003). Others suggest an increased importance of Mediterranean contacts in the transformations during the fifth to third centuries B.C. (González-Ruibal 2009).[1] The Latin term *oppida* also has been applied to the new, aggregated settlements of the period (González-Ruibal 2006; Parcero and Criado 2013; see also Fernández-Götz this volume), perhaps in an attempt to link northwestern Iberia with other European regions. We consider the application of this term in the Iberian context unsuitable and confusing; it is a concept used to characterize multiple and diverse realities (Fumadó 2013; Tarpin 2009; Woolf 1993), which caused lots of problems in regard to interpretations. Moreover, the literary sources barely make use of it in the case of the Iberian Northwest.[2]

The material record of Iron Age *castros* provides no evidence regarding these processes at work, nor foreshadows what was to come in the second century B.C. Our segmentary model, as explained before, emphasizes the inherent stability of the agrarian communities that built and maintained the *castros* in a conflicting, but balanced, complementary opposition. This balance was lost only when the external factor of Roman pressure appeared. We argue that the radical change in settlement patterns was an indigenous response to external pressures, and therefore can only be explained by the appearance of Rome—and its progressive presence and conquest—in the Iberian Peninsula.

The Roman conquest of Iberia started with the defeat of the Carthaginians after the Second Punic War (218–201 B.C.). This victory allowed Rome to control the southern and eastern regions of the peninsula. Over the following years, Rome continued a progressive expansion to the northern and inland parts of *Hispania,* alternating warfare with pacification policy in accordance with political trends and power relations in Italy. During the third and second centuries B.C., the Celtiberian-Lusitanian Wars took place, in the context of Republican civil strife. The first written information regarding northwestern peoples is related to these conflictive moments marked by the progressive submission of communities between the Guadiana and Duero rivers. It must also be taken into account that Hannibal—during the Carthaginian dominion of Iberia—also had undertaken military campaigns in the territories around the Duero Valley. Moreover, exchange relations on the Atlantic coast had taken place during that period and continued for the benefit of Roman allies, mainly Gades (López Castro 1995). The Graeco-Roman literary sources describe the different military operations between the Duero and Miño rivers from the mid-second century B.C. (Currás et al. 2016; Tranoy 1981). Thus, a historical process that occurred over the course of the period progressively put pressure on northwestern communities, following a general direction from south to north, and from coastal and western Meseta areas to inner territories.

In this historical context, new types of settlement appear, disrupting the Iron Age segmentary system in many respects. Above all, large *castros* occur at this time. While the largest Iron Age *castros* occupy 2 to 3 hectares at the most, these new *castros* are more than 10 hectares, including Sta. Trega (Peña 2001), Briteiros (Cardozo 1971), Sanfins (Silva 2007), Monte Mozinho (Almeida 1974), and San Cibrán de Las (López González et al. 2004). They also exhibit a very different spatial organization—with streets dividing the sites into sectors of households (i.e., neighborhoods). The appearance of these settlements goes hand in hand with other novelties in the archaeological record: new weapons, including items derived from the Roman army (*falcatae* and Montefortino helmets: García-Mauriño 1993; Quesada 1992, 2003), plastic art with decorative geometric stone elements in the settlements (Calo 1994), and warrior statues as evidence of new social hierarchies. The first coins in the Iberian Northwest also appear in this period in the southern area and they begin to spread beyond only later, under Augustus's government (Centeno 2012).

Based on the archaeological record, this process is clearly limited to the southern and coastal areas (Figure 13.4), which further illustrates the relevance of Roman presence in understanding the social and territorial changes. The Miño Valley—where Brutus Callaicus turned back his armies during one of the first known Roman campaigns in the region—is the northern limit of the most fundamental transformations. Beyond, the Roman influence is more reduced and belated, although it gradually intensified over time. In the east, similar processes have been documented, with Roman pressure coming from the central part of the peninsula (Orejas 1996). During the end of the Republic era, the Roman dominion was based on bilateral pacts with local communities after their surrender, which gave place to nonregular fiscal systems that responded to a "war economy" as defined by Ñaco (2003), including compensation payments, bounty, possibly hostages, compulsory conscription, and so on. After Brutus Callaicus's campaign (Liv. *Per.* 55; Estr. III, 3, 5; Plin. *Nat. Hist.* IV, 112; Apiano *Iber.* 72; Pap. Oxyr. Año 137; Floro I, 33, 12), a *decemviri* commission was sent to *Hispania* in 133 B.C. in order to organize the conquered territory. Among the tasks of this kind of commission, the imposition of taxes over local communities, distinguishing between the loyals and the rebels, was of great significance (Polybius *Hist.* XXI, 46).

Specific, unambiguous evidence of these Roman actions in northwestern Iberia is rare (Apiano *Iber.* 72), but we argue that the changes in the archaeological record

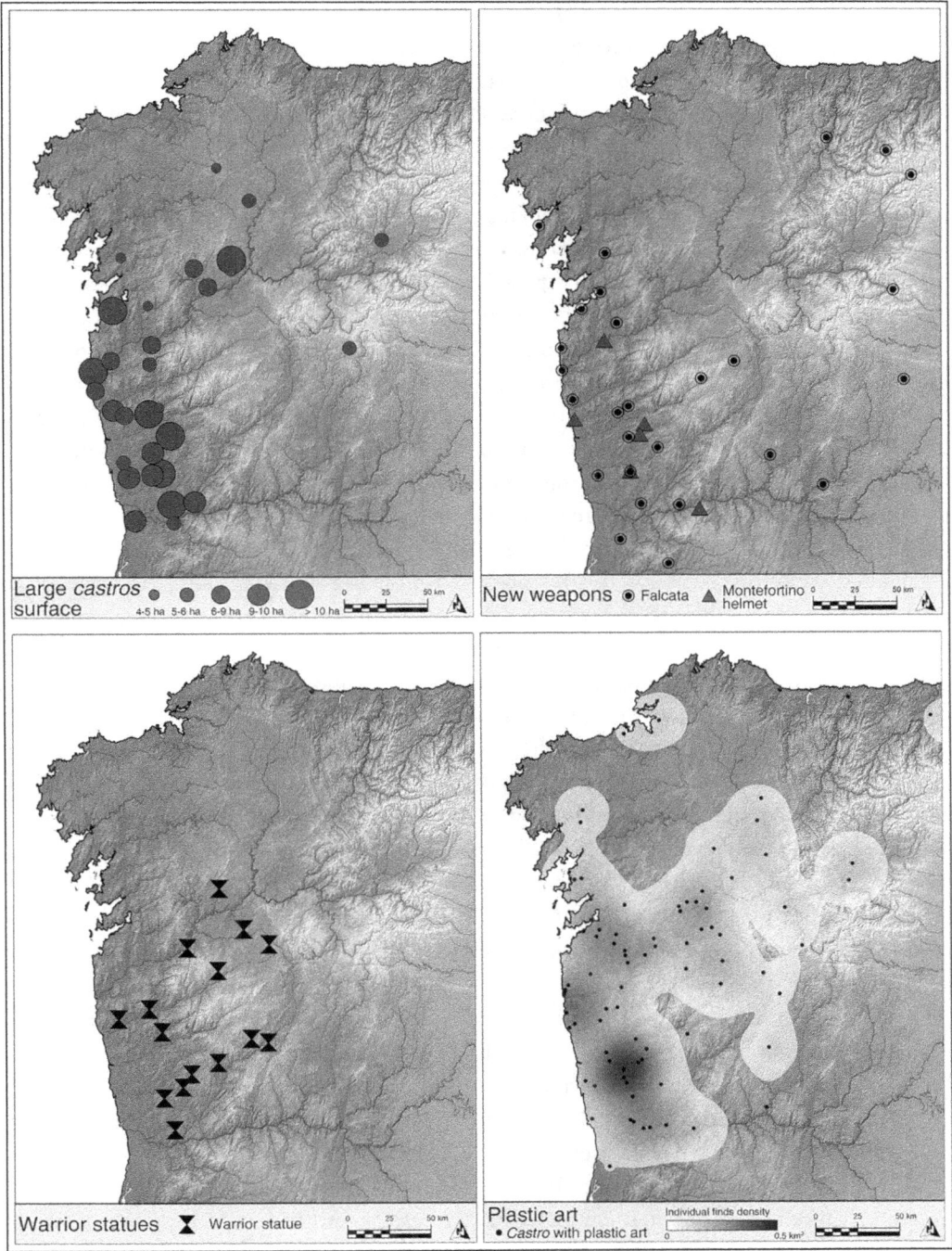

FIGURE 13.4. Changes in the Late Republic period in the northwestern Iberian Peninsula.

described above are the outcome of alterations in sociopolitical dynamics. Some local communities reacted to this process drastically. Large *castros* could be understood as a result of synoecism—the aggregation of small villages to form larger communities, perhaps as an attempt to gain traction in the increasingly unequal relations with Roman generals. A recent GIS analysis of the *citânia* of Briteiros highlights this process: the inhabitants of the *castros* of Sabroso and Santa Iria could have joined the larger *castro* of Briteiros (Fonte et al. 2011:363). On the other hand, newly emerged local elites would serve as middlemen between indigenous communities and the foreign power. All this implies the breakdown of isonomic, segmentary principles and the emergence of unequal relationships between and within individual communities under Roman influence.

Their size and the development of urban characteristics seem to permit the definition of large *castros* as cities (Figure 13.5). But, when we look beyond architectural features, it is necessary to ask whether it is reasonable to consider them as urban centers. Characterizing what constitutes "urban" is not straightforward, and it encompasses a reality that is historically changing and culturally variable. It is plausible, however, to apply a definition borrowed from human geography (Capel 1975; Weber 1966); a foundational aspiration of any social science is to clarify the concepts used, and achieve a validated consensus. It is for this reason that we opt for applying one such concept as established by geographers to the urban environment during the Iron Age—otherwise, we would run the risk of creating a new ad hoc definition, which, instead of clarifying the debate, would only add to the confusion. A city is commonly understood as a nucleus, where there is a substantial concentration of population, and which centralizes the government of a specific territory. It is different from its surrounding settlements because it has functional, economic, and political specialization. Differentiating the "urban" from the "rural" usually has relied on the diverse share that the primary sector (i.e., agrarian activities) has on the economy. An urban area has a population where the greatest share of the economy is carried by nonprimary sectors. We must keep in mind, however, that in the ancient world, farming activities—even in the cities—had a significantly greater importance than in more recent historical periods (Hopkins 1983; Leveau 1983a, 1983b; van Dommelen 1993).

For there to be a city, there has to be an associated territory that is dependent—and over which it must be a seat of power—with a clear political and economic difference. From the archaeological point of view, it is impossible to study urban spaces without carrying out broader regional studies so that the differences between the center and the hinterland can be characterized (see Gyucha this volume).

In short, a city in ancient societies implies a concentration of population as well as functional differentiation when compared to the rest of settlements. Taking into account the importance agrarian activities had in ancient cities, the functional differentiation necessarily has to do with political or religious power, or with market and/or craftwork activities that generate specific urban dynamics. It does not seem to be the case with large *castros*. Despite some interesting recent studies (Cruz 2016; Fonte et al. 2011; Lemos et al. 2011), large *castros* lack comprehensive, in-depth analyses beyond tradi-

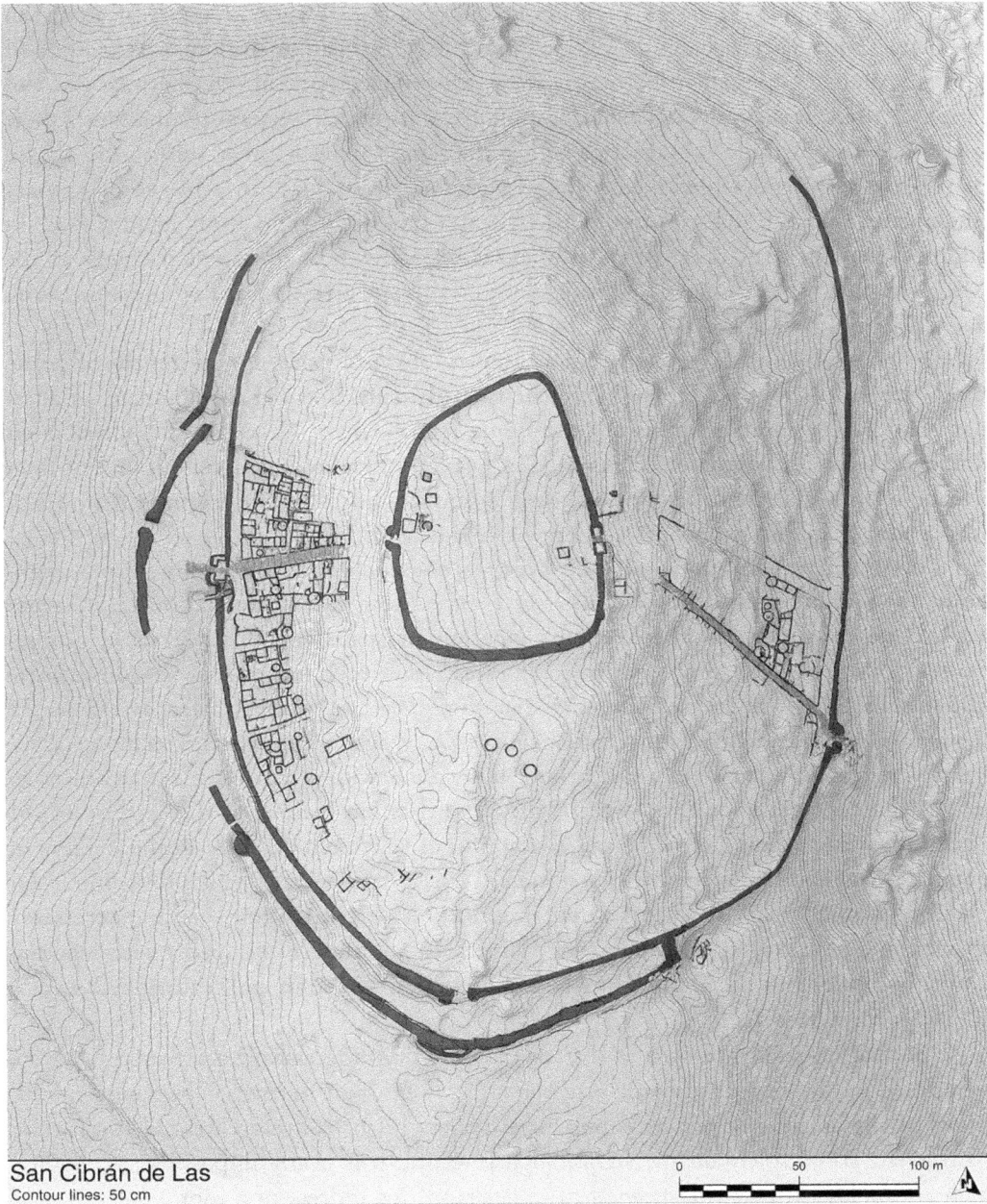

FIGURE 13.5. The *castro* of San Cibrán de Las (after López González et al. 2004).

tional archaeological excavations. But, with our current state of knowledge, despite their size, there is no evidence of large *castros* holding political sway beyond their immediate catchment territory—that is to say, there is no evidence of hierarchy among settlements.

Analysis of the inner space of large *castros* indicates the absence of traces of an urban character (López González et al. 2004; Peña 2001). Similar to the previous period, all domestic units continued to be occupied by self-sufficient peasant families dedicated to farming, there was no specialization confined to particular sectors or buildings, there is no evidence of trade or exchange of a greater scale than at other *castros,* the artisan or productive activities identified in large *castros* also took place in other contemporary settlements, and the material record itself is also hardly different from smaller sites. In addition, any elements associated with social hierarchy from this period—such as the Mediterranean imports, saunas, warrior statues, or plastic art—appear both in large *castros* and ordinary ones.

However, population concentration implies, obviously, the relinquishment of settlement-growth discipline typical of segmentary settlements and the development of alternative and more complex forms of community management. Although underproduction discipline seems to have been maintained in peasant households, the significance of face-to-face relationships remarkably decreased. A similar process was documented by Birch (this volume) in relation to the concept of "coalescence."

Intermediate organizational levels between households and the community—neighborhoods and clusters of households—serve an evident social role. However, it is not easy to make connections between this division of space and possible social groups. Several ideas have been proposed, in some cases rather speculative (Alarcão 2003; Sastre 2004; Silva 2007), but it may be said that these new social units acted as chinks for the growth of inequality within settlements.[3] Once again, Birch's (this volume) argument is remarkably relevant in this regard: individuals with a more stable attachment to place, who controlled local resources, rights, and decision making at the expense of the community as a whole may have played significant sociopolitical roles in the context of population aggregation, potentially resulting in social differences. But it also is important to keep in mind that "increased social stratification or centralization is not necessarily an outcome of aggregation" (Birch this volume). In addition, some spaces with religious Latin inscriptions in the *castros* have been interpreted as communal features (Alvarez et al. 2004; Silva 1999:21).

Be that as it may, the fact is that the large *castros* progressively accumulated power, as attested by the new aristocratic residences that were built in them. They are the indicators of the emergence of a new provincial society in the southern areas of the Iberian Northwest. Based solely on the archaeological record, it is nearly impossible to obtain a high chronological precision needed to understand this process in a more nuanced way. There is sufficient certainty, though, in confining this transitional phase between the later second and the end of the first century B.C., to the era of the Augustan Astur-Cantabrian Wars. Within this period, a subphase also can be identified during the second half of the first century B.C. In that time, most large *castros* were founded or remodeled, and the more profound social and territorial transformations concentrated on the coastal and southern areas of the Northwest. It is also relevant to notice that some houses in the large *castros* contained Latin inscriptions on their lintels—they show indigenous names and the term *domus* (i.e., house).[4] Also, some warrior statues display Latin inscriptions indicating local names (Redentor 2009). These inscriptions date after Augustus's conquest and they correspond to the last phase in the process of indigenous construction of inequality under Roman pressure. In provincial times, some of these large *castros* would indeed consist of large aristocratic houses—as in Armea (Conde-Valvís 1959) and Monte do Padrão (Moreira 2005)—and others would become actual urban centers, such as Tongobriga (Dias 1997, 2013).

In this final period, the founding of some new, small *castros* on flat locations disputes the search for local prominence that characterized Iron Age segmentarity. Moreover, a radically new type of settlement—valley-floor open villages—appears at the end of this era. Along with them, an actual process toward regional settlement hierarchies began.

CENTRALIZATION:
TERRITORIAL ORGANIZATION UNDER AUGUSTUS

When the Cantabrian Wars began at the end of the first century B.C., there was a distinct difference between the southern coastal area and the rest of the study area. Augustus's conquest resulted in novel transformations, which, this time, affected the whole Iberian Northwest. The measures applied after the conquest included a direct intervention of territories and communities, creating a brand new administrative system. Augustus imposed a unified and homogeneous vision of the *oikumene*, and a hegemonic ideology based on the confrontation between civilization (*humanitas*) and barbarism. This went hand in hand with the systematic control and exploitation of resources (Nicolet 1988)—exceeding by far the war economy characteristic of Republican expansion (Ñaco 2003)—and led to a profound territorial transformation throughout the northwestern Iberian Peninsula. These new processes resulted in a radical breakdown for indigenous societies compared to both the Iron Age and the Republican era. Large *castros* were a local response to Roman pressure, obviously conditioned by Roman power, but they followed indigenous dynamics. The forms of territorial hierarchies established after the Augustan conquest, however, were direct external impositions of exogenous administrative, political, and cultural models imported from the Mediterranean. These processes did not lead to actual urban societies but to regional settlement hierarchies with cities that acted as urban "islands" within a rural landscape.

In order to understand this new territorial and social reality, three key factors must be taken into account. First of all, Rome's cultural influence in Northwest Iberia was spread directly by the army and the members of the administration (Sastre 2007). The arrival of foreign population was limited in quantity, formal colonization—for example, foundations of *coloniae*—did not occur. The new urban sites, particularly the conventual capitals, became gathering places of the imperial administration as well as centers of

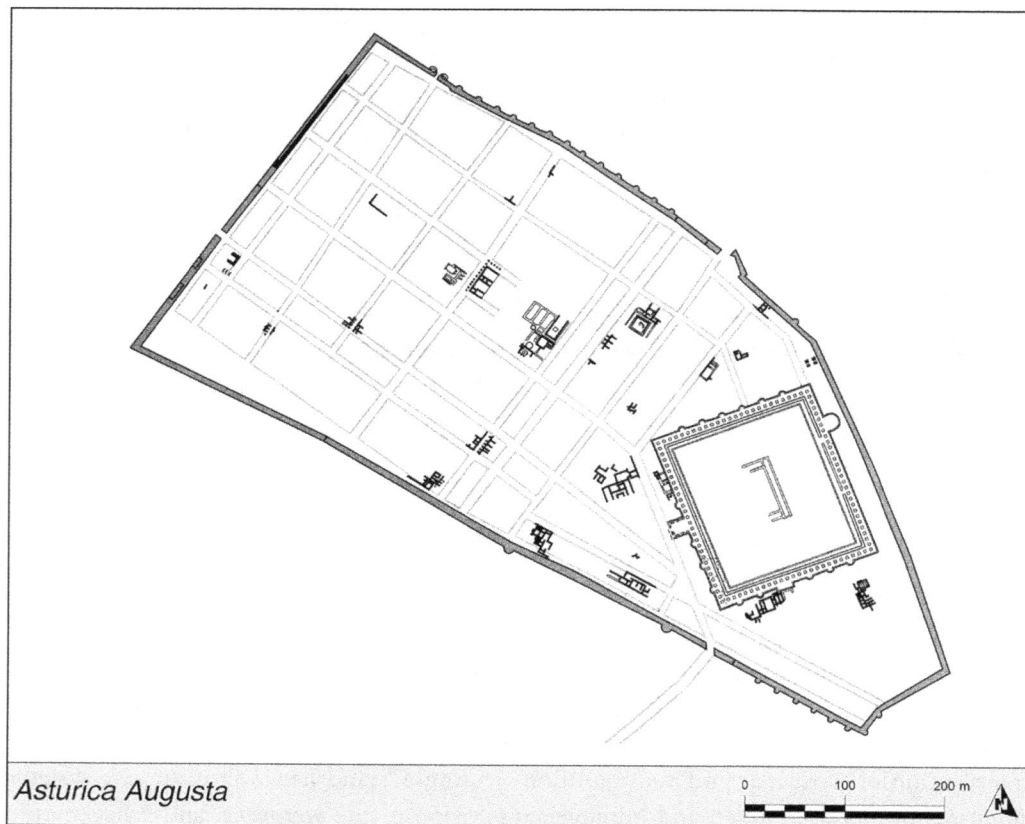

FIGURE 13.6. Plan of the city of *Asturica Augusta* (Astorga, León) (after Orejas and Morillo 2013, and Sevillano and Vidal 2002).

territorial control (Figure 13.6). The population in those new cities was mainly local and regional in origin. A road network, which was essential to ensure control over the region, connected them. Second, an important part of the territories, the mining areas were administered directly by Roman governance (Sánchez-Palencia 2014). Imperial administration used local population for labor as a form of tribute (Orejas and Sánchez-Palencia 2002). Third, domination was enforced through the division and organization of communities and territories into fiscal units called *civitates*. In *De agrorum qualitate*, Frontinus states that the *civitates peregrinae* were the ordinary models for tributary land in Augustan times (France 2001; Orejas and Sastre 1999).[5]

A great deal of attention has been given to urbanization in the study of Roman provinces, and has been seen as a hallmark of Roman-induced changes (Bendala 2006; Le Roux and Tranoy 1983–1984; Revell 2009). However, landscape approaches have revealed the predominance of rural landscapes in many imperial zones (Fleming and Hingley 2007; Mataloto et al. 2014; Orejas et al. 2009), and most *civitates* of the Iberian Northwest do not reflect a classic *urbs et territorium* model either. The new sociopolitical structure imposed by the Roman state generated the emergence of central cores and hierarchical settlement organizations within a process marked by diversity, beyond homogenizing schemes that characterize the models of Romanization.

In this context, the rural world had a strong force in social and territorial relations. The *civitates* were defined and organized by Rome as territorial, political, and fiscal units. Within these units, new forms of settlement developed. During the first century A.D., *castros* still persisted as a form of settlement in many *civitates,* with a special significance in mountain and mining zones. For instance, the La Corona de Quintanilla *castro*—situated in an important gold-mining area (Orejas 1996)—has a layout that reflects the tradition of Iron Age fortified settlements, but it was built in Roman times employing mining techniques (water force) for the delimitation of the site. The intricate trenches surrounding the *castro* were indeed a part of the mining exploitation works (Figure 13.7). The reoccurrence of *castro* settlement morphology, however, should not be interpreted as a survival of pre-Roman social relations because the communal-political *raison d'être* of Iron Age *castros* disappears in the *civitates* (Fernández-Posse 2002). The new construction techniques, new materials, and new forms of spatial organization suggest fundamental modifications within the *castros*. The "overflowing" of population outside the walled enclosures, the occupation of surrounding areas, and the growth of settlements indicate the complete dissolution of Iron Age social parameters. Gradually, *castros* were abandoned and they became exceptional in the regional settlement network by the end of the first century A.D. The few *castros* that persisted—as Roman villages—even until the fourth century A.D. included Viladonga (in Castro de Rei, Lugo; see Arias 2003), Zoñán (in Mondoñedo, Pontevedra; see Vigo 2006), and Monte Mozinho (in Porto; see Almeida 1974; Carvalho and Queiroga 2005).

Other types of rural settlements also appeared in Northwest Iberia during the Augustan era. In the context of intensification of production caused by the imposition of an imperial tributary economy, new settlements dispersed in the landscape related directly with good farming lands and/or territorial hierarchies. Although, in general, there are no monumental cores or large cities during the period, some indigenous settlements—mainly in the southern part of the region—saw urban development (Dias 2011) and/or had a monumental display. From this point of view, *Aquae Flaviae* (modern Chaves, Portugal), with a huge thermal complex, is of great interest; however, only a minority of similar, local capitals developed a monumental core (Costa et al. 2016). The settlement pattern exhibits a predominantly rural and dispersed landscape, with focal settlements in their core areas, which developed administrative and control functions but no monumental features. Some scholars—following the French tradition (Garmy 2012; Leveau 1993)—call them *agglomerations secondaires* (Pérez Losada 2002). These villages show a great diversity, which must be explained as a result of the identity and power expression of local elites within territorial and administrative systems imposed by the imperial government. Of great relevance in this sense is the layout of the road system, which directly affected the new territorial power structure.[6] In the classic model, the city urbanizes the country (centuriations, rural settlements like *vici* that reflect the *urbs*); in our case, the countryside structures itself (Pereira 1984).

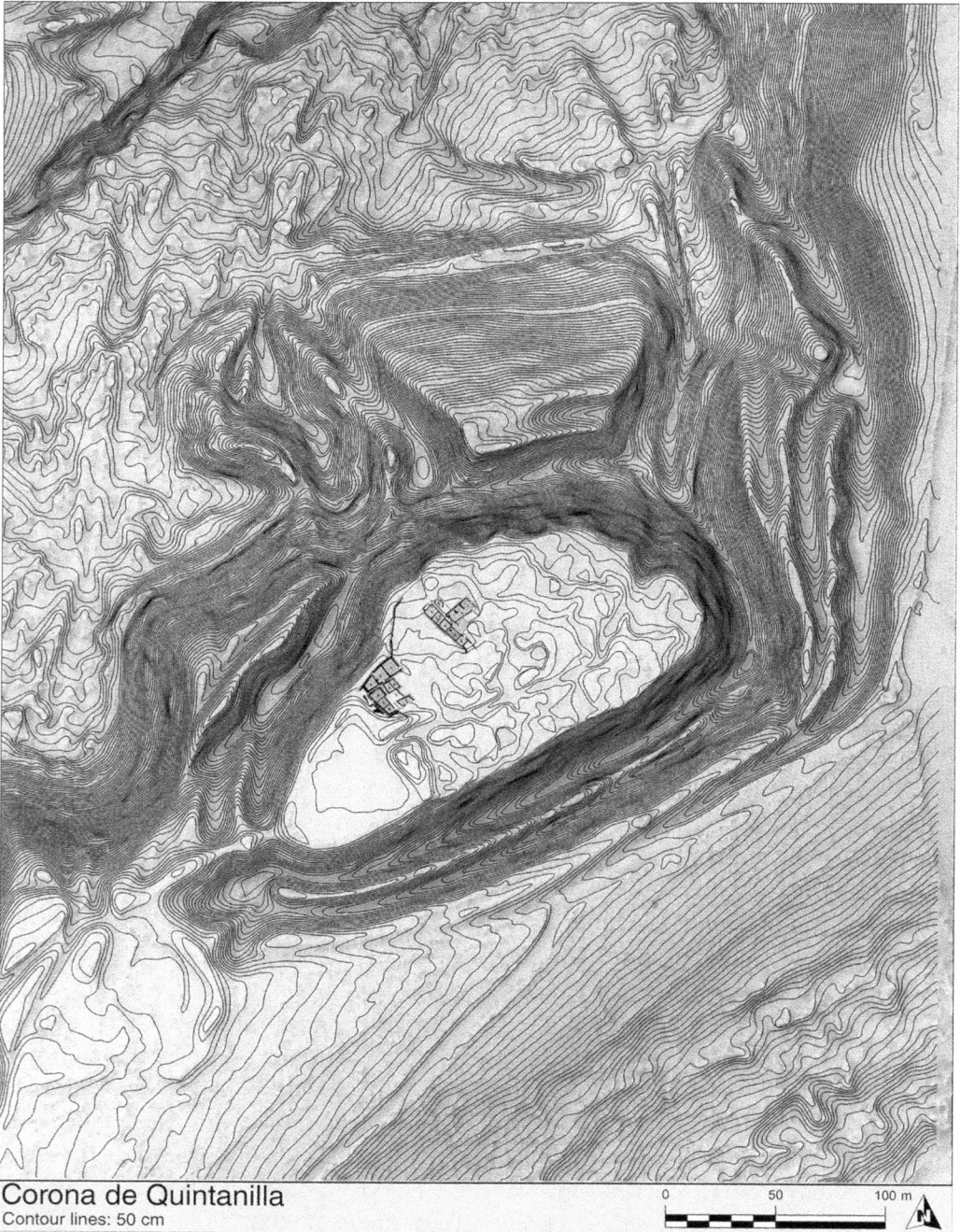

Corona de Quintanilla
Contour lines: 50 cm

0   50   100 m

FIGURE 13.7. The Roman mining *castro* of Corona de Quintanilla (Luyego, León) (after Fernández-Posse and Sánchez-Palencia 1988).

Next, we will explain in some detail some cases of *Asturia Augustana* (Figure 13.6). The capital, *Asturica* (currently Astorga, León)—called *urbs magnifica* by Pliny (Plin. *N.H.* 3, 3, 28)—shows a monumental urban core, with a large number of aristocratic *domus*. This monumental display has been associated with state administration because the general features of urban functions are lacking—neither the public representation of the local elites in epigraphy or sculptures at the site (Orejas and Morillo 2013:99), nor a typical urban integration of the rural hinterland has been documented (Orejas and Morillo 2013:109). In fact, *Asturica* centralized the administration of the *metalla* (mining zones) of the whole Northwest. In this way, the sphere of its political action incorporated a vast territory, even surpassing the boundaries of other *conventus*. *Asturica* differs, for instance, from *Bracara* (modern Braga, Portugal), the capital of the *conventus Bracarensis*. *Bracara* had an important role in the integration of the surrounding rural area, and the existence of an urban *centuriatio* has been proposed (Carvalho 2012; Orejas and Morillo 2013).

The *conventus Asturum,* like the whole Northwest, was divided in *civitates*. El Bierzo (León)—a region that has been the subject of an exhaustive investigation by our research group—makes use of an important document, an Augustan edict from the year of A.D. 15.[7] The document reveals the names of several *civitates* and their role in tribute payment. The *civitates* of Gigurri and Susarri—as well as others, like the Lougei—mentioned in contemporary documents (i.e., hospitality pacts: Balbín 2006) might have corresponded to the areas marked in Figure 13.8. Gold mines also are

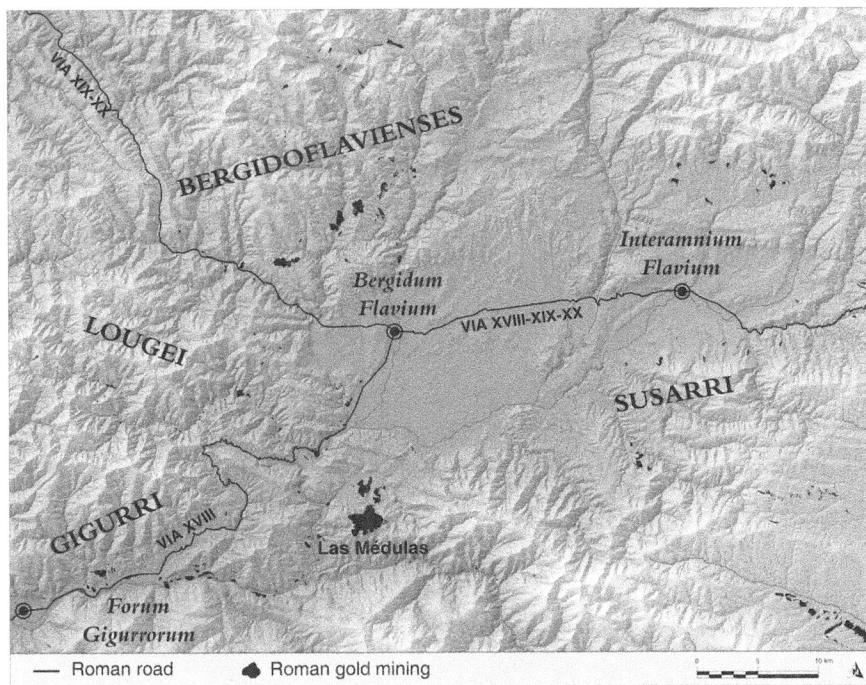

FIGURE 13.8. The *civitates* of El Bierzo (León) during the Early Roman Empire.

represented on the map; at the time of the edict, they were still untapped but would become active during the ensuing century. The *civitates* were populated by *castella*, which were small, rural communities. There are no documented settlements in El Bierzo that could clearly be identified as centers during the first part of the first century A.D. This initial disposition possibly changed during the Flavian reforms. The Roman settlements near the road (via XVIII/XIX/XX from Antonine Itinerary) date from A.D. 50 onward and they probably became central places only under Flavian rule; in the abovementioned Bierzo Edict, these settlements were not yet documented. In the second century A.D., there is a testimony of a *civitas Bergidoflaviensis,* or *Bergidum Flavium. Bergidum* is usually identified with the modern municipality of Cacabelos. The fortified settlement of Castro Ventosa in this area has been dated to pre-Roman times, but most of the material found in the site, as well as its enclosure, is significantly later (from the fourth century A.D. onward; Balboa de Paz et al. 2003). Occupation during the Early Empire is documented at numerous rural, dispersed settlements in the municipality. Among them, the only excavated site is La Edrada. This settlement shows urban development in line with its function as road *mansio,* containing domestic architecture and an Early Imperial sewer system, also serving nearby baths (Díaz Álvarez 2006–2008; Rodríguez et al. 2003).

When the archaeological information available from Northwest Iberia is compared with the social reality revealed from Latin inscriptions, there is a potential for greater understanding. Most inscriptions from the region have a rough aspect, and include simple texts (Figure 13.9). The great majority of them correspond to funerary and votive

FIGURE 13.9. Votive inscription from San Esteban de Toral (León).

epigraphy, including names and the usual *formulae*. These formal characteristics have been interpreted as a symptom of the backwardness and poverty of the dedicants. We argue for an alternative view, based on the idea that literacy and access to monumental scripture are indicative of high status in these rural communities (Sastre 2002). In this context, the limited evidence of civic roles and institutions in inscriptions is very relevant. There is no evergetism and the only honorific inscriptions are related to the army or administrative authorities (García Martínez 1997). These data have important historical implications— the subtle ideological games that permeate civic power were not needed in these rural societies (Pereira 2005), nor monumental features in the urban centers. Peasants remained completely isolated from political or civic activities. Belonging to a *civitas* usually was limited to the "*omni munere fungere*," as the Bierzo Edict states—that is, belonging to a fiscal circumscription and paying taxes in it. The *civitas* organization was not based on urban centers, but rather on regional entities that organized the administration and defined the fields of action for the local aristocratic power. The manifestations of this local power clearly differ from the forms of the expression of elite identity in urban contexts.

Taken together, the Roman society in the Iberian Northwest was a provincial, tributary, and rural society—peasant in the sociological sense—which is reflected in the hierarchically organized countryside. This social organization no way reflects a direct evolution from the pre-Roman world, nor corresponds to the idealized Roman model which historians have minted into the concept of "Romanization." It is not a territory of cities and slaves, but a rural and peasant world that can only be understood within the structure of imperial domination created by Augustus. Archaeology has revealed an indigenous material culture in a new settlement system by this period—communities of this era hardly resembled pre-Roman *castros,* nor the large *castros* forged by the earliest Roman expansion.

CONCLUDING REMARKS

The study of the Iron Age northwestern Iberian Peninsula shows the diversity of change from villages to cities, and its contingency. The emergence of the city is not the result of a linear evolutionary process, and must not be considered as a "necessary" historical development (see Fernández-Götz this volume). The evolutionary models do not explain the resilience of rural and decentralized forms of organization we have documented for this long period, from the beginning of the Iron Age to the second century A.D. Nor have they taken into account the relevance of intercultural contacts that contributed to the end of Iron Age social formations in Northwest Iberia.

Our study has detected a common element, a transversal feature in the long-term perspective—the importance of the rural world and settlement dispersion over the northwestern Iberian Peninsula. As it has been demonstrated throughout this paper, the processes of aggregation and centralization played a secondary role in a landscape deeply marked by rural settlement patterns. The history of ancient landscapes in northwestern Iberia is the history of the rural forms of territorial organization, with internal dynamics marked by the different processes of dispersal, aggregation, and centralization. The keypoint is the way we define societies as the product of social relations—and we can see two different approaches to this, with agrarian communities constructed through segmentary principles versus peasant societies working within a tributary, imperialistic system. So, a fundamental hallmark must be emphasized—the radical change from local dynamics to hierarchical social formations during the end of Iron Age under Roman pressure. Rural dynamics did not vanish, but they suffered a profound reorientation toward inequality and social exploitation.

ACKNOWLEDGMENTS

This essay is part of the research project HAR2015-64632-P *Paisajes rurales antiguos del Noroeste peninsular: formas de dominación romana y explotación de recursos (CORUS),* financed by the Ministerio de Ciencia e Innovación, and carried out in Instituto de Historia (CCHS, CSIC). It is also set in the Fundação para a Ciência e a Tecnologia postdoctoral program (SFRH/BPD/102407/2014).

NOTES

1. Researchers, in general, tend to move the dates forward. A Carthaginian presence in the northwestern Atlantic façade can be taken for granted, but an earlier Phoenician trade, that surely also could have existed, would have had a much more limited impact than commonly assumed.

2. Only two references exist: one referring to the capital of *conventus Bracara Augusta* (Plin. *Nat.* IV, 112), while the other mentions Abobrica (Plin. *Nat.* IV, 112), a place of uncertain location.

3. Surely, an in-depth study on kinship as a tool for construction of inequality should be undertaken in the future. This should be rooted in the approaches that argue that kinship has never been a structural foundation in any society (Godelier 2004, 2009), but a cultural construction determined by social dynamics. Using written Latin sources, a *"societés-a-maison"* model has recently been proposed to interpret the archaeological record of the large *castros* as Iron Age communities (González-Ruibal 2006). This model is only useful for describing particular kinship relations, but it cannot serve as a social model. For an alternative approach to the "house society" model, see Raczky's chapter in this volume.

4. From Briteiros: *[C]oroneri Camali domus* (CIL II 5595), *Camali domi Caturo* (CIL II 5590).

5. "Land has been contained in a survey whose entire area has been allocated to a community, as for example in Lusitania in the case of the people of Salmantica or in Hispania Citerior in the case of the people of Palentia. Moreover, in some provinces land subject to tax has been defined for communities on the basis of its entire area" (Frontinus: *De agrorum qualitate* Th. 1–2).

6. In other Hispanic areas, a *"civitas sine urbe"* model has been proposed in order to explain the existence of some centers, more or less monumentalized, which acted as frameworks of power for the local elites and as administrative, fiscal, and juridical cores (Arrayás et al. 2001; Oller 2011). However, these settlements do not display an urban form—they were not residential sites for the population of the *civitas* which inhabited rural settlements.

7.   "Imperator Caesar Divi filius Augustus holding the tribunician power for the eighth time, proconsul, says: I have learned from all my *legati,* who have been in charge of the *Transduriana provincia,* that the *castellani Paemeiobrigenses,* from the *gens* of the *Susarri,* remained loyal when the others were deserting. Therefore I give to them all perpetual immunity, and I order that they possess without controversy those lands and within those borders which they possessed when Lucius Sestius Quirinalis held that *provincia.* In place of the *castellani Paemeiobrigenses* from the *gens* of the *Susarri,* to whom I have given previously immunity in all matters, I replace at the request of that *civitas* the *castellani Aliobrigiaecini* from the *gens* of the *Gigurri*; and I order the aforesaid *castellani Aliobrigiaecini* to perform all duties along with the *Susarri.* Decreed at Narbo Martius, on the 14 and 15 February, when M. Drusus Libo and Lucius Calpurnius Piso were consuls" (Sánchez-Palencia and Mangas Manjarrés 2000).

REFERENCES CITED

Alarcâo, J. 2003 A organizaçaô social dos povos do Noroeste e Norte da Península Ibérica nas épocas pré-romana e romana. *Conimbriga* 42:5–115.

Albergoni, G. 2003 Anti anti-segmentarisme: pour un modèle rectifié. In *L'anthropologie du Maghreb: Les apports de Berque, Bourdieu, Geertz et Gellner,* edited by L. Addi, pp. 17–38. Awal/Ibis, Paris.

Almeida, C. A. F. 1974 *Escavações no Monte Mozinho (1974).* Centro Cultural Penafidelis, Penafiel.

Arias, F. 2003 Datacións radiocarbónicas do castro de Viladonga. *Gallaecia* 22:193–210.

Arnold, B., and D. B. Gibson (editors) 1995 *Celtic Chiefdom, Celtic State: The Evolution of Complex Social Systems in Prehistoric Europe.* Cambridge University Press, Cambridge.

Arrayás, I., J. Cortadella, T. Ñaco, O. Olesti, and A. Prieto 2001 Civitas y urbs en el nordeste hispánico: algunas reflexiones. In *La Península Ibérica hace 2000 años,* edited by L. Hernández Guerra, L. Sagredo San Eustaquio, and J. M. Solana Sáinz, pp. 311–317. Centro Buendía, Universidad de Valladolid, Valladolid.

Balbín, P. 2006 *Hospitalidad y patronato en la Península Ibérica durante la Antigüedad.* Junta de Castilla y León, Salamanca.

Balboa de Paz, J. A., I. Díaz, and V. Fernández 2003 *Actas de las Jornadas sobre Castro Ventosa.* Ayuntamiento de Cacabelos, León.

Bendala, M. 2006 Hispania y la "romanización." Una metáfora: ¿crema o menestra de verduras? *Zephyrus* 59:289–292.

Bintliff, J. 1999 Settlement and Territory. In *Companion Encyclopedia of Archaeology,* Vol. I, edited by G. Barker, pp. 505–545. Routledge, London.

Bueno, P., A. Gilman, C. Martín Morales, and F. J. Sánchez-Palencia (editors) 2010 *Arqueología, sociedad, territorio y paisaje: estudios sobre prehistoria reciente, protohistoria y transición al mundo romano en homenaje a Mª Dolores Fernández-Posse.* Bibliotheca Praehistorica Hispana 28. Consejo Superior de Investigaciones Científicas, Madrid.

Calo, F. 1994 *A plástica da cultura castrexa galego-portuguesa.* Conde de Fenosa Fund, Pedro Barrie de la Maza, A Coruña.

Capel, H. 1975 La definición de lo urbano. *Estudios Geográficos* 138–139:265–301.

Carballo, L. X. 2001 *A Cultura Castrexa na Comarca de Deza.* Seminarios de Estudios del Deza, Lalín.

Cardozo, M. 1971 *Citânia de Briteiros e castro de Sabroso*. Sociedade Martins Sarmento, Guimarães.

Carvalho, H. P. 2012 Marcadores da paisagem e intervenção cadastral no território próximo da cidade de Bracara Augusta (Hispania Citerior Tarraconensis). *Archivo Español de Arqueología* 85:149–166.

Carvalho, T. P., and F. Queiroga 2005 O Castro do Mozinho: os últimos trabalhos desenvuelto. *Cadernos do Museu (Penafiel)* 11:121–154.

Centeno, R. M. S. 2012 Da república ao Império: reflexões a monetização no Occidente da Hispânia. In *Barter, Money, and Coinage in the Ancient Mediterranean (10th–1st Centuries BC)*, edited by M. P. García-Bellido, L. Callegarin, and A. Jiménez, pp. 355–367. Anejos de Archivo Español de Arqueología 58. Consejo Superior de Investigaciones Científicas, Madrid.

Clastres, P. 1974 *La société contre l'Ètat: Recherches d'anthropologie politique*. Éditions de Minuit, Paris.

Conde-Valvís, F. 1959 Dos villas romanas de la Cibdá de Armeá, en Santa Mariña de Aguas Santas. *Revista de Guimarães* 69(3–4):472–500.

Costa, F. V., M. Martín Seijo, S. Carneiro, and J. P. Tereso 2016 Waterlogged Plant Remains from the Roman Healing Spa of Aquae Flaviae (Chaves, Portugal): Utilitarian Objects, Timber, Fruits, and Seeds. *Quaternary International* 404(A):86–103.

Cruz, G. 2016 Citânia de Briteiros: In the Origins of the Concept of a City. In *Guimarães: Cidade Visível*, edited by P. Pinto, pp. 120–122. Câmara Municipal de Guimarães, Guimarães.

Currás, B. 2014 *Transformaciones sociales y territoriales en el Baixo Miño entre la Edad del Hierro y la integración en el Imperio Romano*. PhD dissertation, Department of Archaeology and Sciences of Antiquity, Universidad de Santiago de Compostela, Santiago de Compostela.

Currás, B., I. Sastre, and A. Orejas 2016 Del castro a la civitas: dominación y resistencia en el Noroeste hispano. In *Celebração do Bimilenário de Augusto: Ad nationes. Ethnous Kallaikon*, edited by R. Morais, M. Bandeira, and M. J. Sousa, pp. 124–135. Câmara Municipal de Braga, Braga.

Dias, L. T. 1997 *Tongobriga*. IPPAR/Ministério da Cultura, Lisboa.

Dias, L. T. 2011 Urbanization and Architecture on the Outskirts of the Roman Empire. In *Roma y las provincias: modelo y difusión*, Vol. II, edited by T. Nogales and I. Rodá, pp. 707–713. Hispania Antigua Serie Arqueológica 3. Universidad de Sevilla, Mérida and Roma.

Dias, L. T. 2013 O momento e a forma de construir uma cidade no Noroeste da Hispânia, periferia do Império romano e fronteira atlântica. *Revista da Faculdade de Letras, Ciências e Técnicas do Património* 12:113–126.

Díaz Álvarez, I. 2006–2008 Bergidum Flavium, encrucijada viaria. Cacabelos (León). *Boletín do Museo Provincial de Lugo* 13:69–78.

Dresch, P. 1986 The Significance of the Course Events Take in Segmentary Systems. *American Ethnologist* 13(2):309–324.

Durkheim, E. 1893 *De la division du travail social*. Félix Alcan, Paris.

Esparza, A. 2009 El significado de los castros del noroeste zamorano. In *Actas III y IV Congreso de Antropología*, pp. 29–37. Instituto de Estudios Zamoranos "Florián de Ocampo," Zamora.

Feinman, G. M. 2011 Size, Complexity, and Organizational Variation: A Comparative Approach. *Cross-Cultural Research* 45(1):37–58.

Fernández-Posse, M. D. 2002 Tiempos y espacios en la cultura castreña. In *Los poblados fortificados del Noroeste de la Península Ibérica: formación y desarrollo de la cultura castreña*, edited by M. A. de Blas and A. Villa, pp. 81–96. Ayuntamiento de Navia, Navia.

Fernández-Posse, M. D., I. Montero, F. J. Sánchez-Palencia, and S. Rovira 1993 Espacio y metalurgia en la cultura castreña: la zona arqueológica de las Médulas. *Trabajos de Prehistoria* 50:197–220.

Fernández-Posse, M. D., and F. J. Sánchez-Palencia 1988 *La Corona y el Castro de Corporales II: Campaña de 1983 y prospecciones en La Valdería y La Cabrera (Leon).* Ministerio de Cultura, Madrid.

Fernández-Posse, M. D., and F. J. Sánchez-Palencia 1998 Las comunidades campesinas en la cultura castreña. *Trabajos de Prehistoria* 55(2):127–150.

Fleming, A., and R. Hingley (editors) 2007 *Prehistoric and Roman Landscapes.* Windgather Press, Oxford.

Fletcher, R. 1995 *The Limits of Settlement Growth: A Theoretical Outline.* Cambridge University Press, Cambridge.

Fonte, J., J. Valdez, F. S. Lemos, and G. Cruz 2011 Citânia de Briteiros e médio vale do Ave (NW de Portugal): SIG e análise arqueológica do território. In *Tecnologías de Información Geográfica y Análisis Arqueológico del Territorio*, edited by V. Mayoral and S. Celestino, pp. 359–366. Anejos de Archivo Español de Arqueología 59. Instituto de Arqueología, Mérida.

Fortes M., and E. E. Evans-Pritchard (editors) 1940 *African Political Systems.* Oxford University Press, London.

France, J. 2001 Remarques sur les "tribute" dans les provinces nord-occidentales du Haut-Empire romain (Bretagne, Gaules, Germanies). *Latomus* 60(2):359–379.

Fumadó, I. 2013 *Oppidum.* Reflexiones acerca de los usos antiguos y modernos de un término urbano. *SPAL* 22:173–184.

García Martínez, S. M. 1997 Evergetismo y propaganda imperial en el noroeste hispanorromano: su manifestación epigráfica. *Lancia* 2:149–164.

García-Mauriño, J. 1993 Los cascos de tipo Montefortino en la Península Ibérica. Aportación al estudio del armamento de la IIº Edad del Hierro. *Complutum* 4:95–146.

Garmy, P. 2012 Les mots et la chose: à propos des agglomérations secondaires antiques. *Revue Archeologique du Centre de la France, FERACF* 42:183–187.

Godelier, M. 2004 *Métamorphoses de la parenté.* Fayard, Paris.

Godelier, M. 2009 No Society Has Ever Been Based on Family or on Kinship. In *In and Out of the West: Reconstructing Anthropology*, pp. 62–79. Translated by N. Scott. University of Virginia Press, Charlottesville.

González-Ruibal, A. 2004 Facing Two Seas: Mediterranean and Atlantic Contacts in the North-West of Iberia in the First Millennium BC. *Oxford Journal of Archaeology* 23(3):287–317.

González-Ruibal, A. 2006 House Societies vs. Kinship-Based Societies: An Archaeological Case from Iron Age Europe. *Journal of Anthropological Archaeology* 25(1):144–173.

González-Ruibal, A. 2009 Past the Last Outpost: Punic Merchants in the Atlantic Ocean (5th–1st Centuries BC). *Journal of Mediterranean Archaeology* 19(1):121–150.

Gwilt, A., and C. Haselgrove (editors) 1997 *Reconstructing Iron Age Societies: New Approaches to the British Iron Age.* Oxbow Books, Oxford.

Hopkins, K. 1983 *Death and Renewal.* Sociological Studies in Roman History 2. Cambridge University Press, Cambridge and New York.

Lemos, F. S. 1993 *O povoamento romano de Trás-os-Montes oriental.* PhD dissertation, Institute of Social Sciences, Universidade do Minho, Braga.

Lemos, F. S., G. Cruz, J. Fonte, and J. Valdez 2011 Landscape in the Late Iron Age of Northwest Portugal. In *Atlantic Europe in the First Millennium B.C.: Crossing the Divide*, edited by T. Moore and X. L. Armada, pp. 187–204. Oxford University Press, Oxford.

Le Roux, P., and A. Tranoy 1983–1984 Villes et fonctions urbaines dans le nord-ouest hispanique sous domination romaine. *Portugalia* 4–5:199–207.

Leveau, P. 1983a La ville antique et l'organisation de l'espace rural: villa, ville, village. *Annales. Histoire, Sciences Sociales* 38(4):920–942.

Leveau, P. 1983b La ville antique, « ville de consummation »? Parasitisme social et économie antique. *Études rurales* 89–91:275–289.

Leveau, P. 1993 Agglomérations secondaires et territoires en Gaule Narbonnaise. *Revue archéologique de Narbonnaise* 26(1):277–299.

López Castro, J. L. 1995 *Hispania Poena: Los fenicios en la Hispania Romana, 206 a.C.–96 d.C.* Crítica, Barcelona.

López González, L. F., M. A. López Marcos, and Y. Álvarez González 2004 Definición y recuperación de estructuras en el Castro de San Cibrán de Lás. *Cuadernos de Estudios Gallegos* 51(117):79–113.

López González, L. F., F. Méndez, B. Albertos, and J. López Alonso 2007 Extracto de la memoria técnica de los trabajos de excavación arqueológica y consolidación en el castro de Borneiro (Cabana de Bergantiños, A Coruña). Campaña 2007. Manuscript on file, Dirección Xeral do Patrimonio Cultural, Xunta de Galicia.

Mataloto, R., V. Mayoral, and C. Roque (editors) 2014 *La gestación de los paisajes rurales entre la protohistoria y el período romano: formas de asentamiento y procesos de implantación.* Anejos de Archivo Español de Arqueología 70. Consejo Superior de Investigaciones Científicas, Mérida.

Mattingly, D. (editor) 1997 *Dialogues in Roman Imperialism: Power, Discourse, and Discrepant Experience in the Roman Empire.* Journal of Roman Archaeology Supplementary Series 23. Journal of Roman Archaeology, Portsmouth, Rhode Island.

Moore, T., and X. L. Armada (editors) 2011 *Atlantic Europe in the First Millennium B.C.: Crossing the Divide.* Oxford University Press, Oxford.

Moreira, A. B. 2005 *O Castro do Monte do Padrão: Do Bronze Final ao fim da Idade Média.* Câmara Municipal de Santo Tirso, Santa María da Feira.

Ñaco, A. 2003 *Vectigal incertum: Economía de guerra y fiscalidad republicana en el Occidente romano: su impacto histórico en el territorio (218–133 a.C.).* BAR International Series 1158. John and Erica Hedges, Oxford.

Nicolet, C. 1988 *L'inventaire du Monde: Géographie et politique aux origines de l'Empire romain.* Fayard, Paris.

Oller, J. 2011 La ciudad sin ciudad: la *ciuitas sine urbe* como elemento de control territorial. *Estrat Crític* 5(1):190–203.

Orejas, A. 1996 *Estructura social y territorio: El impacto romano en la Cuenca noroccidental del Duero.* Anejos de Archivo Español de Arqueología 15. Consejo Superior de Investigaciones Científicas Madrid.

Orejas, A., D. Mattingly, and M. Clavel-Lévêque (editors) 2009 *From Present to Past through Landscape.* Consejo Superior de Investigaciones Científicas, Madrid.

Orejas, A., and A. Morillo 2013 Asturica Augusta: reflexiones sobre su estatuto y su papel territorial (finales del siglo I a. d. C.–principios del siglo III d. C.). In *Debita verba: Estudios en homenaje al profesor Julio Mangas Manjarrés*, Vol. II, edited by E. García and R. Cid, pp. 93–119. Universidad de Oviedo, Oviedo.

Orejas, A., and F. J. Sánchez-Palencia 2002 Mines, Territorial Organization and Social Structure in Roman Iberia: Carthago Noua and the Peninsular Northwest. *American Journal of Archaeology* 106(4):581–599.

Orejas, A., and I. Sastre 1999 Fiscalité et organisation du territoire dans le Nord-Ouest de la Péninsule Ibérique: *civitates*, tribut et *ager mensura comprehensus*. *Dialogues d'histoire ancienne* 25(1):159–188.

Parcero, C. 2003 Looking Forward in Anger: Social and Political Transformations in the Iron Age of the North-Western Iberian Peninsula. *European Journal of Archaeology* 6(3):267–299.

Parcero, C., and F. Criado 2013 Social Change, Social Resistance: A Long-Term Approach to the Process of Transformation of Social Landscapes in the Northwest Iberian Peninsula. In *The Prehistory of Iberia: Debating Early Social Stratification and the State*, edited by M. Cruz Berrocal, L. García Sanjuán, and A. Gilman, pp. 249–267. Routledge, New York and Abingdon.

Peña, A. 2001 *Santa Trega: Un poblado castrexo-romano*. Abano, Ourense.

Pereira, G. 1984 La formación histórica de los pueblos del Norte de Hispania: El caso de *Gallaecia* como paradigma. *Veleia* 1:271–288.

Pereira, G. 2005 *Municipium*, un concepto de economía política. In *La Hispania de los Antoninos (98–180)*, edited by L. Hernández Guerra, pp. 555–566. Centro Buendía 80. Universidad de Valladolid, Valladolid.

Pérez Losada, F. 2002 *Entre a Cidade e a Aldea: Estudio arqueohistórico dos "aglomerados secundarios" romanos en Galicia*. Brigantium 13. Museo Arqueolóxico e Histórico, A Coruña.

Quesada, F. 1992 El casco de Almaciles (Granada) y la cuestión de los cascos de tipo "Montefortino" en la Península Ibérica. *Verdolay* 4:65–73.

Quesada, F. 2003 ¿Espejos de piedra? Las imágenes de armas en las estatuas de los guerreros llamados galaicos. *Madrider Mitteilungen* 44:87–112.

Redentor, A. 2009 Sobre o significado dos guerreiros lusitano–galaicos: o contributo da epigrafía. *Acta Palaeohispanica* 10, *Palaeohispanica* 9:227–246.

Revell, L. 2009 *Roman Imperialism and Local Identities*. Cambridge University Press, Cambridge.

Rodríguez, P., J. C. Alvarez, P. Lomba, and N. Martínez 2003 Campaña de excavaciones arqueológicas en La Edrada 2002. In *Actas de las Jornadas sobre Castro Ventosa*, edited by J. A. Balboa de Paz, I. Díaz, and V. Fernández, pp. 63–82. Patronato del patrimonio cultura de Cacabelos, Cacabelos.

Romero Masiá, A. 1985 Memoria das excavacións arqueolóxicas do castro de Borneiro. Campaña 1985. Manuscript on file, Dirección Xeral do Patrimonio Cultural, Xunta de Galicia.

Sánchez-Palencia, F. J. (editor) 2014 *Minería romana en zonas interfronterizas de Castilla y León y Portugal*. Junta de Castilla y León, Fundación Las Médulas, León.

Sánchez-Palencia, F. J., and J. Mangas Manjarrés (editors) 2000 *El Edicto del Bierzo: Augusto y el Noroeste de Hispania*. Fundación Las Médulas, Ponferrada.

Sastre, I. 2002 *Onomástica y relaciones políticas en la epigrafía del conventus Asturum durante el Alto Imperio*. Anejos de Archivo Español de Arqueología 25. Consejo Superior de Investigaciones Científicas, Madrid.

Sastre, I. 2004 Los procesos de la complejidad social en el Noroeste peninsular: arqueología y fuentes literarias. *Trabajos de Prehistoria* 61(2):99–110.

Sastre, I. 2007 Epigrafía y procesos de cambio en el Noroeste hispánico: la clientela en la formación de la sociedad provincial. In *Acta XII congressus internationalis epigraphiae graecae et latinae (Barcelona, Septiembre 2002)*, edited by M. Mayer, O. Giulia Baratta, and

A. Guzmán Almagro, pp. 1317–1324. Monografies de la Secció Historico-Arqueològica 10. Institut d'estudis catalans, Barcelona.

Sastre, I. 2008 Community, Identity, and Conflict: Iron Age Warfare in the Iberian Northwest. *Current Anthropology* 49(6):1021–1051.

Sastre, I. 2012 Social Inequality during the Iron Age: Interpretation Models. In *Atlantic Europe in the First Millennium: Crossing the Divide*, edited by T. Moore and X. L. Armada, pp. 264–284. Oxford University Press, Oxford.

Sevillano, M. A., and J. Vidal 2002 *Urbs magnifica: Una aproximación a la arqueología de Asturica Augusta (Astorga, León). Museo romano (guía-catálogo)*. Ayuntamiento de Astorga, Astorga.

Sigrist, C. 2004 Segmentary Societies: The Evolution and Actual Relevance of an Interdisciplinary Conception. In *Segmentation und Komplementarität: Organisatorische, ökonomische und kulturelle Aspekte der Interaktion von Nomaden und Sesshaften*, edited by B. Streck, pp. 3–31. Orientwissenschaftliche Hefte 14. Martin-Luther-Universität Halle-Wittenberg, Orientwissenschaftliches Zentrum, Halle.

Silva, A. C. F. 1999 *Citânia de Sanfins: Catálogo Museu Arqueológico da Citânia de Sanfins*. Câmara Municipal de Paços de Ferreira, Paços de Ferreira.

Silva, A. C. F. 2007 [1986] *A cultura castreja no Noroeste de Portugal*. Câmara Municipal de Paços de Ferreira, Paços da Ferreira.

Tarpin, T. 2009 Oppidum, vu par les Romains. In *L'âge du Fer dans la boucle de la Loire: Les Gaulois sont dans la ville*, edited by O. Buchsenschutz, M.-E. Chardenoux, S. Krausz, and M. Vaginay, pp. 183–198. Revue archéologique du Centre de la France 35e supplement. Tours, Paris.

Tranoy, A. 1981 *La Galice romaine: Recherches sur le Nord-Ouest de la Péninsule Ibérique dans l'Antiquité*. De Boccard, Paris.

van Dommelen, P. 1993 Roman Peasants and Rural Organisation in Central Italy: An Archaeological Perspective. In *Theoretical Roman Archaeology: First Conference Proceedings*, edited by E. Scott, pp. 167–186. Worldwide Archaeology Series 4. Avebury/Ashgate, Aldershot.

Vicent, J. M. 1991 Fundamentos teórico-metodológicos para un programa de investigación arqueo-geográfica. In *El cambio cultural del IV al II milenios a.C. en la comarca noroeste de Murcia*, edited by P. López, pp. 31–118. Consejo Superior de Investigaciones Científicas, Madrid.

Vigo, A. 2006 Castro de Zoñán (Mondoñedo-Lugo). Campaña 2005. Avance de resultados. *Gallaecia* 25:65–81.

Weber, M. 1966 *The City*. Free Press, New York.

Woolf, G. 1993 Rethinking the Oppida. *Oxford Journal of Archaeology* 12(2):223–234.

CHAPTER FOURTEEN

Integration and Disintegration

The Role of Kiva Architecture in Community Formation during the Pueblo II and Pueblo III Periods in the U.S. Southwest

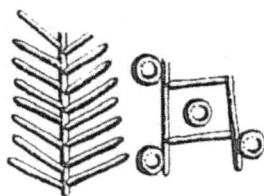

Susan C. Ryan

Abstract *This chapter raises the question of how the built environment reflects identity formation and dissolution during periods of community integration and disintegration. Specifically, this will be achieved through the analyses of ancestral Pueblo vernacular architecture dating from the Pueblo II (A.D. 950–1150) and Pueblo III (A.D. 1150–1300) periods in the northern, middle, and southern San Juan regions in the northern U.S. Southwest in order to shed light on communities of practice as well as their social, temporal, and spatial production techniques. This research examines public and residential kivas to address how architecture emphasized the ways in which structures were actively mediated by production groups, and how their architectural signatures reflect identity during periods of population aggregation and dispersal at the household and community levels. The goal of this study is to contribute to the greater understanding of how social, economic, political, and cultural principles and mechanisms relate to population nucleation in the past and present.*

INTRODUCTION

Researchers in a number of fields have come to recognize the vital importance of the built environment not only as material culture but as symbolic expressions of the larger cultural framework, through which social relations are produced and reproduced. Over the last half-century, studies have demonstrated how architectural characteristics—such as building size, shape, and the presence of various architectural materials, features, and furnishings—have a direct influence on human behavior and interaction, and are material manifestations of worldview ideologies. Some of the most important functions of the various elements within a structure are the encoded messages that convey group identity and provide clues into ancient social organization.

This study raises the question of how the built environment reflects long-term mechanisms of integration in settlement trajectories. Specifically, this will be achieved through the analyses of ancestral Pueblo vernacular architecture dating from the Pueblo II (A.D. 950–1150) and Pueblo III (A.D. 1150–1300) periods in the northern U.S. Southwest. This study examines public and residential kivas—or round rooms used for communal and domestic activities, respectively—to explore the social processes involved in the creation and maintenance of aggregated villages, and the role of the built environment in the mediation of social relationships at diverse scales of integration.

VERNACULAR ARCHITECTURE

All ancestral Pueblo constructions can be described as "vernacular" architecture, or architecture that is built by the people who use it. Vernacular architecture is characterized by the use of locally available materials to produce a form that follows traditional ideologies as well as reflects the local environment (Rapoport 1969:5). Rapoport (1969:8) distinguishes between two types of vernacular architecture—that which is fixed and that which is additive. Fixed vernacular is characterized by very few building types and a model or framework with few individual variations. Additive vernacular is characterized by a greater number of building types and greater individual variation of the model or framework. As Rapoport (1969:4–5) notes, the additive vernacular design process allows for individual variability and differentiation, while the model is held constant. Although additive vernacular has an inflexible framework, users have the ability to communicate particular meanings by adding or subtracting various features that do not constitute the framework (Rapoport 1990:24). Individuals and groups modify architecture to achieve personalization, to establish and express meaning, to display ethnic and group identity, and—most applicable to this volume—to create a sense of social cohesion or integration within communities.

Rapoport's (1969) discussion of vernacular architecture is pertinent to studies of ancestral Pueblo kivas for three reasons. First, and foremost, it directs our attention to which architectural features are fixed or changeable, allowing for an examination of architectural convention and markedness (in the Roman Jakobson sense). Second, it allows for diachronic analyses of which architectural features change and when. Finally, it allows for a spatial analysis of where architectural features change—this can be detected in both domestic and public architecture at the intra- and interregional scales. Given that vernacular architecture is culturally informed, analyzing variations in kiva architecture provides insight into the material manifestation of the various scales of group formation, which, in turn, informs on how aggregation was socially mediated at the household and community levels. In sum, the dialectical relationships created by humans and architecture are socially complex—they are dynamic across time and space, and are reflective of large-scale social, political, economic, and religious ideologies.

SMALL AND GREAT KIVAS

Pit structures have been a hallmark of Pueblo architecture for approximately 1,500 years (Cordell 2007). The architectural form of the kiva originated in pithouses constructed during the Basketmaker II period (500 B.C. to A.D. 500), and transitioned into formalized kivas at approximately A.D. 700–900 throughout much of the northern Southwest. Because kiva production was practiced by households, kin-based groups, or small coresidential groups for hundreds of years, it can be inferred that activities associated with kiva production were undertaken by distinct communities of practice—or groups of individuals who, through the pursuit of a joint enterprise, have developed shared practices, historical and social resources, and common perspectives (Coburn and Stein 2006); a photograph of a modern-day architectural community of practice production group from the Hopi village of Shipaulovi on Second Mesa in Arizona can be found in Page and Page (2009:114–115).

Kiva architecture is exceedingly diverse in small and great houses, and varies according to region, time period, topographic conditions, function, population size, and communities of practice. To simplify matters, archaeologists have typically placed kivas into two typological categories—small kivas and great kivas. For the purpose of this study, I define small kivas as round rooms, less than 10 meters in diameter, in which both domestic and ritual activities took place. Great kivas are defined as round rooms, 10 meters or greater in diameter, in which public, integrative activities took place. These definitions do not rely on the presence of specific architectural features since many were often produced in both small and great kivas during the Pueblo II and Pueblo III periods in the study area.

SMALL AND GREAT HOUSES

SMALL HOUSES

The most common architectural form found throughout the northern and middle San Juan regions is the "unit pueblo." Defined by Prudden (1903, 1914, 1918) as a "unit-type" pueblo, the layout consists of surface rooms located to the north of the kiva and midden deposits located south of the kiva, generally along a north–south axis. In the Chaco area, similar architecture is often referred to as field houses. Although field houses do not always conform to Prudden's definition of a unit pueblo, they do share some common characteristics, including surface rooms, kivas, and middens. For the purpose of this study, I will refer to both unit pueblos and field houses as small houses.

Throughout much of the San Juan Basin, the small house is interpreted as the architectural representation of a nuclear or small extended family (Goodwill-Cohen 2001; Lipe

2006:263; Varien 1999:18). Based on ethnographic data collected from agriculturalist households worldwide, it is assumed that these were inhabited by five to seven people. Given that each household has a kiva, momentary population estimates are generated by multiplying the number of contemporaneous kivas by five to seven people. In some cases, particularly in the Chaco region, small houses composed of up to six households are not uncommon. Small houses may be found independently or in the same community as great houses during the Pueblo II and Pueblo III periods. They remained a consistent architectural tradition until depopulation during the late A.D. 1200s (Bullard 1962; Lipe 1989:55, 2006:263; Varien 1999:18).

Great Houses

Spectacular buildings known as great houses were constructed in Chaco Canyon between A.D. 850 and 1140 (Windes 2003). Collectively, these great houses were the densest concentration of the largest buildings found anywhere in the ancestral Pueblo world. Great houses exhibited characteristics never before seen, including preplanned construction, visually imposing, multiple storied buildings, and buildings with thick walls constructed in a core-and-veneer masonry style (Lekson 1984, 2007a; Lekson et al. 2006; Wilshusen and Van Dyke 2006). Chaco great houses were also—but not always—associated with features, such as great kivas, earthen mounds or berms, and roads (Kantner and Kintigh 2006; Lekson 1984, 2007b; Van Dyke 2003:181; Wilshusen and Van Dyke 2006).

Early great house construction began in Chaco Canyon in the mid-to-late A.D. 800s (Wilshusen and Van Dyke 2006; Windes 2007), and it is at this time that great houses emerge as community centers within the canyon. Early great houses outside of the canyon also appeared during the mid-A.D. 800s to the west, primarily along the Chuska Slope (Van Dyke 2008; Wilshusen and Van Dyke 2006), and in the late A.D. 800s and 900s for the areas south and east of Chaco Canyon (Durand and Hurst 1991; Pippin 1987; Powers et al. 1983; Van Dyke 1999, 2008). Around A.D. 1080, the Chaco regional system expanded to the area north of the San Juan River (Bradley 1988, 2004; Jeancon 1922; Lekson 1999; Malville 2004). There is a consensus that Chaco Canyon was the center of a much larger regional system, although there is a debate about its nature and organization (Earle 2001; Mills 2002). The primary evidence of the regional system is the presence of Chaco-influenced architecture and dozens of "roads" found in an area more than 200 miles in diameter around Chaco Canyon (Kincaid 1983). This area encompasses northwestern New Mexico, southeastern Utah, southwestern Colorado, and northeastern Arizona (Kantner and Mahoney 2000; Roney 1992; Till 2001; Vivian 1990). The intricate Chaco regional system was likely based upon social power concentrated in the hands of the people who occupied the great houses in Chaco Canyon. Although the exact nature of this power is not well understood, it was most likely derived from control over material and ideological resources, such as labor, farmland, water resources, material goods (including exotic goods), and ritual knowledge.

In the late A.D. 1000s and the early A.D. 1100s, connections in the north intensified when Aztec and Salmon Pueblos—the largest great houses outside of Chaco Canyon—were constructed in the area near the confluence of the Animas, La Plata, and San Juan rivers, an area known today as the middle San Juan region (Brown et al. 2008; Reed 2006). The great houses at Aztec Ruins became an equal center—and probably succeeded Chaco Canyon as the primary center—during the mid-A.D. 1100s (Brown et al. 2008; Judge 1989; Lekson 1999; Lipe 2006).

Like small house kivas, great house kivas were a significant element of a household suite comprised of one kiva to approximately six rooms (Lekson et al. 2006:86). At Pueblo Bonito, these suites were linear, and ran from the plaza to the exterior wall of the building; plaza-facing rooms were most likely used for daily activities, and interior rooms were most likely utilized for storage. As is the case with small houses, the number of kivas within a great house directly reflects the number of households. There are 37 households identified at Pueblo Bonito, the largest of the great houses constructed within Chaco Canyon. Approximately half of these households were used contemporaneously (Lekson et al. 2006:86), suggesting a momentary population estimate of between 92 and 130 individuals (one kiva is estimated to have housed between five and seven individuals).

SPATIAL, RELATIONAL, AND COALESCENT COMMUNITIES

Communities have been a crucial component of the southwestern cultural landscape for more than a millennium (Naranjo 2008), but because of the variability of these socially constructed institutions, the concept of community has been difficult to define anthropologically. As Herr and Young (2012:3) note, archaeological definitions of community can range from the functional to the metaphorical and imagined (see also Adler 2002; Canuto and Yaeger 2000; Clark et al. 2009; Isbell 2000; Kolb and Snead 1997; Murdock 1949:82–83; Wills and Leonard 1994). The following discussion will briefly examine spatial and relational community definitions applicable to this study.

Most definitions of "spatial communities" focus primarily on the relationships between individuals and some emphasize place. Adler (1996:98) notes that communities represent the social units in which individuals negotiate land tenure, mobilize labor, resolve disputes, and acquire mates. Adler's definition draws on the relationships between individuals and assumes a secondary focus on place. Another definition, which has a primary focus on individuals and a secondary focus on place, is by Murdock and Wilson who define community as "the number of people who normally reside in face-to-face association" (1972:255; see also Smith this volume). Alternatively, one definition of community with a primary focus on place and a secondary focus on individuals was proposed by Breternitz and Doyel (1987:184). They note that communities can be defined by locating relatively dense clusters of contemporaneous habitations surrounded by zones with few or no settlements. This characterization fits well with how researchers are defining communities throughout the study area of the present chapter. Moreover,

Mahoney suggests the need to distinguish between two scales of community interaction, residential and sustainable, as follows: "Residential communities correspond to spatially distinct clusters of residences, where face-to-face interaction would have occurred on a daily basis. In contrast, sustainable communities correspond to the spatial and demographic scale of the social network required to maintain these residential communities" (2000:20). Given the range of spatial community definitions, it seems appropriate to apply both the residential community and the sustainable community definitions to areas located in the study area. Both involved face-to-face interaction of residents on a daily basis as well as participation in a social network with other "centers" in the region, based on their proximity to each other on the landscape. This definition is especially pertinent to Pueblo II period communities that were developed near public architecture, including great houses or great kivas.

In regards to community formation, we must think about the cultural processes associated with coalescent behaviors. The term *coalescent* was first used in the 1950s in U.S. Plains research to describe the coming together of the Middle Missouri and Central Plains archaeological cultures, forming "what might be called a Coalescent tradition" (Lehmer 1954:147). In a more recent synthetic study, Kowalewski (2006:96, 117) notes that coalescence brings people together to ameliorate tensions that may have existed from social upheavals and/or external pressures. These tensions may stimulate the appearance of corporate political structures (such as councils and confederacies), increasing concern for collective defense, changes in the social means of production, and cultural transformations that emphasize the integration of domestic groups through sodalities, clans, rituals, and settlement layouts designed to promote community integration (Kowalewski 2003, 2006:117; see also Birch this volume). Studies concerned with coalescence tend to focus on the cultural and natural shifts that are thought to have promoted aggregation in large settlements (for a discussion of "nucleated settlements," see also Gyucha this volume). Theses shifts include population growth (Bandy 2004; Warrick 2008), environmental and climatic factors (Adler 1996; Hill et al. 2004), warfare and violence (Arkush 2009; Kuckelman 2000; LeBlanc 1999), and encroachment (Ethridge and Shuck-Hall 2009). These studies focus on how periods of social, political, and cultural realignment are socially mediated. In this sense, the overarching anthropological contribution is not found in the reasons for why people came together, but their behavior in creating and responding to their ever-changing conditions and environments.

Changes in the built environment, including in the layout of architectural plans—like those seen in the growth of Pueblo Bonito over three centuries—or in the uniformity of additive vernacular features within kivas, are particularly suited for research on the ramifications of coalescence behavior. The built environment, composed of domestic and public constructions, directly reflects the relationship between social groups and the collective whole (see also Harrison and Bilgen, Kelly, and Raczky this volume). Alterations in the production of architecture are therefore a direct signal of changing social relationships, and thus, provide us with physical, semiotic indicators of shifting ideologies.

COMMUNITY AND RESIDENTIAL ARCHITECTURAL PATTERNS

In general, Pueblo II communities dating to A.D. 950–1150 consist of dispersed clusters of one or two households located in areas with productive agricultural soils and access to potable water. Roberts (1939) correlated the Pueblo II period "small villages"—outlined in the Pecos Classification—with Prudden's (1903, 1914, 1918) unit-type pueblo as the typical site type of the period. Each habitation included a kiva, a small number of associated surface rooms of *jacal* or masonry, often a small pit structure used as a grinding or mealing room, and a midden area (Lipe and Varien 1999:244). Other architectural features, including extramural pits, small pit rooms, *ramadas,* and/or enclosing stockades, are also typical of the Pueblo II period.

As summarized by Ryan (2013), small house kivas constructed during the Pueblo II period were circular in shape and had internal features, including a bench, central fire pit, and ventilator. Some kivas constructed during this time also had a *sipapu,* floor vault, niches, ash pit, and/or other subfloor pit features. A primary trend in Pueblo II period kiva construction was the use of a masonry lining wall around the diameter of the structure instead of an earthen wall as seen in previous periods. Roof supports were typically masonry pilasters constructed on the kiva bench to support the weight of roofing beams, but some Pueblo II period kivas were constructed with upright posts set into the floor or bench—a practice stemming from the Pueblo I (A.D. 750–950) and Basketmaker II–III (500 B.C. to A.D. 750) periods. A recess in the southern wall at bench level was not a standard feature until the end of the Pueblo II period; however, many kivas constructed within great houses lacked any recess during this period. A deep, well-defined "keyhole" southern recess tended to be common after A.D. 1100, and is often associated with the Mesa Verde cultural tradition.

Often, Pueblo II period villages grew into a community center, identified archaeologically by a great kiva, a great house, a cluster of households, or some combination of these (Lipe and Varien 1999). Additional architectural characteristics that are associated with great house construction are distinctive kivas—they are typically incorporated into the roomblock by enclosing them in a square room, and were often aboveground rather than subterranean. In addition, these kivas typically had subfloor ventilation systems and roof supports that consisted of eight pilasters, often of the radial beam type (Lekson 1984; Van Dyke 2003). Researchers have argued that Chaco culture emerged during the A.D. 800s with the appearance of integrated communities characterized by clusters of small house sites, great kivas, and great houses (Marshall et al. 1979; Plog and Heitman 2010; Powers et al. 1983; Wilshusen and Van Dyke 2006; Windes 2003, 2007). Defining communities as having six contemporaneous small house sites within a 1 square kilometer area, Powers, Gillespie, and Lekson (1983) identified 10 localities in the greater San Juan Basin (this includes the San Juan Basin and portions of the northern San Juan region) that achieved community status during the first part of the Pueblo II period. In addition, Marshall and his colleagues (1979) reported nine possible communities in the southern and western portions of the San Juan Basin. By the end of the Pueblo II period, the number of great houses doubled in communities outside of Chaco Canyon when population densities were the highest of any period in the study area (Powers et al. 1983). Great houses within these communities exhibit extensive variation in their overall shape, plan, and kiva to room ratios (Kantner and Mahoney 2000; Marshall et al. 1979; Powers et al. 1983; Vivian 1990).

The most recognized sites dating to the Pueblo III period in the northern San Juan region include the cliff dwellings of Mesa Verde National Park and Hovenweep National Monument. The organization of settlements changed dramatically during the Late Pueblo III period (A.D. 1225–1300). First, community centers shifted in location from mesatop settings to the heads of canyons and within alcoves, and second, the majority of people began to live in tightly aggregated villages (Lipe and Ortman 2000; Lipe and Varien 1999; Varien 1999).

The shift to highly aggregated canyon-head villages appears to have occurred over a 20–30 year period, and became the dominant organizational layout during the Late Pueblo III period (Lipe and Varien 1999:303). Although some mesatop community centers retained a portion of their population, the majority of households were living in highly aggregated villages by A.D. 1250. These villages tended to be constructed on a canyon rim—usually at the head of the canyon—and below the canyon rim in the rockshelters and/or on the talus slopes.

Most canyon-head community centers share similar architectural elements, including towers, plazas, multiwalled structures, D-shaped structures, and site-enclosing walls—some of which encompassed freshwater springs (Bredthauer 2010; Glowacki 2006, 2015; Lipe 2002; Lipe and Ortman 2000; Lipe and Varien 1999:319; Varien et al. 1996:99). In a study of public architecture located in the northern San Juan region, Churchill, Kuckelman, and Varien (1998) found a consistent decrease in the frequency of great kivas at community center sites, and an increase in multiwalled structures, including circular bi-wall, tri-wall, and D-shaped structures, with most of the latter occurring in the Late Pueblo III period. Great kivas continued to be an architectural element constructed in community centers during the Late Pueblo III period, but were increasingly constructed as roofless, open-air structures as opposed to earlier, roofed versions—perhaps in an effort to make activities increasingly public (Kintigh et al. 1996). Next, I turn to the data used to examine shifting ideologies as detected in kiva production in the study area during the Pueblo II and Pueblo III periods.

DATA AND METHODS

The foundation of this study lies in the analyses of previously collected data from historic and modern publications, site reports—both published and unpublished—and manuscripts. The majority of data were generated from various research projects, including National Historic Preservation Act recording projects, Section 106 compliance-driven cultural resource inventories, archaeological projects conducted on sites protected under the American Antiquities Act, and large-scale excavation projects undertaken by private cultural resource management companies, government, state, and private institutions, and not-for-profit institutions.

Data were collected on 407 small and great kivas from 97 ancestral Pueblo sites dating to the Pueblo II and Pueblo III periods in the northern, middle, and southern San Juan regions (Table 14.1). In Figure 14.1, each archeological site from which data were

TABLE 14.1
REGION, SITE NUMBER, SITE NAME, AND NUMBER OF
KIVAS FROM WHICH DATA WAS COLLECTED

Region	Site Number	Site Name	Kiva Count
Southern San Juan	29SJ395	Bc 51	7
Southern San Juan	NM-G-63-5	West House	1
Southern San Juan	29SJ1912	Bc 192 and Bc 193 (Lizard House)	3
Southern San Juan	29SJ1921	Bc 55	1
Southern San Juan	29SJ1922	Bc 54 (Corn Mother Site)	3
Southern San Juan	29SJ1928	Chetro Ketl	13
Southern San Juan	29SJ1930	Talus Unit #1	8
Southern San Juan	29SJ1947	Pueblo Del Arroyo	18
Southern San Juan	29SJ386	Bc 255 (Casa Rinconada)	1
Southern San Juan	29SJ387	Pueblo Bonito	55
Southern San Juan	29SJ389	Pueblo Alto	16
Southern San Juan	29SJ392	Bc 249 (Kin Nahasbas)	1
Southern San Juan	29SJ394	Tseh So (Bc 50)	4
Southern San Juan	29SJ396	Bc 53 (Robert's Site)	4
Southern San Juan	29SJ397	Bc 57	4
Southern San Juan	NM-G-63-20	NM-G-63-20	1
Southern San Juan	NM-G-63-5	South House	1
Southern San Juan	NM-G-63-5	Rabbit House	2
Southern San Juan	NM-G-63-5	Casa Hormiga	1
Southern San Juan	29SJ393	Kin Kletso	5
Southern San Juan	NM-G-63-34	NM-G-63-34	1
Southern San Juan	29SJ398	Bc 58	2
Southern San Juan	NM-G-63-16	NM-G-63-16	1
Southern San Juan	LA8779	Casamero Pueblo	1
Southern San Juan	LA2757	Guadalupe Ruin	4
Southern San Juan	29SJ753	Bc 56	1
Southern San Juan	29SJ750	Leyit Kin	4
Southern San Juan	29SJ629	Spadefoot Toad Site	1
Southern San Juan	29SJ399	Bc 59 (Tom Mathews's Site)	5

continued on next page

TABLE 14.1 (CONTINUED)

Region	Site Number	Site Name	Kiva Count
Southern San Juan	NM-G-63-36	NM-G-63-36	1
Middle San Juan	LA126581	Tommy Site	1
Middle San Juan	LA45	Aztec West Annex	10
Middle San Juan	N/A	Morris 39	6
Middle San Juan	N/A	Morris 41	10
Middle San Juan	N/A	Morris 42	1
Middle San Juan	AZ-I-26-3	Site AZ-I-26-3	5
Middle San Juan	DCA-83-212	Site DCA-83-212	1
Middle San Juan	LA45	Aztec West	21
Middle San Juan	LA45	Aztec East	1
Middle San Juan	LA45	Hubbard Site	3
Middle San Juan	LA8846	Salmon Pueblo	11
Middle San Juan	NM-H-34-47	Site NM-H-34-47	1
Middle San Juan	NM-H-47-95	NM-H-47-95	1
Northern San Juan	5MT3876	Hanson Pueblo	1
Northern San Juan	5MT2108	Ackmen-Lowry Site 1	1
Northern San Juan	5MT2108	Ackmen-Lowry Site 2	1
Northern San Juan	5MT2148	Dominguez Ruin	1
Northern San Juan	5MT2149	Escalante Ruin	1
Northern San Juan	5MT338	Cannonball Ruin	7
Northern San Juan	5MT1905	Haynie Ruin	5
Northern San Juan	5MT3834	Mustoe Site	2
Northern San Juan	5AA83	Chimney Rock Pueblo	2
Northern San Juan	5MT3892	Seed Jar	1
Northern San Juan	5MT3901	Green Lizard	1
Northern San Juan	5MT4126	Ida Jean	2
Northern San Juan	5MT765	Sand Canyon Pueblo	7
Northern San Juan	5MT3778	Casa de Suenos	1
Northern San Juan	5MT11787	Puzzle House	2
Northern San Juan	5MT10206	Site 5MT10206	1
Northern San Juan	5MT7723	Site 5MT7723	2
Northern San Juan	42SA863	Three Kiva Pueblo	3
Northern San Juan	42SA7660	Site 42SA7660	1
Northern San Juan	42SA7659	Corral Canyon Village	1
Northern San Juan	42SA27838	Carhart Pueblo	1
Northern San Juan	N/A	Prudden Ruin No. 5	1
Northern San Juan	N/A	Prudden Ruin No. 3	1
Northern San Juan	N/A	Prudden Ruin No. 1	1
Northern San Juan	N/A	Prudden Ruin No. VI	1
Northern San Juan	N/A	Ackmen-Lowry Site 4	2
Northern San Juan	5MV01926	Site 1926	1

Region	Site Number	Site Name	Kiva Count
Northern San Juan	5MT10207	Site 5MT10207	2
Northern San Juan	5MV00875	Site 875	2
Northern San Juan	SA-5005	Moon House	1
Northern San Juan	LA44169	LA44169	1
Northern San Juan	5MV640	Spruce Tree House	9
Northern San Juan	5MV625	Cliff Palace	23
Northern San Juan	5MV615	Balcony House	2
Northern San Juan	5MV352	Sun Temple	3
Northern San Juan	5MV01914	Site 1914	1
Northern San Juan	N/A	Ackmen-Lowry Site 3	1
Northern San Juan	5MV01229	Mug House	8
Northern San Juan	5MV01200	Long House	22
Northern San Juan	5MV01104	Site 1104	1
Northern San Juan	5MV01088	Site 1088	2
Northern San Juan	5MV01595	Big Juniper House	3
Northern San Juan	5MV01030	Site 1030	1
Northern San Juan	5MT839	Lowry Pueblo	9
Northern San Juan	5MV00866	Site 866	3
Northern San Juan	5MV00808	Far View House	4
Northern San Juan	5MV00499	Site 499	2
Northern San Juan	5MV00102	Site 102	1
Northern San Juan	5MV0007	Sun Point Pueblo	1
Northern San Juan	5MV00034	Site 34	5
Northern San Juan	5MV00016	Site 16	3
Northern San Juan	5MV00001	Site 1	1
Northern San Juan	5MT8943	Site 5MT8943	2
Northern San Juan	5MV01086	Site 1086	1

collected is represented by a dot. There are 30 archaeological sites from the southern San Juan region, 13 sites from the middle, and 54 sites from the northern San Juan region. It is important to note that only completely excavated kivas were utilized in this study to allow for a holistic examination of internal features in order to provide information on architectural production conventions through time and across the study area.

As illustrated in Table 14.2, architectural data were placed into two main categories: variables and subvariables. The variable category included three main classes of data—temporal assignment, region, and house type—and also included fixed vernacular architectural classes, such as structure type, structure shape, roof type, and so on. The subvariable category included data on the additive vernacular architectural forms produced within the variable classes. For example, a hearth—which I consider a fixed variable—may have

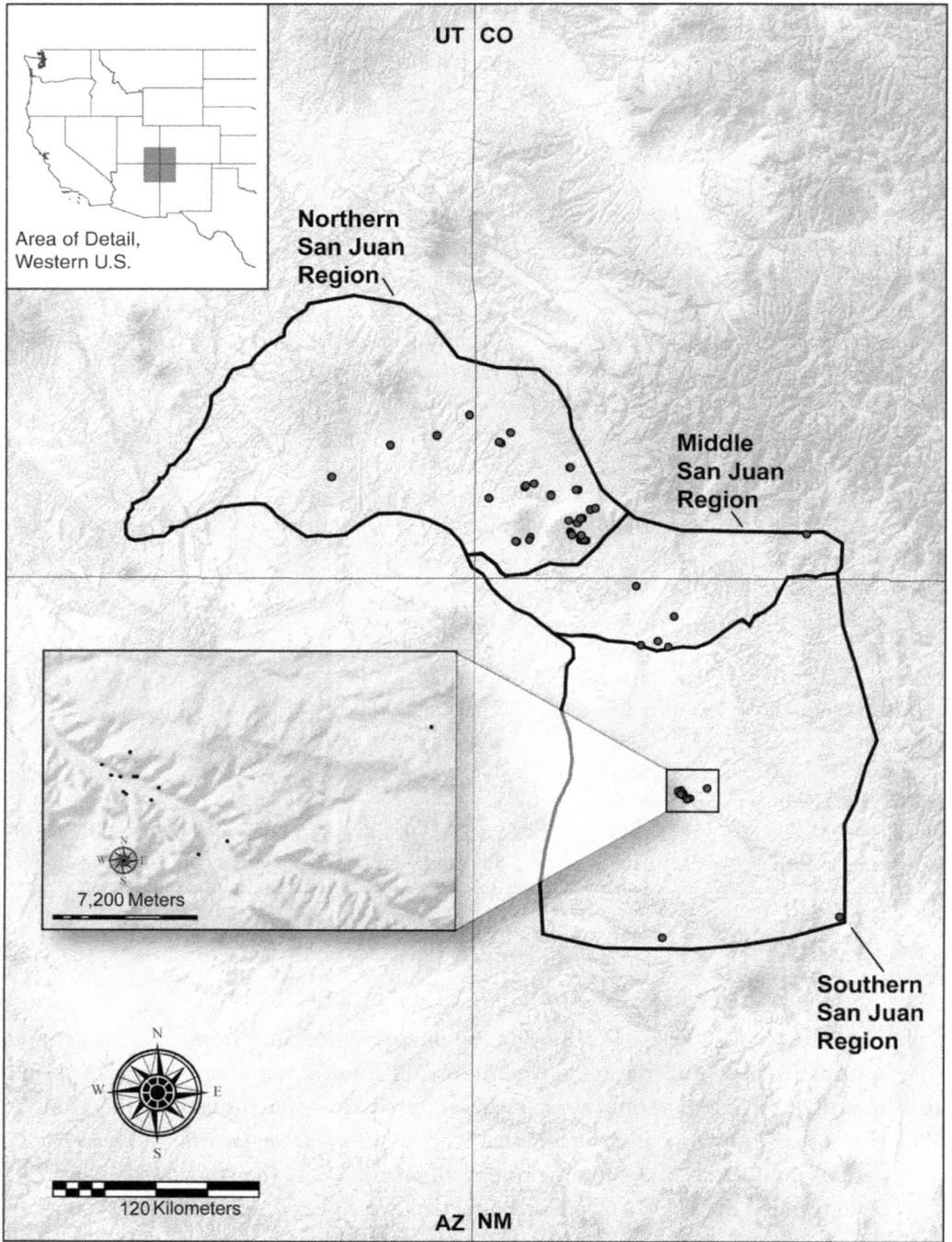

FIGURE 14.1. The study area including the northern, middle, and southern San Juan regions. Each dot represents a site from which architectural data were collected. The lower inset represents sites in Chaco Canyon, southern San Juan region.

Variable	Subvariable
Temporal assignment	Pueblo II (A.D. 950–1150)
	Pueblo III (A.D. 1150–1300)
Region	Northern San Juan Region
	Middle San Juan Region
	Southern San Juan Region
House type	Great house
	Small house
Kiva size	Less than 10 meters
	Greater than 10 meters
Structure type	Tower
	Elevated blocked-in
	Surface blocked-in
	Semisubterranean
	Subterranean
	Great
	Subterranean blocked-in
	Aboveground not blocked-in
Structure shape	Round
	Square
	D-shaped
	Oval
	Square with rounded corners
Structure orientation	North–South
	Northwest–Southeast
	Northeast–Southwest
	East–West
	Southeast–Northwest
	Southwest–Northeast
	South–North
Structure location	Intramural
	Extramural
Roof type	Cribbed
	Cribbed with sockets in the upper lining wall
	Flat
	Cribbed with wainscoting
	Absent
	Posts in floor
	Posts in bench

continued on next page

TABLE 14.2 *(CONTINUED)*

Variable	Subvariable
Roof support type	Pier
	Radial beam
	Oversized
	Squat
	Absent
	Pier with wood
	Radial beam with vertical posts
	Radial beam, no masonry
	L-shaped
	Skinny and small
	Posts
	Stone block
	Radial beam with horizontal posts
	Squat with vertical posts
Recess	Keyhole
	Reduced
	Absent
Sipapu type	Jar lined
	Adobe lined
	Absent
	Slab lined
	Jar and earthen lined
	Masonry lined
Niche orientation	North bench
	South bench
	East bench
	West bench
	Northwest bench
	Northeast bench
	Southwest bench
	Southeast bench
	Absent
	North floor
	South floor
	East floor
	West floor
	Northwest floor
	Northeast floor
	Southwest floor
	Southeast floor
	North face of deflector

Variable	Subvariable
Niche orientation	South face of deflector
	Upper lining wall
	Pilaster
	North face of bin
Niche number	0
	1
	2
	3
	4
	5
	6
	7
	8
	9
	10
	34
Lignite type	Surrounding woodpost
	Below floor
	Below features
	Absent
	Below floor and features
	In pilaster
	Below floor vault
Interstitial shelving	Present
	Absent
Interpilaster shelving	Present
	Absent
Hearth type	Round
	Square
	Oval
	Absent
	D-shaped
Floor vault presence	Present
	Absent
Floor vault type	1-West of hearth
	2-East and west of hearth
	1-East of hearth
	1-North of hearth
	1-South of hearth
Entrance type	Roof hatch
	Pass through

continued on next page

TABLE 14.2 *(CONTINUED)*

Variable	Subvariable
Entrance type	Tunnel
	Stairway
	Doorway
Entrance number	1
	2
	3
	4
	5
	16
Bench number	0
	1
	2
	3
Deflector type	Slab
	Masonry
	Masonry with wing walls
	Masonry with niche
	Masonry with wing walls and niche
	Jacal
	Jacal with wing walls
	Absent
	Masonry with wood poles
	Masonry with jacal wing walls
Ash pit type	Absent
	Round
	Square
	Oval

five subvariable additive forms, including round, square, oval, D-shaped, and absent.

Several software packages were utilized to organize, analyze, and display data, including Access, Excel, R (including poLCA, an "R" statistical package that estimates latent class regression models with covariates), and GIS. Statistical procedures—including Pearson's chi-squared tests (N = 238), bootstrap tests (N = 142), Yate's continuity correction tests (N = 2), and Latent Class Analysis tests (N = 4)—were used to determine variable and subvariable relationships between region, time period, house type, and kiva size. Next, I summarize the results of these tests, starting with house type.

RESULTS

HOUSE TYPE

All fixed vernacular architectural elements produced in small kivas in small houses were also produced in small kivas located in great houses—this includes essential elements, such as a roof, hearth, ventilation system, entryway, and so on. These inferences can be made from this observation. First, small kiva production was similar in both small and great houses across the study area as small kivas were utilized in similar, if not in equivalent, ways—for domestic and ritual purposes. Second, there was a high degree of architectural conventionalism in small kiva production in small and great houses during the Pueblo II and Pueblo III periods, regardless of region. This is not unexpected given that similarities in kiva production indicate a broad-scale ancestral Pueblo ideology or shared architectural practice.

Scholars have illustrated how Pueblo stories, songs, and prayers describe a world in which architecture is not merely an object but is part of a cosmological worldview that recognizes multiplicity, simultaneity, inclusiveness, and interconnectedness. Swentzell notes, "It is an ordered, but flowing, whole that reflects a cosmos strongly biased toward the gentle and inclusive qualities of the universe" (1990:29). Architecture is the place, where the ethereal and nonmaterial qualities of the cosmos are interpreted by ancient architects and emphasized in material form. Pueblo architecture communicates culturally prescribed, and accepted, information to the observer about Pueblo cosmology that results in material culture conformity. This cosmological understanding was no doubt shared across the northern San Juan region during the Pueblo II and Pueblo III periods, and has deep cultural roots that are evidenced in the built environment beginning in the sixth century A.D. (for a discussion of shared ideologies and aggregation, see also O'Shea and Nicodemus, and Raczky this volume).

Having just noted the shared ideologies surrounding the production of fixed vernacular architecture in small kivas, next, I draw attention to the differences in additive vernacular architectural elements produced in residential kivas in small and great houses. Small house kivas were produced with more additive vernacular elements than great house kivas. This indicates that production groups in great houses adhered to a higher degree of social conventionalism than those in small houses, and that the homogeneity of kiva production in great houses was of primary importance, most likely as an effort to integrate individuals with diverse social memberships or backgrounds. Thus, there are notable differences in the integrative qualities of additive vernacular architecture emerging at the residential-private scale between those in large villages versus those in small, dispersed farmsteads. As a result, we must ask the question: Is architectural homogeneity a result of aggregation and increasing demography?

To address this question, I turn to research within archaeology and other disciplines that suggests social conformity is often associated with increasing group size, density, or scale (e.g., Hegmon et al. 2008; Johnson 1982; Kohler et al. 2004; Nelson et al. 2011).

Conformity can assist to facilitate cooperation (Kohler et al. 2004), to reduce scalar stress (Johnson 1982), to establish sameness, to serve as a basis of communication, to promote cohesion in times of economic stress and competition (Hodder 1979), and to reduce transaction costs, such as the amount of individual negotiation or uncertainty (North 1990) (see also Ault and Raczky this volume).

This is well illustrated by Nelson and her colleagues (2011) who assessed the changing relationships among population density, social diversity, and social transformation. Their study examined these relationships across the Southwest by analyzing diachronic data from prehispanic and early historic settlements and the distribution of pottery styles. They hypothesize that social conformity becomes increasingly important as population density intensifies. They found support for this premise in a strong association between low levels of material culture diversity and high levels of population density—concluding that a low diversity of painted designs on pottery was indicative of some degree of shared identity, a component of conformity. Nelson and her colleagues (2011:25) note that material culture conformity served as a means of maintaining social control in the large, densely packed villages that were increasingly isolated from other centers of population in the U.S. Southwest.

Moreover, material culture style is a particularly important component of social relationships in subsistence-based, agricultural economies around the world, most of which can be classified as middle-range societies (Nelson et al. 2011:25). Nearly all social formations in the prehispanic U.S. Southwest fit this classification after A.D. 500. In middle-range societies, material culture similarity—as well as other activities, including participation in rituals (Rappaport 1971)—can serve to establish and maintain social relationships, solidarity, and the capacity for collective action. Conformity in material culture can be attributed to: (1) a direct indicator of worth; (2) a product of tradition; (3) a signal that ties to a group; and/or (4) pressure to conform (Nelson et al. 2011:24–25). Given that the built environment is also a product of material culture production, we can assume that kiva architecture was produced within similar patterns of rationality and behavior. However, as shall be discussed below, although architectural conformity does occur with aggregation, it also reaches a point where it begins to diversify as populations continue to grow. Thus, the answer to the question posed above—Is architectural uniformity a result of increasing population?—is ambiguous.

KIVA SIZE

When examining kiva size—particularly the production of small and great kivas—data suggest small and great kivas shared the same fixed vernacular elements across time and throughout the study area, despite that private and public architecture were utilized in distinct ways. This suggests a broad-scale ideology regarding which elements a kiva must have possessed in order to be considered culturally legitimate, regardless of function. In essence, the great kiva is a much larger version of the residential, household kiva with the exception that loftier corporate groups appropriated the household form—including its symbolic and ideological attributes—and reworked it, turning it into a space used by dozens, and in some cases hundreds, of individuals. It is not surprising, then, that small kivas were produced with more additive vernacular forms than great kivas, given that small kivas were not on public display beyond the extended family. Small kiva production was much less conventional due to the private, residential activities that took place within them. However, this is not the case for large, aggregated great house populations that promoted conformity.

Contrary to the liberties taken when producing small kivas, great kivas displayed a high degree of conventionalism due to the public, integrative activities that took place within them. In this sense, production groups constructing private, residential kivas were not as concerned with expressing integrative architectural characteristics, and we can assume production groups had the license to individualize kivas based on tradition or needs. Alternatively, this highlights the overall necessity for standardization within public architecture in order to fully integrate many different factions within a community. Production groups went to great lengths not to stress architectural differences in public architecture, as this would have detracted from the ability to create a unifying atmosphere. In sum, like the house type results discussed earlier, there are noticeable differences in the scale of integrative qualities of additive vernacular architecture at the nonresidential-public and residential-private scales.

SMALL AND GREAT KIVAS IN SMALL AND GREAT HOUSES

Interestingly, there is one exception to the statement above. Great kivas located in great houses in the southern San Juan region, particularly Chaco Canyon, were produced with more additive vernacular forms than great kivas in the middle and northern San Juan regions; the unique additive vernacular elements produced in great kivas in the southern San Juan region include those listed in Table 14.3. These data are relevant to discussions

TABLE 14.3
SUBVARIABLES UNIQUE TO SOUTHERN SAN JUAN REGION GREAT KIVAS

Two entrances
Masonry-lined sipapus
Masonry deflectors
Above floor ventilators
10 and 34 niche count
North–south axis of orientation
Intramural locations
Surface blocked-in locations
Radial beam roof supports
Round hearths
Three benches
4 and 8 roof supports
Roof hatch entries
North, south, east, west, northeast, northwest, and southwest bench niche locations

of the role of the built environment in recognizing the various scales of integration, as they suggest the emergence of multiple membership groups within large, aggregated populations. This inference seems reasonable in that small house communities generally have a single great kiva that is utilized by all community members in the middle and northern San Juan regions, whereas large-scale great house communities, such as those in Chaco Canyon, often have multiple great kivas per village and/or community. For example, there were three great kivas within Pueblo Bonito. Vivian and Reiter (1965) note that all three—Judd's Kivas A and Q, and Roberts Great Kiva in the west plaza—were contemporaneous.

Based on differences in great kiva additive vernacular architecture, which suggest features were tailored to particular membership groups, it seems likely that residents of Pueblo Bonito were members of, and only participated in, one great kiva as opposed to all three. In order to integrate distinct great kiva groups, one could postulate that the entire residential population of Pueblo Bonito—and perhaps even residents from multiple great and small houses in "downtown" Chaco—may have participated in integrative events at Casa Rinconada, the largest, isolated great kivas in the canyon not directly associated with any one particular great house. This notion suggests that there were at least three primary integrative factions within Pueblo Bonito, and that community integration was occurring at different scales within the village and community in the southern San Juan region. These differences can be identified archaeologically at the residential scale (e.g., in small kiva household groups), at the village scale (e.g., in great kiva membership groups), and at the community scale (e.g., with all kiva membership groups participating in events at an isolated great kiva) (for discussions of scale, see also Ault, Fernández-Götz, Gaydarska, and Kelly this volume).

This notion suggests that populations increased to the point where a different kind of organizational restructuring took place, forming at least three primary integrating factions (for discussions of restructuring see also Ault, Birch, Harrison and Bilgen, and Smith this volume). Kowalewski's (2006) work reminds us that rapid settlement aggregation does not display the emergence of centralized, hierarchical political organization. Instead, we see the development of corporate or collective decision-making entities. I suggest that the built environment in the southern San Juan region supports this concept and illustrates the formalization of horizontal-structuring of social, political, and ritual organizational complexity.

Moreover, Birch (2013:7) notes that aggregation often has a macroregional basis, and that each community develops within a set of uniquely constituted local contingencies. What is true for one aggregated settlement within a particular region will not necessarily be true for another. The example from Pueblo Bonito of the various scales, in which kiva architecture was utilized for integrative purposes, is unique. This mode of organization was an innovative means to structuring an ever-increasingly complex social, ritual, and political system that was growing with each generation for over two centuries. This manifestation did not emerge overnight, it was rooted in existing cultural traditions, rituals, and political institutions (Belfer-Cohen and Goring-Morris 2011; Fowles 2005;

see also Osborne this volume). However, with aggregation and the resulting social pressures, these existing structures were transformed, reconfigured, and given new emphasis to reproduce, transform, integrate, and order new, larger social formations (Kowalewski 2006; see also Gyucha this volume).

CONCLUSION

Data presented in this chapter raise the question of how the built environment encodes communications through the production of architectural features in kivas that affected human behavior and interaction during times of population aggregation and social change. Data suggest that private, nonintegrative kivas were produced with greater architectural variation, and that public, integrative kivas were produced with less architectural variation. Additionally, these data indicate that small kivas located in small houses were produced with more variation than those in great houses. This observation is telling in that distinctiveness—as expressed in architectural variability—was less conventional in great houses, most likely as an effort to promote homogeneity and social cohesion. Interestingly, great houses that contained more than one great kiva appear to have produced public architecture with tailored features, indicating that the residents were members of a specific great kiva group. Because these great kivas served particular portions of the overall community, I further suggest that isolated great kivas—not associated with any one village—may have provided the integrative needs for several villages within the larger community.

As noted above, Kowalewski (2006:96, 117) suggests that coalescence brings people together to alleviate tensions that may have arisen from social upheavals and/or external pressures. These factors may include the appearance of corporate political structures, increasing concern for collective defense, changes in the social means of production, and cultural transformations that emphasize the integration of domestic groups through sodalities, clans, rituals, and settlement layouts designed to promote community integration (Kowalewski 2003, 2006:117). This study lends support for Kowalewski's findings in that the analyses of kiva architecture have revealed specific insights about how social structure and social relationships changed as people adjusted to life in coalescent communities. Social integration meant new architectural design and innovations in material culture production. Residing close together in an aggregated village had different implications for social behavior than living in a single or extended family residence.

Great house architecture—particularly that constructed in the southern and middle San Juan regions—was highly integrated and preplanned compared to that in small house settlements. In a sense, great houses subsumed individual house clusters, replacing them with a singular unit (the great house) that radically aligned domestic architecture around a central plaza space. I subscribe to the notion that the built environment does, in fact, represent imagined ideologies, as Rapoport (1994:488) and Ingold (2000:179) suggest, and people began to identify themselves as an integrated entity prior to the construction of the great houses. Community-based identities had changed preceding the construction of these massive buildings, and identities were consistently renegotiated with each passing generation. Alterations in the physical structuring of the built environment were not necessarily the result of new ritual, political, economic, or social ideologies—they were most likely rooted in Pueblo ideology for centuries. What we have witnessed archaeologically, however, is the alteration in how those ideologies were structured due to changes in social structure as a result of increasing populations.

It is by integrating insights from multiple spatial and temporal scales that we can illuminate the relationships between diachronic processes of cultural change and the lived experience of everyday life. Settlement aggregation was the result of the nucleation of extant communities that had existing relationships and affiliations. While aggregation brought about significant changes, people did not necessarily develop new cultural practices. Existing organizational structures and practices were transformed or reworked, giving materials, ideologies, traditions, and sociopolitical institutions new emphasis to meet the organizational needs of larger population aggregates. Those preexisting relations facilitated aggregation through the strengthening or exploitation of existing ties. Highlighting these relationships provides a framework for understanding how settlements and the social, political, ritual, and economic organization of their inhabitants were transformed in the context of coalescence.

REFERENCES CITED

Adler, M. A. (editor) 1996 *The Prehistoric Pueblo World A.D. 1150–1350*. The University of Arizona Press, Tucson.

Adler, M. A. 2002 The Ancestral Pueblo Community as Structure and Strategy. In *Seeking the Center Place: Archaeology and Ancient Communities in the Mesa Verde Region*, edited by M. D. Varien and R. H. Wilshusen, pp. 25–39. The University of Utah Press, Salt Lake City.

Arkush, E. 2009 Warfare, Space, and Identity in the South-Central Andes. In *Warfare in Cultural Context: Practice, Agency, and the Archaeology of Violence*, edited by A. E. Nielsen and W. H. Walker, pp. 190–217. The University of Arizona Press, Tucson.

Bandy, M. S. 2004 Fissioning, Scalar Stress, and Social Evolution in Early Village Societies. *American Anthropologist* 106(2):322–333.

Belfer-Cohen, A., and A. N. Goring-Morris 2011 Becoming Farmers: The Inside Story. *Current Anthropology* 52(S4):S209–S220.

Birch, J. 2013 Between Villages and Cities: Settlement Aggregation in Cross-Cultural Perspective. In *From Prehistoric Villages to Cities: Settlement Aggregation and Community Transformation*, edited by J. Birch, pp. 1–22. Routledge, New York.

Bradley, B. A. 1988 Wallace Ruin Interim Report. *Southwestern Lore* 54(2):8–33.

Bradley, B. A. 2004 Wallace Ruin and Chacoan Missions. In *Chimney Rock: The Ultimate Outlier*, edited by J. M. Malville, pp. 115–122. Lexington, Lanham, Maryland.

Bredthauer, A. 2010 *A Towering Enigma: An Examination of Late Pueblo II and Pueblo III Towers in the Northern San Juan Region*. Master's thesis, Department of Anthropology, University of Colorado, Boulder.

Breternitz, D. A., and D. E. Doyel 1987 Methodological Issues for the Identification of Chacoan Community Structure: Lessons from the Bis sa'ani Community Study. *American Archaeology* 63(3):183–189.

Brown, G. M., T. Windes, and P. J. McKenna 2008 Animas Anamnesis: Aztec Ruins or Anasazi Capital? In *Chaco's Northern Prodigies: Salmon, Aztec, and the Ascendancy of the Middle San Juan Region after A.D. 1100*, edited by P. F. Reed, pp. 231–250. The University of Utah Press, Salt Lake City.

Bullard, W. R. Jr. 1962 *The Cerro Colorado Site and Pithouse Architecture in the Southwestern United States prior to A.D. 900*. Papers of the Peabody Museum of American Archaeology and Ethnology 44(2). Harvard University, Cambridge, Massachusetts.

Canuto, M. A., and J. Yaeger 2000 Preface. In *The Archaeology of Communities: A New World Perspective*, edited by M. A. Canuto and J. Yaeger, pp. xii–xiv. Routledge, New York.

Churchill, M. J., K. A. Kuckelman, and M. D. Varien 1998 Public Architecture in the Mesa Verde Region. Paper presented at the 63rd Annual Meeting of the Society for American Archaeology, Seattle.

Clark, J., B. J. Hill, D. L. Huntley, and P. Lyons 2009 *Kayenta Diaspora and the Salado Meta-Identity. Hybrid Material Culture: The Archaeology of Syncretism and Ethnogenesis*. Occasional Paper 39. Center for Archaeological Investigations, Southern Illinois University, Carbondale.

Coburn, C. E., and M. K. Stein 2006 Communities of Practice Theory and the Role of Teacher Professional Community in Policy Implementation. In *New Directions in Education Policy Implementation: Confronting Complexity*, edited by M. I. Honig, pp. 25–46. The State University of New York Press, Albany.

Cordell, L. S. 2007 *Archaeology of the Southwest*. Left Coast Press, Walnut Creek, California.

Durand, S. R., and W. B. Hurst 1991 A Refinement of Anasazi Cultural Chronology in the Middle Puerco Valley Using Multidimensional Scaling. In *Anasazi Puebloan Adaptation in Response to Climatic Stress: Prehistory of the Middle Rio Puerco Valley*, edited by C. Irwin-Williams and L. L. Baker, pp. 233–255. Bureau of Land Management, Albuquerque, New Mexico.

Earle, T. 2001 Economic Support of Chaco Canyon Society. *American Antiquity* 66(1):26–35.

Ethridge, R., and S. M. Shuck-Hall (editors) 2009 *Mapping the Mississippian Shatter Zone: The Colonial Indian Slave Trade and Regional Instability in the American South*. University of Nebraska Press, Lincoln.

Fowles, S. M. 2005 Historical Contingency and the Prehistoric Foundations of Eastern Pueblo Moiety Organization. *Journal of Anthropological Research* 61(1):25–52.

Glowacki, D. M. 2006 *The Social Landscape of Depopulation: The Northern San Juan, A.D. 1150–1300*. PhD dissertation, Department of Anthropology, Arizona State University, Tempe.

Glowacki, D. M. 2015 *Living and Leaving: A Social History of Regional Depopulation in Thirteenth-Century Mesa Verde*. The University of Arizona Press, Tucson.

Goodwill-Cohen, L. F. 2001 *A Space Syntax Analysis of Prudden Units in the Mesa Verde Region of Southwestern Colorado: A.D. 750–1300*. Master's thesis, Department of Anthropology, Harvard University, Cambridge, Massachusetts.

Hegmon, M., M. Peeples, S. Ingram, A. Kinzig, S. Kulow, C. Meegan, and M. A. Nelson 2008 Social Transformation and Its Human Costs in the Prehispanic U.S. Southwest. *American Anthropologist* 110(3):313–324.

Herr, S. A., and L. C. Young 2012 Introduction to Southwestern Pithouse Communities. In *Southwestern Pithouse Communities, AD 200–900*, edited by L. C. Young and S. A. Herr, pp. 1–13. The University of Arizona Press, Tucson.

Hill, J. B., J. J. Clark, W. H. Doelle, and P. D. Lyons 2004 Prehistoric Demography in the Southwest: Migration, Coalescence, and Hohokam Population Decline. *American Antiquity* 69(4):689–716.

Hodder, I. 1979 Social Stress and Material Culture Patterning. *American Antiquity* 44(3):446–454.

Ingold, T. 2000 *The Perception of the Environment: Essays on Livelihood, Dwelling, and Skill.* Routledge, London.

Isbell, W. H. 2000 What We Should Be Studying: The "Imagined Community" and the "Natural Community." In *The Archaeology of Communities: A New World Perspective*, edited by M. A. Canuto and J. Yaeger, pp. 243–266. Routledge, New York.

Jeancon, J. A. 1922 *Archaeological Research in the Northeastern San Juan Basin of Colorado during the Summer of 1921.* Edited by F. H. Roberts. State Historical and Natural History Society of Colorado and University of Denver, Denver.

Johnson, G. A. 1982 Organizational Structure and Scalar Stress. In *Theory and Explanation in Archaeology: The Southampton Conference*, edited by C. Renfrew, M. J. Rowlands, and B. A. Segraves, pp. 389–421. Academic Press, New York.

Judge, W. J. 1989 Chaco Canyon—San Juan Basin. In *Dynamics of Southwest Prehistory*, edited by L. S. Cordell and G. J. Gummerman, pp. 209–261. Smithsonian Institution Press, Washington, D.C.

Kantner, J. W., and K. Kintigh 2006 The Chaco World. In *The Archaeology of Chaco Canyon: An Eleventh-Century Pueblo Regional Center*, edited by S. H. Lekson, pp. 153–188. School of American Research Press, Santa Fe, New Mexico.

Kantner, J. W., and N. Mahoney (editors) 2000 *Great House Communities across the Chacoan Landscape.* The University of Arizona Press, Tucson.

Kincaid, C. (editor) 1983 *Chaco Roads Project, Phase I: A Reappraisal of Prehistoric Roads in the San Juan Basin.* Bureau of Land Management, Albuquerque, New Mexico.

Kintigh, K. W., T. L. Howell, and A. I. Duff 1996 Post-Chacoan Social Integration at the Hinkson Site, New Mexico. *Kiva* 61(3):257–274.

Kohler, T. A., S. Van Buskirk, and S. Ruscavage-Barz 2004 Vessels and Villages: Evidence for Conformist Transmission in Early Village Aggregations on the Pajarito Plateau, New Mexico. *Journal of Anthropological Archaeology* 23(1):100–118.

Kolb, M. J., and J. E. Snead 1997 It's a Small World After All: Comparative Analyses of Community Organization in Archaeology. *American Antiquity* 62(4):609–628.

Kowalewski, S. A. 2003 Intensification under Duress. Paper presented at the 68th Annual Meeting of the Society for American Archaeology, Milwaukee.

Kowalewski, S. A. 2006 Coalescent Societies. In *Light on the Path: The Anthropology and History of the Southeastern Indians*, edited by T. J. Pluckhahn and R. Ethridge, pp. 94–122. The University of Alabama Press, Tuscaloosa.

Kuckelman, K. A. 2000 *The Archaeology of Castle Rock Pueblo: A Thirteenth Century Village in Southwestern Colorado.* Electronic document: http://www.crowcanyon.org/castlerock.

LeBlanc, S. A. 1999 *Prehistoric Warfare in the American Southwest.* The University of Utah Press, Salt Lake City.

Lehmer, D. J. 1954 Archaeological Investigations in the Oahe Dam Area, South Dakota, 1950–1951. Smithsonian Institution, Bureau of American Ethnology Bulletin 158. *River Basin Surveys Papers* 7:136–149.

Lekson, S. H. 1984 *Great Pueblo Architecture of Chaco Canyon, New Mexico.* Publications in Archaeology 18B. National Park Service, Albuquerque, New Mexico.

Lekson, S. H. 1999 *The Chaco Meridian: Centers of Political Power in the Ancient Southwest.* AltaMira Press, Walnut Creek, California.

Lekson, S. H. 2007a Great House Form. In *The Architecture of Chaco Canyon, New Mexico*, edited by S. H. Lekson, pp. 7–44. The University of Utah Press, Salt Lake City.

Lekson, S. H. (editor) 2007b *The Architecture of Chaco Canyon, New Mexico.* The University of Utah Press, Salt Lake City.

Lekson, S. H., T. Windes, and P. J. McKenna 2006 Architecture. In *The Archaeology of Chaco Canyon: An Eleventh-Century Pueblo Regional Center*, edited by S. H. Lekson, pp. 67–116. School for Advanced Research Press, Santa Fe, New Mexico.

Lipe, W. D. 1989 Historical and Analytical Perspectives on Architecture and Social Integration in Prehistoric Pueblos. In *The Architecture of Social Integration in Prehistoric Pueblos*, edited by W. D. Lipe and M. Hegmon, pp. 15–34. Occasional Paper 1. Crow Canyon Archaeological Center, Cortez, Colorado.

Lipe, W. D. 2002 Social Power in the Central Mesa Verde Region, A.D. 1150–1290. In *Seeking the Center Place: Archaeology and Ancient Communities in the Mesa Verde Region*, edited by M. D. Varien and R. H. Wilshusen, pp. 202–232. The University of Utah Press, Salt Lake City.

Lipe, W. D. 2006 Notes from the North. In *The Archaeology of Chaco Canyon: An Eleventh-Century Pueblo Regional Center*, edited by S. H. Lekson, pp. 261–314. School for Advanced Research Press, Santa Fe, New Mexico.

Lipe, W. D., and S. Ortman 2000 Spatial Patterning in Northern San Juan Villages, A.D. 1050–1300. *Kiva* 66(1):91–122.

Lipe, W. D., and M. D. Varien 1999 Pueblo II (A.D. 900–1150). In *Colorado Prehistory: A Context for the Southern Colorado Drainage Basin*, edited by W. D. Lipe, M. D. Varien, and R. H. Wilshusen, pp. 242–289. Colorado Council of Professional Archaeologists, Denver.

Mahoney, N. M. 2000 Redefining the Scale of Chacoan Communities. In *Great House Communities across the Chacoan Landscape*, edited by J. W. Kantner and N. Mahoney, pp. 19–27. Anthropological Papers of the University of Arizona 64. The University of Arizona Press, Tucson.

Malville, J. M. (editor) 2004 *Chimney Rock: The Ultimate Outlier.* Lexington, Lanham, Maryland.

Marshall, M. P., J. R. Stein, R. W. Loose, and J. E. Novotny (editors) 1979 *Anasazi Communities of the San Juan Basin.* Public Service Company of New Mexico and New Mexico Historic Preservation Bureau, Albuquerque and Santa Fe.

Mills, B. J. 2002 Recent Research on Chaco: Changing Views on Economy, Ritual, and Society. *Journal of Archaeological Research* 10(1):65–117.

Murdock, G. P. 1949 *Social Structure.* Free Press, New York.

Murdock, G. P., and S. F. Wilson 1972 Settlement Patterns and Community Organizations: Cross-Cultural Codes. *Ethnology* 11:254–295.

Naranjo, T. 2008 Life as Movement: A Tewa View of Community and Identity. In *The Social Constructions of Communities: Agency, Structure, and Identity in the Prehispanic Southwest*, edited by M. D. Varien and J. M. Potter, pp. 251–262. AltaMira Press, New York.

Nelson, M. A., M. Hegmon, S. Kulow, M. A. Peeples, K. W. Kintigh, and A. P. Kinzig 2011 Resisting Diversity: A Long-Term Archaeological Study. *Ecology and Science* 16(1):25.

North, D. C. 1990 *Institutions, Institutional Change, and Economic Performance*. Cambridge University Press, Cambridge.

Page, S., and J. Page 2009 *Hopi*. Rio Nuevo, Tucson, Arizona.

Pippin, L. C. 1987 *Prehistory and Paleoecology of Guadalupe Ruin, New Mexico*. University of Utah Anthropological Papers 107. The University of Utah Press, Salt Lake City.

Plog, S., and C. Heitman 2010 Hierarchy and Social Inequality in the American Southwest, A.D. 800–1200. *Proceedings of the National Academy of Sciences* 107(46):19619–19626.

Powers, R. P., W. D. Gillespie, and S. H. Lekson 1983 *The Outlier Survey: A Regional View of Settlement in the San Juan Basin*. Reports of the Chaco Center 3. National Park Service, Albuquerque, New Mexico.

Prudden, T. M. 1903 The Prehistoric Ruins of the San Juan Watershed in Utah, Arizona, Colorado, and New Mexico. *American Anthropologist* 5(2):224–288.

Prudden, T. M. 1914 The Circular Kiva of Small Ruins in the San Juan Watershed. *American Anthropologist* 16(1):33–58.

Prudden, T. M. 1918 *A Further Study of Prehistoric Small House Ruins in the San Juan Watershed*. Memoirs of the American Anthropological Association 5(1). Lancaster, Pennsylvania.

Rapoport, A. 1969 *House Form and Culture*. Prentice-Hall, Englewood Cliffs, New Jersey.

Rapoport, A. 1990 *The Meaning of the Built Environment: A Nonverbal Communication Approach*. The University of Arizona Press, Tucson.

Rapoport, A. 1994 Spatial Organization and the Built Environment. In *Companion Encyclopedia of Anthropology: Humanity, Culture, and Social Life*, edited by T. Ingold, pp. 460–502. Routledge, London.

Rappaport, R. A. 1971 Ritual, Sanctity, and Cybernetics. *American Anthropologist* 73(1):59–76.

Reed, P. F. (editor) 2006 *Thirty-Five Years of Archaeological Research at Salmon Ruins, New Mexico. Volume I: Introduction, Architecture, Chronology, and Conclusions*. Center for Desert Archaeology, Tucson, and Salmon Ruins Museum, Bloomfield.

Roberts, F. H. 1939 *Archaeological Remains in the Whitewater District, Eastern Arizona. Part 1: House Types*. Bureau of American Ethnology Bulletin 121. Smithsonian Institution Press, Washington, D.C.

Roney, J. R. 1992 Prehistoric Roads and Regional Integration in the Chacoan System. In *Anasazi Regional Organization and the Chaco System*, edited by D. E. Doyel, pp. 123–131. Anthropological Papers 5. Maxwell Museum of Anthropology, University of New Mexico, Albuquerque.

Ryan, S. C. 2013 *Architectural Communities of Practice: Ancestral Pueblo Kiva Production during the Chaco and Post-Chaco Periods in the Northern Southwest*. PhD dissertation, School of Anthropology, University of Arizona, Tucson.

Swentzell, R. 1990 Pueblo Space, Form, and Mythology. In *Pueblo Style and Regional Architecture*, edited by N. C. Markovich, W. Preiser, and F. G. Sturm, pp. 23–30. Routledge, New York.

Till, J. D. 2001 *Chacoan Roads and Road-Associated Sites in the Lower San Juan Region: Assessing the Role of Chacoan Influences in the Northwestern Periphery*. Master's thesis, Department of Anthropology, University of Colorado, Boulder.

Van Dyke, R. M. 1999 The Chaco Connection: Evaluating Bonito-Style Architecture in Outlier Communities. *Journal of Anthropological Archaeology* 18(4):471–506.

Van Dyke, R. M. 2003 Memory and the Construction of Chacoan Society. In *Archaeologies of Memory*, edited by R. Van Dyke and S. E. Alcock, pp. 180–200. Blackwell, Malden, Massachusetts.

Van Dyke, R. M. 2008 Sacred Landscapes: The Chaco–Totah Connection. In *Chaco's Northern Prodigies: Salmon, Aztec, and the Ascendancy of the Middle San Juan Region after AD 1100*, edited by P. F. Reed, pp. 334–348. The University of Utah Press, Salt Lake City.

Varien, M. D. 1999 *Sedentism and Mobility in a Social Landscape: Mesa Verde and Beyond*. The University of Arizona Press, Tucson.

Varien, M. D., W. D. Lipe, M. A. Adler, I. M. Thompson, and B. A. Bradley 1996 Southwestern Colorado and Southeastern Utah Settlement Patterns: A.D. 1100–1300. In *The Prehistoric Pueblo World, A.D. 1150–1300*, edited by M. A. Adler, pp. 86–113. The University of Arizona Press, Tucson.

Vivian, R. G. 1990 *The Chacoan Prehistory of the San Juan Basin*. Academic Press, New York and San Diego.

Vivian, R. G., and P. Reiter 1965 *The Great Kivas of Chaco Canyon and Their Relationships*. Monographs 22. The School of American Research, Santa Fe, New Mexico.

Warrick, G. 2008 *A Population History of the Huron-Petun, A.D. 500–1650*. Cambridge University Press, Cambridge.

Wills, W. H., and R. D. Leonard (editors) 1994 *The Ancient Southwestern Community: Models and Methods for the Study of Prehistoric Social Organization*. University of New Mexico Press, Albuquerque.

Wilshusen, R. H., and R. Van Dyke 2006 Chaco's Beginnings. In *The Archaeology of Chaco Canyon: An Eleventh-Century Pueblo Regional Center*, edited by S. H. Lekson, pp. 211–259. School for Advanced Research Press, Santa Fe, New Mexico.

Windes, T. C. 2003 This Old House: Construction and Abandonment of Pueblo Bonito. In *Pueblo Bonito: Center of the Chaco World*, edited by J. E. Neitzel, pp. 14–32. Smithsonian Institution Press, Washington, D.C.

Windes, T. C. 2007 Gearing Up and Piling On: Early Great Houses in the Interior San Juan Basin. In *The Architecture of Chaco Canyon, New Mexico*, edited by S. H. Lekson, pp. 45–92. The University of Utah Press, Salt Lake City.

CHAPTER FIFTEEN

Settlement Aggregation and Geopolitical Realignment in the Northeastern Woodlands

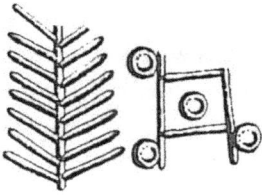

Jennifer Birch

Abstract   *Eastern North American archaeology has benefited from historicized approaches that seek to understand the relationship between the long-term emergence of social and political complexity, and the lived experiences of households and communities. This paper will draw upon archaeological and ethnohistoric datasets pertaining to ancestral Wendat (Huron) society in the Northeastern Woodlands to explore the relationship between coalescence and broader shifts in the geopolitical fabric of Northern Iroquoia. Two subregional site relocation sequences—one located on West Duffins Creek and the other in the Trent Valley—are analyzed in order to understand variability in the processes and outcomes of aggregation. The picture that emerges is one of multilinear adaptations and negotiations taking place amongst local populations and newcomers at multiple social and spatial scales. At the same time, archaeological and ethnohistoric evidence points to a significant degree of asymmetry in sociopolitical relations both at the community level and within the Wendat confederacy council. It is suggested that distinct historical processes of settlement aggregation in each region contributed to these political outcomes.*

During the first and second millennia A.D., the Northern Iroquoian societies of northeastern North America underwent a suite of transformations of general interest to anthropological archaeologists. This includes the adoption of domesticated plants, development of settled village life, warfare, settlement aggregation, and the development of increasingly complex social and political organizations. Iroquoian settlements were generally occupied for 10–40 years before being relocated due to a combination of resource depletion and social factors (Jones and Wood 2012; Warrick 2008), usually only a few kilometers away. The resulting settlement patterns constitute a series of unbroken site relocation sequences that allow us to document the history of contiguous community groups over hundreds of years. Dozens of fully or partially excavated village sites combined with the rich ethnohistoric and ethnographic records make this a significant, yet often overlooked, dataset for studying and theorizing nonstate societies (e.g., Birch 2012, 2015; Creese 2012; Ramsden 1996; Trigger 1990).

At the time of sustained European contact in the early seventeenth century, Iroquoian societies were organized into political confederacies consisting of allied nations (Figure 15.1). Nations were composed of allied communities consisting of palisaded longhouse villages who shared a common territory, endonym, and could act in concert to achieve sociopolitical and economic objectives. Subsistence was based primarily on a combination of maize agriculture, hunting, fishing, and gathering. Many individuals were known to be shrewd traders and diplomats. A lack of differentiation of social classes, marked inequality, or disparities in access to material resources led to the characterization of Iroquoian societies as "tribal" and "egalitarian" despite the recognition that certain individuals and groups occupied positions of considerable influence in societal affairs.

Between the fifteenth and seventeenth centuries A.D., processes of settlement aggregation and the formation of nations and confederacies took place among multiple

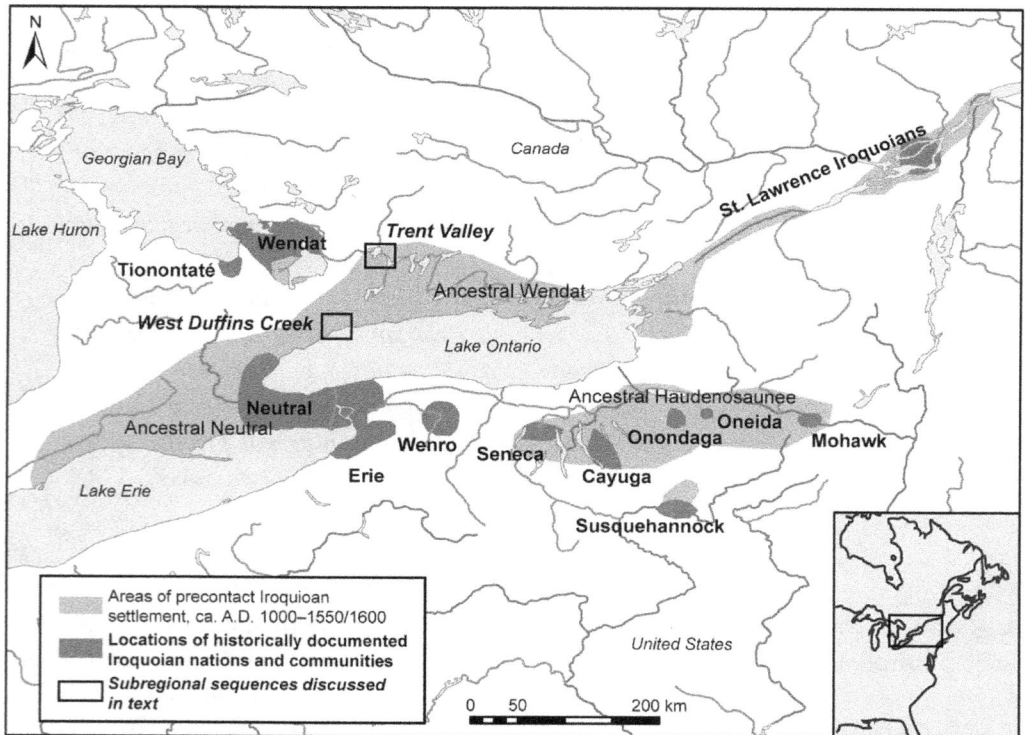

FIGURE 15.1. Locations of pre- and postcontact Iroquoian settlements and confederacies.

Iroquoian societies, including the Haudenosaunee or Iroquois, Neutral, and Erie. In this paper, I consider the developmental trajectories of ancestral Wendat communities and nations, the northernmost Iroquoian peoples. These processes are considered within a broadly historical-processual theoretical framework (Pauketat 2001), with an emphasis on concepts that draw upon alternatives to social evolution (Brück and Fontijn 2013; Feinman and Neitzel 1984; Grinin and Korotayev 2011) to explore the differential pathways and outcomes of coalescence and geopolitical realignment.

Although settlement aggregation and confederacy formation were macroregional phenomena, the specific processes and outcomes of coalescence differed depending on the historical, material, and relational contexts of communities and their constituent parts. To illustrate this, I draw from two well-documented community relocation sequences in the Toronto area and Trent Valley, respectively. These communities in each of these site sequences would go on to become the nations of the Wendat confederacy by the early seventeenth century. Each nation had a different relationship to that larger political body, and some thoughts on why that may have been the case are presented below. The results suggest that the complex negotiations and relationships that developed within and between coalescent communities indicate a degree of organizational complexity and diversity hidden from view in previous anthropological and archaeological constructs of Iroquoian societies as essentially "tribal" and "egalitarian" (see also Birch and Williamson 2013a).

THE HISTORICAL DEVELOPMENT OF ANCESTRAL WENDAT SOCIETY

Between ca. A.D. 900 and 1300, ancestral Wendat settlements developed from small, semisedentary base camps at which a limited amount of maize was cultivated and from which groups would journey to collect seasonally available resources to larger, sedentary villages where maize comprised some 50 percent of the diet (Birch 2015; Pfeiffer et al. 2016; Warrick 2000; Williamson 2014). This increased reliance on maize resulted in a pattern of demographic growth associated cross-culturally with the Neolithic Demographic Transition (Bandy 2008; Bocquet-Appel and Naji 2006), whereby, between ca. A.D. 1300 and 1450, the population of south-central Ontario increased from some 10,000 to 24,000 persons (Warrick 2008).

Population growth influenced the movement of ancestral Wendat populations north into the Simcoe Uplands (MacDonald 2002; Sutton 1999)—what would become historic Wendake—and east into Trent Valley (Ramsden 1990; Sutton 1990). During the 1300s, ancestral Wendat peoples developed practices and institutions that served to integrate their growing population, resulting in a relatively cohesive cultural pattern in south-central Ontario. Archaeologically, these institutions are manifested in semisubterranean sweat lodges (MacDonald 1988; MacDonald and Williamson 2001), ossuary burial (Williamson and Steiss 2003), an elaborate smoking pipe complex (Noble 1979), and widespread homogeneity in ceramic decoration (Ramsden 1977; Wright 1966).

After approximately A.D. 1450, the political situation took a dramatic turn. In the late fifteenth and sixteenth centuries, there is evidence of an increasingly hostile social landscape spreading across Iroquoia. Evidence for conflict becomes widespread in both Ontario and New York State (Birch 2015; Engelbrecht 2003). In Ontario, evidence for conflict includes the defensive situation of sites and construction of multirow palisades and earthworks (Birch 2010, 2012). Human remains bearing signs of violent trauma become commonplace in midden deposits, a pattern that has been interpreted as evidence of prisoner sacrifice and the taking of trophy heads (Williamson 2007). Individual burials and interments in ossuaries are also suggestive of an atmosphere of endemic conflict (e.g., Molto et al. 1986; Williamson 1978; Williamson and Steiss 2003).

During this same period, and almost certainly due in part to this increase in warfare, ancestral Wendat village sites became fewer in number, larger in size, and more widely spaced. This process has been observed in settlement pattern data across the north shore of Lake Ontario (Birch 2012; Birch and Williamson 2013b). Analogous processes were also taking place farther south, in Upper New York State (Bradley 2005; Niemczycki 1984; Snow 1995; Tuck 1971). Because of the limited amount of site-level settlement pattern data available for the Simcoe Uplands and the Lower St. Lawrence River valley, it is unknown if these same processes were playing out there. In the fifteenth century, they appear to have been home to smaller populations (Jones 2010a, 2010b) that may not have experienced the same kinds of social circumscription (LeBlanc 2008) or pressure on resources (Gramly 1977) as did populations to the south, and, in turn, may have experienced relatively less conflict.

In most cases, aggregated settlements have palisades that were extended to accommodate new clusters of longhouses. The extension of palisades suggests that aggregation occurred rapidly, within the average 10 to 40 year life span of village communities. Settlement patterns are characterized by multiple groups of aligned longhouses, which have been interpreted by various scholars as either previously distinct communities (Bamann 1993; Pearce 1984; Tuck 1971; Warrick 2008:136–137) or clan-based groups (Finlayson 1985:172; Trigger 1985:92; Warrick 1984:35), although both may have been the case. The populations of these initial coalescent communities have been estimated to range from 600–1,800 individuals, in some cases ten times the size of the settlements they left behind (Birch and Williamson 2013b). With larger populations composed of unrelated community segments, these formative aggregates would have been settings for the development of more complex internal and external sociopolitical relations than would have existed previously (Birch and Williamson 2013a). In the late sixteenth and seventeenth centuries, coalescent communities would go on to ally themselves into Wendat nations and, ultimately, the confederacy.

POLITICAL EVOLUTION IN COALESCENT COMMUNITIES AND NATIONS

The archaeological signatures of political development in segmentary societies can be difficult to discern. This is because there are multiple organizational levels at which decisions may have been made, including the household, house cluster, clan, moiety, village, nation, confederacy, or any combination thereof. In the absence of structural or wealth-based inequality, direct archaeological signatures of leadership may be faint or absent. As such, broader patterns in the organization of settlements on the landscape or in the organization of the built environment of individual settlements may be more reliable predictors for evidence of sociopolitical change (for various sociopolitical contexts, see Kelly, Fernández-Götz, Osborne, Raczky, Ryan, and Sastre and Currás this volume).

In a number of publications, Birch and Williamson (2013a, 2013b, 2015; also Birch 2012) have unpacked why coalescence gave rise to an increase in organizational complexity at the community level. Prior to A.D. 1450, political action in smaller village communities was likely dominated by lineages or clan segments to which much of the population would have also belonged (Birch 2012; MacDonald 1986; Warrick 2000). The larger populations of coalescent communities would have necessitated more complex decision making, negotiation, and coordination between community segments and mechanisms for achieving consensus—most likely by a village council. The responsibilities of the council and its membership would have included organization for collective defense, decisions about land tenure, maintenance of community infrastructure and waste management, the scheduling of simultaneous labor, decisions about interregional interaction, trade and exchange, alliance formation, and the scheduling and hosting of ceremonial events and feasts. Councils and influential members may have also served important roles in linking communities together into formative tribal nations and confederacies.

It is possible that lineages or clans who were the first to establish settlements, and who had the longest sustained association with villages and their associated territories, may have achieved elevated status. This was the case in the U.S. Southwest where—in the context of population movement and aggregation—local resources, rights, and decision making were controlled by individuals who had the most stable attachments to place, rather than by the community as a whole (Schachner 2012:24; see also Ryan this volume). It is possible that the same process may have played out in the coalescent communities of the Wendat. In the seventeenth century, the Attignawantan (Bear) nation—descendants of the original Iroquoian populations who established themselves in Wendake—held the balance of power in the confederacy council.

In writing about political organization among the segmentary societies of Papua New Guinea, Roscoe (2013) makes an important distinction between the political apparatus and the political community. He argues that the polity as a governing body and the polity as a group are different phenomena, and that the processes that influence their emergence, development, and maintenance should be analyzed as such (Roscoe 2013:59).

In seventeenth-century Wendat society, the ethnographic record indicates that the political apparatus included influential leaders who represented political communities of various sizes. These included lineages, clans, moieties, villages or towns, and nations. Within and between these groups, political relations were fluid. Fluctuations in alliances and factionalism were the norm. Nevertheless, following their formation in the sixteenth century, Wendat nations appear to have permitted the formation of place- and community-based identities that transcended the fission and fusion of settlements and the multiethnic nature of their constituent parts (*sensu* Barthes 1969).

In the remainder of the paper, I will unpack two subregional processes of ancestral Wendat settlement aggregation. Particular focus is placed on the origins of constituent groups, changes in social and political organization encoded in the built environment, material patterning at the inter- and intrasite levels, and the historically contingent circumstances and outcomes for each group as they met the challenges of coalescence, nation building, and incorporation into the nascent Wendat confederacy.

PATHWAYS TO NATION BUILDING

AGGREGATION ON WEST DUFFINS CREEK

Arguably, processes of ancestral Wendat settlement aggregation have been most extensively interrogated in the community relocation sequence located on West Duffins Creek, approximately 30 kilometers east of Toronto, Ontario (Birch 2012, 2016a; Birch and Williamson 2013a, 2013b, 2015; Birch et al. 2016). This drainage contains an unbroken history of human occupation that begins ca. A.D. 1000 and extends nearly into the period of European contact in the seventeenth century. Here, over the course of three to four generations, in the fifteenth and sixteenth centuries, as many as eight small village communities came together to form a single community at the Draper site before relocating as a whole at least twice, to the Spang and Mantle sites (Figure 15.2). The interpretation of this sequence as representing a single population moving through time is supported by site sizes, population estimates, ceramic seriation, and modeling of agricultural catchments and radiocarbon dates (Birch 2012; Birch and Manning 2016; Birch and Williamson 2013a; Finlayson 1985; Warrick 2008).

Until very recently, aggregation at Draper was believed to have occurred in the mid-fifteenth century. However, a suite of new AMS radiocarbon dates and Bayesian modeling of those dates suggests that the initial process of aggregation may have actually occurred in the early sixteenth century (Birch and Manning 2016). There are at least eight small village communities that were abandoned concomitantly with Draper's expansion, suggesting that these people came together at the Draper site. Large quantities of butchered human remains in midden deposits (Williamson 2007), construction of a multirow palisade (Finlayson 1985), and the site's location above a steep break-in-slope all suggest that conflict motivated aggregation at Draper.

The reconstruction of Draper's occupational history (Finlayson 1985) indicates that as each group joined the community, the palisade was expanded to accommodate new clusters of longhouses in a process of aggregation that unfolded over 20–30 years (Figure 15.3a). As each new house cluster was added, they were deliberately constructed in such a way as to keep each group spatially distinct, even when it would have been more practical—in terms of the additional palisade that needed to be constructed—to arrange them parallel within the palisaded enclosure (Birch 2012; Birch and Williamson 2013a, 2013b).

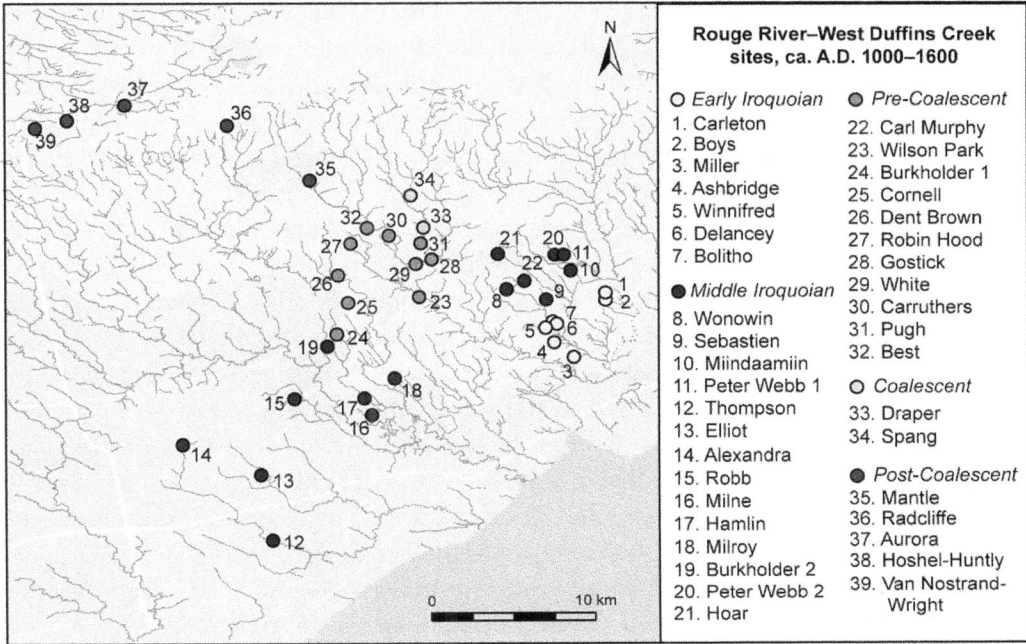

Figure 15.2. Locations of sites in the West Duffins Creek sequence.

Rouge River–West Duffins Creek sites, ca. A.D. 1000–1600

○ *Early Iroquoian*
1. Carleton
2. Boys
3. Miller
4. Ashbridge
5. Winnifred
6. Delancey
7. Bolitho

● *Middle Iroquoian*
8. Wonowin
9. Sebastien
10. Miindaamiin
11. Peter Webb 1
12. Thompson
13. Elliot
14. Alexandra
15. Robb
16. Milne
17. Hamlin
18. Milroy
19. Burkholder 2
20. Peter Webb 2
21. Hoar

● *Pre-Coalescent*
22. Carl Murphy
23. Wilson Park
24. Burkholder 1
25. Cornell
26. Dent Brown
27. Robin Hood
28. Gostick
29. White
30. Carruthers
31. Pugh
32. Best

○ *Coalescent*
33. Draper
34. Spang

● *Post-Coalescent*
35. Mantle
36. Radcliffe
37. Aurora
38. Hoshel-Huntly
39. Van Nostrand-Wright

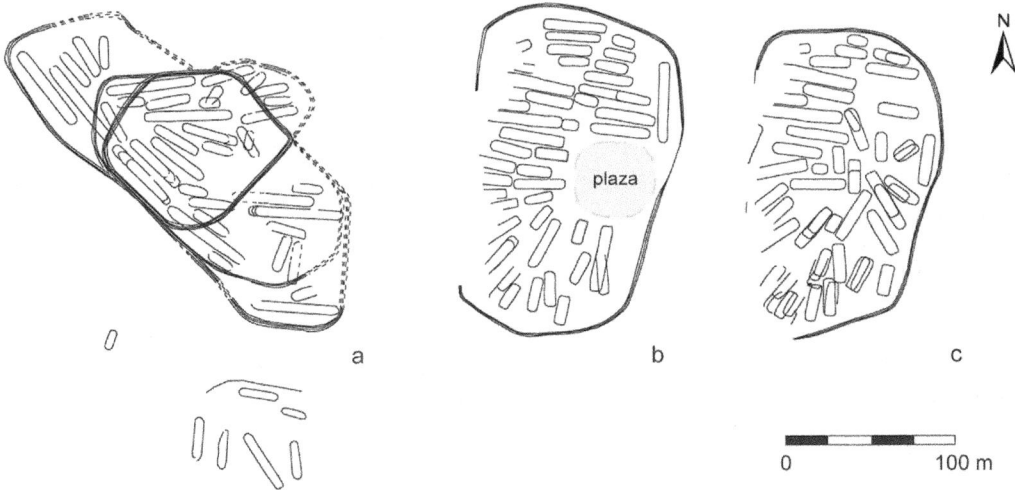

Figure 15.3. Settlement plans, West Duffins Creek sequence: (a) Draper (after Finlayson 1985), (b) Mantle early village, (c) Mantle late village (after Birch and Williamson 2013a).

Because of the clear intention to keep each house cluster separate, it has been interpreted that Draper remained essentially a village composed of multiple, smaller communities—or neighborhoods (e.g., Smith et al. 2014)—sharing a palisaded enclosure (Birch 2012; Birch and Williamson 2013b). Each house cluster also contains one or more "long" longhouses which have been interpreted as the residences of influential lineages (Birch and Williamson 2013b; Hayden 1977). Multiple households contributed to discrete midden deposits located in open areas outside of longhouses (Finlayson 1985). At Draper, there are no material correlates that would suggest the existence of a centralized political organization; however, we can infer that such practices must have been developing in order to manage the more complex sociopolitical and economic functions of this formative aggregate.

It is believed that the Draper community relocated to Spang in the mid-sixteenth century. Less is known about Spang than the villages that are assumed to have preceded and followed it. Limited test excavation in the late 1970s revealed portions of five long-houses, midden deposits, and a five-row palisade (Carter 1981). A recent geophysical survey utilized magnetometry and magnetic susceptibility, together with soil phosphate testing, in an attempt to reveal more detail about the overall site plan. Those data suggest the possible presence of a central plaza, as was identified at its successor village, Mantle (Birch 2016b), however, excavations are required to confirm that inference.

The next iteration of this coalescent community is the Mantle site. Detailed descriptions of the site's settlement patterns, material culture, and occupational history have been reported elsewhere (Archaeological Services Inc. 2014; Birch and Williamson 2013a), and are summarized here. Initially, Mantle was thought to date to the early sixteenth century. Recent chronological modeling suggests that it may in fact date to the late sixteenth century (Birch and Manning 2016). The site has a complex occupational history that involved considerable reorganization of space over time, including the dismantling and construction of longhouses, and the contraction and reinforcement of the site's palisade.

In the early phase of the Mantle settlement plan, houses were arranged in a radial alignment around a single plaza (Figure 15.3b). The construction of such a central space speaks to a well-integrated community, or efforts to encourage such integration. If this was a social experiment, it did not persist over time. Partway through the site's occupational history, the palisade was contracted and the plaza filled with new structures (Figure 15.3c). This included the dismantling of a number of houses in the northern portion of the village. Population estimates, based on the amount of roofed space in the early and later village plans, suggest that the palisade contraction and reorganization coincided with the departure of an estimated 400 residents. While Mantle was heavily palisaded throughout its history, the lack of human remains in midden deposits suggests that regional conflict may have declined during the site's occupation.

Evidence for political centralization includes an organized system for the deposition of refuse that channeled waste out of the village, first into a large, hillside midden, and later, into the borrow trench surrounding the palisade. Two large longhouses—situated on the highest point of land at the site—appear to have played an important role in community affairs. These structures had an enduring place in the village, and were rebuilt and repaired in place multiple times. They correspond to ethnohistoric descriptions of the longest longhouses in a village being the residences of community leaders and venues for public gatherings, including meetings of the village council. It seems clear that one or more households were able to develop and maintain a position of relative influence in the community. It is possible that this group may have been the initial residents of the Draper community. As such, the central plaza, waste management system, and prominent residences serve to materialize more complex social and political relations than are apparent in earlier communities. The Mantle community exhibits evidence for political consolidation that is perhaps not in keeping with traditional models of "egalitarian" political organization which have dominated thinking about the historical development of Iroquoian societies.

The kind of integration and political centralization apparent at Mantle may have been a product of the fact that here aggregation involved the coming together of peoples who already shared a subregional territory, belief system, and, we assume, a common language. This was not the case in the Trent Valley, where we turn our attention next.

AGGREGATION IN THE TRENT VALLEY

Approximately 60 kilometers to the northeast, similar processes of aggregation were taking place set against a somewhat different social and historical backdrop. There is some evidence for a small Iroquoian population occupying the Trent Valley prior to the fourteenth century (Kapches 1987; MacDonald and Williamson 1995). Sizable villages (up to 2 hectares in size) appear after this time, and were joined by an influx of migrants sometime in the late fifteenth century (Sutton 1990) (Figure 15.4). Similarities between

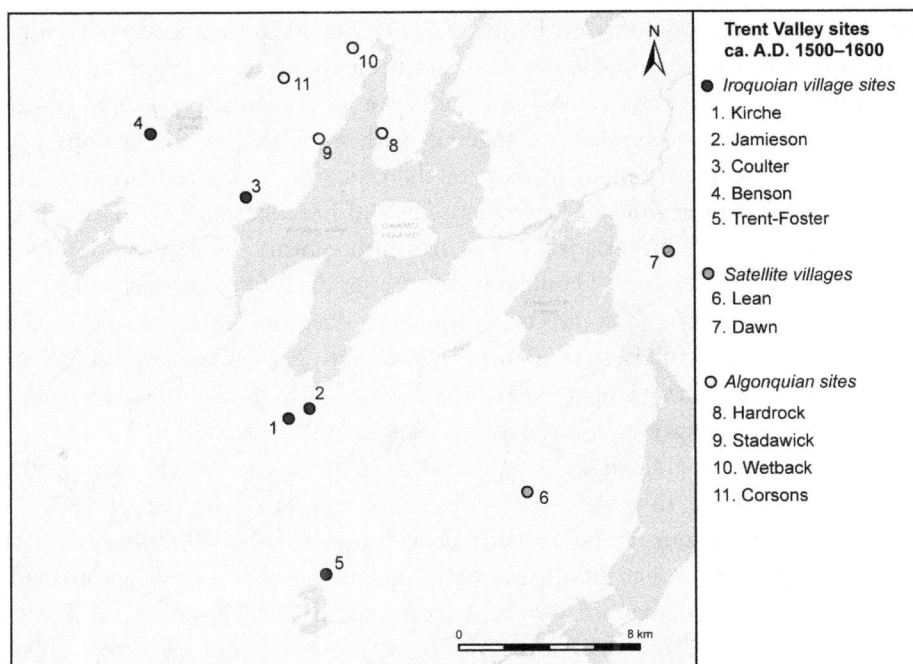

FIGURE 15.4. Locations of sites in the Trent Valley.

early sixteenth-century ceramic assemblages to sites to the west and south make the origins of those immigrants unclear, though they likely came from one or both of these areas.

During the mid-to-late sixteenth century, the gradual abandonment of the Lower St. Lawrence River valley and Jefferson County in upstate New York brought additional immigrants to the valley. These populations are known as St. Lawrence Iroquoians, and possessed distinct ceramic traditions and a complex bone tool industry, which differentiates them archaeologically from ancestral Wendat or Haudenosaunee populations (Engelbrecht and Jamieson 2015; Pendergast 1966). It has been estimated that as many as 800 St. Lawrence Iroquoians settled in the Trent Valley during the mid-to-late sixteenth century (Ramsden 1990; Warrick 2008:195–196). The presence of earthworks and multirow palisades at many St. Lawrence Iroquoian sites in both Ontario and New York suggests this abandonment was driven by either internal or external conflict. It is possible that these populations were unable to develop or maintain strong intraethnic alliances (Engelbrecht 1995), as was the case for the Haudenosaunee and Wendat nations and confederacies, which developed concomitantly with the dispersal of the St. Lawrence Iroquoians.

The late precontact occupation of the Trent Valley also included multiple Algonquian sites and fishing camps. These appear to have been occupied contemporaneously with Iroquoian village sites in the region (Ramsden 2016a). Algonquian peoples were linguistically distinct, seasonally mobile hunter-fisher-gatherers. While it has long been known that Iroquoian and Algonquian peoples were involved in long-term interactions and trade relations (e.g., Trigger 1976), recent research suggests that Algonquian peoples were also living among and within Wendat villages and longhouses in the late sixteenth century (Ramsden 2016a).

So, whereas in the case of West Duffins Creek, aggregation was occurring primarily among homogeneous local populations who had been closely interacting for more than a century prior to coalescence, in the Trent Valley we have a situation where aggregation involved multiple migrant populations, together with a multiethnic indigenous population—a situation that contributed, in part, to the outcomes of coalescence.

Thanks largely to the work of Peter Ramsden and his colleagues, we have a detailed record of excavated village sites dating to the sixteenth century, when the primary occupation of the valley took place (Damkjar 1990; Nasmith 2008; Ramsden 1990, 2009, 2016a, 2016b) (Figure 15.5). A precise chronology does not exist for this sequence, although small quantities of European metals (Ramsden 2016b) suggest that all of the major Iroquoian sites in the Upper Trent Valley date to the mid-to-late sixteenth century—roughly contemporary with the Draper, Spang, and Mantle sites.

The Kirche site originated as a palisaded settlement containing two clusters of aligned longhouses. Some time after the initial establishment of the settlement, a group of longhouses was added outside the palisaded enclosure (Nasmith 2008; Ramsden 1988) (Figure 15.5a). This additional group was never enclosed within the village palisade. A higher proportion of St. Lawrence Iroquoian ceramics in the exterior segment suggests that these houses were occupied by a distinct population with ties to the St. Lawrence Valley (Ramsden 1988:181, 2016a, 2016b).

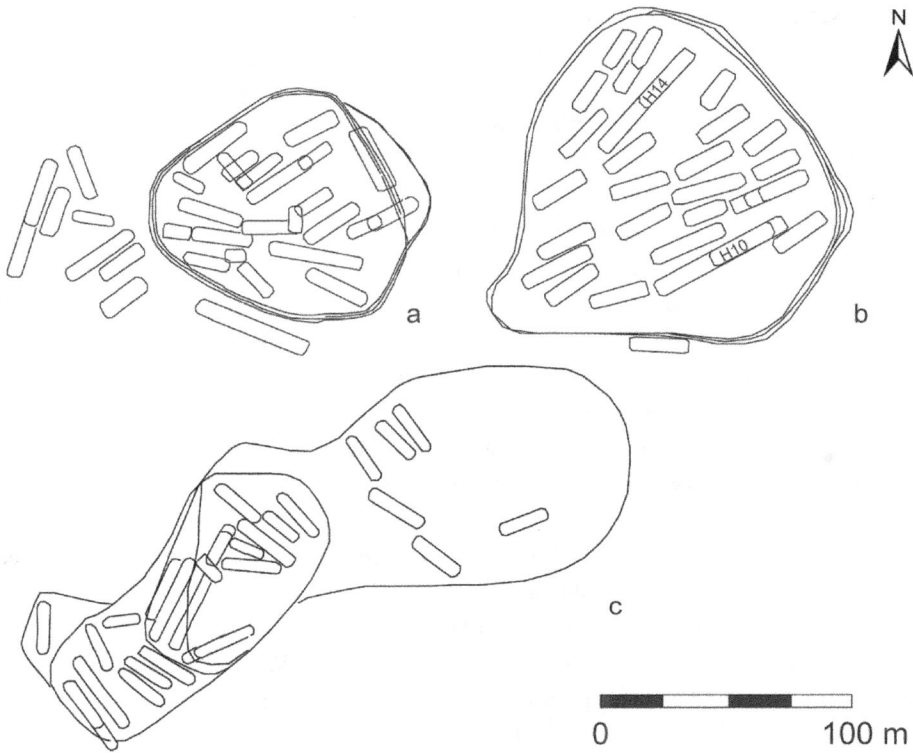

FIGURE 15.5. Settlement plans, Trent Valley sequence: (a) Kirche (after Nasmith 2008), (b) Benson (after Ramsden 2009, 2016a, 2016b), (c) Coulter (after Damkjar 1990).

The most likely successor to the Kirche village is Benson (Figure 15.5b). Benson's political history suggests that it was home to two factions (Ramsden 2009). It is possible, though not certain, that one of these may represent the original Kirche community, and the other represents the newcomers formerly outside the palisade. One faction centered upon House 10 which was found to contain higher proportions of St. Lawrence Iroquoian ceramics and small quantities of European metal. Ramsden (2009) has hypothesized that this group was involved in some manner in the nascent fur trade based on these signatures together with greater quantities of beaver bone than might otherwise be expected in areas of the site also containing European and St. Lawrence Iroquoian material. The other faction was centered upon House 14. These households retained a more traditional material profile and lacked European trade goods. Based on high relative proportions of lithic tools—which are characteristically Algonquian rather than Wendat—Ramsden (2016a) suggests that this portion of the village may also have been home to Algonquian men or families. The footprint of House 10 indicates that it was expanded partway through the site's occupational history. Based on the materials recovered, this is assumed to be related to the incorporation of a St. Lawrence Iroquoian group, possibly bringing with them ties to the French trading posts being established on the St. Lawrence River after 1580. As Ramsden (2009) notes, for every person or group who sought out ties to Europeans for social, economic, or political advantage, there may have been others opposed to it. These political dynamics appear to have played out at the Benson site, with the more traditional faction prevailing. Some time before the complete abandonment of the site, the houses belonging to the faction possessing European goods were dismantled, although the presence of later midden deposits in these areas indicates that the village continued to be occupied.

Those who departed the Benson community may have formed a portion of the population of the Coulter site. Here, settlement aggregation is evidenced through the addition of at least two palisade extensions. The first was a multirow palisade which was completely filled with new houses. The second extension was a single-row palisade that contains only a few houses (Damkjar 1990). Ramsden (1988) has interpreted this pattern as indicating two possible scenarios: either the final number of houses to be enclosed was unknown or the number of houses anticipated did not materialize at the time the single-row extension was built. Trent-Foster, another large late sixteen-century site in the area, is another possible candidate for the relocated Benson community or a portion thereof, although its internal structure remains unknown.

In summary, whereas the community sequence on West Duffins Creek involved the consolidation of closely interacting local village communities into a well-integrated whole, the Trent Valley sequence involved multiethnic local populations, together with multiple migrations to the valley from the north shore of Lake Ontario and from the St. Lawrence Valley. Here, tensions between community segments appear to have been resolved by population relocation and the decision to inhabit at least two incompletely integrated village communities.

GEOPOLITICAL REALIGNMENT:
NATION AND CONFEDERACY FORMATION

Reconstructions of political dynamics in the context of coalescence in each of these site sequences have implications for understanding the sociopolitical landscape of geopolitical realignment, including nation and confederacy formation in the late sixteenth and seventeenth centuries.

The seventeenth-century Wendat (Huron) confederacy was a product of both long-term settlement dynamics and recent migration to the Simcoe Uplands, located between Lake Simcoe and Georgian Bay (Figure 15.6). This area constituted Wendake—the Wendat homeland at the time of European contact. Unlike the Iroquois confederacy, where member nations remained emplaced in their own ancestral territories, physical aggregation seems to have been an important part of becoming Wendat. The Wendat term has been loosely translated as "dwellers on a peninsula" or "people of a floating island" (Steckley 2007)—although this translation remains tentative, it may identify a collection of peoples associated with the landscape of the Simcoe Uplands, as opposed to a singular ethnic identity.

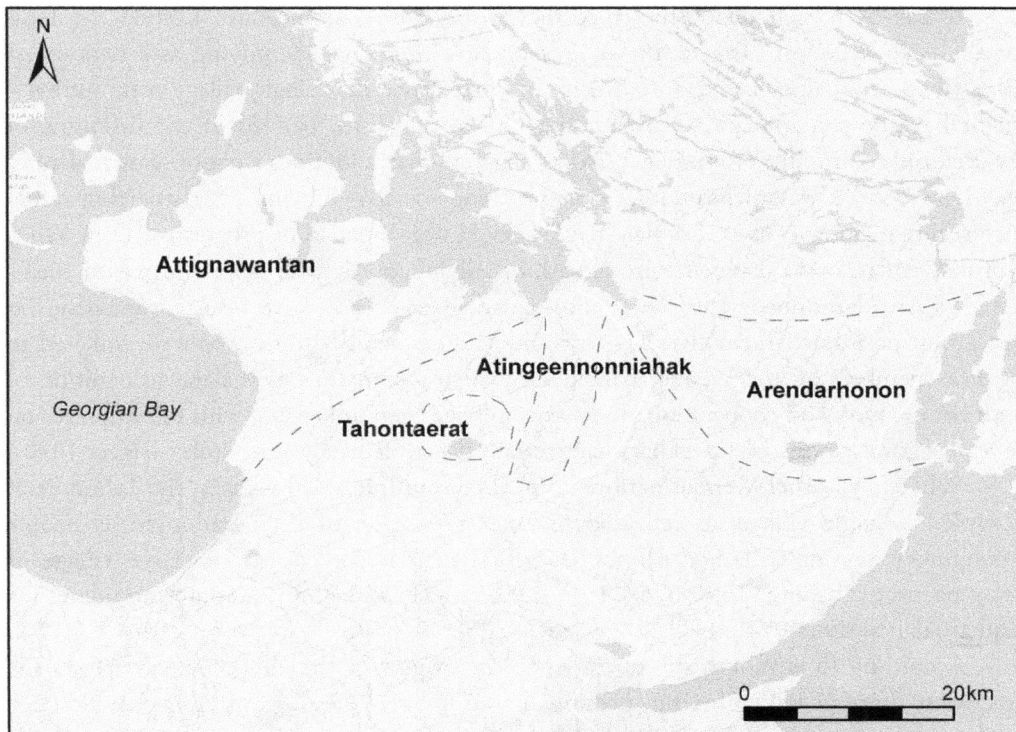

Figure 15.6. Seventeenth-century locations of Wendat nations (after Trigger 1976 and Williamson 2014).

Wendat Nations

At the time of European contact, the Wendat confederacy was composed of four allied nations. The Attignawantan ("of bear country") and Atingeennonniahak ("makers of cord") nations (all endonyms from Steckley 2007) occupied the northern peninsula, and were the earliest inhabitants of Wendake, both groups having originated with the initial fourteenth-century migrants to Simcoe County (Trigger 1976; Williamson 2014). These two nations formed the nucleus of the confederacy, which they claimed dated back to the fifteenth century (Thwaites 1896–1901:16:227–229). Two more nations, the Arendarhonon ("people of the rock/of a rocky country") and Tahontaerat ("two white ears" [Steckley 2007] or "people of the one single white lodge" [Jones 1909]) joined the confederacy around 1590 and 1610, respectively. While the relocation of these groups to Simcoe County occurred immediately before direct European contact and the escalation of conflict with nations of the Haudenosaunee confederacy, the precise reasons for, and mechanisms of, this political and geographic realignment remain unclear.

It has been well established that the Trent Valley communities formed the basis for the Arendarhonon (Trigger 1976). It may have been that identifying as a nation—as opposed to an identity based on ethnicity or coresidence in a single village community—might have been a strategy for overcoming the factionalism that led to the fissioning of the Benson community. Ramsden (2016a) suggests that adopting a nation-based identity may have been "a way of promoting economic and social well-being . . . [whereby] rather than seeing themselves as traditional Trent Valley Huron-Wendat, or progressive Trent Valley Huron-Wendat, or St. Lawrence Iroquoian, or Algonkian, they all agreed to regard themselves as Arendarhonon." This new nation-based identity may have been advantageous as this group positioned themselves vis-à-vis and sought membership in, or were solicited to become members of, the Wendat confederacy. Such a scenario permits the recognition of both competition and cooperation, and seems to have been in keeping with the emphasis on collective governance structures that characterized the confederacy as a whole (Trigger 1990).

Whereas all other Wendat nations comprised multiple allied villages, the Tahontaerat occupied a single village, as reflected by one translation of their endonym as people belonging to a single "lodge" (Jones 1909). This nation occupied the large village of Scanonaenrat (Thwaites 1896–1901:10). The Orr Lake and Ellery sites are candidates for sequential iterations of this village (Warrick 2008:207–208; Williamson 2014).

According to ethnohistoric documents, the origins of the Tahontaerat were on the northwest shore of Lake Ontario, possibly as the Draper-Mantle community, or possibly as that group together with others who occupied other north shore drainages in the early seventeenth century (Birch and Williamson 2013a). While they must have been well aware of the confederacy prior to joining in 1610, it is possible that they may have been reticent to join, or may have had another relationship to the early confederacy. It is possible that pressure or hostilities, as documented in ethnohistoric sources, from their Haudenosaunee enemies to the south forced their relocation, whereby they moved north seeking safety among the more populous Wendat.

Ethnohistoric accounts in the Jesuit Relations suggest that political influence was not equal within the confederacy council (Thwaites 1896–1901:10; Trigger 1976). The Attignawantan—having the greatest population and antiquity in Wendake—retained the balance of power in council where they sat on one side of the longhouse, whereas the representatives of other nations sat on the other. The headman who presided over the proceedings also was Attignawantan. While the precise governance structure of the confederacy council is unclear, the Arendarhonon—at the time the second most populous nation—held the second greatest number of seats on the confederacy council, whereas the Tahontaerat did not appear to have seats on the council as late as 1636.

CONCLUSIONS AND IMPLICATIONS

While these case studies constitute a rough archaeohistorical sketch of the complex socio- and geopolitical dynamics that characterized late pre- and postcontact developments in the Lower Great Lakes region, they demonstrate that there were multiple pathways to coalescence which played out at the community and regional scales. In the context of geopolitical realignment and confederacy formation, greater centralization at the community level for the Tahontaerat may not have conferred a political advantage in the context of geopolitical realignment. Instead, the numerically superior, multiethnic Arendarhonon were able to more securely establish themselves within the Wendat confederacy. This may have been accomplished, in part, because this group possessed more "weak ties" (Granovetter 1973) to both Algonquian groups and French trade connections along the St. Lawrence River, which conferred an advantageous position in the expanding world system of the contact era.

The goal of this exercise has not been to produce generalizing theories about the processes and outcomes of settlement aggregation, but rather to present a case study that highlights the variable pathways to, and strategies employed in, coalescence. This includes the recognition that increased social stratification or centralization is not necessarily an outcome of aggregation (for a similar argument, see O'Shea and Nicodemus this volume). At the same time, the absence of social inequality does not preclude the development of complex, asymmetrical sociopolitical relations. In certain contexts, outcomes of aggregation may favor corporate and collective institutions (e.g., Carballo 2013; Kowalewski 2006; see also Ryan, and Sastre and Currás this volume). The complexity and asymmetry of political relations in the historical development of Wendat society can be explained only through a thorough historicized approach which considers the social histories of community relocation, coalescence, and the formation of nations and confederacies at multiple, intersecting scales of analysis.

References Cited

Archaeological Services Inc. 2014 The Archaeology of the Mantle Site (AlGt-334): Report on the Stage 3–4 Mitigative Excavation of Part of Lot 22, Concession 9, Town of Whitchurch-Stouffville, Regional Municipality of York, Ontario. Manuscript on file, Ontario Ministry of Culture, Tourism and Sport, Toronto.

Bamann, S. E. 1993 Settlement Nucleation in Mohawk Iroquois Prehistory: An Analysis of a Site Sequence in the Lower Otsquago Drainage of the Mohawk Valley. PhD dissertation, Department of Anthropology, State University of New York at Albany, Albany.

Bandy, M. 2008 Global Patterns of Early Village Development. In The Neolithic Demographic Transition and Its Consequences, edited by J.-P. Bocquet-Appel and O. Bar-Yosef, pp. 333–357. Springer, Dordrecht.

Barthes, R. 1969 Ethnic Groups and Boundaries. Little Brown, Boston.

Birch, J. 2010 Coalescence and Conflict in Iroquoian Ontario. Archaeological Review from Cambridge 25(1):27–46.

Birch, J. 2012 Coalescent Communities: Settlement Aggregation and Social Integration in Iroquoian Ontario. American Antiquity 77(4):646–670.

Birch, J. 2015 Current Research on the Historical Development of Northern Iroquoian Societies. Journal of Archaeological Research 23(3):263–323.

Birch, J. 2016a Relations of Power and Production in Ancestral Wendat Communities. In Household Archaeology: A Transatlantic Comparative Approach, edited by C. Chapdelaine, A. Burke, and K. Gernigon, pp. 31–48. P@lethnology 8. Presses Universitaires du Midi, Toulouse.

Birch, J. 2016b Interpreting Iroquoian Site Structure through Geophysical Prospection and Soil Chemistry: Insights from a Coalescent Community in Ontario, Canada. *Journal of Archaeological Science: Reports* 8:102–111.

Birch, J., and S. Manning 2016 Bayesian Modelling and Refinement of Iroquoian Settlement Histories. Paper presented at the 81st Annual Meeting of the Society for American Archaeology, Orlando.

Birch, J., and R. F. Williamson 2013a Organizational Complexity in Ancestral Wendat Communities. In *From Prehistoric Villages to Cities: Settlement Aggregation and Community Transformation*, edited by J. Birch, pp. 153–178. Routledge, New York.

Birch, J., and R. F. Williamson 2013b *The Mantle Site: An Archaeological History of an Ancestral Wendat Community*. AltaMira, Lanham, Maryland.

Birch, J., R. B. Wojtowicz, A. Pradzynski, and R. H. Pihl 2016 Multi-Scalar Perspectives on Iroquoian Ceramics: Aggregation and Interaction in Precontact Ontario. In *Process and Meaning in Spatial Archaeology: Investigations into Pre-Columbian Iroquoian Space and Place*, edited by E. E. Jones and J. L. Creese, pp. 111–144. University Press of Colorado, Boulder.

Bocquet-Appel, J.-P., and S. Naji 2006 Testing the Hypothesis of a Worldwide Neolithic Demographic Transition: Corroboration from American Cemeteries. *Current Anthropology* 47(2):341–365.

Bradley, J. W. 2005 *Evolution of the Onondaga Iroquois*. Syracuse University Press, Syracuse, New York.

Brück, J., and D. Fontijn 2013 The Myth of the Chief: Prestige Goods, Power, and Personhood in the European Bronze Age. In *The Oxford Handbook of the European Bronze Age*, edited by H. Fokkens and A. Harding, pp. 197–215. Oxford University Press, Oxford.

Carballo, D. M. (editor) 2013 *Cooperation and Collective Action: Archaeological Perspectives*. University Press of Colorado, Boulder.

Carter, J. E. 1981 *Spang: A Sixteenth Century Huron Village Site, Pickering, Ontario*. Master's thesis, Department of Anthropology, University of Toronto, Toronto.

Creese, J. L. 2012 The Domestication of Personhood: A View from the Northern Iroquoian Longhouse. *Cambridge Archaeological Journal* 22(3):365–386.

Damkjar, E. 1990 *The Coulter Site and Late Iroquoian Coalescence in the Upper Trent Valley*. Occasional Papers in Northeastern Archaeology 2. Copetown Press, Dundas, Ontario.

Engelbrecht, W. 1995 The Case of the Disappearing Iroquoians: Early Contact Period Superpower Politics. *Northeast Anthropology* 50:35–59.

Engelbrecht, W. 2003 *Iroquoia: The Development of a Native World*. Syracuse University Press, Syracuse, New York.

Engelbrecht, W., and B. Jamieson 2015 Stone versus Bone and Antler Tipped Arrows and the Movement of the St. Lawrence Iroquoians from Their Homeland. Paper presented at the Ontario Archaeological Symposium, Midland.

Feinman, G., and J. Neitzel 1984 Too Many Types: An Overview of Sedentary Prestate Societies in the Americas. *Advances in Archaeological Method and Theory* 7:39–102.

Finlayson, W. D. 1985 *The 1975 and 1978 Rescue Excavations at the Draper Site: Introduction and Settlement Pattern*. Archaeological Survey of Canada Mercury Series Paper 130. Canadian Museum of Civilization, Ottawa.

Gramly, R. M. 1977 Deerskins and Hunting Territories: Competition for a Scarce Resource of the Northeastern Woodlands. *American Antiquity* 42(4):601–605.

Granovetter, M. S. 1973 The Strength of Weak Ties. *American Journal of Sociology* 78(6):1360–1380.

Grinin, L. E., and A. V. Korotayev 2011 Chiefdoms and Their Analogues: Alternatives of Social Evolution at the Societal Level of Medium Cultural Complexity. *Social Evolution & History* 10(1):276–335.

Hayden, B. 1977 Corporate Groups and the Late Ontario Iroquoian Longhouse. *Ontario Archaeology* 28:3–16.

Jones, A. E. 1909 "8endake Ehen" or Old Huronia. 5th Report of the Bureau of Archives for the Province of Ontario, Toronto.

Jones, E. E. 2010a Population History of the Onondaga and Oneida Iroquois, A.D. 1500–1700. *American Antiquity* 75(2):387–407.

Jones, E. E. 2010b Sixteenth- and Seventeenth-Century Haudenosaunee (Iroquois) Population Trends in Northeastern North America. *Journal of Field Archaeology* 35(1):5–18.

Jones, E. E., and J. W. Wood 2012 Using Event-History Analysis to Examine the Causes of Semi-Sedentism among Shifting Cultivators: A Case Study of the Haudenosaunee, AD 1500–1700. *Journal of Archaeological Science* 39(8):2593–2603.

Kapches, M. 1987 The Auda Site: An Early Pickering Iroquois Component in Southeastern Ontario. *Archaeology of Eastern North America* 15:155–175.

Kowalewski, S. A. 2006 Coalescent Societies. In *Light on the Path: The Anthropology and History of the Southeastern Indians*, edited by T. J. Pluckhahn and R. Ethridge, pp. 94–122. The University of Alabama Press, Tuscaloosa.

LeBlanc, S. 2008 Warfare and the Development of Social Complexity: Some Demographic and Environmental Factors. In *The Archaeology of Warfare: Prehistories of Raiding and Conquest*, edited by E. N. Arkush and M. W. Allen, pp. 438–468. University Press of Florida, Tallahassee.

MacDonald, R. I. 1986 *The Coleman Site (AiHd-7): A Late Prehistoric Iroquoian Village in the Waterloo Region*. Master's thesis, Department of Anthropology, Trent University, Peterborough.

MacDonald, R. I. 1988 Ontario Iroquoian Sweat Lodges. *Ontario Archaeology* 48:17–26.

MacDonald, R. I. 2002 *Late Woodland Settlement Trends in South-Central Ontario: A Study of Ecological Relationships and Culture Change*. PhD dissertation, Department of Anthropology, McGill University, Montreal.

MacDonald, R. I., and R. F. Williamson 1995 The Hibou Site (AlGo-50): Investigating Ontario Iroquoian Origins in the Central North Shore Area of Lake Ontario. In *Origins of the People of the Longhouse*, edited by A. Bekerman and G. Warrick, pp. 9–42. Ontario Archeological Society, Toronto.

MacDonald, R. I., and R. F. Williamson 2001 Sweat Lodges and Solidarity: The Archaeology of the Hubbert Site. *Ontario Archaeology* 71:29–78.

Molto, J. E., M. Spence, and W. Fox 1986 The Van Oordt Site: A Case Study in Salvage Archaeology. *Canadian Review of Physical Anthropology* 5(2):49–61.

Nasmith, C. 2008 *The Kirche Site: A 16th Century Huron Village in the Upper Trent Valley*. 2nd ed. Occasional Papers in Northeastern Archaeology 1. Copetown Press, St. John's, Ontario.

Niemczycki, M. P. 1984 *The Origin and Development of the Seneca and Cayuga Tribes of New York State*. PhD dissertation, Department of Anthropology, State University of New York at Buffalo, Buffalo.

Noble, W. C. 1979 Ontario Iroquois Effigy Pipes. *Canadian Journal of Archaeology* 3:69–90.

Pauketat, T. R. 2001 Practice and History in Archaeology: An Emerging Paradigm. *Anthropological Theory* 1(1):73–98.

Pearce, R. 1984 *Mapping Middleport: A Case Study in Societal Archaeology*. PhD dissertation, Department of Anthropology, McGill University, Montreal.

Pendergast, J. F. 1966 *Three Prehistoric Iroquois Components in Eastern Ontario*. National Museum of Canada Bulletin 208. Department of the Secretary of State, Ottawa.

Pfeiffer, S., J. C. Sealy, R. F. Williamson, S. Needs-Howarth, and L. Lesage 2016 Maize, Fish and Deer: Investigating Dietary Staples among Ancestral Huron-Wendat Villages, as Documented from Tooth Samples. *American Antiquity* 81(3):515–532.

Ramsden, P. G. 1977 *A Refinement of Some Aspects of Huron Ceramic Analysis*. Archaeological Survey of Canada Mercury Series Paper 63. National Museum of Canada, Ottawa.

Ramsden, P. G. 1988 Palisade Extension, Village Expansion and Immigration in Trent Valley Huron Villages. *Canadian Journal of Archaeology* 12:177–183.

Ramsden, P. G. 1990 Saint Lawrence Iroquoians in the Upper Trent River Valley. *Man in the Northeast* 39:87–95.

Ramsden, P. G. 1996 The Current State of Huron Archaeology. *Northeast Anthropology* 51:101–112.

Ramsden, P. G. 2009 Politics in a Huron Village. In *Painting the Past with a Broad Brush: Papers in Honor of James Valliere Wright*, edited by D. L. Keenlyside and J.-L. Pilon, pp. 299–318. Archaeological Survey of Canada Mercury Series Paper 170. Canadian Museum of Civilization, Gatineau, Quebec.

Ramsden, P. G. 2016a Becoming Wendat: Negotiating a New Identity around Balsam Lake in the Late Sixteenth Century. *Ontario Archaeology* 96:121–132.

Ramsden, P. G. 2016b The Use of Style in Resistance, Politics and the Negotiation of Identity: St. Lawrence Iroquoians in a Huron-Wendat Community. *Canadian Journal of Archaeology* 40(1):1–22.

Roscoe, P. 2013 War, Collective Action, and the "Evolution" of Human Polities. In *Cooperation and Collective Action: Archaeological Perspectives*, edited by D. M. Carballo, pp. 57–82. University of Colorado Press, Boulder.

Schachner, G. 2012 *Population Circulation and the Transformation of Ancient Zuni Communities*. The University of Arizona Press, Tucson.

Smith, M. E., A. Engquist, C. Carvajal, K. Johnston-Zimmerman, M. Algara, B. Gilliland, Y. Kuznetsov, and A. Young 2014 Neighborhood Formation in Semi-Urban Settlements. *Journal of Urbanism* 8(2):173–198.

Snow, D. R. 1995 *Mohawk Valley Archaeology: The Sites*. Occasional Papers in Anthropology 23. Matson Museum of Anthropology, Pennsylvania State University, University Park.

Steckley, J. L. 2007 *Words of the Huron*. Wilfrid Laurier Press, Waterloo, Ontario.

Sutton, R. E. 1990 *Hidden amidst the Hills: Middle and Late Iroquoian Occupations in the Middle Trent Valley*. Occasional Papers in Northeastern Archaeology 3. Copetown Press, Dundas, Ontario.

Sutton, R. E. 1999 The Barrie Site: A Pioneering Iroquoian Village Located in Simcoe County, Ontario. *Ontario Archaeology* 67:40–87.

Thwaites, R. G. 1896–1901 *The Jesuit Relations and Allied Documents*. 73 vols. The Burrows Brothers, Cleveland.

Trigger, B. G. 1976 *The Children of Aataensic: A History of the Huron People to 1660*. 2 vols. McGill-Queen's University Press, Montreal.

Trigger, B. G. 1985 *Natives and Newcomers: Canada's "Heroic Age" Reconsidered.* McGill-Queen's University Press, Montreal.

Trigger, B. G. 1990 Maintaining Economic Equality in Opposition to Complexity: An Iroquoian Case Study. In *The Evolution of Political Systems,* edited by S. Upham, pp. 119–145. Cambridge University Press, Cambridge.

Tuck, J. A. 1971 *Onondaga Iroquois Prehistory: A Study in Settlement Archaeology.* Syracuse University Press, Syracuse, New York.

Warrick, G. A. 1984 *Reconstructing Ontario Iroquois Village Organization.* Archaeological Survey of Canada Mercury Series Paper 124. National Museum of Man, Ottawa.

Warrick, G. A. 2000 The Precontact Occupation of Southern Ontario. *Journal of World Prehistory* 14(4):415–466.

Warrick, G. A. 2008 *A Population History of the Huron-Petun, AD 500–1650.* Cambridge University Press, Cambridge.

Williamson, R. 1978 Preliminary Report on Human Interment Patterns of the Draper Site. *Canadian Journal of Archaeology* 2:117–121.

Williamson, R. F. 2007 "Ontinontsiskiaj ondaon" (The House of Cut-Off Heads): The History and Archaeology of Northern Iroquoian Trophy Taking. In *The Taking and Displaying of Human Body Parts as Trophies,* edited by R. J. Chacon and D. H. Dye, pp. 190–221. Springer, New York.

Williamson, R. F. 2014 The Archaeological History of the Wendat to A.D. 1651: An Overview. *Ontario Archaeology* 94:3–64.

Williamson, R. F., and D. A. Steiss 2003 A History of Iroquoian Burial Practice. In *Bones of the Ancestors: The Archaeology and Osteobiography of the Moatfield Ossuary,* edited by R. F. Williamson and S. Pfeiffer, pp. 89–132. Archaeological Survey of Canada Mercury Series Paper 163. Canadian Museum of Civilization, Gatineau, Quebec.

Wright, J. V. 1966 *The Ontario Iroquois Tradition.* Bulletin 210. National Museum of Canada, Ottawa.

Contributors

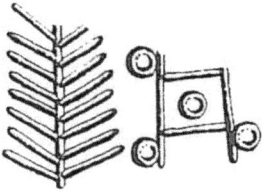

Bradley A. Ault, Department of Classics, University at Buffalo The State University of New York

A. Nejat Bilgen, Department of Archaeology, Dumlupınar University

Jennifer Birch, Department of Anthropology, The University of Georgia

Brais X. Currás, Instituto de Arqueologia, Universidade de Coimbra

Manuel Fernández-Götz, Classics, History and Archaeology Department, University of Edinburgh

Bisserka Gaydarska, Department of Archaeology, Durham University

Attila Gyucha, Integrative Research Center, The Field Museum of Natural History

Laura K. Harrison, Center for Virtualization and Advanced Spatial Technologies, University of South Florida

Alan Kaiser, Department of Archaeology, University of Evansville

John E. Kelly, Department of Anthropology, Washington University in St. Louis

Amy Nicodemus, Department of Archaeology and Anthropology, University of Wisconsin La Crosse

Robin Osborne, King's College, University of Cambridge

John O'Shea, Department of Anthropology, University of Michigan

Daniel J. Pullen, Department of Classics, Florida State University

Pál Raczky, Institute of Archaeological Sciences, Eötvös Loránd University

Susan C. Ryan, Crow Canyon Archaeological Center

Inés Sastre, Instituto de Historia, Centro de Ciencias Humanas y Sociales

Michael E. Smith, School of Human Evolution and Social Change, Arizona State University

Index

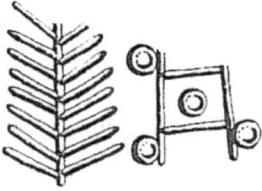

abandonment: causes of, 8, 14, 17, 75, 76, 81, 84, 88–90, 119, 120, 167, 168, 191, 216, 233, 240, 358, 360; followed by aggregation, 2, 10, 15, 37, 76, 175, 193, 354; of nucleated settlements, 16–19, 61, 62, 64, 67, 69, 72, 73, 88, 93, 115, 123, 150, 166, 167, 174, 175, 178, 189, 191, 194, 233, 278, 280, 309, 360; of regions, 7, 73, 118, 120, 150, 151, 324, 358; *see also* collapse, cycles, fission

Abobrica, Spain (site), 314

Academy, Greece (site), 137, 138

Acharnai, Greece (site), 137–140

Acharnians (play), *see* Aristophanes

acropolis: as cult center, 86, 145, 155; as hilltop site, 83, 86, 155; *see also* Athens, citadel

administration: buildings at Seyitömer Höyük, 194, 195, 201, 202; Roman imperial, 307–309, 311–314; *see also* Linear B tablets

Aedui, Gaul (tribe), 97; *see also* Gaul

Aegean: Early Bronze Age, 189–191, 194, 195, 209; Early Iron Age, 150; Early Neolithic, 262; Late Bronze Age, 227, 231–233; *see also* Crete, Cyclades, Greece, West Anatolia

Aeneolithic, Southeast European, 277; *see also* Chalcolithic, Copper Age

aerial photography, 83, 165, 244

Africa, early urbanism in, 106; *see also* Egypt, Ethiopia, Niger River valley, Nile River valley

agathoi, 153; *see also* yeoman farmers

agglomeration, *see* aggregation

agglomerations secondaires, 309

aggregation: causes of, 8–10, 47, 76, 96–98, 108, 112, 114, 123–125, 141, 145, 146, 167, 174, 176–178, 182, 191, 193, 295–297, 301, 304–309, 326, 338, 341, 354, 360, 363; vs. nucleation, 109; processes of, 8–10, 14, 37, 72–75, 83, 110–112, 114, 115, 120–126, 144–146, 192, 215, 270, 272, 273, 275, 277, 278, 280, 281, 304, 313, 328, 340–342, 356–360; socioeconomic consequences of, 1–3, 13–17, 37–41, 43, 44, 46–49, 51–53, 62, 126, 136, 176–180, 189–191, 202, 280, 281, 299, 301, 306, 313, 321–323, 326, 340–342, 349–354, 356–358, 363; *see also* cycles, scalar stress, urbanization

agora: in Athens, 158; role of in Greek city-states, 155, 156

agriculture: Eastern Agricultural Complex, 109, 110; in hinterland, 156, 174; intensification of as a response to population growth, 39, 40, 96, 112, 177; plant domestication, 109; strategies, 70, 109, 116, 118, 141, 145, 170,

in aggregation, 145, 146, 176; *see also* fortification, warfare

Dekeleia, Greece (site), 136, 139

Demeter (Greek god), 141

Demircihöyük, Turkey (site), 190–192, 202; *see also* Anatolian Settlement Model

demography, studies of regional, 8, 15, 108, 110, 111, 116, 175

Deszk, Hungary (site), 65, 67, 72

dietary practices, 8, 16, 75, 351

Dimaina, *see* Vassa

Diomedes (Greek king), 233

Dipylon, Greece (site), 145

DNA studies, 262

Dobrovody, Ukraine (site), 168

Dohack, US (site), 110, 119, 120

Dorfstadt, 156

Draper, Canada (site), 354–357

Dubai, United Arab Emirates (modern city), 19, 239, 240

Duero River valley, Portugal and Spain, 296, 301, 302

Dugan Airfield, US (site), 113, 116

Durkheim, Emile, 44

EAC, *see* Eastern Agricultural Complex

Eastern Agricultural Complex, 109, 110

East Europe, 177, 273

East St. Louis, US (site), 107, 108, 126

economy/economic: elite control of, 71, 74–76, 216, 230, 232; growth as a result of population growth and density, 1, 4, 11, 16, 37–40, 46–51, 153, *see also* energized crowding model; moral, 99; network, 2, 135; political, 40, 44, 98, 99, 168, 231; ritualized, 125; surplus, 152, 153, 299; tributary, 177, 180, 309, 314

Ecsegfalva, Hungary (site), 264

egalitarianism/egalitarian: ideology, 15; political structure, 15, 17, 179, 180, 350, 351, 357; *see also* middle-range societies, tribe

Egypt, Greek trading posts, 153; *see also* Nile River valley

Ehrenbürg bei Forchheim, Germany (site), 82, 86

Eïones, Greece (site), 233

El Bierzo, Spain (region), 296, 311, 312; *see also* Bierzo Edict

electric resistivity tomography, 7

Eleusinian Mysteries, 141

Eleusis, Greece (site), 136–143, 145, 231; *see also* Eleusinian Mysteries

elite: cemeteries, 144, 145; control of economy, 71, 74–76, 216, 230, 232; display and competition, 69, 70, 73, 74, 208, 209, 252–254, 313; ideology, 193, 204, 209; regalia, 69, 73, 74; spatial separation, 71, 73, 144, 207–209, 249; tensions with nonelites, 240; *see also* aristocracy

Ellery, Canada (site), 362

Emborio, Greece (site), 151

Emerald, US (site), 107, 108, 126

enclosure: Central European Neolithic, 273, 274; and identity, 273, 280, 297, 309; intrasite, 44, 66, 67, 70, 226, 270, 272, 273, 276–278, 281, 358; at Kalamianos, 226; Lengyel-type, 273, 274; in Iroquoia, 354–356, 358–360; at *oppida*, 94; at Pecica Şanţul Mare, 66, 67; at Polgár-Csőszhalom, 273, 277; and ritual, 277, 278, 280–281; and settlement growth, 66, 67, 277, 298, 354; and storage, 226; symbolic, 170; at Trypillia megasites, 168, 170; *see also* fortification

Endrőd 39, Hungary (site), 264

energized crowding model, 18, 37–44, 46, 48, 50, 52–53, 90, 136, 142, 143, 145, 242; *see also* scalar stress

environment: and aggregation, 7, 9, 10, 140, 326; change as a result of aggregation, 2, 180; and settlement decline and abandonment, 75, 76, 90, 175; *see also* climate, landscape

Epakria, Greece (site), 136

epigraphy, in Northwest Iberia, 311, 313

Erie (nation), 350, 351; *see also* Iroquoia

Eskişehir, Turkey (region), 195

Ethiopia, and early urbanism, 106

www.ingramcontent.com/pod-product-compliance
Lightning Source LLC
Chambersburg PA
CBHW080410270326
41929CB00018B/2971